MODERN ESSAYS
ON EIGHTEENTH-CENTURY
LITERATURE

Modern Essays on Eighteenth-Century Literature

Edited by

LEOPOLD DAMROSCH, JR.

New York * Oxford

OXFORD UNIVERSITY PRESS

1988

Oxford University Press

Oxford   New York   Toronto
Delhi   Bombay   Calcutta   Madras   Karachi
Petaling Jaya   Singapore   Hong Kong   Tokyo
Nairobi   Dar es Salaam   Cape Town
Melbourne   Auckland
and associated companies in
Beirut   Berlin   Ibadan   Nicosia

Library of Congress Cataloging-in-Publication Data
Modern essays on eighteenth-century literature.
1. English literature—18th century—History and criticism.
I. Damrosch, Leopold.
PR442.M57 1988   820'.9'005   87-5786
ISBN 0-19-504923-3
ISBN 0-19-504924-1

2 4 6 8 10 9 7 5 3 1

Printed in the United States of America
on acid-free paper

Preface

The past two decades have seen an immense expansion of literary scholarship and criticism, accompanied by widening theoretical perspectives that have generated new ways of thinking about the culture of the past. Eighteenth-century literature, though not as exposed as some other periods to the winds of change, has shared in the general revaluation. But the economic history of book publishing has conferred a "classic" status on aging paperback collections that have held the field simply because they are already in print, including the predecessor to this volume, James L. Clifford's *Eighteenth-Century English Literature: Modern Essays in Criticism* (New York: Oxford University Press, 1959). Much that they contain remains valuable, but a great deal has happened since then. The quantity of first-rate work has been remarkable, and no collection can now hope to represent the field as fully as Clifford's did. But that is all the more reason to offer a new selection.

My guiding principle was to choose the best pieces I could, whether widely quoted or less familiar. In practice, 1970 turned out to be an appropriate starting point. I looked for lively, well-written essays that would seem fresh and thought-provoking to specialists and nonspecialists alike; I sought a balance between wide-ranging studies and interpretations of particular texts; and a variety of scholarly and theoretical approaches. It was essential that the essays should not be narrowly focused, which eliminated many otherwise valuable pieces, and that they should stand on their own, which eliminated some excellent books that could not be effectively excerpted. In addition, I have had to omit background essays on history, politics, science, and aesthetics; their usefulness is obvious, but the cost in excluding other pieces would be too great.

The eighteenth century, as this collection conceives it, excludes both the Restoration and Romantic periods. The writers of the 1790s—Godwin,

Wollstonecraft, Blake, even the young Wordsworth and Coleridge—reached maturity during the eighteenth century, but their thought and writings belong more appropriately to a later period.

Each essay is reprinted as it first appeared, except that occasional cross-references have been deleted from pieces excerpted from books, and a few chapter titles have been altered when necessary.

My thanks are due to the many scholars who offered suggestions, and to William Sisler and Kim Scott Walwyn of Oxford University Press for encouraging the project.

College Park, Md.   L.D.
April 1987

Contents

MODERN ESSAYS
ON EIGHTEENTH-CENTURY
LITERATURE

A Tale of a Tub

JOHN TRAUGOTT

Motley in the Brain?

So giddy are the quick changes of Swift's foolery in *A Tale of a Tub* that few readers from his day to ours have been convinced they know the "enemy." The parodies are brilliant and raucous, but they have a habit at odd moments of sounding like Swift himself, and when most thoroughly vulgar and utterly reprehensible they make the keenest comments on the life we must live. Worse by far, as responses to those comments, the serene Augustan assumptions about reason and a gentleman's education, elsewhere encouraged in the reader by the irony towards those lower orders, can come to seem pointless and fatuous. Irony is, after all, a conspiracy of the elite; the reader would seem to have a right to expect from the ironist some regard for class solidarity. Swift seems to delight, however, in leaving the reader, whom he has encouraged to assume his own top-loftiness above the crowd, stranded with what turn out to be merely pompous airs. It is not easy to learn the lesson from a reading of the *Tale* of how not to be a fool among knaves. Officious reason ruins life, but Epicurean dilly-dallying is an idiot illusion; meanwhile madmen and fanatics tell us what the world is really like. Whatever advice we have is a madman's or a fool's, but we ignore it at our peril. The easiest response—which ought to be rejected almost as soon as it is imagined—is that the giddy speaker, being a "persona" parodying literary hirelings or scholarly worms or metaphysical cabbalists or mad world-makers, is the real target of the satire. That tiresome persona of the critics, complained Professor Herbert Davis in a delight-

From *The Character of Swift's Satire: A Revised Focus,* ed. Claude Rawson (Newark: University of Delaware Press; London and Toronto: Associated University Presses, 1983), pp. 83–126.

fully petulant essay,[1] is always getting between us and Swift. We *know* perfectly well that we are in the presence of Swift, not of some novelistic fiction. When we hear, "Last week I saw a Woman *flay'd*, and you will hardly believe, how much it altered her Person for the worse," we shiver with the superb ironist who so easily finds out behind the excellent foppery of the world the bloodiness of us all. He has an ear, this ironist, for picking up in the accents of a vagrant voice in the street an epitome of our existence, mimicking here a smart-talking man-about-town's satisfaction in reporting the latest news that beauty may be a whore and the law a brute. Not very pleasant news. A whore does look better with her paint than without her skin. Better to let such things pass with a knowing giggle and not go about asking discommoding questions. Irony leaves the man who is inclined to look into such things to shift for himself, with the pain of finding out what to do with his knowledge. He is one of the unhappy few cursed with eyes to see, ears to hear, and a tongue to speak. But there are rewards as well as pains in joining the ironist. One takes to oneself the wonderful art of Swift in parodying so perfectly the bloody idiocy of the many and thus one escapes the crowd. Listening carefully to the ring of this irony, we hear also an echo of Lear's rage at the beadle of the law who whips the whore he hotly lusts after. It is rage stylized by Jonathan Swift for an age of reason. The art of it all bestows upon the reader a pleasurable elevation, and there is an instant transfer of allegiance to the author. Few readers have believed themselves superior to this speaker, though in fact he is ostensibly the madman and the object of satire. So distinctions between Swift and his speaker collapse, as they do in all his satires; but here in the *Tale* the problem is especially bedevilling and bemusing as the speaker sets up to wear motley. Presumably Swift does not wear motley in his brain, but even this proposition is not easily demonstrable. The demonic joy with which Swift conjures up his repertoire of voices in the *Tale* and speaks his deepest thoughts in their tongues, the sheer invention and flamboyant virtuosity, seem at times to define a game, civilized though pyrrhonnist and cynical, for would-be ironists, and we could accept it as such were it not for the deadly hatred and rage that show everywhere in odd, sudden bursts that it is not finally a game at all. Even the subject matter, the corruptions in learning and religion, is troubling by its very inconsistency. Corruptions in learning can be taken care of by parody, delivered from a posture of Augustan common sense. We scarcely need be more than snobbish for this sort of thing—or perhaps snobbish with serious artistic purpose, like Pope in the *Dunciad*. But is religion, which assumes the common body and communion, clarified by irony? Satire of the corruptions in religion could hardly be expected to chime with a gentleman's reserve towards the new learning. Though that satire in the *Tale* seems at times to resemble the scurrilous ridicule of a host of seventeenth-century Church polemicists who had less Christianity than Thersites,[2] it goes much deeper, into the inevitable psychology of the religious personality, and raises ultimate questions. Obviously, in reading the *Tale* we need a special attitude of willingness to follow a diabolist personality and to entertain sudden glimpses of realities not comprehended in orthodoxies or class postures. The last thing we need look for is "Sweetness and Light," that shibboleth of Augustan decorum.

Who was Swift, after all, to talk about "Sweetness and Light"? When Matthew Arnold appropriated the phrase in his battle for Culture against Anarchy, he took care to remark, primly but precisely, that the satirist had himself all too little of the first, at least, of these admirable qualities. Although Arnold was willing to incorporate in this way a good deal of the intellectual content of Swift's Spider and Bee allegory of *The Battle of the Books* (and, indeed, like Swift, to spice it with snobbish disdain of the protestantism of the protestant, the dissonance of dissent, and the general hurly-burly of mechanicians, liberals, and people with vulgar names), he did not want to confuse Swift's motives with his own. In effect he did not accept Swift's pretension to the Bee's motives. It is hard to gainsay Arnold.

"Culture hates hatred," says Arnold. "Sweetness and Light" suggests "a finely tempered nature" that "gives exactly the notion of perfection as culture brings us to conceive it: a harmonious perfection in which the characters of beauty and intelligence are both present." With such sweetness what has the violent-tempered satirist to do—he who peeps at the soul of man by way of his breech (to turn, justly, Swift's own figure upon himself)? What has the priest who hates inspiration, the episcopalian who hates bishops, the patriot who hates his countrymen to do? Only too often Swift's idea of religion appears to be a judicious conjunction of punctiliousness with repression. An easy way out from these embarrassing questions for the scholar who thinks to purify Swift of all mixed motives and thus raise his market in academia is to deny, quite baldly, the violence—put it down to satiric technique, while rehabilitating the priest in the most orthodox canonicals by placing him against an historical "background" of Christian ideas, long forgotten but now happily recovered by scholarship.[3] The sociology of this phenomenon of modern academia by which a demonic writer like Swift is "elevated" by being reduced to a proper cleric is beyond the scope of this essay. Suffice it to say that it is a form of the pseudoscientific determinism in scholarship that explains (away) a refractory writer by a system of ideas that were, we are told, his heritage and environment. This Swift comes to seem much like a university lecturer.[4] Nowadays university lecturers, though perhaps atheists, known a good deal more about original sin and other theological puzzles than Swift and his contemporaries cared to contemplate.[5] Such rare knowledge does not lie idle; it is put into the mouth of Swift's ghost, which then responds as obediently as a zombie, easily clarifying the unholy mysteries of the human condition that the living man risked his very sanity to think on. Thus Swift's seeming madness in *A Tale of a Tub*—not only in the bedevilling "Digression concerning Madness" but as well throughout the allegory of the history of the Christian Church—is explained as "Anglican rationalism"; his horror at the Yahoo image of Gulliver in the mirror pool, as "original sin"; his notorious predilection for images of excrement, as traditional Christian denigration of the flesh. Most ingenious of all, the vast abrupt of being that divides the religious personality as manifested in history—Jack and Peter—from reasonable men, or that divides Yahoo from Houyhnhnm, is rationalized as a lesson in the need for "compromise."[6] Little matter that the only wooden figure of the *Tale* is Martin, who represents the compromise, and that the madman of the "Digression concerning Madness" is vital and compelling, the object of every reader's wonder. Little matter that Gulliver, faced with a choice between Yahoo and Houyhnhnm, seems to go as mad as any Platonic dreamer delivered from the Cave to the Light and is the object of every reader's wonder.[7] Little matter—we are delivered to the insipid moral of "compromise" according to a formula called "classical humanism."[8] One cannot resist attempting to apply this moral. When Jack pisses in the eyes of passersby, when Peter pretends to change stale bread into mutton, should Jack piss more moderately, Peter work a more modest magic? When the Yahoos defecate on their own kind, are we to know that "compromise" suggests defecating on only some of our friends, and only moderately?

But a reading of Swift will always constitute an appeal from the scholars to common sense. Thackeray is the *bête noire* of modern scholars of Swift because the sentimental novelist, apologist for female purity and the sanctity of the family, accused Swift of "life-long hypocrisy" for taking a priest's vows when his works show so evidently a "consciousness of his own scepticism." Thackeray is sentimental; he hates Swift for being so thoroughly un-English as to be capable of thinking of ladies at stool; he makes of Swift's life a sentimental drama—two pitiful virgins, Stella and Vanessa, betrayed by an imperious cad who is underneath it all a tragically alienated wretch. Yet for all his genuflecting to the household gods, Thackeray perceives with great clarity Swift's paradoxical qualities—the strange mixture of institutional piety with a subversive and fundamentally pyrrhonistic imagination. Swift, he says, did not "hiccop" Church and State in the simple way of "poor Dick Steele and poor Henry Fielding." "A vast genius . . . to seize, to know, to see, to flash upon falsehood and scorch it to perdition, to penetrate into hidden motives, and expose the black thoughts of men—an awful, an evil spirit" *(English Humorists)*. Without succumbing to Thackeray's nervousness, the common reader will understand this point.

Far from resolving the mysteries of the human condition in a table of doctrines and commandments, the *Tale* is a playhouse of illusions. A harlequin author tells a funny story of three brothers, younkers who come to town to be fops. To get on they do what is required—whore, swagger, tattle, get claps, and join a sect that worships the tailor. Here the harlequin digresses for a speculative game in which he invents a fantastic theology depending on the word *clothes* as Christian theology depends on *cross* (one crazy system among several he spins out before he is done); and then in turns he acts out the postures and struttings of each brother going his way to madness, only pausing occasionally to tell his own sad story as a battered but still pert hireling writer under three reigns, for six and thirty factions, now trying the experiment of writing upon nothing. Being such a shifty fellow, naturally he changes voices and motley from time to time; if he begins as a silly hireling, he soon develops a serious allegory, and seems to conclude as a nihilistic madman. The whole performance of parody, allegory, foolery, sententia, paradoxes, and fantastic imaginings hopelessly confuses profane and sacred subjects. It is a *tour de force* of black humor, and opportunity for Swift to mimic grubs who worm their way and philosophers who hoist themselves into the rare air over the crowd, an opportunity as well to ridicule Roman Catholics and Dissenters. Yet the *Tale's* parody of grubs and sectarians is hardly the continuing interest of this harlequinade. Now as then, it is the mind of Swift dreaming terrible truths, radical and destructive, about our culture, our reason, and the will of God, that captures the reader's imagination. Though speaking in tongues, playing the fool, the author of the *Tale* is always Swift, but Swift relieved of responsibility and its decorums and hence liberated and energized. "Good God, what a genius I had when I wrote that book," said Swift, musing over an entire career of tricks on the world. That genius was a natural gift for parody, and once having hit upon the posture and cant of the parodic figure, a further gift for looking at the world through his eyes, thinking his thoughts, calling into question the fondest orthodoxies. It can only be an inward sympathy with the enemy, for its truest, most incisive, and most radical discoveries of the realities of human life come not as satiric parodies of perverse figures but when the author is speaking in the idiom and guise of those figures. The discoveries are theirs.

At this point one example, only typical, will suffice. Because he has spent his life pursuing the main chance, the hireling author knows, he says, that the trick is not to elbow your way in the crowd but to get above it where there is room. To do that all men are compelled by their nature to invent some machine or other—the pulpit is one, the mountebank's stage another, and even the criminal's ladder to the gallows is a way of asserting the ego. Preachers and criminals fall into one category, the category of humankind, and the allegory of Peter and Jack makes clear the radical realities of religious egotism. These radical realities are elaborately worked out, and worked out to the edge of despair, by the allegory's metaphors. They are Swift's convictions, not the cracked notions of a Grub Street hireling, and the satire falls upon the human psyche, not upon an outrageous fool who is brother to the insupportable Bentley and Wotton. How shall we get above the crowd?—"It being as hard to get quit of *Number* as of Hell" (sec. 1.). Here is the controlling idea of the *Tale:* the problem is likened to the desperation to escape hell; the ego must save itself by escaping "number" and the devil take the hindmost. As with religion, so with other sublimities—learning, glory, philosophy. One is doomed to egotism, to kill off and absorb other egos. The *Tale* is a vast pit (Bedlam Hospital, as it develops) in which desperate figures try to escape over one another's heads. The image and the rigor with which the implications of it are pursued in the whole *Tale* have the intensity of a Bosch drawing of damnation. The psychological nightmare is a secularization of the problem of salvation and for Swift only expressible in his zany's mad style of occult "types and fables." Whenever one of his mad or idiot figures begins to spin fantastic symbols and allegories, Swift is discovering his own truths. The guise is the way to freedom for a proper priest.

In the *Tale,* the trick of playing the fool to speak otherwise unspeakable truths in the service of an "unacceptable" vision of reality is certainly an adaptation of Erasmus's *Folly*. But Erasmus is content that the world should be a playhouse of illusions; Swift is driven wild by the spectacle, though he knows the truth, out of the mouth of the mad author, that "*unmasking,* which I think, has never been allowed faire Usage, either in the *World* or the *Play-House*" (sec. 9). One *must* speak through masks. And all the splendid fabrics of institutions and the noble fabrication of an integral personality with will and reason go glimmering in the course of the *Tale* among the "false lights, refracted angles, varnish, and tinsel." Yet despite all this, against his own evidence and knowledge, Swift makes us feel, with an irrational hatred of irrationality, that there must be a reason for reason. Like Pascal's bet on God when he contemplates the narrow room between nothingness and the infinite, Swift's bet on reason is a spasm of assertion despite his discovery through the eyes of madmen of the illusion of reason. The *Tale*, like the *Argument Against Abolishing Christianity*, the *Modest Proposal*, and *Gulliver*, ends with a desperately felt need of resolution in a situation whose very definition precludes resolution. Such anxiety might well have been, as it was for Pascal, the occasion of religious dedication. It is not, however, and anxiety is the final reality in Swift's satires. Without denying Swift's priestly dedication, which was impeccable—he religiously corrected his choir and put back the bricks in the close wall—I shall try in this essay to account for the emotional intensity of his flirtation, in the guise of his satiric victims in the *Tale*, with a reality entirely different from that prescribed by his confession.

Why is it, first of all, that a satire whose ostensible subject is the quarrels of Anglicans and gentlemen with Puritans, Catholics, and vulgarians, quarrels so antique that they have faded beyond our ability to recall them without scholarly paraphernalia, is as telling today as it ever was? A modern Catholic or Presbyterian, or even a vulgarian, can read it without a thought to his confession, and an Anglican could appreciate it with no greater gusto than an atheist. Surely this is so because its mad voices are to be discovered, not in a scholar's revelation of ancient days, but in the mind of any man. Indeed, our world now being irrevocably topsy-turvy from Swift's point of view—atheistic, pluralistic, individualistic, progressivist—a modern reader, were he to consider only the literal objects of the satire, though admiring of Swift's skill, could not but be indifferent to his attitudes. Even as he wrote the *Tale* (1696–97), Swift must have known that events had passed him by. So quickly had the Williamite toleration evolved, so utterly had men abandoned in a few months' time allegiances they thought the condition of their honor and faith, that neither Jack nor Peter could have been considered a threat when the *Tale* appeared in 1704. Defoe the dissenter, only a few years Swift's senior, remembered as a child copying out the Pentateuch with his family the whole night through against the dawn when King Charles would burn all the Bibles; Anglicans had not forgotten the Puritan's holy text of fire and sword and desolation. But in 1704 such passions were spent, and when Swift appended his "Apology" to the fifth edition (1710), nearly forgotten. Then the dissenter like Defoe was a poor worm and the Catholics for the most part a retiring genteel society. In

1710 Alexander Pope could move in the polite world with little notice, save from Grub Street, of his religion. Although Swift's friends rushed through brutally repressive legislation against dissenters in the last year of Queen Anne's reign, it was an act of political desperation to preserve the Tory ascendancy, to be repealed in the Hanoverian reign. Swift's virulent support of the Test Act in Ireland was an embarrassment rather than a support to successive ministers. The very idea of an integral State-Church at the turn of the century was anomalous and would soon be ludicrous when the Church became scandalously Erastian under the Georges.

It is not, then, in studies of the parochial quarrels of the Restoration that we will find a sufficient account of the evolution of the *Tale*, its success in the early years of the new century and its vitality today, but in an understanding of Swift's radical imagination. Let us begin with the *Tale's* relations to the gentlemanly notions of his patron, Sir William Temple, for here we can grasp the evolution of Swift's peculiar irony of foolery that pervades the work.

From Snobbery to Subversion

An alien in his own country, at Moor Park a poor provincial, by Sir William's grace an amanuensis, Swift naturally smarted under his patron's cold looks. In a remarkable insight, many years later he attributed his hauteur towards great ministers, his refusal to endure their chills and snubs, to that early residence with Temple when he was so painfully unsure of his place.[9] Posthumous child, separated mysteriously from his mother almost at birth ("kidnapped" according to his strange story), poor relation of a dependent family, cut off from all familiar affections and treacherous to natural allegiances, Swift refused to belong to anyone or anything. He was a kind of psychological "bastard." Naturally such a young man, at once superior and self-hating, would identify with the oppressor, adopt his top-lofty attitude, and displace his hatred upon the vulgar. Sir William's mere whim could save him from the fate of living out his life a toady parson to some brutal squire.[10] Sir William being an attractive and accomplished man—as well as a dangerous one—he could not but mimic his manner. He out-snobbed the snob. (Did he acquire then—from knowledge of himself—his lifelong disgust for the Irish character, by his lights only a servile imitation of the English oppressor?) Swift appropriated, in fact, not only Sir William's manner but the ideas and attitudes in which the retired courtier specialized in his declining years. A dabbler in philosophical ideas, Temple loved to expatiate on the way history runs in cycles, on the low ebb of modern times, on the news other ages and times might have for us about our poor pretensions. In short, a kind of dilettante libertine, collecting in diminished times examples of vulgar errors, and, above all, scornful of the search for knowledge. Gentlemen understood the pageant of human life by reading the classics; they could not but smile at the grubs everywhere, in literature, politics, and science, busily trying to bring about "progress" ("Upon Ancient and Modern Learning"). Yet, if Sir William's airs were, by any historical measure, preposterous, he was a man of real talent and reputation, honored for his service in three reigns, respected for his willingness to relinquish ambition. The respectability of his public career was warrant enough to Swift for chiming his snobberies. All ironists begin as snobs, for irony is a trope whose rhetorical effect depends upon the audience's desire to ally themselves with the elite speaker, lest they be counted among the vulgar. They smile archly to signal that they can straighten out his crooked words which mimic the vulgar. Add to this structure Swift's hatred of *arrivistes* (like himself?), this hatred sublimated into high moral purpose; and his alienation from all natural allegiances, this alienation sublimated into intellectual intolerance of clichés and received opinions, or deepened more often than not to a covert nihilism. Such a satirist is as likely to turn the irony back upon his supposed ally as he is to mock the vulgar.

But to begin with the snob, Swift would defend Sir William's wretched mistakes in the Phalaris controversy by tarring his patron's adversaries, Bentley and Wotton, with the same brush he used for grubby writers of the contemporary scene—party hirelings, pamphleteers, smart critics, pedants, theological quarrellers. While he did not know, apparently, that Sir William was utterly wrong-headed, he might have known—had it occurred to him to inquire. Rather, the important thing was to record in the "Apology" how mortified Sir William was to hear Bentley and Wotton termed his "adversaries," they who had had the effrontery to show up a great gentleman in his scholarly errors. Temple had taken up in his casual, aloof way the quarrel in the French court over the relative genius of ancients and moderns. The French quarrel was at once a matter of aesthetics and of court politics. It being assumed by certain courtiers more given to political realism than others that Louis's greatness in political and military realms would naturally be accompanied by a commensurate superiority in the arts, the elevation of the moderns under the aegis of the *Roisoleil* followed. If one may be cynical about these motives, nevertheless the

quarrel had real substance in aesthetics. The questions of progress in per-
fecting ancient forms of literature, or of the just supplanting of those forms
by equally valid modern ones were important, but Sir William had little
interest in such real questions; for him the quarrel was class warfare.
Although his cyclical view of history precluded the absolute superiority of
one age, ancient or modern, over another, in literature he cast his vote for
the ancients on the ground that certain ages might well have a particular
genius. And after all, a gentleman's taste was perfected by reading the
ancients; Sir William's perfected taste enabled him to observe the excellence of the Phalaris Letters, an excellence impossible to any but an
ancient. He had the misfortune to choose a forgery to illustrate his grand
thesis, but that hardly mattered, for what exercised him was the pretension
of the modern age to any accomplishment at all. Just to glance at several
of Temple's egregious opinions is to see how impossible was the position
Swift so eagerly embraced. "But what," asked Sir William, "are the sci-
ences wherein we pretend to excel? I know of no new philosophers, that
have made entries upon that noble stage for fifteen hundred years past,
unless Descartes and Hobbes should pretend to it. . . . There is nothing
new in astronomy, to vie with the ancients, unless it be the Copernican
system; nor in physic, unless Harvey's circulation of the blood. But
whether either of these modern discoveries, or derived from old fountains,
is disputed: nay it is so too, whether they are true or no; . . . But if they
are true, yet these two great discoveries have made no change in the conclusions of astronomy, nor in the practice of physic."[11] He wonders what
has become of ancient skill in magic or in music that could charm the
beasts. Modern music is but fiddling and poetry but rhyming. Though
modern discoverers have introduced to our acquaintance vast continents
and numberless islands, we have done little with this knowledge compared
to what the ancients might have done. How little have we performed in
the exploration of the Northwest Passage to Tartary so long and confi-
dently promised? Does the sun or the earth move? Some astronomers think
the one, some the other. Nor do we know what motion is. Even our tongue
seems to Sir William a poor thing when he remembers his Latin and
Greek.

In this olio of an aristocrat's vulgar errors, there is nothing to be
admired, but one can wonder at the assurance mere accident of birth could
bestow upon a man of Temple's class. But Swift's irony, if it begins in
snobbish sarcasm, elevating the urbane traditionalist over the pert modern,
ends in tragic irony, separating the despairing realist from the desperate

illusionist. Something similar happens with Swift's crass appropriation of certain of Temple's philosophical notions. Slowly, inevitably, they deepen to the most radical conceptions of personality. It is as though a demon came to inhabit Temple's weary mind, pursuing his slight judgments of human insufficiencies until they end in the heart of darkness.

To the bill of indictment drawn here against his silliest postures, Temple would have answered, mildly, that he meant the moderns no injury; it was only that they pretended, with their busy schemes, to improve man's lot, to more importance than the inevitable pattern of life would allow. What can we do? Old wood to burn, old wine to drink, old friends to converse with, old books to read—these are what we need to get through this vale of tears. A characteristic metaphor suggests the reality, the chill, the fatigue: "The abilities of man must fall short on one side or other, like too scanty a blanket when you are a-bed: if you pull it upon your shoulders, you leave your feet bare; if you thrust it down upon your feet, your shoulders are uncovered."[12] We are, Temple would say, all of us, the victims of progress; the discoveries of today are the problems of tomorrow. This weary wisdom must be set in its context, the daily pronouncement of the millenarians.

If Temple was not really serious about any of his vagrant libertine ideas, it was on principle. Tolerant, Epicurean, easily ironic, he surveyed philosophies and civilizations, remote and near, to demonstrate the amusing confusions of the reason. Still more amusing, if reason gives man the prerogative over the rest of creation, it also subjects human nature to troubles, disquiets and miseries. It does little more than create passions and wants, above all restlessness from infinite designs and endless pursuits. Born crying, man lives complaining, and dies disappointed—and the great culprit is his fatal inclination to reason on all things. Again and again, this aristocratic disinclination to meddle in the follies of humanity comes down to three grand objects of scorn. These Swift made his own. The radical human debilities, thought Temple, were restlessness, "sufficiency," and universalism. Restlessness, he sighs, is our fate; our reason will ever destroy our quiet by creating illusions and dissatisfactions. The ego is so perfect that it will seldom stop with mere ameliorations or petty remedies but will push on, busily, to universal schemes intended to answer to all pains and puzzles of life. Worse still, it is only ordinary that one should assume one's own resources quite sufficient for such everyday tasks of worldmaking. Thus "sufficiency." We can hardly hope to escape this fate, but a measure of peace is obtainable if we can but quieten the perplexity of thought by embellishing the scenes of life, making our situation convenient, elegant, and magnificent. This is the Epicurean way. Our game is not to soar after knowledge but to cultivate our garden. And of course this is a literal, not metaphorical, injunction. Temple pays charming tribute to English gardens and the gardener's skill. If philosophers' systems are but jugglers' tricks, we must go a ramble into ancient places where men have built gardens. These are a gentleman's meanderings; the poet's apprehension of the garden, Marvell's or Pope's, is wholly absent. For all its "ease," it is a death-dealing philosophy, for it kills the vital instinct, to know.

How can Swift be so utterly different from his mentor? Did he not appropriate his snobbery and hauteur—including his silliest mistakes; did he not borrow his fundamental ideas? On a superficial level the allegory of the Spider and Bee represents Temple's attitudes—and only slightly below the surface, Swift's idea of himself. Restless, self-sufficient, spinning a universe out of his guts, the Spider is everything Temple could not endure in the modern world. The Bee, the freebooter over all of nature and man's works, is simply a figure for Temple himself. Ranging abroad, sipping but not destroying the flowers, enriching himself and bringing home for others honey and wax, sweetness and light, the Bee comes upon the Spider sitting balefully in the center of his nasty web, spitting and cursing, "*A plague split you, said he, for a giddy Son of a Whore; Is it you, with a Vengeance, that have made this Litter here? Could you not look before you, and be d——n'd? Do you think I have nothing else to do (in the Devil's Name) but to Mend and Repair after your Arse?*" Like Sir William, the Bee is inclined to "droll" and turn back the Spider's venom with urbane quips. "*You boast, indeed, of being obliged to no other Creature, but of drawing, and spinning out all from your self . . . You possess a good plentiful Store of Dirt and Poison in your Breast; And, tho' I would by no means, lessen or disparage your genuine Stock of either, yet, I doubt you are somewhat obliged for an Encrease of both, to a little foreign Assistance.*" Doubtless this is how Swift wanted to see himself, a honey bee, like Temple a gentleman ranging above the vulgar, drolling with them, benignly teaching them a thing or two about civilization. But considering that Temple had little light and Swift less sweetness, the allegory is a travesty. How right Arnold was! Poor Bentley and Wotton, so foolhardy as to be right when an aristocrat was wrong, so earnest, pedantic, and shrill, were perfect victims to bloody with borrowed spurs. As *Don Quixote* destroyed love and valor in Spain, said Temple, pedantry will corrupt the commonwealth of learning. What an opportunity for Swift—to exercise his high-mindedness by saving this commonwealth, to exercise his self-hate, by assuming Sir Williams's drollery. But Swift had no drollery; his was a higher destiny. The Bee is only a bit of pretension. To speak in tongues, wtih the venom and imagination of Spiders, was his genius.

What is remarkable in this vignette is the force and vitality of the Spider's personality, the way in which accent and posture call up a radical individualism, perfect in ego, of demonic energy and endless design. So far as the *Battle of the Books* is concerned, one could put this force and vitality down to the artist's success in picturing forth the object of his satire. Except that, even here, the whole vignette is rather an incongruous intrusion in a weak mock-heroic satiric form, a form that was not congenial to Swift. The reason is not far to search. The mock-heroic form can only picture upstarts as inept flailers at this and that, pert posturers, and that is of course the character of the moderns among the books. But that is Temple's manner, not Swift's. The Spider is neither inept nor pert. In his high blood runs the quickening energy of the race of radical individualists that inhabit Swift's satire from first to last. It is they who inherit the earth. It is in his participation in their imaginations that he knows the truth of human existence and gives up the rationlist game. A strange metamorphosis takes place in Swift's mind. His snobbery, nurtured in the school of Moor Park, reinforces his talent for mimicry and parody, makes him hawk about for the grubs and busybodies who are his natural victims. At this point the worm turns, the parodied vulgarian becomes the radical individualist; his energy and design are not to be put down. The satirist begins to think in the pattern of his victim whose radical notions of life and personality become his own. The satire—a satire fit for gentlemen—turns from the vulgarian back upon the "Christian humanist" with his smug assumptions of reason and order. The provincial Irishman in England, the psychological bastard triumphs. The nihilist asserts his rights against the imitator of Temple, the present snob, the Establishmentarian apologist to be. Self-hate becomes hate; posture becomes art.

When he adopts the pert idiom and cracked fancy of one of the figures the snob in him despises, when he is free of his gentlemanly decorum ("proper words in proper places"—*Letter to a Young Gentleman*) and can speak in the crazy, catachrestical images and metaphor of the busy vulgarian, then Swift's mind is free and his invention at its height. ("The author was then young, his invention at its height, and his reading fresh in his head"—"Apology"). The vaunted simplicity and clarity of Swift's prose style are apparent only when he speaks in official tones—in the *Sentiments of a Church-of-England Man*, in the *Sermons*, in the *Letter to a Young Gen-*

tleman, for example. In the great satires he is not only cruelly complex but even mysterious. In the *Tale* his invention took the form of a discredited sort of wit, a debased metaphysical style of runaway metaphors, pseudological relations established by puns and quibbles, unexpected authorities, and odd learning. In this discredited sort of wit he could indulge himself in the guise of a parodist. The pleasures and insights of the *Tale*, the wild correspondences that destroy familiar categories and set the mind erring in a wilderness of doubt, are in this sense stolen fruits. As he adopts the extravagances of his enemies, his invention takes fire and he becomes his enemy, working out his own sceptical ideas in the enemy's guise. It is at this point that the problem of irony, the trope supposed to separate the sheep from the goats, becomes hopelessly complex. The critics begin to subtilize: is it a "persona" who speaks? is it Swift the Anglican rationalist? is it Swift the diabolist? is it confusion worse confounded? Parody imperceptibly seems to pass into positive statement of what really goes on in the world, and goes on world without end, what really is true of human psychology. Then the critic, like a traffic policeman, shrilly signals which way to go: *here*, for an instant, Swift shows himself through the mask, or is it *there?* or everywhere? or nowhere? *Hic et ubique*, the old mole, the fellow in the cellarage there, moves about. The obvious examples in the *Tale* are the ways in which the parody of the prostitute writer, the hireling of six and thirty factions, now supposedly employed to get up an inane farrago to divert the wits from Church and State—the ways in which this parody becomes a positive account of the reality that the world is a madhouse. Scarcely has he begun his silly stuff when he enunciates the most fundamental proposition of the *Tale*, the controlling motion of the satire, that it is "as hard to get quit of number, as of hell." Scarcely has he metamorphosed himself into a madman when he utters the most famous of Swiftian ironies: "Last week I saw a Woman *flay'd*, and you will hardly believe, how much it altered her Person for the worse." The sentence is never quoted as the remark of a madman. If Swift can be at his most philosophical when he is personating a pert Grub Street writer and at his most typically ironic when he is personating a madman, why should he not bring off his most heartfelt exploration of human psychology when he is spinning out the fantastic conceits of clothes and wind in the guise of a maniac Papist, Peter, and a fanatic Puritan, Jack?

Far from resting in the quietism Temple affected to believe man's only relief from pain, Swift, wholly insensitive to his patron's taste for the gardens of Epicurus, has an obsession to follow the implications of various schemes of power or reason or vision to nihilistic conclusions as he imagines their force in human affairs. Thus the characteristic entrapment of the reader in Swift's irony. Led on by the wonderful assurance of his irony towards pedantic fellows like Wotton and Bentley to indulgence in the Augustan game of baiting (in Temple's fine phrase) the "wonderful pretension and visions of men possessed with notions of the strange advancement of learning and science," the reader finds himself before long puzzling over pyrrhonistic, paradoxical, and despairing conclusions in which the satiric victim somehow seems to triumph. Thus the madman of the *Tale* seems to prove the truth of his assumption that life is a tale told by an idiot; thus Peter and Jack who are set up at the outset to be satiric butts of Anglican rationalism end by convincing the reader that their corruptions of the religious spirit are universal and inevitable. Thus the corruptions of English society that Gulliver discovers are, before we are quit of the Yahoos, seen to abide forever in the human psyche, which is bitterly mocked by the Houyhnhnm's impossible reason. Augustan hauteur towards irrationality and egotism gives way to deep and troubling questions (most of them utterly unanswerable) out of the mouths of the assumed satiric victims, and ends with a conviction of their inevitable triumph. Without any doubt Swift hated pyrrhonism and paradox, and of course his religion forbade despair, but what he wished easily to scorn, his imaginative powers made only too real, far more real than the Augustan myth of order and reason. Thus the great objects of Temple's gentlemanly scorn, restlessness, self-sufficiency, and universalist scheming, are equally the objects of Swift's satire, but strangely, inevitably they become in his thought radical and overwhelming aspects of the psyche, a kind of genetic disease—whether manifested as glory, power, or speculative philosophy, always an example of the instinct to kill, of one ego to absorb another: "For what man, in the natural state or course of thinking did ever conceive it in his power to reduce the notions of all mankind exactly to the same length and breadth, and height of his own?" Swift asks the question, with lipservice to the Augustan norm of common understanding and common forms, but the answer is that examples of men "in the natural state or course of thinking" are nowhere to be found. Rather, the world is a madhouse. Temple would smile serenely at reports of the madhouse that might filter into his garden—ah, the "sufficiency" of man, he would sigh. But Swift imagined "sufficiency" in the figure of the Spider, spinning a poisonous web of a universe out of his own guts, a universe of which he is the only begetter and the only denizen. Dryden and Pope love to dilate on the busy-ness of grubs. "Cool was his kitchen but his brains were hot," Dryden says of Corah, his Puritan malcontent. Pope sets his dunces frenetically spinning their cobwebs over the eye of day. Restlessness, it seems, is a debility of the lower classes, though easily infectious in the whole society. For Pascal the matter is more awesome, touching on the existential misery of the race: "All men's misfortunes spring from the single cause that they cannot rest quietly in one room." Swift, like Temple and Dryden and Pope, has his snobbery; the *Tale* begins with top-lofty scorn of rampant restlessness in Grub Street, and we are to understand that the Wottons and Bentleys smell of the lamp not because they love learning but because they cannot stop concocting absurd and pedantic theories. But in Swift the Augustan snobbery is soon put aside as the examples broaden—from Louis XIV, ever gloriously nervous to sally forth "to fright children from their bread and butter," to Descartes, spinning his "romantick" vortices; from Jack the Puritan to Peter the Catholic; from silly critics and beaux to the pensioners of court and camp and church and city. It is a Hobbesian landscape—every member of the race busily preparing his deadly aggression against his fellow—but a Pascalian overview of the dismal scene, mindful of the desperate office of reason to know the narrow room of dignity. What is unique in Swift is the absolute hatred of pretensions to dignity in busy "scholastic midwifery" that delivers meanings never conceived from "the universal mother," night, which is nothing. Dignity is found in hatred.

The fact is that we should not have Swift at all, his terrible truths, if he were a mere parodist, if his imagination did not work through the psychologies of the outrageous figures he officially hates. Their indecorums, their farfetched metaphors, their absolute egotism free his imagination, defrock the priest, and give us a radical and libertine thinker. The best of Swift is not to be found when he is following his own ideal of "proper words in proper places" or when he is speaking as a priest but when he has forgotten his urbane purview of the hell of lesser creatures, and, speaking in their tongues, can imagine the world they see. Speaking in the tongues of madmen, he had always the excuse that whatever shocking thoughts were expressed were not after all *in propria persona*. That was exactly his defense of himself when the clear implications of the *Tale's* indecorous language and subversive thoughts had aroused suspicions of his orthodoxy and resentment of his improprieties. Then he thought it expedient to append an "Apology" of his orthodoxy to the fifth edition of 1710. Did not those exceptionable opinions and manners come plainly in the voices of "illiterate scribblers, prostitute in their reputations, vicious in their lives, and ruin'd in their fortunes, who to the shame of good sense as well as piety, are greedily read, merely upon the strength of bold, false and impious assertions, mixt with unmannerly reflection upon the priesthood, and openly intended against all religion"? This sort of parody was the way to satirize the "corruptions in religion and learning." "Men of taste" would understand that. And why should any Anglican clergyman be angry to see fanaticism and superstition (i.e., Puritanism and Popery) exposed? Even in this sobersided apology, so different in tone from the rest of the book, he cannot quite stay sober but must play the fool. The book is "calculated to live at least as long as our language"; his original intention was to have had four machines for rising above the crowd rather than the three, for that would have been more cabbalistic; the "chasms" in the work (referring to two of the zaniest passages of Section 9, "A Digression on Madness": "THERE is in Mankind a certain * * * *Hic multa desiderantur* * * * And this I take to be a clear Solution of the Matter," and the passage discussed below) would have been fewer had not the manuscript got out of his hands. In truth, Swift was nearly incapable of saying anything in *propria persona.* That the *Tale* "celebrates the Church of England as the most perfect of all others in discipline and doctrine" is patently absurd— unless we are to believe that what is *celebrated* is insipid, without force or vitality. No reader's interest is in Martin; every reader's interest is in the psychopathology of religious experience figured in Jack and Peter. Doubtless Dr. Swift was perfectly orthodox and wanted to say the best for his Church; it is only when he is someone else—all the time in the *Tale*—that he says the worst.

In a strange way, Swift's worst instincts led him to his most creative work, or to be fair, he had the glory to turn his worst instincts, snobbery and hatred, to the service of his creative mind. Grinding Sir William Temple's axe (a surrogate for his own), mimicking vulgarian types he fancied an affront to Sir William's aristocratic repose, he imagined, when he began to speak in tongues, the madness of all men; driven by an Anglo-Irishman's hatred of dissenters and Catholics, he imagined the destructiveness of the religious personality. Parody, the satiric device encouraged in Swift by the snobberies of the Temple circle, led him to a sympathy (perhaps largely unconscious, though not entirely so) with the enemy he mocked, so that in the grubby or mad postures he affects he is liberated from the decorums of his class and office. He can be as libertine as he pleases speaking in the crazy metaphysical conceits and ingenuities of the character parodied. Catachresis is a sort of franchise.

Here is the crux of the notorious problem of Swift's irony—whether we are to believe the speaking voice, or invert it, or twist it north-northwest, or throw up our hands.

Rabelais in His Right Mind

The fool Swift sets up for is paradox-crammed; he feeds on air, all the winds that blow. He packs up unconsidered trifles and retails them as the heart of the mystery. If he has a lot of the main-chancing Autolycus in him, peddling modern gew-gaws, he has even more of the occultist, seeking the best in the worst, translating excrement to ecstasy. Being so disreputable, he need not be a respecter of persons. Considerations that never trouble the sleep of the orthodox—that historically Christians have a remarkable record as maniacs (he would overstate the case and say an impeccable record), that glorious kings may live to frighten children from their bread and butter, that many people believe that scholastic reasoning can turn a stale crust of bread into a shoulder of mutton—suggest to him the truth of his fondest dream, that the world is a more perfect version of Bedlam hospital. There sit the doctors who should heal us, raking in their own dung. Suddenly the speaker, looking in at the grate of a madman's cell, is so giddy he cannot find words to disclose his secret to the reader. *"Heark in your ear."* A "chasm" in the manuscript and a footnote, *"I cannot conjecture what the Author means here, or how this chasm could be fill'd, tho' it is capable of more than one interpretation."* Left with the chasm—and the stagy machinery of various voices, postures, and costumes, and a choice of fantastic conceits of wind and clothes—the reader can try to make his own paradoxes to fill in the psychology of man, but the poor, bare, forked animal is not to be discovered—only suits of clothes or bags of wind, social conditioning or private self-gratification. Such realities of Swift-the-fool set Swift-the-rationalist in a rage. If the fool's crazy imagination is fun in its parody of men's antic dispositions, it is painful, too, in the knowledge it gives us in nerve and bone that here is the reality of the way men live. Are we in the presence of an aristocratic ironist mimicking egregious idiots or a satanic conjurer calling up the damned human race.?

An obvious and crucial example of Swift's appropriation of the idiot voice to express his own subversive thoughts is his use of sexual imagery. Solemnly, clerically, he tells us in the "Apology" that *"lewd Words, or dangerous Opinions though printed by halves, fill the Reader's Mind with ill Idea's, and of these the Author cannot be accused. For the judicious Reader will find that the severest Stroaks of Satyr in his Book are levelled against the modern Custom of Employing Wit upon those Topicks, of which there is a remarkable Instance in the 153d. Page, as well as in several others, tho perhaps once or twice exprest in too free a manner, excusable only for the Reasons already alledged."* On that page in "A Digression in Praise of Digressions" (*Works,*

1:92–93) the fool "author" complains that modern wit is running dry, including even the vogue of deducing similitudes, allusions, and applications from the pudenda of either sex. The genius of the moderns, like the stature of Indian pygmies, seems to be proportionate to the length of their penises. So much for modern wit, condemned out of his own mouth. The only fly in this ointment for fretted sensibilities is that if we eliminate the raw sexual metaphors that define inspiration, the character of Jack, the glory of kings, we have precious little left. In short, Swift, not the salacious modern, is in need of the pudenda of either sex to deduce similitudes, allusions, and applications, simply because he, Swift, sees sexuality as essential to his explanation of psychology. Like literary fools in a long tradition, he is hardly to be judged by his sincerity.

To digress in the midst of digression, to address the universe ("This, O universe! is the adventurous Attempt of me thy Secretary"), to ape solemn impostors, to spin out catachrestical conceits—these are tricks to relieve oneself of the necessity of logic. When Swift wrote as a sober historian of Queen Anne's last years, he wrote with *parti pris* but with the pretense of logic; in the *Tale* and in *Gulliver* history is treated as though it makes no sense at all, except as a case book in abnormal psychology. Psycho-logic deals with strange and unsuspected correspondences. The fool is free to deal in such correspondences where rational explanations break down. Why did a mighty king for thirty years frighten children from their bread and butter, amuse himself to take and lose towns, beat armies and be beaten, lay waste subject and stranger, friend and foe? All the philosophers dispute the causes natural, moral, and political. The truth lies in his bowels, the vapors from which animate his brain and at last conclude in a *fistula in ano*, in that region especially precious, according to Paracelsus, for furnishing perfume. Here is Swift in idiotic guise, mimicking dark authors, availing himself of their freedom from logic to strike out the connection between glorious history and a man's bowels. Louis XIV's glory is "caused," it seems, by his narcissism and retentivity. The touch about perfume seems exactly right to describe quite literally the pleasure men find in their own bowels. Such mad correspondences may not impress an historian, but in fact Louis's conduct does defy ordinary historical explanations. The historian David Ogg writes ironically of Louis's mysterious attack on Holland in 1672: "Louis was prompted by three motives worthy of a really great King—'religion,' glory, and revenge, motives strikingly contrasted with the economic calculations of Colbert and other Europeans. It was as if seventeenth-century Europe was suddenly transformed into Old Testament Israel, and at no point in the reign did there seem such brilliant justification for the parallel between Jehovah and Louis XIV."[13] On the birth of the Dauphin, Louis had preached to him a sermon in which he was compared with God and the Dauphin with Jesus Christ. The Dauphin's chief characteristic turned out to be, Ogg writes, an insipid lassitude. As for Louis's wars, after years of amusing slaughter, they left the French nation at the boundaries where it began, but starving, and with Europe united against it.

Because Swift's use of the fool bears resemblance to that of Erasmus and Rabelais, we can understand a good deal about his cast of mind by suggesting the similarities and the crucial differences.

No one who has read both these treatises on delusion, *The Praise of Folly* and the "Digression concerning Madness," can doubt that Swift is deliberately parodying Erasmus. Folly is quite as aware of the dregs of life as Swift—his picture of a decaying whore is nearly as withering as Strephon's discovery of Chloe—yet Erasmus knows that Folly's business is not to wither but encourage life. But Erasmus's genial, humanistic scepticism becomes in Swift's mind the ultimate horror rather than the final wisdom. Self-love, always a delusion, has this to be said for it, says Folly, will he who hates himself love anyone? Swift hates his fool and that fool in himself. By reducing the world to a playhouse and the playhouse to a set of masks that the maskers gladly accept in lieu of their real selves, Erasmus's Folly comes in the end to accept Paul's words: "We are fools for Christ's sake" and "Let him that seems to be wise among you become a fool, that he may be wise." Reality exists only in God and even a peroration, a summing up of our folly, is impossible: "I see that you are expecting a peroration, but you are just too foolish if you suppose that after I have poured out a hodgepodge of words like this I can recall anything I have said. There is an old saying 'I hate a pot-companion with a memory.'" Swift's manner is similar ("I my self, the Author of these momentous Truths, am a Person, whose Imaginations are hard-mouth'd, and exceedingly disposed to run away with his *Reason*"—sec. 9) but crazier, being entirely free of any thread of argument; the device, however, is the same—the whirling mountebank upon the stage itinerant (see Holbein's illustration), the quick, inane changes, the mocking seriousness and serious mockery, the deliberate attempt to make received wisdom fade away like a dream in paradoxes and contradictions. But Swift hates this theater of illusion and wants to make the play come out right in this world, not the next (though with no expectation of success). In a Christian world of Erasmus's sort he would have to be counted a man of little wisdom. He knows that satire is resented by none—the world's posteriors are calloused and every man carries with him a racket to bandy the ball from himself into the crowd. The satirist is as great a fool as the fanatic preacher who shouts in the public place "that all are gone astray; that there is none that doth good, no not one . . . ." And yet Swift hates the Epicurean fool who "creams off nature," who teaches the use of "artificial mediums, false lights, refracted angles, varnish and tinsel." That one must play the fool to whip the dog truth out from its kennel when Lady the brach may stand by the fire and stink, this reality is both a source of energy to Swift the artist and of terrible anguish to Swift the rationalist. From this point of view Erasmus's solution of praising delusion is either an act of faith—or a failure of nerve.

What there is of Rabelais in Swift—and what there isn't—shows up another facet of his personality. The search for the oracle, some occult maggot at the center of life, is a futile chase. Swift as well as Rabelais likes to lead on the reader—Rabelais because he believes the verb *trinquer* conveys a sufficient wisdom, Swift because he wants to afflict his reader with his own anxiety. Swift, especially, likes to bait critics, warning them that there is a "superficial Vein among many Readers of the present Age, who will by no means be persuaded to inspect beyond the Surface and Rind of Things; whereas *Wisdom* is a *Fox*, who, after long hunting, will cost you the Pains to dig out. 'Tis a *Cheese*, which by how much the richer, has the thicker, the homelier, and the coarser Coat; and whereof to a judicious Palate, the Maggots are the best . . . 'tis a *Nut*, which unless you chuse with Judgment, may cost you a Tooth, and pay you with nothing but a *Worm*" (sec. 1). What does this mean? Doubtless it satirizes party hacks and small critics who appear wise by hinting at a meaning, but it recalls very explicitly Rabelais's prologue to the first book. "In imitation of a dog, it becomes you to be wise, to smell, feel, and have in estimation these fair goodly books, stuffed with high conceptions . . . you must break the bone, and suck out the marrow,—that is, my allegorical sense . . . signified by these Pythagorean symbols." If you think such tales as I tell, of codpieces, of bacon, of peas are mere foolery, look deeply for the allegorical and sublime sense, says Rabelais. For Plato's philosophical dog worrying a marrow bone, Swift substitutes a fox, a rotten cheese, a hard but wormy nut— fleering replaces fun. Like Diogenes, Rabelais will thump a tub to make a great pother, as though there were some significance in the thumping. Wasn't Socrates, that Silenus, always playing the fool? But what can you believe of a drunkard? (Prologue, bk. 3) Swift throws out his tub to take off attention from others; his work, like other deep pieces such as *Tom*

Thumb or *Tommy Potts* or *The Hind and the Panther,* has its dark Pythagorean meanings. The wisdom of Socrates is to be found in his types and fables. But he is only a hack, threadbare and broken, and (later on) quite mad.

Pope's character of Swift in the *Dunciad*'s invocation—that of a quickchange artist who may choose, among other guises, "to laugh and shake in Rabelais's easy chair"—is less accurate than honorific. Though Swift borrowed much of Rabelais's foolish guise, and often in similar words, he could not have imagined Rabelais's system of strange and exhilarating correspondences that unify and bless life, celebrating scoundrels, pedants, subversives, hobby-horses, and rapists as agents of life, even while informing the whole with a love of humane letters, natural history, and civil law. Rabelais can celebrate, in a sentimental and moving context, the dead Queen Baldebec's acres of *"petit con."* (Contrast Swift's handling of the same image in the vignette of the Brobdingnagian maid of honor's obscene toying with Gulliver.) Gargantua breaks wind so festively that 106,000 little men and women are engendered. (Contrast Swift's handling of the same image in the *Tale*'s description of the communication of spirit among Puritans.) Panurge, tired of amorous flowers of rhetoric, makes an utterly vulgar approach to a grand lady of Paris. Rejected, annoyed by her nice airs, he sprinkles essence of bitch-in-heat over her while she is at prayers and she is assaulted by 600,014 dogs. (Contrast Swift's gruesome story of the Aeolian priests who blow into one another's anuses, thus becoming inspired vessels of the Lord [Acts 9:15], and expel wind to teach, for learning puffeth a man up [I Cor. 8:1], or convey oracular gusts into the genitals of females, thus refining a carnal into a spiritual ecstasy.) Rabelais plays the fool to create a delicious and gay wishfulfillment fantasy that escapes all propriety and brings the backsided part of life into its real relation with the sublime. His cruelty is not oppressive because it remains in the comic domain of wish-fulfillment. Swift, on the contrary, is the master of exhibiting, with hatred, the backsided reality of sublime pretensions. Changing the drunkard for the madman, as befits the change from fantastic comedy to reductive satire, Swift has a cruelty that is owing to his desire to show up the "fantastic" quality of actuality. Fantastic metaphors are moved to the edge of literal statement (or slander). Clearly he wants to suggest that, literally, Puritan fanaticism is a perverse sexuality. The fool's manner in the *Tale* (and in other satires) is in large part a covert way of speaking the unspeakable. Panurge's spinning out of the fantasy of monetary debt that binds all men into a universal commonwealth has been taken for a clown's serious metaphor for the brotherhood of man, under natural and divine law. Swift's generation of the vast system of clothes to explain the universe and the microcosm of man is a bitter parody, funny as it is, of man as a creature made in God's image. That the souls of man are in their clothes is an apparent fantasy that turns out to be only a slight exaggeration.

Voltaire and Coleridge described in remarkably similar terms the paradox of Swift's taking into his bitter imagination the festive manner of Rabelais. For Voltaire, Swift was *"Rabelais dans son bon sens,"* and Coleridge found in Swift "the soul of Rabelais dwelling in a dry place." Both judgments seem impossible contradictions. Had Rabelais been "in his right mind," he would have had nothing to say; had the soul of Rabelais inhabited a dry place, it would have been a dead soul. And yet both judgments are exactly descriptive of Swift. Both Rabelais and Swift invent fantastic images, spun out to the edge of sanity, both play the fool to reduce the sublime to the thing sublimated, but Swift drives the grotesque and the fantastic into the actual, i.e., he rationalizes the fantastic. That is his way with satire, and with life. That is why he can be said to be Rabelais in his right mind, inhabiting a dry place.

Only in the guise of the fool, inventing some fantastic comic fiction, was Swift able to reach the frontier of tragedy. Were he merely a reductive satirist, looking down with Augustan serenity upon the pageant of folly, we should not feel the anguish that pervades all his satires. How shall we account for this anguish except as the tragic conflict of a rationalist personality, seeking everywhere the leaven of good sense that his Anglican confession, its assumption of natural law and civil polity, warrants as the condition of a decent life, but finding nowhere anything but radical egotism, a fatal talent for using the rational faculty for explaining away in sublime terms ordinary instincts for aggression and self-gratification? A conviction, moreover, of the operation of the "spirit" by either social conditioning or necessities of body mechanics, is so overwhelmingly present in every part of the *Tale* that it amounts to a universalism of the kind the satirist attacks in Lucretius and Descartes, among other systemizers. Although Lucretius and Descartes are clearly objects of satire, as their preeminent place in the madhouse shows, their mechanistic systems are simply appropriated to provide the pervasive imagery of sublime perversions. If we read the *Tale* with any regard to what is in the text rather than with a pre-determination of what it *must* or *ought* to mean, considering Swift's holy orders, it is obvious that by Swift's lights the history of Christianity is one of tyranny over mind and body by means of a subtle combination of ingenious rationality and holy mystery (Peter), or of nihilistic and aggressive egotism by means of inner spiritual light and hatred of visible authority. It is obvious as well that this religious judgment is given larger, in fact universal, application to all sublime pretensions in history. We have, then, this paradoxical technique—satire by way of parody, but also a fool's truth about the human condition told in the catachresis and fantasy of the parody. It is useless to try to rationalize these divided aims; they represent a divided soul in Swift. His allegiance to Augustan decorums and to his holy office was never surrendered or betrayed; rather, the undermining of the very assumptions of that decorum and that office is accomplished in such outrageous guises and language that the priest can almost legitimately protest that *he* is innocent of "ill meanings."

The manners of Erasmus and Rabelais afforded him the necessary cover. Like Rabelais he writes about nothing; like Erasmus he forgets what he is saying. One could say that these are Jesuitical subtleties, betraying an hypocrite, were it not for the virulent hate Swift obviously bears the fools through whom he speaks his truth. What he hates is what they know, and, inhabiting them, what he knows. And against what he knows, what he would believe and would have others believe, always a will-o'-the-wisp of an ideal, works to produce his violent irony. This inconsistency is a fault only if one wants doctrine or polemics as the solution to ultimate questions. The inconsistency is, in short, the human fate, as is the self-hatred that animates it. The love of reason is, after all, also a fear of the irrational, and as a sublimation of irrational instincts, naturally subject to all the distortions and perversions Swift is so fond of demonstrating. Although reason in Christian story is subject to various incapacities, according as the believer moves nearer to or further from the pessimism of Augustine and Luther—and Swift in his sermons utters conventional cautions—it nevertheless plays as important a role as in classical thought. For Swift the priest, as for many seventeenth-century Anglicans, reason holds a place only a shade less compelling among the faculties than it does in Arminianism. It is a fool—the libertine idiot of the *Mechanical Operation of the Spirit* and the madman of the "Digression concerning Madness"—that Swift analyzes the reason in a way other than conventional, in a way that goes to the quick of the living man. The fool confuses the frontiers of true and false, sense and nonsense, good and evil, and in metaphors so indecorous that it might seem that the top-lofty Augustan trained in the school of Temple was merely putting us through our paces as gentlemanly ironists, were it not that the confusions bring us to Swift's fundamental insights in the *Tale*. One of the most startling of the fool's images, exploiting metaphysical catachresis (the technique mastered in parody) but illustrating perfectly the tragedy of psyche in which reason and morality serve egotism and aggression, is the famous "bird of paradise" passage (sec. 8). Having got through the scurrilous explanation of female inspiration by way of the genitals, the refining of a carnal into a spiritual ecstacy, the fool explains it all:

> AND, whereas the mind of Man, when he gives the Spur and Bridle to his Thoughts, doth never stop, but naturally sallies out into both extreams, of High and Low, of Good and Evil; His first Flight of Fancy, commonly transports Him to Idea's of what is most perfect, finished, and exalted; till having soared out of his own Reach and Sight, not well perceiving how near the Frontiers of Height and Depth, border upon each other; With the same Course and Wing, he falls down plum into the lowest Bottom of Things; like one who travels the *East* into the *West*, or like a strait Line drawn by its own Length into a Circle. Whether a Tincture of Malice in our Natures, makes us fond of furnishing every bright Idea with its Reverse; Or, whether Reason reflecting upon the Sum of Things, can, like the Sun, serve only to enlighten one half of the Globe, leaving the other half, by Necessity, under Shade and Darkness; Or, whether Fancy flying up to the imagination of what is Highest and Best, becomes over shot, and spent, and weary and suddenly falls, like a dead Bird of Paradise, to the Ground. Or, whether, after all these *Metaphysical* Conjectures I have not entirely missed the true Reason.

Cavalier, bird, geometer, astronomer, mythological creature: all these far-fetched metaphysical metaphors, worthy certainly of Donne, represent the mind of man, all develop from the tragic mystery that good and evil border each other: idealism becomes fanaticism; the straight path turns full circle unawares, merely by its indefinite prolongation; an excess of light on one object obscures another; idealism wearies the spirit and kills. All this is poetry, outwardly of the corrupt metaphysical breed and so stuff of comedy (see Johnson on Cowley), but behind the comic mask a moving image of the inescapable anxiety of being a man. Such a perception is close to religious feeling—this, besides its "metaphysical" account of the psychological origin of God and the devil. The zany license of the fool pose allows the unexpected association, the pert jumps of thought, the imaginative generation. Where satire verges on such human mysteries, it is of course "confused"—assurance yields to description, reductive certainly but only apparently fantastic. Incapable of Blake's vision, Swift had something of his understanding, that God and the devil are ordinarily reversed by the pretense of reason.

Evolution of an Image

The "bird of paradise" image is only typical of metaphysical foolery in the *Tale* that becomes serious symbolic expression. It is a kind of gloss on the four central images—"the mad crowd," the wind mechanics of the Aeolists, the clothes religion, and the madhouse. The clothes and wind religions are metaphysical exfoliations of the fundamental proposition of the *Tale,* that to escape the "mad crowd" is a radical need only to be compared with the hunger for salvation, and the "madhouse" is a generalized version of clothes and wind mechanics. To understand the seriousness of this fool's system, it is helpful to try to reconstruct the evolution of the "wind" image in Swift's mind as he appropriated the systems of Lucretius and Descartes to his own purposes. Here we can see how, in the midst of satire of the spider personality in these great universal philosophers, Swift's irony turns back upon the reader his assumption of Augustan superiority and makes of the system that is supposedly the object of contempt the real explanation of human conduct.

How to get quit of number? Room enough overhead, but how to reach it? Even Socrates, says the zany, suspended himself in a basket to help contemplation. This slight allusion to Aristophanes's *Clouds* suggests the mad train of thought that, ransacking Lucretius and Descartes, spicing the olio with odd bits from scholastic philosophy and Scripture, yoked illustrations, comparisons, and allusions into the grand conceptual metaphor of wind. The process is exactly as Johnson describes metaphysical wit, only here the occult resemblances are so perverse, the industry so "ant-like" (F. R. Leavis's wonderful epithet for Swift's imaginative processes),[14] that Johnson might well have enjoyed the parody of what he thought in any case an unnatural talent, especially so as the working out of the metaphor concludes with an adaptation of Donne's compass image that Johnson singles out for special contempt. Swift's joke, however, is that the joke is serious, creating the devastating analysis of the "inspired" religious personality.

Socrate's great god Vortex is discovered, like the Aeolist's and Jack the Puritan's inspiration, in the bowels. Every man his own wind machine, a fart is perfect evidence of Vortex within. Says Socrates to his pupil Strepsiades (who is practicing farting): "Shalt thou then a sound so loud and profound from the belly diminutive send,/And shall not the high and infinite Sky go thundering on without end?/For both, you will find, on an impulse of wind and similar causes depend." One must rise to ply the philosopher's trade. There is no god but Vortex; all rumbles are holy and by necessity, in the microcosm of the bowels as well as in the macrocosm of the Clouds. Swift would take up the idea of necessity in inspiration, not merely to carry on Aristophanes's scatological joke about the urgency of the intestinal tract, but to illustrate the compulsion under which the brain works, just when pretensions of sublimity, of will and reason, are most elaborate. And like Socrates's explanation of the similarity between internal vapors and the Clouds, the Aeolists have their theory of the microcosm of man and the macrocosm of universe, for as vapors ascend from the lower faculties to water the imagination, so mists may arise from a jakes to form clouds overcasting the face of nature.

The connection of anality with inspiration is so fixed in Swift's mind that he cannot think of the pretensions of philosophers without thinking of defecation. Orators, he says, climb above the crowd so as to let their words drop upon the crowd, which obediently lift up their open mouths in a plane perpendicular to a line from the zenith to the center of the earth, so that no droppings conveyed by gravity will be lost. They are so many jakes. Were the image itself not enough to make clear Swift's idea that the desire to elevate oneself is a desire to dirty others and that respect for the "elevated" is a desire to be dirtied, the explanation of this mechanics by an allusion to Lucretius makes the train of ideas obvious. Sitting in a citadel, alone, aloof, Lucretius watches from his elevation others wandering aimlessly, pitting their wits against one another, struggling to gain the pinnacles (*De Rerum Natura*, 2. 1–61). (The context of Swift's allusion suggests that he developed his image of the "mad crowd" and the hellish struggle to get above it from this reading of Lucretius.) Here Lucretius explains sensation of bodies by the eternal downward stream of atoms, inclined ever so slightly so as to collide occasionally and coalesce. Swift applies this to words and then jumps to 4. 26–521, where Lucretius explains sensation by the penetration of the senses by films of atoms from a distant object. Though hearing is the sense involved, the references to jaws and circles and mouths suggest taste. The auditors like to taste the droppings. And then a prurient joke about ladies in the circle of boxes enjoying lewd wit that runs in a line into a circle makes the imagery "complete"—anal, genital, and oral. At the outset of the *Tale*, then, the associations—suggested only by metaphor—by which later on Aeolist inspiration is defined. Lucretian mechanistic theory will be reduced to anal-genital-oral stimulation and this "psychology" will be equated with various sublimities; the indwelling spirit of the Lord, glory in empire, in philosophy, in religion become wind rushing through tubes and orifices.

The exposition of Aeolist religion beings (end of sec. 6) with an invocation of Lucretius (1. 934) and a parody (sec. 8) of Lucretian cosmology (bk. 5). The accidental concourse of atoms that brought forth land, sea, and sky, stars and sun and the round moon, the vegetables and man himself, must reverse itself and all things perish in an atomic cataclysm. Do not be so superstitious as to think that the gods control this, or that the universe is created for the sake of man. Swift's adaptation (sec. 8) reads, "The Learned *Æolists*, maintain the Original Cause of all Things to be *Wind*, from which Principle this whole Universe was at first produced, and into which it must at last be resolved; that the same Breath which had kindled, and blew *up* the Flame of Nature, should one day blow it *out*. *Quod procul a nobis flectat Fortuna gubernans.*"

Lucretius's prayer to Fortune (5. 107) to spare us this fate is ironic, running contrary to his own principles, since destiny is indifferent to man and it is to inculcate this anti-superstition that he says he writes. Perhaps Swift incorporated the prayer for the same purpose—to mock those who create gods in their own image. To this system he adds a scholastic distinction of the informing form—here, wind—and some word quibbles from hermetic philosophers connecting wind and spirit.

The mock-theology relieves Swift of all decorum and the fool in him, an ingenious modern witling, crazily yokes by force and violence all the possible implications of the metaphor: wind is the material of the universe, spirit, breath of our nostrils, flatulence, farting, belching, prophesying, preaching, the quality of being puffed up by learning (1 Cor. 8:1), the thirty-two points of the compass rose (of the same importance as the thirty-nine articles), the four corners of the world corresponding to the four winds and equivalent to the four points of the body (anus, mouth, left and right arms), the soaring of the mind, the gasping and panting after fame—and more.

With such mystical correspondences in the universe and the little world of man, and between the two, the Aeolists are ready for mysteries and rites. Here Swift is on his own, Lucretius having provided the general idea of materialistic explanations of the mind and spirit and of atomistic winds. (Words are but wind, says Swift; words are but material particles sent steaming in the air, says Lucretius [bk. 4]). Every rite is some sexual application of wind, variations of the oral, genital, anal imagery. The Aeolists have their Communion: " . . . several Hundreds link'd together in a circular Chain, with every Man a Pair of Bellows applied to his Neighbour's Breech, by which they blew up each other" (sec. 8). When replete they belch or fart into one another's mouths, thus becoming vessels of the Lord (Acts 9:15). Since their gods are the winds, they convey wind into the posteriors of their priests, who then belch for their disciples. Female priests of course receive inspiration through "a Receptacle of greater Capacity," thus refining "a Carnal into a Spiritual Extasie."

By resolutely twisting Lucretius's explanation of sensation (bk. 4), Swift is able to extend the sexual implications of inspiration to another sublimity, princely glory. I have shown, says Lucretius, how all things are atoms flying through space, how objects are created (by accidental hookings of atoms inclined this way and that), how mind also is a wind of atoms. What now are images of things but a sort of outer skin perpetually peeled off the surface and flying about, wearing the aspect and form of the object from whose body it has emanated? There follows a complete mechanics of these flimsy atomistic images. By collision of images a centaur may be created, or in sleep a mind so disposed by its particular contexture of atoms may receive an image aimlessly floating in the air. It is not, however, the senses that are deceived but the mind, for the mind gives us a false account of the discrepancies between the films and the objects. So heaven's entire firmament may appear in a puddle no bigger than a finger's breadth. Senses are true and do not lie but reason is fallible. Lucretius is not a man for romance: we do not need tales of Pan piping in the haunted woods but only a theory about rebounding atoms of sound. Our organs were not created to help us, but the organ, having been created by a fortunate conunction of atoms, demands its use.

This sense mechanics being admitted, we have exactly Swift's madman's theory of the imagination: flimsy films "from the superficies of things" are flying about everywhere so that a mind ready to receive particular images, according to its disposition, will find them, and grotesque combinations of them, available in the ambient airs (4.722–822). Now, as to sex, for that instinct most obviously victim of the dangerous prevalence of the imagination, Lucretius has a complete explanation (4.1037–1191). The one stimulus that draws the human seed from the human body is a human form. The seed collecting in the generative organ is ejected in the direction from which the film of a bodily form floats into the mind. Swift (sec. 9) refers to Lucretius (4.1048–65). When the film of a (desired) absent human form strikes upon the senses, the seed of generation is dislodged and swells the sexual organs. Hence follows the will to eject it in the direction of one's lust. The body makes for the source from which the mind is pierced by love. The shafts of Venus create a yearning to transmit the substance of one body into another. Though absent, the object of love will haunt one with these images. Keep such images far off by spilling your seed elsewhere. And then Swift's "madman" explains history by reference to this theory of Lucretius (sec. 9). A certain prince (Henri IV of France) made mysterious preparations for war, alarming the whole of Europe. Crowns trembled, small politicians made conjectures—was it a scheme for universal monarchy? for pulling down the Pope? for subduing the Turk? All this conjecture is resolved when the prince is stabbed by an assassin, his vapors fly out, and it is discovered that it was all owing to a female "whose Eyes had raised a Protuberancy, and, before Emission, she was removed into an Enemy's Country." The collected semen having nothing but the image to go to, turns adust, converts to choler, goes up the spinal duct to the brain. So the same principle that moves a bully to break the windows of the whore who jilts him causes a great prince to raise armies and dream of battles.

But even in the midst of Venus's toils the mind will receive images of other bodies more compelling than the real one over which the hands roam. Naturally this insatiable appetite is most subject to false appearances. A sallow wench is proclaimed a nutbrown maid, a slattern has sweet disorder, a stringy female is lithe as a gazelle; pendulous-breasted, she is Ceres suckling Bacchus, waspish harridans burn with a gemlike flame. How wearisome this delusion, says Lucretius. Truth is that Venus herself is only a human body, smelly and foul, but perfumed and ornamented. Had one the will, one could know this truth—even though a lady's dressing room is said to be inviolate.

How close is all this to Swift, with his talk of ladies' dressing rooms, of happiness as "a perpetual possession of being well-deceived"! It is from the larger context of Lucretius's explanation of sensation and sex (bk. 4) that Swift has borrowed the central conception of this famous passage of the "Digression on Madness" (sec. 9):

> He that can with *Epicurus* content his Ideas with the *Films* and *Images* that fly off upon his Senses from the *Superficies* of Things; Such a Man truly wise, creams off Nature, leaving the Sower and the Dregs, for Philosophy and Reason to lap up. This is the sublime and refined Point of Felicity, called, *the Possession of being well deceived*; The Serene Peaceful State of being a Fool among Knaves. . . .

A little earlier, he had said:

> The Question is only this. . . . Whether Things, that have Place in the *Imagination*, may not properly be said to exist. . . . How fade and insipid do all Objects accost us that are not convey'd in the Vehicle of *Delusion*? How shrunk is every Thing, as it appears in the Glass of Nature? So that if it were not for the Assis-

tance of Artificial *Mediums,* false Lights, refracted Angles, Varnish, and Tinsel, there would be a mighty Level in the Felicity and Enjoyments of Mortal Men.

How are we to read all this parody of Lucretius? Does he stand for all mad systemizers who strike a pompous and pedantic posture above the crowd? Does the speaking voice that spouts his theories represent modern libertine thought (for the revival of atomic philosophy had made Epicurus "modern")? Certainly Epicurus and Lucretius are exemplars of the academicians of Bedlam because they hoped to reduce the notions of all mankind exactly to the same length and breadth as their own (according to Swift's simplistic notion of them, which ignores their pre-eminent good sense and reasonableness). The caricature of Lucretius would seem to suggest only a vivacious version of the Temple snobbery. The Lucretian picture presented notions of a world made up by accidental collision of atoms, indifferent to man, of mental and spiritual processes no more than a jiggling of the atoms of the nerves, of imagination as only a licentious receptivity to films and images floating in the ambient airs, of will and desire as tissues of delusion—these notions are certainly hostile to a Christian's faith. And yet, though the Lucretian picture remains a poetic image, what it symbolizes, a materialistic reality, runs strongly in Swift's mind. It is after all the only basis of the satire of the "abuses" in religion and learning, and those "abuses" are so generalized as to be more properly denominated "the inevitable results of religion and learning." The *Tale* does not reassure the reader of the truths of Christianity. On the contrary, it is a devastatingly convincing attack on the very sublimities that are essential to Christianity. If dissenters and papists are its ostensible object of attack, we should remember that these two groups repesent the mainstream of Christian experience. They represent, moreover, something far more important, the two aspects of religious experience, the inner voice and the authority of the visible community of the Church. Swift's satire does exactly what he condemns revolutionists in empire, religion, and philosophy for doing—it universalizes. "I stay awake nights," says Lucretius, "to give you this look into the heart of hidden things" (4.143). "Since my vein is once opened," says Swift's voice, "I am content to exhaust it at a running . . . for the universal benefit of mankind." Such statements, while certainly parodies of the Augustan universalizing inclination, must be seen as expressing a tendency in Swift himself. His development of the sexual origin of "sublimity" is too pervasive and of too wide an application—both to various aspects of life and to the range of history—to be anything but a dark vision of the human condition. His development of the mechanical operation of the spirit leaves precious little room for genuine spirituality. Certainly, his explanation of glory in empire, philosophy, and religion is utterly serious. The satire does not fall back upon the fool, but the fool is the agent by which Swift freed his imagination and gave vent to his deepest thoughts.

The use of Lucretius is the most pervasive example in the *Tale*—though, as we have argued, there are many others—of the divided aims of parody on the one hand and of serious vision on the other. One can hardly repeat too often that Swift's imagination begins in parody and takes fire from the mad elaborations of metaphor so that catachresis is not only his liberation from Augustan decorums but the sluice gate by which his subversive instincts escape repression. Swift was far too repressive a personality to accept the freedom of a Blake—and, moreover, his age was not propitious for such freedom—but he could think freely of the reversal in men's hearts of good and evil once he gave a sop to his snobbery and that of the class of Temple with which he most wished to identify himself. It is no accident that he became a Churchman "rationally zealous," for the High Church party he chose had the nostalgic authoritarianism of a dispossessed elite and a high-minded disdain of the watery Erastian church then dominant. With this shoring up, this bulwark, he could use the zany characters he parodies to voice his own bitter vision. But it is his unresolved hatred of the realities his fools discover that gives to his satire its tragic overtone.

If Lucretius could set Swift's fantasy going, Descartes would of course be as useful. Swift was not one for fine philosophical discriminations and he deliberately runs together the systems of the ancient and the modern. "*Epicurus* modestly hoped, that one Time or other, a certain Fortuitious Concourse of all Men's Opinions, after perpetual Justlings, the Sharp and the Square, would, by certain *Clinamina,* unite in the Motions of *Atoms* and *Void . . . Cartesius* reckoned to see before he died, the Sentiments of all Philosophers, like so many lesser Stars in his *romantick* System wrapped and drawn within his own Vortex" (sec. 9). If this passage suggests that rational systems are really extensions of the ego of the reasoner, it also shows, as do the actual images of mechanistic sublimity, that Swift had a very particular use for these two philosophers, essentially the same use, to provide an account of life as utterly materialistic that would answer to observable facts. What Swift wanted from Descartes was his materialistic cosmogony by vortices, the mechanics of animal (including human) bodies, and his spider personality. Like Lucretius, Descartes is a world-maker of rather pert assurance. Amused by the welter of opinions of his ancient exemplars and present mentors, resolved to seek all knowledge within himself, in his own self-consciousness, he retired, he tells us in the *Method,* to a warm room to build the "romantick system" Swift parodies. While willing to grant God His mysterious ways, Descartes makes it clear that the Deity might have availed Himself of his system of vortices to create the universe, had He wished. Nor does Descartes wish to deprive the human animal of his traditional, God-given spiritual soul, but he is put to such a fantastic expedient to allow the operation of spiritual substance in a materialistic world that he was suspected of being in fact a materialist. The apparatus of the pineal gland as a valve by which spirit acts upon body not only violates, magically, Descartes's system of mechanics but is so bizarre as to seem almost a Swiftian parody. Descartes's notion of the mechanics of the animal body is more plausible. Like Lucretius, he supposes an agitation of the body by the impact upon the senses of external corpuscles of matter. From the nerve ends, animal spirits transmit these impulses by canals inside the nerves to the brain and pineal gland and thence to the motor centers. A shrewd guess at the operation of the heart and the emotions makes the Cartesian mechanics very much available to Swift as a metaphor for the mechanical operation of the spirit, a metaphor that hovers, as he wished it to do, on the edge of actuality. Here again, as wtih his use of Lucretius, Descartes serves an inherently self-contradictory double purpose—to parody the restless, self-sufficient universalist but also to give voice to Swift's dark vision of the fraud of sublime pretensions, including Christian, in human economy.

Pascal seems again close to Swift's thought. "I cannot forgive Descartes," writes Pascal; "he would gladly have done without God in his philosophy, but he could not spare Him to give [his system of vortices] a little shove to start it going. After that he had no further use for God."[15] Descartes himself observed that life is a war between the infinite will and the finite understanding, which is an exact description of his own predicament and Swift's description of the great ones in empire, religion, and philosophy—in short, the spiders of history. But for Pascal such realities of life were the occasion of spiritual commitment, of a bet born of despair for a desperate hope. For Swift, however, such realities were the occasion only of metaphysical anxiety, being driven as he was to undermine in the guise of a fool the very spiritual pretensions in which officially he placed his faith.

We have only touched on the involutions of thought in the *Tale*, with much emphasis upon its inconsistency, but we have followed through Swift's characteristic imaginative processes. There remains the fantastic metaphor of "clothes," by which Swift defines the corruptions inherent in the religious authority of the visible Church, much as by the metaphor of "wind" he defines the complementary corruptions inherent in the authority of one's inner voice. The allegory of the *Tale,* the development of the personalities of Jack and Peter, the personification of these two corruptions, is a remarkable psychological study. Unless one assumes that the fool speaker represents Swift's most serious thoughts, this entire allegory, these elaborate metaphorical structures of "wind" and "clothes," must be the meaningless patter of an idiot modern. If the argument conducted here is convincing, however, the thought of the *Tale* explores real questions about human pretensions and the answers are not reassuring to the Christian or to the apprentice Augustan rationalist.[16]

"The Self-defeat of Life"

If we listen to the fool and madman as Swift's voice, we cannot but feel the force of the "Digression concerning Madness" as the culmination of Swift's anxiety in the *Tale,* of his satire against pretensions, including his own, that worthies of state and religion and learning can escape the mechanical operation of the spirit. Such a reading is rather different from one in which the in-group joke is that "the author of these momentous truths" is merely a parody of the types Sir William Temple could not abide. The charge levelled by F. R. Leavis,[17] that Swift is wholly negative in this section (and by implication throughout), is at least arguable. The "genius delights in its mastery, in its power to destroy, and negation is felt as self-assertion." This paradoxical vitality, says Leavis, is "the self-defeat of life, life turned against itself." While obviously unsympathetic to Swift's moral attitudes, Leavis was nevertheless the first critic to enter the withering mazes of Swift's irony in the "Digression" and follow faithfully the unpredictable turns of the famous "fool among knaves" passage. Of the secure body of assurances, habits, and assumptions that characterize most ironists he finds nothing at all. Instead, the very intensity of the trickery of expectation, the spontaneity, copiousness, and violence of metaphor continually throw the reader off balance and foil his every attempt to get his bearings from some secure vantage.

Great kings are mad—victims (i.e., beneficiaries) of mechanical internal disturbances such as circulating vapors or atomic films of absent females. Philosophers wishing to reduce the notions of all mankind to their own length and breadth, might in this undistinguishing age be confined to Bedlam. Without enthusiasm—vapors that the world calls madness—the world would be deprived of conquests and systems and all mankind unhappily reduced to the same belief in things invisible. As the vapor strikes we may get a Descartes, Jack of Leyden, or an Alexander. "For the brain in its natural position and state of serenity, disposeth its owner to pass his life in the common forms. . . ."

As Leavis points out, all this is perfectly ordinary Augustan doctrine. Presumably if all mankind were reduced by sanity to the same belief in things invisible, they would all be Anglican rationalists, a religion that teaches people to behave themselves and not examine the mysteries overcuriously. (Swift, his sermons show, had something of the sort in mind, at least as an everyday faith.)

One would suppose that if the author really believed, except as an official stance, that such a Houyhnhnm faith had any reality in this world, he would write a satire of a particular rather than general application. For nothing at all in the picture the *Tale* presents of psychology or of history suggests that men are, or were, or will be other than irrational. The metaphor is of the world as madhouse, but Swift's way with metaphors—the more "fantastic" the better—here as elsewhere in his satires, is to show that fantastically reductive metaphors are nearly indistinguishable from literal truth. From this point on, the "Digression" completely obfuscates the rationalist ideal of common forms. Fancy gets astride the reason. To delude oneself is so easy as to be inevitable; to delude others is no more difficult, for happiness is "a perpetual possession of being well deceived." How insipid is everything not seen with the assistance of false lights! The ironic argument has imperceptibly veered from a commendation of the madness of great schemes in empire, religion, and philosophy to a recommendation of silly credulity, lest one be unhappy. Quite a different matter. And Leavis rightly asks whether "credulity" is not perilously close to the acceptance of "common forms," which, we have already been told, no accomplished madman would accept. And now we are told that "curiosity" is a bad thing for madmen and therefore a good thing for sane men. But "curiosity" is not a virtue in polite circles—the "true [i.e., false] critic" is "curious to observe the colour and complexion of [a writer's] ordure"—and even here is presented as pompous pedantry—"that pretended Philosophy which enters into the Depth of Things, and then comes gravely back with Informations and Discoveries, that in the inside they are good for nothing." Does not "reason" tell us that the outside is preferable to the inside? "Last Week I saw a Woman *flay'd* . . ." And so "reason" may mean "common sense," or "curiosity," or a preference for illusion. "Philosophy" is as dubious. If we do not content ourselves with Epicurean films and images, is the only alternative "to lap up" the Sower and Dregs with Philosophy and Reason? Perhaps this is all quite mad, but if a madman is speaking, why should he claim those who accept his advice to be well-deceived fools among knaves? Clearly the speaker is not a clay pigeon set up for the sport of the gentlemanly fowler but Swift's own voice ironically baiting the reader's serene Augustan assumption that irrationality is only an unfortunate lapse of good taste. Reality is sad and insipid; we do crave tinsel; to be forever cutting is pompous and officious; to accept films and images is to be a fool among knaves but to rest in common forms is somehow desirable; curiosity is bad form but credulity is idiocy.

Are these contradictions in action and thought that must puzzle the will merely "negative" as Leavis complains or do they, like the "bird of paradise" passage, represent Swift's despair of rationality? It is after all the mad metaphors that teach us the terrible truths of the *Tale*. And who are the sane who pass their lives in the "common forms," never forming parties after their own interest, shaping their understanding by the pattern of human understanding, serenely reasonable? Throughout his life Swift raises this Houyhnhnm ideal only to despair of it. It is in his despair that he reaches interesting truths about the human condition. It is to his abandonment of the "common forms" that we owe his fool's voice and his extravagant fictions. "Now, I would gladly be informed, how it is possible to account for such Imaginations as these in particular Men, without Recourse to my *Phænomenon* of *Vapours*, ascending from the lower Faculties to over-shadow the Brain, and thence distilling into Conceptions, for which the Narrowness of our Mother-Tongue has not yet assigned any other Name, besides that of *Madness* or *Phrenzy*." Sometimes Swift's parodies are deeply hidden and seem to represent some inner diabolism, too intimate to question. The passage is a parody of the annunciation (Luke 1:35): "The Holy Ghost shall come upon thee; therefore also that holy thing which shall be born of thee shall be called the Son of God." For Holy Ghose read Vapor; for Highest, the lower faculties; for conceive (Luke 1:31), conceptions; for Holy Thing, madness.

What seems to annoy Leavis is that he cannot find a secure position from which Swift levels his assaults upon the world and his fellow creatures. The bedeviling irony he traces is certainly owing to Swift's habit of changing the perspective of his attacks. The Augustan appeals to simplicity and common sense, the ironist surveys the burrows of busy grubs, the Anglican bows decently to his confession's *via media*, but the radical assaults are upon the sublimities, or as he puts it with such filthy festivity in that out-

house of the *Tale, The Mechanical Operation of the Spirit,* the "ways of ejac-
ulating the soul":

> Too intense a Contemplation is not the Business of Flesh and Blood; it must by
> the necessary Course of Things, in a little Time, let go its Hold, and fall into
> *Matter.* Lovers, for the sake of Celestial Converse, are but another sort of *Pla-
> tonicks,* who pretend to see Stars and Heaven in Ladies Eyes, and to look or think
> no lower; but the same *Pit* is provided for both; and they seem a perfect Moral
> to the Story of that Philosopher, who, while his Thoughts and Eyes were fixed
> upon the *Constellations,* found himself seduced by his *lower Parts* into a *Ditch.*

Although the allusion is to a parable by Socrates in the *Theaetetus,* Swift's
meaning is entirely his own. Socrates merely wishes to illustrate the silly
simplicity of the Philosopher; Swift wishes to say that sublimities are, as
we would say today, a sublimation of the lower parts. Such a potpourri of
attitudes is hardly possible in sensible discourse, nor was Swift's talent in
such discourse. His talent lay in his ear for real voices, his ability to hear
in their fragmentary accents the attitudes of a culture and the psychology
of men; it lay in a vein of poetic fancy, mad metaphors, so outlandish as to
obliterate any question of decorum. A zany patter, parodying grubby, main-
chancing attitudes in modern culture, sets the reader up to play the ironic
Augustan. But, occasionally at first, and characteristically as the *Tale* develops, the zaniness deepens to fantastic and grotesque conceits discovering
radical realities of psychology that wither not only Augustan assumptions
of reason and clarity but also the longer tradition of Christian and humanistic glorification of the higher faculties. It is suddenly clear that the fool
and madman know truths that Sir William Temple could never know. As
in the initial stage of this irony, Swift's playful voice mocks the pompous
universalizing of small "philosophers," so in the next stage the grotesque
conceits which characterize glory in empire, religion, and philosophy turn
back the irony upon the superior reader when it becomes clear that these
assaults are not upon particular objects but upon universal pretensions that
the sublime faculties can ever be more than sublimations of the lower parts.
"The very same Principle that influences a *Bully* to break the Windows of
a Whore, who has jilted him, naturally stirs up a Great Prince to raise
mighty Armies, and dream of nothing but Sieges, Battles and Victories.—
[*cunnus*] *teterimma belli causa* (Horace)." (Another Swiftian misapplica-
tion of a classical author.) The last stage of the ironic process of the *Tale*
grows out of the universal application of the satire: the fantastic and grotesque conceits are shown to be not in the end so much metaphoric as

literally true. Puritan narcissism is not like that of a sexual pervert; it is that of a sexual pervert. Great kings are not prone to make mistakes that make them look like inmates of Bedlam; they are mad.

One has only to deal at the end with the question, what is madness? Clearly Swift answers the question: it is the rock-bottom, universal, and irreducible narcissism and aggression of all men.

It would be an idle work to deny that Swift's politics and religion were for the most part oppressive, and that he himself was a repressive personality, but his salvation as an artist—and sometimes as a politician and Churchman—was his hatred, a hatred like Gulliver's, that compelled him to throw back into men's faces their pompous idealism and pretended rationality and ask them how they liked the smell of it. Faced with their own truth by the bedeviling irony, rational readers are literally created by Swift. His satire is hardly "corrective"—one cannot correct one's being. If "rationis capax" means anything, then it means "capable of reasoning if one knows that when one fixes one's eyes on the constellations, one's lower parts will seduce one into a ditch." It is an improbable possibility, this demand for incessant irony in order to be rational. In this sense only is Leavis's charge of negativism, "the self-defeat of life," a true bill. And it is precisely here that Swift's irony becomes tragic.

But Swift's satire is so festively inventive, so raucous in its humor that the reader's experience of its harlequinade is far more euphoric than lugubrious. The Hobbesian "sudden glory" of mastering life in those mad metaphors and parodying voices is a continuing effect. To triumph over vulgarity and yet to adopt the vulgar voice to express one's own truths is a feat of artistic legerdemain that gives great pleasure, and with this pleasure comes the franchise to participate in Swift's reduction of sublime pretensions to their elemental coprology. One cannot read the *Tale* without laughter that gives dominance to the rational faculties. In short, Swift's rationality is of little avail without its aesthetic component. We honor the artist, not the priest.

The problem of Swift's religion, so far as we can deduce it from the *Tale,* can be only briefly touched on here, but touch on it we must to understand Swift's cast of mind that plays such tricks with our sensibility in the *Tale.* In choosing the *via media* of Anglicanism Swift was not thinking of the predominant latitudinarian current in the Church represented most respectably by Bishop Burnet. This accomplished if garrulous man Swift libeled and ridiculed as though he were an illiterate. A few years after the publication of the *Tale,* and before his "Apology" in the Fifth Edition,

Swift had cast his lot with the Tory lower clergy (and this while still a Whig in politics) and against the Erastian bishops. Such an allegiance does not imply any serious concern for doctrine or spirituality. He was willing that the heathen should be deluded into accepting the faith by suppressing "hard" points in doctrine, points such as the divinity of Christ. (What is shocking in this is not the deception but Swift's ignorance that it would be the mysteries—not the rationalities—that would convert the primitive. Such ignorance must be the consequence of his disinclination to indulge the spiritual dimension of religion.) He is as willing to recommend hypocrisy as a way to faith—for the hypocrite can withstand no better than other men the force of habit. No man, he thought, was responsible for his doubts as long as he kept them to himself. He could insist upon the imposition of mere forms of religion without regard to the belief of the "practitioner."[18] All this adds up not to hypocrisy in Swift but to an anachronistic commitment to the Church of Hooker, though to the form of it rather than the substance. Though liberal in the interpretation of doctrine and ritual, Hooker was absolute in his insistence upon an integral State-Church in which citizenship in the commonwealth was convertible with membership in the Church. Such a society was one manifestation of God's grace, and unlike a Puritan theocracy, was thought to be a blessing to reasoning men, not a curse upon the depraved. By Swift's day, however, it was the individualistic personality that ruled the roost rather than the collectivistic Anglican of Hooker's stamp. Burnet could recognize a reality. Swift's anachronistic attitudes were, therefore, if noble, dry and without real substance. This anachronism accounts for their repressive odor. How else but by repression could they be made to prevail? But more serious, Swift's radical undermining of reason and will brings into question the fundamental assumption of Hooker's Church, which is that the *societas perfecta* is founded on reason, and through reason, law, both effects of God's grace. Such a reasonable theory of human life, respecting God and man, admitting the fall, certainly, but insisting upon the goodness of God in preserving in men sufficient reason for establishing a just society and recuperating their own estate. This ideal seemed hardly compelling after the violence of the seventeenth century, and Swift's own insight into the perversion of rational processes, and, indeed, the inevitability of that perversion, makes it untenable. That Swift was sincere in his support of the faith is not in question. He wanted to rebuild churches in the decayed parishes of London, to establish bishops in the New World, to make the Church a reality in the daily lives of his own parishioners, and yet his obsessive probing of psychological realities that bring assumptions of the glory of the rational faculty into question, his hatred of men's pretensions to spirituality, make of his religion more an anxiety than a faith. The *via media* of Swift is not the gracious and pious way of Herbert. Nothing in the *Tale* makes us believe that the authority of the visible Church can be brought into harmony with the inner conviction of justification. Little wonder that Martin is a manikin when Jack and Peter appear finally not as exceptions to the rule of life but the rule itself. Had he been a saner man, a Burnet or an Addison, Swift would have had little news for us from the frontiers of faith. There, where men ask ultimate questions, the answers are not clear and the guise of the fool was for this Churchman the only way to report back. We come a long way in the *Tale* from the purlieus of Sir William Temple. One can almost imagine that the "fool among knaves" is Temple himself, puttering in the Gardens of Epicurus. As we have seen, Swift takes Temple's ideas but changes them utterly—from ironic amusement at the antics of men to ultimate questions about reason and the will of God. The change from Temple's feeling for life to Swift's is perhaps represented in the *Tale* by the suppression of any mention of the sweet reason of Epicurus, mindful of illusions and physical necessities, but confident of the good life. This true aspect of Epicurus Temple understood. In the place of this sweet reasonableness of Epicurean philosophy, Swift gives us a bitter analysis of the mechanical operation of the spirit by borrowing Lucretius's materialistic system. Instead of representing the truth that Epicurus, while describing the prevalance of films and images in our perception, wanted to provide the reason with defenses against its own deception, Swift simply assumes that men will content themselves with films and images. This change perhaps implies a thoroughgoing criticism of Temple's Epicurean contentment before the amusing spectacle of lesser breeds outside the garden. It would seem to suggest as well the thought processes by which Swift found his own genius after a false start as Temple's minion in the school of gentlemanly irony. Swift's irony simply shatters the values of Christian humanism by showing how they mask the reality of the mechanical operation of the spirit. Far from leaving us in the secure position of the conventional ironist, he leaves us with the burden of anxiety that is his own.

Notes

1. Review of Ronald Paulson's *Theme and Structure in Swift's "Tale of a Tub,"* *Review of English Studies*, N.S. 12 (1961):300–302.

2. For a thorough discussion of the virulence and inhumanity of Anglican ridicule of Puritans, see W. P. Holden, *Anti-Puritan Satire 1571–1642* (New Haven, Conn.: Yale University Press, 1954).

3. Professor George Sherburn complained thirty years ago about "sensational" critical treatments of Swift as "tiger." Not Swift's personality but his rhetoric is the interesting thing, said Sherburn; Swift himself was conventional and orthodox. In the past three decades, academic criticism has indeed followed Sherburn's strictures, endeavoring to remove questions of his personality from consideration of Swift's works. This endeavor has had three main streams: abstract considerations of the demands of the genre of satire, background studies, and a combination of the two first in "persona" studies. The most elaborate example of the last is Ronald Paulson's *Theme and Structure in Swift's "Tale of a Tub,"* which presents the "hack" as a consistent satirical device that Swift sets up in the *Tale* to carry all his animus against hermetists. As Paulson sees it, the "hack" has a long history, going back to the early Christian gnostics. The object of the *Tale's* satire is therefore this "hack" as a vessel of hermeticism. Paulson's view makes of the *Tale* a hermetic work in itself, available only to scholars. His treatment of the long history of hermeticism provides, nevertheless, a valuable understanding of *one* of the objects of Swift's contempt, though it does not account for either the complexity or the emotional impact of the *Tale,* and indeed, as Professor Davis (see n.1) has written, imposes a formidable barrier to the reader's intuitive understanding of the work. A more rigorous treatment of satiric techniques is Edward Rosenheim's *Swift and the Satirist's Art,* and a less polemic discussion of the religious background is Phillip Harth's *Swift and Anglican Rationalism,* both valuable works. It is true, however, that Rosenheim's study is so abstract and rigorously formalistic that it ignores Swift's own quality and meaning, and that Harth's study does not pretend to discuss the peculiar use Swift made of his Anglican heritage. We are led back, then, to Swift's personality and the peculiar quality of his mind, and it is the purpose of the present argument to suggest that Swift studies might usefully return to a humanistic criticism, the apprehension of the *unique* mind and art of Swift. The interesting thing is to see a remarkable personality such as Swift's forging from conventions and tradition its unique world-view. It seems aesthetic and philosophical nonsense to expect, as did Sherburn, that a writer's art and mind can be understood apart from his personality. Where else but from the personality can art come? I have listed the three works that seem best to exploit the currents of Swiftian criticism since Sherburn's complaint. (I do not mean to imply that they derive from Sherburn.) A multitude of articles of various worths in these currents— studies of the satiric genre, of background, and of their combination in the "persona" figure— cannot be listed but point towards the three books mentioned. I should like to think that the present discussion will respond to the question, "How does Swift's *Tale* affect the reader?"; such a discussion must transcend, while respecting, abstract considerations of genre and background.

4. The phrase "university lecturer" is Donald Torchiana's in his study, *W. B. Yeats and Georgian Ireland* (Evanston, Ill.: Northwestern University Press, 1966), ch.4. See also Donald Davie's essay reviewing the methods of Quintana and Bullitt, "Academicism and Swift," *Twentieth Century* 154 (1953).

5. In Swift's day, religion was not a matter of theology but of church-going and moral guidance. Swift and his contemporaries were notoriously hostile to theological subtilizing.

6. "Compromise" is Kathleen Williams's formula for Swift's message in her study, *Jonathan Swift and the Age of Compromise.* My reading of the *Tale* is obviously not in accord with hers, and, indeed, I should say that "compromise" is the most unlikely of messages to attribute

to Swift. In my experience his readers *always* respond to him by remarking his violence and uncompromising pursuit of his argument. It is deadening to tell the reader that if he just knew a little more of what a specialist knows, he would see that Swift is only representative of his age or illustrative of a genre. For the truth is that there is not another Swift either in his age or in the history of the genre of satire. When I insist upon his unique aesthetic quality, I am not of course arguing that he was unconversant with the "art of the possible" in the politics of church and state.

7. I have discussed this unresolvable dilemma in my essay, "A Voyage to Nowhere with Thomas More and Jonathan Swift," *Sewanee Review* 69(1961): 534–65.

8. Williams, *Jonathan Swift and the Age of Compromise.*

9. Letter 19, *Journal to Stella.* The editor, Harold Williams, notes that the reference to Temple may be an editorial interpolation, but we have so many stories of Swift's pride before "great ministers" that the reference seems exactly right.

10. In "On the Fates of Clergymen," Swift writes a fable of the fates of a good and a bad clergyman, which are of course the reverse of justice. The good clergyman seems a thinly disguised description of his own character as he saw it. See Swift's letter to Temple, October 6, 1694.

11. "An Essay upon the Ancient and Modern Learning," in *Five Miscellaneous Essays by Sir William Temple,* ed. Samuel Holt Monk (Ann Arbor: University of Michigan Press, 1963), pp. 56–57.

12. "The Gardens of Epicurus."

13. *Europe in the Seventeenth Century,* ch.7, "The Absolutism of Louis XIV."

14. F. R. Leavis, "The Irony of Swift," *The Common Pursuit* (Harmondsworth: Penguin Books, 1962), p. 81.

15. *Pensées,* "Misère de l'homme sans Dieu," 77. (Brunschvicg edition).

16. I have written on the allegorical implications of the *Tale* and the allegorical habit of mind Swift shows everywhere in "Swift's Allegory: The Yahoo and the Man-of-Mode," *University of Toronto Quarterly* 33 (1963): 1–18.

17. Leavis, "The Irony of Swift," especially pp. 80ff.

18. The best that one can say for Swift so far as his religion is concerned is that he accepted sincerely, by main strength of his will, the assumptions of his faith, but one must say his religious sensibility was nearly nonexistent. He was a Churchman and a zealous defender of the non-Erastian foundation of the Church. He was no toady and no time-server. Bishops, he said, could be installed in episcopal palaces by the government by a tight-rope walking contest, if it so pleased the government, but no government could ordain a bishop or perform ecclesiastical functions *(Remarks on Tindall).* In sum, he fought for the dignity of the Church and its place as an integral part of national life. But it requires religious vision to make the Church effectively a part of national life, and that Swift did not have. His way was authoritarian. Censorship, spying, religious and moral tests, he thought, might bring about some improvement *(Project for the Advancement of Religion).* Would this lead to hypocrisy? he asks. Yes, he answers, and a good thing, too, for by being hypocrites under compulsion people fall into a habit and genuinely accept what they are compelled to do. This is astute psychology for social conditioning (and was the practice of all European churchs) but hardly religion. (His understanding that "religion" is usually a "Pavlov's dog" reflex is in fact the fundamental idea for the satire of Peter in the *Tale.* It takes one to catch one.) In the *Letter to a Young Gentleman, Lately enter'd into Holy Orders,* he suggests that the successful priest should not attempt any explanation of the mysteries—again good advice, but not indicative of theological propensi-

ties. *Thoughts on Religion* contains the advice to missionaries to suppress mention of Christ's divinity. Immediately following this thought is one even more interesting, that argument about opinions fundamental to religion is wicked—whether they be true or false. Naturally, therefore, one should conceal one's want of belief. Swift's lifelong bitter defense of the Test Act in a country where not only the vast majority of the population, but the majority of the protestants, were thereby persecuted is eloquent testimony to his sanguine view of false conformity. When we are aware of these real, as opposed to the scholar's imputed, beliefs, we can understand how the *Tale* can be a revelation of evils fundamental to religion rather than a celebration of the perfection of the Church of England.

Gulliver
and the
Gentle Reader

CLAUDE RAWSON

JILL   You put me in the wrong.
JACK   I am not putting you in the wrong.
JILL   You put me in the wrong for thinking you put me in the wrong.

(R. D. Laing, *Knots*)

"'Tis a great Ease to my Conscience that I have writ so elaborate and use-ful a Discourse without one grain of Satyr intermixt":[1] this, from the Pref-ace to *A Tale of a Tub*, outdoes even Gulliver's claims to veracity in its cheeky outrageousness. That "provocative display of indirectness"[2] which Herbert Read (in a fine though somewhat unfriendly phrase) saw in *Gulliver* governs also the mad parodic world of the *Tale*. The seven prefatory items followed by an Introduction, the signposted chapters of digression (one of them in praise of digressions), the pseudoscholary annotation (with the "commentator" sometimes at odds with the "author"), the triumphant assimilation into the notes of Wotton's hostile exegesis, the asterisks and gaps in the MS., the promise of such forthcoming publications as *A Pane-gyrick upon the World* and *A General History of Ears*, have an exuberance which transcends mere parody and mere playfulness. In such a context, the posturing denial of satiric intention draws a provoking and almost unset-tling attention to itself. We have not yet reached the sudden violences, and the more radical underminings, of the religious allegory or the Digression

From *Gulliver and the Gentle Reader: Studies in Swift and Our Time* (London: Routledge & Kegan Paul, 1973), pp. 1-32.

on Madness, but we are made curiously insecure as to how, exactly, to take the joke.

Nor can we comfortably separate, in our minds, the silly geniality of the putative "author" from Swift's own more astringent presence. Typically, we become aware of a strange interplay of astringency and exuberance, in which it is not always easy to distinguish between narrator and real author. The narrator, or mock-author, is a creature of mad and monstrous egotism, who confides his private problems and draws garrulous attention to his literary techniques. But the *Tale*'s whole marathon of self-posturing cannot be entirely accounted for by its ostensible purpose, which is to mock those modern authors, "L'Estrange, Dryden, *and some others*" (*Tale*, I),[3] who write this sort of book straight. For the *Tale* has at the same time a vitality of sheer performance which suggests that a strong self-conscious pressure of primary self-display on Swift's own part is also at work; the almost "romantic" assertion of an immense (though edgy, oblique, and agressively self-concealing) egocentricity. Swift's descendants in the old game of parodic self-consciousness are Romantics of a special sort, like Sterne and (after him) the Byron of *Don Juan*. If the *Tale*'s "Digression in Praise of Digressions" looks back to, and mocks, things like L'Estrange's "Preface upon a Preface,"[4] it also looks forward to Sterne's "chapter upon chapters," and it is not for nothing that Tristram thinks his book will "swim down the gutter of Time" in the company of Swift's.[5]

Whatever the ancestry of the technical devices as such, the parodic intrusions of Swift's "authors" have a centrality and importance, and are made by Swift to carry a strength of personal charge, which seem to be new.[6] In Sterne and Byron, and in the Norman Mailer of *Advertisements for Myself*, self-conscious forms of parody and self-parody openly become a solipsistic exercise, and oblique mode of self-exploration and self-display much more radical and far-reaching than the playful posturings of Cervantes or Burton, or even Rabelais. Compare the fact that Swift's *Tale* is a satire of advertisements for oneself not only with the title of Mailer's book, but with the fact that Mailer's "advertisements" are exactly the kind of prefatory note and solipsistic digression which Swift parodies. Mailer's coy description of his practice and motives might almost be taken from the *Tale*, with its "admirable desire to please his readers," its typographic self-consciousness, its acknowledgment of the superior attraction of prefaces over the books themselves:

The author, taken with an admirable desire to please his readers, has also added a set of advertisements, printed in italics, which surround all of these writings with his present tastes, preference, apologies, prides, and occasional confessions. Like many another literary fraud, the writer has been known on occasion to read the Preface of a book instead of a book, and bearing this vice in mind, he tried to make the advertisements more readable than the rest of his pages.[7]

It might be argued that Mailer has reached a point where irony, or at least any very fundamental degree of self-mockery, has largely disappeared, and that he provides an impure comparison. Perhaps this fact shows *a fortiori* the special potential of Swiftian parody for turning into a primary self-assertion, and more will be said about Mailer later.[8] In Sterne, where the outward forms of mockery and self-mockery are still almost as prominent as in Swift, and where the style looks back to Swift most directly and avowedly, there is a more immediate guide to certain "unofficial" aspects of Swift's manner.

Swift has in common with Sterne, against most pre-Swiftian practitioners of "self-conscious narration," the imposition of an exceptional immediacy of involvement with the reader. The narrators are not, of course, the equivalents of Swift or even Sterne, but each is an "I" of whose existence and temperament we are kept unremittingly aware, who talks to the reader and seems to be writing the book, and through whom the real author projects a very distinctive presence of his own. Swift and Sterne also share a kind of intimate, inward-looking obliquity which sets them off, say, from their master Rabelais, who, like them, projects a formidable presence, but whose boozy companionable exhibitionism amounts to an altogether different (and more "open") manner. This obliquity (more or less instinctive in Swift, more coyly self-aware in Sterne) perhaps takes the place of an overt self-expression which Augustan decorum, and whatever personal inhibitions, discouraged.[9]

There are, however, important differences also. When Swift's "author" declares in his Dedication to Prince Posterity that "what I am going to say is literally true this Minute I am writing: What Revolutions may happen before it shall be ready for your Perusal, I can by no means warrant,"[10] Swift is exposing the trivial ephemerality of modern writers. Similar remarks from Sterne (or, without any ironic admixture, from Richardson) proudly proclaim the immediacy of their method of writing *"to the Moment."*[11] Swift's mimicry repudiates that intimacy between author and reader which Sterne and Richardson celebrate, but it does not *cancel* such intimacy, as I shall hope to show. Again, when Swift's "author" proclaims in the Preface his determination "to assist the diligent Reader" in "putting himself into the Circumstances and Postures of Life, that the Writer was in, upon every important Passage as it flow'd from his Pen," so that there may be "a Parity and strict Correspondence of Idea's between the Reader and the Author,"[12] Swift is attacking modern garrulities of self-revelation which for him amount to indecent exposure. In Sterne such remarks, however fraught with all manner of Shandean indirection, are genially proffered tokens of relationship. Tristram wants to tell you everything about himself, because he and Sterne enjoy his character (including the irony injected into it by Sterne, and of which Sterne's parodic performance is a part) as a rich fact of human nature. Both want to get the reader intimately involved:

> As you proceed farther with me, the slight acquaintance, which is now beginning betwixt us, will grow into familiarity; and that, unless one of us is in fault, will terminate in friendship.—*O diem praeclarum!*—then nothing which has touched me will be thought trifling in its nature or tedious in its telling.[13]

The difference is not simply a matter of parody, for that exists in Sterne too. Swift's "author," like Sterne's, often addresses the reader and invokes "all the Friendship that hath passed between Us." At the end of the *Tale*, he has no more to say but thinks of experimenting on how to go on writing *"upon Nothing,"* "to let" (in a phrase Sterne might have used) "the Pen still move on":[14]

> By the Time that an Author has writ out a Book, he and his Readers are become old Acquaintance, and grow very loth to part: So that I have sometimes known it to be in Writing, as in Visiting, where the Ceremony of taking Leave, has employ'd more Time than the whole Conversation before.

Neither this, nor Sterne's passage, is quite straight. That both are in some sense ironic need not be labored. But Sterne's irony is of that puppyish, clinging sort which prods, cajoles, sometimes irritates the reader into a participation which may be reluctant and grudging, but which is also primary, direct, and real. Swift's words assert the same intimacy, but the actual effect of the Swiftian acidity at the end of the "author's" innocent sentence would *appear* to be to sever the link, to achieve not intimacy but an alienation. Sterne's irony is one of fond permissive indulgence; the egotism, though mocked, is freely played with, and the reader offered hospitality within it. In Swift's characteristic sting, the friendly egotism freezes into a stark reminder of the fact of mockery or parody of egotism, and (more than parody though by way of it) the claim to friendship with the reader becomes a kind of insulting denial.

But this denial is not an effacement of Swift, nor a suspension of the reader's close sense of his presence. The parody is charged with a peculiarly personal quality of tart defiance (that "self-assertion" of which Leavis speaks in his essay on Swift),[15] which seems to differentiate it from more normal modes of parody, whose formal business it is to mock books. It is a truism that Swiftian parody, like that of many writers who choose to make their most serious statements about life through the medium of allusions to books, is usually more than parody in that, in various directions, it transcends parody's limiting relation to the works parodied. *The Modest Proposal* is both more and other than a mockery of those economic proposals whose form it adopts. The real concern is with matters with which the parodic element as such has no necessary connection: the state of Ireland (rather than economic projectors) in the *Modest Proposal,* human pride (rather than popular travelwriting) in *Gulliver.* The problem sometimes arises of just where the dominant focus lies: a parodic energy may blur a more central intention, and there may be a hiatus between a local parodic effect and the main drift of the discourse. An aspect of this, to which I shall return briefly, is that teasing fluctuation, or bewildering uncertainty, of *genre* which critics have noted in some of Swift's works, and which gives a curious precariousness to the reader's grasp of what is going on. This has an undermining effect which is, in some ways, closely related to the more definite acts of authorial aggression. Beyond the truism that the satire's principal concerns transcend parody stands a further, more disturbing truth: that the nonparodic concerns are themselves transcended by energies which are much less easy to pin down, because they are not "official" or overt.

The *Tale* differs in a formal sense from the *Modest Proposal* and *Gulliver* in that the "modernity" which it attacks finds one of its main symptoms in the kind of book that is being parodied, so that the congruence between parody and the "real" subject is particularly close. Even so, it would be wrong to suggest that this "real" subject is merely a matter of silly or offensive stylistic habits, like garrulousness or digressiveness. The cumulative effect of the *Tale*'s formidable parodic array is to convey a sense of intellectual and cultural breakdown so massive and so compelling that the parodied objects, as such, come to seem a minor detail. This in no case makes the parody expendable. The manner of the hack-author, bland proposer, or truthful boneheaded traveler are essential to the effects Swift is creating, and not merely as means of highlighting satiric intensities through disarming naiveties of style. My last example from the *Tale* shows how parody of friendly gestures from author to reader not only mocks modern garrulousness and all the intellectual slovenliness that goes with it (as well as capturing incidentally a typical social absurdity), but puts the reader himself under attack. This "Satire of the Second Person," in H. W. Sams's useful phrase,[16] is not primarily a matter of *satirizing* the reader, but of making him uncomfortable in another sense, as a person we are rude to is made uncomfortable. Swift, as much as Sterne, is reaching out to the reader, and the alienation I spoke of does not in fact eliminate intimacy, though it destroys "friendship." There is something in Swift's relations with his reader that can be described approximately in terms of the edgy intimacy of a personal quarrel that does not quite come out into the open, with gratuitous-seeming sarcasms on one side and a defensive embarrassment on the other. Such a description can only be a half-truth. And, like many of the examples I shall be discussing, the passage is much lighter than any account of it can be. It is a joke (a good one), and playful. But it is attacking play, and its peculiar aggressiveness is a quality which I believe to be not merely incidental but pervasive in Swift's major satires.

This aggressiveness towards the reader is what chiefly distinguishes Swift from the later writers to whom he can be compared, and who imitate him or are prefigured in his work. It takes many forms, and is not confined to contexts of parody. In the *Tale,* however, parody cannot help being closely involved, and Swift's determined and naked hostility to the targets of his parody has several immediate consequences which differentiate his effects from those of similar passages in Sterne or Mailer. The primacy of the parodic element diverts formal attention (as distinct from our informal sense of Swift's teasing and often explosive presence) away from Swift to his satiric victims. The parody prevents by this means that unSwiftian note of self-cherishing which sometimes creeps into Sterne's, or Mailer's, use of "self-conscious" mannerisms and other "modern" postures, and correspondingly discourages easy complicities in the reader, without freeing the reader from an awkward sense of relationship. But whether parody is present or not, the aggression I speak of is usually quite inescapable in Swift's satire. What is involved is not necessarily a "rhetoric" or thought-out strategy, so much as an atmosphere or perhaps an instinctive tone. This is not to mistake Swift for his masks, but to say that behind the screen of indirections, ironies, and putative authors a central Swiftian personality is always actively present, and makes itself felt.

Consider a scatological passage in *Gulliver.* I do not wish to add here to the available theories about the scatology and body-disgust as such. Psychoanalysts have examined it; C. S. Lewis says, sturdily, that it is "much better understood by schoolboys than by psychoanalysts"; another critic says the "simplest answer is that as a conscientious priest [Swift] wished to discourage fornication";[17] others say that Swift was just advocating cleanliness, mocking the over-particularity of travel-writers, or doing no more any way than other writers in this or that literary tradition. But most people agree that there is a lot of it; and it has been a sore point from the start. Swift knew it, and knew that people knew, and early in book I he has a characteristic way of letting us know he knows we know (I.ii.29).[18] Gulliver had not relieved himself for two days, and tells us how in his urgency he now did so inside his Lilliputian house. But he assures us that on future occasions he always did "that Business in open Air," and that the "offensive Matter" was disposed of "every Morning before Company came" by two Lilliputian servants.[19] Gulliver thinks the "candid Reader" needs an explanation, so he tells us why he tells us this:

> I would not have dwelt so long upon a Circumstance, that perhaps at first Sight may appear not very momentous; if I had not thought it necessary to justify my Character in Point of Cleanliness to the World; which I am told, some of my Maligners have been pleased, upon this and other Occasions, to call in Question.

It is Gulliver and not Swift who is speaking, but it is Swift and not Gulliver who (in any sense that is active at this moment) has had maligners. Gulliver does have enemies in Lilliput, notably after urinating on the palace fire, but the reader does not know this yet, and it is difficult not to sense behind Gulliver's self-apology a small egocentric defiance from the real author. This would be true whether one knew him to be Swift or not, but it comes naturally from the Swift whose writings, and especially *A Tale of a Tub*, had been accused of "Filthiness," "Lewdness," "Immodesty," and of using "the Language of the Stews" (Swift called it being "battered with Dirt-Pellets" from "envenom'd . . . Mouths."[20] Swift's trick consists of doing what he implies people accuse him of, and saying that this proves he isn't like that really: the openly implausible denial becomes a cheeky flaunting of the thing denied, a tortuously barefaced challenge. This self-conscious sniping at the reader's poise occurs more than once: a variant instance of mockfriendly rubbing-in, for the "gentle Reader's" benefit, occurs at the end of II.i, where the particularity of travel-writers is part of the joke.[21]

A related non-scatological passage, which Thackeray praised as "the best stroke of humour, if there be a best in that abounding book,"[22] is Gulliver's final farewell to his Houyhnhnm master, whose hoof he offers to kiss, as in the papal ceremony.[23] (Gulliver seems to have leanings that way: he also wanted to kiss the Queen of Brobdingnag's foot, but she just held out her little finger—II.iii.101.) "But as I was going to prostrate myself to kiss his Hoof, he did me the Honour to raise it gently to my Mouth. I am not ignorant how much I have been censured for mentioning this last Particular" (IV.x.282). Since the passage occurs in the first edition, Gulliver or Swift could hardly have been censured for mentioning this before. "Detractors" would be presumed by the reader to object that human dignity was being outraged, and Swift was of course right that many people would feel this about his book in general. But this is not Gulliver's meaning at all, and the typical Swiftian betrayal that follows gains its real force less from mere surprise than from its cool poker-faced fanning of a reader's hostility which Swift obviously anticipated and actually seemed on the point of trying to allay: "Detractors are pleased to think it improbable, that so illustrious a Person should descend to give so great a Mark of Distinction to a Creature so inferior as I. Neither have I forgot, how apt some Travellers are to boast of extraordinary Favours they have received. But ..." Thackeray's praise ("audacity," "astounding gravity," "truth topsyturvy, entirely logical and absurd") comes just before the famous "filthy in word, filthy in thought, furious, raging, obscene" passage:[24] it is perhaps appropriate that such coarse over-reaction should be the counterpart to a cheerful complacency in the face of the subtler energies of Swift's style.

The mention of travelers in the hoof-kissing passage brings us back to parody, but emphasizes again how readily Swiftian parody serves attacking purposes which are themselves non-parodic. Edward Stone's view that this reference is proof that Swift is merely joking at the expense of boastful travelers misses most of the flavor of the passage.[25] (One might as easily say that the main or only point of the passage is to guy a papal rite. I do not, of course, deny these secondary jokes, or their piquancy.) But parody is important, almost as much in its way as in the *Tale*. Gulliver is an author, who announces forthcoming publications about Lilliput (I.iv.47–8; I.vi.57) and Houyhnhnmland (IV.ix.275)—which is a common enough device— and whose putative authorship of the work we are actually reading, as well as being the source of many of its most central ironies, enables Swift to flaunt his own self-concealment in some amusing and disconcerting ways.[26] A portrait of Gulliver was prefixed to the early editions, and in 1735 this acquired the teasing caption "Splendide Mendax."[27] The elaborate claims to veracity in "The Publisher to the Reader" and in the text itself gain an additional piquancy from this. The 1735 edition also prints for the first time Gulliver's letter to Sympson, which, as prefatory epistles go, is a notably unbalanced document, providing advance notice of Gulliver's later anti-social state and by the same token giving a disturbing or at least confusing dimension to the sober opening pages of the narrative. Gulliver's announcement in the letter that *Brobdingnag* should have been spelt *Brobdingrag* (p. 8) belongs to a familiar kind of authenticating pretense in both fiction and prose satire, but insofar as we remember it later it does make it slightly unsettling to read *Brobdingnag* with an *n* every time it occurs in the book. It is clear that these devices, though not meant to be believed, are not bids for verisimilitude in the manner, say, of Richardson's "editorial" pretense or the countless other tricks of fiction-writers before and after Swift (the correcting footnote, the manuscript partly missing or lost, the discovered diary, the pseudo-biography). Nor are they quite a matter of pure hearty fun, as in Rabelais, meant to be enjoyed *precisely as* too outrageous to be believed. For one thing, Swift's celebrated "conciseness" is too astringent. It is also too close to the idiom of sober factuality, and some people were literally taken in.

We are hardly expected to take *Gulliver's Travels* as a straight (even if possibly mendacious) travel story. But the sea captain who claimed to be "very well-acquainted with Gulliver, but that the printer had Mistaken, that he livd in Wapping, & not in Rotherhith," the old gentleman who searched for Lilliput on the map, the Irish Bishop who said the "Book was full of improbable lies, and for his part, he hardly believed a word of it"[28] (though some of these readers may have been more *ben trovati* than real) do tell a kind of truth about the work. Swift's whole ironic program depends on our not being taken in by the travel-book element, but it does require us to be infected with a residual uncertainty about it; and these instances of an over-successful hoax fulfil, extremely, a potential in the work to which all readers must uneasily respond. This is not to accept the simpler accounts of Swiftian betrayal, which suggest that the plain traveler's, or modest proposer's, factuality lulls the reader into a false credulity, and then springs a trap. With Swift, we are always on our guard from the beginning (I believe this is true of sensitive *first* readings as well as later ones), and what surprises us is not the fact of betrayal but its particular form in each case. But if we are on our guard, we do not know what we are guarding against. The travel-book factuality, to which we return at least at the beginning and end of each book (even the end of book IV, in its strange way, sustains and elaborates the pretense), is so insistent, and at its purest so lacking in obvious pointers to a parodic intention, that we really do not know *exactly* how to take it. What saves the ordinary reader from being totally taken in is, obviously, the surrounding context. (The very opening of the narrative, from the 1735 edition onwards, is colored by the letter to Sympson, but even before 1735 one would have needed to be exceptionally obtuse to think, by the end of the first chapter, that one was still reading a travel-book.) But not being taken in, and knowing the plain style to be parodic, do not save us from being unsure of what is being mocked: travel-books, fictions posing as travel-books, philosophic tales (like *Gulliver* itself) posing as fictions posing as travel-books.[29] Bewilderment is increased by the uncertainty of how much weight to give, moment by moment, to the fact of parody as such and to whatever the style may be mocking, since the parody as we have seen is continuously impregnated with satiric purposes which transcend or exist outside it, but which may still feed on it in subtle ways. And we cannot be sure that some of the plainness is not meant to be taken straight, not certainly as factual truth, but (in spite of everything) momentarily as realistic fictional trimmings: at least, the style helps to establish the "character" of the narrator, though this "character" in turn has more life as the basis of various ironies than as a vivid fictional personality. No accurate account can exhaust the matter, or escape an element of giddy circularity. The proper focus for Swift's precise sober narrative links is paradoxically a blurred focus, because we do not know what to make of all the precision. The accumulation of unresolved doubt that we carry into our reading of more central parts of *Gulliver's Travels* creates, then, not a credulity ripe for betrayal, but a more continuous defensive uneasiness. This undermining of our nervous poise makes us peculiarly vulnerable, in more than the obvious sense, to the more central satiric onslaughts.

The parodic element, though not primary, is never abandoned. At the end of book IV, when any live interest in travel-writers may be thought to have totally receded in the face of more overwhelming concerns, Gulliver keeps the subject alive with some tart reminders of his truthfulness and the mendacity of other travelers. The practice is commonplace, but again there is nothing here either of Rabelais's friendly outrageousness as he refers to his "histoire tant veridicque," or his or Lucian's corresponding frank admission that they are telling monstrous lies, or the honest workmanlike concern with verisimilitude that we find in, say, *Erewhon*.[30] Gulliver says:

> Thus, gentle Reader, I have given thee a faithful History of my Travels for Sixteen Years, and above Seven Months; wherein I have not been so studious of Ornament as of Truth. I could perhaps like others have astonished thee with strange improbable Tales; but I rather chose to relate plain Matter of Fact in the simplest Manner and Style; because my principal Design was to inform, and not to amuse thee. (IV.xii.291)

This passage, which belongs with the well-known (and perhaps somewhat more light-hearted) remark to Pope about vexing the world rather than diverting it, emphasizes Swift's fundamental unfriendliness by a characteristic astringency (that tone is partly Swift's, though Gulliver may overdo it), and by a use of the second person singular, which is aggressively contemptuous. This probably parodies or inverts the common use of "thee" and "thou" in addresses to "gentle readers," where, so far as the pronoun is not merely neutral, intimacy or familiarity is the point. But one can also compare places where an author treats his reader with mild aggressiveness, as when Burton opens his long preface to *The Anatomy of Melancholy* by proclaiming his freedom to tell or withhold information which the reader wants: in fact, the passage hardly has a Swiftian tang, and Burton ends the preface by earnestly requesting "every private man . . . not to take offence" and by presuming "of thy good favour, and gracious acceptance (gentle readers)."[31] Fielding's usages range from warm friendliness (*Tom Jones*, XVIII.i), through a more ruggedly admonishing but still friendly tone (IX.vii), to a partial indentification of the reader with "a little reptile of a critic" (X.i): but even here there is an initial comic relaxation (the comparison with Shakespeare and his editors), and the later concession to the reader that perhaps "thy heart may be better than thy head"; and when Fielding takes stock of his relations with the reader in XVIII.i he warmly disclaims any intention to give offense.[32]

But Swift's use of "thee" is the hostile one ("thou" and "thee" were also often addressed to inferiors),[33] where familiarity, so to speak, has bred contempt. And what we sense in Swift's attack is not the grand public voice of the Satirist, which is, for example, Pope's voice. When Pope uses the hostile "thee" in the *Essay on Man* (e.g., III.27ff., "Has God, thou fool! work'd solely for thy good, . . . Is it for thee the lark ascends and sings? . . ."), it is Man he is addressing, not the reader. Swift's refusal of the "lofty Stile" in the *Epistle to a Lady* rests on an old notion that ridicule is more effective than lambasting ("Switches better guide than Cudgels"), but he has a significant way of describing what the raillery does: it "nettles," "Sets the Spirits all a working." "Alecto's Whip" makes the victims (here specifically "the Nation's Representers") "wriggle, howl, and skip": the satirist makes clear that the whip is to be applied to "their Bums," and that he will not be deterred by the smell.[34] Nothing could make clearer the note of quarrelsome intimacy that is the hallmark of Swift's satire. It may not be very attractive, but it is not meant to be, and it has a unique disturbing effectiveness.

Gulliver's anger (whether nagging tartness, as in the passage under discussion, or ranting fury) reflect a cooler needling offensiveness from the Swift who manipulates the "switch." The chapter, and the volume, end with Gulliver's onslaught on Pride, and his petulant instruction to all English Yahoos "who have any Tincture of this absurd Vice, that they will not presume to appear in my Sight." It is Gulliver and not Swift who is speaking (here it is important not to confuse the two: saying this has almost become a nervous tic among critics), but there is really no sufficiently vivid alternative point of view that we can hang onto at this final moment. I shall return to this, and to what Gulliver actually says, later. What I want to stress here is that the final chapter begins with a needling defiance and the openly unfriendly intimacy of a petty insult, and ends with quarrelsome hysteria. The hysteria is Gulliver's and Swift seems in control. But the quarrel with the reader is one which Swift has been conducting through Gulliver, even though, when Gulliver becomes acutely unbalanced, there is an incomplete (at least a not quite literal) Swiftian commitment to what the quarrel has come to.

Gulliver is sometimes called a gay book. Arbuthnot seems to have started this when he said, "Gulliver is a happy man that at his age can write such a merry work."[35] His letter is joyful about the success of *Gulliver,* and tells of the Captain who claimed to know Gulliver, and the old man who looked up his map. Arbuthnot loved "mischief the best of any Good natured man in England,"[36] and is full of happy complicity in Swift's success and the bonus of a hoax. Pope and Gay were also "diverted" by the reception of the book.[37] Part of the "merry" seems more Scriblerian in-joke than sober description. But the book really can be merry: one thinks of witty fantastications like the joke about the handwriting of ladies in England (I.vi.57),[38] or the charming comedy of the Lilliputian speculations about Gulliver's watch (I.ii.35), which Johnson praised.[39] Such things are very funny, with mild satiric overtones, but without being unduly charged with needling obliquities or any blistering intensity. This is true even in some cases where we should expect Swift to be very hostile. Much of the folly of scientists in book III is treated thus, the flappers, the substitution of things for words, the mathematical obsession which makes the Laputians describe "the Beauty of a Woman . . . by Rhombs, Circles, Parallelograms, Ellipses, and other Geometrical Terms" (III.ii.163) (a joke which is not without bearing on our own habit of reducing women's shapes to "vital statistics"). *Gulliver* has a notably unbuttoned way of giving itself over to local eruptions of mood, but it may be that the very fluctuations of tone invite us (though it will not do to be too solemn) to reconsider the whole nature of the "merriment." Swift obviously enjoyed the comedy of incongruity that runs right through the work (the Lilliputian troop on Gulliver's handker-chief, various Houyhnhnm postures, the She-Yahoo embracing Gulliver): this comes through plainly in his letter to Motte discussing illustrations to the book.[40] But a good deal of this grotesque comedy, notably in Brob-dingnag, is close to being rather painful. The hailstones as big as tennis-balls, the huge frog, the monkey which takes Gulliver for one of its own (II.v.116ff.) have an undeniable science-fiction humor, but Gulliver is throughout in peril of his life. This is even truer of the slapstick comedy of the bowl of cream (II.iii.108): not only is it fraught with painful possi-bilities for Gulliver, but it reflects a crude and bitter malevolence in the court dwarf. J. M. Bullitt speaks well of Swift's "seeming merriment" as reflecting "an almost compulsive desire to separate himself from the inten-sity of his own feelings,"[41] and the margin between high-spirited fun and more disturbing purposes is sometimes a thin one. If notions of the jest as a breaker of tensions, a disguised means of attack, or a showy *(vive la baga-telle!)* shrugging-off of painful feeling seem too ponderous to impose on some (not all) of these passages, they are not foreign to Swift's manner as a whole, and come into his thinking about satire:[42]

> All their Madness makes me merry:
> . . . .
> Like the ever-laughing Sage,
> In a Jest I spend my Rage:
> (Tho' it must be understood,
> I would hang them if I cou'd).

And if the self-humor in these verses forbids us to take the passage at its literal intensity (as it forbids us to take at *their* literal intensity the "hate and detest" and "Drown the World" passages in the letters to Pope expressing the "misanthropy" behind the *Travels*),[43] yet the self-humor is plainly not of the kind that cancels what is said. I imagine, indeed, that the self-humor may in some ways be more disturbing than the plain uncom-promising statement would have been without it. In dissociating the thing said from the full violence of the saying, the ironist both unsettles the reader and covers himself. Since we have here no firm alternative view-point to give us our bearings, we can only know that the ironist means part of what he says, but not exactly how large, or quite what sort of, a part;

and so do not know what defenses are called for. More important, obviously half-meant self-undercutting statements of this kind ("I would hang them if I cou'd," "I hate and detest that animal called man") are more uncomfortable than if they had been wholly meant, for then we might have the luxury of dismissing them as ranting folly. In just this way, our consciousness of Gulliver's folly makes us paradoxically more, not less, vulnerable to the onslaughts on our self-esteem in book IV. Had Gulliver been presented as sane, we should (since again there is no real alternative voice, and no firm norm is indicated) have had to identify him with the satirist behind the mask, and so have been enabled to reject both as totally outrageous. As it is, we reject what comes from Gulliver, and are left with that disturbingly uncertain proportion of it which comes from Swift. It is precisely Gulliver's distance from Swift that permits the Swiftian attack to look plausible. Much of the humor of *Gulliver's Travels* has this effect, not really of attenuating (still less of belying) the Swiftian attack, as some critics hold, but of lending it that self-defensive distancing which makes it viable. Gulliver's solemn habit of trotting and neighing, fully aware of and undeterred by people's ridicule (IV.x.279), releases the whole situation from any possibility of Swift himself seeming solemn.

The same may be said, the opposite way round, of those jokes at the expense of the Houyhnhnms, which are sometimes said to prove that *Gulliver's Travels* has an anti-Houyhnhnm message: their perplexed "Gestures, not unlike those of a Philosopher" (IV.i.226) when they try to understand Gulliver's shoes and stockings, their language which sounds like High Dutch (IV.iii.234), their way of building houses, threading needles and milking cows (IV.ix.274). The first thing I would note is that humor about the Houyhnhnms is never of a destructive tartness: contrast some of the anti-Lilliputian jokes. It also makes the Houyhnhnms (otherwise somewhat stiffly remote, or so some readers feel) seem engagingly awkward and "human," and Swift has a note of real tenderness in some of the passages, the description of the Houyhnhnm dinner-party for example (IV.ii.231-2). Irvin Ehrenpreis, in a fine account of this humor, says that Swift is smiling at his own "whole project of bestowing concrete life upon unattainable abstractions" and "warning the sophisticated reader that [he], unlike Gulliver, appreciates the comical aspect of his own didacticism."[44] The concession conforms to the normal method of the work: one of its effects is to make it more difficult for the reader to answer back.

But the humor has other resonances too. One Houyhnhnm absurdity that some critics make much of is their complacent notion that man's physical shape is preposterous and inefficient for the purposes of life. This is a nice joke when we think of a Houyhnhnm mare threading a needle. But it turns to a cruel irony not at the Houyhnhnms', but at mankind's, expense, when Gulliver's Houyhnhnm master assumes that men are anatomically incapable (despite their impulses) of fighting the destructive wars Gulliver tells him about. Gulliver replies with an exuberant assertion to the contrary that displays a moral fatuity which also has its comic side:

> I could not forbear shaking my Head and smiling a little at his Ignorance. And, being no Stranger to the Art of War, I gave him a Description of Cannons, Culverins, Muskets, Carabines, Pistols, Bullets, Powder, Swords, Bayonets, Sieges, Retreats, Attacks, Undermines, Countermines, Bombardments, Sea-fights; Ships sunk with a Thousand Men; twenty Thousand killed on each Side; dying Groans, Limbs flying in the Air: Smoak, Noise, Confusion, trampling to death under Horses Feet: Flight, Pursuit, Victory; Fields strewed with Carcases left for Food to Dogs, and Wolves, and Birds of Prey; Plundering, Stripping, Ravishing, Burning and Destroying, And, to set forth the Valour of my own dear Countrymen, I assured him, that I had seen them blow up a Hundred Enemies at once in a Siege, and as many in a Ship; and beheld the dead Bodies drop down in Pieces from the Clouds, to the great Diversion of all the Spectators.
>
> (IV.v.247)

This enthusiastic fit is obviously funny. It is funny partly because of the concreteness with which Gulliver generalizes, the entranced particularity with which he evokes not a real battle which happened but some sort of common denominator of war.[45] The effect is instructively different from that of a scene in *Nineteen Eighty-Four* which seems to make some of the same points, and which (like other things in that novel) may have been distantly modelled on Swift.[46] An entry in Winston Smith's diary describes a war-film with a ship full of refugees being bombed, and a "wonderful shot of a child's arm going up up up right into the air," and a greatly diverted audience applauding and "shouting with laughter." Smith says the film is very good, and talks of "wonderful" scenes as Gulliver might. To this extent he is conditioned by the awful world of 1984, but he is struggling for his mental freedom (writing the diary is itself punishable by death), and he suddenly breaks off to think of his account as a "stream of rubbish." The scene does not become funny, because Smith is, in a deeper and partly unconscious sense, disturbed and pained by it, instead of being in Gulliver's fatuous trance of grotesque delight. Orwell drives the painfulness home by having Smith say that there was in the audience a prole woman who "suddenly started kicking up a fuss and shouting they didnt oughter of showed it not in front of kids they didnt." That there should be, within the situation itself, this glimpse of a hurt and protesting normality does not offer much reassurance, but it reaches out to the reader in a kind of complicity of despair. Neither Orwell nor the reader can stand apart from the narartor, or from the rest of the humanity described, and there can be no question of laughing anything off.

The incident in Orwell, however representative (it is in its way as representative as Swift's passage, and of similar things), is a vivid specific occurrence (though only a film), to which a pained immediacy of reaction on Smith's and on the reader's part is natural and appropriate. In Gulliver's account, even when, as at the end, he seems to turn to specific occurrences, there is a comic lack of distinction between the general and the particular, and Gulliver's all embracing celebration has a callous yet oddly innocent absurdity. The comic note, and the fact that the horror is so diffused, ensure that no immediacy of participation by the reader in the things described is possible, or expected. For obvious reasons there is no complicity between the reader and either Gulliver or any member of the applauding crowds. Nor is the grim high-spirited comedy a congenial idiom for any complicity between the reader and Swift: the reader has, rather uncomfortably, to laugh *at* Gulliver, without having anyone very much to laugh *with*. We may speculate whether the exuberance of Gulliver's speech belongs to the moral folly of his original complacent acceptance of mankind; or is an ironic mimicry, after disenchantment, of this early complacent acceptance; or is an exuberant repudiation, proceeding either from righteous indignation or from what some critics might call the *medical* rather than moral folly of Gulliver's final state of misanthropy. On the question of such choices, I shall have more to say.[47] But if we do wish to insist on Gulliver's folly, in *any* sense, in this particular speech, it is clear that there can be no question of such folly, or of Swift's comic sense, canceling or seriously attenuating the point about war and attitudes to war which the passage makes: one of their effects, as with other examples of Swift's humor, is to remove Swift's angry attack from the plane of rant. Yet we are not, I think, very actively horrified at Gulliver's *feelings*, as we should have been if they had been Winston Smith's. In a novel, or in life, we should be revolted by his callousness. But we cannot, here or elsewhere, respond to him as a "character." He is too absurd and two-dimensional. There is a detachment of the character from what he reveals to us which is part of the whole satiric formula of *Gulliver's Travels*, and which the humor here reinforces. We think less about Gulliver than about war, and what Swift is telling us about our attitudes to it. The message is disturbing, and for all the fun, Swift is not, any more than elsewhere, being very friendly.

The tense hovering between laughter and something else, the structural indefiniteness of genre and the incessantly shifting status and function of the parodic element, the ironic twists and countertwists, and the endless flickering uncertainties of local effect suggest that one of Swift's most active satiric weapons is *bewilderment*. It is perhaps not surprising that this weapon should have backfired, and that there should have been so much doubt and disagreement both about the unity of the work, and the meaning of its final section. One of the risks, but also rewards, of the attacking self-concealments of irony is that they draw out their Irish bishops. But we are all, inevitably, Irish bishops in some degree, and the Swift who sought to vex the world may well be deriving a wry satisfaction from our failures to pin him down, although he might not consent to know us in Glubbdubdrib (III.viii.197). What one means by "unity" is too often rather arbitrary, but there is perhaps a broad overall coherence in the consistency and progression of *Gulliver's* onslaught on the reader's bearings and self-esteem. But it is a tense and rugged coherence, and no neatly chartable matter, and any more "external" unities of formal pattern or ideology seem ultimately inseparable from, and possibly secondary to, those satiric procedures and tones which create the commanding impact of the Swiftian voice. An attachment to schematic patterns *per se*, of the kind for which books I and II provide such a brilliant model, seems to have had two results. One has been a tendency to wish either or both the other books away. The other has been a quest to discover in the work as a whole something of the geometrical shapeliness that exists between the first two books. The exercise easily becomes disembodied even when its limitations are partially recognized: it hardly seems to matter much that books I and III deal with bad governments, while books II and IV, in alternating pattern, deal with good governments.[48]
    There are of course some broad structural facts of considerable significance, such as that we are led through three books of allegorical societies which are in principle translatable into real life (with a mixture, as Thomas Sheridan put it, of good and bad qualities "as they are to be found in life"),[49] and which provide a solid background of "realistic" evidence of human vice, into the stark world of moral absolutes of book IV; and that the Struldbrugs at the end of book III are a horrifying climax which prepares us for this. The specific fact that the Struldbrugs give a terrifying

retrospective deepening to the Houyhnhnms' fearlessness of death is only one aspect of their disturbing importance: their chief force, at first meeting, is to put the concerns of the narrative once and for all on an entirely new plane. Again, the fact, noted by Case and others,[50] that the incidental persons in the narrative links between the four main episodes tend to become nastier and nastier, provides an important progression, not perhaps because the reader senses it as a progression (unless it happens to be pointed out), but because the evil of sailors and others (the "real" men) in books III and IV provides a relevantly documented and depressing background to the main preoccupations of those books. (The Portuguese Captain and his crew are an exception to which I shall come later.) The point about these patterns is not that they are neat and flawlessly progressive (they are not), and not merely that they fit in with the "themes" (though they do): it is that they have an effect *as we read*, without our necessarily being aware of them *as patterns*. After all, the real point about even the special relationship between books I and II is not the series of arithmetical piquancies, but the unfolding irony about human self-importance.

This self-importance, or pride, is at the center of the work's concerns. A principle that is sometimes overlooked in discussions not only of structural shape but of ideological themes is that these things make themselves felt, if at all, through the reader's continuous submission to *local* effects, which means in this case exposure to the Swiftian presence at close quarters. Ideologically, *Gulliver's Travels* revolves round the familiar Augustan group of concepts, Nature, Reason and Pride. Its position is basically a commonplace one, but it bears some restating because some ironies of characteristic force and stinging elusiveness proceed from it. Nature and Reason ideally coalesce. Nature is ideal order, in all spheres of life: moral, social, political, aesthetic. Deviations from this are unnatural, as murder or any gross misdeed might, in our own idiom, be called an unnatural act. If one said that the deed came naturally to one, one would be using the term in a different sense. Such other meanings were also of course available to Swift, and I shall argue that the interplay between ideal and less ideal senses provides an important irony. Reason is the faculty which makes one behave naturally (in the high sense), makes one follow Nature and frame one's judgment (and behavior) by her just and unerring standard. So More's Utopians (in some ways ancestors of the Houyhnhnms) "define virtue to be life ordered according to nature, and that we be hereunto ordained of God. And that he doth follow the course of nature, which in desiring and refusing things is ruled by reason,"[51] and the Houyhnhnms believe a somewhat secularized version of the same thing (IV.v.248). The terms Nature and Reason are often in fact interchangeable. Where this is not so, they may complete one another: Nature teaches the Houyhnhnms "to love the whole Species," Reason to distinguish between persons on merit (IV.viii.268). The Houyhnhnms, etymologically *"the Perfection of Nature"* (IV.iii.235), combine Nature and Reason in the highest sense. Their virtues are friendship, benevolence, decency, civility, but they have no ceremony or foolish fondness (IV.viii.268). This means that they have both emotions and propriety, but that neither is misdirected or excessive. They would have understood Pope's phrase in *The Temple of Fame* (l. 108) about "that useful Science, to be *good.*" Their morality is pervaded by an uncompromisingly high (and instinctive) common-sense and utilitarianism, and what might be called an absolute standard of congruity or *fittingness.* Thus they cannot understand lying, because speech was made to communicate (IV.iv.240), or opinion, because there is only one truth and speculation is idle (IV.viii.267). It follows that behavior which offends against this unerring standard is readily seen as deviation or perversion. (This is a suggestion which Swift exploits very fully and painfully.) Even physically, the Houyhnhnms are rational-natural, for (thanks partly to their simple diet, Nature being, as Gulliver knows from some "insipid" meals, "easily . . . satisfied"—IV.ii.232) they are never ill, illness being a deviation from the natural state of the body. For a comic boiling-down of this mind–body ideal, one might cite Fielding's deist Square, who "held human nature to be the perfection of all virtue, and that vice was a deviation from our nature, in the same manner as deformity of body is."[52] Swift has his tongue in his cheek about some Houyhnhnm notions of the "natural" standard of mind–body integration, as when the Houyhnhnm master, in a passage of not very flattering but entirely delightful comedy, considers our physical shape unsuited for the employment of Reason in "the common Offices of Life" (IV.iv.242), but Swift *is* seriously suggesting that luxurious eating habits are a cause of human physical degeneracy, so that morality and physical health are causally related and not only (as apparently for Square) by analogy. Nature ideally is one, and her laws pervasive.

In *Gulliver's Travels,* however, there is a gap between Nature and "human nature," in an actual sense, which would make Square's complacency untenable, though his *rationale* is perfectly applicable to the Houyhnhnms. The Houyhnhnms are not complacent in Square's sense because in them the ideal and the actuality are fully matched. Actually, Square's remarks also concern an ideal and, like other forms of philosophical "optimism," logically allow for an uglier reality, but, given the ugly facts, Swift (and Fielding) would see a monstrous impropriety in putting the matter that way at all. Mankind is guilty of a collective deviation from Nature and Reason at every level, and this Unreason, by the familiar buried pun, becomes in *Gulliver* (as in *A Tale of a Tub* or the *Dunciad*) a vast and wicked madness: the congruence between madness and moral turpitude is one of the most vivid and inventively resourceful themes of Augustan satire. Scientists, or those of a certain sort, are one of the traditional examples. They delve into what Nature keeps hidden, and they seek to pervert Nature (in such cases the word slides easily from an ideal sense to something approaching "things as they are") into something other than it is, "condensing Air into a dry tangible Substance," "softening Marble for Pillows and Pin-Cushions," arresting the growth of wool on sheep (III. v.182).[53] The phrase "natural philosophy" provides an exploitable pun (Fielding said in *Tom Jones*, XIII.v, that natural philosophy knew "nothing of Nature, except her monsters and imperfections"), and when Gulliver explained to the Houyhnhnm master "our several Systems of *Natural Philosophy*, he would laugh that a Creature pretending to *Reason*, should value itself upon the Knowledge of other Peoples Conjectures, and in Things, where that Knowledge, if it were certain, could be of no Use" (IV.viii.267–8). Science becomes divorced from usefulness and good sense. The Laputians are "dextrous" mathematicians on paper but have no idea of "practical Geometry" (III.ii.163). Natural philosophy is thus at least doubly unnatural, in that it variously violates Nature, and in that it is the irrational pastime of creatures who pretend to Reason. This is routine perversion, built-in to the situation. It exercised Swift, and Pope, *as* perversion. But there are further perversities. One is the encroachment of science on government. The Brobdingnagians stand out from the "Wits of *Europe*" in not having "reduced *Politicks* into a *Science*." Unlike us, they have no books on "the *Art of Government*," and despise mystery, refinement (a term which, as in many other satires of Swift and Pope, has familiar suggestions of dishonesty and other vices, as well as folly: "heads refin'd from Reason")[54] and intrigue (II.vii.135). The Laputians, on the other hand, like our Mathematicians, have a "strong Disposition" to politics (III.ii.164), and the Academy of Lagado has a school of political projectors (though that, by some characteristic reversals, has crazed professors trying to do genuine political good, as well as schemes which hover uncertainly between outright folly and a sort of mad good sense—III.vi.187ff.). What, Gulliver asks, is the connection between mathematics and politics? Perhaps it is that "the smallest Circle hath as many Degrees as the largest," so that it might be thought that managing the world requires "no more Abilities than the handling and turning of a Globe." But he thinks the real explanation is "a very common Infirmity of human Nature, inclining us to be more curious and conceited in Matters where we have least Concern, and for which we are least adapted either by Study or Nature" (III.ii.164). This professional perversion or unnaturalness has connections with a whole series of ironies about perversity in the professions and occupations of men. The Yahoos are of a "perverse, restive Disposition" (IV.viii.266), and Swift seems to see human perversity as a thing of almost unending coils of self-complication. But before coming to this, the main outline may be summarized thus.

In this Nature–Reason system at its simplest and purest, every vice is readily resolved into a violation of nature, and therefore into a peculiarly culpable form of unreason. The greed, quarrelsomeness, ambition, treachery, and lust of men, as we encounter them throughout the *Travels*, are in an elementary sense unnatural by definition. This unnaturalness is prone to almost infinite refinements, and therefore as we shall see open to a painful and varied series of ironic expositions. But the overriding unnaturalness, which becomes unbearable to Gulliver at the end, is that the "Lump of Deformity, and Diseases both in Body and Mind" called man, should be "smitten with *Pride*": pride, in the assumption itself, in the face of so much folly, that man is a rational animal, the pride of having any self-esteem at all (as Gulliver, though perhaps not Swift, might more extremely put it), and (in the special case of scientists and their like) the pride of impiously tampering with God's creation and the normal state of things. Pride, which governs the mad scientists of book III (and the philosopher experts in the earlier books, I.ii.37, II.ii.103–4); the puny self-importance of the Lilliputians in book I, who play at men; and that of men, which emerges by extension in book II, is the most deeply unnatural of all the vices because, as the other vices prove, there is nothing to be proud of.

This diagnosis of mankind is an Augustan commonplace, and many important elements of it may be found not only in an earlier humanism but also in various old traditions of classical and Christian thought. But Swift refines on it by a number of characteristic ironies which serve to undermine any comfort we might derive from having to contend with a simple categorical indictment of mankind, however damaging. Whichever way we interpret book IV, man is placed, in it, somewhere between the rational Houyhnhnms and the bestial Yahoos. He has less reason than the former, more than the latter. The Houyhnhnms recognize this in Gulliver, though they think of him, and he eventually thinks of himself, as basically of the Yahoo kind. A Houyhnhnm state may be unattainable to man, but there are norms of acceptable, though flawed, humanity which do not seem, in the same way, beyond the realm of moral aspiration: one-time Lilliput (I.vi.57ff.), modern Brobdingnag, the *"English"* Yeoman of the old Stamp" (III.viii.201), the Portuguese Captain. These positives must be taken gingerly. Ancient Lilliput and the old Yeomen are no more; Brobdingnag is hardly a European reality, there are not many like the Portuguese Captain and his crew, although some other decent people make fleeting unremarkable appearances. Still, they are there, and at worst, we reflect, we are still better than the Yahoos. But in conceding this assurance, Swift also takes it away. This is not just in the dramatic strength of the parallels between them and us, which culminate in the "objective" test of the female Yahoo's sexual craving for Gulliver (IV.viii.266–7). There are qualities in which Gulliver is actually inferior: "Strength, Speed and Activity, the Shortness of my Claws, and some other Particulars where Nature had no Part" (IV.vii.260). Swift can be more or less playful with those "usual Topicks of *European* Moralists' (II.vii.137) about man's physical inferiority to animals, and an earlier speech of the Houyhnhnm master, already referred to, has its rich comic side (IV.iv242–3). But it is a point meant to be taken note of, and recurs with some insistence. There is no mistaking the tartness with which we are told, in a further twist, that the Yahoos (to whom men are physically inferior!) are superior in agiliby to asses, though less comely and less useful in other respects (IV.ix.272–3). This is a Houyhnhnm view, but we need not suppose that Swift meant it literally in order to sense that he is having another snipe at the human form divine.

But more important is the assertion that man's portion of Reason, which theoretically raises him above Yahoos in non-physical matters, is in fact something "whereof we made no other Use than by its Assistance to aggravate our *natural* Corruptions, and to acquire new ones which Nature had not given us" (IV.vii.259). The notion that men use their reason to make themselves worse rather than better was not invented by Swift,[55] but it disturbingly weakens the contrary assurance that it is after all by virtue of our reason that we are better than the Yahoos. It is a Houyhnhnm comment, but so are the contrary ones (IV.iii.234; IV.vi.256; IV.ix.272). No one else tells us much either way. It recurs in various forms. Gulliver comes to realize that men use Reason "to improve and multiply those Vices, whereof their Brethren in this Country had only the Share that Nature allotted them" (IV.x.278). When men are under discussion, linguistic usage on the subject of Reason and Nature tends to change: Reason multiplies vices, Nature allots them. In an earlier passage there is even an unsettling doubt as to whether Reason in this case really *is* Reason. It occurs after the cruel irony in which the Houyhnhnm master supposes that, odious as men are, Nature has created their anatomy in such a way as to make them "utterly uncapable of doing much Mischief" (IV.v.247), to which Gulliver replies with the account of war which I discussed earlier. The master then says he hates Yahoos but cannot *blame* them any more than he would blame "a *Gnnayh* (a Bird of Prey) for its Cruelty,"[56] but as to man,

> when a Creature pretending to Reason, could be capable of such Enormities, he dreaded lest the Corruption of that Faculty might be worse than Brutality itself. He seemed therefore confident, that instead of Reason, we were only possessed of some Quality fitted to increase our natural Vices.   (IV.v.248)

This possibility, that man's Reason is not Reason, is not entertained. It goes against the run of the book's argument. But it is characteristic of Swift to place it before us, as an alternative (if only momentarily viable) affront. Either we have no Reason, or what we have is worse than not having it. The irresolution saps our defenses, for we need to answer on two fronts.[57] At the same time, neither point is true to the book, which does concede (notably through several comments of the Houyhnhnm master himself) that Gulliver is both better and more rational than the Yahoos. Swift is needling us with offensive undermining possibilities even while a moderately comforting certainty is being grudgingly established. Of the two negative, undermining streams of argument, the dominant one is that which says we do have Reason, but that it makes us worse. Its most intense manifestation occurs with Gulliver's description of the Yahoos' horrible smelly sexuality. The passage incidentally shows how germane the term Reason is, in ways we might not automatically expect, not merely to the concept "good morals" but also to the concept "virtuous passions." It drives home how the most unlikely vices tend to equal unreason (or, in the perverted human sense, not *unreason* but Reason):

> I expected every Moment, that my Master would accuse the *Yahoos* of those unnatural Appetites in both Sexes, so common among us. But Nature it seems hath not been so expert a Schoolmistress; and these politer Pleasures are entirely the Productions of Art and Reason, on our Side of the Globe.   (IV.vii.264)

Though this has special resonances in the context of *Gulliver's Travels*, and a true Swiftian tang, it is also the classic language of primitivism, which is in fact a minor theme of the work. The Houyhnhnms are in some respects prelapsarian innocents, ignorant of at least some forms of evil, and with no bodily shame or any idea of why Gulliver wears clothes. They also have no literature, but a high oral tradition in poetry and knowledge (IV.iii.235; IV.ix.273–4). Utopian Lilliput and the old English Yeomen are idealized pre-degenerate societies, and Swift's concern with the idea of the degeneration of societies has often been noted. But there is the contrary example of Brobdingnag, an advanced and largely good society which, by a shaming and pointed contrast with Lilliput and England, has emerged from an earlier turpitude (II.vii.138).[58] The Yahoos prove that there is no idealization of the noble savage, and though the Houyhnhnms do have a primitivist element, the high ideal of Nature associated with them embodies some key values of civilized Augustan aspiration. This may partly proceed from a not fully resolved duality in the conception of Reason both as civilized achievement and as corrupting force, not to mention the sense, perhaps tending against both others, of a spontaneous rightness which "strikes . . . with immediate Conviction" (IV.viii.267).

But, if so, the confusion is not really Swift's. The fact is that both the language of ideas on these matters, and ordinary English idiom, make available these various senses. Nature and Reason were all-purpose terms, and Swift, who was not writing a logical treatise (although it has been shown that he was, in a manner, refuting logical treatises),[59] was only too ready, as we have seen, to exploit the ironic possibilities offered him by the language. His whole style in this work thrives on what from a strictly logical point of view is a defiant (and transparent) linguistic sleight of hand. The textbook definition of man as *animal rationale* simply refers to that reasoning faculty which was supposed to distinguish men from beasts. Swift's "disproof" consists of tacitly translating a descriptive definition into a high ethical and intellectual ideal, and then saying that man's claim to Reason is fatuously and insufferably arrogant.[60] The often-quoted formulation in the sermon "On the Trinity" that *"Reason* itself is true and just, but the *Reason* of every particular Man is weak and wavering, perpetually swayed and turned by his Interests, his Passions, and his Vices"[61] shows that Swift is perfectly aware of semantic distinctions when he wants to be. It can also stand as an acceptable boiling-down of much that is said about human unreason in *Gulliver's Travels.* Swift's concern here, however, is not to boil the issue down to its commonplace propositional content, but to exploit the damaging ironies by all the verbal means which the language puts at his disposal.

The double standard by which the words Nature and Reason tend to be used in a debased sense when they refer to men, and an ideal sense when they refer to Houyhnhnms, lies at the heart of this. The dreadful thing is that man is neither natural in the high sense, nor (like the Yahoos, as the quotation about "politer Pleasures" showed) in the low. If we then grant that this double unnaturalness is itself natural to man, we find him becoming unnatural even to this nature. Suggestions of multiple self-complicating perversity exist in the accounts of all men's occupations and professional activities. One might instance the Laputian reasoners, who are "vehemently given to Opposition, unless when they happen to be of the right Opinion, which is seldom their Case" (III.ii.163); the Admiral who "for want of proper Intelligence . . . beat the Enemy to whom he intended to betray the Fleet" (III.viii.199); the kings who protested to Gulliver in Glubbdubdrib

> that in their whole Reigns they did never once prefer any Person of Merit, unless by Mistake or Treachery of some Minister in whom they confided: Neither would they do it if they were to live again; and they shewed with great Strength of Reason, that the Royal Throne could not be supported without Corruption;
> (III.viii.199)

the politician who "never tells a *Truth*, but with an Intent that you should take it for a *Lye*', and vice versa (IV.vi.255).[62] Most elaborate is the chain of ironies about the unnaturalness of the law. It is unnatural that laws should exist at all, since Nature and Reason should be sufficient guides for a rational creature. Other related perversities are: that while meant for men's protection, the law causes their ruin; that (for a variety of discreditably tortuous reasons) one is always at a disadvantage if one's cause is just; that lawyers use irrelevant evidence, and a jargon which no one can understand (which among other things runs against the reiterated principle that speech is only for communication); that lawyers, who are expected to be wise and learned, are in reality "the most ignorant and stupid" of men (IV.v.248–50). A major irony running through this is that man is unnatural even to his own natural unnaturalness. Assuming that moral perversion is natural to the species, it becomes, in this sense, natural for judges to accept bribes. But it is even more natural for judges to be unjust, so that "I have known some of them to have refused a large Bribe from the Side where Justice lay, rather than injure the *Faculty*, by doing any thing unbecoming their Nature or their Office" (IV.v.249).

One becomes unnatural to one's lesser natural iniquities when a deeper iniquity competes with them. The concept of Nature is debased by an ever-declining spiral into whatever depths mankind might perversely sink to.

Whatever these depths, Gulliver can follow the spiral downwards and (both in his naive complacent phase and in his later disenchanted misanthropy) accept them as natural. The spiral has almost endless possibilities, and the reader for much of the time has not even the comfort of feeling that there is a rock-bottom. But there is, at the end, something like rock-bottom, a final insult to the nature of things which Gulliver finds completely unbearable:

> My Reconcilement to the *Yahoo*-kind in general might not be so difficult, if they would be content with those Vices and Follies only which Nature hath entitled them to. I am not in the least provoked at the Sight of a Lawyer, a Pick-pocket, a Colonel, a Fool, a Lord, a Gamester, a Politician, a Whoremunger, a Physician, an Evidence, a Suborner, an Attorney, a Traytor, or the like: This is all according to the due Course of Things: But, when I behold a Lump of Deformity, and Diseases both in Body and Mind, smitten with *Pride*, it immediately breaks all the Measures of my Patience; neither shall I be ever able to comprehend how such an Animal and such a Vice could tally together. The wise and virtuous *Houyhnhnms*, who abound in all Excellencies that can adorn a rational Creature, have no Name for this Vice in their Language, which hath no Terms to express any thing that is evil, except those whereby they describe the detestable Qualities of their *Yahoos;* among which they were not able to distinguish this of Pride, for want of thoroughly understanding Human Nature, as it sheweth it self in other Countries, where that Animal presides. But I, who had more Experience, could plainly observe some Rudiments of it among the wild *Yahoos.*   (IV.xii.296)

Pride, the complacency of thinking that man is a rational animal, now becomes the "absurd Vice" which is the final aggravation of all our iniquities, the ultimate offense to Nature. Yet even Pride, the ultimate unnaturalness, is itself part of "Human Nature" ("for so they have still the Confidence to stile it,"[63] says Gulliver to Sympson, p. 7), so that we may wonder whether we really have after all reached rock-bottom, or whether there is yet another opening for still deeper unnaturalness to be revealed. The suspicion arises that if things do stop here, it is only because the book must close somewhere, rather than because the subject is exhausted. And in this final impasse the only possible response, dramatically, is Gulliver's mixture of insane hatred and impotent petulance as he forbids any English Yahoo with "any Tincture of this absurd Vice" ever to appear in his sight.

The book ends here, with Gulliver a monomaniac and his last outburst a defiant, and silly, petulance. We are not, I am sure, invited to share his attitudes literally, to accept as valid his fainting at the touch of his wife

(IV.xi.289) and his strange nostalgic preference for his horses. He has become insane or unbalanced, judged by standards of ordinary social living, and I have already suggested one reason why, in the whole design of the work, this is appropriate: it makes his rant viable by dissociating Swift from the taint of excess, without really undermining the attack from Swift that the rant stands for. It is Gulliver's manner, not Swift's, which is Timon's manner, as critics are fond of noting, which means that he (like Lucian's or Plutarch's or Shakespeare's Timon),[64] and not Swift, is the raging recluse. But his are the final words, which produce the taste Swift chose to leave behind: it is no great comfort or compliment to the reader to be assaulted with a mean hysteria that he cannot shrug off because, when all is said, it tells what the whole volume has insisted to be the truth.

It is wrong, I think, to take Gulliver as a novel-character who suffers a tragic alienation, and for whom therefore we feel pity or some kind of contempt, largely because we do not, as I suggested, think of him as a "character" at all in more than a very attenuated sense: the emphasis is so preponderantly on what can be shown through him (including what he says and thinks) than on his person in its own right, that we are never allowed to accustom ourselves to him as a real personality despite all the rudimentary local color about his early career, family life and professional doings. An aspect of this are Swift's ironic exploitations of the Gulliver-figure, which to the very end flout our most elementary expectations of character consistency: the praise of English colonialism in the last chapter, which startingly returns to Gulliver's earlier boneheaded manner, is an example. The treatment of Gulliver is essentially *external*, as, according to Wyndham Lewis, satire ought to be.[65] Nor is Gulliver sufficiently independent from Swift: he is not identical with Swift, nor even similar to him, but Swift's presence behind him is always too close to ignore. This is not because Swift approves or disapproves of what Gulliver says at any given time, but because Swift is always saying something *through* it.

Gulliver in his unbalanced state, then, seems less a character than (in a view which has much truth but needs qualifying) a protesting gesture of impotent rage, a satirist's stance of ultimate exasperation. Through him, as through the modest proposer (who once offered sensible and decent suggestions which were ignored), Swift is pointing, in a favorite irony, to the lonely madness of trying to mend the world, a visionary absurdity which, in more than a shallow rhetorical sense, Swift saw as his own. At the time of finishing *Gulliver*, Swift told Pope, in a wry joke, that he wished there were a "Hospital" for the world's despisers.[66] (If Gulliver, incidentally, unlike the proposer, does not preach cannibalism, he does ask for clothes of Yahoo-skin [IV.iii.236] and uses this material for his boat and sails [IV.x.281].) But Gulliver does not quite project the noble rage or righteous pride of the outraged satirist. The exasperated petulance of the last speech keeps the quarrel on an altogether less majestic and more intimate footing, where it has, in my view, been all along. Common sense tells us that Swift would not talk like that in his own voice, but we know disturbingly (and there has been no strong competing voice) that this is the voice he chose to leave in our ears.

Still, Gulliver's view is out of touch with a daily reality about which Swift also knew, and which includes the good Portuguese Captain. Gulliver's response to the Captain is plainly unworthy, and we should note that he has not learnt such bad manners (or his later hysterical tone) from the Houyhnhnms' example. But we should also remember that the Captain is a rarity,[67] who appears only briefly; that just before Gulliver meets him the horrible mutiny with which book IV began is twice remembered (IV.x.281; IV.xi.283); that the first men Gulliver meets after leaving Houyhnhnmland are hostile savages (IV.xi.284); and that just after the excellent Portuguese sailors there is a hint of the Portuguese Inquisition (IV.xi.288). The Captain does have a function. As John Traugott says, he emphasizes Gulliver's alienation and "allows Gulliver to make Swift's point that even good Yahoos are Yahoos."[68] But above all perhaps he serves as a reasonable concession to reality (as if Swift were saying there *are* some good men, but the case is unaltered), without which the onslaughts on mankind might be open to a too easy repudiation from the reader. In this respect, he complements the other disarming concessions, the humor and self-irony, the physical comicality of the Houyhnhnms, Gulliver's folly, and the rest.

Even if Swift is making a more moderate attack on mankind than Gulliver, Gulliver's view hovers damagingly over it all; in the same way that, though the book says we are better than the Yahoos, it does not allow us to be too sure of the fact. (The bad smell of the Portuguese Captain, or of Gulliver's wife, are presumably "objective" tokens of physical identity, like the She-Yahoo's sexual desire for Gulliver.) This indirection unsettles the reader, by denying him the solace of definite categories. It forbids the luxury of a well-defined stand, whether of resistance or assent, and offers none of the comforts of that author–reader complicity on which much satiric rhetoric depends. It is an ironic procedure, mocking, elusive, immensely resourceful and agile, which talks at the reader with a unique quarrelsome intimacy, but which is so hedged with aggressive defenses that it is impossible for him to answer back.

Finally, a word about the Houyhnhnms. It is sometimes said that Swift is satirizing them as absurd or nasty embodiments of extreme rationalism. Apart from the element of humor discussed earlier, with which they are presented, they are, it is said, conceited and obtuse in disbelieving the existence or the physical viability of the human creature. But, within the logic of the fiction, this disbelief seems natural enough. The Lilliputians also doubted the existence of men of Gulliver's size (I.vi.49), and Gulliver also needed explaining in Brobdingnag (II.iii.103-4). In both these cases the philosophers are characteristically silly, but everybody is intrigued, and we could hardly expect otherwise. Moreover, Gulliver tells Sympson that some human beings have doubted the existence of Houyhnhnms (p. 8), which, within the terms of the story (if one is really going to take this sort of evidence solemnly), is just as arrogant. More important, the related Houyhnhnm doubt as to the anatomical viability or efficiency of the human shape (apart from being no more smug than some of Gulliver's complacencies *in favor* of mankind) turns to a biting sarcasm at man's, not at the Houyhnhnms', expense when, as we have seen, the Houyhnhnm master supposes that man is not capable of making war (IV.v.247).

The Houyhnhnms' proposal to castrate some younger Yahoos (IV.ix.272-3) has also shocked critics. But again this follows the simple narrative logic: it is no more than humans do to horses. Our shock should be no more than the "noble Resentment" of the Houyhnhnm master when he hears of the custom among us (IV.iv.242). To the extent that we *are* shocked, Swift seems to me to be meaning mildly to outrage our "healthy" sensibilities, as he does in the hoof-kissing episode. But in any event, the Houyhnhnms get the idea *from* Gulliver's account of what men do to horses, so that either way the force of the fable is not on man's side. The fiction throughout the man–horse relationship: horses are degenerate in England (p. 8 and IV.xii.295), as men are in Houyhnhnmland. Again, I think man comes out of it badly both ways: the Yahoos of Houyhnhnmland make their obvious point, but the suggestion in reverse seems to be that English horses are poor specimens (though to Gulliver better than men) because they live in a bad human world. At least, a kind of irrational sense of guilt by association is generated. We need not suppose that Swift is endorsing Gulliver's preference of his horses to his family in order to feel offended about it. At many (sometimes indefinable) points on a complex scale of effects, Swift is getting at us.

The Houyhnhnms' expulsion of Gulliver belongs to the same group of objections. It seems to me that some of the sympathy showered on Gulliver by critics comes from a misfocused response to him as a full character in whom we are very involved as a person. The Houyhnhnm master and the sorrel nag are in fact very sorry to lose Gulliver, but the logic of the fable is inexorable: Gulliver is of the Yahoo kind, and his privileged position in Houyhnhnmland was offensive to some, while his rudiments of Reason threaten (not without plausibility, from all we learn of man's use of that faculty) to make him a danger to the state as leader of the wild Yahoos (IV.x.279). The expulsion of Gulliver is like Gulliver's treatment of Don Pedro: both episodes have been sentimentalized, but they are a harsh reminder that even good Yahoos are Yahoos.

The main charge is that the Houyhnhnms are cold, passionless, inhuman, unattractive to us and therefore an inappropriate positive model. The fact that we may not like them does not mean that Swift is disowning them: it is consistent with his whole style to nettle us with a positive we might find insulting and rebarbative. The older critics who disliked the Houyhnhnms but felt that Swift meant them as a positive were surely nearer the mark than some recent ones who translate their own dislikes into the meaning of the book. But one must agree that the Houyhnhnms, though they are a positive, are not a *model*, there being no question of our being able to imitate them. So far as it has not been grossly exaggerated, their "inhumanity" may well, like their literal *non*-humanity (which tells us that the only really rational animal is not man), be part of the satiric point: this is a matter of "passions."

They are, of course, not totally passionless.[69] They treat Gulliver, in all personal contacts, with mildness, tenderness and friendly dignity (IV.i.224ff.). Gulliver receives special gentleness and affection from his master, and still warmer tenderness from the sorrel nag (IV.xi.283). Their language, which has no term for lying or opinion, "expressed the Passions very well," which may mean no more than "emotions" but does mean that they have them (IV.i.226). In contrast to the Laputians, who have no "Imagination, Fancy and Invention" (III.ii.163), but like the Brobdingnagians (II.vii.136), they excel in poetry (IV.ix.273-4), though their poems sound as if they might be rather unreadable and are certainly not of a very rapturous kind.

But their personal lives differ from ours in a kind of lofty tranquility, and an absence of personal intimacy and emotional entanglement. In some aspects of this, they parallel Utopian Lilliput (I.vi.60ff.), and when Gulliver is describing such things as their conversational habits ("Where there was no Interruption, Tediousness, Heat, or Difference of Sentiments"), a note of undisguised wishfulness comes into the writing (see the whole passage, IV.x.277). W. B. Carnochan has shown, in a well-taken point, that such freedom from the "tyrant-passions" corresponds to a genuine longing of Swift himself.[70] I do not wish, and have no ability, to be psychoanalytical. But in a work which, in addition to much routine and sometimes rather self-conscious scatology (however, "traditional"), contains the disturbing anatomy of Brobdingnagian ladies, the account of the Struldbrugs, the reeking sexuality of the Yahoos and the She-Yahoo's attempt on Gulliver, the horrible three-year-old Yahoo brat (IV.viii.265–6), the smell of Don Pedro and of Gulliver's family and Gulliver's strange relations with his wife, one might well expect to find aspirations for a society which practised eugenics and had an educational system in which personal and family intimacies were reduced to a minimum. Gulliver may be mocked, but the cumulative effect of these things is inescapable, and within the atmosphere of the work itself the longing for a world uncontaminated as far as possible by the vagaries of emotion might seem to us an unattractive, but surely not a surprising, phenomenon.

But it is more important still to say that the Houyhnhnms are not a statement of what man ought to be so much as a statement of what he is not. Man thinks he is *animal rationale,* and the Houyhnhnms are a demonstration (which might, as we saw, be logically unacceptable, but is imaginatively powerful), for man to compare himself with, of what an *animal rationale* really is. R. S. Crane has shown that in the logic textbooks which commonly purveyed the old definition of man as a rational animal, the beast traditionally and most frequently named as a specific example of the opposite, the non-rational, was the horse.[71] Thus Hudibras, who "was in *Logick* a great Critick," would

> undertake to prove by force
> Of Argument, a Man's no Horse.[72]

The choice of horses thus becomes an insulting exercise in "logical" refutation. The Yahoos are certainly an opposite extreme, and real man lies somewhere between them. But it is no simple comforting matter of a golden mean. Man is dramatically closer to the Yahoos in many ways, and with all manner of insistence. While the Houyhnhnms are an insulting impossibility, the Yahoos, though not a reality, are an equally insulting *possibility.* Swift's strategy of the undermining doubt is nowhere more evident than here, for though we are made to fear the worst, we are not given the comfort of knowing the worst. "The chief end I propose to my self in all my labors is to vex the world rather than divert it," and whatever grains of salt we may choose for our comfort to see in these words, "the world," gentle reader, includes *thee.*

Notes

1. *Works: The Prose Writings of Jonathan Swift,* ed. Herbert Davis et al. (Oxford: Blackwell, 1939–68) I.29. See also I.32.
2. Herbert Read, *Selected Writings* (London, 1963), p. 127.
3. *Works,* I.42n.
4. See Edward W. Rosenheim, Jr., *Swift and the Satirist's Art* (Chicago and London, 1963), p. 62.
5. *Tristram Shandy,* IV.x; IX.viii.
6. For a most useful survey of this "self-conscious" mode of writing, see Wayne C. Booth, "The self-conscious narrator in comic fiction before *Tristram Shandy,*" *Publications of the Modern Language Association of America,* LXCII (1952), 163–85. There is a good deal of this kind of writing shortly before Sterne, not necessarily derived from Swift, and my point does not *primarily* concern an "influence." See also Booth, *The Rhetoric of Fiction* (Chicago and London, 1965), p. 229.
7. Norman Mailer, *Advertisements for Myself* (London [Panther Books], 1970), p. 7.
8. See pp. 140ff., and chapter V, passim, in *Gulliver and the Gentle Reader.*
9. It is noteworthy that in some of his *private* correspondence with Stella, Swift frequently used what we now recognize as Shandean mannerisms: coy spontaneities of self-reference, playfully affectionate bits of private nonsense and of intimate double-entendre, broken sentences and even the sort of non-verbal and sub-verbal communication ("little language," grunts and cries) which is part of the everyday world of Tristram and Walter Shandy and Uncle Toby, but which Swift was quick to satirize in its more public manifestations (e.g., the sub-verbal communion, through looks and sighs and belches, of the worshippers in the *Mechanical Operation of the Spirit, Works,* I.183, etc.). See the examples from the *Journal to Stella* cited in Herbert Davis, *Jonathan Swift: Essays on his Satire, and Other Studies* (New York, 1964), pp. 82ff., and Davis's pertinent comment on p. 93 "that the letters of Swift from which I have been quoting, were first published at various times between 1745 and 1767, that the account of the life and character of Stella first appeared in 1765, and the *Journal to Stella* partly in 1766, and partly in 1768; they were all therefore first read by those who had delighted in the novels of Richardson and Sterne, and who were enjoying the sentimental comedies of Kelly and Cumberland."
10. *Works,* I.22. Here again Swift is prepared privately to practise the things whose *public* manifestation he reproves. A. B. England has recently shown how in the private *Journal to Stella* Swift is concerned that his writing should suggest "that nothing which comes into his consciousness is irrelevant," and that the moment by moment reporting of facts and feelings, even if they turn out to be erroneous, must stand as the true record of "the incoherent, discontinuous movement of his experience and his thoughts," citing comments like "I must say every sorry thing that comes into my head," "Mr. Lewis's man came in before I could finish that word beginning with a W . . . ," etc. ("Private and public rhetoric in the *Journal to Stella,*"

Essays in Criticism, XXII (1972), 133; *Journal to Stella*, II.568, 371). Like other critics, Mr. England rightly argues that the spontaneities and discontinuities are themselves part of a deliberate rhetoric. So, of course, were Sterne's. The points of interest in the present context are that Swift was both drawn to a proto-Shandean style and at the same time reserved his nonsatiric uses of it for his *private* writings.

Compare Swift's narrator's claim that his statements are "literally true this Minute I am writing," whatever the next moment may bring, with the Mailerian hipster's doctrine that "there are no truths other than the isolated truths of what each observer feels at each instant of his existence . . . the truth is not what one has felt yesterday or what one expects to feel tomorrow but rather truth is no more nor less than what one feels at each instant in the perpetual climax of the present" (*Advertisements for Myself*, pp. 285-6).

11. Richardson, Preface to *Sir Charles Grandison*.

12. *Works*, I.27.

13. *Tristram Shandy*, I.vi.

14. *Works*, I.131, 133.

15. F. R. Leavis, "The irony of Swift," *The Common Pursuit* (Harmondsworth, 1962), p. 80.

16. H. W. Sams, "Swift's satire of the Second Person," *ELH. A Journal of English Literary History*, XXVI (1959), 36-44.

17. C. S. Lewis, "Addison," in *Essays on the Eighteenth Century Presented to David Nichol Smith* (Oxford, 1945), p. 1; Irvin Ehrenpreis, *The Personality of Jonathan Swift* (London, 1958), p. 39, on *A Beautiful Young Nymph Going to Bed*. Ehrenpreis also lists parallels from other writers. See also Roland M. Frye, "Swift's Yahoo and the Christian symbols for sin," *Journal of the History of Ideas*, XV (1954), 201-17, and Deane Swift's *Essay* (1755), pp. 221ff.

18. This notation gives the book and chapter reference to *Gulliver's Travels* and the page in *Works*, XI.

19. For an amusing passage about indoor as against outdoor defecation, see "A. Panegyrick on the D———n," II.229ff. (*Poems*, ed. Harold Williams (Oxford, 1958), III.894ff.).

20. William King, *Some Remarks on the Tale of a Tub* (1704) cited by Ricardo Quintana, *The Mind and Art of Jonathan Swift* (New York and London, 1936), p. 75; William Wotton, *A Defense of the Reflections upon Ancient and Modern Learning . . . With Observations upon The Tale of a Tub* (1705), in *A Tale of a Tub*, ed. A. C. Guthkelch and D. Nichol Smith, 2nd edn. (Oxford, 1958), pp. 322, 323, 326; *Works*, I.5. Swift was not at first known to be the author.

21. The tartness of these jokes in *Gulliver* may be contrasted with the protracted and elaborate geniality with which Norman Mailer descirbes "an overwhelming urge to micturate" in *Armies of the Night* (New York, 1968), pp. 42-4, with its vacuous mock-concern about what people would think of his "pissing on the floor" if the attendant reported it to the police or the press got hold of the news (p. 43), and with its fussily self-delighting returns to the episode, and to Mailer's coy feelings of guilt, later in the book (pp. 63, 71).

22. Thackeray, *The English Humourists of the Eighteenth Century* (Everyman's Library, London and New York, 1949), p. 32.

23. For other satirical-treatments of the papal ceremony, see *Tale*, IV (*Works*, I.71), and Rabelais I.ii; I.xxxiii; II.xxx.

24. *English Humourists*, pp. 34-5.

25. Edward Stone, "Swift and the Horses: Misanthropy or Comedy?," *Modern Language Quarterly*, x (1949), 374n.

26. Real concealment seemed a necessity, with such a subversive book, though Pope told Swift on 16 November 1726 that people were not worried by "particular reflections," so that

he "needed not to have been so secret upon this head" (*Correspondence*, III.181). In any case, *simple* anonymity or pseudonymity would have served the practical purposes. Swift's authorship soon became fairly well known anyway.

27. Horace, *Odes*, III.xi.35.

28. *Correspondence*, ed. Harold Williams (Oxford, 1963–65), III.180, 189. See also Mario M. Rossi and Joseph M. Hone, *Swift or the Egotist* (London, 1934), pp. 330, 441.

29. See Ricardo Quintana, *Swift: An Introduction* (London, 1962), pp. 53ff., 158f.

30. Rabelais, II.xxviii, et passim; Lucian, *True Story*, I.2ff.; Butler, *Erewhon*, ch.ix, ad fin.

31. "Democritus Junior to the Reader," *Anatomy of Melancholy*, Everyman's Library (London and New York, 1932), I.15, 123.

32. Contrast Gulliver's use of this convention: "I never suffer a Word to pass that may look like Reflection, or possibly give the least Offence even to those who are most ready to take it. So that, I hope, I may with Justice pronounce myself an Author perfectly blameless; against whom the Tribes of Answerers, Considerers, Observers, Reflecters, Detecters, Remarkers, will never be able to find Matter for exercising their Talents" (IV.xii.293). This hardly pretends to be a friendly, or even a plausible, gesture from Swift, though it is, of course, amusing.

33. For both these uses, see *Oxford English Dictionary*, "Thou," *pers. pron.*, *Ib*, and "Thou," *verb*.

34. Swift, *Epistle to a Lady*, II.139ff. (*Poems*, II.634–7).

35. *Correspondence*, II.179.

36. Ibid., 120.

37. Ibid., 181, 182.

38. The clinching joke, though not the passage as a whole, is Swift's. See R. W. Frantz, "Gulliver's 'Cousin Sympson,'" *Huntington Library Quarterly*, i. (1938), 331–3.

39. Boswell, *Life of Johnson*, ed. G. B. Hill and L. F. Powell (Oxford, 1934), II.319.

40. *Correspondence*, III.257–8.

41. *Jonathan Swift and the Anatomy of Satire* (Cambridge, Mass., 1961), p. 7.

42. *Epistle to a Lady*, II.164–70 (*Poems*, II.635).

43. *Correspondence*, III.103, 117.

44. Irvin Ehrenpreis, "The meaning of Gulliver's last voyage," *Review of English Literature*, iii (1962), 35.

45. The passage seems to some extent to conform to Erasmus's prescription for amplifying a description with appropriate graphic detail: see *De Copia*, Book II, Fifth Method, especially the examples from Quintilian, VIII.iii.67–69, and Lucan, III (*On Copia of Words and Ideas*, trs. and ed. Donald B. King and H. David Rix [Milwaukee, 1963], pp. 47–50. Quintilian is describing how to make vivid the capture of a city; Lucan is describing a particular battle. Neither passage has nor seeks the crazy and generalized exuberance of Gulliver's headlong list.

46. George Orwell, *Nineteen Eighty-Four*, part I, ch.i (Harmondsworth, 1954), pp. 10–11.

47. See pp. 50–2 of *Gulliver and the Gentle Reader*.

48. A. E. Case, *Four Essays on Gulliver's Travels* (Gloucester, Mass., 1958), p. 110.

49. Thomas Sheridan, *The Life of the Rev. Dr. Jonathan Swift*, 2nd edn., (1787), p. 433.

50. Joseph Horrell, "What Gulliver knew," *Sewanee Review*, li (1943), 492–3; Case, *Four Essays*, p. 121; Samuel H. Monk, "The pride of Lemuel Gulliver," *Sewanee Review*, lxiii (1955), 56.

51. More, *Utopia*, trs. Ralph Robinson, Everyman's Library (London and New York, 1951), p. 85. For an excellent discussion of More and Swift, see John Traugott, "A voyage

to Nowhere with Thomas More and Jonathan Swift: *Utopia* and *The Voyage to the Houyhnhnms'*, *Sewanee Review*, lxix (1961), 534–65. A somewhat different comparison is made by Brian Vickers, "The satiric structure of *Gulliver's Travels* and More's *Utopia*," *The World of Jonathan Swift*, ed. Brian Vickers (Oxford, 1968), pp. 233–57.

52. *Tom Jones*, III.iii. I hasten to say that I do not believe that the Houyhnhnms are therefore a satirical skit on the deists (or that Square, as one might just as easily "prove," was a skit on the Houyhnhnms), though the rationalisms have points in common. A. O. Lovejoy's "The parallel of Deism and Classicism," *Essays in the History of Ideas* (New York, 1960), pp. 78–98, makes abundantly clear that many basic assumptions about Nature and Reason were the common property of deists and non-deists alike. (My discussion here is indebted to this and other essays in Lovejoy's book.) This may be the place to say categorically that in my view Swift treats the Houyhnhnms mainly seriously and not mockingly, and that the recent arguments to this effect by Sherburn, Crane, Rosenheim, W. B. Carnochan, and others have put criticism of *Gulliver's Travels* back on the right lines.

53. These wonderfully apt examples are adapted from Rabelais, V.xxii, as is noted in W. A. Eddy, *Gulliver's Travels: A Critical Study* (New York, 1963), pp. 161–2. Jean Plattard's notes to the *Cinquiesme Livre* (Paris, 1948), pp. 324–5, show that Rabelais was literalizing a series of adages of Erasmus. See also the account of Lucian's *True Story* in Eddy, p. 16.

54. Pope, *Dunciad*, III.6.

55. See for example Roland M. Frye (above, n.17), pp. 208–9.

56. This is an illuminating parallel to Swift's remark to Pope on 26 November 1725 about the kite (*Correspondence*, III.118). I have briefly discussed interpretations of this controversial letter in a review in *Notes and Queries*, ccix (1964), 316–17.

57. There are certain analogies between this mode of attack, and those strategies of aggression *either way*, of putting one's victim in an "untenable position" or "double bind," some of whose manifestations in the domain of psychopathology are described in R. D. Laing, *Self and Others* (Harmondsworth, 1971), ch. ix, esp. pp. 141ff., 147. And see Peter Sedgwick in *Laing and Anti-Psychiatry*, ed. Robert Boyers and Robert Orrill (Harmondsworth, 1972), pp. 22–4.

58. The passage runs pointedly against the Lilliputian (I.vi.60) and English (III.vii.201–2) examples. All rather strikingly have grandfather-grandchildren references. The contrast may reflect Swift's interest, noted by some critics, in a cyclical theory of history (e.g., III.x.210), but such force as it has on the reader *as a contrast* is simply to the discredit of England.

59. R. S. Crane, "The Houyhnhnms, the Yahoos, and the history of ideas," *Reason and the Imagination*, ed. J. A. Mazzeo (New York and London, 1962), pp. 231–53.

60. See Ehrenpreis, op. cit., *Review of English Literature*, iii (1962), 34. In some ways, *animal rationis capax* is not really very different from *animal rationale* in the low-pitched textbook sense. Bolingbroke may have this partly in mind when he says the distinction "will not bear examination" (*Correspondence*, III.121).

61. *Works*, IX.166.

62. Physicians provide a monstrously concrete example of Nature turned upside down. The basis of the reversal is the perfectly fair notion, discussed earlier, that health is the "natural" state of the body: "these Artists ingeniously considering that in all Diseases Nature is forced out of her Seat; therefore to replace her in it, the Body must be treated in a Manner directly contrary, by interchanging the Use of each Orifice; forcing Solids and Liquids in at the *Anus*, and making Evacuations at the Mouth" (IV.vi.254).

63. But this parenthesis may refer to the word "degrading," and not to the phrase "human Nature."

64. Lucian, *Timon, or the Misanthrope;* Plutarch, *Life of Antony,* LXX; Shakespeare, *Timon of Athens.* Or it may be that when Swift professed his misanthropy in *Gulliver's Travels* to be "not [in] Timons manner" (*Correspondence,* III.103) he was merely saying that he was just as misanthropic, but would avoid Timon's "manner" only, i.e., his style of ranting grandiloquence, a version of that "lofty Stile" (*Epistle to a Lady,* II.140, 218, *Poems,* II.634, 637), which Swift almost invariably refused to use.

65. Robert C. Elliott, *The Power of Satire* (Princeton, 1960), pp. 225–6.

66. *Correspondence,* III.117. See W. B. Carnochan, "The complexity of Swift: Gulliver's fourth voyage," *Studies in Philology,* lx (1963), 32ff.

67. "O, if the World had but a dozen Arbuthnetts in it I would burn my Travells" (*Correspondence,* III.104). Don Pedro may, in this sense, be an Arbuthnot.

68. Traugott, op. cit., *Sewanee Review,* lxix (1961), 562. For another useful perspective, see R. S. Crane, "The rationale of the fourth voyage," *Gulliver's Travels. An Annotated Text with Critical Essays,* ed. Robert A. Greenberg (New York, 1961), pp. 305–6.

69. See also George Sherburn, "Errors concerning the Houyhnhnms," *Modern Philology,* lvi (1958), 94–5, and Carnochan, op. cit., *Studies in Philology,* lx (1963), 25–6.

70. Carnochan, op. cit., p. 27.

71. *Reason and the Imagination,* pp. 247ff.

72. *Hudibras,* I.i.65, 71–2. See Ehrenpreis, op. cit., *Review of English Literature,* iii (1962), 23ff., for further illustration of the relevance of logic books. Another specified example of the non-rational animal was the ape. That Gulliver should have been taken by a Brobdingnagian monkey for one of its kind (II.v.122) gains an additional piquancy from this. Swift uses the horse, unlike the monkey, as an opposite, not as a parallel, but man is the loser both ways.

Rhetoric and Poems:
The Example of Swift

WILLIAM K. WIMSATT

I

"Cousin Swift, you will never be a poet." Words supposedly uttered by Dryden on the occasion of Swift's first publication, his Pindaric *Ode to the Athenian Society* (1692). If the story is an invention, we may well think it a happy one.

We have the four ungainly Odes, written to the sober norm of his patron and Covering Cherub Sir William Temple, and the two pentameter couplet poems: *To Congreve* and *On Temple's Illness*. The *To Congreve* is especially instructive—a creaky adulatory buttonholing, a supposed love affair with the encomiastic muse, a savage presumptive fancy of his own power and calling as a satirist. *Saeva indignatio* without much evidence that it has been earned. "How easy it is to call rogue and villain," Dryden was saying in this very year, 1693, "and that wittily! But how hard to make a man appear a fool, a blockhead, or a knave, without using any of those opprobrious terms!" Swift all his life would be a rebel to this rule, but he had not yet found an idiom which could make the defiance interesting.

We entertain the image of an obscure young country versifier, who, except for the external testimonies of authorship, we might well hesitate to identify with the man-about-town and political writer, aged about forty-six in 1713, who could produce, in tetrameter couplets, the darkly lustrous myth of dalliance *Cadenus and Vanessa*, or, in his later years and bereave-

From *The Author in His Work: Essays on a Problem in Criticism*, ed. Louis L. Martz and Aubrey Williams (New Haven: Yale University Press, 1978), pp. 229–44.

ment at Dublin, could contrive *Verses on the Death of Dr. Swift* (1731) and
On Poetry: A Rapsody (1733).

II

Much earlier he had demonstrated, if only for a moment, a successful way
of writing even the pentameter couplet, in his two London poems of 1709
and 1710, *A Description of the Morning* and *A Description of a City Shower*.
These are witty burlesque poems, but it is worth saying that they are not
written in witty couplets, not like Pope or Dryden.

> The Slipshod Prentice from his Masters Door,
> Had par'd the Dirt, and Sprinkled round the Floor.
> Now *Moll* had whirl'd her Mop with dext'rous Airs,
> Prepar'd to Scrub the Entry and the Stairs.
>
> [5-8][1]

The sentences avoid rhetorical pointing. The structure is studiously flat—
a sort of soft-mat photo texture. This is the quiet anti-poetic, the bathetic.
This ineloquent mock-pastoral-aubade, as Claude Rawson[2] points out,
invites definition by contrast with the vibratory ethos or personal projection of such romantic city poets as Baudelaire and Eliot. *Morning* is the
flatter of the two poems. It is a *very* flat poem, and hence short. This style
could not be sustained long. The *Shower* is more rhetorical.

> Here various Kinds by various Fortunes led,
> Commence Acquaintance underneath a Shed.
> Triumphant Tories, and desponding Whigs,
> Forget their Fewds, and join to save their Wigs.
>
> [39-42]

They said it was the best thing Swift "ever writ," and he too thought so.
This city rainstorm, so elaborately derived from Dryden's Virgil, the First
Georgic, and the Second and Fourth *Aeneids,* is described ingeniously by
Brendan O Hehir as "an oblique denunciation of cathartic doom upon the
corruption of the city."[3] The closing triplet and alexandrine are *not* low
burlesque, not a mere travesty of Dryden's style, despite Swift's much later
note on the passage (1735) and his letter to a friend. As there is really
nothing wrong with either a triplet or an alexandrine, nothing prevents us
from reading these as the climax of the poem's high burlesque or mock-

georgic-heroic, raising low matter to a focus of ample and pregnant realization.

> Sweepings from Butchers Stalls, Dung, Guts, and Blood,
> Drown'd Puppies, stinking Sprats, all drench'd in Mud,
> Dead Cats and Turnip-Tops come tumbling down the Flood.
>
> [61–63]

All the life of the farm, says Irvin Ehrenpreis, appears as decayed garbage, yet still in action.

III

But even earlier Swift had made another and even better discovery. If it was an accident that he found his true idiom, the tetrameter or short couplet, during his *Wanderjahre,* the ten years of his unsettlement, from 1699, shuttling between England and Ireland, yet it may be seen as an emblematic accident. The immediate and chief antecedent of Swift's anti-sublime and anti-pathetic idiom is usually and correctly enough placed in the short, harsh couplets in stringy sequences and the absurdly manufactured rhymes of Samuel Butler's *Hudibras* (a very long poem which Swift is *said* to have known by heart and which indeed is present here and there in his *Tale of a Tub*).[4] This spavined mock epic, however, has its own antecedents, in English and continental literature, and difficult as they may be to trace, we can say something about the overall view.

The long couplet as perfected by Dryden and Pope came from the classical Roman hexameter and elegiac couplet,[5] and its basic theoretical formula can be found in the figures of parallel, antithesis, metaphor, and turn described in book 3, chapters 9–11 of Aristotle's *Rhetoric.* Add only such refinements as zeugma (described with the other figures in Puttenham's *Arte of Poesie,* 1589), chiasmus, and the vernacular figures of accentual meter and rhyme. The Popean couplet, in which Swift was always to experience a relative discomfort, was Ovid with the impasto of rhyme. Marvell's short couplet, as in the *Coy Mistress* and *The Garden,* may be described in the same mainly classical terms. But the short couplet in its laughing mode was something broader and coarser, distinctly late Latin, vernacular, and anti-classical. It was a revolt against and a vagabond swerve away from the ancient decorum. Its genius may be illustrated characteristically, at one of its peaks, in the deviant Latin poets of the high Middle

Ages—the *vagantes (vagi clerici)*, refugees from Parisian discipline, irreverent, scoffers, ribalds, ironists, parodists: Golias, Primate, Bishop, Archpoet. We know that these poets, having flourished for their brief heyday, lay long out of sight, beneath the horizon for some six centuries. Even by Chaucer's time a Goliardeys was no better than a coarse jester, a jangler, the quarrelsome Miller of the Canterbury prologue. In the Victorian mid-nineteenth century, the antiquarians Thomas Wright and Andreas Schmeller were performing acts of resurrection when they brought out their editions of the poems ascribed to Walter Map (1841) and of the Benedictbeuern manuscript, *Carmina Burana* (1847). During Swift's lifetime, it is true, we find the *Historia Poetarum et Poematum Medii Aevi*, edited by the Helmstadt scholar Polycarp Leyser at Halle in 1721. And Pope in a satiric squib alludes to Blackmore as an ArchPoet. The tradition was no doubt carried all along in student drinking songs, such as the *Gaudeamus igitur*, which emerges in Germany during the later eighteenth century. But there is no likelihood that either Swifr or Pope knew any Goliardic poetry.

I am speaking synchronically of poetic affinities. "Deep within I seethe with anger," confessed the twelfth-century Archpoet to his patron the Archchancellor of the Empire. "In my bitter mind I'm talking. . . . I'm like a dead leaf on the wind."

> Aestuans intrinsecus ira vehementi
> in amaritudine loquar meae menti:
> factus de materia levis elementi
> folio sum similis de quo ludunt venti.

The four-plus-three medieval Latin septenary and the trochaic tetrameter *(Dives eram et dilectus)* were contemporaries of the French octosyllabic, and the French was the model for the English. The Goliardic rhyming was the last expressive burst of Latin as a spoken language.[6] It is Latin hovering on the verge of vernacular: a verse written in clanging contrast to the quantitative measure of the classical tradition, and revelling in a verbal chime that is a barbaric opposite to the logical homoioteleuton of classical prose. Rhyme in the Goliardic-Skeltonic-Scarronian-Hudibrastic tradition is all that Gothic, rude, and beggarly jingle deplored by such civilized theorists as Campion, Milton, and Roscommon. In that short-couplet tradition Swift found his own voice, his characteristic freedom and crashing energy. Thwarted *Episcopus*, actual *Decanus*, Swift was an Augustan *Archipoeta Redivivus*—not a libertine singer of wine, woman, and song, nevertheless exuberant in the license of rhyming irreverence, "the sin of Wit, no venial crime."

> The Language *Billingsgate* excel
> The Sentiments resemble *Hell.*
> [*A Panegyric* (1729–30), ll. 108–9]

It is a familiar enough idea that Swift made poetry out of anti-poetic materials, or simply that he made poetry that was anti-poetry. I myself might prefer to say that the anti-poetry of that age was only the anti-classical, and that the paradox of the anti-poetic, in our own age of postexpressionism, has lost most of its force. After the cruelty, the blackness, the obscenity, the absurdity, the suicide, the zero level of our modern comic experience, Swift is no longer a radical instance of inversion as such. I proceed to some rhetorical observations, moving, perhaps unadventurously, within the established demonic frame of reference. Details, I believe, are likely to win against outline in any account of the episodic, spotty, staccato career of Swift in verse. Nevertheless, I have a central and fairly simple aim in this paper. That is, to show some of the main ways in which the short couplet, rather than the long, emerged as his appointed expressive instrument.

IV

The long couplet in the classical tradition, and especially that couplet as it is refined by Swift's friend Alexander Pope, is a structure composed of *processed words,* words manipulated into new, momentary phrases—ellipses, compressions, inversions, zeugmas, extraordinary junctures, suspensions:

> Where Wigs with Wigs, with Sword-knots Sword-knots strive.
> Where *Nature moves,* and *Rapture warms* the Mind.
> A hero perish, or a sparrow fall.
> And now a bubble burst, and now a world.
> The sot a hero, lunatic a king.

Pope's unit of wit is the half-line. His rhymes depend very much on the very special syntactic mechanism which brings them into conjunction. "Each Atom by some other struck," Swift himself wrote in a poem to Pope, "All Turns and Motion tries; Till in a Lump together stuck, Behold a *Poem* rise!" (*Dr. Sw————to Mr. P————e*, 1727). Even in Pope's use of the starkest everyday language, he arranges with atomic care; he maximizes in very exact, if excited and unusual, sequences.

> Shut, shut the door, good *John!* fatigu'd I said.
> Tye up the knocker, say I'm sick, I'm dead.
> [*An Epistle to Dr. Arbuthnot*, 1–2]

The short couplet, a release and freedom for Swift, was a hobble for Pope. Swift did not think Pope imitated his couplet very well. He disparaged Pope's imitation of his style in supplying the episode of the town mouse and the country mouse to fill out the Horatian *Satire* 2. 6. Probably we could not always, under any circumstances (that is, if not told the authorship in advance), be sure of seeing in Pope's lines something essentially different from the plainer and in a sense heavier phrasing of Swift. Lines 9–28 of this poem are debated, the external evidence failing. But from line 133 on we are certain about Pope. And thus:

> O charming Noons! and Nights divine!
> Or when I sup, or when I dine,
> My Friends above, my Folks below,
> Chatting and laughing all-a-row,
> The Beans and Bacon set before 'em,
> The Grace-cup serv'd with all decorum:
> And even the very Dogs at ease!
> Which is the happier, or the wiser,
> A man of Merit, or a Miser?
> Whether we ought to chuse our Friends,
> For their own Worth, or our own Ends?
> [*Satire* 2. 6. 133–50]

The half-line chiming units and with them a certain buoyancy and sprightliness, a graceful soaring, fit conveniently with our knowledge on external evidence that these lines were written by Pope.[8]

V

The earliest surviving short-couplet poem by Swift, the *Verses Wrote in a Lady's Ivory Table Book* (1698?), is a sharp example of his peculiar love for what we can best, I think, call live *whole* phrases.

> Here you may read *(Dear Charming Saint)*
> Beneath *(A new Receit for Paint)*
> Here in Beau-spelling *(tru til deth)*
> There in her own *(far an el breth)*
> Here *(lovely Nymph pronounce my doom)*
> There *(A safe way to use Perfume)*
> Here, a Page fill'd with Billet Doux;
> On t'other side *(laid out for Shoes)*
> *(Madam, I dye without your Grace)*
> (Item, *for half a Yard of Lace.*)
>   [7–16]

Add the following from the Horatian *Epistle* 1.7, to Lord Oxford, purporting to narrate Swift's first encounter with him:

> Swift, who could neither fly nor hide,
> Came sneaking to the Chariot-side,
> And offer'd many a lame Excuse;
> He never meant the least Abuse—
> *My Lord—The Honour you design'd—*
> *Extremely proud—but I had din'd—*
> *I'm sure I never shou'd neglect—*
> *No Man alive has more Respect—.*
> [*To Lord Oxford* (1713), ll. 63–70]

Swift's short couplets are composed, characteristically, of ready-made phrases, from the colloquial and stereotype repertory, pieces of stock language laid together in bundles, clattering parallels. He rattles the literal commonplaces, brandishes the living speech. We are close to the specimens of fatuity which he collected so lovingly in his *Polite Conversation* (in modern American parlance, *The Cliché Expert Takes the Stand*). The lines largely lack internal figural structure. The wit may come in the contrast between phrases drawn from different fonts, as that of the beau and that of the lady so systematically rhymed in the *Ivory Table Book*. Johnson said of Swift's prose *(The Conduct of the Allies)*, "He had to count ten, and he has counted it right." Of Swift's verses, Johnson said, "there is not much upon which the critic can exercise his powers."

One may have felt the same kind of literalism, or fidelity to real speech, in the hexameter couplets of the greatest French comic writer, Molière. It is tempting to draw this proportion: as Pope, especially in his Homer, is to Racine, so Swift, in his short couplets, is to Molière.

VI

Swift found Berkeley's *Alciphron* "too speculative."[9] Swift was anti-meta-physical, anti-speculative. His orientation toward *things*— hard objects, such as can be set on a shelf, put in a box, or carried in pocket or hand (a "rhyming and chiming" universe, yet how unlike the dappled cosmic vision of the poet Hopkins)—reminds us of the philosophers in the Grand Academy of Lagado, who conceived the notion of carrying *things* about with them, to use instead of words. One of Swift's most reliable poetic devices (as we might expect in general from the author of *Gulliver*) is the catalogue or "inventory" of miscellaneous physical things or of verbal things: the *Furniture of a Woman's Mind* ("A Set of Phrases learnt by Rote; A Passion for a Scarlet Coat"—[1727], 2. 415); the key literal items of millinery concern, *lace, stuff, yard, fan* (in rhyming positions), the samples of card-table talk, the cheats, complaints, and accusations, all the splattering enumerations of a cluttered life that make the *Journal of a Modern Lady* ("I but transcribe, for not a Line / Of all the Satyre shall be mine. . . . Unwilling Muse begin thy Lay, / The Annals of a Female Day"—[1729], II.28–29, 34–35); the verbal trash that composes the cliché mind of a *Grisette* (1730); the list of false parts removed by *A Beautiful Young Nymph Going to Bed* (1731); the disgusting clutter of *A Lady's Dressing Room* (1730): "Of all the Litter as it lay; . . . An Inventory follows here."

> The various Combs for various Uses,
> Fill'd up with Dirt so closely fixt,
> No Brush could force a way betwixt.
> A Paste of Composition rare,
> Sweat, Dandriff, Powder, Lead and Hair.
> [8, 10, 20–24]

The imputation of slovenly vice or, at the mildest, of helter-skelter frivolity conveyed in these catalogues represents a juncture of couplet rhetoric and a certain kind of sexism which I am not concerned to develop in this paper.

Such verbalized and inventoried objects are most conspicuous when they occur as rhymes. Rhyme is the most brilliantly attractive feature of Swift's verse. "Rhyme," says Butler in *Hudibras*, "the rudder of verses" (I.I.403). So much of Swift's line, says Martin Price "is absorbed into the rhyme."

In a cunning blend of prudence and artistry, Swift sometimes teases us with a rhyme word left blank—either a scatological word ("Celia, Celia, Celia————") or the name of some dangerous political target.

> How the Helm is rul'd by ———
> At whose Oars, like Slaves, they all pull.
> *[To a Lady* (1733), ll. 159–60]

If we have any doubt how the music of that rhyme goes, we can consult its complement in another poem of about the same date.

> But why wou'd he, except he *slobber'd,*
> Offend our Patriot, Great Sir R———?
> *[The Life and Character of Dean Swift* (1733), ll. 107–08]

The first poem quoted just now, the *Epistle to a Lady, Who desired the Author to make Verses on Her, in the Heroick Stile,* exhibits, I believe, the most sustained instance of this unheroic device that Swift ever achieved.

> I, WHO love to have a Fling,
> Both at Senate-House, and ———   King
>
> . . . .
> If I treat you like———   a crown'd Head
> You have cheap enough compounded.
> Can you put in higher Claims,
> Than the Owners of *St. J*———*s.*   James
> You are not so great a Grievance
> As the Hirelings of *St. St*———*s.*   Stephens
> You are of a lower Class
> Than my Friend Sir *R*———*Br*———*s.*   Robert Brass
> [221–22, 239–46]

That kind of rhyming is the complementary opposite of a French diversion described by Addison in *Spectator* 60, the game of *bouts-rimés*—where only the rhyme words are given, and the player is challenged to fill in the blank lines to his fancy. Swift's extraordinary rhymes sometimes seem to invite being extracted from his verse for use in that way too. A few of his most bravura passages might make almost manageable parlor games. What might we not make, for instance, of such a series of expressions as:

dupes us
Peri Hupsous,
Longinus,
outshine us.

over-run ye,
for love or money,
translation,
Quotation.

Words combined into makeshift rhymes play a large part here. In many, perhaps in most, of Swift's comic two-syllable rhymes, we find one makeshift (sometimes with forced accent, and better if the first of the couplet) combined with one ready-made, the excuse or occasion for the couplet. In the passage I have just dismembered, we note, along with the excellent *Peri Hupsous* and *Longinus,* the no less ready-made cliché or tag phrase "for love or money." The closing couplet, formed on the Latinate *translation* and *Quotation,* may be said to take advantage of a very easy linguistic opportunity.

> A forward critic often dupes us
> With sham quotations *Peri Hupsous*
> And if we have not read *Longinus,*
> Will magisterially outshine us.
> Then, lest with Greek he over-run ye,
> Procure the book for love or money,
> Translated from Boileau's translation,
> And quote *Quotation* on *Quotation.*
> [*On Poetry: A Rapsody*
> (1733), ll. 255–62]

A more minute rhetorical examination of this passage might choose for special remark such a word as *magisterially,* unrolling itself so magisterially that, although only one word of four, it manages to usurp three of the line's four metrical ictuses; it illustrates what we might have been suspecting, that Swift's apparently flat and plain bundles of simple phrases are susceptible of very nice tilting within the metrical frame. The last couplet, with its easy rhyme of *translation* and *quotation,* is fortified internally in each line by an anagnorisis or "turn" upon the rhyming word.

It is difficult to make significant statistical statements about Swift's rhyme. The most florid passages stand out in the memory and color the whole. Broaden the base for a moment and think of the English tradition, most notably Butler, Swift, and Byron. Swift, said Byron, "beats us all hollow, his rhymes are wonderful."[10] Byron shows himself a true Swiftian when he joins Aristotle with Longinus via the word *bottle.*

————"Longinus o'er a Bottle,"
Or, "Every Poet his *own* Aristotle."
[*Don Juan*, I. 204]

The English comic rhymes are poetic *objets trouvés*, a flotsam and jetsam, jumble and tumble, of miscellaneous prefabricated linguistic objects, conspicuous curiosities, bric-a-brac, trophies hauled in, a polyglot litter, gravels, seaweed, driftwood, of a language and culture—classical adjuncts, history, proper names, tags, quotation on quotation, a world of partial assimilations to the native English stock, a collage of newspaper scraps, a Table Book of the real and the verbal world, where the poet finds scrawled his heterogeneous chiming vocabulary. Think of Stephen Dedalus on the beach at Sandymount, meditating the "ineluctable modality of the visible." "Signatures of all things I am here to read. . . . Seaspawn and seawrack, the nearing tide, that rusty boat."

The homonyms of a language sometimes offer each other so much mutual support as hardly to be realized for the different words which they actually are. Thus *light* in weight and *light* in color. Or they clash and compete, and one of a pair may win, the other surviving only in some formalized and redundant phrase ("without *let* or hindrance") or in a classic quotation ("By heaven, I'll make a ghost of him that *lets* me"). The feat of rhyming verse is to find and focus a context where a clash of partially homonymous expressions is rendered harmonious—an illustration of the Jakobsonian rule that in poetry the axis of selection (the range of equivalence which is put to one side in straight prose) is projected onto the axis of combination, which in poetry is an axis of analogy. Swift's short-couplet rhymes are a maximum demonstration of this feat, not verbal music but paronomastic meaning. "Longinus" becomes a new signature; it reveals a latent aspect of its meaning as it evokes "outshine us." *Peri Hupsous* gives up a secret through its affinity for "dupes us."

VII

Swift persisted in experiment with varied verse forms throughout his career. He returned often enough to the pentameter couplet. He wrote anapests. He tried ballad stanzas, songs, Skeltonic dimeters. He scored such successes as the breathless gabble meter of *The Humble Petition of Frances Harris* and *Mary the Cook Maid's Letter to Dr. Sheridan*, or the squalid stanzas of the *Pastoral Dialogue* of Dermot and Sheelah. But it is fair to say that the poetic virtues which I am trying to celebrate are exerted at their maximum in the jabbing four-stress couplet (sometimes trochaic, more often iambic) which Swift made so specially his own voice.

One of the conveniences which he discovered through the use of his couplet was speed. The extraordinary speed of which this idiom was capable appears perhaps most strikingly in some of his shorter narrative poems. *The Progress of Marriage* (1721–22), for instance: how to begin a story.

> Aetatis suae fifty two
> A rich Divine began to woo
> A handsome young imperious *Girl*
> Nearly related to an Earl.
> [1–4]

Or *The Progress of Love* (1719): how to execute a turn in the middle of a story.

> Suppose all Partyes now agreed,
> The Writings drawn, the Lawyer fee'd,
> The Vicar and the Ring bespoke:
> Guess how could such a Match be broke. . . .
> [Guess how! She had run off with John the butler.]
> For truly John was missing too:
> The Horse and Pillion both were gone
> Phillis, it seems, was fled with John.
> [21–24, 40–42]

Or the principle of metamorphosis. Parallels (or similars) in general make for similitude, analogies, puns, metaphors, even metamorphoses—and even the latter a speedy operation in the short couplet. In an early couplet poem, *Baucis and Philemon* (1708–9), the metamorphosis, as Ehrenpreis observes, is like a "series of answers to riddles. How is a cottage like a church? How is a kettle like a bell?"[11]

> The chimny widen'd and grew high'r.
> Became a Steeple with a Spire:
> The Kettle to the top was hoist
> And there stood fastn'd to a Joyst. . . .
> [95–98]

Or the disappearing trick. How to make two trees disappear, gradually yet completely, in six lines.

> Here *Baucis*, there Philemon grew.
> Till once, a Parson of our Town,
> To mend his Barn, cut *Baucis* down;
> At which, 'tis hard to be believ'd,
> How much the other Tree was griev'd,
> Grew Scrubby, dy'd a-top, was stunted:
> So, the next Parson stub'd and burnt it.
>
> [172–78]

One hazard of the short line, the short, straight syntax, is that this structure may produce too many antithetic reversals, parentheses that get out of hand, digressions, loquacity—a sort of scrappiness. Swift's lesser poems are often enough notable as paragraphic assortments rather than as continuous movements. But segmentation can also produce the radiantly disjunct concentrations, the movement as of a series of shrapnel bursts, in such passages of Swift as the opening paragraphs of the *Verses on the Death of Dr. Swift* (1731).

> Dear Honest *Ned* is in the Gout,
> Lies rackt with Pain, and you without:
> How patiently you hear him groan!
> How glad the Case is not your own!
>
> What Poet would not grieve to see,
> His brethren write as well as he?
> But rather than they should excel,
> He'd wish his Rivals all in Hell.
>
> [27–34]

A term used very frequently by appreciators of Swift—whether of his verse or of his prose—is "energy." Energy—in his short verse a kind of direct insistence, an urgent announcement, a raw shock. The diapason of disgusting energy, for instance, that permeates the group of poems in which Cassinus and Peter and Strephon and Chloe and Corinna and Celia pursue their malodorous adventures. Or the energy of smiling outrage, the art of "obliging Ridicule," as he himself termed it (*Poems*, I. 216), which he found so congenial in his poems of compliment to the other sex.

> WHY, *Stella*, should you knit your Brow,
> If I compare you to the Cow?
>
> [21–22][12]

Another term which the critics have favored and which applies very well to a somewhat different range of energy in Swift is "exuberance." A nearly equivalent word might be "bumptiousness." Under this head I present a concluding contrast between Swift and his kindred spirit Pope. *On Poetry: A Rapsody*, from which we have already quoted, shows Swift in a maximum parallel to Pope—to Pope in the Horatian *Epistle to Augustus*, of course, an apology for poetry, with satire on the contemporary scene and salute to a reigning dunce. Swift did not, like Pope, write a close imitation of Horace, but he clearly had the classic model in mind (*Poems*, 2. 658). Swift's poem anticipated Pope's by four years (1733). Consider the end of each poem. Pope's so remarkable for innuendo and subtlety:

> But Verse alas! your Majesty disdains;
> And I'm not us'd to Panegyric strains:
> The Zeal of Fools offends at any time,
> But most of all, the Zeal of Fools in ryme.
> Besides, a fate attends on all I write,
> That when I aim at praise, they say I bite.
> A vile Encominum doubly ridicules;
> There's nothing blackens like the ink of fools.
> [*Epistle to Augustus*, 2, 404–11]

(The poem, we know, was mistaken by some for a panegyric upon the administration.) Add a certain kind of literalness in Pope which invites special illustration from another poem: "Three thousand Suns went down on *Welsted's* Lye" (*Epistle to Arbuthnot*, l. 375). Not exuberance! Pope means that more than ten years had passed before he answered Welsted in *The Dunciad*.

How different all that from the cheerfully over-obvious ironies of Swift! (The *Rapsody* on poetry deceived Queen Caroline. But several printers and publishers of the poem at Dublin were taken into custody; *Poems*, 2.640.)

> Say, Poet, in what other Nation,
> Shone ever such a Constellation.
> Attend ye *Popes*, and *Youngs*, and *Gays*,
> And tune your Harps, and strow your Bays.
> Your Panegyricks here provide,
> You cannot err on Flatt'ry's Side.
> Above the Stars exalt your Stile.
> You still are low ten thousand Mile.
> On *Lewis* all his Bards bestow'd

Of Incense many a thousand Load;
But *Europe* mortify'd his Pride,
And swore the fawning Rascals ly'd:
Yet what the World refus'd to *Lewis*,
Apply'd to *George* exactly true is:
Exactly true! Invidious Poet!
'Tis fifty thousand Times below it.[13]
[2.656–57, ll. 465–80]

"Overshooting the mark," said Longinus, "ruins the hyperbole."[14] "Those hyperboles are best, in which the very fact that they are hyperboles escapes attention." But Swift's way was to invert all those rules enunciated by classical authorities on the heroic or the sublime. His finesses came by extravagance—inventive extravagance. It takes a genius to go so joyfully wrong. This is the open door into the sunlight of laughter which Swift discovered when he moved from the murky constraints of his pentameter metaphysics on the illness of Temple into the abandoned fun of the *Lady's Ivory Table Book*.

Notes

1. Swift's verse is quoted throughout my essay from *Swift's Poems*, ed. Harold Williams (Oxford, 1958), vols. 1, 2, 3.
2. It is a pleasure to acknowledge the kindness of Professor Rawson in allowing me to study an eloquent chapter on the poems, from his forthcoming book on Swift.
3. Brendan O. Hehir, "Meaning of Swift's 'Description of a City Shower,'" *ELH* 27 (1960): 194–207. Cf. David M. Vieth, "*Fiat Lux:* Logos versus Chaos in Swift's 'A Description of the Morning,'" *Papers on Language and Literature* 8 (1972): 302–7.
4. Laetitia Pilkington, *Memoirs* (London, 1748), 1:136; Harold Williams, *Dean Swift's Library* (Cambridge, 1932), pp. 87–88.
5. William Bowman Piper, *The Heroic Couplet* (Cleveland, 1969), chaps. 2–3.
6. Jakob Schipper, *A History of English Versification* (Oxford, 1918), pp. 126, 182, 192; F. A. Wright and T. A. Sinclair, *A History of Later Latin Literature* (London, 1931), pp. 234, 296, 305–6, 319, 323, 324, 330; F. J. E. Raby, *A History of Secular Latin Poetry in the Middle Ages* (Oxford, 1957), 2:173, 183, 278, 362; *The Oxford Book of Medieval Latin Verse*, ed. F. J. E. Raby (Oxford, 1959), pp. 251, 485, 486, *Psalterium Profanum, Weltliche Gedichte des lateinischen Mittelalters*, ed. Josef Eterle (Zurich, 1962), pp. 534–36, 579–81.
7. Pope is quoted from *The Twickenham Edition of The Poems of Alexander Pope* (London, 1939–69), vols. 1–11.
8. Pope's Horatian *Epistle* 1.7, "Imitated in the Manner of Dr. Swift," seems to betray his hand far less clearly. On the other hand, Pope, adding only ten scraps from another poem by Swift, transformed the conclusion of the *Verses on the Death of Dr. Swift* from a curiously straight and inflated (if in part ironic) panegyric of the Doctor to what has been described as

a "rapid-fire" antithetic dialogue, on the Horatian and Popean model. See Arthur H. Scouten and Robert D. Hume, "Pope and Swift: Text and Interpretation of Swift's Verses on His Death," *PQ* 52 (April 1973): 207–8, 215.

9. *The Correspondence of Jonathan Swift*, ed. Harold Williams (Oxford, 1965), 1:16.

10. E. J. Trelawney, *Recollections of the Last Days of Shelley and Byron* (Boston, 1858), 1:37.

11. Another early poem, *Van Brug's House* (1703–6), executes some remarkable metamorphoses of poetry and heraldry into architecture.

12. With a burst of laughter, and in the presence of his victim (Lady Acheson, an "agreeable young Lady, but extremely lean"), Swift once boasted: "That Lady had rather be a *Daphne* drawn by me, than a *Sacharissa* by any other pencil" (*Poems*, 3:902). His awareness of another possible sensibility is expressed in an earlier poem censuring some freedom in raillery taken by his crony Sheridan.

> If what You said, I wish unspoke,
> 'Twill not suffice, it was a Joke.
> [*To Mr. Delany*, 1718, ll. 65–66]

13. Other examples of hyperbolic number in Swift: *On Censure* (1727), l. 27; *Journal of a Modern Lady* (1729), l. 139; *Strephon and Chloe* (1731), l. 99; *Apollo* (1731), l. 20.

14. *Peri Hupsous*, chap. 38. Translation of W. Rhys Roberts.

Pope: Bipolar Implication

IRVIN EHRENPREIS

Near the source of Pope's work is an anxiety understandable in terms of his health and religion. As a Roman Catholic in a Protestant nation, Pope suffered maddening penalties. He could not attend a university or hold a civil office. He paid double the normal tax on land, and the law forbade him to reside within ten miles of London. All Roman Catholics were exposed to charges of conspiring against the government.

But Pope's worst affliction was tuberculosis of the spine, which gave him rickets and a progressive, lopsided curvature of the back. It made him grotesquely short and gradually weakened his thin limbs. It produced much languor, a susceptibility to bad colds, and other painful or unpleasant symptoms which worsened as he aged. Pope had to wear a stiff corset, warm clothes, and (over the skinny legs) three pairs of stockings. Normal sexual relations were out of the question.

Frail, vulnerable, and (in effect) impotent, it was natural for the poet to desire the security of well-placed friends. One of the mainsprings of his imagination was the need to protect himself. Still he was conscious of his genius and wanted fame. He yearned to exercise heroic power over others through the gift of poetry.

To gain the recognition he longed for, Pope had to mask many emotions. As an adolescent, he began a career of seeking out men of talent, rank, or power, winning their friendship and making them serve him. To do so, he learned to charm them with tact and wit, paying careful compliments and accommodating himself to the moods of the mighty.

From *Acts of Implication: Suggestion and Covert Meaning in the Works of Dryden, Swift, Pope and Austen* (Berkeley: University of California Press, 1980), pp. 83–111.

Not only in his poems but also in his letters and conversation, Pope systematically maintained careful representations of himself that would uphold an appearance of strength, independence, and natural benevolence, all in keeping with the doctrines he recommended in verse. What records we have of his conversation suggest that he hoped his sentiments would be repeated. The rhetoric of Pope's most familiar letters sometimes sounds like that of a senator emitting platitudes for his own obituary. A second reader—Posterity—normally looked over the poet's epistolary shoulder.

I assume that the constraints, added to those of health and religion, nourished a deep resentfulness which compounded the original anxiety. The poetic instinct bent itself to please those whom Pope needed, while the very impulse to create started from subterranean discomforts. Words are a common resource of those who cannot act, but Pope's words had many duties. They vented painful emotions which the poet dared not express simply. They conveyed an air of assurance to cloak a fundamental unease. They made up for a lack of sexual authority. They rewarded friends and punished enemies.

Pope devised methods of attracting and reassuring those who might be hostile to his brilliance, and yet of challenging subtle readers by offering them dangerous thoughts. Wit and irony are known ways of accomplishing these ends, and good critics have examined Pope's use of them. He found other ways as well, which are less familiar.

If we agree that sex, religion, and politics are themes which invite indirection, we may also agree that religion, for Pope, was too risky a subject to experiment with. He did venture on opinions that might trouble his coreligionists, especially a tolerance of non-Catholic positions. He blamed great ecclesiastics for time-serving, avarice, and other vices. But he did not indulge in satire on allegedly false doctrines, as Dryden and Swift had done. In *The Messiah* and *An Essay on Man*, Pope tried, explicitly and implicitly, to avoid controversy.

Sexual themes were treacherous too. The poet's obvious incapacity drove him to adopt conventional poses for fear of becoming too easy a mark for ridicule. Whether he used a rake or a moralist as his mouthpiece, he could hardly afford to sound innovative. Yet if sexual themes particularly excite wordplay, they must have exerted a special charm upon a poet. Pope felt the charm, and characteristically offered both conformist and subversive treatments of those themes.

The association of sexuality with creative power is natural. Keeping this connection in mind, one must notice Pope's tendency to maintain it and yet to separate the imagery of conception from that of sexual intercourse.

He liked to refer to his works as his progeny and to the muse as a wife, but not to lovemaking between the creative pair.

In these misty crossings we touch the depths of Pope's identity. He offered several distinct representations of the poetic character. The most familiar is the public idealization of an uncorrupt spokesman for patriotic and social virtue. This is the character he liked to give his own career. Yet implicitly, the ideal public figure depreciates another, viz. the inspired artist celebrated by Horace and recommended by Pope in *An Epistle to Augustus:*

> 'Tis he, who gives my breast a thousand pains,
> Can make me feel each passion that he feigns,
> Inrage, compose, with more than magic art,
> With pity, and with terror, tear my heart.
>
> (lines 342–45)

In these lines "poet" clearly means seductive playwright rather than didactic satirist.

But there is still another figure, for which Pope voices contempt and which he embodies in the persons of failed or inept authors. This, alas, is the one that excites his greatest energy, his most imaginative language. Therefore, although it alludes normally to writers whom Pope disliked, one may speculate that it also reflects Pope's doubts about his status. He might be a uniquely gifted genius, but putting aside traditional hyperboles, what did the laurel crown amount to when it topped his crazy carcass?

So one may also speculate about the scenes of grotesque fantasy that break out in Pope's best work. Underground, cavernous, and obstetric images, tinged with sexuality, suggest that literary parenthood compensated the poet for the loss of voluptuous pleasure. Pope designed deeply coherent masterpieces around heroines deprived of normal sexual relations: *Eloisa to Abelard, An Elegy to . . . an Unfortunate Lady* ("Of the Characters of Women"). Even Dulness, in *The Dunciad,* is an unwed or parthenogenetic mother. Yet Pope produced no episode of admirable and fulfilled passion.

Two of his most polished works deal sympathetically with women penalized for subversive lust. In *Eloisa to Abelard* the lover has been castrated and the mistress consigned to a nunnery. In the *Elegy . . . to an Unfortunate Lady* a noble heiress has stabbed herself after eloping to a foreign country with a lover whom her guardian uncle had rejected. In both these poems the author encourages us to pity the lawbreaker: "Is it, in heav'n a crime to love too well?" he asks.

In *An Epistle to a Lady* the poet compliments his spinster friend Martha Blount (whom he briefly endows with a mythical husband and daughter) by opposing her to a series of corrupt, passionate mistresses or wives. In *The Rape of the Lock* the male figures are ridiculed and defeated, while the females remain unsatisfied.

Against this pattern it seems significant that the scenes of grotesque fantasy depend on images of unpleasant confusion and procreation. I am thinking of the Cave of Spleen in *The Rape of the Lock,* the Cave of Poverty and Poetry in Book One of *The Dunciad,* the bowers of the mud nymphs in Book Two of *The Dunciad,* and similar material.

Spleen of course means melancholy; and in the seventeenth century, it was commonplace to regard melancholy as the "balm of wit" and the "breath of poetry." When the gnome Umbriel descends to the Cave of Spleen, he is visiting a spring of creative imagination. Here Spleen herself is a goddess who can inspire the "poetic fit." Although the details of this allegorical cave are traditional, Pope colors them with phallic and erotic lights, with hints of perverse coition and gestation. So we get a linking of creativity with displaced sexuality and pain:

> Men prove with child, as pow'rful fancy works,
> And maids turn'd bottles, call aloud for corks.
> (*Rape of the Lock,* IV, 53–54)

In Book Three of *The Dunciad* we meet the laureate Cibber lying with his head in the lap of the goddess Dulness while a dark, soporific dew falls and "raptures" overflow (lines 1–5)—a titillating scene. Two-thirds of the way through Book Three, another genius of false imagination appears— John Rich, producer of pantomimes. Here Pope brings in imagery of miraculous transformations of the universe echoing the representation of Christ in *The Messiah* and suggesting genesis and doomsday at once (lines 229–36). The chaos reaches its climax with an egg from which the human race is hatched. Again the work of creative imagination carries hints of asexual conception or parthenogenesis.

We have to notice how often Pope connected the act of composition with discomfort, muddle, misshapen birth and growth, delusive transformation. We do not meet order, dignity, and reality, but chaos, monsterhood, and illusion: "the chaos dark and deep, / Where nameless somethings in their causes sleep" (*Dunciad,* I, 55–56, 59, 93–94). Attacking the decline of humanistic education, Pope deplores the standard practice of training schoolboys to compose Latin verses: "We hang one jingling padlock on the mind: / A poet the first day, he dips his quill; / And what the last? a very poet still" (*Dunciad*, IV, 163–64).

These examples of disrespect for his vocation are from the last years of Pope's career and refer to bad poetry, not good. In his early work we read similar lines:

> Still run on poets in a raging vein,
> Ev'n to the dregs and squeezings of the brain;
> Strain out the last, dull droppings of their sense,
> And rhyme with all the rage of impotence.
>
> (*Essay on Criticism*, lines 606–9)

This linking of composition to a hard stool and a limp penis also belongs to an attack on bad writing. But the images have too much power to rest in the boundaries prescribed by explicit meaning. When he refers directly to his own career as an author, Pope says, "I've had my purgatory here betimes, / And paid for all my satires, all my rhymes" (*Donne*, IV, 5–6). It was only half-jokingly that he once said of the poet's calling, "Must one not be prepared to endure the reproaches of men, want and much fasting, nay martyrdom in its cause" (*Correspondence*, II, 227). The pleasure of creation loses itself in the toil and humiliation.

If one puts aside the link with authorship and considers unsublimated sexuality, the material points one along a more direct road but not to marriage, parenthood, and stability. The poet offers conventional denunciations of vice. But he also provides vivid descriptions of frustrated passion, titillating coquetry, tenderness outside marriage, and misery born in wedlock. The frailty and quick alterations of carnal appetite strike him more than its fruitfulness. He conveys a deep sympathy with the voluptuous impulse and deep uncertainty as to its consequence.

In *The Rape of the Lock*, disorderly lust glances at us from the first couplet; and it pounds on us in the final canto. "Die" for sexual climax, "thing" for vagina, "hair" displaced from the groin to the head, all remind one that the proper study of nubile girls is men.

"What dire offence from am'rous causes springs, / What mighty contests rise from trivial things, / I sing," says Pope as he begins a story connecting love with theft and war. The couplet sounds plain enough until we hear an echo of Horace joining the same themes and calling the vagina (or lust) a most shameful cause of war (*cunnus taeterrima belli / causa—Satires* I, iii, 107). Once we remember that Pope would translate "cunnus" as "thing," the language of decorum becomes a screen for impropriety.

In Canto Five of *The Rape of the Lock*, the battle of the sexes takes a more liberal form; and when Belinda defeats the Baron with a pinch of snuff, he says,

> Thou by some other shalt be laid as low.
> Nor think, to die dejects my lofty mind;
> All that I dread, is leaving you behind!
>
> (lines 98–100)

Here the poet openly, if indelicately, sympathizes with the natural impulse of young blood. So also in the early cantos of *The Rape of the Lock*, Pope celebrates the delight of Belinda in her own sexually provocative beauty:

> Now awful beauty puts on all its arms;
> The fair each moment rises in her charms,
> Repairs her smile, awakens ev'ry grace,
> And calls forth all the wonders of her face.
>
> (I, 139–42)

So also the sylphs—spirits whose job it is to guard Belinda's defensive and offensive weapons—are represented with wholehearted (though smiling) approval. Their humble work is to "tend the fair"; so long as the heroine refrains from matrimony, they strive to protect the arsenal of her beauty—

> To save the powder from too rude a gale,
> Nor let th'imprison'd essences exhale,
> To draw fresh colours from the vernal flow'rs,
> To steal from rainbows ere they drop in show'rs
> A brighter wash; to curl their waving hairs,
> Assist their blushes, and inspire their airs;
> Nay oft, in dreams, inventions we bestow,
> To change a *flounce*, or add a *furbelo*.
>
> (II, 93–100)

Belinda makes us live among changing appearances, unfixed emotions, fascinating discords, elegant but furious rivalries, stylized and comic wars. There is nothing placid, domestic, or parental about *The Rape of the Lock*. Its few snatches of security only prepare us for long passages of delightful uneasiness.

Yet in some masterful lines of elevated reasoning, one of Belinda's friends, named Clarissa, warns her of the transience of voluptuous pleasure and belligerent beauty. She reminds us that courtship ought to fix its goal in stable domesticity, marriage and motherhood:

> Since painted, or not painted, all shall fade,
> And she who scorns a man must die a maid;
> What then remains, but well our pow'r to use,
> And keep good humour still whate'er we lose.
>
> (V, 27–30)

This is sane as well as eloquent. Only, as it happens, when the Baron wished to snip off a lock of Belinda's hair, it was the same Clarissa who gave him the scissors.

In *The Rape of the Lock* the poet's obsession with time and change heightens a brief joy in youthful ardor. But ultimately it implies that creative imagination alone can triumph over age and death. The familiar theme of *monumentum aere perennius* brings together the sexual aspect of authorship and the lure of misdirected passion. Elsewhere Pope belittled the theme. Here, by invoking it ironically to close a battle of the sexes, he momentarily resolves his own doubts.

So at the end of the poem, yet once more reviving the exhausted pun on "die," once more identifying the eye of beauty with the eye of heaven, Pope brings nature and art together as he immortalizes the maiden whom he cannot enjoy. Here we meet that ideal of the poet as artist which enabled Pope to transcend his private self-disgust and his public role as guardian of the nation's morals.

> For, after all the murders of your eye,
> When, after millions slain, your self shall die;
> When those fair suns shall set, as set they must,
> And all those tresses shall be laid in dust;
> *This lock,* the muse shall consecrate to fame,
> And mid'st the stars inscribe *Belinda's* name.
>
> (V, 145–50)

Years later, Pope took up the burden of sexuality with rather less of an effort to sound decorous. This was in *Sober Advice from Horace,* published anonymously in 1734. Here, however, the theme of lust itself becomes part of a political argument; and one should meet that argument before going on to the poem. To Pope, the most challenging aspect of implicit meaning presented itself in his criticism of the highest levels of English vice. From about the time he was forty, and continuing about fifteen years, the poet's judgment of his nation deepened in severity, and he invented subtler, yet keener, ways to reveal it.

The port of embarkation for these expeditions into outrage is unusually appparent in *An Essay on Man*. Here, in the third epistle, the poet displays a vision of the primitive condition of human society. This vision embraces a harmony between various realms of morality and value: private duty and public responsibility, virtue and power, the order of social privilege and the order of natural talent. In the *Essay* Pope represents humanity in the state of nature as embodying the ideal harmony. Kingship, virtue, piety, and wisdom stand united:

> 'Till then, by Nature crown'd, each Patriarch sate,
> King, priest, and parent of his growing state;
> On him, their second Providence, they hung,
> Their law his eye, their oracle his tongue.
> He from the wond'ring furrow call'd the food,
> Taught to command the fire, controul the flood,
> Draw forth the monsters of th'abyss profound,
> Or fetch th'aerial eagle to the ground.
> . . . .
> *Love* all the faith, and all th'allegiance then;
> For Nature knew no right divine in Men,
> No ill could fear in God; and understood
> A sov'reign being but a sov'reign good.[1]

It was from the contemplation of this empyrean that Pope came to judge the rich and the great. What he found of course was that English social order rarely disclosed the corerspondences he admired. The directors of the nation set more examples of vice than of virtue. The wealthy class largely overlapped with the frivolous class. The circle of talent bowed to the circle of corruption. Spokesmen for the houses of learning were vain and pedantic; at the head of religious institutions stood worldly, ambitious prelates.

To express his anger or disappointment, Pope used a categorical rhetoric that suited his poetic style. He juxtaposed group to group, example to class, ideal to reality. When he condemned, he described the evil as typical. When he praised, he handled the subject as a rare brightness in a world of shadows.

Pope's methods of satirical implication, therefore, gain strength from the contrast the poet habitually makes between style—including rhetorical forms—and meaning. As a satirist he gave extraordinary attention not only to nuances of implication but to the patterns of sound and rhythm in which he embodied them. These elements he fitted inside the parallels and antitheses of phrase or clause and the analogies or contrasts that shaped his paragraphs. His figures of speech could be pointedly brief, or they could expand the length of a paragraph or even (as a reiterated motif) of a poem, deepening the categorical tendencies of the rhetoric and poetic. So also his arguments moved discursively from general to particular, from example to universal and back. One poem balanced or opposed another, as the first *Moral Essay (To Cobham)*, on male psychology, balanced the second *(To a Lady)*, on female.

On all these levels Pope's constant effort is to redefine, regroup, to undermine old congruities and establish or hint at new ones. In his explicit arguments Pope seldom tried to inculcate fresh doctrines, but relied on traditional wisdom, on commonly accepted moral principles, or formulae. Maynard Mack has demonstrated the fullness of the tradition behind the sentences of *An Essay on Man*. "Its materials," he says, "are painstakingly traditional."[2] Earl Wasserman and Miriam Leranbaum have shown how much the third and fourth *Moral Essays* (*Bathurst* and *Burlington*) owed to Aristotle.[3] Thomas Maresca has argued persuasively that in the imitations of Horace, Pope leaned heavily on the uncontested principles of pagan and Christian ethics which commentators elicited from the text of the ancient poet.[4] Yet in the freshest way Pope's genius built sparkling, challenging designs out of these common properties.

The chief effect of style on meaning in Pope's satires of the 1730s and 1740s is to group persons and ideas in discomforting ways. Since the clusters assembled and disconnected are based on moral relationships, the outcome is a questioning of assumptions often put forward and widely credited. Among these Pope's special tendency is to cast into doubt the proper association of rank with merit, virtue, or even good manners. Again and again in his poems the author invokes a natural hierarchy of established families who benevolently control the landed wealth and the government of the country—recalling the harmonious vision of *An Essay on Man*. But he implies that the social and moral boundaries can no longer be congruent. They have broken down; a heterogeneous mob has replaced the ordered community; and it takes in

> Whate'er of mungril no one class admits,
> A wit with dunces, and a dunce with wits.
> (*Dunciad*, IV, 89–90)

A simple example is Pope's imitation of Horace *Satires* I, ii *(Sober Advice from Horace)*, to which I now return. The Latin poem is a jocular mock-sermon on the dangers of adultery committed with respectable women. Horace directs his satire against men who feel dissatisfied with the sexual opportunities afforded them by slaves, freedwomen, or courtesans, and who insist on pursuing matrons. The individuals whom Horace singles out for explicit reproach are all male. Though he opens by illustrating the theme of excess with instances of prodigality and avarice, once he arrives at the matter of adultery, he focuses his poem on it. While Horace dealt with persons of consequence, he did not draw attention to their rank.

Pope gives roughly equal representation to both sexes but makes his most scandalous examples female. He draws attention to the rank of his characters and connects lust with gluttony and avarice. In a mock-apparatus, Pope ridicules the scholarship of Richard Bentley (whose emendations he was nevertheless willing to adopt) and endows him with a prurient sensibility.

The reason for the difference between the two poets is that under the appearance of ridiculing adulterers, Pope is busy endowing the great of the land with the worst vices. He deals with a king's mistress (line 81), a prime minister's infidelities (line 88), the venereal disease of a duchess (line 95), the lust of an archbishop (line 44). Even Bentley, enlisted as annotator *malgré soi*, was himself master of a great college and a cultivator of the Whig ministry in power.

We observe that several of Horace's types of masculine vice turn feminine in Pope's lines. Tigellius the singer becomes Mrs. Oldfield the actress (line 4); Fufidius changes into Fufidia (line 18); Rufillus, Rufa (line 29); Maltinus, Jenny (line 33). In other words, the poet refuses to let the women appear passive, or to imply that only the males of the ruling class are corrupt. Horace had assumed that men were the instigators of vice, and women the persons seduced (though not always resisting). Pope implicitly breaks down the barrier between the sexes, suggesting that on the highest levels women become unnaturally aggressive. To those readers who compared the imitation with the Latin original, Pope would have implied that English ladies of fashion differed from ancient Roman matrons in starting rather than responding to acts of lust. In a sense, this poem leads into Pope's second *Moral Essay, To a Lady*.

Far more broadly, Pope suggests that corruption makes strange bedfellows; and that vice brings together groups that ought to be kept apart. Where Horace blames a few men for disgracing their ancestors, Pope hints that the natural hierarchy which underpins civilized society has yielded to moral chaos. This is also what the effects of style and structure suggest. In his opening lines, the poet uses rhythm and sound patterns to clarify the irony of his tone:

> The Tribe of Templars, Play'rs, Apothecaries,
> Pimps, Poets, Wits, Lord Fanny's, Lady Mary's. . . .

The catalogue of lawyers, poets, etc., makes the kind of set one might expect to gather in a theater district that lies near the inns of court. But high-placed lords and ladies should have no close ties with actors, pimps, and the healers of venereal disease. Pope marks off "Lord Fanny's, Lady Mary's" with a caesura but places them at the climax of his catalogue. In rhythm and sound patterns they are unlike the earlier series but tied to it. Yet they are, in sound, curiously like each other. Thus Pope implies the ambiguous sexuality of Hervey—the couplet has feminine endings—and the scandalous association of both him and Lady Mary with dubious characters.

Two aspects of the language of the poem add to such effects. Where Horace uses plain words like *inguina, cunnus,* and *muto* (all mistranslated in the Loeb edition), Pope enlists either a suggestive euphemism like *part* (line 87) or a pun like *frigate* (line 62). The consequent dazzle of ambiguities (*rise,* line 88; *stiff,* line 152; above all, *thing,* passim) enriches the suggestion of barriers breaking down. Maynard Mack has pointed out an exquisite instance. When Pope writes,

> Suppose that honest part that rules us all,
> Should rise, and say—"Sir Robert! or Sir Paul!"
> (lines 87–88)

the reference to a prime minister and a statesman evokes question time in the House of Commons; "part" suggests a genital "member," and therefore Member of Parliament; and so a fornicating phallus invades the high process of legislation.[5] Another pair of realms that should be kept apart, merge.

The categories that fascinated Pope, in the satires, were those of public and private, high rank and low. Against these he pitted other categories like good and bad, tasteful and vulgar. Often his rhetoric moves from the personal and private world to that of public responsibility, or from the latter to the former. Invariably, he assumes that a harmony between these worlds is natural.

Such modulations depend on Pope's starting from familiar doctrines (what I should call formulae) and identifiable examples. As a moralist, he may state his doctrine in a paradox, but the teaching itself is likely to be conventional, not difficult and not too subtle. Pope still has a tendency of his own which differentiates him from the usual preacher of Christian doctrine and from most satirists. In searching for models of virtue, he looks instinctively to actors who are offstage—of middle rank or out of favor. If he must have virtuous kings, statesmen, or bishops, he likes to secure ancients, foreigners, or Englishmen long dead.

By these means Pope can imply harsh judgments on the most powerful figures of his own age without endangering himself. The judgment grows more severe, and the class of corrupt persons more extensive, until we arrive at the *Epilogue to the Satires, 1740,* and the last book of *The Dunciad.* Finally, as in *The Dunciad* (Book IV), Pope was willing to blacken the character of whole orders of humanity. Earlier, he tried to appear selective; for his selectiveness was carefully weighted. Thus in picking names to celebrate, the poet did not always avoid men of rank. Among the subjects of his eulogies are Bathurst, Cobham, Oxford (father and son), and Bolingbroke. But he picked his noble heroes from the files of Jacobites, Tories, and opposition Whigs. Otherwise, he favored commoners of middle rank, like Kyrle,[6] Martha Blount,[7] and Dr. Arbuthnot.

Pope usually mentioned bishops only in order to blame them.[8] But when he wished to display his impartiality and bestow compliments on them, he named four, starting with one indeed close to the court but ending climactically with Berkeley, who had been sponsored by the Tory Swift, had been chaplain to the Jacobite Duke of Wharton, and had gained his elevation in spite of his connections:

> Ev'n in a Bishop I can spy Desert;
> Secker is decent, Rundel has a heart,
> Manners with Candour are to Benson giv'n,
> To Berkeley, ev'ry Virtue under Heav'n.
> (*Epilogue to the Satires,* II, 70–73)

Only the tribute to Berkeley is unequivocal. If we collect all the epithets, the poet drives us into separating the order of bishops from the moral order of decency, charity, candor, and virtue in general. "Ev'n" and "spy" suggest a minute search for the few exceptions to the rule. Berkeley has a strong place in his line, emphasized by the caesura and enriched by the echo of his name's sound and rhythm in "virtue" *(vartue)*. Though he ends the series, he makes a contrast to the preceding trio, two of whom divide a line and the third occupies a weak place in a slow line of bathetic compliment.

So also if Pope did praise a very rich government official in Ralph Allen, he went out of his way to call him "low-born";[9] and as Erskine-Hill says, Allen's career rested on genuine service to the nation and was independent of Walpole or party.[10] Although I dwell on the subtle or indirect conveyance of meaning, Pope could be perfectly open at the same time. His gift for innuendo did not keep him from declaring explicitly what he was busy implying:

> But does the Court a worthy Man remove?
> That instant, I declare, he has my Love:
> I shun his Zenith, court his mild Decline. . . .
> *(Epilogue to the Satires,* II, 74–76)

Pope's distaste for kings and conquerors is too obvious to need mention. Recently even his respect for the Emperor Augustus as an admirable alternative to the degenerate Georges has been persuasively doubted by meticulous scholars.[11] Miriam Leranbaum pointed out the large number of "great" men alluded to in the first *Moral Essay (To Cobham):* "The emphasis is upon rulers, kings, statesmen—exalted figures of all kinds."[12] She observed further that the matching poem, *To a Lady,* also abounds in high personages, and that for part of the poem Pope uses "queen" as a synonym for "woman."[13] Leranbaum connected these poems with the fourth epistle of *An Essay on Man,* which again has a good many allusions to kings in general and to certain rulers and tyrants in particular: Alexander, Caesar, Titus, Marcus Aurelius, Charles XII of Sweden—of whom two are treated as admirable (Titus and Marcus Aurelius) and the others as baneful. The same epistle of *An Essay on Man* opens and closes with a panegyric of Bolingbroke, and the first epistle opens with an apostrophe to him. In all three places he is opposed to kings. Bolingbroke was of course the intellectual leader of the opposition to Walpole's government and to George II's court.

We may infer that the most exciting subject for Pope's ridicule was George II. An analysis of the methods applied to his majesty's character will bring out Pope's methods in general. The operations begin at the level of common nouns. In poems published during the dozen years beginning in 1731, the word "king" constantly appears to point the generalizations about human nature and morality. But somehow the poet uses the name seldom with respect and often with contempt: "the pride of kings," "a lunatic king," "public spirit its great cure a crown."[14] A couplet like that in the fourth epistle of *An Essay on Man* gives the direction of Pope's pressure on the word:

> Struck o'er with titles and hung round with strings,
> That thou may'st be by kings, or whores of kings. . . .
> (lines 205–6)

In the *Epistle to Burlington* the poet foresees that some future king will follow the example of the earl, whose ideas are "worthy kings" (lines 195, 204). The notion of the future implicitly excludes the present; and if the projects are suitable for kings, it strikes us that the monarch in power has not seen fit to carry them out. We might infer therefore that kingship as such is a concept excluding George II.

In the *Epistle to Bathurst* the word "king" appears only in connection with avarice (lines 72, 78, 401). The poet suggests that bribes are welcomed by a king and may determine royal policy. In his imitation of Horace *Satires* II, i, Pope uses the word "king" only once and then ambiguously, to say that he himself writes sober, moral poems such as a king might read (line 152). The remark exudes irony because near the beginning of his poem Pope says that George II does not read poetry (line 35). A few weeks later, in the second epistle of *An Essay on Man* (published in February, 1733), "kings" are an instance of presumption (line 244), and "king" is what a lunatic thinks himself to be (line 268).

If we now skip to the last epistle of *An Essay on Man*, we see the process speed up, and discover a concentration of "kings" used with offputting connotations: fools fight for kings, wish to be kings, are ennobled by kings, become the favorites of kings.[15] The poet draws a contrast between the immortal fame of his hero Bolingbroke and the short-lived reputation of kings (IV, 387). The process does not pause here but goes on to the last book of *The Dunciad*, where Pope lets himself ridicule the "*Right Divine* of kings to govern wrong" (line 188).

When the poet's text failed him, as being too exposed, he could seek refuge in his mock-commentary. In this sanctuary (like Swift in the notes to the fifth edition of *A Tale of a Tub*) he could conjure up not one but two editors quarreling with one another over the meaning of a line, and by this device could produce with safety insinuations against George II. In *The Dunciad* (IV, 181–82) there is a commentators' quibble over a supposed allusion to verses by Claudian that describe liberty as flourishing under a good king. In the course of the disagreement, "Scriblerus" observes that liberty is often confused with monarchy; but "Bentley" retorts that "Liberty was never *lost*, or *went away* with so good a grace, as under a good king!"

In *An Epistle to a Lady* ("Of the Characters of Women") the use of "queen" suffers a similar deformation. Here, in a gallery of female portraits, the only picture of a queen is a flatterer's deception (lines 181–86). Pope declares that women generally want power and pleasure: every lady would be queen for life (line 218). Thus he makes the word itself into a term of abuse for vicious, megalomaniac females; and we hear the contemptuous phrase, "a whole sex of queens" (line 219).

As a common noun, of course, "king" easily alternates with its near synonyms. "Tyrant" and "prince" appear alongside it. But all these are mingled with the proper names of various rulers, from Alexander the Great to George II—or with allusions plainly identifying them. Except for Titus and Marcus Aurelius, the names receive ambiguous or sinister overtones. In the *Epistle to Cobham* (lines 146–53)—published during the same month as the last epistle of *An Essay on Man*—Pope has a passage assembling an ugly gang of individual rulers, as if to balance the use of the common noun in the *Essay*. Although explicitly chosen to illustrate the inconsistency of human nature, almost every one is dispraised in an epithet: buffoon, perjur'd, godless, bigot, faithless, duped, fool.[16]

This example hardly misleads one. Pope's satires do provide momentary glimpses of a king's behaving himself decently, but such acts tend to appear out of character for the particular monarch; and in representing them, the poet seems to want a contrast to the inactivity of George II. Thus Pope describes Charles II, James II, and Louis XIV as tolerating satirical poetry. But he does so in response to a friend who warns him against enraging the present powers,[17] and he treats the phenomenon as contrary to what one might expect of each king. The greatest concentration of admirable royal gestures, in the *Epistle to Augustus*, invites us to set the heroism or patronage of half a dozen kings against the lack of those qualities in King George.[18] And yet several of these examples are themselves ambiguous: Charles I pensioned Quarles (line 387); Charles II "debauch'd" the muses (line 152); William III knighted Blackmore (line 387).

In the late poems generally, miscellaneous rulers are named to be censured or ridiculed. Pope gives special attention to wicked or stupid figures:

kings, usurpers, and emperors whom the poet might freely identify, yet who, by association with the class of kings, would stain the mantle of George II. By admitting his exceptions, the poet strengthens the innuendo against the type.

As early as the *Epistle to Burlington* (published in December, 1731), Pope contrasts the good taste of his lordship with the doubtful taste of Louis XIV and Nero (lines 71–72). In *An Essay on Man*, Epistle IV, along with the common noun, the poet sneers at Caesar three times, as well as Alexander the Great and Charles XII of Sweden.[19] Alexander and Caesar had already been stigmatized in Epistle I as natural disasters (lines 159–60). Midas, in the *Epistle to Arbuthnot,* is cursed by Apollo with the ears of an ass (lines 69–82).

As one reads through the poems, it becomes clear that Pope intends us to refer back and forth among them in order to perfect identifications which are hinted at in separate places. Lord Fanny, Sporus, and Narcissus are thus united.[20] So also the names for Lady Mary Wortley Montagu and her husband. She alone may be Fufidia, Sappho, or simply Lady Mary,[21] which is to say, lustful, unclean, avaricious, and bluestocking. (Sir Edward and she together are Gripus, Shylock, or Avidien and his wife—all usurers.)[22] So when readers are not linking the ambiguous sexuality of Hervey to the florid style of his prose, they may be blending the stinginess ascribed to Lady Mary with her alleged carnality. Alternatively, they may assure themselves that various names allude to the same person because they notice a cluster of traits circulating unchanged. The style of wit and the courtly prominence of Sporus in the *Epistle to Arbuthnot* persuade us that Hervey is the reference of "H——vy" in the *Epilogue to the Satires.*[23]

Even so with Caesar: Pope openly alluded to George II as "Caesar" in an imitation of Horace.[24] A year later, in the last epistle of *An Essay on Man*, he mentioned "Caesar with a senate at his heels," and juxtaposed him to Marcellus in exile—thus inviting us to set George II against Bolingbroke.[25] At the very same time, when he refers to Caesar retreating from Britain and risking his empire for a punk, we may perhaps think of the king leaving England to join Madame Walmoden in Hanover.[26]

Alternatively, Pope may suppress the word "king" and bring together traits well known as marks of his majesty: bearishness, the habit of kicking when angry, the domination of the royal mind (such as it was) by Queen Caroline, the prime minister's power over his master. "'Tis a bear's talent not to kick, but hug," may be an allusion to George II.[27] The following lines (gathering in six of the seven cardinal sins!) certainly are such an allusion:

> Know, there are Rhymes, which (fresh and fresh apply'd)
> Will cure the arrant'st Puppy of his Pride.
> Be furious, envious, slothful, mad or drunk,
> Slave to a Wife or Vassal to a Punk,
> A Switz, a High-dutch, or a Low-dutch Bear—
> All that we ask is but a patient Ear.[28]

One of Pope's most mischievous devices is to insult George and Caroline by reviling their flatterers. The obvious example occurs in the earliest imitation of Horace. Here, Pope's friend Fortescue advises the poet to write something in praise of the king. Pope replies with some lines of parody of what Blackmore, Budgell, and Cibber have written in praise of William III and George II. Fortescue suggests that he praise the queen and the royal children. The poet replies that the ears of majesty are too "nice" to bear his verses. But the satire on bad poets irresistibly attaches itself to the royal persons, and in a closing ambiguity, Pope deliciously evokes his monarch's indifference to literature of all sorts:

> And justly *Caesar* scorns the Poet's Lays,
> It is to *History* he trusts for praise.[29]

Queen Caroline undergoes a similar blackwash in the second *Moral Essay (To a Lady)*, when Pope ostensibly despairs of finding an honest portrait of her, because flattering authors and artists adorn her always and mechanically with conventional virtues:

> One certain Portrait may (I grant) be seen,
> Which Heav'n has varnish'd out, and made a *Queen:*
> The same for ever! and describ'd by all
> With Truth and Goodness, as with Crown and Ball:
> Poets heap Virtues, Painters Gems at will,
> And show their zeal, and hide their want of skill.
> (lines 181–86)

The innuendo is of course that the artists must manufacture the virtues because Caroline has none of them.

This device can be pointed, as when, in the *Epilogue to the Satires,* the poet denounces those who "make saints of queens, and gods of kings" (II, 225). But it can easily be generalized to apply to other persons of consequence, and in one of the most dazzling passages of his poetry, Pope brings in bishops, judges, and statesmen. This is the first *Moral Essay, To Cobham.*

Here, in a justly famous paragraph, Pope argues that most poets (or artists) turn, for their examples of virtue, to the upper levels of society. He then transforms the fact into satire by recommending the practice. Actually, he says, it is so hard to be virtuous in a great position that whoever succeeds in doing so deserves unusual praise:

> 'Tis from high Life high Characters are drawn;
> A Saint in Crape is twice a Saint in Lawn;
> A Judge is just, a Chanc'lor juster still;
> A Gownman, learn'd; a Bishop, what you will;
> Wise, if a Minister; but, if a King,
> More wise, more learn'd, more just, more ev'ry thing.
> Court-virtues bear, like Gems, the highest rate,
> Born where Heav'n's influence scarce can penetrate:
> In life's low vale, the soil the virtues like,
> They please as Beauties, here as Wonders strike.
>   (lines 87–96)

The method of implication derives again from the way the technique of verse divides and unites categories: lower clergy and episcopacy are separated instead of being united as the church; so also are a lower justice and the chancellor, who ought to be collected in the law. "Saint in crape" and "saint in lawn" are parallel in form and rhythm. Yet the parson might be a saint while the bishop could only gain promotion through corruption. "Judge-just," as alliteration, balances "chanc'lor-juster," with its repeated endings and sibilants. But the judge is far likelier than the chancellor is to keep his integrity. The categories of true and specious goodness are thus closely joined precisely as they are set apart. "Crape" opposes "lawn" in sound as "judge" opposes "chanc'lor." In the paragraph as a whole the ideas of high and low are similarly split and rejoined.

Such operations bring the whole relation of example to postulate into doubt. Pope can illustrate an aphorism with an instance that weakens it, as when he says that poets want only to enjoy their garden and book "in quiet," and then praises Swift for saving "the rights a court attack'd."[30] More abstractly, he even challenges the distinction between reality and fiction. Thus Pope offers us historical examples, identified by name or otherwise, along with veiled pseudonyms which can be penetrated by a give-away trait or association, and, as well, with utterly imaginary examples which discourage speculation. Sometimes he combines these various procedures, by using the real name harmlessly and then following it at once with a pseudonym and satiric characterization of the same person: the

Addison-Atticus passage in the *Epistle to Arbuthnot* is a cunning example (lines 192–214). At his boldest, in dealing with the king, Pope can use the very name of George, but so ambiguously that one reader might think the reference innocuous (or complimentary) while another could see it as an insult:

> I sought no homage from the Race that write;
> I kept, like Asian Monarchs, from their sight:
> Poems I heeded (now be-rym'd so long)
> No more than Thou, great *George!* a Birth-day Song.
>
> (*Epistle to Arbuthnot*, lines 220–23)

(That is, the king is so indifferent to poetry that he cannot notice it even when it is in praise of himself.) The magnificent climax of this technique is of course the opening and closing lines of the *Epistle to Augustus* (Horace *Epistles* II, i, 1–30, 390–419). Both these passages may be read as either eulogy or vituperation.

If we consider the entire range of such innuendoes and the classes of men and ideas to which they are applied, we may say that ultimately, Pope establishes two realms of implication in his satires—one, conventionally didactic; the other, boldly subversive. One shares the orientation of the explicit meaning and develops it in the usual way by imagery, analogy, irony, etc. The other has a different center, different coordinates, from the explicit meaning, which it employs as a code or a screen. Maynard Mack calls the one thematic and the other topical.[31]

Thus, although I have made much of the subversive implications of the first *Moral Essay (To Cobham)*, that poem has a familiar orientation as well, implicitly supported by Pope's choice of images. This design starts from the explicit question whether or not one can secure a true knowledge of the inner characters of men.

Pope offers two points of view, the scepticism of Montaigne and the effort made by Locke to establish an area of demonstrable knowledge. Pope claims that he can arrive at true knowledge by way of the concept of a ruling passion. But for two-thirds of the poem he illustrates the sceptical position.

The imagery of the epistle to Cobham opposes effects of light to elements drawn from external nature: landscape, plants, animals. Pope implies that light and color are more deceptive than line and shape. He implicitly links human deceitfulness with the ancient principle that line is more reliable than color. He associates virtue with things that grow naturally, vice with things that blaze.

On this level the poem is not dangerous but quite satisfactory, with the images implicitly bearing out the argument. It is when we shift our attention from the pattern of images to the choice of human examples that the subversive implications rise to trouble us.

The same analysis applies to the last epistle of *An Essay on Man*. Here the poet discusses the best ways for men to achieve happiness, and says that "fled from monarchs, St. John, [it] dwells with thee" (line 18). Conventionally, this verse alludes to expressions like "happy as a king," and implies that kings are not in fact happy. But subversively, it implies that the corruption of George II is less likely to produce happiness than the integrity of his opponent, Bolingbroke.

So also, expounding the principle that God works in orderly ways and does not often suspend the rules governing the universe, Pope observes that adherence to order may sometimes subject virtuous persons to illness and pain:

> Think we, like some weak prince, th'Eternal Cause
> Prone for his fav'rites to reverse his laws?
>
> (lines 121–22)

Conventionally, here, Pope is implying that divine justice is the model for earthly justice. But subversively, he implies that under George II, royal mistresses and favored courtiers may commit crimes with impunity.

One of the strongest examples of what I may call the bipolarity of Pope's implications is a passage in the *Epilogue to the Satires*. It illustrates his fascination with the connection between private and public realms. Pope starts from the assumption that domestic virtue has a direct relation to public performance, that a faithless husband cannot be an honest statesman. He then proceeds to dissolve the line between the realms, and blame a corrupt politician as if his infidelities sprang from the same cause as his misgovernment. The well-known lines about Vice owned by Greatness make the process splendidly visible:

> *Vice* is undone, if she forgets her Birth,
> And stoops from Angels to the Dregs of Earth:
> But 'tis the *Fall* degrades her to a Whore;
> Let *Greatness* own her, and she's mean no more:
> Her birth, her Beauty, Crowds and Courts confess,
> Chaste Matrons praise her, and grave Bishops bless:
> In golden Chains the willing World she draws,
> And hers the Gospel is, and hers the Laws. . . .
>
> (*Epilogue*, I, 141–48)

The explicit meaning is deepened by the association of vice with the Scarlet Whore; and as James Osborn has shown, the particular scarlet whore intended was the Empress Theodora. Yet, as Osborn has also shown, there was a hidden, far more scandalous allusion, in these lines, to the marriage of Walpole with his mistress Maria Skerrett; and the description of Vice represents her triumph.[32]

The poem does not call upon us to choose between these implications. Conventionally, Pope associates the career of vice with the fall of angels and the rise of the Whore. Subversively, he ties it to the marriage of Molly Skerrett. Neither implication excludes the other, but the two move in different directions. The failure to accept such bipolarity has led some scholars to disregard the topical meaning for the thematic or the latter for the former, whereas the poet usually is playing with both at once, and letting the second peep out from behind the first.[33]

I think we can apply a similar analysis to Pope's concept of heroism. Scholars have noticed his habit of setting up the moral and social values traditionally belonging to the country house as vastly superior to those traditionally assigned to a royal court.[34] This opposition blends with an old political tradition of a country party, based in the gentry, which resisted the measures of the court. When the Tory–Whig alignments emerged in the late 1670s, they cut across the court-and-country alignments, which endured along with them. In poems that seem to place rural contentment before urban activity, Pope is often invoking as well the old political antithesis between country and court. Like Swift, he could distinguish unproductive stockbrokers or financiers from productive merchants or tradesmen. It is the former that he liked to merge with Walpole and the court. If Pope habitually embodied his own values in a cultivated, politically active country gentleman like Arthur Browne,[35] he also assumed that such a figure would for patriotic reasons resist the government in power. Here then is a concept of heroism in keeping with that of Dryden after the Revolution and of Swift after the death of Queen Anne.

In the late satires, however, Pope's bipolarity also shows itself in his treatment of this sort of hero. Ostensibly, he may place the uses of retirement before those of public office during a reign of corruption. The country gentleman may therefore appear to be a truly heroic figure, reminding us of Dryden's cousin John Driden. Yet as T. R. Edwards suggests, the poet as such can be recognized as Pope's hidden hero; and it is for this reason that, so early as *An Essay on Criticism*, we see the poet described as a warrior.[36] I find it significant that in this youthful, hopeful poem, Pope was willing to draw an analogy between writers and monarchs or conquerors:

> Like Kings we lose the Conquests gain'd before,
> By vain Ambition still to make them more. . . .
>   (lines 64–65)
> A prudent Chief not always must display
> His Pow'rs in *equal Ranks*, and *fair Array*,
> But with th' *Occasion* and the *Place* comply,
> *Conceal* his Force, may seem sometimes to *Fly.*[37]
>   (lines 175–78)

In the pessimistic *Epistle to Augustus* the parallel becomes an antithesis:

> Yet let me show, a Poet's of some weight,
> And (tho' no Soldier) useful to the State. . . .
> I scarce can think him such a worthless thing,
> Unless he praise some monster of a King. . . .
>   (lines 203–4, 209–10)

For now it is precisely as an independent gentleman that the poet is heroic. It is by resisting the blandishments of pensions and offices, by refusing to serve a corrupted crown, that the poet shows his virtue:

> I cannot like, Dread Sir! your Royal Cave;
> Because I see by all the Tracks about,
> Full many a Beast goes in, but none comes out.
>   (Horace, *Epistles*, I, i, 115–17)

Thus on the one hand, Pope recommends and identifies himself with "chiefs, out of war, and statesmen, out of place."[38] He celebrates Cobham as a gardener,[39] Bathurst "unspoil'd by wealth,"[40] and the Man of Ross making grandeur blush.[41] He implicitly praises himself for being the friend of men like Caryll and Bethel.

On the other hand, Pope exalts his own heroic character as bold moralist in verse, driving vice before him—"un-plac'd, unpension'd, no man's heir, or slave."[42] It is Pope in his own right who feels proud "to see / Men not afraid of God, afraid of me."[43] As the voice of heroic virtue, or even as "God's deputy" (in the words of T. R. Edwards),[44] he implicitly congratulates men like Burlington for being chosen among the poet's friends:

> Enough for half the Greatest of these days
> To 'scape my Censure, not expect my Praise:
> Are they not rich: what more can they pretend?
> Dare they to hope a Poet for their Friend?
> *(Epilogue to the Satires, II, 112–15)*

Not only does he become the standard of merit; he records it. So Pope holds the authority that makes Hough and Digby immortal,[45] that damns Sporus and annihilates King George. In this ancient sense it is he who assigns the most splendid rewards for true greatness; honor derives from him as the fountain, and not from the king:[46]

> Sages and Chiefs long since had birth
>   E're Caesar was, or Newton nam'd,
> These rais'd new Empires o'er the Earth,
>   And Those new Heav'ns and Systems fram'd;
>
> Vain was the chief's and sage's pride
>   They had no Poet and they dyd!
> In vain they schem'd, in vain they bled
>   They had no Poet and are dead!
> (Horace, *Odes*, IV, ix, 9–16)

From such a height it becomes feasible for the poet to connect the two poles of his ideal. By depicting himself as independent gentry, winning his power from being out of the great world, he implicitly brings both heroisms together:

> Content with little, I can piddle here
> On Broccoli and mutton, round the year;
> But ancient friends, (tho' poor, or out of play)
> That touch my Bell, I cannot turn away.
> 'Tis true, no Turbots dignify my boards,
> But gudgeons, flounders, what my Thames affords.
> To Hounslow-heath I point, and Bansted-down,
> Thence comes your mutton, and these chicks my own:
> From yon old wallnut-tree a show'r shall fall;
> And grapes, long-lingring on my only wall,
> And figs, from standard and espalier join:
> The dev'l is in you if you cannot dine.
> Then cheerful healths (your mistress shall have place)
> And, what's more rare, a poet shall say *grace*.
> (Horace, *Satires*, II, ii, 137–50)

In these genial lines, offering old-fashioned, rustic hospitality, the poet who can speak with the voice of God, who defies prelates, politicians, and tyrants—

> Ye tinsel insects! whom a court maintains,
> That counts your beauties only by your stains—
> *(Epilogue to the Satires,* II, 220–21)

wears his other mantle, that of an honest country gentleman.[47] Simultaneously, by cherishing the title of "poet" and echoing the language of Horace, he reminds us that it is his creative genius—the power that immortalized Belinda as well as Bolingbroke—which confers such authority upon Pope.

Notes

1. *Essay on Man* III, 215–22, 235–40. The last four lines quoted allude bitterly to the court's easy control over Parliament at the time when the poem was published (May 1733).

2. Introduction to *An Essay on Man,* in Pope, *Poems,* III (i), p. xlii.

3. Earl R. Wasserman, *Pope's "Epistle to Bathurst"* (Baltimore: Johns Hopkins Press, 1960), p. 37 et passim; Miriam Leranbaum, *Alexander Pope's "Opus Magnum"* (Oxford: Clarendon Press, 1977), pp. 111–12, 117, 121, 125–26.

4. Thomas E. Maresca, *Pope's Horatian Poems* (Columbus: Ohio State University Press, 1966).

5. See Mack, *The Garden and the City* (Toronto: University of Toronto Press, 1969), p. 166.

6. *Moral Essays* III *(To Bathurst),* lines 249–90.

7. *Moral Essays* II *(To a Lady),* lines 249–92.

8. For contemptuous or ambiguous allusions to bishops in general or particular, see the following: *Moral Essays* I *(To Cobham),* lines 88–90; Horace *Satires* II, i, 152; Horace *Satires* I, ii, 39–44; *Epistle to Arbuthnot,* line 100; *Epilogue to the Satires* I, 132, 146, and II, 33, 70–74; *Dunciad* I, 28; IV, 593.

9. Original reading of *Epilogue to the Satires* I, 135.

10. *Social Milieu of Alexander Pope* (New Haven: Yale University Press, 1975), p. 237.

11. Howard Weinbrot, "History, Horace, and Augustus Caesar," *Eighteenth-Century Studies* 7 (1974): 391–414; Malcolm Kelsall, "Augustus and Pope," *Huntington Library Quarterly* 39 (1976): 117–31.

12. *Alexander Pope's "Opus Magnum,"* p. 72.

13. Ibid., p. 74.

14. *Essay on Man* I, 2; II, 268; IV, 172.

15. Ibid., IV, 157, 160, 206, 289.

16. Caesar, Otho, Louis XIV; Charles V, Philip II, and Philip V of Spain; Cromwell, Victor Amadeus II of Sardinia, and the Duke of Orleans (Regent of France).

17. Horace *Satires* II, i, 111–14.

18. Horace *Epistles* II, i, 7, 8, 140–42, 375, 380–83.

19. Lines 146, 220, 244.

20. Horace *Satires* II, i, 6; II, ii, 101; *Epistle to Arbuthnot*, lines 149, 305–33; *Dunciad* IV, 103.

21. Horace *Satires* I, ii, 18, and II, i, 83; *Moral Essays* II, 24; *Epistle to Arbuthnot*, line 101; Horace *Satires* I, ii, 2; Horace *Epistles* I, i, 164.

22. *Essay on Man* IV, 280; Horace *Satires* II, i, 103, and II, ii, 49.

23. *Epilogue to the Satires* I, 72.

24. Horace *Satires* I, ii, 21.

25. *Essay on Man* IV, 257–58.

26. *Moral Essays* I *(To Cobham)*, 81–84.

27. Horace *Satires* II, i, 87.

28. Horace *Epistles* I, i, 58–64. For the seventh sin, see line 56. For detailed evidence, see Mack, *The Garden and the City*, pp. 128–41.

29. Horace *Satires* II, i, 35–36.

30. Horace *Epistles* II, i *(To Augustus)*, 198–99, 221–24.

31. *The Garden and the City*, p. 163.

32. James M. Osborn, "Pope, the Byzantine Empress, and Walpole's Whore," *Review of English Studies*, n.s., 6 (1955): 372–82.

33. Cf. Barbara Lauren's quarrel with T. E. Maresca in her essay, "Pope's *Epistle to Bolingbroke*," *Studies in English Literature* 15 (1975): 419–30.

34. G. R. Hibbard, "The Country House Poem of the Seventeenth Century," *Journal of the Warburg and Courtauld Institutes* 19 (1956): 159–74; Mack, *The Garden and the City*, pp. 77–115; Erskine-Hill, *The Social Milieu of Alexander Pope*, pp. 279–317.

35. Horace *Epistles* II, ii.

36. *This Dark Estate* (Berkeley and Los Angeles: University of California Press, 1963), p. 16.

37. Cf. lines 508–14, 715–18.

38. Horace *Satires* II, i, 126.

39. *Moral Essays* I.

40. *Moral Essays* II, 226.

41. Ibid., line 281.

42. Horace *Satires* II, i, 116.

43. *Epilogue to the Satires* II, 208–9.

44. *This Dark Estate*, p. 92.

45. *Epilogue to the Satires* II, 240–41.

46. Cf. *Epilogue to the Satires* II, 234–47.

47. Mack, *The Garden and the City*, pp. 188–231.

Alexander Pope:
The Political Poet
in His Time

HOWARD ERSKINE-HILL

In his moving imitation of Horace's epistle to Florus (II.ii), Pope gives us
a political and historical view of his own early life:

> Bred up at home, full early I begun
> To read in Greek, the Wrath of Peleus' Son.
> Besides, my Father taught me from a Lad,
> The better Art to know the good from bad:
> (And little sure imported to remove,
> To hunt for Truth in *Maudlin*'s learned Grove.)
> But knottier Points we knew not half so well,
> Depriv'd us soon of our Paternal Cell;
> And certain Laws, by Suff'rers thought unjust,
> Deny'd all Posts of Profit or of Trust:
> Hopes after Hopes of pious Papists fail'd,
> While mighty WILLIAM's thundring Arm prevail'd.
> For Right Hereditary tax'd and fin'd,
> He stuck to Poverty with Peace of Mind;
> And me, the Muses help'd to undergo it;
> Convict a Papist He, and I a Poet.
>
> (52–67)[1]

From *Eighteenth-Century Studies*, 15 (1981–82), 123–41.

In an age when, as Pope himself suggested, to be a papist was to be a reputed rebel (Pope to Harcourt, May 1723),[2] it was harder to say these things openly than, for example, to make his better-known declaration that in his early poems "pure Description held the place of Sense."[3] We should take this the more seriously, therefore; and my aim in this paper is to use it as a vantage point for a brief survey of Pope's career in relation to his time.

The lines I quote are interesting on several counts. They stress that Catholics were discriminated against by law, imply that papists had hoped for a better position under James II, intimate that Pope thought William III prevailed less by law than force, and recognize that Pope's father was penalized as a Jacobite (that is the plain sense of line 64 with its preposition "For").

With what picture of Pope's age should we connect this passage of autobiography? Historians have recently been giving a report rather different from the traditional one. While the new trend may eventually be revised or rejected it seems sensible at least to listen to what recent historians are saying. In the old view the papist James II attempted to impose Roman Catholicism on Britain by an archaic resort to royal prerogative and divine right. For this violation of contract with his people most of them were happy to depose him and set up the Protestant and explicitly contractual monarchy of William and Mary, Anne, and the Hanoverians. After experiments with coalitions and with one Tory administration, a succession of Whig governments, notably under the twenty-one-year premiership of Sir Robert Walpole, established political stability. The only challenge came from unrepresentative groups of Roman Catholics who wanted a papist king, and of Tories who still believed in divine right. These, drawing on the strength of the still primitive Scottish Highlands, mounted a series of brave but small-scale Jacobite risings, never more than a forlorn hope.[4] A literary corollary of this account might be that if the writers of the time assailed "the present happy establishment" (a term much favored by that establishment) their motives were probably either impractical idealism, constitutional misanthropy or malevolence, or disappointed ambition. In the last connection, few apologists for Walpole and the Hanoverians claim they were much concerned with the promotion of literature.[5]

In the new view we see a nation less congratulating itself on a glorious revolution than reeling from an event which few had sought to bring about in the form it finally assumed, few understood, and few could justify by the standards of the time. Lock's stress on contract was generally unrepresentative. Unable to deny that James was king in law, to affirm that a contract existed before 1688, or to concede the dangerous claim that William gained his throne by force of arms, the majority of the political nation settled for the argument that James had in effect abdicated. This James himself denied by both word and arms. The image of rape, violent seizure of what belonged to another, was used by both Williamites and Jacobites, though more often by the latter.

Dissatisfaction with William and his wars soon set in. William seemed as much an autocrat as James. Many desired and more expected James to return. There were even a few Jacobites of a Whiggish cast of thought who urged that James be restored to reestablish the liberties of the nation. One of these, Charlwood Lawton, friend of William Penn, defended James's plan for a civil comprehension of churches, and spoke up for the now intensely vulnerable Roman Catholic community. Under Anne the situation changed. Britain once again had a native prince. The Act of Settlement provided for the family of Hanover to succeed Anne if she died childless, but as her reign progressed and the Tories came to power, many looked with disfavor on the prospect of a further foreign prince and hoped that some means could be found to return Britain to her native royal line. The Sacheverell Trial of 1709–10 was a kind of shadow replay of the Revolution, and the whole episode was profoundly disquieting for the Whigs.[6]

Anne's death, however, caught the overlapping groups of Tories and Jacobites unprepared. George came over and put the Whigs in power. He knew he could not trust the Tories. What now happened has been described as "a whole social revolution." "Half the nation was driven into the wilderness"—the Tories were as effectively proscribed from political office and its patronage as the Roman Catholics were by law debarred from "Posts of Profit or of Trust." The de jure claim of the native line was now less important than the Tories' recognition, clearer as the years went by, that only a Stuart restoration and a free parliament could give them back what they had once shared with the Whigs.[7] Lord Hervey, a Court Whig and nobody's fool, said in 1737 that "the majority of the Tories are certainly Jacobites"[8] and recent scholarship accords greater importance to Jacobitism. It may be more useful to think of a nation divided between two parties, each with its own candidate for the throne, the Whig king and party holding a tight monopoly of power, the Tory king and party driven into exile, conspiracy, or silence, than of a nation ruled by the Whigs but with a loyal Tory opposition. Bolingbroke and Wyndham, however, tried to create such an opposition with Tory and Whig elements. They had some success, yet the Tories did not get office again till 1760. Walpole spoke of Britain as a "divided country," and Hervey said in 1737 that

George II's "character with all ranks of people" had fallen so low that the "open manner in which they expressed their contempt and dislike, is hardly to be credited."[9] To the question, "Why then did none of the Jacobite risings succeed?" some answer is given in the recognition that the English were not now a military nation whose civilians could readily take up arms, that the Tories hoped for a peaceful restoration as in 1660, and that Walpole helped secure the Hanoverian succession by his alliance with France, and his efficient and ubiquitous secret service.[10]

A final point should be added to this newer view of the political situation. It was not by the standards of the time old-fashioned of the Tories to hope for a second restoration. Few thought that the British constitution was evolving away from monarchy; indeed, few believed in indefinite political progress. The grand aim of both parties was, no doubt, to secure, if possible in their interests, a wise, effective, and respected monarchy.

We may draw closer to Pope by considering some of the key figures in these events who were close to him. Pope told no more than the truth when he claimed to "live among the Great."[11] When we consider the great with whom he was on terms of friendship it is striking how many of them were committed and important Jacobites at one time or another. His most-esteemed noble friend, Bolingbroke, was secretary of state to the Pretender during the 1715 Rebellion. Allowed to return to Britain in 1723, he detached Sir William Wyndham, another friend of Pope, from the Jacobite cause, to set up a non-Jacobite opposition to Walpole. In 1732–33, made restless by their lack of success, they formed new plans for a Stuart restoration.[12] Francis Atterbury, bishop of Rochester, on whose behalf Pope testified at the political trial at the House of Lords, was leader of the English Jacobites before their plot broke in 1722, and secretary of state to the Pretender after being sent into exile.[13] Robert Harley, first earl of Oxford, directed from the Tower the Plot of 1716–17, in which Charles Caesar, husband of Pope's friend, Mrs. Caesar, was crucially involved.[14] Lord Lansdowne, the Tory statesman and poet to whom Pope dedicated *Windsor Forest*, was Jacobite until 1725.[15] Lord Bathurst was Jacobite until after the Atterbury Plot. The Duke of Buckingham, whose *Works* Pope edited, was Jacobite. The second earl of Oxford and the fifth earl of Orrery, close correspondents of Pope, were Jacobite. Lord Cobham, to whom Pope addressed his *Epistle on the Characters of Men* with its politically suggestive conclusion, was included in a proposed Jacobite council of regency for Prince Charles Edward in 1743. Lord Cornbury visited the Pretender in 1731 to discuss in secret a plan for restoration, but broke with him in 1735. Pope subsequently praised him for his patriotic integrity.[16]

Pope's much-admired friend, the Earl of Peterborough, was considered by the poet to be "well inclined" and fit to have headed the proposed Jacobite rising in 1714.[17] All these were Tory and Protestant. The small Roman Catholic community was in general too intimidated to meddle with Jacobitism, but two of Pope's Catholic friends of old standing, John Caryll and Father Thomas Southcote, were certainly Jacobite.[18]

Of Pope's closer friends, a relatively smaller number supported the Whig governments and the court. The Earl of Burlington was one, William Fortescue another; Pope addressed a poem to each of them. The younger James Craggs is in this category. Pope refused the pension Craggs offered him, but paid generous tribute to his memory. Sir William Trumbull, an important early friend who died in 1716 had, so far as I know, no Jacobite connections. Hugh Bethel had none, while Ralph Allen had a strongly anti-Jacobite record. Lord Lyttelton, an important opposition friend in Pope's later years, was a Patriot Whig. That something like two to one of Pope's closer friends should turn out to be Jacobite at one time or another may seem surprising. We have long discarded the picture of Pope reclining in the bosom of the establishment, but the general view is still that his connections were chiefly with Hanoverian Tories. It seems we must revise this view.

Of the names listed, Southcote, Caryll, Lansdowne, and Trumbull have a bearing on Pope's earliest work. So, surely, have his father and home background. Pope was also born into a literary tradition fraught with affairs of state. Men like Granville and Caryll afforded Pope a link with its great exemplar, the eventually Roman Catholic Dryden. It would be surprising if Pope's own phrase from *To Arbuthnot*—"pure Description"—proved the whole truth about his earlier work, however convenient the claim might later be. It now seems probable that his earliest published lines are a short lampoon on William and Mary, alleging that prince's lack of lasting conquest, whether in love or war. It brings out with a bitter triumph that "mighty WILLIAM" got no child to succeed him.[19] It is surely interesting that the subject of Pope's juvenile epic, *Alcander, Prince of Rhodes*, was "a prince, driven from his throne," however slavishly it imitated the *Aeneid*, the *Odyssey*, and other ancient poems.[20] The *Pastorals*, closest, no doubt, to "pure Description," contain in "Spring" allusions to the Royal Oak, and also—in a packed yet graceful riddle—to Anne's victories over France, the Act of Union, and her Royal Arms. These nicely managed signals are Tory but certainly not Jacobite. *Windsor Forest*, however, seems all one would expect of a poem dedicated to Lansdowne, a Tory Jacobite waiting for his moment. The oblique criticism of William III in the guise of William I as a warrior king, the rejected but recorded lines against "a foreign master's rage," the potent image of rapine, have been sufficiently remarked; this is certainly a covertly anti-Williamite poem, and the reference to "wrongs yet legal" points straight forward to the "certain Laws, by Suff'rers thought unjust" of the passage I began by quoting.[21] The conspicuous line: "And Peace and Plenty tell, a STUART reigns" (line 42) has some notable implications in a poem published twelve years after the Act of Settlement gave the succession (after any children of Anne) to the House of Brunswick, at a time when the aging and childless queen was in ill health, and when over the water an English Stuart prince claimed the throne of his fathers. Certainly this line had a special significance for the Jacobite Mrs. Caesar, who quotes it more than once with great approbation in later years, in her so far unpublished journal.[22] Pope's *First Book of STATUS his Thebais* (which probably goes back to the time of the William III lampoon but was published at the time of the first version of *The Rape of the Lock*) may, it has been suggested, allude to the unhappy state of Britain, torn between two claimants to the throne, one in possession, the other poised to enforce his claim.[23]

The Rape of the Lock has not usually been thought to contain political meanings, save for its affectionately ironical bow to "Great *Anna*" taking counsel and *"Tea."* The argument that this poem, published in the wake of the Sacheverell Trial, may allude to the rape of a kingdom, as well as to the ravishing away of youth and beauty by time, of virginity by men, of reputation by gossip—and of a shining lock of hair by the Baron—is one I have put more fully elsewhere than I shall here.[24] Suffice to say here that to read Pope's famous heroicomical poem in the tradition of poems on affairs of state so prominent in the previous thirty years is to feel that a whole system of signals in the work has been activated. At least, the poem is contrived to remind us of historical and political matters; the heroicomical focus on Belinda's small social world is so managed as to allude to a larger world of state. Thus the chief action is set in a royal palace, Anne distantly presides over the poem, and the sylphs "guard with Arms Divine the *British Throne.*" Thus we hear of "Foreign Tyrants" as of "Nymphs at home" and thus, after the rape, we are reminded that "Triumphal Arches" and "Imperial Tow'rs" yield to what the Jacobites alleged James II's England had yielded to: "The conqu'ring Force of unresisted Steel" (III, 179). But above all, it is the Game of Ombre, carefully placed by Pope in the five-canto version just before the rape, which brings affairs of state to our mind. The form of the game at cards, including ombre, was at this time a well-understood mode for witty comment on political affairs.

It was in March 1714 that the five-canto version of the poem came out. In September 1714 George I crossed from Hanover, next March Bolingbroke fled to France, and in April Pope completed his satirical pamphlet, *The Key to the Lock*, in which he mocks the idea of finding political and treasonable meanings in his poem.[25] Swift, when he sees *The Key*, says, "I think that you have changed it a good deal, to adapt it to the present times."[26] In 1717, when the Jacobite Rebellion of 1715 and the Conspiracy of 1716–17 had both failed, Pope added to his poem Clarissa's speech in Canto V "to open more clearly the MORAL of the Poem." Whatever we think *The Rape of the Lock* is about, this speech changes its meaning. The 1714 version dramatized the protests and scuffles after the rape with great comic *brio*, caused the lock to be lost in the confusion, and be subsequently transformed into a star by the "quick poetic eyes" of the Muse. There seems almost a providence in the conflict, for if Belinda hadn't put up a fight, the Baron would have kept the lock. When Pope "opened the MORAL" he balanced (though did not cancel) this significant sequence by a speech advocating the heroism of submission. One cannot help wondering, after seeing how *The Key to the Lock* sought to deflect political interpretation, whether the speech too was not adapted "to the present times." If so, the poem is in no way injured, for Pope brilliantly gave the speech advocating submission to the lady who originally connived at the violence, and proffered to the Baron his "conqu'ring . . . Steel" (III, 127–28).

Accusations of Jacobitism which the *Key* anticipated came in due time. "That little High-Church Rhimer, Poet P[o]pe" was depicted with Ormond and Sacheverell grouped round the Pretender, and in a discarded prologue to Addison's *Drummer* it seems to be suggested that he was alarmed at the Jacobite allusions of his own works.[27] Pope's deeper thoughts during this period of Jacobite unrest may never be fully known. Direct references to affairs of state are usually lighthearted, as when he cheerfully reports the rumor that the Pretender is coming.[28] His graver or more moving letters, as when he recounts how "We here bid our papist-neighbours adieu, much as those who go to be hanged do their fellow-prisoners,"[29] did not need to specify their occasion. Bolingbroke was in exile, Oxford and Lansdowne in the Tower, and the Marquess of Seaforth, to whose sister Caryll had married his eldest son, was in arms for the Pretender. Legislation was passed requiring papists to register their estates for punitive taxation. No doubt this occasioned the Popes' decision to sell their house and land in Binfield (as much, perhaps, the "Paternal Cell" of my opening quotation as Pope's original home in Lombard Street, London) and put themselves under the protection of the Whig Lord Burlington at

Chiswick. The Dancastles and Englefields (Pope's "papist-neighbours" in Berkshire) refused the Oaths and registered their estates, the latter with a clear and impressive preamble explaining that this was for religious and not political motives.

Apart from the registration of estates, the Popes should in any case have been summoned to take the Oaths. Pope later speaks of his father as not having "dar'd an Oath."[30] He himself (not unnaturally) ridiculed papists who took the Oaths just to keep their horses, and since he got rid of his own horse at this time[31] and speaks of being double-taxed,[32] the usual assumption that he refused the Oaths may be correct. Much later in his life, in 1739, he was accused by the government press of refusing them.[33] However, while the Popes' kinsfolk, Mrs. Elizabeth and Mrs. Margaret Rackett of Hammersmith, are duly recorded as having been summoned to take the Oaths and having refused them,[34] no record of the Popes' position survives in those archives which should hold them. Conceivably (though I am not very satisfied with the explanation) the issue of the summons in Binfield could be in some way controlled by Dancastle, the papist Lord of the Manor; and by the time the Popes reached Burlington's protection at Chiswick the justices were perhaps only interested in papist property-holders. One certainly has the impression of adroit footwork on the Popes' part.

By contrast with 1715–17, Pope's letters at the time of the Atterbury Plot in 1722–23 show his deep emotional engagement in the situation opened out by the imprisonment and trial of his admired friend Atterbury.[35] At the same time, Pope's edition of the *Works* of the Jacobite Duke of Buckingham came out. "They had no sooner Appear'd," reports Mrs. Caesar in her Journal, "but all the Rest was seiz'd at Jacob Tonson's. Mr. Pope was question'd About them [,] As the Publisher, that they Dropt but the Books were no more to be sold in Full Beauty."[36] Pope, it seems, was in danger of arrest. At the same time his kinsfolk, the Racketts of Hallgrove in Surrey, fell under suspicion of Jacobitism.[37] Endangered on several fronts, Pope bravely affirmed his personal loyalty to the arrested Jacobite leader, Atterbury, and though his evidence cannot have been of much significance, spoke in his favor in his trial at the House of Lords. Today we know more than Walpole could prove, but everyone suspected the bishop's complicity. Considering the public speeches made, and Pope's own personal contacts, I think it hardly credible that Pope really believed Atterbury innocent of Jacobite conspiracy.[38] His protestation of Atterbury's innocence must then be construed either as legalistic (a passionate deial that Walpole and his agents had assembled adequate evidence for the prosecution) or political (a veiled affirmation that Atterbury had worked to restore the true king). Sherburn raises the question of perjury, which Pope was certainly charged with in contemporary newspapers.[39] The term must certainly be read in the political context. It may be right to remember that while those who refused the Oaths were usually conscientious religious individuals, active Jacobites often took them, on the grounds that they were more useful to their cause if less under public suspicion. Highminded political perjury was not unknown.

The stress of events in this, the second great political crisis of Pope's life, drew from him his affirmation to Lord Harcourt (whom Mrs. Caesar considered Jacobite at heart) that he held no "Tenets of faith" "averse to, or destructive of, the present Government, King, or Constitution."[40] He thus repudiated the common charge against papists, but his statement still warrants the strictest scrutiny. Nor was he yet free of embarrassment on the score of his poems. In No. 65 of the *True Briton* (13 January 1724), the young Jacobite Duke of Wharton, who had defended Atterbury in print and speech, and was now Pope's neighbor at Twickenham, wrote a clever essay on political innuendo. It proclaimed its innocence of this art and instructed the reader in it at the same time. Citing *The Rape of the Lock* and *The Key to the Lock* as its great example, it urges that the *True Briton* is as innocent of political innuendo as Pope's poem. Since the *True Briton* is certainly not innocent of political innuendo, where (Pope may have felt) did that leave *The Rape of the Lock?*

At the height of the crisis, Pope wrote as if he expected to follow Atterbury into exile.[41] He emerged from it, mysteriously enough, on good social terms with Walpole. It is a moment in Pope's life worthy of a little thought. It has been noticed that between the Plot and the appearance of *The Dunciad* Pope wrote nothing political. It has been suggested that Walpole had a hold on him during these years, and this may be.[42] Mrs. Caesar's journal displays the terrifying jocularity with which Walpole kept his finger on those who were politically vulnerable. A Tory protested to Walpole in 1730 that he was safe from being "found in Plots. Sir Robert said he believ'd so. But [,] Turning to Mr. Caesar. Here's one we once Came Very Near."[43] Walpole may have sought to silence Pope, if he could not win him over, by a characteristic blend of friendliness and threat. Pope was not a big political fish, but celebrated poets were important in the state, and from Walpole's point of view this one had kept very bad company. Whatever the case, Pope continued to express his loyalty to Atterbury. In the carefully arranged secret correspondence between the exiled bishop and his son-in-law, William Morrice—a correspondence which, of course, eventually arrived on Walpole's desk and survives in his papers—the behavior of their Tory friends to them is faithfully reported. Bathurst, for example, cools off and stays away; he has abandoned the cause. For a time there is no clear report of Pope. Then on 5 March 1727, "our Twittenham Friend . . . constantly speaks of you [Atterbury] in terms of ye greatest friendship and Regard." On 25 March 1731, he expresses his "Friendship & Veneration" for Atterbury. His "Regard is not at all lessened by Time or Absence." Around 1728–29, Morrice had thought Pope was growing cool. This was when it was becoming known that Atterbury was giving up his post of secretary of state to the Pretender, though there may not necessarily be a connection.[44]

By 1731 the political opportunities had changed. Walpole indeed remained in power under the new king, but Bolingbroke, who returned from exile as Atterbury went, had now launched his non-Jacobite campaign against Walpole's administration, and his influential opposition journal, *The Craftsman.* If Pope was intimidated after the Atterbury crisis, the personal influence of Bolingbroke will have helped to embolden him again. At the same time a new sort of protection was available. Bolingbroke sought to unite all sorts of opposition under his banner, from Whigs out of office to sometime Jacobites. To be part of this campaign did not necessarily involve a current Jacobite commitment. Yet to compare Wharton's Jacobite *True Briton* with Bolingbroke's *Craftsman* is to see that there is a considerable overlap in the character of their rhetoric. Each makes powerful use of the idea of corruption as a political process leading to slavery and ruin; each sets against that dark prospect, as a real hope, the ideal of an active and patriotic integrity. The *Craftsman* launched, and the two great Tory satires, *Gulliver's Travels* and *The Beggar's Opera,* engaging the public's attention, Pope was able to find his own subtle route back to freedom of poetic political expression. This was of course the 1728 and 1729 *Dunciad,* a poem on the face of it concerned primarily with the state of literature. Bearing traces of the anti-Hanoverian satire apparently present in the early drafts,[45] it was actually presented by Walpole to the king and queen on 12 March 1729. Was this extraordinary episode Pope's revenge on Walpole for imposing on him a period of silence? If so, it was both daring and potent—as the comic time-bomb went off and readers detected the anti-Hanoverian subtleties of the poem.

Pope's next major poem, *An Essay on Man,* may not seem to touch the political lines I have been exploring in this paper. One of its few political references, a couplet glancing at Walpole's parliamentary difficulties and praising Shippen,[46] "the head of the veteran staunch Jacobites,"[47] was excised before publication, perhaps because Pope did not want the public to guess the authorship of his new poem. *An Essay on Man* has often been related to contemporary deism, but it has been less often observed that the *Universal Prayer*, which seems to be the germ of the religious doctrine of *An Essay on Man*, appears to go back to the early date of 1703.[48] Yet in 1711 Pope was attacking the Socianianism and atheism, alleged, of the "Foreign Reign" of William III (*An Essay on Criticism*, 544–55).[49] I suggest that Pope's universalism had nothing to do with a Socinian, deist, or atheist rejection of the divinity or atonement of Christ, but much to do with his experience of sectarian narrowness and upbringing in a persecuted church. A great part of those hopes of "pious Papists," which failed with the coming of William, were bound up with James II's ill-fated project for a civil comprehension of the churches. Pope is, of course, an endlessly eclectic poet. But as a matter of biographical hypothesis, this may, I suggest, be what lies at the root of Pope's ecumenical impulse.

By 1734, according to Lord Hervey, Pope was recognized by the court as a public critic of the king and royal family.[50] He was thus a committed and important member of the opposition to Walpole, an orientation which is felt throughout the *Imitations of Horace*, though by no means to the exclusion of personal introspection, and a sense of the subtle and unprogrammatic nature of human experience. This is a phase of Pope's career which has been brilliantly explored by Maynard Mack in *The Garden and the City*. We should, however, be aware of the specific political movements going on behind Pope's increasingly bold poetry of opposition. Bolingbroke had by now given Walpole some hard knocks, but he and Wyndham had not really managed to hold their forces together. In 1730 the Pretender had shown he was as effective as Bolingbroke in determining how the Tory M.P.'s should vote,[51] and this may have occasioned Bolingbroke's interest in the Jacobite initiatives of 1732–33. Discouragement at his general lack of success, and the fact that Walpole had discovered something of his latest veering toward Jacobitism, caused him to withdraw to France in May 1735.

For nearly two years Pope published no major poems. Then in April 1737 there appeared the retrospective imitation of Horace's epistle to Florus. Not only in the lines I have quoted but throughout the poem there is a harking back to Pope's earlier political preoccupations. The image of conquest and theft, recalling the public literature about the events of 1688, is now used as a way of understanding Pope's whole life as papist and poet.[52] Publication of the epistle *To Augustus* rapidly followed, and here Pope went further than he had ever yet done in direct political challenge

to the court. Alluding to Swift's successful campaign against Walpole's circulation of debased currency in Ireland, Pope asserts the constructive
moral role of the poet in the state:

> Let Ireland tell, how Wit upheld her cause,
> Her Trade supported, and supply'd her Laws;
> And leave on SWIFT this grateful verse ingrav'd,
> The Rights a Court attack'd, a Poet sav'd.
>
> (221–24)

According to Swift's and Pope's friend, the Jacobite John Barber, these
lines were discussed in the King's Council, and it was proposed that Pope
should be arrested. Since, however, the allusion was to the previous reign
it was decided to avoid a confrontation, and the government press would
appear to have been held back.[53] Pope was undeterred. Nothing more
appeared that year, but in 1738 were published the epistle *To Mr Murray*
with its unforgettable portrait of a corrupt minister (97–109), the epistle
To Lord Bolingbroke with its even more defiant attack on court and
government:

> Adieu to Virtue if you're once a Slave:
> Send her to Court, you send her to her Grave.
>
> (118–19)

and the two Dialogues of the Epilogue to the Satires.

All this was in the absence of Bolingbroke, who returned to England and
took up residence with Pope in July 1738. He found a situation in which,
with Queen Caroline dead, Walpole's position was weakening, but the
opposition was fragmenting back into its original components. Walpole
said that concealed Jacobites had succeeded beyond expectation, and Bolingbroke wrote that the spirit of Jacobitism "rises anew among the
Tories." In October 1739 Walpole was to tell Dudley Ryder that Prince
Frederick's supporters, a new opposition group, had proposed "a revolution in favour of the Prince, saying that the King's interest was entirely
lost . . . but the Jacobites said if there was to be an alteration, it should be
a restoration."[54] To look closely at this moment of British history is not to
be impressed with the growth of stability so much as with a sense of crisis.

It is in this context that we should read Pope's 1738 poems, especially
the Epilogue to the Satires, and Bolingbroke's *Idea of a Patriot King*, written later in 1738, circulated among Prince Frederick's supporters, and

secretly printed by Pope. Each writer is reacting to seeing Walpole on the defensive, yet the opposition too disunited to pursue its advantage. Each seeks to distance and understand the political confusion by the governing concepts of corruption versus patriotism. The Epilogue to the Satires combines a not altogether comfortable Horatian intimacy with some of the desperate gestures of actual Jacobite conspiracy in 1722. This is not to say that Pope was now a Jacobite, or writing Jacobite poems, but that he was drawing on what he must have known was a part of the language and stance of Jacobitism. Inevitably there was much overlap between the rhetoric of Jacobite and non-Jacobite Toryism. If one compares with these poems the Tory opposition poetry of David Morgan in his *Country Bard* (1739, 1741), a poem which praises Bolingbroke and Pope, we shall not see a wide difference in the kind of rhetoric and judgment, only in the degree of literary skill. Morgan was certainly a Jacobite, however; he joined Prince Charles Edward in 1745 and was subsequently executed.[55]

Bolingbroke draws a picture of the Patriot King as an ideal, rhetorically rather than philosophically conveyed, *praecipere laudando*. As a test it is, I suggest, like panegyric without the prince. By circulating it among Prince Frederick's supporters, Bolingbroke suggested that this was the man. Whatever else, this was prudent. But bearing in mind Bolingbroke's changeable political career, constant to the Tories but not to any one royal line, one cannot but wonder whether his rhetoric of corruption and patriotism was not a political weapon nicely judged to turn in either direction, as the opportunity offered, Hanover or Stuart. Certainly the Pretender's agent at the French court in 1740 observed of Bolingbroke and Wyndham that "they both seem to dread that any business of the King's [i.e., the Pretender's] should be thought of without them."[56]

Describing the great procession of Dullness summoned by "Fame's posterior Trumpet" in *Dunciad* IV, Pope included among those who "Roll in her Vortex":

> Not those alone who passive own her laws,
> But who, weak rebels, more advance her cause.
>
> (IV, 85–86)

The allusion is to the Tory doctrine of Passive Obedience, abandoned by most Jacobites in regard to the House of Brunswick, and, unmistakably, to the only rebels Pope knew in his time, the Jacobites themselves, whose armed risings, conspiracies, and initiatives, because of their weakness, increased rather than diminished the power of the Hanoverian court and

its governments, and thus, in the myth of Pope's poem, the power of Dullness, that great selfish and collective power which survived the death of
Caroline and the fall of Walpole, to be the mighty goddess of a falling
civilization. The couplet is another sign of Pope's awareness and concern
with these political issues, and we are left with an equivocality absolute
characteristic, I suggest, of Bolingbroke, Wyndham, the majority of
Tories, and all who in an unmartial country, governed by a thoroughly
corrupt electoral system, could hope for radical political change only by a
revolution. The political message against Dullness is: rebel powerfully, or
not at all. In the last year of his life Pope neutrally remarked to the unsympathetic Spence that the great men might be more for a restoration then
than before, if there were any likelihood of it succeeding.[57] A year later, in
the autumn of 1745, an anonymous Jacobite seems to have quoted from
Pope's Epilogue to the Satires in an appeal to the English to join the army
of Prince Charles Edward Stuart.

I have tried to trace Pope's career in its historical context. This context
is not one in which a "present happy establishment" is contentedly
evolved, but ruthlessly imposed and corruptly maintained—or so "the
suff'ring Party" (Pope's phrase) saw it.[58] Whether with the lightest obliquity or the bravest plainness, Pope always reminds us of this issue. This
is the value for him of his two most suggestive political images, that of
conquest, rapine, forcible deprivation, "certain laws by suff'rers thought
unjust," and that of corruption, slow moral and political decay, by which
a "happy establishment" might buy a man's voice, and cause him to become
a singing or a dancing slave.

In the margin of this passage of Pope's Montaigne (translated by
Cotton):

For it is lawful for a Man of Honour to say as the *Lacademonians* did, having
been defeated by *Antipater*, when just upon the point of concluding an agreement, *You may impose as heavy and ruinous Taxes on us as you please, but to command us to do shameful and dishonest things, you will lose your time, for it is to no
purpose.*

Pope wrote "The case of those who pay double Taxes."[59] Pope thus
affirmed his inner resistance to conquest and oppression, and his resolve,
"tho' no soldier" and "not a Giant quite" to make his independent voice
heard. What did he use it to say? He told Swift that he was no enemy to
the present constitution, and Atterbury that he hoped George I would not
be a King of Whigs, or a King of Tories, but a King of England.[60] Partisan

like Bolingbroke in that he saw his original party proscribed, like Boling-broke he aspired to the ideal of a nonparty, national, and patriarchal mon-archy. His opposition to the relation between Walpole and the Hanoverian court, therefore, is not loyal opposition in a two-party system, but a protest against the supplanting of one party system by another of a new and nar-rower kind. It is a voice warning that a comprehensive national constitu-tion is being subverted into a one-party state. To arrest that subversion was the great aim of both Bolingbroke and Pope, and if at times it seemed that a Stuart restoration would achieve this end, Pope was, we may infer but not demonstrate, not utterly averse. In a period of deceptive calm, treacherous currents, and sudden storms, Pope navigated with skill. True, he trimmed his sails at times, but he also sailed near the wind.

Notes

1. The same passage was with good reason chosen by John M. Aden as the starting point for his essay, "Pope and Politics: The Farce of State," in Peter Dixon, ed., *Alexander Pope* (London: G. Bell and Sons, 1972), pp. 172–99. While my picture shows the life in a different light, Aden has since deepened his view: first in his article, "The Change of Sceptres and Impending Woe" (see note 24, below), and second in his book *Pope's Once and Future Kings* (Knoxville: Univ. of Tennessee Press, 1978).

2. *The Correspondence of Alexander Pope*, ed. George Sherburn (Oxford: Clarendon, 1956), II, 171–72.

3. *To Arbuthnot*, lines 147–48, *The Twickenham Edition of the Poems of Alexander Pope*, gen. ed. John Butt (London: Methuen, 1939–67), IV, 106.

4. Basil Williams, *The Whig Supremacy* (Oxford: Oxford Univ. Press, 1939); J. H. Plumb, *Sir Robert Walpole*. Vol. I: *The Making of a Statesman*, and Vol. II, *The King's Minister*. (London: Cresset, 1956 and 1960); J. H. Plumb, *The Growth of Political Stability in England, 1675–1725* (London: Macmillan, 1967).

5. The most recent survey is Bertrand A. Goldgar, *Walpole and the Wits: The Relation of Politics to Literature, 1722–1742* (Lincoln: Univ. of Nebraska Press, 1976), which gives, pos-sibly, too much weight to this point.

6. J. P. Kenyon, *Revolution Principles: The Politics of Party, 1689–1720* (New York and London: Cambridge Univ. Press, 1977); Geoffrey Holmes, *British Politics in the Age of Anne* (London: St. Martin's, 1967); Holmes, *The Trial of Dr. Sacheverell* (London: Eyre Methuen, 1973). On the use of the image of rape, see Howard Erskine-Hill, "Literature and the Jacobite Cause," *MLS*, 9 (Fall 1979), 15–20.

The intellectual aftermath of 1688 has been considerably illuminated by the recent work of Mark Goldie. For the use of conquest theory to justify the Revolution, see "Edmund Bohun and *Jus Gentium* in the Revolution Debate, 1689–1693," *Historical Journal*, 20, No. 3 (1977), 569–86. For the survival of radical Whiggism, see "The Roots of True Whiggism, 1688–94," in *History of Political Thought*, 1 (June 1980), 195–236. For an assessment of the balance and combination of argument, see "The Revolution of 1689 and the Structure of Political

Argument: An Essay and an Annotated Bibliography of Pamphlets in the Allegiance Controversy," *Bulletin of Research in the Humanities,* 5 (Winter 1980), 473–564. In "'Abdicate' and 'Contract' in the Glorious Revolution," *Historical Journal,* 24, No. 2 (1981), 323–37, Thomas P. Slaughter seeks to reinstate something of the old Whig view of 1688 by pointing out that the word 'abdicate' was ambiguous in the 1689 discussions: it might not mean 'voluntarily renounce' but 'capitulate to force.' It is true that the ambiguity of the word was useful in political debate, but this in turn only underlines the general unacceptability among supporters of the Revolution of the argument that James II had been deposed by force. Scholars of the period will wish to consult J. C. D. Clarke's ambitious and important article, "A General Theory of Party, Opposition and Government, 1688–1832," *Historical Journal,* 23, No. 2 (1980), 295–325, which offers something of a new light on the political writers of the time.

7. Eveline Cruickshanks, *Political Untouchables: The Tories and the '45* (London: Holmes and Meier, 1979), pp. 4–5, and Ch. i, passim.

8. Romney Sedgwick, ed., *Lord Hervey's Memoirs,* selected ed. (London: Batsford, 1952; rev. ed. 1963), p. 191.

9. Ibid., pp. 153, 169.

10. Cruickshanks, *Political Untouchables,* passim.

11. *To Fortescue,* lines 133–34, Twickenham ed., IV, 19.

12. H. T. Dickinson, *Bolingbroke* (London: Constable, 1970), pp. 240–41; Cruickshanks, *Political Untouchables,* pp. 12–13.

13. G. V. Bennett, *The Tory Crisis in Church and State, 1688–1730* (Oxford: Oxford Univ. Press, 1975), pp. 205–310.

14. Cruickshanks, *Political Untouchables,* p. 8.

15. Elizabeth Handasyde, *Granville the Polite: The Life of George Granville, Lord Lansdowne, 1666–1735* (Oxford: Oxford Univ. Press, 1933), pp. 215–16, and Chs. v, vii–viii, x–xii passim.

16. Cruickshanks, *Political Untouchables,* pp. 12–13; Pope, *To Mr. Murray,* lines 60–62, Twickenham ed., IV, 241.

17. Joseph Spence, *Observations, Anecdotes and Characters of Books and Men,* ed. J. M. Osborn (Oxford: Clarendon, 1966), item 257.

18. Howard Erskine-Hill, *The Social Milieu of Alexander Pope: Lives, Example and the Poetic Response* (New Haven: Yale Univ. Press, 1975), Chs. ii and iii passim; Spence, *Observations,* items 69, 70, and Appendix to 70.

19. David Nokes, "Lisping in Political Numbers," *N&Q,* NS 24 (June 1977), 228–29.

20. Spence, *Observations,* item 38.

21. Twickenham ed., I, 159; J. R. Moore, "Windsor Forest and William III," in *Essential Articles for the Study of Alexander Pope,* ed. Maynard Mack, rev. and enl. ed. (Hamden, Conn.: Archon, 1968), pp. 242–46.

22. Bodleian MSS, Microfilm 740, Vol. III. I am most grateful to Dr. Linda Colley of Christ's College, Cambridge, for drawing my attention to this source.

23. John M. Aden, "The Change of Sceptres and Impending Woe," *PQ,* 3, No. 4 (1973), 728–38. Aden's argument is now incorporated into his book *Pope's Once and Future Kings.*

24. Erskine-Hill, "Literature and the Jacobite Cause."

25. Norman Ault, ed., *The Prose Works of Alexander Pope* (Oxford: Basil Blackwell, 1934), pp. 173–202. Aden (*Pope's Once and Future Kings,* pp. 123–24) and Erskine-Hill ("Literature and the Jacobite Cause," p. 20) take the view that *The Key* was written as a deliberate blind.

26. Swift to Pope, 28 June 1715, *Corr.,* I, 302.

27. George Sherburn, *The Early Career of Alexander Pope* (Oxford: Clarendon, 1934), pp. 160–61.

28. Pope to Teresa Blount, 23 July 1715, *Corr.*, I, 308.

29. Pope to Caryll, 20 March 1716, *Corr.*, I, 336–37.

30. *To Arbuthnot*, line 397, Twickenham ed., IV, 126.

31. Pope to Teresa and Martha Blount, 23 July 1715, *Corr.* I, 309; John Dancastle to Pope, Summer 1717, *Corr.*, I, 404.

32. *To Bethel*, line 152, Twickenham ed., IV, 67.

33. By the *Gazetteer*, 9 January 1739, cited in Howard Weinbrot, *Augustus Caesar in "Augustan" England* (Princeton: Princeton Univ. Press, 1978), p. 145.

34. Greater London Record Office, Middlesex Records, MR RR 23, fol. 2; MR RRE 2, fol. 4v; MR RR 19/7.

35. *Corr.*, II, 134–206; Sherburn, *Early Career*, pp. 228–30.

36. Sherburn, *Early Career*, pp. 224–28; Bodleian MSS, Microfilm 740, Vol. I.

37. E. P. Thompson, *Whigs and Hunters: The Origin of the Black Act* (London: Allen Lane, 1975), Appendix 2.

38. Erskine-Hill, *The Social Milieu of Alexander Pope*, pp. 158–60.

39. Sherburn, *Early Career*, p. 229.

40. Pope to Harcourt, 6 May 1722, *Corr.*, II, 171–72.

41. Pope to Atterbury, 20 April 1723, *Corr.*, II, 167.

42. *Corr.*, II, 368, 441, 530; III, 11, 53, 112; E. P. Thompson, *Whigs and Hunters*, p. 287. However, Aden's remarks on Pope's *Odyssey* translation (*Pope's Once and Future Kings*, pp. 170–75) would, if accepted, modify this view.

43. Bodleian MSS, Microfilm 740, Vol. II.

44. Cambridge University Library, Cholmondely (Houghton) Papers, 1406, 1823, 1835, 1604, 1542.

45. The content of these drafts was expounded by Maynard Mack in his paper to the American Society for Eighteenth-Century Studies in Victoria, B.C., Canada, in May 1977. See Goldgar, *Walpole and the Wits*, pp. 77–78.

46. Maynard Mack, ed., *An Essay on Man: Reproductions of the Manuscripts in the Pierpont Morgan Library and the Houghton Library* (Oxford: Oxford Univ. Press, 1962), p. xxxiii.

47. Hervey's phrase, *Memoirs*, ed. Sedgwick, p. 7.

48. R. W. Rogers, "Alexander Pope's Universal Prayer," in *Essential Articles*, ed. Mack, pp. 375–91. See also G. Douglas Atkins, "Pope and Deism: A New Analysis," in Maynard Mack and James A. Winn, eds., *Pope: Recent Essays by Several Hands* (Hamden, Conn.: Archon, 1980), pp. 392–415.

49. Twickenham ed., I, 300–304.

50. Hervey's *Memoirs*, ed. Sedgwick, p. 73.

51. Cruickshanks, *Political Untouchables*, p. 12.

52. Aubrey Williams, "Pope and Horace: The Second Epistle of the Second Book," in Carroll Camden, ed., *Restoration and Eighteenth-Century Literature: Essays in Honor of Alan Dugall McKillop* (Chicago: Univ. of Chicago Press, 1963), pp. 309–21.

53. Twickenham ed., IV, 213.

54. Cruickshanks, *Political Untouchables*, pp. 15, 17; Dickinson, *Bolingbroke*, p. 258.

55. Cruickshanks, *Political Untouchables*, pp. 91, 99, 101, 105; Howard Erskine-Hill, "Literature and the Jacobite Cause: Was There a Rhetoric of Jacobitism?" in *Ideology and Conspiracy: Aspects of Jacobitism 1690–1759*, ed. Eveline Cruickshanks. (Edinburgh: John Donald).

56. Cruickshanks, *Political Untouchables*, p. 23.
57. Spence, *Observations*, item 257.
58. Pope to Arbuthnot, 26 July 1734, *Corr.*, III, 420.
59. Maynard Mack, "Pope's Books: A Biographical Survey with a Finding List," in Maximillian Novak, ed., *English Literature in the Age of Disguise* (Berkeley and Los Angeles: Univ. of California Press, 1977), p. 278.
60. Pope to Swift, 28 November 1729, *Corr.*, III, 81; Pope to Atterbury, 20 November 1717, *Corr.*, I, 454.

"A Double Capacity": *The Beggar's Opera*

IAN DONALDSON

> For the generality of men, a true Modern Life is like a true Modern
> Play, neither Tragedy, Comedy, nor Farce, nor one, nor all of these.
> Every Actor is much better known by his having the same Face, than
> by his keeping the same Character: For we change our minds as often
> as they can their parts, & he who was yesterday Cesar, is to day Sir J.
> Daw. So that one might, with much better reason, ask the same Ques-
> tion of a Modern Life, that Mr. Rich did of a Modern Play; Pray do
> me the favor, Sir, to inform me: Is this your Tragedy or your Comedy?
>
> (Pope to Cromwell, 29 August 1709[1])

I

The Beggar's Opera has had a remarkable stage history, in respect both of
its enduring popularity and of the wide variety of ways in which it has been
interpreted. Its popularity in modern times derives very largely from two
famous and quite different productions of the 1920s. Nigel Playfair's long-
running London production (which in turn set off a train of critical and
scholarly works and small editions of the plays) was pretty and porcelain,
its music (arranged by Frederick Austen) decorative, sweet, pathetic. Ber-
tolt Brecht's adaptation, *Die Dreigroschenoper,* presented in Berlin in 1928,
was quite another thing, its caustically unsentimental tone perfectly conveyed by the music of Kurt Weil. Neither production could be said to have
interpreted *The Beggar's Opera* very faithfully, and it is understandable that
Empson should have spoken tartly in his splendid essay on the play in the
early thirties: "It is a fine thing that the play is still popular, however stu-

From *The World Upside-Down: Comedy From Jonson to Fielding* (Oxford: Clarendon, 1970),
pp. 159–82.

141

pidly it is enjoyed."[2] And yet there has seldom been a period in which *The Beggar's Opera* has not been, in some sense, "stupidly" enjoyed, and this tendency to provoke a wide range of responses and interpretations is not the least intriguing aspect of the play. Eighteenth-century performances of the play were quite as various as those in modern times. In 1777—to take just one instance—*The Whitehall Evening Post* found occasion to complain with equal tartness of the two productions of *The Beggar's Opera* then running at the two main London theaters; at one house Lucy was being played as high tragedy, at the other she was played as low comedy, and "we scruple not to pronounce them both wrong."[3] Not tragedy, not comedy; then what do you call it? In an earlier rehearsal play, Gay had put that question in his very title: *The What D'Ye Call It*. The play defied all categories; it was, said Gay, "A Tragi-Comi-Pastoral Farce." There is a well-known letter in which Pope and Gay speak delightedly of the bewildering effect *The What D'Ye Call It* has had upon its audiences. Some of the town, they write, have taken the play as "a mere jest upon the tragic poets," others have seen it as a satire on the late war; the deaf Mr. Cromwell, hearing none of the words, was much surprised to see the audience laughing at such apparently tragical action; those who came to hiss were so diverted that they forgot the purpose of their visit. The "common people of the pit and gallery," Pope and Gay go on, "received it at first with great gravity and sedateness, some few with tears; but after the third day they also took the hint, and have ever since been loud in their clapps."[4] It was a perfect Scriblerian victory; a victory for what Hugh Kenner has well described as the art of counterfeiting.[5] Counterfeiting is quite different from hoaxing; the puzzlement set up by *The What D'Ye Call It* or *The Beggar's Opera* is of quite a different order from that temporary puzzlement aroused by, let us say, Ireland's *Vortigern*. Even after long familiarity with Gay's work, even after taking "the hint," one is still likely to feel the variousness of its appeal, its odd ability to be at once ironical and sentimental, risible and grave.

A small cross-section taken from near the end of *The Beggar's Opera* will show how Gay's kind of counterfeiting works, and how complex its effects may be. A writer in the first number of *The Sentimental Magazine* in 1773 observed that the principal difficulty of approaching Gay's work was to know how seriously it was intended, as simplicity and "the real pathetic" are so intermingled with the humorous and parodic that "one is at a loss whether to take it as jest or earnest—whether to laugh or cry." "Indeed," he went on, after discussing this difficulty in relation to *The Shepherd's Week,* this effect is also produced in this two dramatic burlesques, the Beggar's Opera and What d'ye call it; for how ludicrous soever the general character of the piece may be, when he comes so near to hanging and shooting in good earnest, the joke ceases; and I have observed the tolling of St. *Pulcre's-bell* received by an audience with as much tragical attention and sympathetic terror as that in Venice Preserved.

The testimony about eighteenth-century audience reaction to the final moments of *The Beggar's Opera* is of some interest; so too is the fact that the writer should turn instinctively for his comparison to a similar effect in Otway's *Venice Preserv'd*. For it seems highly probable that Oway's scene was just the one which Gay here intended to burlesque. Pierre's heroic ascent to the scaffold in Act V of *Venice Preserv'd* was one of the most celebrated tragic moments of the Restoration and eighteenth-century stage. As Pierre awaits his execution, the *Passing-bell tolls*; assured by his friend Jaffeir that his death will be honourable—Jaffeir will stab him, then stab himself, at the gallows—Pierre proudly presents himself to his execution-ers with the measured words, *Come, now I'm ready*. That bell had been gently mocked by Addison in the forty-fourth *Spectator* paper as early as 1711; and the year after the first performance of *The Beggar's Opera* Pope was also to speak dryly of the tolling bell as "a mechanical help to the Pathetic, not unuseful to the modern writers of Tradegy."[6] Gay's use of the tolling bell in the last act of *The Beggar's Opera* as Macheath, standing between Polly and Lucy, also awaits Jack Ketch ("Would I might be hanged!") just as clearly mocks this highly popular dramatic device. Sud-denly confronted with four more wives, with a child apiece, Macheath reaches desperately for the dignity of Pierre's own phrase: "Here—tell the Sheriffs officers I am ready." (An extra relish was given to the allusion by the fact that Walker, the actor playing Macheath in the original production at Lincoln's Inn Fields, had also played Pierre at the same theater a few weeks earlier.)[7] No gallows joke, I suppose, is likely to be simple in its effects; that this one should compel an audience to "tragical attention and sympathetic terror" does suggest, however, an abnormal emotional com-plexity, an abnormal success at the counterfeiter's art. "Sublimity," wrote Goldsmith, "if carried to an exalted height, approaches burlesque...."[8] Gay's art reverses the process; his burlesque, carried to an exalted height, approaches sublimity.

Gay's counterfeiting is different not only from mere hoaxing but also from mere literary parody and ridicule. His style of burlesque is quite unlike that of Buckingham. "Our Poets make us laugh at Tragoedy / And with their Comedies they make us cry," Buckingham had written in the prologue to *The Rehearsal,* stating what was to become the commonest of eighteenth-century theatrical jokes, that it was impossible nowadays to tell comedy and tragedy apart. Behind this joke lay the neo-classical premise that comedy and tragedy ought to be firmly kept apart; the premise of Goldsmith's *Essay on the Theatre,* in which he complains that comedy and tragedy, traditionally kept in "different channels," had lately encroached upon each other's provinces. Gay converts a stock joke into a new art-form. "*The whole Art of* Tragi-Comi-Pastoral Farce," he wrote in his Preface to *The What D'Ye Call It, "lies in interweaving the several kinds of the Drama with each other, so that they cannot be distinguished or separated.*" And in his "interweaving" of the dramatic kinds Gay gently challenges the old neo-classical premise that insists that the kinds be kept pure and distinct. In *The Beggar's Opera,* heroic tragedy, Italian opera, pastoral, popular ballads, and sentimental comedy merge bizarrely together, continually awakening ironical memories of other kinds of literary experience, yet nevertheless forming a whole which is in some ways curiously life-like. "By the assumed licence of the mock-heroic style," Hazlitt wrote perceptively, Gay "has enabled himself to *do justice to nature*."[9] What is "natural," perhaps, is the sense which Gay stimulates of the manifold possible ways of looking at any set of actions: as in life itself, an act may be heroic, or laughable, or sad; the plays are unclassifiable, open-ended. And in this respect they may strike us as being peculiarly modern.

The challenge to neo-classical principles was also being made about this time by other and more serious campaigners. Steele had argued in *Tatler* 172 that one really ought to be able to write tragedy not only about "the history of princes, and persons who act in high spheres," but also about "such adventures as befall persons not elevated above the common level." The common man is potentially as much of a tragic figure as is the prince. It is little wonder that eighteenth-century audiences were confused as to the proper way of responding to the echoes of *Venic Preserv'd* as Macheath went to the gallows at the end of *The Beggar's Opera,* for such echoes of heroic tragedy were a common device in the new bourgeois tragedy. Only three years after the first performance of *The Beggar's Opera,* George Lillo in the final act of *The London Merchant* was to imitate closely the final act of *Venice Preserv'd:* as George Barnwell awaits his execution at the scaffold, the passing bell tolls once more, and Barnwell, like Macheath, prepares to meet his death with a half-quotation from Otway on his lips: "I am summoned to my fate. . . . *Tell 'em I'm ready.*" The fate of a London prentice, Lillo implies, should hold the same poignancy for us as the fate of Macbeth or Faustus or Pierre. If a prentice may take on heroic stature, why may not a highwayman too? In his Preface to *The What D'Ye Call It*, Gay had gravely repeated the arguments of the propagandists for the new bourgeois tragedy. To the "objection" that the sentiments of the play are *"not Tragical, because they are those of the lowest country people,"* he answered: " . . . that the sentiments of Princes and clowns have not in reality that difference which they seem to have: their thoughts are almost the same, and they only differ as the same thought is attended with a meanness or pomp of diction, or receive a different light from the circumstances each Character is conversant with." Gay puts a new ironical edge on the sentimentalists' proposition. It is only "circumstances" and the artificial conventions of "diction" (high style for princes, low style for clowns) which disguise the basic truth that all men are alike, that those in low life are no worse than those in high, that those in high life are no better than those in low. All men may therefore be seen as heroes; or, if you prefer all men may therefore be seen as rogues. As so often in Gay's work, the question is left open: we may look at it which way we please. Yet what we cannot forget—and the fact is important to an understanding of *The Beggar's Opera*—is the general sense of the interchangeability of men. Despite all appearances, one man will turn out to be much the same as another.

II

The Beggar's Opera, wrote Pope, was "a piece of Satire which hit all tastes and degrees of men, from those of the highest Quality to the very Rabble."[10] All classes and all men come within the arc of its satire; no one is left unscathed. Yet it is the method of Gay's irony to keep maintaining the illusion that this is not so at all; that although things are in a bad way in this society there must surely be exceptions somewhere to the general rule; someone must be kind, someone must be honest, someone must be heroic. Throughout the play Gay keeps suggesting possible exceptions to the general rule of bourgeois possessiveness and self-interest, possible avenues of romantic freedom and escape, possible evidence of a primitive honesty; only regretfully, ironically, to dismiss such possibilities, to shut off the avenues and to reject the evidence as we approach more nearly.

The method is seen at its broadest in the opening song of the play:

Through all the employments of life
Each neighbour abuses his brother;

> Whore and Rogue they call Husband and Wife:
> All professions be-rogue one another.
> The Priest calls the Lawyer a cheat,
> The Lawyer be-knaves the Divine;
> And the Statesman, because he's so great,
> Thinks his trade as honest as mine.

Peachum's song pictures a society in which all men are reduced to a common level: husbands and wives stand on the same footing as rogues and whores; priests and lawyers are as bad as each other; all men are "brothers" in that they are all united in knavery. Yet there is one exception to this cheerless general rule, one honest man in this corrupt society: Peachum. And Peachum's "trade" is that of an informer and receiver of stolen goods. Peachum explains how his trade might be said to be honest: "A Lawyer is an honest employment, so is mine. Like me too he acts in a double capacity, both against the Rogues and for 'em; for 'tis but fitting that we should protect and encourage Cheats, since we live by 'em." "A double capacity," Peachum implies, is twice as useful as a single one; the phrase suggests a sophisticated professional versatility, like that of the lawyer, who can now prosecute, now defend, using the law as a rapier or as a shield as the need arises. No one needs to be told that Peachum's "capacity" is in fact that of the double agent, that he is as great a rogue as everyone else in his society. The phrase "double capacity" might also be said to describe the way in which Gay's own irony works, saying one thing and implying another, shaping a double picture of Peachum and (in turn) of every other character in the play.

The ironical method in this opening passage is enjoyably broad and easy; no one could be fooled by Peachum. Yet it is worth watching even at this stage of the play how Gay creates an awareness that things may be seen in a multiplicity of ways. Here is how Peachum resolves to secure the release from Newgate of some female members of the gang: "I love to let the women scape. A good sportsman always lets the Hen-Partridges fly, because the breed of the game depends upon them. Besides, here the Law allows us no reward; there is nothing to be got by the death of women— except our wives." Sportsman's heartiness, old-fashioned gallantry to the ladies, and financial shrewdness are nicely blended. The passage invites us to see Peachum as soft-hearted, and to see him as callous; to see women as objects of chivalry, and to see them as mere "game"; to see them as being of value, because they are breeders, and as being of no value, for the law allows no reward for information against them. Everything depends upon your viewpoint. Like hen-partridges the women are allowed to escape, but like hen-partridges they are at the same time captive within the lord's domain; the image of the bird which is apparently free but in fact captive runs throughout the play. Then the perspective shifts once more; women are praised, in a barbed phrase, as the educators of men and their rewarders ("We and the surgeons are more beholden to women than all the professions beside"), then instantly condemned as the seducers of men:

> 'Tis woman that seduces all mankind,
>   By her we first were taught the wheedling arts:
> Her very eyes can cheat; when most she's kind,
>   She tricks us of our money with our hearts.
> For her, like Wolves by night we roam for prey,
>   And practise ev'ry fraud to bribe her charms;
> For suits of love, like law, are won by pay,
>   And Beauty must be fee'd into our arms.

It is not the men who trap the women—thus runs the argument of Filch's song—but rather the women who trap the men, as they have done since the time of Eve, the archetypal wheedler and betrayer. The men are betrayed by the softness of their hearts. The betrayal is not that the women are unfaithful, but that they demand cash. Hence men are turned into predatory *"Wolves,"* against their better natures. What should be noticed is the revolution of images here as men and women take it in turns to be hungry predators and innocent victims, wolves and partridges, confusing in our minds the notion of who is hunting whom, but suggesting obliquely that everyone may be seen as acting in a double capacity, that no one is simply a hunter or simply a prey, that society is at war with itself, and that that war is at its most deadly in the relationship between the sexes. Tempering such suggestions is the gaiety of the dramatic moment; the predominant mood is set by the light, darting melody to which the song is set. The final effect is thus one of incongruity: the incongruity of a sharpster protesting that he had been undone, yet at the same time educated, by the ladies; the incongruity of words and music, as this unsettling vision of society is unfolded with such gay charm.

   This ironic revolution of images continues throughout the play; it is typical of Gay's method that within one song (Air XLV) he should have Lockit picturing himself first as a gudgeon, the "easy prey" of his treacherous daughter, next as a trapper, catching one innocent bird (Macheath) with another unwitting decoy (Lucy). It is in the case of Macheath and

Polly that this confusion of role is most delicately suggested, and once again the predominant images are those of hunter and hunted. Mrs. Peachum's wish is to save Macheath from the predatory company of lords and gentlemen; "he should leave them to prey upon one another." Yet it is more logical (as Samuel Butler had suggested) to see a highwayman himself as an animal of prey: "Aristotle held him to be but a kind of huntsman; but our sages of the law account him rather a beast of prey, and we will not allow his game to be legal by the forest law."[11] We are to learn in due course (III.ii) that the image is an apt one for Macheath, who keeps company with lords and gentlemen in their gaming-houses merely so as to know who is worth setting upon on the road. And yet (as Empson's analysis makes clear) there is also the suggestion that Macheath may indeed be a victim, in his relationship with Polly:

> I know as well as any of the fine ladies [says Polly] how to make the most of my self and of my man too. A woman knows how to be mercenary, though she hath never been in a court or at an assembly. We have it in our natures, papa. If I allow captain *Macheath* some trifling liberties, I have this watch and other visible marks of his favour to show for it.

For a new wife to claim that she knows how "to make the most" of her husband suggests that she has a concern for advancing him in the world. What Polly has in fact been doing (the syntax glides us demurely over the point) is getting what she can out of her husband in order to line her own pockets.

The imagery of Polly's songs continues the doubt as to who is hunting whom:

> I, like a ship in storms, was tost;
> Yet afraid to put in to Land;
> For seiz'd in the port the vessel's lost,
> Whose treasure is contreband.
> The Waves are laid,
> My duty's paid.
> O joy beyond expression!
> Thus, safe a-shore,
> I ask no more,
> My all is in my possession.

"Duty" is both a tax, and a moral obligation; the word chimes ironically throughout the play. For other characters than Polly, it seems, "duty" is something one owes to oneself, and is closely connected with the idea of self-interest. "If she will not know her duty," says her mother, "we know ours"; the duty is to hang Macheath before he hangs them. For the ladies of the town, love is the "duty" which they owe to themselves in their youth (Air XXII); the gain go "upon duty" on the heath in order to make themselves rich. Polly's duty, on the other hand, appears to be directed outwards; there seems to be something endearingly old-fashioned about her ideas of social responsibility. And yet the song also pictures Polly as a smuggler; the contraband "treasure" is Macheath (Gay has given a specific sense to the colloquial phrase, "you treasure"), who is reduced to a mere possession which Polly is now free to enjoy. She is free, Macheath is a mere possession; the highwayman, whose job it is to capture other people's treasure, is himself captured by Pirate Polly. The point is again made with a sweet obliqueness (quite lost in Brecht's "Pirate Jenny"), the whole conceit of the song apparently arising out of an innocent imitation of a favorite operatic simile ("the ship") which the Beggar has warned us earlier he will introduce by way of heightening. The adventurer and the turtle-dove; such is Polly's double capacity.

It is this controlled confusion of imagery which causes, in turn, our confusion of response as we watch the play. It is perhaps as important that the sentimentality of the play can hold the irony in check as it is the other way about; Brecht's version of the play shows how much is lost by the removal of this sentiment counterweight. There is nothing in *Die Dreigroschenoper* which manages to strike a note quite like this:

> Now I'm a wretch indeed—Methinks I see him already in the cart, sweeter and more lovely than the nosegay in his hand!—I hear the crowd extolling his resolution and intrepidity!—What vollies of signs are sent from the windows of *Holborn*, that so comely a youth should be brought to disgrace!—I see him at the tree! the whole Circle are in tears!—even Butchers weep!—*Jack Ketch* himself hesitates to perform his duty, and would be glad to lose his fee, by a reprieve.

In 1770 Francis Gentleman, writing in *The Dramatic Censor*, praised this speech for its pathos and simplicity: " . . . the breaks are fine, the sentiments tender, the description lively, all dressed in a naiveté of language, which finds a passage to the heart, by nature's aid alone."[12] Gay's counterfeiting is such that it is possible to believe that one is watching an orthodox sentimental drama. "Those cursed Play-books she reads have been her ruin," Mrs. Peachum has said of her daughter, and Polly's speech is a creditable imitation of the way in which the heroines of the play-books deliver themselves. Polly sees life as like a play, and the assumption that underlies her speech is that in real life people will behave as they do in theaters: "the whole Circle are in tears," butchers will weep and hangmen melt, everyone will wish for a happy ending. Yet this *is* a play which we are watching, and Macheath *will* be saved (just as Polly hopes) by a reprieve; hence for those (like Francis Gentleman) used to the sentimental traditions, the speech seems to work "by nature's aid alone."

Though Gentleman was quick enough to spot particular touches of literary parody throughout the play, he was evidently prepared to regard certain whole scenes as genuinely pathetic. The first encounter between Polly and Macheath he seemed to regard in this light. "His reluctance to fly, and her tender resolution to part for a time rather than hazard his safety," he ventured, "raise delicate feelings."[13] This scene is, of course, partly intended to ridicule the hackneyed stock scenes of parting lovers; but there is some kind of justification for Gentleman's remarks: certainly the parody is not forced upon us in the way it had been in Cibber's *The Comical Lovers* or as it was to be in the equally ludicrous parting scene in Sheridan's *The Critic*. Such concealment of the parodic tactics heightens the whole scene between Polly and Macheath. *"Were I laid on* Greenland's *coast"* pictures an idyllic lovers' escape, in the style of "Come live with me and be my lover" or "If you were the only girl in the world," but is actually—as Empson pointed out—a reply to a question about transportation. And at least some members of the audience must have recalled the last time hey had heard that tune on stage, in Farquhar's *The Recruiting Officer,* where both words and context were very different; what Kite and his recruits were celebrating there was their proposed escape from the very domestic ties in which Macheath is now entangling himself:

> We all shall lead more happy lives
> By getting rid of brats and wives,
> That scold and brawl both night and day—
> Over the hills and far away.

The total effect is—as Boswell remarked of another song earlier in the play—"at once . . . painful and ridiculous."[14]

Throughout the play each character in turn speaks kindly about his *heart.* Peachum finds that "it grieves one's heart to take off a great man"; and Mrs. Peachum pleads with him that he be, like herself, not "too hard-hearted." Polly's heart, she tells us at once, yields very readily:

> Though my heart were as frozen as Ice,
> At his flame 'twould have melted away.

And throughout the play Polly's heart, like Lucy's contrives to melt, bleed, split, burst, and break: "I know my heart," she modestly remarks. Macheath in his first song announces the "My heart was so free," but now it is "riveted" to Polly's; before long, Macheath is in search of the "free-hearted ladies" of the town. The variation in the depth of the irony means that some of these claims to free- or tender heartedness are likely to win a temporary credibility. But we can never quite forget the talk of *double capacity* with which the play began; people are likely to play more roles than one; soft hearts may turn to hard; the man who professes himself the lovable victim of society may turn out to be a predator and oppressor. The second act opens with a new mirage of the free life, created by Macheath's gang. Like everyone else, the gang speak well of their hearts: money "was made for the free-hearted and generous, and where is the injury of taking from another, what he hath not the heart to make use of ?" Here is their apologia for the highwayman's profession:

Jemmy Twitcher. Why are the laws levell'd at us? are we more dishonest than the rest of mankind? what we win, gentlemen, is our own by the law of arms, and the right of conquest.
Crook-finger'd Jack. Where shall we find such another set of practical philosophers; who to a man are above the fear of Death?
Wat Dreary. Sound men, and true!
Robin of Bagshot. Of try'd courage, and indefatigable industry!
Nimming Ned. Who is there here that would not dye for his friend?
Harry Padington. Who is there here that would betray him for his interest?
Matt of the Mint. Show me a gang of Courtiers that can say as much.
Ben Budge. We are for a just partition of the world, for every man hath a right to enjoy life.
Matt. We retrench the superfluities of mankind. The world is avaricious, and I hate avarice.

This variant of the levellers' plea—beginning with the claim "we're no worse than our betters," and edging quickly to the larger one, "we're better than our betters"—has an interesting contemporary analogue: namely, the formal apologias for the merchant's profession commonly found in the new middle-class drama of the day. Steele's Mr. Sealand in *The Conscious Lovers* (IV. ii), and Gay's own Mr. Barter in *The Distress'd Wife* (IV. xvi), champion the merchants against their "betters," the landed gentry, in very similar style; Lillo's Thorowgood and Trueman in *The London Merchant* were likewise soon to present a panegyric of the merchant as one who relieves nations of their "useless superfluities," delivering them to other nations in need (III. i). As the merchants justify their occupation, so with equal reasonableness the gang justify theirs. Their defense is attractive, just as Polly's pathos is attractive, and, like Polly, the gang win their admirers: one modern critic seems prepared to take them at their word, considering the passage to represent Gay's own views on the desirability of the even distribution of wealth throughout society.[15]

Yet it is impossible to forget both the context of the passage and the whole ironical movement of the play. For all their fine free-heartedness, for all their Robin Hood air of disinterested charity, the gang acts, as everyone else does, in a double capacity. For Macheath, friendship is nowhere to be found save with the gang:

> The modes of the Court so common are grown,
>   That a true friend can hardly be met;
> Friendship for interest is but a loan,
>   Which they let out for what they can get.

Corruption has spread outwards from the Court to infect all society; "interest"—a complex word of the time, signifying both financial interest and self-interest of the kind spoken of by Hobbes[16]—rules everywhere. But Macheath clings to the one exception to the general rule: "But we, gentlemen, have still honour enough to break through the corruptions of the world." Yet, to Macheath's astonishment, it is finally a member of the gang, Jemmy Twitcher, who betrays him—"a plain proof that the world is all alike, and that even our Gang can no more trust one another than other people." Locke, in his *Essay Concerning Human Understanding* (Bk. I, Ch. 2, §2), discussing whether or not there could be said to exist any innate moral principles, had interested himself particularly in the moral code of highway men. "Justice and truth are the common ties of society; and therefore even outlaws and robbers, who break with all the world besides, must keep faith and rules of equity amongst themselves; or else they cannot hold together."[17] Finally, Macheath's gang are shown to lack even that faith and those rules of equity; like everyone else, they are governed solely by "interest."

Behind the charm and sentiment of the play is a Hobbesian vision of a world dominated by universal interest. And it is with Hobbes in mind that we should look at the play's central cluster of images, those which compare and contrast human and animal life. Throughout both his dramatic and his non-dramatic work Gay continually glances back and forth between the world of men and the world of beasts, implying continually that that of the beasts is preferable to that of men:

> But is not man to man a prey?
> Beasts kill for hunger, man for pay.
> (Fable X)

> Here *Shock*, the pride of all his kind, is laid;
> Who fawn'd like Man, but n'er like Man betray'd.
> ("Elegy on a Lap-Dog")

This contrast is thoroughly traditional to both pastoral and satire, yet in *The Beggar's Opera* it appears to take on a specific coloration from a still-current philosophical debate. Lockit's speech in the third act of the play should be the starting-point here: "Lions, Wolves, and Vultures don't live together in herds, droves, or flocks.—Of all animals of prey, man is the only sociable one. Every one of us preys upon his neighbour, and yet we herd together." The background of this well-known speech is worth investigating.

Up until about the middle of the seventeenth century, one of the popular "proofs" of God's benign ordering of the universe was the fact that animals of prey hunted alone or in pairs, while grazing animals and those necessary to man's comfort and well-being grouped themselves together conveniently in herds. Were the predators to move about in herds, remarked Henry Peacham (the author of *The Compleat Gentlemen*) in mild alarm in 1622, "they would undo a whole country."[18] This "proof" about the habits of herding animals and solitary animals was adduced to support a generally optimistic theory about the efficient organization of the human and animal kingdoms, and of the relationship between them. It was a natural corollary of this theory that human beings themselves, who came together in "herds" to form towns and cities, were to be reckoned more like cows than like wolves, being pacific rather than warlike. Aristotle had put this even more flatteringly: like ants and bees, men come together naturally and for the common good, yet they are by nature superior to those creatures, because of their knowledge of languages, of justice, of good and evil.[19] This theory was devastated by Hobbes at the middle of the century. Men do not come naturally together for the common good (Hobbes argued), but rather for a variety of selfish reasons: for honor, dignity, passion, glory, gain. Man is more like a wolf than he is like a cow or a bee. The human community is unique in that it is the only "herd" which is composed of animals of prey: therefore its laws and government must be powerfully devised and powerfully imposed.[20] Shaftesbury in his various replies to Hobbes tried to attack this proposition; in his "An Inquiry Concerning Virtue or Merit" in 1699 he refined the old argument about wild animals living on their own and tame ones sheltering together, and in *"Sensus Communis:* An Essay on the Freedom of Wit and Humour" in 1709 he insisted upon the naturalness and the mutual usefulness and pleasure of human herding: "If eating and drinking be natural," he wrote, "herding is so too. If any appetite or sense be natural, the sense of fellowship is the same."[21]

Two distinct views of man as a "sociable animal" were therefore current at the time at which Gay wrote *The Beggar's Opera:* the skeptical Hobbesian view, and the more optimistic view of Shaftesbury, which argued that sociability, like the other human passions, was both instinctive and conducive to the common good; that self-interest and social interest might be the same. There is little doubt, I think, that the Hobbesian view pervades *The Beggar's Opera,* but Gay's achievement is to throw up as an ironical alternative the sentimental Shaftesburian view of things, appearing, as it were, to weigh the two social theories judiciously in the balance, hinting that there *might* be exceptions to the general Hobbesian rule. The Peachums and Lockits, the lords and the gamesters of London come together as Hobbes reckoned men always did in cities, out of self-interest and a desire for mutual plunder. "If you would not be look'd upon as a fool," says Lockit to his daugher, "you should never do anything but upon the foot of interest. Those that act otherwise are their own bubbles." The gamesters are

> Like pikes, lank with hunger, who miss of their ends,
> They bite their companions and prey on their friends.

"Man is a herded animal, and made for Towns and Cities," says one of the characters in Shadwell's *Bury Fair;* and Gay's vision of the city is the same Hobbesian vision as Shadwell had presented in that play: "So many Pens of Wild Beasts upon two legs, undermining, lying in wait, preying upon, informing against, and hanging one another: A Crowd of Fools, Knaves, Whores, and Hypocrites." Yet Gay never puts things quite so bluntly. Possibly (he suggests) the dominant passion is not interest but love, which finally conquers all: *"Can love be controul'd by advice?"* Polly sings; "How the mother is to be pitied who hath handsome daughers!" Mrs. Peachum complains, "Locks, bolts, bars, and lectures of morality are nothing to them: they break through them all." But then, by gradual steps, Gay closes off that sentimental possibility. As Empson's fine account of the play demonstrates, Polly's passionate love for Macheath is subtly presented as being as self-interested and destructive as the tradesman's or the criminal's passion for financial advancement; the tightening of the marriage knot can be as deadly as the tightening of the hangman's. In her ardent quest for the sociability of marriage Polly can look like a beast of prey.

To see how Gay gently subverts the sentimental Shaftesburian premise about the benign workings of the human passions, we may explore a little further the sources and implications of his literary parody in the final scene of the play. The memories of *Venice Preserv'd* in this scene I have already noted. Overlaying these, however, are other memories of another equally famous heroic tragedy. Polly and Lucy, standing imploringly on either side of Macheath, may well (as earlier critics have suggested) have put an audience in mind of Robert Walpole's wife and mistress struggling for the great man's attention, or even conceivably of Handel's two leading sopranos, Cuzzoni and Faustina, to whom the beggar obliquely alludes in the play's introduction. Yet they would also probably have reminded an audience of Dryden's Octavia and Cleopatra, competing in that famous scene in Act III of *All for Love* for the affection of Antony.

> Which way shall I turn me—how can I decide?
> Wives, the day of our death, are as fond as a bride

is how Macheath expresses the struggle, echoing the words of Antony before him: "O Dolabella, *which way shall I turn?*" Antony's struggle is expressed in tears and blushes, the simple appearance of the two women being sufficient to draw forth all his instinctive, though conflicting, affections of pity, shame, and love: the scene might be described as heroic-sentimental. Macheath's struggle is very different:

> One wife is too much for most husbands to hear,
> But two at a time there's no mortal can bear.

Macheath's dilemma is a dry and intellectual one: how do I get out of this fix? In *Spectator* 44—the same number in which he had mocked the stage device of tolling bells—Addison examined other "Artifices to fill the Minds of an Audience with Terrour" which were then in popular use, and descended with particular and merciless wit upon this very scene in *All for*

Love. Dryden's Octavia, it will be remembered, makes her entrance in this scene *"leading* ANTONY'S *two little daughters."* A disconsolate mother with a child in her hand, Addison remarks, is a convenient device to draw compassion from an audience. "A Modern Writer," he goes on, observing the fact and "being resolved to double the Distress," introduced a princess on stage leading a couple of children by the hand; this was such a success that a third writer, not to be outdone, resolved to introduce three children, thus scoring an even greater triumph; and, says Addison, that is not all:

> ... as I am inform'd, a young Gentleman who is fully determin'd to break the most obdurate Hearts, has a Tragedy by him, where the first Person that appears upon the Stage, is an afflicted Widow in her Mourning-Weeds, with half a Dozen fatherless children attending her, like those that usually hang about the Figure of Charity. Thus several Incidents that are beautiful in a good Writer, become ridiculous by falling into the Hands of a bad one.

With the sudden production at the end of *The Beggar's Opera* of four more wives for Macheath—making six in all on stage—all four bearing "a child a-piece," Gay clinches the same comic point that Addison had made in *The Spectator.* The fallacy which Gay's parody implicitly attacks is not simply that of believing that pathos can be increased mechanically, like troops in a stage-army; it is also the sentimental fallacy of believing that the mere presence of wives and children will reduce us, mechanically, to tears and hugs and blushes. The affections do not operate with quite the happy regularity with Dryden and Shaftesbury, in their different ways, had suggested. There are times when one would rather stick one's head in the hangman's noose than be sociable any longer.

The final escape-route can only be to death, but that "the taste of the town" will not allow, and Macheath is saved by a reprieve. The last and cruellest irony is that the sentimental passions will not only drive a man to drink and to the gallows, but that they will also rescue him from those final avenues of freedom with an ominous promise of the nuptial bliss which awaits him:

> But think of this maxim, and put off your sorrow,
> The wretch of to-day, may be happy to-morrow.

It is characteristic that the play should close upon such an ambiguous promise of happy days.

Gay's ironical concession to "the taste of the town" at the end of *The Beggar's Opera* reminded Colley Cibber of Jonson's similar ironical concessiveness in *Bartholomew Fair*,[22] and on this point, as on other points, the two plays are indeed alike. Each uses similar methods of comic leveling and inversion, bringing before us the fact that, despite all evidence to the contrary, all men are alike; were it not for the reprieve, says Gay's Beggar regretfully, his play would have carried a most excellent moral, "that the lower sort of people have their vices in a degree as well as the rich: And that they are punish'd for them." Both plays operate on a double level, entertaining their audiences so agreeably that their ironical undercurrents are not always fully discernible. Both plays move genially to their conclusions, with a wry knowledge of the way in which the theatrical public will like events to be resolved. Both plays—but most of all, *The Beggar's Opera*—maintain to the end an element of tease, of take-it-which-way-you-will. In its various and seemingly contradictory ways, for its pathos and its bathos, as a sentimental lollipop and as a terse social fable, *The Beggar's Opera* will no doubt continue to give equal delight. To deceive us so variously and so well is a triumph of the counterfeiter's art.

Notes

1. *The Correspondence of Alexander Pope*, ed. George Sherbrun (Oxford, 1956), i. 71.
2. William Empson, *"The Beggar's Opera,"* in *Some Versions of Pastoral* (2nd imp., London, 1950), p. 250.
3. *The Whitehall Evening Post*, Tuesday, ll November 1777; cited in W. E. Schultz, *Gay's "Beggar's Opera"* (New Haven and London, 1923), pp. 76-7.
4. *The Letters of John Gay*, ed. C. F. Burgess (Oxford, 1966), p. 19 (letter of 3 March 1714 - 15).
5. Hugh Kenner, *The Counterfeiters* (Bloomington and London, 1968).
6. *The Dunciad* (1729), ii. 220 n.
7. *The London Stage, 1660–1800*, ed. Emmett L. Avery; Part 2: *1700–29* (Carbondale, Illinois, 1960), p. 950.
8. "An Enquiry into the Present State of Polite Learning in Europe," in *The Collected Works of Oliver Goldsmith*, ed. Arthur Friedman (Oxford, 1966), i. 288.
9. *The Complete Works of William Hazlitt*, ed. P. P. Howe, after the edition of A. R. Waller and Arnold Glover (London and Toronto, 1930), iv. 65.
10. *The Dunciad* (1729), iii. 326 n.
11. Samuel Butler, *Characters and Passages from Note-Books*, ed. A. R. Waller (Cambridge, 1908), p. 227.
12. *The Dramatic Censor* (London, 1770), i. 117. The passage was also admired by Hazlitt: ibid, iv. 65.
13. *The Dramatic Censor*, i. 117–18.
14. *Boswell's Life of Johnson*, ed. G. B. Hill, rev. L. F. Powell (Oxford, 1934), ii. 368.
15. Sven M. Armens, *John Gay, Social Critic* (New York, 1954), p. 56.

16. For a discussion of some contemporary usages of the word see Felix Raab, *The English Face of Machiavelli* (London and Toronto, 1964), pp. 157–68.

17. *An Essay Concerning Human Understanding*, ed. A. C. Fraser (Oxford, 1894).

18. Henry Peacham, *The Compleat Gentleman*, ed. Virgil B. Heltzel (New York, 1962), p. 79.

19. Aristotle, *Politics*, ed. Ernest Barker (Oxford, 1946), I. ii, §10 (pp. 5–6).

20. See especially *DeCive*, II, V, §5; *Leviathan*, ii. 17.

21. Shaftesbury, "An Inquiry Concerning Virtue or Merit," in *Characteristics*, ed. John W. Robertson (London, 1900), i. 237–338; "*Sensus Communis:* An Essay on the Freedom of Wit and Humour," in *Characteristics*, i. 74.

22. *An Apology for the Life of Mr. Colley Cibber*, ed. Robert W. Lowe (London, 1889), i. 245.

Generic Transformation
and Social Change:
Rethinking the Rise of the Novel

MICHAEL McKEON

Twenty-five years after its first appearance, Ian Watt's *The Rise of the Novel* continues to be the most attractive model we have of how to conduct the study of this crucial literary phenomenon.[1] The phenomenon is crucial because it is modern. If the novel originated in early modern Europe, it should be possible to observe and describe its emergence within a historical context whose richness of detail has no parallel in earlier periods. But of course this is no coincidence: it is the rise of an unprecedented historical consciousness, and of its institutional affiliates, that has both encouraged the preservation of historical detail, and legitimated contextual methods of study which use that detail as a mode of understanding. Watt's book is attractive because it is fully responsive to the call for a historical and con- textual method of study that seems somehow implicit in his subject. Thus his concern with the rise of a distinctive set of narrative procedure—"for- mal realism"—is informed by a concern with a parallel innovation in phil- osophical discourse, and these he connects, in turn, with a set of socio- economic developments at whose center are the rise of the middle class, the growth of commercial capitalism, and the concomitant eclipse of feudal and aristocratic modes of intercourse. The analogy between these histori- cal strands is most succinctly accounted for in their shared "individual- ism"—that is, in their common validation of individual experience—a term that allows Watt at various points to argue the importance to his sub-

From *Cultural Critique*, 1 (1985), 159–81.

ject of a fourth major strand of historical experience, the Protestant Reformation.

Watt's account of the unity of the historical context in which the novel arose is far more subtle, as all readers know, than this bald outline can suggest. And its general persuasiveness is evident in the fact that the sort of criticism to which it has seemed most vulnerable has aimed not to refute the relevance of historical context, but to complicate Watt's version of it. The problem is perhaps most notorious in the social strand of his context. Where is the evidence, critics have asked, for the dominance of the middle class in the early eighteenth century? How is it distinguished from the traditional social categories of the nobility and gentry, which clearly survive the rapid social mobility of the seventeenth century and persist into the eighteenth with considerable power and prestige? Don't the novels of Henry Fielding, an indispensable figure in the rise of the novel, evince a social attitude much closer to that of a middling gentry than to that of a putatively flourishing commerical middle class? But even in the literary realm, critics have also been preoccupied with a problem of persistence. The narrative procedures of Daniel Defoe, Samuel Richardson, and Fielding may explicitly subvert the idea and ethos of romance, but they also draw, without apparent irony, on many of its stock situations and conventions. Although Watt pays little attention to it, and then only as a superseded genre, romance can be seen to inhabit both the form and the content of these early eighteenth-century narratives. And once again it is Fielding who points the problem most acutely, since he has little use for several of those narrative procedures that have been advanced as the *sine qua non* of the new form.

From this brief summary it is clear that the two central problems with Watt's account of the rise of the novel are versions of each other. His treatment of the early modern historical context, because of its very richness, has sensitized us to what has been left out: the romance and the aristocracy. By the end of the eighteenth century, the conceptual categories of "the novel" and "the middle class" will be sufficiently stable to enjoy the stability of that nomenclature. But it is of course precisely in the period that we wish most definitively to understand—the period of crucial transformation—that such categories are most unstable and most resistant to being strictly identified either as what they are going to be, or as what they once were. What is required, then, is an understanding of how conceptual categories, whether "literary" or "social," exist at moments of historical change: how new forms first coalesce as tenable categories by being known in terms of, and against, more traditional forms that have thus far been taken to define the field of possibility. We must begin, in other words, with the very fact of categorial instability in the later seventeenth century. Let me pause for a moment before entering my argument, in order to summarize it. What I have to say is based on a set of terms and relations that will recur from time to time throughout the essay. They are not particularly complicated, but I think it will be helpful to lay them out as quickly and clearly as possible. I plan to describe the two great instances of categorial instability that are central to the rise of the novel. The first sort of instability has to do with generic categories; the second with social categories. The instability of generic categories registers an epistemological crisis, a major cultural transition in attitudes toward how to tell the truth in narrative. For convenience, I will call the set of problems associated with this epistemological crisis, "questions of truth." The instability of social categories registers a cultural crisis in attitudes toward how the external social order is related to the internal, moral state of its members. For convenience, I will call the set of problems associated with this social and moral crisis, "questions of virtue." Questions of truth and questions of virtue concern different realms of human experience, and they are likely to be raised in very different contexts. Yet in one central respect they are closely analogous. Questions of truth and virtue both pose problems of signification: What kind of authority or evidence is required of narrative to permit it to signify truth to its readers? What kind of social existence or behavior signifies an individual's virtue to others?

As we will see, the instability of generic and social categories is symptomatic of a change in attitudes about how truth and virtue are most authentically signified. But for both questions, we can observe the process of change only if we break it down into its component parts. Let me summarize this break-down: first, for questions of truth. At the beginning of the period of our concern, the reigning narrative epistemology involves a dependence on received authorities and a priori traditions; I will call this posture "romance idealism." In the seventeenth century, it is challenged and refuted by an empiricist epistemology that derives from many sources, and this I will call "naive empiricism." But this negation of romance, having embarked on a journey for which it has no maps, at certain points loses its way. And it becomes vulnerable, in turn, to a counter-critique that has been generated by its own over-enthusiasm. I will call this counter-critique "extreme skepticism." As we will see, in refuting its empiricist progenitor, extreme skepticism inevitably recapitulates some features of the romance idealism which it is equally committed to opposing. For questions of virtue, the terms alter, but the two-part pattern of reversal is very much the same as for questions of truth. We begin with a relatively stratified social order, supported by a reigning world view which I will call "aristocratic ideology." Spurred by social change, this ideology is attacked and subverted by its prime antagonist, "progressive ideology." But at a certain point, progressive ideology gives birth to its own critique, which is both more radical than itself, and harks back to the common, aristocratic enemy. I will call this counter-critique "conservative ideology."

Needless to say, contemporaries did not articulate these several positions as consciously-formulated and coherent doctrines. I have abstracted these ideologies and epistemologies from a large body of early modern discourse, in order to isolate the principal stages in the process of historical change that we refer to when we speak of "the rise of the novel." By this means, I think, we may come closer to conceiving how change occurs: how the past can persist into the present, and help to mediate the establishment of difference through the perpetuation of similarity. Let me now proceed to fill in the spaces in my argument.

I

I will begin with questions of truth and the instability of the system of narrative genres in the seventeenth century. Evidence for the unstable usage of terminology lies everywhere, but it is most striking in explicit attempts to categorize the several genres of narrative. In 1672, the bookseller John Starkey advertised his list of publications in a catalogue divided into the following categories: Divinity; Physick; Law; History; Poetry and Plays; and Miscellanies. Under the heading of "history" he includes Suetonius, Rabelais, what he calls the "Novels" of Quevedo, biographies, travel narratives, and a contemporary work that we would be likely to see as a popular romance.[2] By modern standards, the most pressing problem raised by such usage is the absence of any will to distinguish consistently between "history" and "literature," "fact" and "fiction." But on the other hand, the catalogue of William London, printed fifteen years earlier, obligingly separates "History" from "Romances, Poems and Playes."[3]

What is most significant about this sort of usage is that it is not entirely foreign to us. Unlike traditional generic taxonomies, it evinces a real, but markedly inconsistent, commitment to comprehend its categories within a basic discrimination between the "factual" and the "fictional." Indeed, it is the inconsistent imposition of this recognizably "modern" concern on a more traditional system that makes the usage of this period look so chaotic.

What it represents, I think, is a movement between opposed conceptions of how to tell the truth in narrative. Another sign of this movement is the transformation which the term "romance" has undergone in the past hundred years. Despite the neutral usage that I have just quoted, by the end of the seventeenth century the ascendant meaning of "romance" is both far broader, and far more pejorative, than before. Increasingly, the idea of romance dominates the thought of the Restoration and early eighteenth century as a means of describing, and most often of discrediting, a particular, idealist way of knowing. Romance comes to stand for a species of deceit that undiscriminatingly includes lying and fictionalizing, and the category to which it is most often opposed is not "the novel," but "true history."

Many cultural movements contributed to the naive empiricist championing of "true history." Three of the most important are also closely intertwined: the scientific revolution, the typographical revolution, and the Protestant Reformation. Moreover, in all three of these movements we can see both the dominant influence of naive empiricism, and the stealthy emergence of a subversive, extreme skepticism. I will begin with the new science. In his history of the founding institution of the new science, Thomas Sprat compares unfavorably the ancient mode of natural history with that of his fellow moderns: it "is not the true following of *Nature* . . . It is like *Romances,* in respect of *True History.* . . ."[4] The new science was dedicated, of course, to objective observation, experiment, and related principles of empirical method. And it was deeply interested in trying to embody these principles in literary technique and form. According to the *Philosophical Transactions* of the Royal Society, "we have more need of severe, full and punctuall Truth, than of Romances of Panegyricks."[5] To this end, the Society even undertook to instruct foreign travelers in the best literary techniques for ensuring what we might call the "historicity" of their journals. It enlisted the aid of Robert Boyle and the mathematician Lawrence Rooke to formulate directions not only for how to keep a travel journal, but also for how to turn it into a narrative without diluting its crucial historicity.[6]

It is not too much to say that these directions amount to one of the most important, explicit bodies of literary theory composed in conjuction with the origins of the English novel. They prescribe a preferred style and rhetoric that correspond to a new type of the man of letters, the ethically and socially humble recorder of reality who is enable to master the new knowledge by his very innocence of the old. In Sprat's words, the new breed are "plain, diligent, and laborious observers: such, who though they bring not much knowledg [sic], yet bring their hands, and their eyes uncorrupted: such as have not their Brains infected by false Images. . . . "[7] One such observer is described by the editors of the multi-volume collection of travel narratives in terms that might collectively be called the convention of the claim to historicity: "This Narrative has nothing of Art or Language, being left by an ignorant Sailor, who, as he confesses, was in no better a Post than Gunner's Mate, and that to a *Greenland* Fisher; and therefore the Reader can expect no more than bare matter of Fact, deliver'd in a homely Stile, which it was not fit to alter, lest it might breed a Jealousy that something had been chang'd more than the bare Language."[8] According to another, equally conventional, traveler, "it would be no difficult Matter to embellish a Narrative with many Romantick Incidents, to please the unthinking Part of Mankind, who swallow every thing an artful Writer thinks fit to impose upon their Credulity, without any Regard to Truth or Probability. The judicious are not taken with such Trifles; . . . and they easily distinguish between Reality and Fiction."[9]

At the heart of the claim to historicity is the assertion that what one is describing really happened. And it is not hard to hear in these sober claims the naive empiricism of Defoe and Richardson, both of whom pretend to be only the editors of authentic documents whose plain and artless truth is above question. But if we permit the sobriety of the voices slightly to extend into self-parody, we also can detect the extreme skepticism of Swift and Fielding, subverting the claim to historicity by carrying it to absurdity. This is one example of how naive empiricism generates its own, radically skeptical, critique. Let me turn now to another example, one related not to the new science but to the new typography.

To a certain extent, we owe the very notion of comparative and competing accounts of the same event to the opportunity for comparison uniquely provided by print. Printing produces documentary objects that can be collected, categorized, collated, and edited. Like science, it promotes the norm of "objective" research, and it favors criteria of judgment that are appropriate to discrete and empirically apprehensible "objects": singularity, formal coherence, and self-consistency. Finally, print encourages a test of veracity that accords with the process itself of typographical reproduction, namely, the exact replication of objects or events in their external and quantitative dimensions.[10] Contemporaries were conscious of the epistemological powers of print. William Winstanley describes "some I have known (otherwise ingenious enough) apt to believe idle Romances, and Poetical Fictions, for Historical Varieties [i.e., verities], . . . and for this only reason, *Because they are Printed*."[11] But only a slight extension of this awe brings us to the satiric stance of Cervantes, who has a great deal of fun at the expense of characters—including Sancho Panza—who naively believe everything they see in print. In fact much of the self-reflexive pleasure of Part II of *Don Quixote* lies in watching its characters compare the documentary objectivity of Part I (which has already been printed) with the more fallible standard of truth upheld by private memory and experience.[12] Cervantes himself naively claims that his book is a "true history" dedicated to the critique of chivalric romance. But we know to read this affiliation, as well as his playful attitude toward print, as at least in part a skeptical critique of naive empiricism.

My third and final example concerns the contribution of Reformation thought to naive empiricism and its subversion. Protestantism, like the standard of "true history," elevates individual and closely observed experience over the a priori pronouncements of tradition. But Protestantism is also the religion of the Book, of the documentary object, and as such it inevitably tends to elevate the truth of Scripture as the truth of "true history." This documentary and empiricist emphasis is clear in the great works of the Protestant tradition. The central aim of John Foxe's *Acts and Monuments* (1563, 1570) is the documentation of the Protestant martyrs, and the task is achieved in an aura of scrupulous historicity and with a battery of editorial procedures that are dedicated to the critical authentication of every historical detail.[13] Such authenticating procedures may also be found in John Bunyan's *Life and Death of Mr. Badman* (1680), even though its protagonist is a palpable fiction. Bunyan claims that it is based on "True stories, that are neither *Lye*, nor *Romance* . . . All which are things either fully known by me, or being eye and ear-witness thereto, or that I have received from such hands, whose relation as to this, I am bound to believe."[14] By the same token, Protestant spirituality encouraged individual saints to a scrupulous documentation of their own "true histories." When Ralph Thoresby first went up to London, his father sent him a typical directive: "I would have you, in a little book, which you may either buy or make of two or three sheets of paper, take a little journal of any thing remarkable every day, principally as to yourself . . ."[15]

So from the beginning, Protestantism was deeply invested in the materialistically-oriented techniques of naive empiricism as a useful means to its spiritual and otherworldly ends. The potential contradiction between worldly means and otherworldly ends is most apparent in writings like the "apparition narratives" of the later seventeenth century; Defoe's *A True Relation of the Apparition of one Mrs. Veal* (1706) is the best-known of them today. These narratives use the evidence of the senses in order to prove the extra-sensory world of spirit. They deploy an extraordinary arsenal of authenticating devices—names, places, dates, events, eye- and ear-witness testimony, etc.—in order to prove the reality of the invisible world. Richard Baxter explained his own important contribution to the form in terms that poignantly convey the dilemma of a culture divided between two competing standards of truth that still seem somehow reconcilable: "Apparitions, and other sensible Manifestations of the certain existence of Spirits of themselves Invisible, was a means that might do much with such as are prone to judge by Sense."[16] But it is a very short distance from Baxter's earnest and spiritualizing dependence on the evidence of the senses to the realm of conscious satire. Consider those moderns in Swift's early satires who mistake their own bodily wind for the spirit of intellect and divinity.[17] Once again, that is, the counter-critique of extreme skepticism is involuntarily extruded by naive empiricism itself as a form of subversive self-parody.

But over time, extreme skepticism emerges as a self-conscious and autonomous stance in its own right. Its premises are the same as those of the naive empiricism which it undertakes to negate. It is equally critical, that is, of "romance," but it is so thoroughly skeptical as to discredit empiricist skepticism itself as nothing more than a new, and artfully modernized, species of the old romance. It is this counter-critique that will issue eventually in Fielding's narrative form. Along the way we may observe certain milestones, narratives—like William Congreve's *Incognita* (1691)— which elegantly achieve the double negation that is characteristic of the form: first, of the fictions of romance, and then of naive empiricism itself. But like its antagonist, the counter-critique of extreme skepticism undergoes a considerable development; I have space only to offer several exemplary quotations.

Richard Steele is an important figure in the attack on naive empiricism. Echoing pamphleteers of the mid-seventeenth century, for example, he argued in one of his periodical letters that newspapers were to England what books of chivalry had been to Spain.[18] Steele was also critical of the claim to historicity in the genre of the secret memoir, which was especially popular among what he called "some merry gentlemen of the French nation." The secret memoir claimed, as Steele observed, to give the true history of military campaigns or court intrigues even though their mendacious authors had really been cowering behind the lines or scribbling in a draft garret.[19] Writing of the same phenomenon, Pierre Bayle observed that thus "the new romances [that is, these supposedly historical memoirs] keep as far off as possible from the romantic way: but by this means true history is made extrememly obscure; and I believe the civil powers will at last be forced to give these new romancers their option; either to write pure history, or pure romance . . . "[20] Henry Stubbe compared the natural histories of the Royal Society to "the story of *Tom Thumb*, and all the *Legends* or *falsifications of History*, which the *Papists* obtrude upon us."[21] The language is striking: whether implicitly or explictly, over and over true history is discredited as the new romance. The skeptical critique of travel historicity was similarly acerbic. The dubious reader of a typically authenticated travel narrative of 1675 confuted the pamphlet's overheated claims by coolly writing on its title page: "By a new fashion'd Romancer."[22] The most thorough and trenchant critique of travel historicity was made by the Third Earl of Shaftesbury, who began, as Steele did, with the remark that "these are in our present Days, what *Books of Chivalry* were, in those of our Forefathers."[23] As the critique of naive empiricism gained momentum toward the end of the century, parodic impersonation seemed to offer itself as the most likely means of subversion. Another dubious reader of travel narratives wrote the following parody of a rival's fashionably plain style of objective narration: "*We cast Anchor: We made ready to Sail. The Wind took Courage. Robin is dead. We said Mass. We Vomited.* [Then he continues in his own, sarcastic voice.] Tho' they are poor Words any where else, yet in his Book which is half compos'd of them, they are Sentences, and the worth of them is not to be told."[24]

But if this kind of extreme skepticism was to become more than an (admittedly liberating) act of subversion, it was obliged, like the subversive stance of naive empiricism before it, to elaborate an alternative, positive, and coherent conception of how to tell the truth in narrative. And here its position was quite as unstable as that of its opponent. For if the claim to historicity is naively posited as the negation of the negation of romance idealism, how tenuous must be that secret sanctuary of truth, distinct both from romance and from too confident a historicity, which is defined by the meta-critical act of double negation? With hindsight we might want to say that the counter-critique of extreme skepticism was groping toward a mode of narrative truth-telling which, through the very self-consciousness of its own fictionality, somehow detoxifies fiction of its error. But the ingenuity of this maneuver could itself look more like a mast for the stealthy recapitulation of romance lies. Consider Fielding's ostentatious indulgence in romance conventions, or Swift's obviously parabolic narratives. Indeed, the sheer defensiveness of this counter-stance makes it parasitic upon, and reproductive of, the errors of the enemy. If naive empiricism is too sanguine regarding its own powers of negating romance fiction, its critique is too skeptical about that possibility, and it risks, through its reactive method of parodic impersonation, the effectual affirmation of what it is equally committed to replacing.

Both epistemologies, in other words, are unstable. I would argue that they attain stability not in themselves but in each other, in their dialectical relationship, as two competing versions of how to tell the truth in narrative, which, in their competition, constitute one part of the origins of the novel. The paradigmatic case is *Pamela* (1740) vs. *Shamela* (1741), since it is then that the conflict emerges into public consciousness and is institutionalized as a battle over whether it is Richardson or Fielding that is creating the "new species of writing." My argument is that it is, rather, the conjuction of the two. But I would also point out that the logic of our progress through the seventeenth century into the middle of the eighteenth argues against trying to pinpoint "the first novel," or even its first dialectical engagement. Before *Pamela* and *Shamela,* for example, there is the tacit but crucial confrontation between *Robinson Crusoe* (1719) and *Gulliver's Travels* (1726), a confrontation to which I will return. The novel rises not in the isolated emergence of a great text or two, but as an experimental process consisting of many different stages.

II

So far our attention has been focused on epistemological instability, and the series of critiques by which questions of truth are propounded. We must now turn to the analogous questions of virtue, to the instability of socioeconomic categories, and to the interaction between what I have called the aristocratic, progressive, and conservative ideologies. In the seventeenth century, the traditional imprecision in the use of status categories is complicated by an unprecedented rate of social mobility. The effects of this mobility are suggested by the fact that it is at this time that attempts begin to be made to assess the population not according to a traditional, status stratification, but by annual income and expenditures. This amounts to the first, systematic emergence of the modern impulse to classify society according to the fundamentally economic criteria of class.

The form taken by these population tables is quite relevant to our purposes, because they provide the sort of evidence of instability, on the subject of social categories, that we found in publishers' book lists on the subject of generic categories. Gregory King's celebrated table of the 1690s ostensibly aims to give a continous financial, and therefore quantitative, progression from the top to the bottom of English society. But he is obliged to work with both honorific and occupational categories, and around the middle of his table the two sorts of category become intermixed in a way that undermines the purpose of the project. For in several cases, King lists status categories above occupational ones, even though the crucial standard of average yearly income should reverse the orders. In other words, King's abiding respect for the traditional status hierarchy momentarily overrules his modernizing aim to create a hierarchy of incomes. The qualitative criteria of status infiltrate and disrupt the effort at a quantitative categorization.[25] Half a century later, in 1760, Joseph Massie carried over King's six traditional categories of elevated status to the top of his own table. But they repose there aloof and untouched, a kind of honorific gesture that has nothing to do with the real work of economic discrimination, for which Massie uses completely different categories in the rest of his table. In other words, status categories persist here as a vestigial remnant of a mode of thought which, however useless in the definitive description of contemporary English people by class, still appears indispensable.[26]

In both men, the instability of social categories owes to a discrepancy between two standards of classification, that of "status" and that of "class." It reflects what we might call a crisis of "status inconsistency," a divergence of power, wealth, and status widespread and persistent enough to resist the methods by which stable societies traditionally have accommodated the instances of non-correspondence that occasionally must arise. One such method is the traditional granting or selling of honors to newly enriched but ignoble families. To speak of "traditional" societies is also to speak of societies dominated by what I have called an "aristocratic" ideology. In aristocratic culture, it is not only that power, wealth, and honorific status most often accompany each other; honor also is understood to imply personal merit or virtue. Thus the social hierarchy is a great system of signification: the outward forms of genealogy and social rank are taken to signify an analogous, intrinsic moral order. The seventeenth-century crisis of status inconsistency therefore strikes at the moral foundations of aristocratic ideology. The sale of honors became, in Lawrence Stone's phrase, an "inflation," and the latent tension between honorific and monetary criteria became a glaring contradiction for contemporaries.[27] The word "honor" itself acquired a more complicated import. As a neutral term of description, its meaning was, in effect, internalized, changing from "title of rank" to "goodness of character."[28] But "honor" in the more traditional sense of the term, like "romance," had fallen on very hard times.

We can hear this in the genial contempt expressed by Bernard Mandeville. For Mandeville, honor "is only to be met with in People of the better sort, as some Oranges have kernels, and others not, tho' the outside be the same. In great Families it is like the Gout, generally counted Hereditary, and all Lords Children are born with it. . . . But there is nothing that encourages the Growth of it more than a Sword, and upon the first wearing of one, some People have felt considerable Shutes of it, in Four and twenty Hours."[29] The aristocratic system of signification held no illusions for Stephen Penton, either. For "if Merit were to be the Standard of Worldly Happiness, what great desert is there in being born Eldest Son and Heir to several Thousands a Year, when sometimes it falls out, that the Person is hardly able to Answer Two or Three the easiest Questions in the World wisely enough to save himself from being Begg'd?"[30] William Sprigge plausibly argued that "the younger Son is apt to think himself sprung from as Noble a stock, from the loyns of as good a Gentleman as his elder Brother, and therefore cannot but wonder, why fortune and the Law should make so great a difference between them that lay in the same wombe, that are formed of the same lumpe; why Law or Custome should deny them an estate, whom nature hath given discretion to know how to manage it."[31] And Defoe draws the versified conclusion:

> What is't to us, what Ancestors we had?
> If Good, what better? or what worse, if Bad?
> . . . .
> For Fame of Families is all a Cheat,
> 'Tis Personal Virtue only makes us great.[32]

In the realm of social change, the idea of "personal virtue" occupies the place that "true history" does in epistemology. For progressive ideology, elevated birth is an arbitrary accident which should not be taken to signify worth. If it is, it becomes a fiction, an imaginary value, like "honor" a mere "romance." Thus Defoe observes that when gentlemen "value themselves as exalted in birth above the rest of the world . . . ," it is upon the basis of a strictly "imaginary honour."[33] *Real* honor, honor of *character,* attaches to personal virtue. And Defoe heartily approved of the assimilationist practice whereby the meritorious and newly-risen crowned their merit through the purchase of titles of rank.

But what were Swift's views on questions of virtue? Swift was as caustic as Defoe on the subject of aristocratic pretension. But he was far more inclined to see the ideas of inherited honor and gentle birth as useful fictions that had an instrumental social value. "Suppose there be nothing but

Opinion in the Difference of Blood," he wrote. "Surely, that Difference is not wholly imaginary. . . . It should seem that the Advantage lies on the Side of Children, born from noble and wealthy Parents . . . [And] Ancient and honorable Birth[,] . . . whether it be of real or imaginary Value, hath been held in Veneration by all wise, polite States, both Ancient and Modern."[34] It may seem puzzling that men like Swift should return to half-embrace the very fiction they have rejected. But we already have seen this sort of movement in the return of extreme skepticism to a form of self-conscious romancing. For progressives like Defoe, aristocratic ideology was subverted and replaced by a brave new view of social signification. Virtue is signified not by the a priori condition of having been born with status and honor, but by the ongoing experience of demonstrated achievement and just reward. Thus the status inconsistency endemic to aristocratic culture is rectified, in this progressive view, by upward mobility through state service, private employment, or any other method of industrious self-application. To conservatives like Swift, this progressive model of the career open to talents was deeply repellent, as we will see. But the negation of both aristocratic and progressive ideology left conservative ideology without a positive and stable view of how the social injustice of status inconsistency ever might be overcome.

From the conservative point of view, progressive ideology only replaced the old social injustice by a new and more brutal version of it, unsoftened now by any useful fictions of inherited authority. At the heart of this new system was the naked cash nexus. For the conservative, the archetypal progressive upstart rose by exploiting the capitalist market, and especially the new mechansims of financial investment and public credit which were established at the end of the seventeenth century. For men like Swift, only landed property had real value. All other property was, as he put it, "transient and imaginary," but most of all that of exchange value.[35] Defoe also recognized that the modern world of exchange value was ruled by, in his phrase, "the Power of Imagination."[36] And he perceived that in some mysterious sense, capitalist credit was only a secularization of aristocratic honor. But Defoe was convinced that the circulation of money and the opportunity for capital accumulation were essential if individual merit were to be dependably signified and rewarded. For Swift, the market exchange of commodities only established a new elite of the undeserving on the grounds of a new, and far more dangerous, species of corruption. That is, it only institutionalized a new form of status inconsistency: namely, wealth and power without virtue. As for honorific status, the situation had become hopelessly confused. To the conservative mentality, there was an obvious corruption in those progressive upstarts who sought to legitimate their rise by the purchase of a title. But the system of honors was itself corrupted, and many ancient landed families were as thoroughly indebted to the capitalist market for the improvement of their estates as anyone.

Here, as on questions of truth, the doubly critical posture of men like Swift left very little ground for the affirmation of any positive social signifier of merit and virtue. With the triumph of Whig oligarchy in the eighteenth century, the aristocratic order seems to regain its stability after the rapid social mobility of the previous century. But the status category of "aristocracy" has altered considerably, even if the terminology has remained the same. The status orientation itself has been complicated by a class orientation—by individualistic and monetary criteria and by capitalist practices. The rise of the middle class, in other words, was not the rise of a discrete and determinate social entity, but a historical process in which traditional status groups were altered as much from within as from without. And the rise of the middle class is inseparable from the rise of a class orientation toward social relations. Men like Swift knew this; they knew that the enemy was not so easily distinguished as an ungentle, upstart invader from without. Nevertheless, for lack of a more dependable signifier, they retained in their minds the possession of land and gentle status as a self-consciously conventional signification of what seemed an increasingly embattled virtue.

Why should narrative, in particular, be suitable for the representation of progressive and conservative ideologies? The term "ideology" often is used to suggest a simplistic reduction of human complexity. But as I intend the term, "ideology" is discourse whose purpose is to mediate and explain apparently intractable social problems—in this case, the problematic questions of virtue. To explain the condition of status inconsistency is not to explain it away, but to render it intelligible. In fact, the very plausibility of ideological explanation depends on the degree to which it appears to do justice to the contradictory social reality that it seeks to explain. In the present context, ideological explanation works by telling stories. The question of how virtue is signified has an inherently narrative focus because it is concerned with genealogical succession and individual progress, with how human capacity is manifested in and through time. This concern can be seen in the "macro-narrative" of seventeenth-century history itself, which provided writers with an important model for their novelistic micro-narratives. Seventeenth-century England was vitally concerned with the problem of political sovereignty and its sources. At the beginning of the century, sovereignty seemed to rest with the king and to be validated by, among other things, his genealogical inheritance of royalty. In 1642, Charles I warned that parliament's challenge to royal sovereignty threatened the very continuity of the historical succession. The great danger, he said, was that at last the common people would "destroy all rights and proprieties, all distinctions of families and merit, and by this means this splendid and excellently distinguished form of government end in a dark, equal chaos of confusion, and the long line of our many noble ancestors in a Jack Cade or a Wat Tyler."[37] Charles was not entirely wrong in this apocalyptic prophecy: seven years after it he was decapitated. And before the end of the century, the nation had joined together to depose another rightful monarch and to exclude the next fifty-seven prospective heirs to the throne. In their place was crowned a foreigner, and in the place of sovereignty by genealogical inheritance was affirmed sovereignty by achievement: the simple and pragmatic fact that a peaceful and stable settlement had been achieved.[38]

In the language of questions of virtue, the fall of Charles I is the most infamous instance of status inconsistency in the century. And after the Battle of Worcester in 1651, prince Charles wandered the land in disguise like nothing so much as a romance hero destined, after much travail, to be discovered and restored to his aristocratic patrimony.[39] But to readers of a progressive persuasion, the triumphs of Oliver Cromwell and William of Orange showed, in different ways, the superiority of industrious valor to mere lineage. Progressive ideology even entered into the making of Cromwell's New Model Army. In 1643 he declared: "I had rather have a plain russett-coated captain that knows what he fights for, and loves what he knows, than that which you call a gentleman and is nothing else. . . . Better plain men than none, but best to have men patient of wants, faithful and conscientious in the employment . . ."[40]

Cromwell's language here reminds us that Calvinist Protestantism has an important relevance to progressive ideology, for God's mark of inner nobility was superior to any external social elevation. Speaking of divine election, Cromwell asked: "May not this stamp [of God] bear equal poise with any hereditary interest . . . ?[41] And, as a coreligionist affirmed, "It is not the birth, but the new birth, that makes men truly noble."[42] If Calvinist election argued a new aristocracy alternative to that of birth, Calvinist discipline dictated a spirit of service and reform that worked both to glorify the works of God and to signify one's possession of grace. But what are the narrative implications of this dovetailing of Protestant belief and progressive ideology? As early as Foxe's *Acts and Monuments*, the apocalyptic battle between the Roman Catholic hierarchy and God's saints is colored by the progressive contest between corrupt noblemen and industrious commoners. Foxe's "Story of Roger Holland, Martyr," for example, is the tale of an apprentice who is idle and licentious until the moment of his Protestant conversion. Thereafter he prospers wonderfully as a merchant tailor. So when the reformed apprentice is finally called up before his papist inquisitor, he is able to manifest, through a spirited resistance and a serene martyrdom, that spiritual grace which already has been apparent in his labor discipline and his material prosperity.[43]

Calvinist doctrine encouraged in progressive narrative the self-serving conviction that divine grace could be internalized as virtue, and externalized once again as worldy achievement. But Calvinism also counselled against the proud sufficiency of human desire, and it sharpened the conservative critique of enthusiasm and the Protestant ethic. The adventures of Robinson Crusoe exemplify both the ethical obstacles to progressive ideology, and the power of that ideology to drive all before it. Robinson Crusoe is an industrious younger son whose worldly success at first signifies nothing more than acquisitiveness and ambition. But once he is shipwrecked, his island turns out to be a progressive utopia. Because it excludes all human society, it provides an arena in which the anti-social passions of avarice and domination can be indulged without suffering the consequences. Thus Robinson can accumulate goods without creating exchange value. He can exercise absolute sovereignty without incurring the wrath of a greater authority. And when human society finds him, and it comes time to leave the island, he is able to naturalize the artificial, laboratory conditions of his utopia because he has learned to internalize divinity, to identify his own passions with the will of God. A slighter version of this progressive, utopian plot is given by Henry Neville, whose George Pine is an industrious city apprentice who happens to stumble into a travel narrative.[44] Stranded with four women on an Edenic desert island where productive labor is unneeded, Pine resourcefully proceeds to manifest his merit through reproductive labor, populating the island with offspring who then constitute a new genealogy and social order, of which he is the unquestioned sovereign.

But the progressive battle between aristocratic corruption and industrious virtue could of course be waged in a setting closer to home. Often it was embodied in plots that pitted aristocratic seducers, rapists, and dunderheads against chaste and canny young women of the middle and lower orders. The obvious exemplar is Richardson's *Pamela* (although it is by no means the rule that virtue should be so ostentatiously rewarded as hers is). Behind Pamela lies a succession of Pamela-like heroines, including the sister of Gabriel Harvey (Spenser's college friend), who left a manuscript account of her pert resistance to seduction.[45] The most important development of this particular progressive plot model was achieved by Aphra Behn, whose ingenious variations include a female aristocratic oppressor who is pathologically fixated on nobility of birth as the trigger of sexual desire, and who is finally reformed by falling in love with an apparent nobleman who turns out to be the son of a Dutch merchant.[46]

Whatever their differences, progressive plots have in common the aim to explain the meaning of the current crisis of status inconsistency, and, in the symbolic realm of fictional action, to overcome it. How do conservative plots manage this explanation so as to subvert progressive ideology itself? One method is by making the oppressor an aristocrat not by birth but by purchase, and his ruling corruption not sexual desire, but the lust for money and power. But the villains of conservative plots need not be aristocrats at all. Fielding's undeserving upstarts, like Shamela and Jonathan Wild, show an obvious debt to the assorted rogues, highwaymen, and pirates of criminal biography. When Charles Davenant undertook to describe the fall of English virtue under the Whigs, he cast his macrohistory in the pseudo-autobiographical form of a micro-narrative about the rise of the rogue figure Mr. Double, "now worth Fifty thousand Pound, and 14 years ago I had not Shoes on my Feet." Mr. Double's story is that of a bad apprentice whose vice is not idleness but too much industry, and he ends his allegorical autobiography by comparing himself to "most of the Modern Whigs ... Did they rise by Virtue or Merit? No more than myself."[47]

When conservative protagonists are sympathetic, they are victims of the modern world—either comically ingenuous innocents, or sacrifices to its corrupt inhumanity. One of the striking achievements of *Gulliver's Travels* is that its protagonist is able to fill both of these conservative roles. Like Robinson Crusoe, Lemuel Gulliver begins as a naive and industrious younger son, a quantifying empiricist and an upwardly-mobile progressive. In Lilliput he falls into the role of the obsequious new man, hungry for royal favor and titles of honor (recall his assimilationist vanity at being made a Nardac, the highest honor in the land). But Gulliver in Lilliput is also a hardworking public servant who ruefully learns, like Lord Munodi later on, the conservative truth about modern courts and their disdain for true merit. However, in his final voyage Gulliver so successfully assimilates upward that he goes native, believes he is a Houyhnhnm, and is forced to endure the comic rustication of an unsuccessful upstart, bloated with pride and uncomprehendingly indignant at his failure to make it.

In this final character of Gulliver (or in that of Shamela) we see the industrious virtue of the progressive protagonist pushed to its limits, so that it breaks open to reveal an ugly core of hypocritical opportunism. This technique of parodic impersonation is typical both of conservative ideology, and of its epistemological counterpart, extreme skepticism. It is the mark of a stance so intricately reactive as to be hard to pry loose, at times, from what it opposes. Moreover, unlike progressive narrative, conservative plots are far from hopeful about the overcoming of the social injustice and status inconsistency which they explain with such passion. Their frequent pattern is a retrograde series of disenchantments with all putative resolutions, and conservative utopias tend to be, as Houyhnhnmland is and as Robinson Crusoe's island is not, hedged about with self-conscious fictionality, strictly unfulfillable and nowhere to be found.

Let me now briefly summarize this attempt to rethink the rise of the novel. In order to overcome some deficiencies in the reigning model of what this movement amounted to, I have isolated, as its central principle, two recurrent patterns of "double reversal." Naive empriricism negates romance idealism, and is in turn negated by a more extreme skepticism and a more circumspect approach to truth. Progressive ideology subverts aristocratic ideology, and is in turn subverted by conservative ideology. It is in these double reversals, and in their conflation, that the novel is constituted as a dialectical unity of opposed parts, an achievement that is tacitly acknowledged by the gradual stabilization of "the novel" as a terminological and a conceptual category in eighteenth-century usage. But we have also been concerned with a pattern of historical reversal that is of broader dimension than this movement, and from whose more elevated perspective the conflicts that are defined by our double reversals may even appear to dissolve into unity. For as we have seen over and over again, the origins of the English novel entail the positing of a "new" generic category as a dialectical negation of a "traditional" dominance—the romance, the aristocracy—whose character still saturates, as an antithetical but constitutive force, the texture of the category by which it is in the process of being replaced.

Of course the very capacity of seventeenth-century narrative to model itself so self-consciously on established categories bespeaks a detachment sufficient to imagine them *as* categories, to parody and thence to supersede them. And with hindsight we may see that the early development of the novel is our great example of the way that the birth of genres results from a momentary negation of the present so intense that it attains the positive status of a new tradition. But at the "first instant" of this broader dialectical reversal, the novel has a definitional volatility, a tendency to dissolve into its antithesis, which encapsulates the dialectical nature of historical process itself at a critical moment in the emergence of the modern world.

I have argued that the volatility of the novel at this time is *analogous* to that of the middle class. But it is clear that in a certain sense, the emerging novel also has *internalized* the emergence of the middle class in its preoccupation with the problem of how virtue is signified. From time to time we can observe the distinct questions of virtue and truth being raised simultaneously by writers of the most diverse aims and formal commitments. At such times we sense that writers wish to "make something" of the analogous relation between these questions, if only through their tacit juxtaposition. And occasionally the analogy will even be explicitly asserted. In this way, questions of truth and virtue begin to seem not so much distinct problems, as versions or transformations of each other, distinct ways of formulating and propounding a fundamental problem of what might be called epistemological, sociological, and ethical "signification." And the essential unity of this problem is clear from the fact that progressive and conservative positions on questions of virtue have their obvious corollary positions with respect to questions of truth. What this means is that epistemological choices come to have ideological significance, and a given account of the nature of social reality implies a certain formal commitment and procedure. Moreover we may conceive these correlations of truth and virtue also in terms of narrative form and content, so that the way the story is told, and what it is that is told, are implicitly understood to bear an integral relation to each other.

But I do not mean to suggest that the conflation of questions of truth and virtue occurred easily or quickly. On the contrary, it is the result of much thought and experimentation, a very small portion of which I have described here, expended over a considerable period of time. And the conflation itself begins to occur when writers begin to act—first gingerly, then systematically—upon the insight that the difficulties of one set of problems may be mediated and illuminated by the reflection of the other. This insight—the deep and fruitful analogy between questions of truth and questions of virtue—is the enabling foundation of the novel. And the genre of the novel can be understood comprehensively as an early modern cultural instrument designed to confront, on the level of narrative form and content, both intellectual and social crisis simultaneously. The novel emerges into consciousness when this conflation can be made with complete confidence. The conflict then comes to be embodied in a public controversy between Richardson and Fielding—writers who are understood to represent coherent, autonomous, and alternative methods for doing the same thing. At this point—in the mid-1740s, after the first confrontation between Richardson and Fielding—the novel has come to the end of its origins. And it begins then to enter new territory.

Notes

1. *The Rise of the Novel: Studies in Defoe, Richardson and Fielding* (Berkeley: University of California Press, 1957). The following essay summarizes one central argument of my book. *The Origins of the English Novel, 1600–1740* (Baltimore: Johns Hopkins University Press, 1987).

2. *The Annals of Love, Containing Select Histories of the Armours of divers Princes Courts, Pleasantly Related* (1672), sig. Dd7^v Ee4^v. Except where noted, place of publication of early modern works is London.

3. *A Catalogue of The most vendible Books in England . . .* (1657).

4. *The History of the Royal-Society of London . . .* (1667), 90–91.

5. *Philosophical Transactions*, 11 (1676), 552.

6. See *Philosophical Transactions*, 1 (1665–66), 141–43, 186–89. Boyle's instructions are excerpted from his *Some Considerations of the Usefulness of Experimental Natural Philosophy* (1663).

7. *The History of the Royal-Society of London . . .* 72.

8. Awnsham and John Churchill, eds., *A Collection of Voyages and Travels . . .* (1704), I, viii.

9. Edward Cooke in ibid., II, xix.

10. See in general Elizabeth L. Eisenstein, *The Printing Press as an Agent of Change: Communications and Cultural Transformations in Early Modern Europe* (Cambridge: Cambridge University Press, 1979), Chap. 2 and passim.

11. *Histories and Observations Domestick and Foreign . . .* (1683), sig. A5^v, A6^r.

12. E.g. see *Don Quixote*, II (1615), ii–iv.

13. See the discussion of William Haller, *The Elect Nation: The Meaning and Relevance of Foxe's Book of Martyrs* (New York: Harper & Row, 1963), 122, 150–60, 213–14.

14. Bunyan, *Life and Death*, 326, sig. A4^v.

15. *The Diary of Ralph Thoresby, FRS, Author of the Topography of Leeds (1677–1724)*, ed. Rev. Joseph Hunter (1830), I, xv, quoted in George A Starr, *Defoe and Spiritual Autobiography* (Princeton: Princeton University Press, 1965), 10.

16. *The Certainty of the Worlds of Spirits . . .* (1691), sig. A4^r.

17. E.g., *A Discourse concerning the Mechanical Operation of the Spirit . . .* (1704).

18. *Tatler*, No. 178, May 27–30, 1710.

19. *Tatler*, No. 84, Oct. 22, 1709.

20. *The Dictionary Historical and Critical of Mr. Peter Bayle* (1697), 2nd ed. (1734–38), IV, "Nidhard," n. C, 366.

21. *The Plus Ultra reduced to a Non Plus* . . . (1670), II.

22. See the copy of [Richard Head,] *O-Brazile, or the Inchanted Island* . . . (1675) reproduced in *Seventeenth-Century Tales of the Supernatural*, ed. Isabel M. Westcott, *Augustan Reprint Society*, No. 74 (1958).

23. "*Soliloquy:* or Advice to an Author," (1714), in *Characteristicks of Men, Manners, Opinions, Times*, 2nd ed. (1714), I. 344.

24. [François Mission,] *A New Voyage to the East-Indies, by Francis Leguat and His Companions* . . . (London and Amsterdam, 1708), iv. The rival is the Abbot of Choisy.

25. See the discussion in David Cressy, "Describing the Social Order of Elizabethan and Stuart England," *Literature and History*, No. 3 (March 1976), 29–44.

26. See Peter Matthias, "The Social Structure in the Eighteenth Century: A Calculation by Joseph Massie," in *The Transformation of England: Essays in the Economic and Social History of England in the Eighteenth Century* (New York: Columbia University Press, 1979), 176, 186, 188.

27. See Lawrence Stone, *The Crisis of the Aristocracy, 1558–1641* (Oxford: Clarendon Press, 1965), Chap. 3. For a discussion of "status inconsistency" and reference-group theory in the context of seventeenth-century historiography, see Stone's *The Causes of the English Revolution, 1529–1642* (London: Routledge & Kegan Paul, 1972), Chap. 1.

28. A generalization based on the use of the term in dramatic contexts: see C. L. Barber, *The Idea of Honor in the English Drama, 1591–1700*, Gothenburg Studies in English, 6 (Göteberg: Elanders, 1957), 330–31.

29. *The Fable of the Bees* (1714), ed. Phillip Harth (Harmondsworth: Penguin, 1970), "Remark (R)," 212–13.

30. *New Instruction to the Guardian* . . . (1694), 135–36.

31. *A Modest Plea for an Equal Common-wealth Against Monarchy* . . . (1659), 62–63.

32. *The True-Born Englishman. A Satyr* (1700), 70–71.

33. *The Compleat English Gentleman* (written 1728–29), ed. Karl D. Bülbring (London: David Nutt, 1890), 171.

34. *Examiner*, No. 40, May 10, 1711; (Irish) *Intelligencer*, No. 9 (1728).

35. *Examiner*, No. 34, Mar. 29, 1711.

36. *Review*, III, No. 126, Oct. 22, 1706.

37. "Answer to the Nineteen Propositions," June 18, 1642, in J. P. Kenyon, ed., *The Stuart Constitution 1603–1688: Documents and Commentary* (Cambridge: Cambridge University Press, 1966), 23.

38. See Gerald M. Straka, *Anglican Reaction to the Revolution of 1688*, State Historical Society of Wisconsin (Madison, Wi.: University of Wisconsin Press, 1962).

39. See *Charles II's Escape from Worcester: A Collection of Narratives Assembled by Samuel Pepys*, ed. William Matthews (Berkeley: University of California Press, 1966), 40, 42, 44, 50, 74, 96.

40. To Suffolk County Committee, Aug. 29, Sept. 28, 1643, in *The Writings and Speeches of Oliver Cromwell*, ed. Wilbur C. Abbott (Cambridge, Ma.: Harvard University Press, 1937), I, 256, 262.

41. Quoted in Michael Walzer, *The Revolution of the Saints: A Study in the Origins of Radical Politics* (Cambridge, Ma.: Harvard University Press, 1965), 266.

42. Thomas Edwards, "The Holy Choice," in *Three Sermons* (1625), 63–64, quoted in ibid., 235.

43. See *Acts and Monuments*, ed. S. R. Cattley (London: Seeley and Burnside, 1839), VIII, 473–74.

44. See *The Isle of Pines* ... (1668).

45. See "A Noble Mans Sute to a Cuntrie Maide," in *Letter-Book of Gabriel Harvey, 1573–1580*, ed. Edward J. L. Scott, Camden Society, N. S. 33 (London: Nichols and Sons, 1884), 144–58.

46. See *The Fair Jilt: or, the History of Prince Tarquin, and Miranda* (1696), in *The Histories and Novels of the Late Ingenious Mrs. Behn* ... (1696).

47. The *True Picture of a Modern Whig* ... , "6th ed." (1701), 14, 32.

Life as Pilgrimage
and as Theater

RONALD PAULSON

My text is taken from *The Spectator*, that great mediator between cultures, or at least between the learned and the new reading public. In no. 219 (1711)[1] Addison says that according to one metaphor, from Scripture, men are "Strangers and Sojourners upon Earth, and Life is a Pilgrimage," but according to another, Epictetus's metaphor, the world is "a Theatre, where everyone has a Part allotted to him" and is judged by how well he plays his part.[2] Addison prefers the second, and I am going to show what his preference means in a few narratives of the 1720s to '40s. These are narratives in that they connect two or more points in time, but they are, to be more precise, a spiritual autobiography, a ballad opera, a graphic series called a "progress" and a "comic epic in prose." These are all works that in one way or another avoid being what the time would have considered "high art,"or if "avoid" is too strong a word, some of them ask us to redefine "high art" to include lower, more popular forms. In these narratives the metaphor of life as a journey, with its emphasis on sequential actions and a lone protagonist, begins to be augmented and radically altered by the metaphor of life as a stage, in which a role-playing protagonist has to interact with other actors; and this change is reflected in the major novels of the following decades.[3]

In the passage I have quoted, Addison uses the metaphors of pilgrimage and theater as alternative models of providential design. The pilgrimage

From *Popular and Polite Art in the Age of Hogarth and Fielding* (Notre Dame: University of Notre Dame Press, 1979), pp. 115–33.

stresses teleology: whether the Christian pilgrimage or the epic journey, whether the travels of Adam or Odysseus or Aeneas, it must have a destination. The aspects of divine providence Addison found in the theatrical metaphor were its apparent arbitrariness, inscrutability, and incalculable distance from our everyday concerns. This metaphor, he says, is "wonderfully proper to incline us to be satisifed with the Post in which Providence has placed us" (Epictetus himself, he reminds us, was a slave), for there may well be a discrepancy between the way the drama ends or the fate of the dramatis personae and the fate of the actors who played them. When the play is over and the roles relinquished, the actors are all equal; or, as Addison suggests, there may be new roles assigned in heaven commensurate with our performance in the assigned roles on earth.[4]

> The great Duty which lies upon a Man is to act his Part in Perfection. We may, indeed, say that our Part does not suit us, and that we could act another better. But this (says the Philosopher) is not our Business. All that we are concerned in is to excell in the Part which is given us. If it be an improper one the Fault is not in us, but in him who has cast our several Parts, and is the great Disposer of the Drama.

Whenever Addison discusses providential design he describes it in terms of a visual spectacle. Here in the present the pattern is seen as in a glass darkly; in heaven we will be able to look down, so to speak, and appreciate the pattern, which he describes as "an Entertainment" or "a Scene so large and various" offering "so delightful a Prospect" (no. 237).

But the example he gives is a grim one: Moses on Pisgah is shown by God a scene on a roadway, a spring where a soldier on his journey stops to drink and forgets his purse. When he has departed, a child comes up, sees the purse he has dropped, and takes it; and then an old man arrives ("weary with Age and Travelling") and rests under the tree, the soldier returns to seek his purse, assumes the old man has taken it, and kills him. This scene causes Moses to fall on his face "with Horror and Amazement," but God explains that what he has seen is divine justice, for some years ago the old man had murdered the child's father. Addison is far from denying a providential pattern, but he distances it far beyond man's reach, portraying life as a journey interrupted by a scene in which three travelers come together in various roles, from the past as well as the present. To these people life is a journey, but to Moses, the human consciousness who observes them, it is a scene, and moreover one that has to be interpreted by the playwright himself.[5]

For Addison, the theatrical scene seems necessary to replace the determinedly teleological pilgrimage with a series of provisional structures, roles, and scenes, which are more appropriate to man's life in society. He can make use of both Plato's metaphor of "every living being as a puppet of the gods" and the idea that you "either learn to play it, laying by seriousness, or bear its pains," with its overtones of the immediate moment-to-moment functioning of the individual in society.[6] It is a metaphor quite different from the traditional one we associated with Jacque's speech in *As You Like It* that begins, "All the world's a stage." The emphasis now is on the willful adopting of roles (not the inevitable movement from one to the next, as from whining schoolboy to sighing lover) in order to control or conceal feelings in a polite society, to restrain natural instincts, and to distinguish social classes by tone of voice, gesture, and stance. For *The Spectator* creates a "Fraternity of Spectators," as Mr. Spectator tells us early on (no. 10)—"every one that considers the World as a Theatre, and desires to form a right Judgment of those who are actors on it." This is the theatrical situation, and these are the elements we find reflected in English novels from *Pamela* to *Joseph Andrews* onward—spectators, role players, frames and scenes, and a playwright. The journey does not disappear, but, no longer the steady forward flow of a Defoe novel, it is segmented: the lone hero does not vanish, but he becomes part of a configuration of characters, a group, often a family.

The situation is already implicit in the spiritual autobiography—a nonfictional narrative that becomes fictive or exemplary in the telling. Certainly in *Robinson Crusoe* (1719) the straight diachronic narrative of Crusoe's life is compromised by the fact that it is told by the aged, the converted, and so the new and different Crusoe. The pattern is seen by—written down by—the converted Crusoe, whose language makes it clear that the waves that bear the young Crusoe are the providence of God, to which he must entrust himself if he is to be safely borne to shore. The tradition of spiritual autobiography exploits the knowledge that people do *not* full see the truth about themselves at the moment; the reason for writing such autobiographies is that the writer, in recording the information and later observing it, discovers some patterns that eluded him when the experience was new. Thus the convert can easily become the spectator of his own drama, or even the playwright, imposing providential roles upon those existential events.

At any given moment Crusoe is caught within typological or allegorical patterns relating him to Adam and the Prodigal Son, or to Jonah or merely to the spiritual pilgrim, but also to the selves projected in the alternative actions he contemplates as he moves along: what it would have been like had he never wandered, had he not been saved from the shipwreck, or had the ship sunk with all its provisions. His linear movement forward is structured by signs, suggesting another, a vertical system of analogues with an equally strong causal gravitation.

The important fact that connects Hogarth's "progresses" of a Harlot and a Rake (1732, 1735) with Defoe's narratives is that both center on the problem of the self and the process of an individual's defining and redefining himself in time. Hogarth, to the extent that he derives from the popular graphic tradition, emphasizes the left-to-right movement of causality from action to consequence and from crime to punishment, manifest in each plate and in the sequence of six or eight. But the story he has made of these elements is the spiritual pilgrimage, once concerning the search for a true identity. Brought up like Defoe on Nonconformist devotional literature, he shows an awareness that consciousness itself—and so the narrative flow—is not simply linear but layered. The distinction is between an allegorical world with allegorical figures and an allegorical world in which a Crusoe or a Harlot or a Rake moves about uneasily, trying on types or figures. Both Defoe and Hogarth produce spiritual allegories *manqué*.[7]

Hogarth, however, makes clear that his terms are theatrical. In the second plate of *A Harlot's Progress* the mask, monkey, and mirror are straight out of Ripa's *Iconologia*, where the description of imitation includes "a woman holding a bundle of brushes in her right hand, a mask in her left, with an ape at her feet." The ape is present, Ripa says (1709 translation), because of "its aptitude for imitating man with its gestures" *(ars simia naturae)*, and the mask to suggest "the imitation, on and off the stage, of the appearance and bearing of various characters." Certainly "aping" and "masking," verbally and metaphorically, are present in the scene. On the level of story, the mask also alludes to a masquerade as the place where the Harlot has met her new lover: she has *worn* this mask, and so the metaphorical relationship is almost one of identity. The monkey too is a fashionable acquisition (like the black slave-boy) which has been made either by the Jewish merchant or by his mistress, and is itself an aping of fashion, which applies to both: she with her clothes and young lover, a "lady"; he with his old-master paintings and Christian mistress, a "gentleman." The monkey is shown trying on attire that resembles the Harlot's before a dressing table; and his expression of surprise at her kicking over the table (to divert her keeper from the retreat of her lover) is parallel to the Jew's.

In these terms, and in terms of those stage-set scenes through which she moves, we must say that the Harlot proceeds surrounded by alternative roles, indicated by the pictures (painted simulations from the brush of Imitation herself) which she and her keeper hang on their walls and by the poses, compositions, and iconography in which she places herself. These alternatives include, for example, the life patterns of the clergyman or the bawd, the ego ideal of a gentlewoman in keeping (which recalls Defoe's change from religious to social terms in *Moll Flanders*), and even the sentimental illusion of living the life of the Virgin/Magdalen and enjoying the successful criminal careers of Captain Macheath and Dr. Sacheverell. A nicely schematic example is the Rake, in the oblivion of a brothel, breaking the mirror, destroying his own identity, and cutting out the faces of all the portraits of Roman emperors on the wall with the single exception of Nero—who becomes thereby his new identity.

We should remember the Puritan doctrine that one must scrub away his own image from the mirror and replace it with Christ's. "We all with open face beholding, as in a glass, the glory of the Lord, are changed into the same image."[8] But the difference between the world of Hogarth and Defoe is that Hogarth, totally accepting the metaphor of roles, shows his protagonists, far from finding Christ, completely losing themselves. By implication there is something untouched and pure—or at least authentic—about the original nature, back in the country, of the girl who *becomes* the Harlot. The reverse of the spiritual autobiography, his "progress" shows the closing off of awareness, as the Harlot's or Rake's models lead not to conversion but to self-annihilation. For Hogarth makes it clear that he has no doubts about the theatrical behavior of humans in the vacuum created by the inscrutability of unequal providence. The two examples of divine justice, pictured above the Harlot's head on the wall of her Jewish keeper's room (or the one he has furnished for her), choose the moment when God has withdrawn and spared Nineveh and it is Jonah who is still cursing the wicked city; and in the story of Uzzah touching the Ark of the Covenant, it is not God's thunderbolt but a human priest who stabs Uzzah in the back. The allegory has been humanized, and the providential structure removed, or rather displaced to human agents.

On the one hand, the order of divine providence has been reduced to the natural law of causality. It has been dismissed by the humans themselves insofar as they ordered the mutilated copies of the paintings.[9] But (except for one theatrical lightning bolt)[10] Hogarth never gives an indication of it either; and even his clergyman friend John Hoadly (son of the Latitudinarian bishop), who wrote the verses to accompany the *Rake's Progress*, refers only to the natural law of act and inevitable consequence.[11] While Hogarth demonstrates horizontal causality, however, he also shows the vestiges of vertical causality, which should be the divine pattern, but now consists only of humans imitating the models or the roles of the Biblical stories and classical myths, and the vertical pull is that of puppet strings. When a priest stabs Uzza and Jonah curses the sinners of Nineveh, beneath the picture the Jewish keeper prepares to curse the unfaithful Harlot and cast her into outer darkness.

The picture the Harlot hangs on her own wall (in imitation of her late keeper) above the portraits of Macheath and Sacheverell demonstrates the process by which spiritual autobiography becomes drama. This is a print of the angel staying the hand of Abraham about to sacrifice his son Isaac. The Harlot, who associates herself with Macheath and Sacheverell, criminals who were reprieved and lived happily ever after, sees the Biblical scene as a comforting promise of mercy and reprieve for herself. The hand of the avenging father is stayed by divine intervention. But there is also the whore-hunting magistrate who has come to arrest her, and he associates himself not with Isaac but with Abraham. And the print is also, of course, an address to the audience, whose response is different from the Harlot's and perhaps parallel to the screaming admonitory choric face made by the knot in the Harlot's bed curtain: mercy, we tend to read, is better than rigorous Old Testament justice. My point is that once an object is interpreted in different ways by different characters, those characters have moved from the function of mere "others" (or objects) to subjects in their own right, with the capability of symbolizing their own "others." Defoe characters see the world outside as threat or providence, but for the Harlot and Rake the people around them are not only projections but real threats—cannibals who *do* devour Crusoe, as he fears they will. This is the other half of the Hogarth progress—the world in which the Harlot and the Rake find themselves, full of clergymen interested only in promotion or what's under young ladies' skirts, or magistrates who take too much pleasure in hunting down and punishing pretty young prostitutes.

It was not just any drama that picked up Addison's theatrical metaphor, but one which derived from the tradition of the rehearsal play, and so emphasized the elements of audience and playwright as well as the distinction between actors and roles in the drama on stage. Materializing precisely *The Spectator*'s metaphor, Gay's *Beggar's Opera* (1728) carried Hogarth from Defoe's portrayal of a subject encountering only objects to a dramatic model in which subjects encounter other subjects, who perhaps regard *them* as objects.

The year 1728 saw the final flowering of the old Stuart world in Pope's *Dunciad*, which looks back and sees it all gone, but just a month earlier, Gay's play had been produced, and within the year Hogarth executed his two major versions of *The Beggar's Opera* in oil, which set him on his course toward *A Harlot's Progress* and *Strolling Actresses Dressing in a Barn*. In the same year Fielding produced his first play, and by the end of the following year he had learned enough from *The Beggar's Opera* to write *The Author's Farce*. This conjuction of events represents, in its variety of visual and verbal forms, the transition from the literary world of the "Augustans," Dryden, Swift, and Pope, to that of Fielding, Richardson, Hogarth, and Johnson. Together, Gay and Hogarth showed Fielding how the Augustan elements of satire, irony, allusion, and analogy, from the protected position of a social and intellectual elite, could be modified into a more generous and wide-ranging—in some ways more sentimental but in others more questioning and skeptical, perhaps more "democratic"— mode. They showed, at the moment of political and social disillusionment, when it had become clear that the "Augustan Age" was a sham, the Stuarts gone for good, and the Age of Walpole (one of whose nicknames was "the Screen") there to stay—new ways in which cultural forms could continue to develop in England.

Gay's ballad opera and Hogarth's two main representations of it demonstrate the alternative solutions of a parody of high art and a viable substitute for it. The smaller version shows large figures dominating the picture space and explores Gay's play as a popular, English version of opera—and of history painting. There is a small, intimate stage, subdued set, contemporary costumes, and a subject concerned with play acting. The larger version puts a great deal more emphasis on the play as parody of high art, reducing the size of the players in their contemporary dress and playing up the operatic theatricality of the trappings that surround them. The effect is more clearly mock-heroic, reflecting Gay's intention to make thieves sound like opera singers playing gods and heroes.

One norm Gay and Hogarth have chosen is the bare, forked animal man—or the *tabula rasa* or even perhaps the Noble Savage. Then comes the criminal, who serves as another layer, a superimposition on the original, which if not good is authentic, and after that the courtier, politician, aristocrat, or merchant whose roles the criminal attempts to mimic. The second norm is the visual, the immediately seen and experienced. In both play and paintings the visual element relates back to Addison's emphasis on *seeing* as superior to what is *said*. "Every Passion gives a particular Cast to the Countenance," writes Mr. Spectator, "and is apt to discover itself in some Feature or other. I have seen an Eye curse for half an Hour together, and an Eyebrow call a Man Scoundrel" (no. 86). He concludes that he believes "we may be better known by Looks than by our Words; and that a Man's Speech is much more easily disguised than his Countenance." This is an emphasis on the visual to correct the verbal that derives from the stage and gives Hogarth many of his terms of reference.[12] Hereafter, as Fielding shows, we will have to watch the expression as we listen to the words; we will be participating in both a drama and a spiritual autobiography, observing an object while listening to a subject.

The dramatic scene is summed up by Mr. Spectator in an account of one of his participations in a spectacle (no. 19):

> Observing one Person behold another, who was an utter Stranger to him, with a Cast of his Eye, which, methought, expressed an Emotion of Heart very different from what could be raised by an Object so agreeable as the Gentlemen he looked at, I began to consider, not without some secret Sorrow, the Condition of an Envious Man.

One man looks at another "with a Cast of his Eye"; Mr. Spectator sees "one person behold[ing] another"; looking at the second, Mr. Spectator sees an "agreeable" object (perhaps he knows his "character"), and, looking at the first responding to the second, he sees "a Cast of his Eye." He then raises these emprirical observations to the status of generalization by concluding, but subjectively (and sentimentally), "not without some secret Sorrow," that the first is "an Envious Man." The interaction of spectator and scene, or of these three men, produces the general reflection on "the Condition of an Envious Man," but with no illusions on Mr. Spectator's part that this is more than a generalization raised by personal and perhaps idiosyncratic observation.

This scene will become eventually, in Mackenzie's *Man of Feeling* (1771), a situation in which the reader is a spectator to an editor, who responds to the author of the manuscript, who responds to the manuscript's protagonist Harley, who himself is responding to people and events he encounters (to understand which he sometimes needs an interpreter). In *The Beggar's Opera*, however, Addison's scene takes its definitive form as actors on a stage playing roles of criminals, who themselves play roles of "gentlemen," "merchants," and "ladies"; and these are observed by spectators in the audience who are no less part of the play because they are meant to read their own values into the models the criminals use as wish fulfillment, special pleading, and rationalization—and so include participants as well as spectators, some of whom talk among themselves and ignore the performance; and finally by the Beggar, who has written the play and revises it shamelessly in the light of the respectable audience's desires.

Hogarth's painting in its final version perfectly conveys this reading of the play, with the respectable spectators sitting on the stage, exchanging glances and roles with the actors themselves, and among them the lover of one of the actresses and both Rich the stage manager and Gay the playwright.[13] In the *Harlot's Progress,* then, the actor-spectator-playwright relationship remains in the clergymen and rakes and magistrates, who range from bored spectators to interested participants to models and authors of her "progress," which is (we have noted) a selection of roles. The first plate was already summed up by Mr. Spectator (no. 266), who plays the role himself of the clergyman who watches "the most artful Procuress in the Town, examining a most beautiful Country-Girl, who had come up in the same Waggon with my Things," but—and this is the point Hogarth makes—he does nothing more than remain a spectator. The causal pull of the Hogarthian plate slows down to comparison and contrast, or "this leads to that" becomes "this is like or unlike that," as within the scenes of a play. The structure of admonition or morality, which takes the form of crime leading to punishment, becomes one of definition of interpersonal relations.

Gay's *Beggar's Opera* was attacked as subversive because there were political references to Walpole, and because London lower-class types were said to be emulating the model of Macheath and falling into a life of crime. The second reason may have been an excuse for the first, but behind the Harlot's pin-up of Macheath was the fear, publicized in the newspapers, that people would imitate his charming, successful example.[14] In *The Beggar's Opera* the roles are no longer merely assigned by a stage manager, but chosen within the play by the individual himself, and so have become models.

The element of the theatrical metaphor given greatest emphasis by Addison is precisely this one, and the relation between a copy and an original:

Instead of going out of our own complectional Nature into that of others, 'twere a better and more laudable Industry to improve our own, and instead of a miserable Copy become a good Original.   [No. 238]

Quite different from Defoe's insistence on the need for rebirth or conversion into another role, Addison's assumption of an original nature that is good in the sense of authentic leads to the imminent danger of losing one-self, which I believe Gay and Hogarth describe. Epictetus' paradigm, in which roles are deterministic facts, has become *The Spectator's* primary awareness that there are human agencies which we *can* fathom behind actions: the fashions of gentlemen and ladies, the plays and novels, the social as well as the literary conventions, of the time. "Consider all the different pursuits and Employments of Men," says Mr. Spectator,

> and you will find half their Actions tend to nothing else but Disguise and Imposture; and all that is done which proceeds not from a Man's very self is the action of a Player. For this Reason it is that I make so frequent mention of the stage.
> [No. 370]

In *Strolling Actresses Dressing in a Barn* (1738), Hogarth shows the goddess Diana played by an actress who is caught backstage with her petticoats around her ankles, ignoring (fortunately, both he and Fielding would have agreed) her onstage role of Diana. Both aspects of the theatrical metaphor are implied: an actor plays the role, well or poorly, and we observe him behind the scenes, where we can clearly see the irreducible reality he is concealing in order to play the role.

Hogarth follows one way of playing *The Beggar's Opera*, in which there is only one system of roles/models, all bad. Fielding in his mature fiction plays it another way, as a misalliance of different model systems, one drawn from the Bible, another from the stage or fictional romance. In *Joseph Andrews* (1742) the comedy is generated when the innocent Christian models that govern Adams and Joseph come into contact with the models centered around affectation. Joseph sees himself as a male Pamela and as the Biblical Joseph resisting Potiphar's wife—but in fact acts because (we learn later) love of Fanny Goodwill is in his heart. Lady Booby's models are something else again: "She held my hand," says Joseph, writing to his sister and model Pamela, "and talked exactly as a lady does to her sweetheart in a stage-play." She sees herself not as Potiphar's wife but as a Dido entangling a reluctant Aeneas—a tragic heroine who will end in self-immolation. The focus in the *Harlot's Progress* is on the relationship of the individual and his/her models; in the Joseph—Lady Booby scenes it is on the interpenetration of different model systems which never quite mesh. Joseph is unaware that Lady Booby is not Potiphar's wife, or a female version of Mr. B., and Lady Booby is unaware that Joseph is not a reluctant Aeneas.

Fielding comes fresh from rehearsal plays of his own in which the unit of narrative is the scene as observed by spectators, as well as by critics and by the author himself.[15] There is already a script, but in the rehearsal situation the author and his audience can collaborate and make changes even at this point, aware as they are of the characters as actors in their roles and out of them. The playwright's presence, nearby and ready to comment and explain, if not revise, is something with which Hogarth does not complicate his scene. For it is this amiable author who, like Gay's Beggar, feels responsible for pleasing as well as instructing his audience. The question of providential design in the structure of the narrative is therefore very differently solved by Fielding. The design is plainly present in *Joseph Andrews* and not explained away in terms of a convert looking back and seeing the divine pattern in existential events. The peddler *does* keep turning up at the right moment, and Adams or somebody else *does* appear just in time to save Fanny, who has called upon providence for aid. But this is also the story in which Slipslop, however grotesque, is just as she is described, because we recognize the literary conventions from which Fielding has constructed her. And the narrator is constantly explaining and demonstrating to the reader the literary artifice of the narrative he is writing. The providential structure is virtually congruent with the romance or comedy plot in this book which is being written to answer *Pamela*, a literary work that tries to conceal its literariness and pass as real as well as exemplary.

The graphic narrative is a very different tradition to be associated with than the tradition of romance or comedy. Herein lies the profound difference, despite so many similarities, between the worlds of Hogarth and his friend Fielding. In one, even in church *"Dieu"* is out of sight and only *"et mon droit"* remains in control (as in *The Sleeping Congregation*). In the other, human fates are still to a large extent governed by providence, a presiding comic Genius, or the author-historian who is creating the book. Whereas Hogarth imitates the *Beggar's Opera* structure, in which the respectable criminals are present as spectators and models and are always pardoned, Fielding incorporates this structure within a larger romance plot with happy ending and rewards and punishments respectively for the good and evil.[16] The plot he follows is a spiritual pilgrimage, but he brings with him enough sense of the Beggar's forced ending or of the rehearsal play to hint that behind those happy endings can be either a sure knowledge of correspondence with providential pattern *or* a bitter awareness of the distance—of the conventional quality of a play's ending.

Tom Jones is Fielding's most complete manifestation of the theatrical metaphor. But by this time the density of reference to theaters and the theatrical model has become remarkable. We recall the jestbooks with their actor-personae (no longer court jesters) converging on the poker-faced Joe Miller and the theatrical game of roles and play projected by Hoyle, whose concern with the reading of significance in expressions and gestures of partners and opponents is as great as Addison's or as Fielding's in his "Essay on the Knowledge of the Characters of Men" (1743). Then there is Thomas Blackwell, who in his *Letters concerning Mythology* (1748) treats the metaphor of "the world's a stage" as of equal substance and significance as that of Prometheus' theft of the gods' fire or any other Greek "metaphor."[17] Even David Hume describes the mind (in his *Treatise* [1739]) as "a kind of theatre, where several perceptions successively make their appearance; pass, repass, glide away, and mingle in an infinite variety of postures and situations"—and yet we have not "the most distant notion of the place where these scenes are represented, or of the materials of which it is composed."[18] In Hume's hands the metaphor lends itself to a radical skepticism about the possibility of rationally understanding reality itself, which was only faintly adumbrated in Addison's *Spectator*, no. 219.

The chapter in *Tom Jones* called "A Comparison between the World and the Stage" (bk. VII, chap, i) makes explicit the metaphor which permeates the novel. The journey—Tom's pilgrimage—is interrupted and broken into segments which are Tom's actions (climaxing in the bedroom farce at Upton in book IX), each involving an interaction with another person and the responses and observations of spectators inside the scene, various groups of spectators (readers) outside it, and the author himself. The climax is both Tom's arrival in London and his participation as spectator and actor in a puppet show, a performance of *Hamlet*, and a dangerously close rehearsal of *Oedipus*.[19]

The "Comparison between the World and the Stage," however, moves the emphasis from the stage (Fielding recalls Epictetus' analogy of men and actors)[20] to the audience, its divisions, different responses, and tendency to confuse actor and role. The audience becomes the most important part of the metaphor. Most of the characters in the novel, as well as its readers, fall into the category of audience, ranging from the credulous, the Partridges—who cannot tell the difference between Garrick and Hamlet and attribute human actions to divine providence (the audience to whom Fielding addressed himself exclusively in his "examples" of the *Interposition of Providence in the Detection and Punishment of Murder* [1752])—to the Blifils and Thwackums and Squares, who consciously mininterpret events, to the intelligent few who are expected to understand the ironies and, like some of the viewers of the rehearsal play, contribute to the construction of the fiction itself. These are the privileged members of the audience, like the author himself, who

> admitted behind the scenes . . . can censure the action, without conceiving any absolute detestation of the person, whom perhaps Nature may not have designed to act an ill part in all her dramas; for in this instance life most exactly resembles the stage, since it is often the same person who represents the villain and the hero.

It appears that Epictetus' god, the playwright, has been replaced by Nature, or human nature, and the Passions "are the managers and directors of this theatre (for as to Reason, the patentee, he is known to be a very idle fellow and seldom to exert himself)", and these managers "often force men upon parts without consulting their judgment, and sometimes without any regard to their talents." The author himself is merely a privileged spectator, whose only advantage over his reader is his ability to see behind the masks of the characters, whose role playing is self-determined and socially-determined.

He does emerge, however, as a "comic writer" who, by the conventions of poetic treatises, is entitled to use supernatural assistance for special occasions (XVII, i), and for a moment he is the "Creator" himself, though well aware of the discrepancy in his analogy (X, i). In *Tom Jones*, where peddlers only forward the plot when the hero has shown them a kindness, the outcome of the comic action is dependent on the freedom of characters like Tom, and the question is in what sense the "author" is governor of, and in what sense governed by, the unfolding pattern of events. The ambiguity lies, I believe, in the fact that while in the journey metaphor he is the *raconteur* of the tale, in relation to the theatrical metaphor he is only a privileged spectator (very like Addison's). He opens his last book (XVIII): "We are now, reader, arrived at the last stage of our long Journey," which is both Tom's journey along the road on foot and the journey of the author and reader alongside "like fellow-travellers in a stage-coach," with the author "an entertaining companion." ("Our pen," he writes earlier, " . . . shall imitate the expedition which it describes, and our history shall keep pace with the travellers who are its subject" [XI, 9].)

The activities of writing and living were, of course, in a sense parallel in the spiritual autobiography: Crusoe's act of writing was part of the incantation; his life was meaningless to him and to others until it was written down, materialized in words. The metaphor of journey, Fielding suggests in *Tom Jones*, remains as a means of explaining the process of living, writing, and reading the unfolding romance, with its clear-cut beginning, middle, and end; while the metaphor of theater must be resorted to in order to examine objectively and understand the problematic actions of both living and writing. The journey metaphor remains associated with the subject, who sees himself as a pilgrim (as both writer and protagonist), while. the theatrical metaphor emerges when it is necessary to explain something about these figures in relation to the world—that is, in terms of custom, roles, and disguises. This is the metaphor they unconsciously live by.

Goldsmith was following Fielding's model in *The Vicar of Wakefield* (1766) when he had Dr. Primrose, his first-person narrator, tell us he sees life as a journey:

> Almost all men have been taught to call life a passage, and themselves the travellers. The similitude still may be improved when we observe that the good are joyful and serene, like travellers that are going towards home; the wicked but by intervals happy, like travellers that are going into exile.[21]

The Primrose family migrates to a new parish and begins to fragment as son George departs, daughter Olivia disappears, and Dr. Primrose sets out alone on the road to find her. The climax of his providential metaphor of life as a journey is reached, ironically, when his family is completely broken up and he is confined to prison (chap. XXIX, p. 163). In his sermon preached to the prisoners he asks them to take comfort, "for we shall soon be at our journey's end," and "the weary traveller" will "lay down the heavy burthen laid upon" him and find his heavenly (versus earthly) reward. The point is that reward is distanced into the afterlife from this point of immobility in the present. Earlier, when he sent George off into the world, Dr. Primrose had advised him to remember the 37th Psalm, "never saw I the righteous man forsaken, or his seed begging their bread" (v. 25, p. 26). The context of the quotation he chose is a journey: "The steps of a man are from the Lord, and he establishes him in whose way he delights" (or, "he holds him firm and watches over his path"); "though he fall, he shall not be cast headlong, for the Lord is the stay of his hand" (vv. 23–24). Though it appears the Dr. Primrose is intended to be in some sense educated, demonstrating a progress by his statement of the doctrine of unequal providence to the prisoners, the fact is that at the end of the novel a shower of earthly rewards vindicates his *first* interpretation (to George) of providence as justice on this earth. The fact that Primrose's progress is analogous to Job's may, as Battestin has suggested, help to explain why he too was returned his lost possessions. [22] But I suspect that the answer is involved in the other metaphor that informs Dr. Primrose's progress, and of which he is seemingly unaware.

On his travels in search of Olivia he encounters George, performing in a troupe of actors, and the progress George recounts takes the form of a journey, from the Primrose vicarage to London to Amsterdam to Louvain to Paris, and so on, each in a different profession: gentleman usher, writer, English teacher, Greek teacher, tutor, rhetor, and finally actor. "I was driven for some time from one character to another," George tells his father, and we recall that in each case he was given the idea of what profession to adopt by a friend. It becomes clear that Goldsmith has seen his journey as a series of roles adopted, and the metaphors of life as journey and theater have coalesced.

Once generated, however, by the recognition scenes with Arabella Wilmot and George and with George's performance in *The Fair Penitent*, the theater metaphor takes over: we are hurried into the grotesquely theatrical recognition of the lost Olivia and the revelation of her seduction (a fair penitent), the Vicar's arrival home with her just as his house bursts into flames, his imprisonment by the wicked seducer of his daughter, and so on to the final reversals, recognitions, and unmasking—a blaze of theatrical metaphor with which the providential resolution is expressed.

Only in the denouement of a play can the lowly find hope and the mighty beware (*Sperate miseri, cavete faelices*, according to the book's epigraph). The fairy tales and ballad romances, even the model of Primrose's life as Job's, are part of the system of analogies that becomes, with the appearance of George and his troupe of actors, specifically theatrical, with Dr. Primrose another actor. The members of the Primrose family are "all equally generous, credulous, simple, and inoffensive," and (like George) they pick up any role offered them. At the moment when Dr. Primrose is preaching life as a journey to an eternal reward, he is locked in a prison which soon turns into a set for *The Beggar's Opera*, with the Beggar himself virtually materialized to set things right. Even Job's story, parallel at many points to the Vicar's, is not a journey but a drama in which a puppet master takes away and restores possessions in a most theatrical way. Sir William Thornhill, like the duke in *Measure for Measure*, is merely the great Puppet Master's surrogate on earth.

The only scholar who has connected Dr. Primrose with the primrose *path* has cited *Macbeth* ("the primrose path to the everlasting bonfire"). [23]

The germ of the Vicar and his antagonist Squire Thornhill, however, as well as the novel's conjuction of metaphors, is in *Hamlet*—in Ophelia's speech to Laertes as he departs on *his* journey:

> But, good my brother,
> Do not, as some ungracious pastors do,
> Show me the steep and thorny way to heaven,
> Whiles, like a puff'd and reckless libertine,
> Himself the primrose path of dalliance treads,
> And recks not his own rede.
>
> (I, 3, 45–51)

Here is the pastor, the "thorny way to heaven" and the "primrose path of dalliance" in which the pastor does not heed his own counsel.[24] Here is the Vicar, the subject who needs to see his life as the hard journey of a Job with an inevitable reward for virtue, and the Vicar, the object whose life is actually a theater with provisional roles and apparent rewards and punishments distributed at the denouement.

The *Vicar* sums up the various uses of the theatrical metaphor and serves as a retrospect on the period it closes. It shows us the two ways the theatrical metaphor was used by the contemporaries of Hogarth and Fielding. The patricians staged one form of theater for the lower orders, consisting of paternalistic gestures and costumes, and another for themselves, this one interposing masks between themselves and bodily contact with coarse realities (such as the lower orders). Both Squire Thornhill and Dr. Primrose (and his family) carry out these charades in their related ways. The Primroses imitate the Thornhills, as the hapless dwarf in the fable follows the giant into giant-battles.

The norms of self-control and protective masks to conceal the feelings reached to the satirists themselves. Swift and Pope, with their personae and ambiguous identities, eventuated in Goldsmith as "Primrose," who simultaneously criticizes the phenomenon and partakes of it. Addison saw role playing in society as essential (if not natural); the Augustan satirists largely echoed this—or rather Addison echoed them; and the earl of Chesterfield in his *Letters to His Son* merely overformulated Addison's formulation. But the generation of John Gay, Hogarth, and Fielding asks the question: When does the playing of roles become the imitating of models, which may not be provisional but prescriptive and self-enclosing? They attack role playing as pretense and as the loss of one's own identity in disguises. They share the belief that the original identity is probably better than the assumed ones (a notion Swift and Pope would have questioned). Goldsmith muddles these various positions and produces his magnificently ambiguous portrait of Dr. Primrose.

The case of the lower orders is analogous. For them the metaphor of life as theater—Epictetus' way of living with his slavery—was a form of effigy-making of themselves and thereby coming to terms with the harsh realities of their life. On the other hand, one of their few strategies for coming to terms with their rulers was to stage a series of theatrical threats for their benefit. Thus again one drama is staged for oneself and another for the "others." Or perhaps it is rather that the poor saw themselves within a normative theatrical metaphor of provisional identities and employed it to keep up a dialogue with the other group that mattered to them, the polite world. Perhpas they always took the roles less seriously than their betters did theirs.[25]

Imagine a country house picture gallery with portraits of Cicero, Sir Robert Walpole, and Jesus Christ. A Whig lord would see them as models for emulation—as would probably also a successful merchant or financier. A moralist would see such imitation as a loss of self, and a pious dissenter would agree, excepting the portrait of Jesus, which allows for an *imitatio Christi*. But Moll Flanders—someone below the level of official culture—would see such costume pictures as a means of personal transcendence or of escape. Her disguises, seen from above, are an obscuring or distorting of her true, absolute identity, but seen from below they are an opportunity for carnival, though outside the socially-acceptable forms of the calendar of crowd rituals. Even the moralist could not interpret Moll's desperately prudential costuming as social-climbing or an attempt to emulate her betters. The artist, on the other hand, could see his own adopting of personae as in some ways as desperate as Moll's.

For with the poor there was yet another dimension. The artists and writers—Gay, Hogarth, and Fielding—felt that they were themselves simultaneously living the metaphor and seeing through it, as part of a subculture of the artist in a hostile society they called the Age of Walpole. They therefore saw the subculture of the lower orders parodying the official acts of the official culture (as in *The Beggar's Opera*) and also regarded it as in some ways behaving itself *without* affectation, emitting vulgar laughter when it felt like it and not concealing its feelings by manners.

When Edward Young, in his *Conjectures on Original Compositon* (1759), exclaims, "Born originals, how comes it to pass that we die *Copies?*" and refers to "that medling Ape Imitation" who "snatches the Pen, and blots out nature's mark of Separation, cancels her kind intention, destroys all mental Individuality," he is only materializing in Addison's metaphor the argument of his whole book:

> ... illustrious Examples *engross, prejudice,* and *intimidate.* They *engross* our attention, and so prevent a due inspection of ourselves; they *prejudice* our Judgment in favour of their abilities, and so lessen the sense of our own; and they *intimidate* us with the splendour of their Renown, and thus under Diffidence bury our strength. [P.17]

The concern with masking is only the obverse of a yearning for authenticity, which can be sought either in the high-art form of the retirement theme or Roman Republican virtue (another form of play acting), or in the low form of types who are outside the social structure altogether (or seem to be).

Notes

1. For the *Spectator,* see Bond ed., II, 351–54.
2. For Epictetus, see *Encheiridion,* 17; also Seneca, *Epistulas morales,* 77, 20, and E. R. Curtius, *European Literature and the Latin Middle Ages* (New York, 1953), pp. 138–44.
3. Addison includes, between the two metaphors I have mentioned, a third: life as an inn, "which was only designed to furnish us with Accommodations in this our Passage." This metaphor Addison seems to mix with life as journey (as does Fielding in *Joseph Andrews,* where some of the most elaborate scenes are in the inns along the path of Joseph's journey). Later, in the nineteenth century, drawing upon the tradition of the Symposium (and the satiric dinner parties in Horace and Petronius), writers begin to depict a weekend in a country house as a microcosm of life—a structure most clearly seen in the classical whodunits laid in an isolated house or railway carriage.
4. An alternative was rewards and punishments *at the end of the play;* but even here, as in Ralph Cudworth's use of the metaphor, the emphasis is on "at last," suggesting the Last Judgment. See Cudworth, *The True Intellectual System of the Universe* (2d edn., 1743), II, 879–80.
5. See also no. 483.
6. Plato, *Laws,* I, 644de; Palladas, *Greek Anthology,* X, 72; quoted in Curtius, p. 138. Elsewhere Addison tells us that discretion "is like an Under-Agent of Providence to guide and direct us in the ordinary concerns of Life" (no. 225). On "the theatre of the great" in contemporary society, see E. P. Thompson, "Patrician Society, Plebeian Culture," *Journal of Social History,* VII (1974), 382–405. On the more general rhetorical sense of role playing, which would include Jacques's speech, see Richard Lanham, *Motives of Eloquence: Literary Rhetoric in the Renaissance* (New Haven, 1976), esp. chaps. 1 and 2.
7. As Homer Brown nicely puts it, "the point is not that writers like Defoe tried and failed to write novelistic allegories but that life could not be reduced or raised to a spiritual meaning" ("The Displaced Self in the Novels of Daniel Defoe," *ELH,* XXXVIII [1971], 562–90). Moll Flanders is, of course, Defoe's most flamboyantly play-acting heroine, accompa-

nying new roles with costumes as well as gestures, and in the preface to *Moll Flanders* (1721) Defoe makes one of his infrequent allusions to the stage (as an analogue to his defense of the portrayal of vice in his novel). In a large sense, we could say that Defoe himself is "impersonating" his protagonists—if we wished to limit "impersonate" to the theatrical metaphor ("dramatic monologue").

8. 2 Corinthians 3:18, cited in Sacvan Bercovitch, *The Puritan Origins of the American Self* (New Haven, 1975), p. 14. One has to recall the way Hogarth deals with threats to his own identity, as in the replacement of his face with Charles Churchill's in *The Bruiser*. For the problem of the Harlot as the Virgin Mary, see above, p. 19.

9. In the first plate of *Marriage à la Mode*, a *Martyrdom of St. Agnes* after Domenichino omits the heavenly host and Christ crowning the martyr. In *"Rake,"* plate 5, divinity has been expunged from the church, only the human-centered commandments remain; and in *The Sleeping Congregation*, *"Dieu"* is omitted from the royal motto on the wall, leaving in effect only *"et mon droit."* In *Marriage à la Mode*, when a St. Luke appears in a pictue above the murder of Earl Squanderfield, he is only a spectator, and can only stare but not intervene.

10. The only indication of providence in "modern moral subjects" is the lightning bolt aimed at White's Gambling House in *Rake*, plate 4 (which is shown burning in pl. 6), and this is an addition which is precisely balanced by a group of dice-playing boys and their game of chance. The parallelism is between White's and Black's gambling establishments, of course, but as an addition the lightning bolt becomes a second kind of chance, parallel with the boys' game.

11. In plate 4, when consequences begin to descend, we read: "Approaching the poor Remains / That Vice hath left of all his Gains." No mention is made in plate 6, where there is a possibly providential figure, and the verses to plate 8 end admonishing the poor Rake to "cure they self, & curse they Gold."

12. One example among many is the *Plain Dealer* in 1726: "The *Painter* informs the Understanding, and warms the Imagination, by striking the *Sight* stongly, and giving it the Height of Pleasure; while all that can be done, of that kind, by the greatest Poet that ever liv'd is to make us merely *imagine*, that he sets Things before our Eyes" (collected edn. [1730], II, 26–27).

13. Hogarth frequently relates his works to the theater: "The figure is the actor / The attitudes and his actions together with which / The face works an expression and the words must speak to the Eye and the scene . . . "; "I have endeavourd to weaken some of the prejudices belonging to the judging of subjects for pictures, by comparing these with stage compositions [,] the actors in one suggesting whats to the spectator [in the other]"; "We will therefore compare subjects for painting with those of the stage . . . "; and, above all, "my Picture was my Stage and men and women my actors who were by Mean of certain Actions and expressions to Exhibit a dumb shew" (Autobiographical Notes," in *Analysis of Beauty*, ed. Burke, pp. 203, 211, 209). The recognition of Hogarth's use of visual structures in terms of theatrical conventions was immediate among his contemporaries. Aaron Hill compares his art with the stage as early as 1736, praising him as a reformer; unlike his "rival theatre-managers," he gives purpose and propriety to his "dramas" (*Prompter*, 27, Feb. 1736); see also Arthur Murphy in *The Gray's Inn Journal* (9 Mar. 1754) and Reynolds in his *Fourteenth Discourse*.

14. See J. B. Guerinot and Rodney D. Jilg, eds., *The Beggar's Opera, Contexts* (New Haven, 1976), pp. 118–41.

15. The subject of the relationship between Fielding's rehearsal plays and his novels has been dealt with in my *Satire and the Novel in Eighteenth-Century England* (New Haven, 1967), pp. 85–99; see also J. Paul Hunter, "Fielding's Reflexive Plays and the Rhetoric of Discov-

ery," *Studies in the Literary Imagination*, V (1972), 65–100, reprinted in *Occasional Form* (Baltimore, 1975), pp. 48–75.

16. Fielding's history of Mr. Wilson, for example, is the progress of Hogarth's Rake up to the point of despair and madness; but Fielding has the truly Christian Harriet Hearty intervene, which awakens the would-be rake to the errors of his ways, and converts him. In Hogarth's progress there is only the ineffectual version of Harriet, Sarah Young, and no chance of reprieve.

17. Blackwell, p. 70. On sight, emprirical evidence, and stage presentation as opposed to history painting, see p. 32.

18. Hume, *Treatise*, ed. A. D. Lindsay (London, 1959), I. 239–40.

19. For Partridge's reaction to Garrick's Hamlet, cf. *Miller's Jests*, no. 188, where the yokels at the London theater are enjoying all the goings on, from music to orange wenches, until the curtain goes up and three actors begin the play—"upon which one of them cry'd to the other, Come, Hodge, let's be going, ma'haps the Gentlemen are talking about business."

20. In this chapter Fielding quotes from Samuel Boyse's poem *Deity* (1740), which calls the world "the vast Theatre of Time": "Perform the parts Thy providence assign'd, / Their pride, their passions, to Thy ends inclin'd"—emphasizing the Epictetus version. (He also quotes from the poem in *The Champion*, 12 Feb. 1739–40.) For one view on Fielding and divine providence, see Martin C. Battestin, *The Providence of Wit: Aspects of Form in Augustan Literature and the Arts* (Oxford, 1974), chap. 5. I do not want to suggest an exclusive causal relationship between Fielding's novels and *The Beggar's Opera*. The metaphor of the theatre is, of course, central to part II of *Don Quixote*—in the theatrical performance for Sancho on his island, in the puppet show, and in the role playing carried on for Don Quixote's benefit. It continued in the more specific terms of a troupe of actors in Scarron's *Roman comique*. The relationship between journey and theatrical performance was already implicit in one strain of the picaresque.

21. Arthur Friedman, ed., *Collected Works* (Oxford, 1966), IV, 135.

22. Battestin, op. cit., chap. 7.

23. K. Eichenberger, *Oliver Goldsmith, das Komische in den Werken seiner Reifeperiode* (Bern, 1954), p. 78; see also Sven Bäckman, *This Singular Tale, a Study of "The Vicar of Wakefield" and Its Literary Background* (Lund, 1971), pp. 94 and 131 n. 33.

24. The primrose is also, of course, used by Goldsmith in *The Deserted Village* to suggest rural innocence and simplicity; but even here it is "Sweet as the primrose peeps beneath the thorn" (l. 330 [*Works*, IV, 299]).

25. Thompson (in "Eighteenth-Century English Society," p. 157) sees the plebeian culture" as essentially "picaresque"—"not only in the obvious sense that more people are mobile, go to sea, are carried off to wars, experience the hazards and adventures of the road. In more settled ambiences—in the growing areas of manufacture and of free labor—life itself proceeds along a road whose hazards and accidents cannot be prescribed or avoided by forethought; fluctuation in the incidence of mortality, of prices, of employment, are experienced as external accidents beyond any control. . . . " My own definition of picaresque depends on the shifting relation of a servant to a master—to the moments of stability sought (or imposed) on the wanderer. The moments of stability tend to assume that relationship, which of course leads to theatrical impersonation. See my *Fictions of Satire* (Baltimore, 1967).

Robinson Crusoe:
The Self as Master

JOHN J. RICHETTI

You are not to take it, if you please, as the saying of an ignorant man, when I express my opinion that such a book as Robinson Crusoe never was written, and never will be written again. I have tried that book for years—generally in combination with a pipe of tobacco—and I have found it my friend in need in all the necessities of this mortal life. When my spirits are bad—Robinson Crusoe. When I want advice— Robinson Crusoe. In past times, when my wife plagued me; in present times, when I have had a drop too much—Robinson Crusoe. I have worn out six stout Robinson Crusoes with hard work in my service. On my lady's last birthday she gave me a seventh. I took a drop too much on the strength of it; and Robinson Crusoe put me right again. Price four shillings and sixpence, bound in blue, with a picture into the bargain.

(Wilkie Collins, *The Moonstone*)

Near the very end of his *Farther Adventures,* Robinson Crusoe visits China and allows himself to describe it as a poor, ignorant, and barbarous nation. That description strikes Crusoe as a departure from his usual procedure and he apologizes:

As this is the only excursion of this kind which I have made in all the account I have given of my travels, so I shall make no more descriptions of countrys and people; 'tis none of my business, or any part of my design; but giving an account of my own adventures, through a life of inimitable wandrings, and a long variety of changes, which perhaps few that come after me will have heard the like of; I

From *Defoe's Narratives: Situations and Structures* (Oxford: Clarendon 1975), pp. 21–62.

shall therefore say very little of all the mighty places, desart countrys, and numerous people I have yet to pass thro', more then relates to my own story, and which my concern among them will make necessary.[1]

Such limitation is exactly why we now read Defoe. His achievement, as Ian Watt has rendered it fairly, was to assert the "primacy of individual experience" by a "total subordination of the plot to the pattern of the auto-biographical memoir."[2] Crusoe sees more of the world in his sequel than any ordinary eighteenth-century person could even hope to see, and yet he calmy denies his readers extensive knowledge of that extraordinarily varied world in order to deliver himself. This audacity accords perfectly with the egocentric preferences of the novel as a genre which really cares only for personality and its triumph over environment and circumstances. As Ortega y Gasset once remarked, characters in novels "interest us not because of what they are doing; rather the opposite, what they do interests us because it is they who do it."[3] Such paradox seems borne out by the dismal fate of Crusoe's continuation. The tremendous variety of scene the sequel features is, perhaps, part of the reason for its failure. Crusoe himself tends to fade out of sight and the exotic locales take over to a degree. In the original, Crusoe is himself the actor and the stage, the whole theater.

But even in Part One, it may be argued, there are events, actions of a fairly spectacular and clearly external kind. Crusoe, after all, is not ironically self-contained in the manner of modern heroes. The point is that those acts and events are subordinate to the special event we call literary personality of character. The events do indeed seem to draw out personality, for some kind of event (or the deliberate absence of one) is clearly necessary to provide a field for achievement or externalization of personality. But we always feel as we read that personality is radically primary, that it existed before events and continues to exist in spite of circumstances that seek to change or even to obliterate it. Finally, in fact, we are led back to Ortega's paradox when we realize that the result of the narrative is to convert events into vehicles for character; or, more exactly, that events gradually accommodate themselves to the emerging self as its power to deal with events increases. It is not simply that the self learns to manage events. Rather, events become as we read an appropriate expression of the self. Thus, what we are chiefly conscious of as readers of the first part of *Robinson Crusoe* is a world of initially controlling circumstances and events in which the narrative self somehow manages not simply to survive but to make survival a form of autonomy. That autonomy is acceptable because it is disguised, not presented as a simple heroic assertion but residing in the kind of complex and elusive being that the novel as such is uniquely equipped to create. In that being, the self does not dominate the world but manages to produce a version of the world which is perfectly aligned with itself and its desires.

As an archetypal personage of the last two hundred and fifty years of European consciousness, Crusoe seems to have achieved his popularity by virtue of precisely that versatility and adaptability, able as Wilkie Collins's Betteredge says to provide sage advice "in cases of doubt and emergency."[4] As the accumulated reports of more serious Crusoe watchers make clear, he seems at various times to be the embodiment of various ideologies. On the one hand, for observers from Marx to Ian Watt, he is a representative of capitalist ideology, driven to acquire, control, and dominate. On the other hand, if we read with patience the actual text of his story and listen to recent commentators such as J. Paul Hunter and G. A. Starr, he is quite convincing as a man intent upon discovering his ultimate limitations by seeking spiritual definition and divine pattern in his life. His goal is from this point of view to abdicate responsibility, to give God the glory and take whatever shame there is upon himself. I think we must concede the accuracy of *both* these decriptions; Crusoe is in my view neither exclusively a masterful economic individual nor a heroically spiritual slave. He inhabits both ideologies in such a way that he manages to be both at once and therefore to reside in neither. What we may call the real Crusoe, the existential Crusoe that the novel aspires instinctively to deliver, is the personal energy that experiences the contradiction implicit in mimetic narrative: control in a context of helplessness and helplessness in a context of control. Crusoe can be called a converter, turning an ideology to the uses of survival and autonomy by using what it gives and neutralizing its possessive effects. He survives physically on the island, as we shall see, by means of a resourcefulness and cunning well beyond probability, but the narrative tries to assure us in various ways that his control is a mere response to circumstances. For the sake of what we must call psychological survival, to get away from the destructive effects of isolation, he realizes on the island that he is a part of providential design. He experiences and accepts divine control but that control can only be realized in the free context he has himself created. And that free context, the narrative makes us remember, is itself the result of determining circumstances stretching back to Crusoe's adolescence. In *Robinson Crusoe*, a position is always relative; the freedom and defining autonomy of the narrative self is in the consciousness (or, better, the enactment) of this dynamic relativity.

Robinson Crusoe begins with an advertisement which is a remarkably accurate adumbration of that structure of relations as it introduces some key terms and oppositions:

> If ever the story of any private man's adventures in the world were worth making publick, and were acceptable when publish'd, the editor of this account thinks this will be so.
>
> The wonders of this man's life exceed all that (he thinks) is to be found extant; the life of one man being scarce capable of a greater variety. (1)

We are used to valuing private experience. Much fiction since the mid-nineteenth century has explicitly and self-consciously set out to show how reality resides in subjective states and how public realities are mere super-structures, attenuated forms of institutions. The value of making such experience "public" in a novel is really to deny the category of public experience[5] and to exalt the aggressively unique nature of private experience. This preface claims that Crusoe has connected the public and the private, implying that in being himself he has lived the kind of private existence that is of "public" interest. But, as the next sentence of the preface makes clear, that interest does not arise because Crusoe's life resembles those of his contemporaries, not because he is the typical private man. Rather, his life is one of "wonders" unparalleled, "variety" without precedent. How, then, is Crusoe's story so worthy of public notice? It is, obviously, being sold as an extravaganza to people who, like all of us, value the exotic and the various as a pleasurable relief from the humdrum and uniform quality of daily life. Crusoe, however, domesticates wonder by industry and skill and discovers common providential arrangement in variety. He lives in an uncommon common fashion. His life is public, that is, attractive and meaningful to the typical private person, because he introduces private and common order into thrilling and uncommon events.

This special "commonness" which Crusoe exemplifies is evident at once in the opening paragraph of the narrative. It is at once unique and conventional in the history of English narrative in its brief but exact attention to sociological detail. Seventeenth-century criminal biographies supplied sociological location for their heroes and speculated briefly on why they left conventional pursuits for lives of crime. Travelers sometimes did the same. We remember that Gulliver was the third of five sons of a father who had a small estate in Nottinghamshire.[6] But Crusoe supplies information which is at first merely neutral—date of birth, details of European immigration, and naturalization in England—undifferentiated data whose purpose is to certify Crusoe not simply as a real person but as a private person, one whose life begins in random, shapeless facts.

That opening goes on to record, again with a unique attention to exact sociological data, how these facts provide an explanation of Crusoe's subsequent behaviour which is the root of his story. He is a third son, bred to no trade and *therefore* given to "rambling thoughts." These facts provide something like an explanation of behavior rather than an exact determinant of it. The issue remains uncertain. Young Crusoe is partly the result of these factors, partly the victim of a compulsive inner "propension of nature" to wander. Crusoe, from the start of his narrative, is both in and out of its circumstances. The narrative seems to reserve a part of him which is really beyond social determinants, merely natural but triggered somehow by social factors.

Now we know, as Ian Watt has put it, that Crusoe's "propension of nature" is really the internalized ideology of capitalism,[7] or rather, that dangerously dynamic aspect of capitalist ideology which must in the context of the early eighteenth century be denied and suppressed.[8] By its location here partly in circumstances and partly in the unruly nature of the individual, such desire can be presented but disavowed. Moreover, it can provide a plausible motion for its own eventual banishment to Crusoe's island, where it will be able to surface and work itself out fully but benignly. This wavering pattern of the opening pages of the book is crucial in every respect. Not only Crusoe but the nature of his world are being defined. It is a world where "nature" (a personal, internal reality, somehow given) and circumstances (that is, external in some way, historical, social facts) seem to be complementary causes of action. Again, the self must in such a situation be both in and out of circumstances. Its "nature" becomes a shifting and complex thing, sometimes given, sometimes partly "caused," sometimes private, and sometimes sliding over into public patterns like the generalized figures of fiction (the rebellious son, the ambitious traveler, the heroic castaway, the repentant sinner). In his opening paragraphs, Crusoe is infected mysteriously by nature, but this nature is at least partially rooted in the personal circumstances Crusoe has just described. He himself tells us so, although he puts it in such a way that circumstances seem responsible primarily for the earliness of the desire to leave home: "Being the third son of the family and not bred to any trade, my head began to be fill'd very early with rambling thoughts" (5).

"Rambling" is, then, a natural tendency which in Crusoe's case is triggered or aggravated by circumstances. Young men, psychological truisms permit us to agree with Crusoe, are always potentially attracted to "rambling," that is, to repudiating their fathers and establishing themselves as independent beings. The destruction of the father implicit in such an establishment seems to be what lies behind Crusoe's desire to go to sea, that is, to become rich above his father's station. To surpass him economically is in a real sense to destroy him. Capitalist ideology may be said to encourage this natural tendency much more strongly than other ideologies, but at the same time it preserves a hesitancy about the destructive implications of such ambitious energies. The official and sanitized version of capitalist ideology represented by Crusoe *père* formally disapproves of a radical separation of son from father and of the consequent destruction of father by son in surpassing him. So Crusoe's father and Crusoe himself in this narrative portray as unruly nature and/or unfortunate circumstance what is really the central energy of capitalist ideology. Crusoe is a culture hero in the literal sense because he enacts this destructive separation by means of his narrative complexity, taking on himself and deriving from himself and his circumstances the responsibility for it. The long haul toward the island and back eventually is a journey into "nature" to bring back an acceptable version of official ideology. Crusoe appropriates nature for his culture by experiencing it, that is, by deriving it simultaneously from personal reality and circumstances. The formal ambitions of his narrative to find the exact measure of will and circumstances which make up a life are a means to that cultural end. Moreover, that relativity whereby the self is presented creates by implication the autonomous self that masters the paradox.

Those formal ambitions are especially evident in the opening pages of the book. As we read we are confronted with a dance among various sorts of explanations—social, moral, and psychoreligious—for Crusoe's desire to roam. Crusoe's perspective is, of course, above these levels as analytic reporter, concerned, as his tone and manner inform us, primarily with reporting causes and conditions exactly. As his father concludes his homily, Crusoe reports rather stiffly but exactly: "I observed in this last part of his discourse ... I say, I observed the tears run down his face very plentifully, and especially, when he spoke of my brother who was kill'd" (7). He reports further that he "was sincerely affected with this discourse, as indeed who could be otherwise" (7). But the next sentence records the wearing off of this impression in a few days. Crusoe notes the irrelevance of moral discourse in the face of irrational desire; in fact, he implies in his capacity as neutral recorder the primacy of mysterious internal impulse. The deliberate and impressive circumstantiality of his account is a means of proving the compulsive nature of that internal impulse.

But young Crusoe is hardly impulsive, and his compulsion seems furthered by craft. He tries to create conditions which will be favorable for his going away, working on his mother: "However, I did not act so hastily neither as my first heat of resolution prompted, but I took my mother, at a time when I thought her a little pleasanter than ordinary" (7). He plans, in short, to go away, but neither impulsively nor formally and definitively. He wants his father's consent, he reasons with his mother, and will agree to a bargain: "if she would speak to my father to let me go but one voyage abroad, if I came home again and did not like it, I would go no more, and I would promise by a double diligence to recover that time I had lost" (7). Such diplomatic cunning is perfectly plausible psychologically and reinforces our belief in Crusoe's real desire to go to sea. But it does lessen considerably our belief in the irrationality of Crusoe as agent or executor of his desires. Crusoe is effectively separated from his desires by his cunning in executing them. To put it another way which can serve as the cryptic summary of his secret as a successful character and culture hero, he acts but does not act.

That is precisely how he first goes to sea. Despite his manipulations, his actual departure is a matter of accident: "But being one day at Hull, where I went casually, and without any purpose of making an elopement that time" (8). Even though he has been planning and resolving to go for over a year, he is finally moved by immediate impulse and circumstance. His career begins (as it is to continue) as mediation between action and control. His voluntary–involuntary beginning is a rough example and exemplar of his later career. He is both responsible and not responsible, and the convincing and specifically novelistic complexity thus evoked is a way to have action without full responsibility.

We need, perhaps, to remember the dangers and discomforts of seventeenth- and eighteenth-century sailing; most of us would choose gaol with Dr. Johnson. Understandably, Crusoe takes to the sea very slowly. And again, Defoe's commitment to the plausible is a means towards the structural consistency we are after. Crusoe in bad weather repents dramatically; when the storm subsides he responds to these new circumstances with equal complacence, only to return to even greater repentance when the storm returns. All this pathetic vacillation establishes Crusoe as the absolute dupe of circumstances, a veritable weather-vane. Such a characteristic effectively weakens the subversive independence he aspires to and will eventually achieve. Paradoxically, it also establishes the irresistible force of his compulsion to go to sea, for he resolves to continue even in the face of absolute terror not only of violent death but of his own revealed moral weakness.[9] Psychologically, Crusoe is possessed by an imperious desire which is strengthened by his own weakness; structurally, this psychological plausibility is in the service of the contradiction his story seeks to enact.

Weakness and strength, active control and passive submission are the antinomies being suspended by his narrative.

The ship sinks and Crusoe is provided with a substitute father to draw the moral. His comrade's sea-faring father warns him that these are palpable tokens of divine will. That traditionally transparent world of religious meaning, complete with Biblical figure, presented by the old sailor is followed directly in the narrative by a world of casual but pressing social and psychological particulars. Crusoe explains that he had some money with him, so he went to London by land, and that fear of ridicule kept him from taking the divine warning. The commonplace realities of psychosocial circumstance are, however, endowed by Crusoe with a mysterious significance. They are part of that inscrutable inner drive which Crusoe the narrator can only account for at this point by speculating about "a secret overruling decree that hurries us on to be the instruments of our own destruction, even tho' it be before us, and that we rush upon it with our eyes open" (13). Crusoe is tentative in offering this; he says that nothing else seems quite adequate to explain the persistence of his drive. He rejects, as we perhaps do not, the merely random and self-serving psychosocial particulars which lead him on and with which he cooperates. We know from our historical perspective what those energies are up to; we realize that the trivial facts and circumstance of personality are ultimately governed by a will to power which lies behind narrative and dream. Crusoe's baffled explanation is an instinctive and protective reversal of that will to power into a self-destructive internal mechanism or an external fate.

Throughout this first voyage and its aftermath, Crusoe remains "ignorant" in the literal sense. During the shipwreck, he is just a passenger, does not quite understand what is happening to the ship because nautical terms like "founder" mean very little to him, cannot help the crew fight the storm, and sits quaking in his cabin. He even swoons, frightened and bewildered by a gun the ship fires as a distress signal (11–12). During his second voyage, his first real trading voyage, this ignorance continues. In retrospect, Crusoe regrets that he sailed as a gentleman-adventurer-trader rather than as a sailor, in which "tho I might indeed have workt a little harder than ordinary, yet at the same time I had learn'd the duty and office of a fore-mast man; and in time might have quallified my self for a mate or lieutenant, if not for a master" (14).

Preliminary ignorance of self is a prerequisite for autobiographical protagonists; unlike picaros, who begin with infinite cunning and thorough cynicism, they exist to show us the self growing and expanding in one way or another. Crusoe is thus required to be ignorant that we may experience his acquisition of wisdom. And yet, we know that Crusoe's subsequent wisdom is fully implicit in his initial desire to go to sea. In this light, Crusoe's ignorance is a strategy for ideological coherence as well as narrative satisfaction; indeed, in *Robinson Crusoe* these two ends are always exactly parallel. It is not necessary to worry about which came first; the technique of autobiographical narrative of this kind is the working out of the implications of the ideological position it describes. The urge to acquire is given, as Marx noted, by the structure of market society, where the individual incorporates within himself the idea of private property. But the narrative is out to establish a pattern whereby the self can gradually discover outside itself that which it carries within. Thus, the assertion of a preexisting self is always what is meant by the development of the self. Crusoe is necessarily ignorant of the implications of his will to power, and his overt technical ignorance of seamanship is an intensifier which covers up those implications, or at least distracts us from them. The real task of this kind of narrative seems to be not the development of a new self but the discovery or establishment of an environment where the self can emerge without blame as a response to reality rather than as the creator of it.

In spite of his ignorance, Crusoe prospers on his voyage and learns navigation into the bargain. He acquires social identity for the first time: "this voyage made me both a sailor and a merchant" (15). The security and stability are temporary, and the next trip ends in Moorish captivity. On one level, this captivity is part of the variety of event to which the book is committed.[10] On the level of structure, it is part of the shift which takes place in Crusoe's situation from internal to external compulsion. An objective and technical problem of survival and freedom replaces the subjective need for powerful self-assertion implicit in Crusoe's original desire. In escaping from Sallee, Crusoe is free to master his environment without apologies. In narrative terms, this liberates the story to elaborate that environment with precision, not simply because it is exotic but because it is morally neutral. It is only at this point in the story that Defoe begins to place before us in any abundance the fascinating details for which he is famous. That precision is the most obvious manifestation at the level of language of the will to power that informs the book. The environment is handed over to Moors and monsters and can therefore safely be dominated and elaborated by Defoe's language and Crusoe's acts.

This is not to say that there is a melodramatic shift from that novelistic ambiguity we have observed to heroic simplicities. Here and indeed throughout *Robinson Crusoe*, what we experience as readers is that sense of freedom only within circumstances already observed. Consider the escape itself. Crusoe meditates for some two years but forms no definite plans. Specific plans involve the arrival of proper circumstances, of what Crusoe calls "an odd circumstance . . . which put the old thought of making some attempt for my liberty again in my head" (17). Out fishing one day with Crusoe and another slave, his master finds himself nearly lost at sea. He resolves for the future to refurbish a captured English longboat with a cabin, a compass, and provisions against an emergency. Crusoe, by virtue of his dexterity in taking fish, always accompanies him. It happens further and more particularly that his master is to go out in this boat "with two or three Moors of some distinction in that place, and for whom he had provided extraordinarily" (17). So the boat this time has extraordinary provisions, guns as well, since they plan to shoot as well as fish. The last crucial circumstance arrives when Crusoe's master finds that his friends are unable to go and orders him to go out in the ship thus provisioned and catch some fish for their dinner that night. Crusoe's escape is a matter of hugely fortunate circumstances combined with his eye for the main chance. This set of circumstances (a regular set-up) anticipates those that surround his survival on the island a little later in the narrative and announces his central talent: an ability in the midst of captivity to act at precisely the right moment. The structure of this escape is the same as that implicit in his "escape" from paternal restriction and the landlocked "upper station of low life," a question of waiting patiently for the inevitable fortunate moment.

A key transition is at stake here. Moorish captivity and escape mark the first conversion of Crusoe's original impulse to dominate into a will to survive. The inevitability of such a conversion and justification of the will to power is a commonplace for anyone who looks at a competitive market society. Crusoe must be taken out of the way and placed in an environment whose inhuman (or non-European) hostility converts self-aggrandizing dominance into a completely justifiable will to survive. The real function of the exotic locales in the book is to provide a suitable ground for Crusoe's energies. The process forms what Roland Barthes in another context has called the naturalization of the social and historical which is behind what he calls bourgeois myth.[11]

The capture and escape thus function as a means of setting Crusoe free for the first time from the negative responsibilities of his internalized drive to power. His story once started cannot be stopped. His inner compulsion is largely transferred to the series of external accidents and coincidences which constitute the rest of his adventures. His initial capture creates a chain of events with their own inevitable sequence. Nature and narrative logic create a liberating circle of compulsion within which Crusoe can act with an innocent desperation which gives him great power.

That power seems almost too great and the escape situation seems a melodramatic study for the more plausible and even struggles to come on the island. Here, doubtless responding to convention in such matters, Defoe drags in mysterious monsters, hideous howlings which keep Crusoe and Xury awake at night.[12] Crusoe is obtrusively original and boldly self-conscious as he fires his gun at these monsters: "But is is impossible to describe the horrible noises, and hideous cryes and howlings, that were raised, as well upon the edge of the shoar as higher within the country, upon the noise or report of the gun, a thing I have some reason to believe those creatures had never heard before" (21). Similarly, when he and Xury meet friendly Negroes, Crusoe asserts himself by shooting a monster which is about to attack them. The Negroes then skin the brute, taking the meat and giving Crusoe the skin. They display in the process their skills and native crafts; they bring water in "a great vessel made of earth, and burnt as I suppose in the sun" (25). Once Crusoe establishes his power and technological superiority, anthropological observations are possible. Clearly, all this anticipates the sequence of events on the island, although in hasty, crude, and sketchy form. Such repetition and elaboration of pattern are signs of the story's affinities with myth so often remarked upon. What is novelistically crude is appropriate in myth, where, as Levi-Strauss observes, "the function of repetition is to render the structure of the myth apparent."[13]

However, Crusoe is a crypto-hero and his story true rather than mythical; his power and autonomy are only permitted to emerge within the world of circumstances that the novel specialized in and myth excludes. So he is "delivered" by a Portuguese ship and returned to the chain of circumstances that constitute his life. Luck and accident in this case complete heroic escape and European self-establishment among beasts and savages, as indeed they are to conclude matters later on in the story. These conclusions point to a recurring problem. The central fantasy of the book has to be grounded somehow in those social and psychological realities to which the book is committed. Crusoe therefore is given solid reason to continue in his quest for satisfaction in the facts surrounding his prosperity as a planter in Brazil. He describes with characteristic clarity how he and his neighbor planned their crops and cleared their ground but also how his old desires thereby returned: "I had no remedy but to go on; I was gotten into an employment quite remote to my genius, and directly contrary to the life

I delighted in, and for which I forsook my father's house and broke thro' all his good advice; nay I was coming into the very middle station or upper degree of low life, which my father advised me to before" (28). The repetition which myth requires is here the plausible result of the reawakening of Crusoe's initial desires among the social realities of farming in Brazil, cunningly turned into the acceptable cycle of psycho-social probability. The indefatigable desires of the self that Crusoe so clearly if casually describes are not gratuitously asserted but made to grow out of the handy and opposite circumstances which repeat his original situation in England. In a sense, the circumstances exist to provoke the self and return it to its mythic direction without violating the mimetic decorum of the novel, indeed by paying exact attention to it.

This survey of the preliminary situations of Crusoe's career reveals, I think, the central and essentially double view the narrative takes toward its incidents. Reality is richly served, and my commentary necessarily violates the thick texture of inner and outer circumstance the narrative delivers. But that convincingly tangled surface invariably resolves itself into situations which propel Crusoe forward, which seem to be obstacles but which are as we read remarkably similar occasions for self-display. Beneath the mimetic fullness and apparent variety, there is what can only be called an energy which may be said to turn each situation toward a variation on the theme of self-assertion.

That energy and its capacity for turning the randomly varied world of mimetic narrative into a self-expressive structure emerge in their fullness on the island, where fidelity to mimetic decorum is naturally more prominent than ever. On the island, Defoe's exact rendering of things and events is at its clearest and most intense, partly because exactness becomes most necessary here as an opposite to the formlessness of the island. In other words, the technique of self-analysis combined with scrupulous external observation that Defoe gives his hero reveals itself here clearly for what it is: a means of blameless self-assertion. That technique is often praised as an end in itself; an achievement that speaks for itself; but I think it is more important and critically relevant to analyse Crusoe's talents as analytic reporter in the context of their function in the narrative considered as a whole. Crusoe isolated so dramatically is in a position to speak about himself and his circumstances in a new way which eventually allows him that maximum of freedom and virtual autonomy as a character that his narrative aspires to achieve for him. I think we can say that in time he becomes on the island a contemplative consciousness who can literally observe himself at work, resembling in that fruitful split the master in Hegel's formulation who interposes the slave between the thing and himself and thereby achieves freedom.[14] Indeed, the point of my commmentary from here on is to observe Crusoe's expanding but carefully qualified power, to see how precisely he extracts control within the limitations of circumstances.

To be sure, Crusoe's control is partly an aspect of the retrospective narrative position which he shares with Defoe's other autobiographers. They are writing their own stories, and we are conscious of them as master of their autobiographies, above events in that elementary sense. But Crusoe's relationship to events has a dynamic quality that we have already experienced if we have read this far in his book, but which becomes more regular and even obtrusive when he reaches the island. Consider the shipwreck itself, a rush of meticulously rendered descriptive details but preceded and indeed punctuated by a phrase which is characteristic of Defoe's narratives at moments of stress. The ship in the storm suddenly strikes a sand bar: "It is not easy for any one, who has not been in the like condition, to describe or conceive the consternation of men in such circumstances" (33). What is implicit in such a statement is a world of pure compulsion *as experienced*, that is, of the frenzied simultaneity of a reality which admits of no human mediation at all and which taxes the limited linear resources of the novel. Crusoe's next step is to violate the blurred reality of such a sentence by outlining the situation as a set of possibilities: " . . . we knew nothing where we were, or upon what land it was we were driven, whether an island or the main, whether inhabited or not inhabited; and as the rage of the wind was still great, tho' rather less than at first, we could not so much as hope to have the ship hold many minutes without breaking in pieces, unless the winds by a kind of miracle should turn immediately about" (33). To provide shape and calm sequence in the middle of the disasters of experience is a function of any retrospective narrator, but Crusoe is also aware of the desirability of conveying the emotional immediacy of the situation. His recourse to the initial formula of the impossibility of rendering experience is evidence of that. What he is in fact doing is establishing a narrative point between the world of experience and the world of narrative, that is, between the unruly and actually incommunicable world of reality as experienced and the lucid, controlled world of narrative. Throughout his narrative, Crusoe will continue to allude to that inchoate world of experience and indeed succeed in making us see it to some extent, but only by constantly giving up the attempt to describe it and rendering it in the solid sequences of orderly narrative. What we read is not simply the sequence but the sequence offering itself again and again as a partial description and evocation of the experience itself. The eventual result of that delicate balance is to give us the world of experience as such where the "slave" exists and to allow us at the same time to occupy the privileged position of the "master."

To continue the example: Crusoe's ability to evoke confusion and render a convincing and potentially involving version of experience is beyond question here in the shipwreck scene. (Compare Gulliver's calm and totally emotionless descriptions of similar disasters.) But in that rush of detail, we observe signs of the control that keeps us sufficiently in control to read and sufficiently out of control to participate. "Nothing can describe the confusion of thought which I felt when I sunk into the water" (34), says Crusoe at once. He leaves us to insert or to charge what follows with the appropriate turmoil, but the invocation of that turmoil is necessary. What follows is an almost completely objective description of action, of how Crusoe survives, what he does and the tactical reasons for doing it: "I had so much presence of mind as well as breath left, that seeing my self nearer the main land than I expected, I got upon my feet and endeavoured to make on towards the land as fast as I could" (35). At this point in the paragraph, there occurs the only metaphor for several pages, one of the few figurative moments in the language of the shipwreck scene: "I saw the sea come after me as high as a great hill, and as furious as an enemy which I had no means or strength to contend with" (35). His business, he tells us, is not to contend but to co-operate, to hold his breath and try to maintain the kind of neutral position which will use the force of the surf as a propellant towards the shore. The simile is exactly appropriate at this point: its first part is a way of measuring and describing and its second has a tactical rather than emotional content. It is a way of figuring Crusoe's refusal to over-step himself either in action or in language. Even this figurative moment is of a piece with the rigorously descriptive and analytic function of these paragraphs. The figurative surface contributes to the deeper opposition between control and participation, reminds us of the initial compulsion and confusion, and reinvokes the emotional tone set some sentences before at the beginni..ₒ of the sequence.

We are conscious here and elsewhere in the book of a world of unruly and therefore fascinating forces—experience, in short. But in the midst of all that welter of observation are the occasional analytic details which establish human understanding and implicit control of that world. That is the discernible shape and disposition of Defoe's narrative prose: a series of descriptive clauses and then the analytic phrase, the clarifying insight which makes the previous clauses cohere. "I stood still a few moments to recover breath and till the water went from me, and then took to my heels, and run with what strength I had further towards the shore. But neither would this deliver me from the fury of the sea, which came pouring in after me again, and twice more I was lifted up by the waves and carried forwards as before, the shore being very flat" (35). Crusoe's understanding of the relationship between surf and shore anticipates his shrewd understanding in time of the island. We are conscious in the very arrangements of Defoe's prose of a continuous and dynamic movement between experience exactly observed and the experiencing and narrating self, and that swing in the prose is a metonymic reflection of the substance of the narrative in its most profound sense.

The dynamic substance is clearest in what Crusoe tells us about how he came to keep a journal, only beginning to keep it after he had achieved some mastery of himself and the island. If he had kept it from the first, the journal would have been full of what he calls "many dull things."

> For example, I must have said thus: "Sept. the 30th.
>
> After I got to shore and had escap'd drowning, instead of being thankful to God for my deliverance, having first vomited with the great quantity of salt water which was gotten into my stomach, and recovering my self a little, I ran about the shore, wringing my hands and beating my head and face, exclaiming at my misery, and crying out, I was undone, undone, till tyr'd and faint I was forc'd to lye down on the ground to repose, but durst not sleep for fear of being devour'd." (52)

In this passage from the journal that he chose not to write Crusoe is merely what other historically authenticated lone survivors became. This hysterical, formless, and naturally self-destructive aspect of Crusoe is only touched upon, although it is the threatening chaos implicit in his subsequent ordering of things. His paranoia, of course, continues unabated, but it is as much a fear of this formless, self-destructive self as it is of external enemies.[15]

Nature and the natural self are overcome by a form of self-assertion of which the journal is only the most obvious manifestation. Crusoe's gradual discovery of God and his acquistion of what he identifies as spiritual consciousness of God's presence and operation in his life are ways to enforce that self, to acquire a self which is, like God, beyond nature and yet in nature. Crusoe's spirituality does not, therefore, contradict his talents as survivor; it is a formalization, in effect, of his own masterful relationship to the environment.

If we look at Crusoe's survival after the initial shocked stupidity of being thrown upon the beach, it is a continuation of his behavior in the water: clear-eyed cooperation with circumstances. As the Spaniard remarks after hearing of all this in the *Farther Adventures,* this is a remarkable achievment: "'had we poor Spaniards been in your case, we should never have gotten half those things out of the ship, as you did: nay,' says he, 'we should never have found means to have gotten a raft to carry them, or to have gotten the raft on shore without boat or sail; and how much less should we have done,' said he, 'if any of us had been alone!'" (294). Crusoe works with unbelievable care, and the secret of his success lies in watching the tides and co-operating with their flow. But even in the middle of heroic ingenuity and improbable steadiness, there are unstable forces at work, a portion of that formless and hysterical self that threatened him when he landed. In the middle of his tidewatching and planning, Crusoe begins to wonder "why Providence should thus compleatly ruine its creatures, and render them so absolutely miserable, so without help abandon'd, so entirely depress'd, that it could hardly be rational to be thankful for such a life" (47). But "something always return'd swift upon me to check these thoughts" (47). Crusoe casts up an account at this point and ends rumination with a proverb: "All evils are to be considered with the good that is in them, and with what worse attends them" (48). By themselves, such ruminations are uninteresting; proverbs like this one are normally excuses for inaction. But in the context of Crusoe's remarkable feat of survival, the division of experience into good and bad, useful and destructive, and the analysis of circumstances implicit in the proverb are heroic acts which are the center of Crusoe's character. Just As God cooperates with natural process and even employs disasters to further his mysterious ends, Crusoe finds meaning in flux, holds back his own potential hysteria, and converts disaster and accident into fortune and plan.

His casting of accounts is as admirable a feat in his context as mastering the tides and building a raft to get the goods from the ship. Both are analytic acts, both involve a separation of the self from circumstances in order to master them by cooperating with their flow. It is no accident that Crusoe begins to speak at this point as if he operated on himself as well, as if he had a self which dealt in various ways with another part of himself. This is perhaps an existential inevitability which is perceived in common speech: "I made myself do it," we say, meaning really that there is a part of us that is self-consciously apart from our functioning self. Crusoe exists at this point in his narrative in that world of self-consciousness that we ordinarily conventionalize; indeed, it is for him a means of survival rather than a manner of speaking: " . . . as my reason began now to master my despondency, I began to comfort my self as well as I could, and to set the good against the evil, that I might have something to distinguish my case from worse, and I stated it very impartially, like debtor and creditor, the comforts I enjoy'd against the miseries I suffer'd" (50). In the context of his exertions, such reflections are more than pious platitudes; the "I" that performs this operation has asserted itself impressively and coherently. The other self that is negated is like the potentially destructive world of tides and winds that surrounds him.

Crusoe's techniques of self-assurance can be derived from the methods of Protestant self-consciousness, but the meaning and ultimate function of these spiritual techniques are inseparable from Crusoe's position in his book and on his island. Although Crusoe has to learn certain specific techniques such as building, pot-making, baking, etc., he is essentially knowledgeable in the over-all technique and internal disposition for physical survival. He seems to know *how to learn*. He tells us that such is not the case when it comes to spiritual survival; he pictures himself as insensible to God's mercy and goodness, occasionally confused by his bad fortune and indifferent the rest of the time to God's role or presence in his life. The casting of accounts is an effective but temporary stay against confusion, that is against the psycho-spiritual uncertainty that Crusoe tells us was a real danger until his "conversion." That conversion occurs slowly, surrounded by the continuing details of survival, and, given the efficiency of Crusoe's proceedings, we may wonder why that conversion is necessary at all. We may easily be tempted and forgiven for dismissing all this religious rigmarole as Defoe's cunning or boring insertion of piety. But Crusoe's story is coherent and whole and the religious experience is part of his total survival. The answer to our unease with it lies, I think, in his solitude, an untenable human situation but a necessary one for the needs of this particular narrative. In our context as readers of the narrative, "conversion" is an informative pun on what really happens. To be that delicately powerful master-slave the narrative requires, Crusoe has to be converted in part into a passive figure who is delivered by God, that is, whose active survival and the identity which that involves have to be guaranteed by some outside force beyond the random flow of circumstance, some force that is on the side of order and pattern and meaning. Crusoe's competence at survival is a sign of his potentiality for virtual autonomy, but he can hardly be the only one who establishes order and pattern and meaning. Thus, before his conversion he suffers from what we may call with R. D. Laing a form of "ontological insecurity." Laing's description of that state is useful and relevant here:

> The individual in the ordinary circumstances of living may feel more unreal than real; in a literal sense, more dead than alive; precariously differentiated from the rest of the world, so that his identity and autonomy are always in question. He may lack the experience of his own temporal continuity. He may not possess an over-riding sense of personal consistency or cohesiveness. He may feel more insubstantial than substantial, and unable to assume that the stuff he is made of is genuine, good, valuable. And he may feel his self as partially divorced from his body.
> ... the ontologically insecure person is preoccupied with preserving rather than gratifying himself: the ordinary circumstances of living threaten his *low threshold* of security.[16]

Now Crusoe is not in "ordinary circumstances"; his singular situation makes him liable to the symptoms of schizophrenia that Laing describes but at the same time facilitates by its externality his ability to correct those symptoms. To that end, he established identity and his own temporal continuity: he makes his own calendar and his own house and clothing and so on. He is forced to be preoccupied with survival, so that, to use Laing's terms, surviving becomes a form of gratification. But in order, finally, to feel more substantial than insubstantial and to establish his value and worth, in order definitively to avoid the schizophrenia Laing describes, he needs a God who enforces his new way of living, whose ways are his ways. He has already left behind the God of his father back in England, a God who rewards complacency in a complacent fashion. This new God is to be an ingenious artisan, a force who in fashioning Crusoe's life is both in and out of nature, like Crusoe in building and expanding continuously. Looking at the economy of the novel, we can say that what happens is Crusoe's conversion of God from an antagonist into an ally.

That kind of God begins to be revealed to Crusoe early in his journal. There he records how he was astounded to find one day ten or twelve ears of green barley growing by his cave and how he took this for a miracle:

" ... that God had miraculously caus'd this grain to grow without any help of seed sown, and that it was directed purely for my sustenance on that wild miserable place" (59). But then the world of mere circumstance is discovered to be responsible; the barley has grown from some chicken feed Crusoe shook out of a bag he wished to use. Crusoe's "religious thankfulness to God's providence" abates "upon the discovering that all this was nothing but what was common" (59). Now the mature Crusoe of a bit later in the narrative learns to see this as a virtual miracle. God has used this devious chain of circumstances to provide corn, "as if it had been dropt from heaven" (59). The mature Crusoe learns to see the dialectic between secular detail and divine order and to see that God works his uncommon ways with common things. It is miraculous that some corn should have remained unspoiled, that Crusoe should throw it out at that place, "it being in the shade of a high rock . . . whereas, if I had thrown it anywhere else at that time, it had been burnt up and destroy'd" (59). The world of mere circumstance is not transcended, but rather intensified in its importance. Just as Crusoe survives physically by watching for favorable forces in the chaotic appearance of nature, he survives on a psycho-spiritual level by learning to see God's presence in the minutest disposition of his circumstances. For us as readers, this is effectively a reinforcement and validation of our delight in the details of the narrative. Our attention is a means of participating in that world of richly satisfying order at every level, from Crusoe's domestic arrangements to the divine arrangements Crusoe perceives.

Crusoe's need for that God as something which validates his solitary being and provides an analogue for his order becomes evident in the next sequence as he falls ill with a fever and describes a dreadful dream of religious warning in which he sees a powerful and mysterious figure who threatens him with death. But the nightmare does not precipitate his religious crisis; it is simply a symptom of his bodily and spiritual confusion. Defoe makes Crusoe travel towards his conversion through the clinical reports of his physical illness. It is impossible even for us (practised as we are at such reactions) to experience that illness as a reductive comment on his spirituality, mainly because the narrative is so firmly committed to the factual aspects of Crusoe's survival and this "spirituality" is so manifestly a necessary consequence of that factual survival. For the main conversion experience is not the dream, which as such belongs to the shapeless and potentially unmanageable aspect of experience that the book is out to dominate. The dream is clearly presented as the kind of experience that can be evoked but not described: the destroying angel in the dream is "all over as bright as a flame, so that I could but just bear to look towards him; his countenance was most inexpressibly dreadful, impossible for words to describe" (65). What actually effects the conversion is Crusoe's search for tobacco, which he explains, with the solid verification the book specializes in, the Brazilians take "for almost all distempers" (69). He finds the tobacco, along with a Bible, and then tells us in great detail how he experimented with taking the tobacco and, in a fuddled condition from his fever and the tobacco, opened the Bible "casually" and read, "Call on me in the day of trouble, and I will deliver, and thou shalt glorify me" (70). Even at so dramatic a moment, Crusoe continues to report circumstances and to describe alternatively his physical treatment and its results and the accompanying clarity and leisure for religious meditation: "while I was thus gathering strength, my thoughts run exceedingly upon this scripture, *I will deliver thee*" (71). Crusoe delivers himself at last by meditating upon the situation and the text; he has been delivered from sickness, if not from the island.

Once again, Crusoe's immersion in the minutest facts of his existence provides the solution and enables him to survive. Sickness, the most obvious kind of victimization of an individual by circumstance, becomes a means of self-knowledge and eventual freedom. Sickness gives Crusoe the opportunity to report his symptoms, to distance himself from his physical and psychological self, for his sickness induces a kind of delirium. Crusoe is able in his narrative to treat himself as a thing, as something which because of its weakness can enter into the flow of objects and events which constitutes natural reality. Once in that reality, Crusoe can be led by an exact and complicated but entirely visible chain of circumstances stretching back in his history towards the tobacco and the Bible; he can observe himself getting better and see himself in the process of regaining health as participating in the partially benign forces that God inserts into nature. Heretofore, Crusoe observed for his own survival, marked carefully how external phenomena can be made to yield human direction and bent carefully to human purpose. Now he himself, body and soul, joins that company of natural phenomena. He observes "himself," he achieves by sickness the perspective that Hegel called the "master." Part of himself remains the "slave," indeed the point is that part of him becomes for the first time entirely perceived in his narrative as the slave of circumstance, committed fully and clearly to a chain of events going back to his origins. He has always been part of that chain, but as readers of the sickness–conversion sequence we are being involved in the operative reality of that chain and in the simultaneous freedom implicit in our and Crusoe's consciousness of that necessity and cooperation with it. We and Crusoe join God in cooperating with that chain of circumstances, for God inserts his purpose (i.e. Crusoe's conversion) into circumstances without violating their natural logic.

Crusoe's exact description of his return to health and his examination of the word "deliverance" are worth looking at, since they reveal quite explicitly how he achieves freedom by perfect submission to those circumstances:

> But as I was discouraging my self with such thoughts, it occurr'd to my mind that I pored so much upon my deliverance from the main affliction, that I disregarded the deliverance I had receiv'd; and *I was, as it were, made to ask my self* such questions as these, viz. Have I not been deliver'd, and wonderfully too, from sickness? from the most distress'd condition that could be, and that was so frightful to me? and what notice had I taken of it? Had I done my part? God had deliver'd me, but I had not glorify'd Him; that is to say, I had not own'd and been thankful for that as a deliverance; and how cou'd I expect greater deliverance?
>
> This touch'd my heart very much, and immediately I kneel'd down and gave God thanks aloud for my recovery from my sickness. (71, my italics)

Necessarily, Crusoe talks to himself, but it is circumstance that forces him to ask the crucial questions of himself. He is no longer casting an account, as we observed him earlier in a more independent and crude ethical phase; he is himself part of an account. Before, Crusoe had balanced circumstances, splitting them into positive and negative, debit and credit. Here he becomes part of God's ledger, owing certain services for certain services. It is a tremendous relief, a validation of what had been an entirely personal survival. And the next day, while reading the New Testament, Crusoe reads another text whose relevance completes the conversion experience: "*He is exalted a Prince and a Saviour, to give repentance, and to give remission.* I threw down the book, and with my heart as well as my hands lifted up to heaven, in a kind of extasy of joy, I cry'd out aloud, 'Jesus, thou son of David, Jesus, thou exalted Prince and Saviour, give me repentance!'" (72). Crusoe is "converted" into a petitioner, changed from an omnicompetent engineer into a primitive and fearful supplicant. But we know as readers that he experiences this extravagant and conventional dependence in a postion of radically complete security. He does not, we remember, fall ill until his habitation is complete and secure: his walls have been finished; the wrecked ship has been systematically stripped of all that can be used and we hear no more of it. Structurally, his sickness can be regarded as a guilty response to his assertive survival, the complete opposite of the miracle of independent action, a kind of compensatory withdrawal into formless passivity and a desire for validation of the order established by the self.

The conversion, in fact, enables Crusoe to leave his paranoid seclusion and to convert his island from a prison into a garden. From this point on, Crusoe turns to the island itself, exploring it, domesticating it, and indeed enjoying it in various ways. The self, liberated from survival by a reciprocal relationship with an "other," is free to gratify itself. Crusoe experiences power for the first time, "a secret kind of pleasure (tho' mixt with my other afflicting thoughts) to think that this was all my own, that I was king and lord of all this country indefeasibly, and had a right of possession" (74). Now the countryside appears "so fresh, so green, so flourishing, every thing being in a constant verdure or flourish of spring, that it looked like a planted garden" (74). In all this, the structure emerges only as something which is suspended in the tentative resolutions of the narrative. Crusoe's condition "began now to be, tho' not less miserable as to my way of living, yet much easier to my mind" (72). In time (eleven days we are told) and within the qualifications of psychological relativity, he takes a survey of the island and begins to enumerate its positive side. Like Marvell's sojourner in the garden, he finds "mellons upon the ground in great abundance, and grapes upon the trees; the vines had spread indeed over the trees, and the clusters of grapes were just now in their prime, very ripe and rich" (74). But quite unlike Marvell's Adam, he notes that this is an equivocal paradise, the grapes are dangerous if eaten as they are. He remembers several Englishmen in Barbary killed by "fluxes and feavers" from eating such. Crusoe converts them into raisins by drying them, "wholesom as agreeable to eat" (74).

That detail of Crusoe's Eden can stand as a perfect example of Crusoe's new condition: the recipient of divine deliverance, he understands that God is only partially present in what he gives, and so he converts or refines nature into that which sustains and nourishes. Having himself experienced pure activity and pure passivity, he can now in his lordship of the island set about reconciling or balancing the contradiction to be found everywhere upon it. It is a new step from the cunning observation and defensive building he did when he first arrived, and it is also unlike the passive stasis of his sickness. His new condition is the synthesis which results from the thesis and antithesis of pure action and pure passivity. This part of the book can therefore display Crusoe as the perfect mediator. Having reconciled contradiction in himself, he moves among contradictions, resolving them. He discovers that the island has wet and dry seasons, he builds a "villa" for pleasure to balance his secure fortress for survival, he tames wild things (a parrot, then goats), he despises the surplus value of his gold and celebrates useful things but keeps his gold anyway, in effect reconciling the two systems of value. He is able to speak jauntily "of my reign or my captivity, which you please" (101). Such activities enable us to see a meaning in Crusoe's new condition which makes it more than the simple religious tranquillity he claims it is. Crusoe sings a *contemptus mundi* tune even while we rejoice in his expanding and ever more orderly island world. Crusoe's independence is really his achievement of the Hegelian mastership; he has done with the thing and is not contained in its being as a thing but "enjoys it without qualification and without reserve. The aspect of its independence he leaves to the servant, who labors upon it."[17] There is a part of Crusoe which "labors" upon the island in these various and fascinating ways, but the true gratification Crusoe derives from it is a matter of his freedom from the fact of the island, the island as a constellation of forces and things which threaten his being in their natural formlessness, their character as undifferentiated and (as we know) potentially dangerous phenomena. It is his mastership and the authentic gratification it implies that are being asserted when Crusoe describes his spiritual indifference:

In the middle of this work [he has been building what will be an unusable boat], I finish'd my fourth year in this place, and kept my anniversary with the same devotion, and with as much comfort as ever before; for by a constant study and serious application of the word of God and by the assistance of His grace, I gain'd a different knowledge from what I had before. I entertain'd different notions of things I look'd now upon the world as a thing remote, which I had nothing to do with, no expectation from, and indeed no desires about: in a word, I had nothing indeed to do with it, nor was ever like to have; so I thought it look'd as we may perhaps look upon it hereafter, viz. as a place I had liv'd in, but was come out of it, and well might I say, as Father Abraham to Dives, *Between me and thee is a great gulph fix'd.*   (94–5)

Significantly, it is at this point that Crusoe's self-consciousness develops to the extent that he is able to think in coherent autobiographical terms. Previously, he had only been able to look back at flashes of his past, to regret this or that imprudence or to bewail a present deficiency. Now he reviews his life, considers the causes of his wandering and of his relative indifference to God and finds at last that God has forgiven him and is in process of showing him mercy. His new sense of self, his new mastership, provides access to the Puritan world-view, with its emblems, types, allusions, and metaphors,[18] and that scheme provides his autobiography with a shape by giving him a coherent past. But that world-view is in Crusoe's case expression of an inner coherence which can now recapture the past and enjoy the spectacle of the self surviving into the present. He spends, he tells us, "whole hours, I may say whole days' thinking what would have become of him without the goods from the ship. The picture that holds Crusoe's attention is his significant anti-type, either dead or worse, a "meer savage; that if I had killed a goat or a fowl, by any contrivance, I had no way to flea or open them, or part the flesh from the skin and the bowels, or to cut it up; but must gnaw it with my teeth and pull it with my claw like a beast" (96). The graphic insistence of this vision in the context of Crusoe's order and what we know of its establishment tells us that Crusoe's thankfulness is an indirect expression of his triumph and satisfaction over avoiding that hideous alternative. Crusoe can safely invoke Elijah's survival as a type of his own; he intends no irony and considers the relative benignity of his environment as quite the equivalent of the prophet's ravens. Praising the mildness of his God-given environment is a way of neutralizing what Crusoe fears most, what he stands most clearly against and what we have already defined as the turbulent world of experience *per se* that the novel posits and then refines: "I found no ravenous beast, no furious wolves or tygers to threaten my life, no venemous creatures, or poisonous, which I might feed on to my hurt, no savages to murther and devour me" (98). What is chiefly of interest, what we as readers experience through Crusoe's thankful autobiographical pause, is the antithesis between Crusoe as atavistic savage or beast and Crusoe as orderly master of himself and his island. That is the opposition that informs this section, and our calm experience of it is the culmination of our experience so far as readers and satisfied onlookers. In fact, what Crusoe really learns to do in every way through his conversion is to experience by means of contradiction, to keep before himself (in his terms) what he might have been if God had indeed abandoned him. To experience anything properly, that is to see through it and understand its meaning, the event must be doubled, seen as part of a system of alternatives. Of course, what that comes to for Crusoe is keeping before himself the image of various anti-Crusoes, the beast and savage at his fiercest, but also the Crusoe who fails to plan (building a boat too large to move to the water) or the "rash and ignorant" pilot who finds his boat carried out to sea. In this temporarily hopeless state, Crusoe looks back at the island and reproaches himself with his "unthankful temper, and how I had repin'd at my solitary condition; and now what would I give to be on shore there again! Thus we never see the true state of our condition till it is illustrated to us by its contraries, nor know how to value what we enjoy, but by the want of it" (102–3).

We are never very far from that central antithesis, especially in that stretch of the book from Crusoe's conversion to his discovery of the footprint. Crusoe in that time provides us with the most extensive descriptions of his technology: making clothes, boatbuilding, pot-making, basket weaving—culminating, within his own hierarchy, in the taming of wild goats. This last achievement is crucial for his comfort if not his survival, because his powder has run out. In his context, meat or game is not only an important food but a defining food; it is culturally superior to fish and grain and is part of his sustaining order. Crusoe's informal recapitulation of the history of civilization appears here at its most coherent, and the transition from the hunting to the domestication of animals for food is a momentous one in terms of establishing human control and regularity. It is at this point that Crusoe can speak, jokingly to be sure, of political power and of total domination of his island. In taming the goats, he possesses nature in a thoroughgoing way, exceeding the dominance implicit in agriculture, which is after all something of a cooperation with natural forces. "It would have made a stoick smile to have seen me and my little family sit down to dinner; there was my majesty the prince and lord of the whole island; I had the lives of all my subjects at my absolute command; I could hang, draw, give liberty, and take it away, and no rebels among all my subjects" (109).

But to attend to the symmetry of this act and its place in the narrative is to see another and even more coherent principle in operation. Like all his technology but more clearly than any other act, the taming of the goats repeats Crusoe's own story; it is a re-enactment of the conversion of his own unruly nature (that fatal propension for wandering which began it all) by God, who catches Crusoe on the island and tames him the same way that Crusoe catches goats in a pit and tames them. Crusoe's entire career on the island as a bringer of order is, by extension, a taming of his externalized self. I am not suggesting that Defoe intended the goats as a "symbol," or that Crusoe in any way transfers his guilt to them as scapegoats. As elsewhere in this study, I am positing a level of coherence which is below the consciousness or explicit intention of author and character and which is, rather, implicit in the reader's experience and which constitutes the system or language by which the book exists.

And it is precisely at this point in the narrative, when the island has been totally possessed by Crusoe, when it is fully an extension of himself, that he discovers the footprint on the beach. Crusoe has all along feared others, although his paranoia has diminished with his growing powers. That he should now find that he had indeed been in danger all along, that his possession and rule of the island are in some sense illusory is a recapitulation of the primal bourgeois scene. The free individual discovers that he is threatened by other individuals whose claim to freedom is as total as his own. Crusoe's fear and ultimate rage are compounded of classic Hobbesian aggression and jealousy. Moreover, those rivals will turn out to be cannibals, that is, nothing less than full-fledged embodiments of the antitype of himself that haunts Crusoe's imagination and sustains him in his drive for order and towards civilization. Crusoe has established "culture" in nature, but nature returns with a vengeance in the person of the cannibals.

It is worth noticing that there is no novelistic preparation for the footprint, no transition is offered, merely an abrupt new topic: "But now I come to a new scene of my life" (113). The abruptness is appropriate in several ways, the first and most obvious one of which may be described as psychological. It is accurate and inevitable that Crusoe's serenity should lead to turbulence, that he should face the greatest danger when he is totally secure. But the inevitable irony of desire thus uncovered is really a way of proving the inevitability of bourgeois society: serenity need not be eternally followed by its psychological opposite, but it must always be so in a bourgeois society where the price of freedom, as politicians still say, is eternal vigilance. Psychological patterns are insisted upon when they coincide with social patterns.

On another level, the abruptness reveals the structure I have been talking about. *Robinson Crusoe* deals in extremes; it presents a world where one state is transformed into its opposite and where the secret of survival is a talent for changing violent transpositions into gradual adaptations. Crusoe is here once again literally hurled back onto the world of mere nature, and that thrust from absolute solitude to dangerous society, from pastoral isolation and mock empire to a realistic state of war, is enacted and heightened dramatically by this violent shift in the action. What Crusoe must learn to do in this section is to repeat the stabilizing and possessive operation he has performed first upon himself and then upon his island, and now upon others, that is, upon society.

That situation and the beginnings of the controlling operation are implicit in Crusoe's rendition of his shock upon seeing the footprint:

But after innumerable fluttering thoughts, like a man perfectly confus'd and out of my self, I came home to my fortification, not feeling, as we say, the ground I went on, but terrify'd to the last degree, looking behind me at every two or three steps, mistaking every bush and tree, and fancying every stump at a distance to be a man; nor is it possible to describe how many various shapes affrighted imagination represented things to me in, how many wild ideas were found every moment in my fancy, and what strange unaccountable whimsies came into my thoughts by the way. (113)

Characteristically, Crusoe refuses to reproduce confused emotions and delivers a careful rendition of the external facts of behavior; he sketches a scenario of movements and alludes to internal disorder too vast to render. Note the apology ("as we say") for the imprecise, colloquially figurative expression he needs to describe the physical feeling of terror: "not feeling . . . the ground I went on" (113). He is out of himself and surrounded by others; the most intense subjectivity induced by the fear of others eliminates the balanced, "objective" subjectivity Crusoe has painfully acquired, and he experiences himself as a subject pure and simple, a wildly erratic collection of responses to the threatening stimuli. The re-introduction of "spontaneous" subjectivity reveals definitively for us and Crusoe the dangers and the persistence of nature.

The ensuing long debate that occupies Crusoe for many pages until the last defeat of the cannibals is still another kind of accounting whereby Crusoe seeks to escape this destructive spontaneity, to exhaust reality by listing its alternative formulations, hoping to stand at last quite apart from their world of cause and effect. What Crusoe really seeks, in short, is to reenact the mastery he has already achieved. The beginning of that distancing, the theoretical underpinning for his autonomy, is laid out at the beginnings of the internal debate: "How strange a chequer work of providence is the life of man! and by what secret differing springs are the affections hurry'd about as differing circumstances present! To day we love what to morrow we hate; to day we seek what to morrow we shun; to day we desire what to morrow we fear, nay, even tremble at the apprehensions of; this was exemplify'd in me at this time in the most lively manner imaginable" (114–15). On one level, this is mere sententious verbalizing, Christian stoicism of an uninteresting sort. But in the imaginative context of Crusoe's problem within the narrative, it is an anatomy of experience which enables him to stand both in and out of experience, to be in those contraries and eventually to stand apart from them in the moment of action which is a magical combination of both.

For what Crusoe does in the debate is to explore those contradictions by verbalizing them intensely. After seeing the cannibals, he jumps rapidly from violent and eloquent moral disgust and elaborate schemes for destroying them to impeccably enlightened anthropological and historicist tolerance to clear-headed self-preservation. He embraces all these positions with equal fervor, seems to hold them all with equal if temporary conviction. His final decision is to do nothing, to leave it all to God, to obey impulse: in his words, to obey "a secret hint . . . a strange impression upon the mind, from we know not what springs" (128). Thus, when the moment for action finally comes, none of the coherent plans or postures is quite relevant. Crusoe acts, to be sure, but he acts because of the totally unforeseen and purely haphazard circumstances he is by this time so at home in. Action is a reflex which has little to do with consciousness. Action, in fact, is a matter of watching the unpredictable flow of events for an opening, of cooperating with events at the moment when they will serve, that is, of observation and submission such as Crusoe has used in his previous triumphs. Throughout this long period of suspenseful watching and contradictory planning, Crusoe is changed from a planter-colonist into a fearful observer as much of his own shifting desires and fantasies as of the coastline for cannibal enemies. He comes close to disastrous action, almost reverts to his first condition as a man of naively aggressive action: "All my calm of mind in my resignation to providence, and waiting the issue of the dispositions of Heaven, seem'd to be suspended, and I had, as it were, no power to turn my thoughts to any thing, but to the project of a voyage to the main, which came upon me with such force, and such an impetuosity of desire, that it was not to be resisted" (144). Such direct human assertion is a vulgar surrender to nature; it reduces reality to a simple challenge issued by nature and places the actor in an impossible heroic situation in which he must struggle directly with oppressive circumstances. Survival in Defoe's narratives typically involves a strong temptation towards such action. Indeed, the central problem of all narratives is to find a mode of action which mediates between the impossible heroic and the untenable actual.

Crusoe is saved from the novelistic disaster of simple heroism by a dream, a remarkably prophetic one. He dreams of "two canoes and eleven savages" who bring another one to kill and eat. The prisoner escapes and Crusoe takes him in: " . . . he came running into my little thick grove before my fortification, to hide himself; and that I seeing him alone, and not perceiving that the others sought him that way, show'd myself to him, and smiling upon him, encourag'd him; that he kneel'd down to me, seeming to pray me to assist him; upon which I shew'd my ladder, made him go up, and carry'd him into my cave, and he became my servant" (145). In his dream, Crusoe hopes this servant will guide him to the mainland and escape. His dream strengthens him in his resolve to do nothing directly, for it is a curiously unreal dream in which Crusoe does not really participate but simply watches action with a cool detachment totally foreign to normal dream experience. Crusoe's smile in the dream is a sign of the serenity he is about to achieve, a pleased instinctive recognition of the resolution of his dilemma: doing nothing will involve him in the ultimate act of control—escape. The frantic internal debate over a course of action is resolved by the dream; the ultimate danger represented by the cannibals is to be converted into the source of ultimate deliverance. by standing still and watching the most extreme of his circumstances, Crusoe will be liberated from them. Awake, he realizes that planning is useless, circumstances will provide: "But as I could pitch upon no probable means for it, so I resolv'd to put myself upon the watch, to see them when they came on shore, and leave the rest to the event, taking such measures as the opportunity should present, let be what would be" (146).

Crusoe's resolution is the most explicit statement of the central satisfaction of his book. His strategy for survival is a means of establishing a relationship between the free self and the determined event so that the self can act upon events and in reaction to events without losing its autonomy. Indeed, the deep fantasy that Crusoe and his story serve is the dream of freedom perfectly reconciled with necessity, the self using necessity to promote its freedom. Crusoe builds up at this point to his greatest and most daring exploit in the enactment of the dream of freedom, and the pervasive antithesis between circumstances and freedom is here at its sharpest. What he proposes (fittingly in a dream, proposing without asserting) is the startling exploitation of his own anti-type, for the cannibals are an externalization of an anti-Crusoe, the natural man he has repressed by various means.

For once, Crusoe is eager, and his readiness endures through the year and a half he tells us he had to wait. Time of this sort is meaningless in *Robinson Crusoe;* the "years" serve as breaks and transitions between crises. As readers, we feel the stress of ordering experience which rushes by Crusoe: a world of moving details and obstacles rather than the lingering static existence he claims he endured. But even Crusoe's record at this point is of impatience: "*But* the longer it seem'd to be delay'd, the more eager I was for it; in a word, I was not at first so careful to shun the sight of these savages, and avoid being seen by them, as I was now eager to be upon them" (146).[19]

The long break in Crusoe's personal time between his resolve and his opportunity does work, however, to make him surprised when the cannibals actually appear. Moreover, opportunity when it comes never matches plans, so Crusoe finds not the eleven of his dream but thirty. These and subsequent events Crusoe perceives through his telescope, and he reports everything he sees by that means in suitably distanced language, full of the tentative and objective features of vision from a distance. He is really in this scene physically apart from events even as he is tremendously concerned in them; his perspective is literally necessary but structurally coherent as well. Crusoe is on his way to enacting literally what he has been doing thus far in various indirect ways. He becomes at the moment of Friday's deliverance exactly like the deity who delivered him: suddenly visible, powerful, and obviously mysterious in that power. He acquires at the moment of action, that moment when he sees the lone savage pursued by two others, a sense of divine purpose, or, better, his impulses are for the first time in his story fully acceptable as divine urges. Crusoe here begins his final transformation into a quasi-divine, autonomous hero whose desires are no longer self-destructive in their determinate independence but fulfilling and self-constructive in their free dependence on reality. Friday swims from his pursuers (two of them), and at that precise moment when the unmanageable three pursuers are reduced to a workable two, Crusoe is struck with the inevitability of his action: "It came now very warmly upon my thoughts, and indeed irresistibly, that now was my time to get me a servant, and perhaps a companion or assistant; and that I was call'd plainly by Providence to save this poor creature's life" (147). The universe has been dramatically realigned; the inevitable is now exactly parallel to Crusoe's desires and needs. By mastering the art of observation, by rejecting in effect all assertive and personal action, Crusoe (telescope in hand) achieves a divine perspective and his action coincides perfectly with the bizarre swing of events.

As a reconstructed cannibal, Friday in his conversion repeats the taming of the goats. He is Crusoe's heretofore menacing anti-type now completely domesticated, and Crusoe is now literally the master in acquiring an actual slave. The split whereby part of him worked on nature is now healed, as Friday is easily taught the various techniques for running the island's economy that Crusoe had previously mastered. Crusoe retains the mastery, of course, in every sense. They are his techniques and his island; Friday works, but Crusoe possesses the labour and its meaning. Moreover, Friday retains enough of his ferocity and tribal hatred to assist Crusoe in his last acquisition of real political power in the defeat of the cannibals when they return with European captives.

Having in a real sense defeated the last recalcitrant part of himself in domesticating Friday, Crusoe is now able to treat the cannibals who return as an objective force which can be freely destroyed. In terms of the coherence of the narrative, it is for this reason that the cannibals appear this time with European captives. The sight of a white man bound and awaiting horrid consumption galvanizes Crusoe into action. He is released by his total mastery of himself from the complicating moral alternatives he posed when he first saw the cannibals. True, he gives us a highly condensed repetition of those moral alternatives when he first learns of the cannibals' arrival from Friday. But he places himself with new confidence in an aggressively close position (within range of his weapons) to their feast, "that I might observe their barbarous feast, and that I would act then as God should direct; but that unless something offer'd that was more a call to me than yet I knew of, I would not meddle with them" (169). To say that Crusoe's immediate and impetuous attack to save a white man is a racist instinct is true but not the whole truth. The hapless Spaniard about to be devoured is a surrogate Crusoe in a way, for Crusoe can now view the island as entirely his, and an attack on another white man is an attack on himself, on a community that he is now fit to preside over by virtue of his mastery. He recognizes himself in that bearded man, for at that moment he becomes the proprietor of the island and his sovereignty is threatened by the atrocity. Friday hates these cannibals already; he is, Crusoe notes, "in a state of war with those very particular people; and it was lawful for him to attack them" (169). Crusoe enters into a state of war with those cannibals because he has achieved the requisite freedom for meaningful opposition to them, what Friday has by means of his history and membership in a community. Crusoe now has his own equivalent to that history, a coherent being in his island rather than a mere defensive relationship to it.

The huge battle with the cannibals and their bloody defeat is only the first in the climactic series of consistently one-sided triumphs which marks this last phase of Crusoe's career.[20] Crusoe admits that his enemies are so surprised and so frightened by the action of the fire-arms that they "had no more power to attempt their own escape, than their flesh had to resist our shot" (171). In other words, Crusoe's triumph is not really or at least not completely the result of bravery but of the power and surprise he commands and the technological world over which he alone on his island presides. He moves, once again, like his God, unexpectedly and irresistibly. On the surface, Crusoe's new political power which follows the battle is adventitious; he refers to it in jest: "My island was now peopled, and I thought my self very rich in subjects; and it was a merry reflection which I frequently made, how like a king I look'd" (175). His real power is in his confident movements: his absolutely sure sense of what to do and where to station himself in relation to events and phenomena. His power has the technological-natural inevitability of the bullets which pierce the flesh of the terrified cannibals.

When his last great adventure on the island arrives, when a ship suddenly appears in his harbor, Crusoe's caution is thus appropriately a divine instinct: "I had some secret doubts hung about me, I cannot tell from whence they came, bidding me keep upon my guard" (182). He argues darkly that such intuitions are proof of a world of supervising spirits. No matter that Crusoe's reasons for caution are absolutely sound: "it occurr'd to me to consider what business an English ship could have in that part of the world, since it was not the way to or from any part of the world where the English had any traffick; and I knew there had been no storms to drive them in there, as in distress; and that if they were English really, it was most probable that they were here upon no good design; and that I had better continue as I was, than fall into the hands of thieves and murtherers" (182). Crusoe is able to jump neatly from the natural cunning explicit in such observation to the ideological coherence with transforms such sagacity into a link between heaven and earth. Crusoe feels his power, feels a kind of current of energy running through him from natural fact and random circumstance to divine ordering. He is the center, a heroic mediator of a special kind at this point.

That mediation is nowhere clearer than in the subsequent events. Crusoe sees three men put ashore by mutineers, and their condition, he remarks, is exactly like his when he first landed on the island. He is now in a position to rescue them just as he was rescued by providence in various ways; he becomes providence in effect. When he confronts them, the marvellous audacity implicit in Crusoe's new part of the drama of deliverance surfaces in the dialogue:

> "Gentlemen," said I, "do not be surpriz'd at me; perhaps you may have a friend near you when you did not expect it." "He must be sent directly from heaven then," said one of them very gravely to me, and pulling off his hat at the same time to me, "for our condition is past the help of man." "All help is from heaven, sir," said I. (185)

Naturally, Crusoe disavows his powers and expresses only formal confidence in God's wisdom. But the serene efficiency with which he masterminds the fight against the mutiny is an unmistakable token of the power he now embodies. Crusoe invokes desperation as the psychological source of that serenity, but we know that he has long ago in our experience of him passed through desperation, that his entire story is an effort to exclude the kind of frantic movement within circumstances that desperation implies. His very description of desperation changes it into the calm power we as onlookers are given. Crusoe senses that he is part of a larger pattern, that his story has taken its final shape and established its inevitable direction, and that his and God's purposes are inseparable. The captain is apprehensive, but Crusoe smiles.[21]

> I smil'd at him, and told him that men in our circumstances were past the operation of fear: that seeing almost every condition that could be, was better than that which we were suppos'd to be in, we ought to expect that the consequence, whether death or life, would be sure to be a deliverance. I ask'd him what he thought of the circumstances of my life, and whether a deliverance were not worth venturing for. "And where, sir," said I, "is your belief of my being preserv'd here on purpose to save your life, which elevated you a little while ago? For my part," said I, "there seems to be but one thing amiss in all of the prospect of it." "What's that?" says he. "Why," said I, "'tis that as you say, there are three or four honest fellows among them, which should be spar'd; had they been all of the wicked part of the crew, I should have thought God's providence had singled them out to deliver them into your hands; for depend upon it, every man of them that comes a-shore are our own, and shall die or live as they behave to us." (189)

We know from following the sequence of Crusoe's career and watching his successive elevation to higher and higher forms of mastery (the self, the environment, animals, natives, and now Europeans) that he is speaking out of more than a desperate need to leave the island. What we enjoy most as readers and what is truest in all this sequence against the mutineers is our sense of Crusoe's serene omnicompetence, his ability to be above circumstances while immersed in them. Crusoe is so much the master in this passage that he can speak of their situation as only superficially dangerous; it looks dangerous only to the ignorant observer: "almost every condition that could be, was better than that which we were *suppos'd to be in.*" Crusoe knows his power so exactly that he wonders that some of the mutineers on shore are honest fellows who must be spared. The whole lot, in his view, seem clearly meant to be instruments in his plan rather than individuals with their own fates and power to save themselves.

The actual battle with the mutineers repeats the strategies and satisfactions of the two encounters with the cannibals, although here the manœuvres are appropriately more complicated and extensive, given the higher sophistication of his adversaries. In directing this battle, Crusoe is still quite recognizable as a human imitation of providence: distant, inscrutable, and omnipotent. Matters are arranged so that the captain represents Crusoe as the "governor and commander" of the island; the effectiveness of their counter-attack depends upon Crusoe's exactly engineered fiction of irresistible power, both military and legal: "In a word, they all laid down their arms, and begg'd their lives; and I sent the man that had parley'd with them, and two more, who bound them all; and then my great army of 50 men, which, particularly with those three, were all but eight, came up and seiz'd upon them all, and upon their boat, only tht I kept myself and one more out of sight, for reasons of state" (194–5).

The pretense continues past the victory. We and Crusoe and his allies from the ship are all in on the elaborate masquerade in which Crusoe is not only transformed for immediate strategic purposes from castaway hermit to colonial proprietor but in which he is given the ship as his political right, clothed by the captain in appropriate European garb, and in which he even extends these outward ceremonies to actual judicial power over the mutineers. Crusoe's transformation is utterly complete; he dispenses justice as it was, in a sense, dispensed to him at the beginning of the island episode. He gives the mutineers the penance of island exile: "I accordingly set them at liberty, and had them retire into the woods to the place whence they came, and I would leave them some fire arms, some ammunition, and some directions how they should live very well, if they thought fit" (200). Through all this, Crusoe's acting is suspiciously perfect. He shows them (twice) as evidence of his power the captain of the mutiny hanging at the yard-arm of the ship. He pretends to correct the real captain and reminds him that these men are "my prisoners, not his; and that seeing I had offered them so much favour, I would be as good as my word; and that if he did not think fit to consent to it, I would set them at liberty, as I found them; and if he did not like it, he might take them again if he could catch them" (200). Crusoe plays at power and never has to take it quite seriously, simply because he has achieved so much of it. One must never admit to one's power and freedom, since that would falsify their essentially dynamic and relational nature. Power and freedom are states of equilibrium between the self and a constantly unruly and threatening environment and/or society. The elaborate games that Crusoe plays as he ends his story are not only strategies for managing the mutineers. They represent an awareness in the narrative of the nature of freedom. They repeat on that trickiest and most difficult level of reality—the social and political—the games that Crusoe has had to master all through his story in order to "survive," that is, to achieve a special kind of autonomy.

Once Crusoe leaves the island (now a full-fledged colony), the rest is rather tedious accounting of the wealth he richly deserves for his extraordinary feat of survival and mastery. It is wealth which has earned itself in Crusoe's absence. He has only innocently fought for his life but has been rewarded with great wealth he did not directly seek. That is a perfect and beautifully appropriate conclusion for a capitalist hero, combining freedom and innocence in a manner rather difficult to achieve in the real economic world. But Crusoe is faced with a dilemma now that he is back in the world where that innocence can hardly hope to be preserved: "I had more care upon my head now, than I had in my silent state of life in the island, where I wanted nothing but what I had, and had nothing but what I wanted: whereas I had now a great charge upon me, and my business was how to secure it. I had ne'er a cave now to hide my money in, or a place where it might lie without lock or key . . . on the contrary, I knew not where to put it, or who to trust with it" (207). Crusoe never solves that problem. In his sequel, he goes wandering and trading, moving incessantly to maintain his (and our) sense of innocent mastery. But having lost the island and its free space, he loses our interest.

Notes

1. *Robinson Crusoe* (Everyman edition, ed. Guy N. Pocock), p. 387. All further page references in the text are to this edition.
2. *The Rise of the Novel,* (Berkeley, 1962), p. 15.
3. "Notes on the Novel," in *The Dehumanization of Art and Other Writings* (New York, 1956), pp. 61–2.
4. *The Moonstone* (Modern Library edition), p. 15.
5. The decline in the belief in the worth of such experience since antiquity is discussed by Hannah Arendt in definitive fashion. See *The Human Condition* (New York, 1958), p. 175.
6. Gulliver has entirely rational and overt motives, at first certainly, for his travels. He, after all, has a legitimate and limiting professional identity as a ship's doctor. His later and more compulsive journeys come out of personal inclination and not out of that mixture of personality and social circumstance that the beginning of *Robinson Crusoe* tries to grasp.
7. *The Rise of the Novel,* p. 65.
8. C. B. Macpherson remarks on this pervasive hesitation in the face of new implications: "And however one interprets the Restoration and the Whig Revolution it cannot be said that support for traditional values had become entirely insignificant by the end of the century, or even later. Locke tried to combine traditional and market morality; so did Burke, in a more fundamental and more desperate way, a century later." *The Political Theory of Possessive Individualism,* p. 86.
9. "But if I can express at this distance the thoughts I had about me at that time, I was in tenfold more horror of-mind upon account of my former convictions, and the having returned from them to the resolutions I had wickedly taken at first, than I was at death it self; and these, added to the terror of the storm, put me into such a condition, that I can by no words describe it." (11)
10. The narrative convention to which this part of the book belongs has been isolated by G. A. Starr in "Escape from Barbary: A Seventeenth-Century Genre," *Huntington Library Quarterly,* 29 (Nov. 1965), 35–52.
11. *Mythologies,* trans. Annette Lavers (New York, 1973), p. 141. All of Defoe's stories,

but especially *Crusoe,* fit Barthes's notion of "myth" very well, for they may all be said to convert the historical world they describe into "natural" arenas where survival is the defining problem.

12. See Starr, "Escape from Barbary."

13. "The Structural Study of Myth," in *Structural Anthropology,* trans. Claire Jacobson and Brooke Grundfert Schoepf (New York, 1963), p. 229.

14. *The Phenomenology of the Spirit,* trans. J. B. Baille, in *The Philosophy of Hegel,* ed. C. J. Friedrich (Modern Library edition), p. 405.

15. Here is one passage among various that illustrates the presence of a disorder which is potentially threatening, constricting, and stifling as this description implies: "I have already observ'd how I brought all my goods into this pale, and into the cave which I had made behind me. But I must observe too, that at first this was a confus'd heap of goods, which as they lay in no order, so they took up all my place, I had no room to turn my self; so I set my self to enlarge my cave and works farther into the earth, for it was a loose sandy rock, which yielded easily to the labour I bestow'd on it; and so when I found I was pretty safe as to beasts of prey, I work'd side-ways to the right hand into the rock, and then turning to the right again, work'd quite out and made me a door to come out, on the out-side of my pale or fortification." (51). The disorder of the goods is overcome by the elaborate and intricate system of Crusoe's tunnels, not just a large space in which to range goods but a larger space in which Crusoe himself can participate in his externalized order.

. 16. *The Divided Self* (London: Penguin edition, 1965), p. 42.

17. *The Phenomenology of the Spirit,* p. 405.

18. Crusoe comes to these meanings only gradually, but J. Paul Hunter is certainly justified in complaining that past emphasis upon Defoe's "realism" has "obscured the emblematic meaning of Crusoe's physical activities." Hunter's point, however, that Defoe's realism "continually makes his hero express his spiritual condition by physical actions" is implicitly reductive and neglects the situation in which the self comes to earn the right to indulge in such exegesis. See *The Reluctant Pilgrim: Defoe's Emblematic Method and Quest for Form in Robinson Crusoe* (Baltimore, 1966), pp. 189–90.

19. In one sense, this is a mere psychological truism, the natural shape of behavior for a person in Crusoe's circumstances. But the psychological truth of Crusoe's moments is merely the top layer of his reality for us. The ultimate source of his excitement is the hope of deliverance, and that deliverance in the light of his status as a hero of narrative must be a deliverance with freedom. Crusoe, I think we have to remind ourselves, cannot be experienced simply as a man on an island; he is *the* man on *the* island. The critical *locus classicus* for that point is Watt's chapter in *The Rise of the Novel,* "Robinson Crusoe, Individualism and the Novel," pp. 60–92.

20. Crucial throughout this analysis is the simple fact that things happen in *Robinson Crusoe* in a certain sequence rather than in any other order. The sequence we read yields a coherent progression of transformations, much as a sentence is what linguists call a transformation of raw information into the resolving order of language. Crusoe's book presents a series of experiences—both the events themselves and the narration which delivers those events to us—and that series constitutes a coherent sequence, an extended sentence. The trouble up to now is that critics have used the partial perspectives of religion, economics, psychology, and literary history and missed or blocked out important parts of that sequence.

21. J. R. Moore notes that "Defoe smiled often and laughed rarely" and attributed that habit to many of his characters. See *Daniel Defoe: Citizen of the Modern World* (Chicago, 1958), p. 73. Crusoe, at least, only smiles at moments of power.

Defoe's Prose Style:
The Language of Interpretation

G. A. STARR

CAIN   Have you then seen the venerable Tents
        Where dwell the Heaven born, the Angelic Pair,
        To whom all human Reverence highly due,
        Is and ought always to be humbly paid?
DEVIL   We have.
CAIN   Did you, together with my grand Request,
        A just, a humble Homage for me pay
        To the great Sire and Mother of Mankind?
DEVIL   We did.
CAIN   Did you in humble Language represent
        The Griefs and Anguish which oppress my Soul?
DEVIL   We did, and back their Blessing to thee bring.
CAIN   I hope with humblest Signs of filial Duty
        You took it for me on your bending Knees?
DEVIL   We did, and had our Share; the Patriarch
        Lifting his Hands to Heaven express'd his Joy
        To see his spreading Race, and bless'd us all.
CAIN   Did you my solemn Message too deliver,
        My Injuries impartially lay down,
        And due Assistance and Direction crave?
DEVIL   We did.
CAIN   What spoke the Oracle? he's God to me;
        What just Command d'ye bring, what's to be done?[1]

Why this lumbering blank verse at the head of an essay on Defoe's prose style? To make the preliminary point that we should probably begin by

From *Modern Philology*, 71 (1974), 277–94.

enumerating styles, not generalizing about a style. The fact is that these lines appear here as verse for the first time; until now they have always been printed as prose.[2] Whether or not I am correct in surmising that they originated as blank verse, previous commentators have noticed nothing anomalous about them. They have always passed as normal Defoean prose, yet they are clearly at odds with the prevailing view of his style. Critics are unanimous in stressing the plainness of Defoe's language, but this passage aspires to elevation through epithet and periphrasis; his syntax is usually characterized as loose and sprawling, and thus as structurally equivalent (or at least appropriate) to the homely naturalness of his vocabulary, but this passage strives for formality through metrical regularity, and through various figures of speech and thought.[3]

Nor is this passage altogether idiosyncratic: although its inversions of normal word order are rarely found elsewhere in Defoe's prose; some of its other schemes of construction recur both in the fictional and nonfictional writings. They are less frequent in narrating action than in expounding ideas, but even in the tales of adventure there is more exploring of states of mind, and more deliberate, balanced prose, than criticism has yet recognized. One notable specimen is the slave-tutor's elaborate speech to Colonel Jack, comparing the prosperous wickedness and guilty anxiety of his former life in England with the physical hardships and virtuous calm he now experiences in Virginia.[4] Toward the end of *The Farther Adventures of Robinson Crusoe*, when a Russian grandee explains his decision to remain in Siberian exile, Defoe exploits the oxymorons of "miserable greatness" and "blessed confinement" in a similar series of carefully turned paradoxes.[5] With their sustained antitheses and parallelisms, such passages smack too much of artifice to represent Defoe's prose at its best. Used on a more limited scale, these schemes of balance can seem impressively artless, especially when they bring to an aphoristic point a loosely strung series of thoughts or events: one celebrated example is Moll's summary of the joint career of two fellow criminals: "In short, they robb'd together, lay together, were taken together, and at last were hang'd together."[6] My object, however, is not to vindicate Defoe's endeavors toward stylistic balance and formality, let alone to maintain that they are the most common or distinctive feature of his prose, but simply to suggest, by calling attention to their existence, that immethodical homespun garrulity is not Defoe's only style.

A second preliminary point is that no valid stylistic comments can be based on nuances of punctuation, capitalization, italicization, or spelling in the texts of Defoe's novels. His only major work of which a manuscript survives is *The Compleat English Gentleman;* its editor observes that "the close and hurried writing, the indistinct characters, which may very often mean different letters, the great number of emendations, additions, and deleted passages, the extensive use of contractions and of shorthand and other abbreviations, and the uncommon, irregular, and often curious and faulty spelling make it difficult and sometimes perplexing to read . . . Defoe scarcely puts any commas, and only very rarely puts a full stop or other mark; . . . he puts [capitals] quite at random."[7] There is no reason to suppose that this manuscript differs from those of the fictional writings of the half-decade between *Robinson Crusoe* (1719) and *Roxana* (1724). As occasional critic, Defoe was aware of the importance of correct "pointing," but as practicing novelist he seems to have disregarded the matter entirely.[8] Analysis of the early printings of *Moll Flanders* indicates that he had little to do with the accidentals in this typical text.[9] We can asume that every word in a Defoean first edition corresponds (however erroneously) with some mark in his manuscript, but no such assumption can be made about the accidentals; in *Moll Flanders,* at any rate, they largely represent compositorial guesses at Defoe's intended meaning. If this is generally true of the novels, then such features of the texts can provide no firm basis for further interpretations.

This point can be clairifed by a glance at critical commentary on the famous passage in *Robinson Crusoe* where the hero finds some money in the cabin of the wrecked ship: "I smil'd to my self at the Sight of this Money, O Drug! Said I aloud, what are thou good for, Thou are not worth to me, no not the taking off of the Ground, one of those Knives is worth all this Heap, I have no manner of use for thee, e'en remain where thou art, and go to the Bottom as a Creature whose Life is not worth saving. However, upon Second Thoughts, I took it away; and wrapping all this in a Piece of Canvas. . . ." The penultimate clause, Coleridge observes, is "Worthy of Shakespeare;—and yet the simple semi-colon after it, the instant passing on without the least pause of reflex consciousness is more exquisite and masterlike than the touch itself. A meaner writer . . . would have put an '!' after 'away,' and have commenced a new paragraph." In *The Rise of the Novel,* Ian Watt quotes these passages and questions the validity of Coleridge's praise: he faults Coleridge for using the 1812 edition of the book, which "had put a good deal of order into Defoe's haphazard punctuation," whereas "the early editions actually give a comma, not a semi-colon, after 'I took it away,'"[10] But whatever punctuation the early editions "act⏤lly give" has little foundation in what Defoe wrote; rather, it constitutes an attempt to put order, not into Defoe's own virtually nonexistent punctuation, but into his narratives by means of punctuation, supplied zealously but often inconsistently and uncomprehendingly by the compositors. In short, Watt's comma probably has no more authorial sanction than Coleridge's semicolon; neither his reading, Coleridge's, nor anyone else's can be sustained or refuted by an appeal to the accidentals of Defoe's texts.

A third and final preliminary point is that historical evidence can sometimes help to illuminate Defoe's prose style. The *Crusoe* passage just quoted, for instance, has an allusive resonance missed by past commentators. Crusoe's apostrophe to the gold may be typical, as Watt maintains, "of Defoe the economic publicist ever on the alert to enforce the useful truth that goods alone constitute real wealth;" but it does not follow that the monologue is not "really suited to Crusoe's character or his present situation,"[11] for Defoe is using a classical *topos* to characterize the hero and his predicament. Elsewhere in the book similarities or direct references to the Prodigal Son, Elijah, Balaam, Adam, etc., help to define, evaluate, or intensify Crusoe's situation;[12] in the background of the present scene stands the cock in Aesop's first fable: "As a *Cock* was turning up a Dunghill, he spy'd a *Diamond*. Well (says he to himself) this sparkling Foolery now to a Lapidary in my place, would have been the Making of him; but as to any Use or Purpose of mine, a *Barley Corn* had been worth Forty on't."[13]

What matters here is not the role of Aesop's fable as possible source or influence, but its usefulness in highlighting certain stylistic features of Crusoe's language when the two passages are juxtaposed. For one thing, the effect of Crusoe's apostrophe to the gold—his "sudden removing from the third person to the second," the "turning of [his] speech to some new . . . thing, that [he himself] gives show of life to"[14]—becomes clearer when compared with the Aesopic cock's monologue: from wry amusement ("I smil'd") analogous to the cock's facetious detachment ("this sparkling Foolery"), Crusoe shifts to vigorous denunciation, and eventually condemns the money, by now exalted to the status of a human adversary, "to the Bottom as a Creature whose Life is not worth saving." The cock had made his paradoxical point through simple contrast ("a *Barley-Corn* had been worth Forty on't"), as does Crusoe ("one of those Knives is worth all this Heap"), and the cock had made explicit the linking quality of his contrast ("Use or Purpose of mine") as does Crusoe ("I have no Manner of use for thee"). But Crusoe submerges this crux of his argument in the surrounding reiteration of "not worth . . . no not [worth] the taking . . . not worth saving," and although these purport to be answers to the rhetorical question "what are thou good for," they actually answer no question, nor do they qualify or extend an argument, for example, "the useful truth that goods alone constitute real wealth." Instead, they serve chiefly to do what Watt says the passage fails to do—that is, they give a "useful truth" rhetorical substance by projecting human qualities onto the money, by making it and Crusoe momentary antagonists, and thus by dramatizing an economic paradox as a clash of personalities.

So much for preliminaries: we should beware of generalizing prematurely about Defoe's prose, of basing our arguments on the shaky evidence of accidentals, and of neglecting the relevance of literary history to discussions of style.[15] Here now is my thesis. Defoe's prose is indeed "realistic," but in a special and limited sense: his characters tell us directly rather little about themselves or their external world, but they create an illusion of both by projecting themselves upon their world in the act of perceiving it. This is to say that the monologue just considered is not only "suited to Crusoe's character [and] his present situation," but epitomizes in a crude yet striking way Defoe's main technique for rendering both character and situation. Character is revealed through response to the other, the external thing or event encountered; at the same time, the external thing or event is described less in objective terms, as it is in itself, than in subjective terms, as it is perceived by the narrator. Nor is the very act of perception a passive state but an outgoing process, in which Defoe's narrators imprint their own nature on the world around them, by imputing to it human qualities not inherently "in" it at all.

I agree with all the commentators, for instance, that *A Journal of the Plague Year* seems impressively realistic in its evocation of what life must have been like in the stricken city. Yet when we come to examine the sources of its lifelikeness, we find that this effect depends less on a vivid or precise rendering of the grim spectacle surrounding the narrator than on his interpretative responses to it. "We hear again," says J. H. Plumb, "the shrieks of the dying and the lamentations of the living;"[16] but in what sense do we "hear" them? The narrator repeatedly mentions the "dismal Shrieks and Out-cries of the poor People;" the "terrible Shrieks of Skreekings of Women, who in their Agonies would throw open their Chamber Windows, and cry out in a dismal Surprising Manner;" the "most grievous and piercing Cries and Lamentations;" "the most horrible Cries and Noise the poor People would make;"[17] and so on. Perhaps words like "Shrieks" and "Skreekings" do convey through onomatopoeia some sense of the sounds the narrator tells us he heard, but for the most part these are not auditory descriptions at all: they specify nothing about the sounds themselves, but refer instead either to the inpact they made on the narrator, or cumstances under which he infers they were uttered. Defoe represents a given cry as expressing emotion A in the crier, or generating emotion B in the hearer; by predicating either A or B of the sound itself, he is "reading into it" human values, interpreting its significance in the very act of recording it.

Since the emphasis is more on how things are perceived than on what they are in themselves, Defoe's narrative style tends to be more adverbial than adjectival, and many words classifiable grammatically as adjectives are in effect functioning as adverbs. Thus "terrible," "grievous," "horrible," etc., appear to modify the shrieks and cries, but refer to these sounds only indirectly; what they primarily tell us is how H. F. the saddler was affected, for the terror, grief, and horror are his.[18] By this I do not mean that Defoe fails to make us "hear again the shrieks of the dying and the lamentations of the living;" my point is that things and events are rendered *as* perceived, as in some sense transformed and recreated in the image of the narrator.[19]

Defoe's rendering of visual experience furnishes abundant evidence of this procedure. The following passage is Robinson Crusoe's initial description of Friday:

He was a comely, handsome fellow, perfectly well made, with straight strong limbs, not too large, tall, and well-shaped, and, as I reckon, about twenty-six years of age. He had a very good countenance, not a fierce and surly aspect, but seemed to have something very manly in his face; and yet he had all the sweetness and softness of an European in his countenance too, especially when he smiled. His hair was long and black, not curled like wool; his forehead very high and large; and a great vivacity and sparkling sharpness in his eyes. The colour of his skin was not quite black, but very tawny; and yet not of an ugly, yellow, nauseous tawny, as the Brazilians and Virginians, and other natives of America are, but of a bright kind of a dun olive colour, that had in it something very agreeable, though not very easy to describe. His face was round and plump; his nose small, not flat like the negroes; a very good mouth, thin lips,a nd his fine teeth well set, and white as ivory.[20]

In *The Rise of Modern Prose Style,* Robert Adolph analyzes this passage as a specimen of "The New Prose of Utility." In the older prose of Nashe and Overbury, Adolph argues, "the details reflect the narrator's own attitudes," whereas "Defoe's emphasis is all . . . on the difficulty of exact, objective description, . . . not on the author's momentary feelings toward the subject. . . . Defoe seems to aspire toward an objective report on a laboratory specimen."[21] In earlier chapters Adolph had maintained that both in theory and practice, the chief aim of the new prose that emerged after the Restoration is "utility," and that "the escape from subjectivity is universal."[22] However valid these contentions may be with respect to the evolution of seventeenth-century prose as a whole, their applicability to the present passage is questionable. Nor does this passage seem to bear out Adolph's further contention that "Crusoe's only important interest in Friday is utilitarian": Crusoe's language is heavily evaluative, but his values here are not primarily, let alone exclusively, utilitarian. Up to this point the "savage wretches" have posed a mortal threat to Crusoe, and their "inhuman, hellish brutality" has been labeled the worst "degeneracy of human nature," so that we have been led to expect an individual savage to present a "horrid spectable," a countenance expressive of the "abominable and vitiated passions" of these "monsters."[23] But Crusoe's description of Friday is clearly designed to counter these expectations, for this alien creature is rapidly made to appear attractive. This is not achieved through "an objective report on a laboratory specimen," by avoiding the author's or narrator's "feelings toward the subject," but the reverse: what is rendered is the narrator's interpretative response to the external object, and particularly certain character traits which Crusoe infers from (or imputes to) Friday's physiognomy. The presence of such qualities as manliness, sweetness, and softness—and the absence of fierceness and surliness-is not, strictly speaking, observed on but read into Friday's face. Tawny skin is no more "ugly" or "nauseous" to a scientist reporting on a laboratory specimen than it is, presumably, to a Brazilian or Virginian endowed with it; to Crusoe it is disagreeable aesthetically and emotionally, just as to him there is "something very agreeable" in skin "of a bright kind of dun olive colour"—whatever shade that may be. The entire passage is ethnocentric (which is to say subjective) in its intimation that Friday embodies the virtues of Indians and Negroes without their moral, temperamental, or aesthetic drawbacks; its recurrent pattern is to assign Friday mildly exotic features, but to associate them with the grace and delicacy of civilized Europeans rather than the gross animality of African or American natives. Of course this effect is not created by language alone; syntax plays an equally important part, but consideration of the structural aspects of Defoe's prose must be reserved for a separate study.

It would be a mistake to overstate the case against Defoe's concern with utility, or with describing things exactly; my point is that in this passage, the expression of both concerns is to a striking extent personal and subjective rather than scientific or objective. In Defoe's novels utility is not the mere shibboleth of a moral, social, or economic theorist; the question is commonly one of usefulness to a specific person in specific circumstances. As we have seen, the gold-finding passage in *Robinson Crusoe* poses not only the abstract thesis that economic value is determined by utility, but also the dramatic paradox that the very thing most prized by one person may be of no use to another (the lapidary and Defoe's reader versus the cock and Defoe's hero), or to the same person in a different situation (Crusoe in civilization versus Crusoe insulated). In the present passage Crusoe may in part be "sizing up Friday as a slave," as Adolph asserts, but he also seems to be doing something more interesting and less sinister. Crusoe is here seeing for the first time an individual fellow man where he had hitherto thought to find only monsters. His very "seeing" involves the projection of his own feelings and values onto Friday, so that through this initial act of perception, Crusoe in a sense endows Friday with his own humanity. It is not, in other words, a matter of scientific observation, though, as we shall see in a moment, scientific prose of the period was itself often far less impersonal and objective than Adolph's account of it indicates.[24]

At all events, it is curious that Adolph should regard *Robinson Crusoe* or any other novel as the "logical culmination" of the post-Restoration development of an impersonal, objective prose; there would seem to be stronger grounds for regarding the novel as proceeding in an opposite direction— toward rather than away from subjective consciousness and personal interpretation—with regard both to its content and its prose style. In view of what the novel was subsequently to become, it cannot be claimed that Defoe carries this process very far; but if the present argument is correct, his prose does considerably more subjective interpreting of the external world than critics have recognized. By the mid-nineteenth century, according to J. Hillis Miller, "everything is changed from its natural state into something useful or meaningful to man. Everywhere the world mirrors back to man his own image, and nowhere can he make vivifying contact with what is not human."[25] It is perhaps debatable whether man can ever perceive the external world—or at any rate can communicate his perceptions—without transforming it from its natural state into something meaningful to him, and thus in some measure imposing upon it his own image; but in any case, Defoe's narrators often make contact with what is not human precisely *by* vivifying it, by discovering in it values and meanings which are not its own but theirs.[26]

Does Defoe's style show an indebtedness, or even a resemblance, to "scientific" prose? The Royal Society is sometimes cited as having supplied a model or precedent for Defoe's factual plainness. Without claiming that there was any direct influence, Ian Watt observes that "certainly Defoe's prose fully exemplifies the celebrated programme of Bishop Sprat: "a close, naked, natural way of speaking; positive expressions; clear sense; a native easiness; bringing all things as near the mathematical plainness as they can; and preferring the language of artisans, countrymen, and merchants before that of wits and scholars."[27] But it is usually Sprat's description (or prescription) of the Royal Society's ideal, not an actual specimen of scientific prose by one of the "Royal So-So's," that is compared with Defoe's literary practice, and this prose sometimes turns out to be stylistically different from what Bishop Sprat's formula might lead us to expect. The following passage, for instance, is on a down-to-earth subject—clay—yet the clarity and plainness which it achieves is anything but mathematical, for its crucial device is *prosopopoeia*, an insistent humanizing of the inanimate. Although its style is typical of the scientific prose of John Evelyn (1620–1706), who in turn is an unusually distinguished but quite representative Restoration virtuoso, I quote the passage here because it exhibits, in a charmingly extreme form, the anthropomorphizing tendency already noted in Defoe. There is a kind of clay, writes Evelyn in *Terra*, which is "so obstinate and ill-natured, as almost nothing will subdue; and another so voraciously and greedy, as nothing will satiate, without exceeding industry, because it ungratefully devours all that is appplied to it, turning it into as arrant clay as itself. Some clays are . . . in dry seasons costive, and . . . most of them pernicious and untractable. . . . Clay is, of all other [soils], a cursed stepdame to almost all vegetation . . . whether it be the voracious, hungry, weeping, or cold sort. In these cases, laxatives are to be prescribed."[28]

No doubt Evelyn's values here can be described as utilitarian. But to do so is not very illuminating stylistically unless one goes on to observe that man, not utility, is Evelyn's ultimate norm; that it is not only *to* man that Evelyn deems clay useful or worthless, but *from* man that he draws these and other categories for meaningfully perceiving it; and that his main descriptive and evaluative strategy, like Defoe's in the gold-finding episode, is to project human (and specifically moral) qualities onto the inanimate thing, so that it becomes a dramatic adversary rather than an object of detached, impersonal, "scientific" scrutiny. Marjorie Nicolson and others have made us aware of the importance to belles lettres of imagery drawn from science in the late seventeenth and eighteenth centuries;[29] less widely recognized is the extent to which scientific prose of the period was itself metaphorical and poetic—qualities conspicuous in Evelyn's treatment of clay.[30] More generally, this passage points to what may be a fallacy in Adolph's conception of post-Restoration prose, for it reminds us that the more an author of this period is preoccupied with the utility of a thing, the less his account of it is likely to resemble "an objective report on a laboratory specimen;" in other words, the two tendencies may often be inversely proportional, not directly proportional as Adolph maintains.

But let us suppose that Evelyn is attempting to treat his subject according to Sprat's program: if we were to set aside the adjective "mathematical," might we not conclude that he has succeeded? When the phenomena to be described are unfamiliar, or when there is as yet no settled vocabulary with which to describe them, then the writer would seem faced with a choice between inventing new terms or applying existing terms in a more or less metaphorical fashion to the new subject matter. The problem is more complex than this, both theoretically and historically, but such a scheme may help to clarify Evelyn's position (and ultimately Defoe's) relative to the stylistic ideals of the Royal Society. A preference for "the language of artisans, countrymen and merchants before that of wits and scholars" might authorize the use of specialized terms of art, were they available, but when they are not, the ideals of the Royal Society may best be served by representing the unfamiliar metaphorically, in terms of the familiar.[31] The question then becomes, How far can prose go in this direction without falling into the proscribed language of "wits?" To this, the answer appears to have been that when metaphor attracts attention to itself or is pursued for its own sake, when it leads to "amplifications, digressions, and swellings of style," when it is a source of "luxury and redundance of speech" or a "superfluity of talking"—in short, when metaphor is a mere ornament, tending to obscure rather than clarify—it constitutes a stylistic vice, and by the same token a philosophical and moral vice. These phrases are from the two paragraphs in Sprat's *History* immediately preceding the positive program cited earlier, and indicate that Sprat's real target of attack is not metaphor per se but the verbose "extravagance" and "excesses" of traditional eloquence—as is also evident from his one specific reference to metaphor in the series: "this vicious abundance of phrase, this trick of metaphors, this volubility of tongue." That his rejection of metaphor is not complete is shown further at the end of the *History*, when Sprat comes to defend—quite consistently, in my opinion—a kind of metaphor "founded on such images which are generally known, and are able to bring a strong, and sensible Impression on the *mind*."[32] In other words, Sprat himself, though generally regarded as a staunch enemy to metaphor, recognizes that it may be legitimate as well as necessary insofar as it makes for clarity, ease, and naturalness. It can therefore be maintained that Evelyn's lines on clay carry out in their own peculiar way the essential spirit of Sprat's program—assuming (as I think we must) that Evelyn introduced his anthropomorphic imagery not as a sustained conceit, to be relished for its own sake, but as a body of "images which are generally known" by means of which he could make his observations intelligible to his contemporaries.

Returning to the language of Defoe, we may now be in a better position to assess both Watt's contention that it has "a certain 'mathematical plainness,' a positive and wholly referential quality," and the relation he sees between it and "the attempt of the Royal Society to develop a more factual prose." On the latter question, Defoe may be said to share the stylistic ideals of the Royal Society, with the caveat that neither he nor Sprat is as radically opposed to figurative language as is usually supposed.[33] Defoe may seek to put things simply and exactly, but is evidently aware that the dry impersonality we now associate with scientific prose is not necessarily the best way to achieve this, and that the more Crusoe and H. F. the saddler project themselves into their descriptions, the better we will understand not only their subjective states but the objects and events they encounter. As to Watt's general description of Defoe's prose, a necessary qualification would seem to be that much of Defoe's rendering of things is not "factual" or "referential" at all, but creates this illusion by ascribing to the object qualities which the narrator comes upon, not through simple observation, but through processes of ego-, ethno-, or anthropocentric interpretation. In his fictional prose, to be sure, Defoe cannot afford to call attention to such devices. The illusion that the things and events he is describing are real depends to some extent on our not noticing the fundamental artificiality—the "fictiveness" if not arbitrariness—of his humanizing the external world in this way. Nevertheless this illusion is created in part by an essentially symbolic activity, the metaphoric ascription of human traits to external objects.

This is by no means the sole source of Defoe's realism, and if its role had not been overlooked or denied by most previous commentators, there would be less need to insist here on its importance. It will be useful to examine at this point some features of Defoe's writing which are more commonly regarded as contributing to its realism. I shall continue to confine my attention to language, and to base most of my remarks on passages which other critics have chosen to discuss, not only to avoid culling evidence which happens to fit my views, but to make clear how these views differ from existing accounts of Defoe's prose style.

It is often said that Defoe's realism owes a great deal to the sheer abundance of *things*. One modification of this thesis has already been proposed: namely, that Defoe often presents not things but people perceiving things, so that both the existence and the nature of the things are established by indirection, by showing us people in the act of perceiving them. A second modification might be introduced here in the form of a rhetorical question: how many of Defoe's things are *un*familiar? As soon as representation calls for more than simple naming, there comes into play some such technique as I have been describing. What should be stressed at once, though, is that much of Defoe's realism is on the elementary level of naming: many objects and places take on whatever fictional reality they possess, and make whatever contribution they do to the realism of their narrative contexts, simply because we happen to know what their names stand for.

In Lancashire, Moll Flanders is courted by an Irish fortune hunter who "talk'd as naturally of his Park, and his Stables; of his Horses, his Game-Keepers, his Woods, hisTenants, and his Servants, as if we had been in the Mansion-House, and I had seen them all about me."[34] Jemmy actually owns these things no more than Moll does, but he beguiles her in the same way that she and Defoe's other narrators often beguile us, for the passage epitomizes Defoe's realism at its simplest. The naming of a great many commonplace objects creates the illusion that we are amidst them; or to speak more accurately, our own imaginations, fastening on the familiar names, create such an illusion. In this context the scope of "imagination," of "illusion," and ultimately of "realism" itself, is quite limited. Here as elsewhere Defoe's chief concern is with objects not in themselves but in relation to human actions and values—in relation to the person perceiving them or, in this case, alluding to them "as naturally . . . as if" they were there to be perceived. The real point of this passage, after all, is that these things are *his:* note the cumulative force of "*his* Park, and *his* Stables; of *his* Horses, *his* Game-Keepers, *his* Woods, *his* Tenants, and *his* Servants." That they exist follows a fortiori from the "fact" that he owns them, and this order of priorities is very characteristic of Defoe's realism. It is usually a significant relationship to the narrator that confers imaginary existence on external people, places, and things, rather than a rendering of the kind of inherent, individual qualities which would give them an existence independent of the narrator. Needless to say, Defoe regards the relationship of owner to property as a particularly meaningful one, but it does not follow that this is the only one he is capable of conceiving, as some of his critics have maintained.

In Defoe's novels, God and the Adam of Genesis 1:19–20 tend to become one: things are not called into being and then named, but often called into being *by* being named. Certainly this is what Jemmy does here;

the bulk of the passage consists of his catalog of squirely appurtenances, and it deserves emphasis that these things are only said, not "shown," to exist. Moll's imagination is not aided, so far as we are told, by his vivid or detailed descriptions. That Moll can imagine Things when she hears bare Names is owing rather to her own experience—not only of language but of life. For the modern reader, in turn, much of Defoe's realism depends on the historical accident that so many objects named in the stories, which were commonplace at the time, happen to remain familiar today. When Moll speaks elsewhere of pieces of "Holland" (p. 8), or of "Lac'd-heads" (p.14), or of a "Suit of Knots" (p. 184), the latter condition is not met: lacking special knowledge of the history of English dress, the modern reader is likely to find such details *un*realistic, in the sense that the names evoke no memory of corresponding objects in his own experience. True, a book might be filled with casual naming of vanished customs, objects, and locales, and still have a valid title to be called realistic in some genetic or mimetic sense, as a document of social history; but in affective terms such materials do not make for realism, and may in extreme cases (e.g., some of the *hapax logomena* in Old English) result instead in impenetrable obscurity.

To put it another way, there are no cassowaries in Jemmy's park. I am not maintaining that the scene would have been *ipso facto* less realistic had he chosen to put them there, although the very ordinariness of Jemmy's inventory—just what we would expect of a country gentlemen, and nothing more—no doubt helps to prevent suspicion on Moll's part or ours.[35] What I am suggesting is that if he had fancied laying claim to an aviary, merely naming his exotic birds would not have sufficed. Some indications of what they were like, and particularly of why he had them, would also be called for, and it is information of the latter kind—about their meaning and value to Jemmy himself—which Defoe would be most likely to marshal to make them realistic.[36] At all events, unless Moll and the reader were already acquainted with them, simply naming them would not increase but reduce the realism of the passage.

As to Defoe's presentation of things beyond merely naming them, the following two statements sum up—and were influential in establishing—what has come to be the prevailing view on this matter. Dorothy Van Ghent observes: "What is important in Moll's world of things is the counting, measuring, pricing, weighing, and evaluating of things in terms of the wealth they represent and the social status they imply for the possessor.

What is unimportant (and we learn as much by what is unimportant as by what is important) is sensuous life, the concrete experience of things as they have individual texture."[37] Ian Watt also regards these socioeconomic indicators as more crucial to Defoe's rendering of the "world of things" than the "individual texture" of objects as the narrators "concretely experience" them. But he sees Defoe's bias as having a distinctive epistemological foundation as well. "Defoe's style," he says, "reflects the Lockean philosophy in one very significant detail: he is usually content with denoting only the primary qualities of the objects he describes—their solidity, extension, figure, motion, and number—especially number: there is very little attention to the secondary qualities of objects, to their colors, sounds, or tastes."[38]

Neither formulation is entirely at odds with the thesis which has been advanced here. In calling attention to an element of constant interpretation—Defoe's habit of treating things "in terms of" what they "represent" or "imply"—Van Ghent makes a valid and important point, but just as Adolph narrows Defoe's interpretative range unduly by regading utility as his sole evaluative category, so Van Ghent distorts Defoean evaluation by reducing it to a question of wealth or social status. It is clear, from the *Journal of the Plague Year* and *Robinson Crusoe* passages already considered, that psychological, aesthetic, and moral as well as socioeconomic values enter into the language with which Defoe renders the "world of things;" considerations of utility are often uppermost in Crusoe's mind, and of wealth and social status in Moll's, but what is stylistically significant is the process by which these and other values are ascribed *to* a world of external things *by* Defoe's narrators. To the extent that Defoe describes things at all (rather than merely naming them), it is their significance—in the widest sense, their position in relation to the narrator—that he is chiefly concerned to establish.

Watt has chosen for analysis the following passage in *Moll Flanders:* "The next thing of moment was an attempt at a gentlewoman's gold watch. It happened in a crowd, at a meeting-house, where I was in very great danger of being taken. I had full hold of her watch, but giving a great jostle as if somebody had thrust me against her, and in the juncture giving the watch a fair pull, I found it would not come, so I let it go that moment, and cried as if I had been killed, that somebody had trod upon my foot, and that there was certainly pickpockets there, for somebody or other had given a pull at my watch." Watt quotes more, but his comment on these lines is most relevant here: "It is very convincing. The gold watch is a real object, and it won't come, even with 'a fair pull.' The crowd is composed of solid bodies, pushing forwards and backwards. . . . All this happens in a real, particular place. It is true that, as is his custom, Defoe makes no attempt to describe it in detail, but the little glimpses that emerge win us over completely to its reality."[39]

What seems to me most important in this passage is the element that Van Ghent would deny—Moll's "sensuous life." This consists largely of active contact with things: having hold, giving a jostle, giving a pull, being balked, letting go. Moll cannot afford to linger over the "individual texture" of external objects, but she does convey the sensations of a body and mind energetically in touch with them. People, places, and things concern her less in themselves than in their bearing on what she does and undergoes. This attempt happened, Moll tells us, "*in* a crowd, *at* a meeting house." Watt speaks of "a real, particular place," but these adverbial and prepositional phrases scarcely realize or particularize the place itself: they modify Moll's experience, which they situate less in actual time and space than in its own patterns of spatial movement and temporal sequence. What matters most to Moll about these surroundings is that they are "where [she] was in very great danger of being taken," and I am not sure her sense of danger would have seemed more convincing if she had indeed specified "a real, particular place" (e.g., St. Anne's Church, Soho)[40] as the setting. Similarly, such phrases as "in the juncture" or "that moment" locate fresh developments in relation to other fragments of Moll's experience, not according to an objective chronology of clocks or calendars.

As to the focal object in the episode, it does not seem to me that its reality (such as it is) can be accounted for adequately in terms of Defoe's concentration on Lockean "primary qualities." The watch is gold; it is a gentlewoman's (though only accidentally, not essentially, according to Moll's traditional philosophy), and Moll wants it. The lines quoted are about Moll's strenuous efforts first to get it, then to avoid being caught, and neither the watch nor the other external things—gentlewoman, crowd, meeting house—have any independent reality worth speaking of. Eventually an illusion of solidity may be imparted indirectly to the watch by the unavailing "fair pull," but once again it is an act or perception of the narrator's, not the external object, which is rendered directly. In this connection it is worth noting that in Moll's long third sentence, the phrases "*as if* somebody had thrust me against her" and "*as if* I had been killed" furnish not facts but Moll's commentary on the facts. Unobtrusive as they may be, such metaphorical devices are important; they contribute not to what

Watt calls the "immediate presentation" of the scene, but to a presentation constantly mediated by Moll's imagination.

It was suggested earlier that Defoe's presentation of any given thing depends a good deal on whether it is already familiar to readers; that when it is, simple naming often suffices, and that when it it not, Defoe relies more on a metaphorical approach to the unknown via the known than on an objective specification, Lockean or scientific, of its distinguishing qualities. These contentions are borne out interestingly by Defoe's handling of Captain Singleton's trek across Africa. Here Defoe had a splendid opportunity to invest exotic objects with solidity and particularity, and ample factual information was available to him, had he wished to make the African settings convincing in Watt's terms. But as Gary J. Scrimgeour points out, Defoe makes very limited use of such material: "Those elements which are specifically African were matters of common knowledge and were often handled with equal or greater concreteness by other writers on Africa. . . . Much of the realistic atmosphere is in fact not African, but English. One of Defoe's favorite tricks is to compare an African bird, animal, or river with its English equivalent—a device which, in the mouth of the unlettered Singleton, often does produce an illusion of verisimilitude."[41] Yet what Scrimgeour regards as a limitation on the realism of *Captain Singleton*, and the "trick" with which he sees Defoe as disguising this inadequacy, are characteristic of Defoe's narratives whenever more than mere naming of familiar objects is called for, and it is not only in the hands of "unlettered" narrators that they "produce an illusion of verisimilitude." Nevertheless, Scrimgeour's illustrations of the device are pertinent here: "Vegetables of various kinds are brought to the Europeans by the natives, but they are then described either by reference to the nearest English equivalent or in the vaguest terms: "a great heap of roots and plants for our bread, such as the Indians gave us" or "we met with a little negro town, where they had growing a sort of corn like rice, which ate very sweet." The beasts of burden consume a plant "like thistles" in place of water and a root "not much unlike a parsnip, very moist and nourishing." . . . [Defoe's] sole monster "seemed to be an ill-gendered kind, between a tiger and a leopard." . . . The only serpent in *Captain Singleton* is the one of "a hellish ugly deformed look and voice" that the men mistake for Satan."[42] Scrimgeour contends that Defoe's attempt at realism "was totally subordinated to other interests"—namely, a demonstration of the opportunities open to "The Compleat English Tradesman" in Africa—and concludes that "both aesthetics and reality bow their heads before commerce."[43] This seems to me an exaggeration, analogous to Adolph's narrowing of Defoe's values and purposes to the purely utilitarian. Profit and utility are important themes in *Captain Singleton*, but they are not the only considerations that affect Defoe's rendering of the African scene: as the serpent description indicates, other values are clearly present.

Scrimgeour is a sensitive reader, and it is instructive that he should equivocate on the question of whether *Captain Singleton* is realistic. On the one hand, he suggests that the book is considerably less realistic than it might have been, had Defoe stocked it more abundantly with African *realia*.[44] In other words, he shares Watt's view that particularized things make for realism, but holds that Defoe's achievements in this line are not at all "impressive" in *Captain Singleton*, and finds the vagueness and paucity of Defoe's Africana somewhat "surprising." On the other hand, he recognizes that the narrative does achieve a "necessary though meretricious authenticity," through what I have called the projection of familiar English categories and values onto the alien landscape; yet he regards this aspect of realism with suspicion, twice labeling it "simply a device, almost a trick," denying that it is "in any sense created by an artistic or ethical ideal," and finding it "necessary" only because of Defoe's "preoccupation with certain attitudes unrelated to literature"—that is, as a vehicle for economic propaganda. But by now it should be clear that this "trick" is characteristic of Defoe's imaginative writings in general, and that it is "necessary" not only to the propounding of ideological theses, but to the meaningful experiencing and communicating of all kinds of "strange surprising adventures," which is made possible by interpreting the strange in terms of the familiar.

We praise *Robinson Crusoe* for its hero's demonstration that, thrust into a "waste, howling wilderness," man can create order. This is usually put in economic terms: we are fascinated (and perhaps reassured) by Crusoe's capacity to conquer and regulate his physical environment. A similar process takes place within the soul of the hero: in religious terms, divine grace subdues and redeems errant human nature, and several recent critics have found Crusoe's spiritual progress as striking as his mastery over external nature.[45] A Freudian critic might admire *Robinson Crusoe* for tracing an attainment of psychological order as well: initially torn between the anarchical demands of a powerful id and the constraints of superego, Crusoe eventually pieces together not only an economic utopia, not only a spiritual salvation, but an ego. The implication of the present argument is that all these processes are reflected in, and in some sense dependent on, the nature of Crusoe's language, for it is on this level that the ordering of experience most fundamentally takes place. Externally, wild animals are domesticated, the wilderness is enclosed, Friday is Europeanized, and so on; internally, the hero's own chaotic, wasteful, and sinful impulses are sublimated, disciplined, or converted into methodical, productive, and virtuous industry: my point is that Crusoe's language not only describes these processes, but enacts or embodies them. By animating, humanizing, and Anglicizing the alien things he encounters, Crusoe as narrator achieves verbally exactly what Crusoe as hero achieves physically, spiritually, and psychically. In the poetry of the period, personification constantly implies a relation between man and the external world; in *Robinson Crusoe*, the hero not only makes contact in this way with what is foreign and threatening to him, but by imposing on it his own values, he attains through the act of narration a mastery over it. In the same way, Captain Singleton may be said to conquer Africa, and H. F. to overcome the Plague.[46] It is in this general sense that it seems to me most meaningful to speak of the "functional" quality of Defoe's prose. His characters are not secure, detached observers of the world, but actors in it, vulnerable to it and intent on triumph over it; even at the supposed time of writing, in affluent retirement, they remain somewhat unsure of themselves. As a consequence, the act of recounting their lives, no less than the struggles they narrate, represents an effort to achieve control over experience, to formulate a conception of themselves as stable and respectable as the place they have outwardly attained in the world.

There are other ways, of course, of approaching Defoe's language. One can calculate statistically the relative frequency of different parts of speech, or of words derived from Romance or Germanic stock.[47] One can examine the social, political, economic, and religious milieux reflected in Defoe's vocabulary, or one can analyze this element rhetorically rather than genetically, in terms of the class, party, occupational, and denominational interests which his vocabulary serves to articulate or advance.[48] Formally, one can weigh the fitness of Defoe's language to the personalities and situations of his various fictional narrators, or one can attempt to isolate certain terms or clusters of words which Defoe habitually uses in an insistent or unusual way.[49] The present essay has dwelt instead on certain interpretative and figurative qualities which Defoe's language shares with most poetry and much other prose; it has deferred the task of defining Defoe's stylistic individuality until the structural aspects of his prose have also been considered. In the meantime, examination of his language has indicated that Defoe's realism has to do primarily with his narrators' perceptions, only second-

arily with the "world of things" on which most previous criticism had
focused; that apart from simple naming, Defoe is less concerned with rendering external things directly than with presenting them as experienced
by or related to his narrators, and less concerned with rendering them
objectively than with assigning them human significance, and that this significance is broader, in some respects, than most commentators on Defoe
have acknowledged.

In other respects, however, it is curiously narrow. In a Defoe novel,
everything and everyone mentioned matters to the narrator, and it makes
for a certain kind of realism that all should be so plausibly filtered through
the narrator's consciousness—or at any rate that so little should seem interpolated by an authorial consciousness independent of the narrator's. Whatever contradictions there may be in the characterization of Defoe's heroes
and heroines, most critics do not seem to feel that these inconsistencies
make his characters less lifelike. On the contrary, modern readers are more
likely to balk at the opposite aspect of Defoe's characters—to feel that
individually and collectively their personalities embrace not too much but
too little to be entirely realistic. They share an anxious egoism which tends
to give unity and meaning to the episodic materials of adventure stories,
but which at the same time confines them and their capacity for experience.
If it helps them to see life steadily, it prevents them from seeing life whole.
Important dimensions of both human and nonhuman nature are closed to
them. Such mastery as the Defoean hero achieves over himself and his
world is quite precarious: it involves insulation and repression rather than
openness and liberation, an imposing of order on everything alien and
threatening rather than that benign acceptance of the facts of otherness and
disorder (or order beyond man's contriving) which we find at the conclusion of a Sophoclean or Shakesperean tragedy. We may regard man as
capable of more expansiveness and love than Defoe's heroes and heroines
ever attain—our classic drama offers a vision of what man can potentially
become, alongside which they seem somewhat stunted figures—but the
fact that they are limited people, according to various poets', moralists',
and psychoanalysts' ideals of human development, does not limit their reality or interest. What it does mean is that there are some things Defoe's
characters can encompass and some things they cannot, and the same is
true of Defoe's style. His prose cannot render other people and things as
they are in themselves, since his narrators must recast the world in their
own images in the very act of perceiving it. They may scrutinize their
surroundings as attentively as one of Robbe-Grillet's narrators, but their
gaze is obsessively purposeful, seldom coolly contemplative: in a sense they

see only what they want to see, and what they want to see is chiefly how things stand in relation to themselves. Nor do we in turn see as much through their eyes as through their busily analyzing and combining, imagining and judging minds. "In my dear self I center everything:" [50] this line of Rochester's may not exhaust Defoe's theories about human motivation, but it does sum up accurately his narrator's habitual mode of experiencing and describing their world.

Notes

1. *The Political History of the Devil* (London, 1726), p. 119; capitals added to first words in lines.

2. "If Defoe . . . did write a supplement to Milton's epic, the world has been spared further knowledge of it" (John Robert Moore, *Daniel Defoe, Citizen of the Modern World* [Chicago, 1958] p. 231). But this dialogue between Cain and Satan—which continues for another forty lines—would seem to be a fragment of such a supplement, or a draft for one of its scenes; in either case, it gives us a glimpse of the form this project might have taken.

3. Alliteration, anaphora ("Did you," "We did," "Did you," "We did," etc.), an other forms of repetition abound (e.g., *traductio:* "humbly," "humble," "humble," "humblest;" and *conversio:* "paid," "pay"); note also, among schemes of construction, the frequent parallelism, appositions, and anastrophes (e.g. Cain's penultimate speech)—the latter constituting, in my opinion, the strongest evidence that the passage was composed as blank verse rather than prose.

4. *Colonel Jack*, ed. Samuel Holt Monk (London, 1965), pp. 166–67; for comment on the style of this passage, see my *Defoe and Casuistry* (Princeton, N.J., 1971), pp. 83–84.

5. In *Romances and Narratives of Daniel Defoe*, ed. George A. Aitken (London, 1895), 2:307–8.

6. *Moll Flanders*, ed. G. A. Starr (London, 1971), p. 209.

7. Karl D. Bülbring, Introduction to *Compleat English Gentleman* (London, 1890), pp. xvii, xix; see also George H. Healey, Preface to *Letters* (Oxford, 1955), pp. vii–viii.

8. In *Applebee's Journal* for November 6, 1725, Defoe says of a pedant: "His Stile was all rough Laconicks, thronged with Colons and Full-Points; and he seldom made his Paragraphs above a Line and a half" (in William Lee, *Daniel Defoe: His Life, and Recently Discovered Writings* [London, 1869], 3:438).

9. See "Note on the Text" to my edition of *Moll Flanders*, pp. xxvi–xxviii.

10. Ian Watt, *The Rise of the Novel* (London, 1957), pp. 119–20, quoting *Coleridge's Miscellaneous Criticism*, ed. Thomas M. Raysor (London, 1936), p. 294.

11. Watt, p. 119.

12. See my *Defoe and Spiritual Autobiography* (Princeton, N.J., 1965), and J. Paul Hunter, *The Reluctant Pilgrim* (Baltimore, 1966), passim.

13. Roger L'Estrange, *Fables, of Aesop and Other Eminent Mythologists*, 6th ed. (London, 1714), p. 1. In the *Little Review*, August 17, 1705, Defoe had said: "We may find a Diamond in a Dunghil" (facsimile, ed. Arthur W. Secord [New York, 1938], in *Colonel Jack*, when the hero and a fellow pickpocket successfully make off with a pocketbook full of bills, notes, and

diamonds, but find this "Booty too great . . . to Manage" and are "puzzl'd," Jack sums up their situation by saying, "Now, were we something like the Cock in the Fable" (p. 47).

14. From the definitions of *aversio* in Henry Peacham's *Garden of Eloquence* and John Hoskins's *Direccions for Speech and Style*, as quoted in Lee A. Sonnino, *A Handbook to Sixteenth-Century Rhetoric* (London, 1968), p. 34. My argument does not depend on Defoe's having studied traditional rhetoric, but for evidence that he did, compare his use of technical terms like "antiperistasis" in *The Storm* (London, 1704), p. 3, and in *Some Remarks on the First Chapter in Dr. Davenant's Essays* (London, 1704), p. 3.

15. The latter point could have been argued on other grounds than those briefly touched on here: see Michael Riffaterre, "The Stylistic Approach to Literary History," *New Literary History* 2 (1970):39–55.

16. H. Plumb, Foreward to *A Journal of the Plague Year* (New York, 1960), p. x.

17. *A Journal of the Plague Year*, ed. Louis A. Landa (London, 1970), pp. 55, 80, 163, 178.

18. Locke's remarks on "simple ideas of sense" are relevant here. There are a great many more "particular simple ideas," he says, "belonging to most of the senses than we have names for. The variety of smells, which are as many almost, if not more, than species of bodies in the world, do most of them want names. Sweet and stinking commonly serve our turn for those ideas, *which in effect is little more than to call them pleasing or displeasing* [italics added]. . . . Nor are the different tastes, that by our palates we receive ideas of, much better provided with names. Sweet, bitter, sour, harsh, and salt are almost all the epithets we have to denominate [a] numberless varieties of relishes" (*Essay concerning Human Understanding*, bk. 2, chap. 3, sec. 2, ed. A. C. Fraser [New York, 1959], 2:149. Locke thus recognizes that in reporting even the simplest sensations, we specify more about our responses than about the objects eliciting them; more important for our present purposes, he suggests here that in articulating our response, we perform an act of interpretation, and resort to a conceptual framework (or at any rate a terminology) which is evaluative, not merely descriptive.

19. This differentiates the *Journal* from formal history, for Defoe's language stresses what many historians have sought to minimize—the subjective nature of the act either of apprehending or recounting one's experience. Not that all pretense to objectivity is abandoned; on the contrary. But an air of objectivity is not cultivated directly, by distancing the material through a detached, impersonal manner; rather, it is sought indirectly, by characterizing the narrator as a bourgeois sage who embodies rationality and piety in an ideal balance. H. F. the saddler takes what is in fact a thoroughly engaged position toward his subject matter, but because he presents himself as open-minded, conscientious, and deliberate, we accept his tendentious interpretation of the plague as moderate and just. This reading is developed more fully in my *Defoe and Casuistry*, pp. 51–81.

20. *Robinson Crusoe*, in *Romances and Narratives*, 1:228–29.

21. Robert Adolph, *The Rise of Modern Prose Style* (Cambridge, Mass., 1968), pp. 280–81.

22. Ibid., pp. 245 and passim.

23. *Robinson Crusoe*, in *Romances and Narratives*, 1:183, 189, 186.

24. It should be added that Crusoe's description of Friday is somewhat anomalous: Defoe seldom tells us much about the physical appearance of his characters, and his narrators' own bodies are probably the least personalized "things" in their whole range of perceptions. For the would-be illustrator of Defoe there is plenty of helpful wardrobe information, so that Crusoe's goatskins, Roxana's finery, Moll's disguises, etc., can be drawn vividly, and can convey a good deal about the creatures inside them; yet no narrator offers a self-portrait to compare with Crusoe's sketch of Friday, and it is no accident that Defoe's illustrators present

costume-dummies in characteristic situations, rather than faces individualized on the basis of textual evidence.

25. *The Disappearance of God: Five 19th-Century Writers* (New York, 1965), p. 5.

26. To the Victorians whom Miller so ably discusses, this "transformation of the world" may have marked a loss, but to Defoe it represented a gain—one which he celebrates especially in the *Tour,* the *Plan of the English Commerce,* and other writings on trade. Nor, of course, was Defoe alone in this view. For a discussion of how this transformation, instead of coming "as a severe blow to humanity," tended in Defoe's lifetime "to release a tidal wave of energy and enthusiasm that carried mankind forward in the greatest creative activity of its history," see Ernest L. Tuveson, *The Imagination as a Means of Grace* (Berkeley and Los Angeles, 1960), pp. 9–10 and passim.

27. Watt, p. 101, quoting Sprat's *History of the Royal Society* (1667), p. 113.

28. *Terra: A Philosophical Discourse of Earth ... Presented to the Royal Society* [1675], in *Silva,* ed. A. Hunter, 4th ed. (York, 1812), 2:7, 38, As the knowledgeable proprietor of a brick and tile works in Essex, Defoe may have read this work, either in Evelyn's original version, or as excerpted in *Husbandry and Trade Improv'd.* a popular compilation by another F.R.S. [Fellow of the Royal Society] John Houghton (d. 1705), several times reedited by a third F.R.S., Richard Bradley (d. 1732) (4th ed.) [London, 1727], 1:181–83). Over a century later, Thomas Batchelor says that potatoes "love the taste of new ground," that "it is quite a treat to fresh land to sow clover upon it," that clover is not charged with *"tiring or sickening* the milder species of clays," and that certain crops are sown with a view of *"resting the soil" (General View of the Agriculture of the County of Bedford* [London, 1808], pp. 426, 427, 428, 433).

29. Marjorie Nicolson, *Newton Demands the Muse* (New York, 1946); cf. William Powell Jones, *The Rhetoric of Science: A Study of Scientific Ideas and Imagery in Eighteenth-Century English Poetry* (Berkeley and Los Angeles, 1966).

30. See, however, Donald Davie's brief but illuminating *The Language of Science and the Language of Literature, 1700–1740* (London and New York, 1963), and his earlier essay, "Berkeley's Style in *Siris,*" *Cambridge Journal* 4 (1950):427–33.

31. So long as the writer must rely on words, and cannot simply produce the things themselves, it is hard to see how he can proceed otherwise—how he can deal with the unknown except in terms of the known. When you see a cassowary in St. James's Park, Locke points out, you can recount your experience readily enough if you and your listener already know the name "cassowary" and what it stands for; if not, you can make yourself understood only by describing a kind of bird "about three or four feet high, with a covering of something between feathers and hair, of a dark brown colour, without wings, but in the place thereof two or three little branches coming down like sprigs of Spanish broom, long great legs, with feet only of three claws, and without a tail" (*Essay concerning Human Understanding,* bk. 3, chap. 6, sec, 34 [2:85]).

32. *History of the Royal Society,* p. 413; cf. Jackson I. Cope's valuable introduction to his edition of the *History* (Saint Louis, 1958), pp. xxix–xxx.

33. In seeking "plainness," both Sprat and Defoe reject metaphorical ornament, but in seeking "naturalness" they eschew the appearance, not always the fact, of metaphorical artifice. On this subject see the passages quoted and discussed by James T. Boulton in his excellent introduction to *Defoe* (New York, 1965), pp. 4–5.

34. *Moll Flanders,* p. 143.

35. It is also important that Jemmy be able to fantasize so "naturally:" his casualness and apparent lack of design operate as strongly on Moll as the substance of what he says, and this

is true in turn of her effect on us. The contemporary critic who referred scornfully to "the little art which [Defoe] is truly master of, of telling a lie with the air of truth," was presumably struck by these same qualities in Defoe's total fictional manner. See James Sutherland, *Defoe*, 2d ed. (London, 1950), pp. 249–50.

36. In *Religious Courtship* an English merchant is said to have "the finest Collection of Paintings of any Merchant in Leghorn:" "he is a great Lover of Art, and has a nice Judgment, which are the two only Things that can make buying so many Pictures rational; for his Pieces are so well chosen, that he may sell them when he pleases for above a thousand Pounds more than they cost" (2d ed. [London, 1729], p. 233). We also learn that the man is a Papist, and that the pictures are objects of his superstitious devotion—but practically nothing about the pictures themselves.

37. Dorothy Van Ghent, *The English Novel: Form and Function* (New York, 1961), p. 35.

38. Watt, p. 102.

39. Ibid., pp. 96–97. Watt quotes *Moll Flanders* from Aitken's edition, *Romances and Narratives*, 8:19. Watt's reading of this passage and his treatment of the problem of realism in general are heatedly assailed by David H. Hirsch, "The Reality of Ian Watt," *Critical Quarterly II* (1969): 164–79.

40. It was here that Moll King, on whom Moll Flanders was partly modeled, stole a gold watch from a gentlewoman in 1718. Defoe's extensive use of actual place names, elsewhere in this book and the other novels, often seems designed not so much to enhance the reality of settings in themselves as to suggest, by a kind of shorthand, an element of spatial progression analogous to such elementary notations of temporal progression as: "At length a new scene opened" (*Moll Flanders*, p. 149).

41. "The Problem of Realism in Defoe's *Captain Singleton*," *Huntington Library Quarterly* 27 (1963):29.

42. Ibid., pp. 25–26, 28, quoting the Aitken edition, *Romances and Narratives*, 5:97, 63, 75, 89, 93.

43. Scrimgeour, p. 37 and passim.

44. Ibid., p. 28.

45. See n. 12 above.

46. Indeed, the *Journal of the Plague Year* is a noteworthy instance of this procedure. The epidemic is so destructive of human order, so overwhelming in scale, and so impervious to all efforts to combat or contain it, that it represents in an unusually recalcitrant form the "otherness" of the external world which each of Defoe's heroes must contend with as actors. At the same time, it is so impersonal, and so baffling in its mode of operation, that it is unusually resistant to the attempt which H. F. must make as narrator to give it human significance and value. H. F. responds by positing a divine providence superior even to the plague, thus subordinating the plague to a mind and will analogous to man's own. Before such cataclysms, human reason may be as helpless as the human body, but the faithful can detect in them the hand and purpose of providence. Interpreting the plague as a scourge wielded *by* hand *for* a purpose, H. F. can master its inscrutability if not its physical threat. At times he personifies the plague directly, like the gold in *Robinson Crusoe*, but his most telling strategy is to humanize the plague indirectly—as ministering to providential ends, which are themselves conceived anthropomorphically.

47. See Stephen H. Dill, "An Analysis of Some Aspects of Daniel Defoe's Prose Style" (Ph.D. diss., University of Arkansas, 1965); Gustaf L. Lannert, *An Investigation into the Language of Robinson Crusoe as Compared with That of Other 18th Century Works* (Uppsala and Cambridge, 1910).

48. See Bonamy Dobree, "Some Aspects of Defoe's Prose," in *Pope and His Contemporaries: Essays Presented to George Sherburn*, ed. James L. Clifford and Louis A. Landa (Oxford, 1949), pp. 171–84; and especially Boulton (n. 33 above).

49. See Mark Schorer, Introduction to *Moll Flanders* (New York, 1950), and Denis Donoghue, "The Values of Moll Flanders," *Sewanee Review* 71 (1963):287–303; both stress the mercantile aspect of Moll's language. In recent articles on "Defoe and Crusoe," *ELH* 38 (1971):377–96, and on "Language and Character in Defoe's *Roxana*," *Essays in Criticism* 21 (1971): 227–35, Everett Zimmerman challenges this "reductive economic interpretation of Defoe," and very persuasively argues that the language (and behavior) of Defoe's narrators reveals more deep seated "metaphysical terrors," against which their "materialism" is merely one kind of defense.

50. See "To a Lady That Accused Him of Inconstancy," in *The Compleat Poetical Works of Robert Wilmot, Earl of Rochester*, ed. David M. Vieth (New Haven, Conn., 1970), p. 107.

Penetration and Impenetrability
in *Clarissa*

LEO BRAUDY

That was the devilish part of her—this coldness, this woodenness,
something very profound in her, which he had felt again this morning
talking to her; an impenetrability.

(Virginia Woolf, Mrs. Dalloway)

"Say what strange Motive, Goddess! cou'd compel / A well-bred *Lord* t'assault a gentle *Belle?*" The questions posed by *Clarissa* and *The Rape of the
Lock* are remarkably similar. What cultural changes could have occurred in
the thirty-odd years between their first publications so that a situation
which in one major work is the object of Olympian poetic satire could in
the second major work be the subject of tragic fictional involvement? What
could turn Pope's savage depiction of the social repression of natural sexual instincts (symbolized in the Cave of Spleen) into the praise of the necessary repression of sexuality that characterizes *Clarissa?* What connection
is there between the barren Baron and the loveless Lovelace, between the
social imperatives of the poem and the personal imperatives of the novel?

To a certain extent, *Clarissa* continues *The Rape of the Lock* (as *The Rape
of the Lock* may continue *The Country Wife*), and Pope seems presciently
aware that his poem could not include a solution to the problem he posed
in it. No matter how brilliantly in effect the poem might laugh the real life
participants together (and the Baron was already dead from smallpox the
year before it was published), in the more severe world of the poem itself,
the conflict is not resolved. The battle stops in mid-gesture, resolvable per-

From *New Approaches to Eighteenth-Century Literature: Selected Papers from the English Institute*, ed. Phillip Harth (New York: Columbia University Press, 1974), pp. 177–206.

haps in the couplet but not on any social or psychological level. Pope seems to see no narrative device by which the conflict he so accurately describes can be resolved by the characters themselves in a way that the reader will recognize as valid and possible. "Trust the Muse," says Pope, and the ringing in of that Horatian topos, have-faith-in-the-poem-to-transfigure-the-story-it-tells, marks the point where Pope's genius ends its search for a form that might more fully express his new subject matter. *The Rape of the Lock* is aware of the forces of a newly emerging definition of the inner life that threatens to change Belinda's world of social banter into the more terrifying conflicts of the world of Clarissa. But Pope is writing poetry, not prose, and part of his greatness arises from the collision between his new themes and his old forms. He understands the inadequacy of this kind of poetry to express and develop to the full the ideas about character that fascinate him; in the *Moral Essays* and *Arbuthnot* he takes his insight even further, moved in part perhaps by Donne's lyric energies to personalize his own more public form. Like Swift in the creation of Gulliver, Pope in the *Moral Essays* and *Arbuthnot* seems poised between a satiric and fictional view of character, between character viewed from the outside, in analogy to painting, with the goal of caricature and simplification, and character expressed from within, through an essentially non-visual exploration of the potentials of inconsistency and uncertainty.

The perception of cultural change may outrun the formal means at the writer's disposal to express that change. The creation of fictional character seems to arise from a feeling that earlier attitudes toward character are deficient psychologically, and therefore rhetorically, to face the newly perceived problems of self-definition. Seventeenth-century character, with its varied hagiographic, theophrastan, and satiric strands, is essentially character constructed by rhetoric and viewed from without. When such characters are placed on a stage, in the context of others, their rhetorical balance is transformed into psychological self-containment. We may be asked to laugh at the self-containment (Jonson's Morose) or with it (Wycherley's Horner). But even in the triumph of such a character, there is a necessary human loss that is one of the main themes of Restoration comedy. "The satirist satirized" expresses in rhetorical terms the psychological truth embodied in Horner's final rejection of the affection of Margery Pinchwife in order to preserve the myth of his impotence. Style and language become an end in themselves, and the desire to feed one's ego by the control of others unavoidably leads to personal isolation and despair. But, within traditional literary forms, the entrapped satirist or the entrapped satiric character is as far as the author can go. Wycherley's insight is presented with the traditional impersonality of the dramatist. Pope's use of poetry, with its traditions, precedents, and forms, its natural desire to bring the new into the frame of pre-existing order, similarly leads him to the "solution" of detachment and distance, character viewed once again from the outside. "Trust the Muse," forget the terror beneath, remember instead "the moving toyshop of the heart," In *The Dunciad* Pope returns to the definition of the poet that he seemed to have left behind in *The Rape of the Lock:* the Olympian detached voice, contemplating with equal measure intricacy and grandeur, beauty and foulness, triviality and apocalypse. Strange that a poet who considered himself to be the latest in a line of great poets stretching back to Homer should spend so much of his last years casting and recasting a more complex and more elaborate version of *Mac Flecknoe.* By turning Pope into MacDryden, *The Dunciad* implicitly announces the failure of detached poetic Olympianism, failed perhaps because it never distinguished clearly enough between the vices and virtues of the personal voice in literature, its mixed portion of fragmentation, empathy, and energy. When Pope attacks more and more by name, at a stage in his career when one might expect Horatian detachment, he is stating quite distinctly that the problem is not action, nor institutions, nor faulty generalizations, nor immoral principles; the problem is in individuals, in their weak sense of themselves and in that necessary corollary, the weakness of the written, self-justifying word.[1]

Personal identity is just as vexed a problem in seventeenth- and eighteenth-century philosophy as it is in literature. But the terms of the problem are generally less complex because conflict is not the philosopher's immediate concern. Descartes' elaboration of medieval distinctions between mind and body was a necessary prelude to his theories of perception and knowledge that could also allay a potential religious hostility. Hobbes, Locke, and Hume, in their own ways, similarly recognize that the problem of personal identity cannot be separated from general problems of knowledge, and they discuss questions of consciousness, memory, and bodily continuity with sometimes lesser and sometimes greater intensity. But their questions all aim toward decisions about what each considers to be larger matters. They ask "what is identity in general?" and "how do we understand the term identity when it appears in other contexts?" They wonder "what is a person?" and "how is one person not another person?" Hobbes and Locke, for example, are especially interested in personal identity within society. Hobbes wants to define the limits of individuals so that no man encroaches too much on the next and he therefore seeks to dispense with the unquantifiable and uncontrollable in human nature. His model for the state is a mechanical being, and his model for human nature is a completely socialized being. Unsocialized thoughts, like unsocialized behavior, must be either brought into the frame of society or expunged:

> The secret thoughts of a man run over all things, holy, prophane, clean, obscene, grave, and light, without shame, or blame; which verball discourse cannot do, farther than the Judgement shall approve of the Time, Place, and Persons. An Anatomist, or a Physitian may speak, or write his judgement of unclean things; because it is not to please, but profit: but for another man to write his extravagant, and pleasant fancies of the same, is as if a man, from being tumbled into the dirt, should come and present himselfe before good company.[2]

Locke is similarly interested in the social extensions of the self and defines consciousness in such a way that he can answer the later questions "what is a person in law?" and "how do we determine responsibility for action?" He calls the question of personal identity a "forensic" one and discusses such problems as the difference between a person drunk and a person sober, a person sleeping and a person waking.[3] Hobbes and Locke would basically like to purify the definition of personal identity by connecting it only with one's personal responsibility for action within society: any antisocial or non-social component of personal identity was an aberration. Even though, for example, at one point Locke seems to anticipate the use of psychiatry in courts of law, he also assumes that it will not be used to exonerate or explain but to assign reward and punishment with more precision.

Since Hume is more sensitive to the phenomenology of everyday life than Hobbes and Locke, he does not demand the same fixity of personal identity. He basically attacks any idea of a substantial self that remains unchanging through life and experience. personal identity, he says, is a "grammatical" fiction that serves to connect the "republic" or "commonwealth" of one's impressions and ideas. Memory is insufficient to provide total continuity because it "does not so much produce as discover personal identity, by shewing us the relation of cause and effect among our different perceptions,"[4] Hume finds no difficulty in asserting that our perceptions are always our own, never anyone else's, and that we are always ourselves, whether conscious or not, whether we remember or forget. One might expect that Hume would then argue for bodily continuity as the main criterion of personal identity. but he does not take that step, no matter how he may imply it. Hume's attack is better than his explorations. His pages on personal identity tend to refer more to mind than to body, and more to identity than to person. In one of his first references to personal identity in the *Treatise*, Hume remarks that "'Tis certain that there is no question in philosophy more abstruse than that concerning identity, and the nature of the uniting principle, which constitutes a person." But, in the Appendix to Book I of the *Treatise*, after saying that consciousness seems to come from "reflecting on past perceptions," Hume can go no further: "But all my hopes vanish, when I come to explain the principles, that unite our successive perceptions in our thought or consciousness. I cannot discover any theory, which gives me satisfaction on this head."[5]

The final pun indicates Hume's real interest. When the first book of the *Treatise* is rewritten as *An Inquiry Concerning Human Understanding*, the discussion of personal identity is essentially dropped. Despite his attack on a static concept of the self, Hume does not want to pursue the discussion of personal identity any further, into, for example, a definition that might combine process and bodily continuity. Like the other philosophers, whatever range of definitions they offer, Hume seems to consider personal identity a point of vantage from which to view the world outside.

By comparison, the novelists deal instead with the anxiety about identity. With Defoe's first-person narratives or Richardson's epistles (which, unlike Pope's, separate correspondents rather than link them), the pressure of self-definition, the pressure on the working out of problems *now*, intensifies both formally and thematically. There can be no invocation of the traditional topoi of superior poetic insight, no turning aside to more pressing philosophical problems, to be asserted as saving solutions. Fiction identifies the mind and the page, making the creation of a book into an act of self-justification; self-expression becomes inextricably linked to personal identity. Pope may not go further because it is within the novel, as defined by Defoe and Richardson, that a new sense of human separateness is best analyzed and explored—all our basic attitudes towards ourselves, our minds, our bodies, and our relationships with other people, especially male-female relationships. In the uncertainties of prose fiction, with its uncertain grasp on the expository and ordered, all the questions have to be asked again and again, formulated and reformulated; they cannot be provisionally locked into some traditional aesthetic form. Neither muse nor machinery nor philosophic system can be trusted to provide a safe literary refuge. Everyone, author and character alike, must tell his own story. As Anna Howe reports to us after Clarissa's death, " . . . it was always a matter of surprise to her that the sex are generally so averse as they are to writing; since the pen, next to the needle, of all employments, is the most proper, and best suited to their geniuses; and this as well for improvement as amusement."[6]

Pen and penetration. Richardson is not usually considered to be a writer who uses figurative language. He is a plain writer: steeped in common speech, unpoetic, unsoaring. But within *Clarissa* repetitions of certain words and their cognates build patterns that contain a force larger than any immediate context. One such word is *penetration,* as used to characterize the wit and understanding of both Clarissa and Lovelace. Another is *impenetrable,* used to describe the barriers put up by both Clarissa and Lovelace. Still another is *prepossession,* frequently used by the Harlowes to characterize what they believe is Clarissa's predilection for Lovelace. Add to these the varieties of will, legal and personal: *good will, ill will,* and *willful. Character,* of course, is yet another, not only the social nature Pope speaks of in *To a Lady,* but the elements of writing as well, the cryptographical form Lovelace uses for his secret letters, his "cursed algebra." All these words have many interrelations, and in this paper I would like to concentrate on *penetration* and *impenetrable,* with an implicit nod at the others, because the poles of penetration and impenetrability express most clearly what I take to be Richardson's main theme: the efforts of individuals to discover and define themselves by their efforts to penetrate, control, and even destroy others, while they remain impenetrable themselves.

Almost everything that happens to Clarissa she perceives to be a diminishment of her freedom. In *Pamela,* the urge toward marriage and children implied a sense of continuity, a commitment to society, an effort to bring Pamela's values to bear upon a corrupt social world and hopefully reform it. In *Clarissa* society has effectively vanished and the battleground is inside the self. Clarissa enters the novel believing that there are timeless social relations that insure her personal security. She quickly finds that her assumptions are untrue and in the process becomes aware of what she had unconsciously assumed. Her own desires, she finds, will be sacrificed to the desires of her father and brother in order to aggrandize the family wealth and perpetuate the family name. The family good is superior to her own. The first threat to the self comes therefore from what had seemed to be the most secure part of Clarissa's life. She has discovered that familial roles and relations will not bear the moral weight she had placed upon them. She first tries to convince her family that she is not subversive. But she is unsuccessful. They lose their legitimacy for her as keepers of value not because they do not understand her position but because they understand too well the point where family and individual values fatally clash, and on this issue Mrs. Harlowe is as much Clarissa's opponent as Mr. Harlowe, or James, or Arabella. But Clarissa's basic value is singleness, as defined by the relations between both men and women and between parents and children. The novel therefore details the process of Clarissa's disappointment with the traditional ways identity has been defined outside the self. Rationality has failed; legal and religious institutions have failed; and finally the family has failed. What then does "I"mean in a world without the traditional contexts of institutional and intellectual order? Clarissa will finally found her personal continuity and substantiality solely upon the purity of her principles—and in such self-definition deny her less certain past selves, her treacherous heart and body, and her fallible need for other people.

Clarissa's primary fear about marriage, and her objection to Solmes, the suitor her family forces upon her, is the loss of identity it entails:

> *Marriage* is a very solemn engagement, enough to make a young creature's heart ache, with the *best* prospects, when she thinks seriously of it! To be given up to a strange man; to be ingrafted into a strange family; to give up her very name, as a mark of her becoming his absolute and dependent property; to be obliged to prefer this strange man, to father, mother—to everybody: and his humours to all her own—or to contend perhaps, in breach of a vowed duty, for every innocent instance of free-will. To go no-whither: to make acquaintance: to give up acquaintance: to renounce even the strictest friendships perhaps; all at his pleasure, whether she thinks it reasonable to do so or not: surely, sir, a young creature ought not to be obliged to make all these sacrifices but for such a man as she can love. If she be, how sad must be the case! How miserable the life, if to be called *life!*[7]

As the novel makes clear, you must distrust society and the world around you, even your own family and the one you love. They all want to steal your self away, to penetrate your ideas, to prepossess your feelings, to bend your will to their own. The only answer is to trust the principles you find within: "Principles that *are* in my mind; that I *found* there; implanted, no doubt, by the first gracious Planter: which therefore *impel* me, as I may say, to act up to them, that thereby I may, to the best of my judgment, be enabled to comport myself worthily in both states (the single and the married), let others act as they will by *me*" (II, 306). But how is that *me* to be defined?

For Clarissa, as for Lovelace in his own way, the true self is everything that everyone else is not. Self-definition excludes the rest of the world, and, when it does find its values, finds them either in the innate principles of "the first gracious Planter" or in the values of the past. Fred Weinstein and Gerald Platt, in *The Wish to be Free*, have argued that insecurity arises from an attack on contemporary systems of value and the concomitant fear of building a new system of values solely from within. The revolutionary then seeks the sanction of older forms to legitimize his rebellion.[8] As Robespierre reintroduced many feudal and patriarchal values and practices, so Clarissa, whose radical idealism rejects even such primitive social forms, will gradually define herself as an example, an anti-physical saint. And so she is accepted by her admirers, notably Belford, her prime disciple, who writes to Lovelace:

> ... I have conceived such a profound reverence for her sense and judgment, that, far from thinking the man excusable who should treat her basely, I am ready to regret such an angel of a woman should even marry. She is in my eye all mind: and were she to meet with a man all mind likewise, why should the charming qualities she is mistress of be endangered? Why should such an angel be plunged so low into the vulgar offices of domestic life? Were she mine, I should hardly wish to see her a mother, unless there were a kind of moral certainty that minds like hers could be propagated. For why, in short, should not the work of bodies be left to *mere* bodies?   (II, 243–44)

Clarissa explores and helps define the cultural moment when the self-willed isolation of the individual that insures a security against the world becomes first an opposition between self and society and finally a mutually exclusive definition of the images of male and female. Weinstein and Platt have further argued that, with the industrial revolution, the formerly undifferentiated roles of husband and wife—both controlling and both nurturing—separated into the controlling father and the nurturing mother, the one who comes home only to command and the other who stays home, without commanding and with only ameliorative power. This division is already present in Mr. and Mrs. Harlowe: the unapproachable God-like tyrant and the wheedling, sympathetic, and subordinated mother. None of Clarissa's experience in the novel does anything to contradict this definition of male and female roles. In fact, she expands and institutionalizes it—as Belford's remarks indicate—into a general denial of sexuality. Like Richardson when he writes the novel, Clarissa separates herself into masculine and feminine parts and defines them against each other into even greater purity. In search of the anti-masculine self Clarissa desires, Richardson has taken the first step towards the concept of "the opposite sex" and the rigidification of male and female roles that would be the heritage of the nineteenth century and our own.

Pen, penetration, prepossession, impenetrable. Obviously the sexual nuance is there in the abstract language. But, without undervaluing sexuality, I think that its function in *Clarissa* should be seen in a larger context.

The fear of sexuality in *Clarissa* constitutes only the most obvious expression of a general fear of relationship and vulnerability that characterizes both Clarissa and Lovelace.[9] Here are two passages, both from the third volume of the novel, and both remarks by Lovelace. In the first, to Belford, Lovelace describes an incident during which he had grabbed Clarissa's hand and implored her to accept him as a lover: "And I snatched her hand, and more than kissed it; I was ready to devour it. There was, I believe, a kind of frenzy in my manner which threw her into a panic like that of Semele perhaps, when the Thunderer, in all his majesty surrounded with ten thousand celestial burning-glasses, was about to scorch her into a cinder" (II, 98).

The unbowdlerized story, of course, is that Semele desired Zeus to come upon her in all his godhead, undisguised, and that the intercourse itself destroy her, except for the fertilized germ that would become Dionysus. Whose coyness then is the ten thousand celestial burning-glasses, Richardson's or Lovelace's? It certainly suits with Lovelace's character, for, in its avoidance of the actual myth, it expresses Lovelace's simultaneous desire to assert sexual power and to shrink from that power's destructive potential. His own remark in this situation, as Clarissa has reported it to Anna Howe a few pages earlier, is much more passive: " . . . take me, take me to yourself; mould me as you please; I am wax in your hands; give me your own impression, and seal me for ever yours" (II, 80). How precarious is that self-assertion by which Lovelace defines himself! Precarious in the same way as Clarissa's, for both fear the weakness and vulnerability that they blame on their sexuality. To compensate for his weakness, Lovelace makes his sexuality into a weapon, and Clarissa's refusal of sexuality is the shield she fashions from the same impulses. Because of his disguises, Clarissa calls Lovelace the "perfect Proteus" and insists to Anna Howe that she is not being herself contradictory, but only reporting Lovelace's self-contradictions. Yet Lovelace's uncertainties awaken a "divided soul" in Clarissa as well, and to his changeability she gradually opposes her self-purification. Clarissa becomes clarissima.

Far from being the expression of an abstract, semi-allegorical opposition between flesh and spirit, the relationship between Clarissa and Lovelace develops into a set of polarized self-images because the characters believe those responses are increasingly appropriate to the situations in which they find themselves.[10] Clarissa and Lovelace further elaborate the balance-sheet self that so preoccupied Robinson Crusoe and Pamela, in which goods and evils, benefits and demerits, were entered in parallel columns. But identity in *Clarissa* can no longer be the combination or even the choice of one or the other side of the equation. One must choose absolutely; there is no third term. Using Lovelace to define herself (as he uses her), Clarissa believes that she is a totally interior being, while he is totally exterior. The true self, as she defines it, is a purging of the external world—the theatrical, role-playing definition of identity Lovelace embodies—as well as the divisions he excites within her, her "divided soul." In order to achieve true singularity, there can be no ambivalence, no past vacillations. Each step along the way to Clarissa's self-willed death is a sloughing away of the snakeskin of some past self. In Richardson's profound paradox, Clarissa believes that her justification will come through the opinion of others about her inner worth, and she becomes pure to justify the exemplary view of her others hold. Like so many Enlightenment figures, torn between the desire for autonomy and the anxiety of rejecting traditional standards, Clarissa seeks her justification in the future, from those who will learn from her story and her example.[11] Samuel Johnson tried to purge some of his own anxiety about self-assertion by coming as a grown man to bare his head in the public square of Uttoxeter, there to expiate a childhood disobedience of his father. But Clarissa turns her will inward and expresses her self-sufficiency by destroying the self that dared assert itself.

Since physicality is the most obvious barrier to that self-definition, Clarissa turns more and more against her own body. The body, she decides, is the weak barricade before the mind, the will, and ultimately the soul. The eye first allows the breach in that barricade: another's eye, which attempts first to possess one visually, then physically, and finally psychically; or your own eye, which must necessarily be deluded by the specious beauty of external form. As Anna Howe writes to Clarissa, "The eye, my dear, the wicked eye, has such a strict alliance with the heart, and both have such enmity to the understanding! What an unequal union, the mind and body! All the senses, like the family at Harlowe Place, in a confederacy against that which would animate, and give honour to the whole, were it allowed its proper precedence" (II, 116–17). That which would animate is, of course, the anima, the soul. Anna Howe's parallel invokes neither Locke's legal definition of identity, self as the name for the individual acting in society, nor Hume's conglomerate identity, self as the name for all that is you. It implies instead a need to purge oneself of the senses, as Clarissa must purge herself of her family, to gain true self-identity. Passion, Clarissa writes to Anna Howe, is the same in both sexes: "Those passions in our sex which we take no pains to subdue, may have one and the same source with those infinitely blacker passions which we used so often to condemn in the violent and headstrong of the other sex; and which may be only heightened in *them* by *custom,* and their *freer education.* Let us both, my dear, ponder well this thought; look into ourselves, and fear" (II, 236).

Lovelace, too, is preoccupied with the threat to his eyes. He claims that his antagonism toward women, the revenge he seeks, dates from a youthful jilt. But in a more violent passage, he gives a clue to the depths beneath his attack: "How usual a thing is it for women as well as men, without the least remorse, to ensnare, to cage, and torment, and even with burning knitting-needles to put out the eyes of the poor feathered songster . . . which, however, in proportion to its bulk, has more life than themselves (for a bird is all soul), and of consequence has as much feeling as the human creature!" (II, 247). I could here detail the many analogies in *Clarissa* between caged birds and caged human beings or recall Clarissa's remark about the suitability of the pen and the needle to the talents of women. But it is enough to note the importance that both Clarissa and Lovelace give to the eyes.[12] Richardson has in effect transformed a Renaissance trope into a psychological compulsion. Lovelace may owe his existence to the precedent of Wycherley's Horner. But this time lives and not just maidenheads are at stake. Visibility is not a metaphor for sexuality, just as sexuality is not a metaphor for identity. They are interlocked concepts for Richardson, and the general rejection of metaphor by the eighteenth-century novel underlines its search for what might be called a rhetoric of essences rather than surfaces. Clarissa's refusal of physicality parallels the almost non-visual world of Richardson's novel. Were Adam and Eve blind in Eden? Clarissa supposes her story to show first of all that "the eye is a traitor" (II, 313), indicating the treasonous nature of the visual world, that world of otherness, that the frail eye opens us to. The division between mind and body that Descartes developed as an epistemological assumption has in *Clarissa* become an ontological imperative.[13]

What feminine roles are available to Clarissa in her relationship with Lovelace? Possible models are her mother's relation to her father and Anna Howe's to Hickman, the former an abdication to masculine authority and tyranny and the latter a genial subordination in which the woman has the actual control. There is no continuum of relationship between men and women like that which can exist between persons of the same sex.[14] Especially for the woman who wants to exercise her will morally and personally, there seem to be no real alternatives, only either a total acceptance of the myth of male-female relations or a split between mind and body, in which the body is defined as male and therefore rejected. When Clarissa decides to die after she has been raped by Lovelace, he does not understand. Since Clarissa had been drugged and her mind is therefore inviolate, why should his physical violation of her be so important? (Anna Howe makes the same point in IV, 18.) But Clarissa knows the truth of her frailty: *weakness comes from within*. It is not a diabolical imposition from the outside. The mind is its own place—and the body as well. Against Lovelace she defines her will as a totally mental and spiritual entity, not only separate from desire but opposed to it as well. In the process of her self-definition she rejects both memory, the psychological criterion for the continuous self, and body, the physical criterion for the continuous self. She holds to herself only the timeless assertion of spirit and will. Once again Richardson has psychologized rhetoric. This is no longer the Renaissance topos of the battle of the sexes, the military images of love poetry, but a definite statement about the incompatibility of the masculine and feminine egos, the warfare between their essential self-definitions. Lovelace believes that the mind and body are separate. But Clarissa believes they are connected as well, to the death of the soul, if the taint of the physical goes too far.[15]

With little sense of the historical background or the way their researches had been foreseen by Richardson among many other writers, R. D. Laing and A. Esterson have systematized and thereby made familiar the pattern of family relationships so clearly portrayed in *Clarissa*. Clarissa first seeks to preserve her will inviolate when her family tries to force her to deny her grandfather's bequest. The social and economic pressures felt by the Harlowes are translated into a pressure upon the one member of the family they believe to be the weakest and most tractable, like Cordelia and Cinderella, a younger daughter. The bond of the Harlowes is their anger against a world they believe is about to attack them. By isolating one person and identifying all the family's problems with that person's actions or refusal to act, the rest of the family is saved from insecurity and conflict. Through the example of the Harlowes we can see how the structure of the modern nuclear family may have been insensibly created as a response to otherwise intolerable social and economic realities. Clarissa responds by setting her mind against her body, becoming the spiritual ancestor of the young girls Laing and Esterson describe in *Sanity, Madness, and the Family*. But one aspect of Clarissa's character prevents her from being a case: her assertion of will and freedom, the step outside the garden gate that ends in her death. What is schizophrenia in the younger daughters of weak will described by Laing and Esterson defines itself in Richardson, thanks to the strength of Clarissa's will, as a psychic ideology. Richardson in *Clarissa* could perhaps justifiably consider Clarissa's response to be necessary and appropriate in a new and increasingly anonymous world. In our own time it has become one of the main elements in a self-limiting, self-destructive response to the world around us.[16]

Clarissa's desire to purify her sense of self bears many similarities to Gulliver's. Compressed between the demands of her family on one side, Lovelace on another, and the injunctions and coaxings of Anna Howe on still a third, Clarissa seeks to define herself to the exclusion of all others: purity of self shall become an example to all around her. Here is the point where satiric simplicity and saintly purity can intersect, in the belief that the most accurate vision of human nature involves the successive shedding of complexity and ambivalence so that character may be defined by exclusion rather than inclusion. Faced with the hostile world around her, Clarissa adopts Gulliver's method, separating her personal identity from the contamination of body in search of a definition of character based on inner principles and order. Both consider the body to be a weak defense against the necessary incursions of the world. Gulliver, true to his theatrical ancestors, defines the threat in terms of the violation of his reputation, not in the "rakish annals" that Lovelace always worries about, but in the annals of cleanliness. In Book I of *Gulliver's Travels* he attempts to "vindicate" himself against hypothetical attacks on his excesses, both sexual and scatological. In the context of Swift's work his overreaction is absurd. But underneath is a dark dilemma about the nature of the self that parallels Clarissa's desire to see herself solely as a being of mind and spirit. Look within and fear; look outside and fear as well. The mingled impression of caricature and characterization we receive from *Gulliver's Travels* conveys the way Gulliver stands between the comic concerns of Restoration drama and the psychological dilemmas of the novel.[17] I use Gulliver here as a foil to Clarissa because I do not want to consider Clarissa's situation to be totally that of a woman in a male world. It is also a human situation, and that is the source of its power.

Lovelace reflects Gulliver's worries over reputation even more directly. Servants, Clarissa says at one point, are bad nowadays because they imitate stage servants (IV, 164). That remark is a small version of the difficulty of Lovelace, who models his character on the stage libertine—Don Juan, Horner, Dorimant—even though his personal nature does not really fit the role. Lovelace is less the descendant of these stage figures than their victim. Like Clarissa, Lovelace puts a great weight on his own consistency. She attempts to define and regulate her sense of personal identity by what she believes to be innate principles of virtue. He attempts to rule his life in accordance with pre-existing literary and theatrical stereotype—the "rakish annals" he so frequently invokes. Lovelace therefore represents a type of character and a type of human being very important to the history of the novel—the person warped or ruined by his experience of art.[18] In the history of literature, the novel marks a transition in literature from theatrical and satiric definitions of character—character apprehended from without—to fictional character—character apprehended from within. When critics believe that Clarissa is superior to Lovelace because he seeks external approval while she cultivates the inner life, they accept the attack Richardson's fiction seems to make on the role-playing self and embrace the assumption that hidden things are necessarily superior to visible ones. But Clarissa is as enslaved to the moral attitudes of others in her desire to become an example as Lovelace is enslaved to older forms of literary character. In fact both Lovelace and Clarissa act out of fear that they will themselves disintegrate if they do not first annihilate or by dying obviate the existence of others. In their search for wholeness neither will admit the need for others. The myths of survival that animate Robinson Crusoe, Moll Flanders, Gulliver, Lovelace, and Clarissa assert that the only acceptable self is a self-sufficient one. The only way to avoid the control of others is to control yourself. The response therefore to the threat of penetration, whether physical, mental, or spiritual, is to become impenetrable, to become independent by making others dependent upon you.

Whatever the symbiosis of Clarissa and Lovelace, the novel is still Clarissa's. In the early novel, men tend to be the main characters when vocation and society are the main themes. The issue in such novels is often "what place in society is suitable to his merits?" In novels that have a woman for the central character, the basic question is usually "how is the self to be realized, whether society exists or not?"[19] We first can learn about the relations between men and women in a particular era from direct statements about masculine and feminine behavior, the legal situation, and other factual sources. But more important, more pervasive, and more elusive, is the symbolic situation of men and women: how do masculine and feminine stand for different aspects of a total individual, whether that individual is actually a man or a woman? how do new myths emerge from old? what other cultural forces accompany their creation?

Clarissa marks the definite reversal of the classical and medieval psychomachia of temperate man and emotional woman, for Clarissa's psychic independence and sense of personal identity are linked directly with her denial of a physical being that has responded too precipitately to the lure of a man. Belford reports to Lovelace: "The lady has been giving orders, with great presence of mind, about her body . . . "(IV, 340). And, in the elaborate will she writes toward the end of the novel, Clarissa declares "I am nobody's," affirming the interpenetrating relationship of self-possession and self-denial: "In the first place, I desire that my body may lie unburied three days after my decease, or till the pleasure of my father be known concerning it. But the occasion of my death not admitting of doubt, I will not, on any account, that it be opened; and it is my desire that it shall not be touched but by those of my own sex" (IV, 416).

Clarissa lasts a year, but the yearly cycle is unrenewed. Without physicality, without sexuality, there are no bodies, no children, and no continuity. Clarissa's world is a dead end, and the only thing to do is quickly to get out of it. Clarissa has triumphed by reducing her individual human nature to a purified personal identity. As Lovelace says to Belford shortly before death, " . . . I admire her more than ever; and . . . my love for her is less *personal*, as I may say, more *intellectual*, than ever I thought it could be to woman" (IV, 262). Or, as Belford describes the deathbed of Mrs. Sinclair, with the prostitutes surrounding it: " . . . as much as I admire, and next to adore, a truly virtuous and elegant woman: for to me it is evident, that as a neat and clean woman must be an angel of a creature, so a sluttish one is the impurest animal in nature" (IV, 381). Need I mention that Belford has referred to Swift's Yahoos in the previous sentence? The Gulliverian hatred of the body and its messes has Clarissa as its ideologue and Belford as her acolyte. Sydney Shoemaker in *Self-knowledge and Self-Identity* described Descartes's argument that "since he could doubt the existence of bodies, but could not doubt the existence of himself, he could not be a body."[20] The bodily continuity that Hume implied was part of the definition of a person is summarily rejected in Clarissa's idea of herself. She has domesticated Descartes (although Richardson would have been upset at the suggestion) to create a self that exists without conflict or change, bound neither to time nor to society, expressing in her own way what Locke called "the sameness of a rational being."[21]

The parameters within which Richardson's characters seek for a firm sense of identity have much to do with the ways in which the English novel subsequently explores characters as well as with the narrative structures that guide that exploration. Novelistic attitudes toward character both reflect and lead the way people think about themselves and their world. When literature on all levels of sophistication becomes the primary link between people, the main bridge between individuals and society, then self-images will be greatly controlled by literary images. Until the advent of film, it is the word that structures the self. Any discussion of penetration and impenetrability in character must necessarily lead finally to a discussion of the act of writing itself.

The will that Clarissa writes towards the end of the novel makes clear that it is not will alone which controls one's identity and relation to others, but will as embodied in writing. Once again, Clarissa bears comparison to Gulliver: both parallel their search for personal purity with a search for linguistic purity; Clarissa as immediate letter writer stands next to Gulliver as plain-speaking voyager. The work of recent literature most alluded to in *Clarissa* is not actually *Gulliver*, but *A Tale of a Tub*, and *A Tale of a Tub* not as a religious tract, but as a work about writing. Language helps one to possess the potentially fragmented self and keep it whole. Pamela itched to write and hid her writings by sewing them into her petticoats to swathe her virginity from Mr. B. Clarissa not only protects herself, she also objectifies and distances herself by writing. Throughout the early parts of the novel she worries about the pride involved in being an example. But, as the novel moves on, she gradually accepts her exemplary status, in great part because of the self-objectification created by her own writings. The woman with the pen confronts the man with the penis. Clarissa changes not so much by Lovelace's attacks on her as she does by the sense of self-sufficiency and self-enclosure writing has helped to give her. Whereas Lovelace uses writing as a disguise, Clarissa uses it as an inward stay— another re-enactment of the competition between the belief that the self is enriched through role-playing and stylization and the belief that the truly strong self is purified and sincere. Once again, Clarissa and Lovelace are similar in their sensitivities, if not in their final positions. In volumes one and two of the novel, they have both been established as adroit and polished users of words. Often admired, they are also often attacked by other characters who complain that they use language as wit, to penetrate, even while they remain personally impenetrable. Like Fielding's ideal in *Joseph Andrews*, they cannot be looked into like a simple book, even for a few pages.[22]

What happens when the two impenetrable penetrators meet? In the early pages of the novel they are both optimistic about their ability to use words for their own best ends. They seem to preserve a Hobbesian belief in the humanness of language and its suitability as a medium for explanation and correspondence. Unlike *A Tale of a Tub*, *Clarissa* seems to imply that language can work: letters can be ways to communicate and justify. Swift calls on the violence of satiric language to renovate and revitalize the dead language around him, preventing it from slipping further into non-meaning. Richardson, in his commitment to plainness and clarity, shows a self-consciousness about language, without questioning its basic nature. At the point where self-justification and communication finally conflict, Richardson chooses to explore while Swift is content to mock. The existence of language may imply the existence of society. But it also implies the existence of self-conscious persons.

The problem of linguistic definition and clarification (to found a true science, to establish a workable society, to express basic religious truths) is therefore necessarily tied to the problem of personal identity: the fears about linguistic fragmentation that plague writers like Swift stand kin to the fears of psychic fragmentation and loss of identity that characterize the speaker of *A Tale of a Tub*. Pope's optimism in the 1730s about the poet's ability to reform language parallels his optimism about the new possibilities for human character. Clarissa in her turn implies that prose is the only medium possible for spiritual meaning and promulgates an anti-physical mysticism based not on ineffability but on language. Clarissa's will assigns destinies and meaning to all, and she designs her coffin as well, imposing her own meaning on her life:

> The principal device, neatly etched on a plate of white metal is a crowned serpent, with its tail in its mouth, forming a ring, the emblem of eternity; and in the circle made by it is this inscription:
>
>
>
> CLARISSA HARLOWE
> April x
> [Then the Year]
> AETAT. XIX.
>
>
> For ornaments: at top, an hour-glass winged. At bottom, an urn.   (IV, 257)

The snake with its tail in its mouth, emblem of eternity, but emblem as well of Clarissa's "reptile pride," the unchanging mind, the necessity for impenetrability and self-sufficiency, the rejection of inconsistency and division. As Belford rails shortly afterward, "what wretched creatures are there in the world! What strangely mixed characters! So sensible and so silly at the same time! What a *various*, what a *foolish* creature is man!" (IV, 299). The "infinite variety" so prized by Moll Flanders has become the single-mindedness of Clarissa. Purified language will make up for the fragmented self. The self-sufficiency through writing that Swift mocks in *A Tale of a Tub* becomes Clarissa's mainstay against the fear of self-annihilation. Through the pen the deepest self is both realized and corrected. As Clarissa writes to Anna Howe early in the novel, "I am almost *afraid* to beg of you, and yet I repeatedly *do*, to give way to that charming spirit, whenever it rises to your pen, which smiles, yet goes to the quick of my fault. What patient shall be afraid of a probe in so delicate a hand?" (I, 345).

Richardson in *Clarissa* therefore finally rejects the possibilities of psychological "inconsistency" and change that Pope explored so brilliantly in the *Moral Essays* and *Arbuthnot*. Pope had firm roots in a literary past and had achieved economic self-sufficiency with his translations of the *Iliad* and the *Odyssey*. Even as he saw the shape of culture changing around him, he could explore and criticize those changes as a kind of secure outsider in his society. Richardson was an insecure insider, a figure of the new world, part aesthete and part businessman. In a period of rapid social and economic change, he perceived the sympathy his audience would feel for characters who needed to maintain a strict hold on the essential of self, to deny vulnerability, to become impenetrable, at the same time that they insured their self-sufficiency by penetrating and hopefully puncturing everyone who came near enough to threaten the fragile sense of personal identity that lay within them. Self-sufficiency and self-creation is the general message of the novel, and Richardson spoke to a world ready for the message. Clarissa's desire for self-containment closely resembles the personal rigidity of Samuel Johnson, his fear of sloth, his need to purge himself of fault and his works of personality. To speak a *Rambler,* as Mrs. Thrale tells us Johnson could do on request, reflects the same subordination of self to work that Sterne worries in another way, by recognizing the form that self can project rather than fighting against it. Through Clarissa's rejection of the body, the devil within, and society, the devils without, Richardson articulated better than any writer of his time a group of attitudes toward personal identity and relations with other people that still influence us. Perhaps in our time we can finally cease to believe in those devils and continue Pope's exploration of the values of inconsistency and ambivalence. After all, as we can now see, Freud did not begin a new age. He was the prelude to the end of the old one—an age that the genius of Richardson helps us to define in all its literary fruitfulness and it psychic barrenness.

Notes

1. In *Samuel Richardson and the Eighteenth-Century Puritan Character* (Hamden, Conn., 1972), Cynthia Griffin Wolff attempts to relate Richardson's ideas to still another aspect of seventeenth-century attitudes toward personal identity, the Puritan conception of the self. But she glosses over the difficulty, pointed out by Sacvan Bercovitch, that "precisely because spir-

itual autobiography highlighted the solitary confrontation between man and his Maker it came to form a powerful countercurrent to Renaissance individualism." Unlike Clarissa, the Puritans desire to escape the willful self: " . . . self-consciousness functions in these writings to erode individuality." (In a review of *The Puritan Experience: Studies in Spiritual Autobiography* by Owen C. Watkins, *SCN* (Spring 1973), p. 1.)

2. *Leviathan*, ed. C. B. Macpherson (Harmondsworth, 1968), p. 137. Hobbes later compares madness with drunkenness as similar effects of excessive (anti-social) passion: "For, (I believe) the most sober men, when they walk alone without care and employment of the mind, would be unwilling the vanity and Extravagance of their thoughts at that time should be publiquely seen: which is a confession, that passions unguided, are for the most part meere Madnesse" (p. 142). We might look forward here to Gulliver, Roderick Random, Doctor Slop, and the many other medical men who populate the eighteenth-century novel.

3. *An Essay Concerning Human Understanding*, ed. John W. Yolton (London, 1965), 1, 287–90. Hobbes says dreams "are caused by the distemper of some of the inward parts of the body" (p. 91), and are therefore connected to other unsocializable behavior. Perhaps the same assumption from a different point of view animates the form of *Pilgrim's Progress*, "delivered under the Similitude of a DREAM,"

4. *A Treatise of Human Nature*, ed. L. A. Selby-Bigge (Oxford, 1888), pp. 261, 262. Derek Parfit has recently argued that Hume's concept of personal identity could accommodate schizophrenia, brainwashing, and identity crisis, because he seems to allow for discontinuous selves within the same body. "Personal Identity," *Philosophical Review*, 80, no. 1 (January 1971), pp. 3–27. See also in the same issue the responses by Terence Penelhum and Fraser Crowley, with a rejoinder by Parfit.

5. *Treatise*, pp. 189, 635–36. Perhaps Hume does not pursue the issue because he is unwilling to take the time necessary for a full attack on the Cartesian assumption of the dependence of body on mind: " . . . j'avais déjà connu en moi très clairement que la nature intelligente est distincte de la corporelle, considérant que toute composition témoigne de la dépendance, et que la dépendance est manifestement un défaut . . ." *Discours de la méthode*, ed. Geneviève Rodis-Lewis (Paris, 1966), p. 62.

6. Samuel Richardson, *Clarissa*, introd. John Butt (London, 1932), IV, 495. Further citations will be included in the text. For a more extended discussion of non-traditional relations between form and narrator, see Braudy, "The form of the Sentimental Novel," *Novel*, 7, no. 1 (Fall 1973), pp. 5–13. The use of the word "self-justification" brings to mind the printing use of "justify," that is, to bring out to the edge of the page. The OED records such a usage in 1683, and Richardson the printer would certainly have known it. Wolff, in *Samuel Richardson and the Eighteenth-Century Puritan Character*, has an interesting discussion of the passage from diary to autobiography in terms of self-presentation. See especially Ch. 2, "Richardson's Sources." Diderot, in his *Éloge de Richardson* (1761), remarks that when he meets a friend who has been to England, he always asks first if he saw Richardson and then if he saw Hume, perhaps creating an emblem of his own effort to combine the two.

7. I, 152–53, the copy of a letter from Clarissa to her Uncle John Harlowe that she sends to Anna Howe. Compare Gibbon on Blackstone: "The matrimonial union is so intimate according to our laws; that the very legal existence of the wife is lost in that of the husband, with whom in general she composes but one person . . . She is however sometimes considered as a separate but inferior being . . ." *The English Essays of Edward Gibbon*, ed. Patricia B. Craddock (Oxford, 1972), pp. 83, 84. See also Christopher Hill's classic article on the social and economic situation, "Clarissa Harlowe and her Times," reprinted many times, perhaps most handily in *Samuel Richardson*, ed. John Carroll (Englewood Cliffs, N.J. 1969), pp. 102–

23. Clarissa's metaphorical use of "ingrafted" bears strong resemblance to her invocation of "the first gracious Planter" in the next quotation.

8. *The Wish to be Free: Society, Psyche, and Value Change* (Berkely and Los Angeles, 1969), pp. 108-36.

9. Ian Watt, for example, emphasized sexuality more exclusively and makes a dichotomy between Clarissa and Lovelace without discussing their similarities. See *The Rise of the Novel* (Berkely and Los Angeles, 1957), pp. 230-38. On 232, Watts says, "Even so, Clarissa dies; sexual intercourse, apparently, means death for the woman." Here Watt glosses over both Clarissa's will and Lovelace's fears.

10. Compare, for example, Alan Wendt's statement that Lovelace is the "appeal of the flesh" to Clarissa, while Clarissa is the "appeal of the spirit" to Lovelace; in "Clarissa's Coffin," *PQ*, 39 (1960), 485. But Lovelace's fear of sexuality is strong—"How does this damned love unman me!" (II, 526)—and he generally avoids any real consummation (IV, 297). See also Gregory Bateson's discussion of "double bind," especially the way two people in a relationship will begin to caricature themselves each in oposition to the other (in *Steps to an Ecology of Mind* [New York, 1972], especially Part III, "Form and Pathology in Relationship").

11. R. D. Laing in *Self and Others* remarks: "To live in the past or in the future may be less satisfying than to live in the present, but it can never be as disillusioning" (Harmondsworth 1971), p. 48.

12. One could, of course, also bring to bear Sandor Ferenczi's demonstration of the parallels between blinding and castration, the eye and the testicle. See "On Eye Symbolism," *Sex in Psycho-analysis* (New York, 1956), pp. 228-33.

13. It is no mistake, then, that Belford twice identifies Clarissa with Socrates, and, I would say, Socrates as opposed to Christ. The belief in the resurrection of the body constituted the most important difference between Christianity and the neoplatonism it sought to reject and replace. But even an idealized body is not sufficient for Clarissa. Socrates exemplifies a sense of self that considers its highest end to be a sublimation up the ladder of being to become . . . perhaps a bird, that being made almost entirely of soul that Lovelace aspires to as well. For further discussion of resurrection as a problem in Christian thought, see Terence Penelhum, *Survival and Disembodied Existence* (New York, 1970).

14. To make himself known to Belinda, the Baron must act in such a way that he totally alienates her. Does the creation of Thalestris require the creation of Sir Plume to do her bidding?

15. Both Clarissa and Lovelace are considered to have a "reptile pride," making the usual identification of Lovelace and Satan a little too facile. Satanhood is not an objective symbolization for the literary reader to make, but a psychological observation of impenetrability and recalcitrance. Such similar phrases and images break down the seeming polarities of Clarissa and Lovelace. Watt, for example, makes much of the Lovelace-spider, Clarissa-fly, formula. But Lovelace also characterizes himself as a fly (II, 140). The satanic possibilities of both their prides may be the most recurrent example of this tendency in the novel.

16. R. D. Laing and A. Esterson, *Sanity, Madness, and the Family* (Harmondsworth, 1970).

17. Gulliver's worry about reputation is also paralleled by Clarissa's fear of crowds (III, 436). Defoe gives a realistic dimension to the solitary's fear of others in *A Journal of the Plague Year*.

18. In later works, however, it is more often women than men who are supposedly affected. Richardson considered Lovelace to be an original creation: "I intend in him a new Character,

not confined to usual Rules." Quoted by T. C. Duncan Eaves and Ben D. Kimpel, in *Samuel Richardson* (Oxford, 1971), p. 211.

19. This distinction reflects that made by Pope in *To a Lady* between the private nature of women and the public nature of men.

20. *Self-Knowledge and Self-Identity* (Ithaca, N.Y., 1963), p. 17.

21. *Essay*, I, 281.

22. Clarissa and Lovelace therefore both share Satan's powers of language. But, while Lovelace revels in being Proteus, Clarissa tries to repress such changes. Yet in the process they are both consummate users of language, and, again like Satan, they use their language to enclose themselves still further.

Tom Jones:
Irony and Judgment

JOHN PRESTON

Plot as Irony

Those who admire the plot of *Tom Jones* often find themselves in some embarrassment. To become engrossed in what Professor Kermode calls "the Swiss precision of the plotting"[1] seems only to increase the difficulty of gauging the novel's imaginative scope. In this sense we must agree that, as Arnold Kettle says, "in *Tom Jones* there is too much plot."[2] Fielding's smooth stage-managing of the action may well be thought to trivialize the book. This, indeed, is what Andrew Wright in effect concedes when he maintains that Fielding's art is serious because it is play, "a special kind of entertainment."[3] His reading of the plot supports the view that we should "take *Tom Jones* on an ornamental level," that Fielding provides "a kind of ideal delight."[4] But, granted that comedy depends on our feeling able to reshape life, and that the delight we take in this is properly a function of art's "seriousness," yet it may seem that this reading of *Tom Jones* gives away too much. After all, any achieved work of art takes on the status of play. That is what art is, in relation to life. And it may be that the works we recognize as "playful" (the Savoy operas for instance) are just those in which play forfeits its seriousness. So, whilst appreciating the ease with which Fielding turns everything into delight, we have still to explain how he can, as James thought, "somehow really enlarge, make everyone and

From *The Created Self: The Reader's Role in Eighteenth-Century Fiction* (New York: Barnes & Noble, 1970), pp. 94–132.

everything important."⁵ We know that Fielding's presence as narrator contributes to this impression. Can we say that the plot of the novel confirms it?

It may be thought that to do so we should need to be more convinced that the plot was sensitive to the inner experience of the characters. We are not usually satisfied with plot which does not emanate from some "inwardness," some subtlety in attending to the growth of consciousness. Forster's distinction between plot and story will help to show why this is so. Story is to be considered "a very low form" of art because it offers a sequence which has no meaning apart from that given by the sense of time. This significance of a train of events, the sense that it is "caused," arises when we discover in it the signs of personal will, of motives and desires and of the adjustments they call for. This is the kind of causality Forster illustrates: "The kind died, and then the queen died of grief."⁶ Causality without these signs may be as trivial and meaningless as story. Consider "The king died, and then the-queen dyed all the curtains black." This too is a plot: it answers the question "why?" But does not take that question seriously. And it looks as if the plot of *Tom Jones* is unserious in this way. That is why there is something self-defeating about the attempts to analyse it: Fielding has answered the questions of the plot facetiously. Yet I do not think we are justified in deducing from this, as Ian Watt does, "a principle of considerable significance for the novel form in general: namely, that the importance of the plot is in inverse proportion to that of character."⁷ In fact, Fielding makes it quite clear that he has been deliberately unserious about the plot. It is not typical; it has been designed specifically to serve his own special and rather subtle purpose.

There is no doubt that he means to draw attention to the artificiality of the plot. Why else, towards the close of the novel, recommend us to turn back "to the Scene at *Upton* the Ninth Book" and "to admire the many strange Accidents which unfortunately prevented any Interview between *Partridge* and Mrs. *Waters*" (XVIII, ii)? "Fielding," says Frank Kermode, "cannot forbear to draw attention to his cleverness."⁸ But is this likely? Fielding expected his readers to know what sort of writer would do this. He had already presented several such on the stage in his "rehearsal" plays. Trapwit is a good example. He is the vain author of an incoherent and unfunny comedy ("It is written, Sir, in the exact and true spirit of Molière," *Pasquin*, I, i); and he too is particularly proud of the plot.

Now, Mr. Fustian, the plot, which has hitherto been only carried on by hints, and open'd itself like the infant spring by small and imperceptible degrees to the audience, will display itself, like a ripe matron, in its full summer's bloom; and cannot, I think, fail with its attractive charms, like a loadstone, to catch the admiration of every one like a trap, and raise an applause like thunder, till it makes the whole house like a hurricane.　　　　　　　　　　　　　*(Pasquin, III, i)*

Fielding means us to see that in *Tom Jones* the sequences are those of farce and that the real skill consists in using them in a certain way, to get at some truth about human nature. The plot not only does not develop character, it actually subdues character to the demands of comic action. It will have to be in the shape of this action that we discern the shape of human behavior. And Fielding wants to make sure that we get the right impression of that shape.

We would do well, then, not to take Fielding's self-congratulation at face value. In reminding us of Book IX he intends us to be more subtle about it than he himself claims to be. We find there, of course, "a plot-node of extraordinary complexity,"[9] but may too easily assume, as Kermode does, that this is exactly what robs this and subsequent actions of "the full sense of actual life—real, unpredicatable, not subject to mechanical patterning."[10] Actually the succeeding events *are* unpredictable. We could not possibly foresee from Book IX that Fitzpatrick and Mrs. Waters would go off together as "husband and wife," that Tom would be attacked by Fitzpatrick (though for his supposed affair with Mrs. Fitzpatrick, not his actual one with Mrs. Waters), or that this would involve him again with Mrs. Waters, or in what way. When we look back on the completed sequence, it is true, we see it differently: the unpredictable suddenly appears to have hardened into the arbitrary. After all, we think, it *was* only a trick of the plotting. But, really, the plot faces two ways. From one side it looks like a forced solution, from the other an open question. In one way it looks arbitrary and contrived, in another it not only makes the reader guess but *keeps* him guessing at what has happened. The latter aspect of the plot is sustained by what Eleanor Hutchens calls "substantial irony:" "a curious and subtle means used by Fielding to add irony to a given detail of plotting is to leave the reader to plot a sequence for himself."[11] The reader has not, in fact, been told everything and is sometimes as much in the dark as the characters themselves. But irony of this kind is only contributory to the ironic *shift* by means of which the whole direction of the novel is reversed, and the plot has to sustain two contradictory conclusions simultaneously.

It is left to the reader to make this irony work. Fielding suggests as much by placing the reader in a dilemma. He draws him into the middle of the action, which then looks free-ranging, unpredictable, open-ended. If the plot is to behave like life, the reader must be unable to see his way before him. But he can only play this game once. On re-reading the novel he knows in advance the answer to all riddles, the outcome of all confusions. The plot thus poses questions about the way it should be read. Is it impossible to read the book more than once? Or is it necessary to read the book at least twice in order to understand it? On second reading do we reject the first, or are we in some way expected to keep them both in mind at once? This last is, I think, the only possibility Fielding leaves open for us, and it is this dual response which secures the ironic structure of the plot.

I think we can see why this must be so if we examine more closely the two "faces" of the plot, and consider first what the book looks like when we can take the action as a diagram, or "architecturally," as Dorothy Van Ghent does. She writes of it as a "Palladian palace perhaps; . . . simply, spaciously, generously, firmly grounded in Nature, . . . The structure is all out in the light of intelligibility." This, she considers, diminishes its scope: "since Fielding's time, the world has found itself not quite so intelligible . . . there was much in the way of doubt and darkness to which Fielding was insensitive."[12] Ian Watt offers a similar reading: "it reflects the general literary strategy of neo-classicism . . . (it makes) visible in the human scene the operations of universal order." Its function, he claims, is to reveal the important fact "that all human particles are subject to an invisible force which exists in the universe whether they are there to show it or not." The plot must act like a magnet "that pulls every individual particle out of the random order brought about by temporal accident and human imperfection."[13] Read in this way it will appear as a paradigm of the deistic world picture:

> All Nature is but Art, unknown to thee;
> All Chance, Direction, which thou canst not see
> (*An Essay on Man*, i, 289–290)

Is this likely to be Fielding's meaning? it is true that in *The Champion* he asserts (against the deists in fact) his belief in "this vast regular Frame of the Universe, and all the artful and cunning Machines therein," and denies that they could be "the Effects of Chance, of an irregular Dance of Atoms." But he is still more concerned to deny that the Diety is "a lazy, unactive Being, regardless of the Affairs of this World, that the Soul of Man, when his Body dieth, lives no more, but returns to common Matter with that of the Brute Creation" (Jan. 22, 1739–40). As James A. Work has shown,[14] the concept of universal order was nothing for Fielding if it was not the evidence of God's providence and a support for personal faith. In fact Fielding's essay on Bolingbroke brings out specifically the moral and intellectual impropriety of reducing the Divine order to the status of a work of art. Bolingbroke, Fielding reasons, must be making game of eternal verities in considering "the Supreme Being in the light of a dramatic poet, and that part of his works which we inhabit as a drama." It is the impiety that is offensive of course, the "ludicrous treatment of the Being so universally . . . acknowledged to be the cause of all things." But involved in this is the mistrust of those artists who "aggrandize their profession with such kind of similies."[15] (*Works*, viii, 499–500). Fielding's own procedure, if Ian Watt were right, would be uncomfortably close to this, and it may be that, once more, we should not take him literally when he claims to be in this position.

The beginning of Book X is an occasion when he does so:

> First, then, we warn thee not too hastily to condemn any of the Incidents in this our History, as impertinent and foreign to our main Design, because thou dost not immediately conceive in what Manner such Incident may conduce to that Design. This work may, indeed, be considered as a great Creation of our own; and for a little Reptile of a Critic to presume to find Fault with any of its Parts, without knowing the Manner in which the Whole is connected, and before he comes to the final Catastrophe, is a most presumptuous Absurdity. (X, i)

This is equivocal. It may be taken to indicate that this is the structural center of the novel, the peripeteia. It occurs at the height of the book's confusion and may be necessary to reassure the reader that the author is still in control. Yet it would be naive of Fielding to think that this was the way to do so, especially as he adopts a tone that suggests otherwise. He sounds touchy and self-defensive and tries to browbeat the reader. To claim that the work is "a great Creation of our own" is arrogant in the way that the essay on Bolingbroke indicated, and the arrogance is blatant in the reference to "a little Reptile of a Critic." Fielding clearly wants to discredit the narrator and, in the process, to make fun again of the pretensions of the plot. He makes a similar point in a different way in the introduction to Book XVII. Now he is asserting that affairs have got beyond his control.

> . . . to bring our Favourites out of their present Anguish and Distress, and to land them at last on the Shore of Happiness, seems a much harder Task; a Task indeed so hard that we do not undertake to execute it. In Regard to *Sophia*, it is more

than probable, that we shall somewhere or other provide a good Husband for her in the End, either *Blifil,* or my Lord, or Somebody else; but as to poor *Jones,* . . . we almost despair of bringing him to any Good. (XVII, i)

He cannot invoke supernatural assistance: "to natural Means alone we are confined; let us try therefore what by these Means may be done for poor *Jones*" (XVII, i). But this again is a kind of boast. At any rate it draws attention to the hard work and (paradoxically) the artifice necessary to reach a "natural" outcome. It is another way of claiming that the design is intact. His pride in his own skill is obtrusive here as elsewhere. But this can hardly mean that Fielding had the kind of vanity which is the mark of the bad writer, unsure of his own powers.

We must conclude, I think, that to pose as a bad writer will help Fielding to avoid slipping into shallow rationalism. If he poses as the invisible Divine presence behind events, it is with a full sense of the kind of error this would be. What in one sense is an ironic parody of a form is, in a more profound way, an ironic repudiation of spiritual arrogance. In the same way the plot is less an assertion of Augustan rationality than a recognition of the confusion the rationalist can hardly tolerate. It is in fact a vehicle for what is self-contradictory, what is emotionally as well as intellectually confusing in human experience.

This is an aspect of the plot that Eleanor Hutchens admirably describes:

Substantial irony is an integral part of the fabric of *Tom Jones.* Just as the straightforward plot moves from misfortune to prosperity along a tightly linked causal chain but brings the hero full circle back to the place of beginning, so the concomitant irony of plot turns things back upon themselves transformed. This larger structure is repeated in multitudinous smaller ironies of plot, character, and logic. . . . The reversal of truth and expectation accompanies plot and theme as a sort of ironic *doppelgänger.*[16]

Her main concern is to identify the specific episodes ("ironies of the plot . . . so numerous as to defy complete cataloguing"[17] which add an ironic dimension to the whole narrative. But what she calls the "concomitant irony of plot" can be taken to refer to a reversal of meaning in the plot as a whole, and it is in this way that it produces the effect we noted, of seeming to face two ways at once. The "causal chain" that "Fielding-as-narrator" boasts about seems to strengthen the possibility of a comprehensible order in human experience. But the plot also moves through a causal sequence of a different kind, a sequence of coincidences, chance meetings and meetings missed, good luck and bad, unplanned and unforeseen events. From this point of view it is easier to see that Fielding is dealing with the unpredictable, not in character or motive—his theory of "conservation of character" leads in quite a different direction—but, to use his own term, in the "history," the shape of events. The meaning of history, as Philip Stevick has shown,[18] interested Fielding profoundly, and the plot of *Tom Jones*, set against actual historical events, helps to define that meaning.

The episode of Sophia's little bird (IV, iii), which Eleanor Hutchens cites as an example of irony of substance,[19] is even more interesting as a model of this ironic meaning in the action as a whole. The causal links are firm: the bird is a present from Tom, therefore Sophia cherishes it, therefore Blifil lets it escape, therefore Tom tries to catch it and fails, therefore Sophia raises the alarm, therefore Allworthy and the rest come and eventually pass judgment on the two boys. The sequence does, it is true, depend on character and motive; but, like the plot as a whole, it finds these less interesting than their consequences in the actions and opinions of others. The episode is trimmed to the requirements of parable: it moves from personal predicament to moral judgment. In this way the episode suggests how the whole plot will be designed to exercise and refine the faculty of judgment, an aspect of the book I wish to examine later. At this stage, however, it is more to the point to note that the action in this episode can be traced through another kind of sequence. It springs from a paradoxical situation: the affection of Tom and Sophia is expressed in the captivity, Blifil's malicious envy in the releasing of the bird. There is truth to feeling in that situation; it is carefully staged, no doubt, but does not seem forced. Yet the subsequent action is quite fortuitous. Tom's actions could not have been predicted, for we had not even been told that he was near at hand; the branch need not have broken; there was no reason to expect that the bird would be caught and carried away by "a nasty Hawk." The events no longer seem to explain each other. What seemed to have an almost mathematical logic now defies rationalization. Actions cannot be foreseen, nor can their consequences be calculated: Blifil's malice, for instance, is better served by chance than by design. And intention, will, desire, all are overruled by Fortune.

This is one essential meaning of the plot. It is designed to tolerate the random decisions of Fortune. If Fielding has an arbitrary way with the plot, this is not in order to square it with some concept of Reason or Nature, the "one clear, unchang'd and universal light," but to reflect our actual experience. "I am not writing a System, but a History," he reminds his readers, "and I am not obliged to reconcile every Matter to the received

Notions concerning Truth and Nature" (XII, viii). And in *The Champion* he argues that the historian especially should be prepared to allow for the effects of chance. "I have often thought it a Blemish in the works of *Tacitus*, that he ascribes so little to the Interposition of this invincible Being; but, on the contrary, makes the Event of almost every Scheme to depend on a wise Design, and proper Measures taken to accomplish it." (Dec. 6, 1739.) He goes so far as to assert that wisdom is "of very little Consequence in the Affairs of this World: Human Life appears to me to resemble the Game of *Hazard*, much more than that of *Chess;* in which latter, among good Players, one false Step must infallibly lose the Game; whereas, in the former, the worst that can happen is to have the odds against you, which are never more than two to one" (ibid.). No doubt this extreme position is offered with due irony. Fielding briskly corrects it in the opening chapter of *Amelia:* men accuse Fortune "with no less absurdity in life, than a bad player complains of ill luck at the game of chess." Also, as Irvin Ehrenpreis observes, Fielding can see a way to resist Fortune: he "opposes Christian providence to pagan Fortune. Since it operates by chance, fortune may indeed advance vice and obstruct virtue. . . . But steady prudent goodness will attract the blessing of the Lord, and wisdom is justified of her children"[20] Yet this is not to argue that Fielding rejects the role of Fortune, or does not feel its force. On the contrary, he implies that Fortune is the term we must use to describe the human condition, the element in which human qualities are formed and human virtues and vices operate. This is in fact the source of his moral confidence. *Amelia*, as George Sherburn points out, is intended to cure the hero of "psychological flaccidity" and of thinking that in an often irrational world "moral energy is futile."[21] And *Tom Jones* celebrates "that solid inward Comfort of Mind, which is the sure Companion of Innocence and Virtue" (Dedication), and which will not be at the mercy of Fortune. A "sanguine" temper, says Fielding, "puts us, in a Manner, out of the Reach of Fortune, and makes us happy without her Assistance" (XIII, vi).

There are, then, qualities of mind which rise above Fortune; but Fortune is the medium in which they operate. And, above all, Fortune is the medium of comedy. This, certainly, is what more than anything makes it tolerable. But, particularly because it is the source for comic complication, we shall want to see how it opposes the idea of a benevolently ordered world. Since comedy does in the end fulfil our expectations, it may after all persuade us that Fielding is tampering with events and trying to make the plot act "as a kind of magnet." But in fact Fielding creates his comedy out of the way his characters try to dominate Fortune and fail. They try to make things turn out as they want them to, but neither the narrator nor the reader can be persuaded that the desired conclusion has been reached by trying. It is itself a gift of Fortune. The beauty of the comedy is not that it establishes a coherent universe, but that for the time being it allows the reader to believe in *good* Fortune.[22]

The basis of the comic action is the "pursuit motif," which Dorothy Van Ghent has identified with such clarity.[23] It is implicit in the story of Sophia's little bird, and later comes to dominate events. Sophia follows Tom, Squire Western chases Sophia, Tom later pursues Sophia, Fitzpatrick pursues his wife, Allworthy and Blifil follow the Westerns to town, where Blifil will pursue Sophia. In the Upton scenes the theme comes to a climax, in an intricate comic entanglement. And Fielding turns to "epic" simile to underline what is happening. "Now the little trembling Hare, whom the Dread of all her numerous Enemies, and Chiefly of that cunning, cruel, carnivorous Animal Man, had confined all the Day to her Lurking-place, sports wantonly o'er the Lawns; . . ." (X, ii). The simile of the hunt is used again in Book X, Chapter vi, to describe Fitzpatrick's pursuit of his wife: "Now it happens to this Sort of Men, as to bad Hounds, who never hit off a Fault themselves . . ." And Fielding makes sure that we notice what he is doing: "Much kinder was the [Fortune] to me, when she suggested that Simile of the Hounds, just before inserted, since the poor Wife may, on these Occasions, be so justly compared to a hunted Hare." Immediately afterwards, "as if this had been a real Chace," Squire Western arrives "hallowing as Hunters do when the Hounds are at a Fault." Later, Mrs. Fitzpatrick uses the image to describe her own situation: she "wisely considered, that the Virtue of a young Lady is, in the World, in the same Situation with a poor Hare, which is certain, whenever it ventures abroad, to meet its Enemies: For it can hardly meet any other." (XI, x.) These images bring out an element of crudity in the motif: "we have got the dog Fox, I warrant the Bitch is not far off" (X, vii). The chases are anything but rational; they are headlong, indiscreet, urged on by primitive instinct. Thus, when Western is easily diverted from one pursuit to another, from the chase of his daughter to the chase of a hare, Fielding quotes the story of the cat who was changed into a woman yet "leapt from the Bed to her Husband" to chase a mouse. "What are we to understand by this?" he asks. "The Truth is, as the sagacious Sir *Roger L'Estrange* observes, in his deep Reflections, that "if we shut Nature out at the Door, she will come in at the Window; and that Puss, tho' a Madam, will be a Mouser still'" (XII, ii). Dorothy Van Ghent, who notes that "instinctive drives must . . . be emphasized as an important constituent of 'human nature,'" does not in fact observe that

Fielding explicitly links them in this way with the theme of pursuit. Her idea is that the book is based on "a conflict between natural, instinctive feeling, and those appearances with which people disguise, deny, or inhibit natural feeling."[24] This is not convincing. It seems better to follow Fielding's hints that the action, a series of rash pursuits, shows human behaviour to be irrational, governed chiefly by instinct, not reflection, and therefore particularly exposed to Fortune.

These factors in human behavior are above all what bring about the loosening of the causal chain and frustrate the intentions of the characters. In Book XII, Chapter viii, Fielding acknowledges that it must seem "hard," indeed "very absurd and monstrous" that Tom should offend Sophia, not by his actual unfaithfulness but by his supposed "indelicacy" in cheapening her name. Some, he thinks, will regard "what happened to *Jones* at *Upton* as a just Punishment for his Wickedness, with regard to Women, of which it was indeed the immediate Consequence;" and others, "silly and bad Persons," will argue from it that "the characters of men are rather owing to Accident than to Virtue;" but the author himself admits no more than that it confirms the book's "great, useful and uncommon Doctrine," which, however, "we must not fill up our Pages by frequently repeating." He proceeds to show the absurdity of trying to adjust our behavior to a system of cause and effect. Tom becomes totally unlike himself, no longer a creature of appetite but a romantic lover, as Partridge tells him: "Certainly, Sir, if ever Man deserved a young Lady, you deserve young Madam *Western;* for what a vast Quantity of Love must a Man have, to be able to live upon it without any other Food, as you do" (XII, xiii). Yet this does not make Tom immune from Fortune; when he reaches Mrs. Fitzpatrick's house in London he misses Sophia by ten minutes. "In short, these kind of hair-breadth Missings of Happiness, look like the Insults of Fortune, who may be considered as thus playing Tricks with us, and wantonly diverting herself at our Expence" (XIII, ii). In the end his romantic persistence leads him to the most discreditable episode of the book: after hanging round Mrs. Fitzpatrick's door all day, he finally enters her drawing room to meet Lady Bellaston.

Similarly, the dénouement, the solving of all the riddles, is brought about by chance, indeed by mistake. Tom can do nothing to help himself. In the end it is Mrs. Waters who is able to explain matters. But she herself is at first ignorant who Tom is. She only discovers that Jones is Bridget Allworthy's child when she is visited by the lawyer Dowling. He in turn has been sent by Blifil to say that she "should be assisted with any Money [she] wanted to carry on the Prosecution" against Jones. It is his malice, apparently so obstructive, which in spite of his intentions, leads to the ending we desire. Our expectations are realized only by being contradicted.

It is now possible to see why the reading of the plot should be able to sustain a large irony. We shall be tempted into a choice of readings. But, if we think ourselves objective, surveying a complete design which has been distanced by its past tense and assimilated into "history," we may well find in it a degree of order that Fielding hardly intended. If, on the other hand, Fielding is trying in many ways to undermine our sense of objectivity and privilege, we must find ourselves drawn into the confusion and hazard of the action, aware now of "history" as a process in which we are involved, moving toward effects we cannot predict: we are not allowed to understand more of the course of events than the characters do. Yet, as we have seen, this kind of involvement is only possible on the first reading. Fielding has written into the narrative an assumption that must be contradicted by subsequent readings. Indeed, one cannot read even once through the book without finding that many passages have come to take on an altered meaning.

Irvin Ehrenpreis sees this as confirming that, like *Oedipus Rex,* the book is essentially a sustained dramatic irony. Behind the many moments of "discovery," of "sudden understanding," which he regards as really the action of the book, there is, he says, "the supreme recognition scene disclosing the true parentage of Tom Jones. The opening books of the novel are permeated with ironies that depend on his being Bridget Allworthy's proper heir," What we admire, what Coleridge must have been praising, is "the cheerful ease with which Fielding suspends his highest revelation till the end, the outrageous clues with which he dares assault our blindness in the meantime."[25] This seems to me an important truth about the novel. But it seems also to imply other more complex truths which Mr. Ehrenpreis does not consider. Apparently Fielding can, even on a second reading, be supposed to be "suspending" the final revelation; we can be held to retain our "blindness" in spite of what we have discovered. That is, we have a sense of duality not only in the book itself, but in our own response to it. We recognize our "blindness" just because we no longer suffer from it. We know and do not know simultaneously: we are both outside and inside the pattern of events. Like Eliot's Tiresias, we "have foresuffered all," yet are still capable of being surprised. If the book has a core of dramatic irony, it is one in which the reader knows himself to be caught, or of which he knows himself to be the source. He is the observer of his own ironic mistakes. Our responses to the book are, we may say, part of the reason for Fielding's laughter, a laughter in which we share. We are, in short, never quite ignorant nor yet entirely omniscient. In this way the book leads us to one of the most rewarding experiences of comedy: it simultaneously confuses and enlightens, it produces both question and answer, doubt and reassurance.[26] This is a far cry from the imitation of Universal Reason; yet it offers a way out of the confusion of human experience. The book suggests the power of control in the very act of undermining that power; or, from another point of view, can play with the possibilities of confusion because the sense of control is never lost. It can accept the reality of fortune because it has achieved the wisdom that an acceptance of fortune gives.

Chapters vii, viii, and ix of Book V are a notable example of this procedure. Allworthy is ill and is not expected to live. This is the situation as the other characters understand it, and Fielding says nothing that would allow us to understand more of it. Our only advantage over them is in our emotional detachment, as, for instance, when we see them betray their dissatisfaction at Allworthy's legacies. When the attorney from Salisbury arrives, we know no more than they do who he is or what news he brings. (In fact we know less than Blifil; like the other characters we also are his dupes.) Fielding gives no sign that there is anything more in the situation; indeed, by depicting at some length the disappointed greed of Allworthy's dependents he implies that the scene can only carry this limited and obvious irony. Yet when we have read the rest of the novel we know that there is much more to be seen. For instance, we know already that Allworthy's illness will not be fatal; this, in fact, is what keeps the scene within the limits of comic decorum. This is what enables R. S. Crane to say that as the novel progresses things become both more and more, and less and less serious, that it offers a "comic analogue of fear."[27] Also we know, what Fielding apparently thought we should not know, that the attorney is the lawyer Dowling and that he brings Bridget Allworthy's own dying words, "Tell my Brother, Mr. *Jones* is his Nephew—He is my Son.—Bless him," words that are not recorded in the novel until Book XVIII, Chapter viii. Thus the scene at Allworthy's death-bed is superimposed on the silent, unacknowledged presence of that other death-bed. Fielding deliberately chose *not* to present this as a dramatic irony. The scene as he renders it takes all its significance from information he has denied us, from knowledge we import into the scene, as it were without his consent. The words that are not spoken reverberate thus throughout the novel. But, as they have *not* been spoken, their sound is produced in one part of the reader's mind whilst he is deaf to it with the other. In fact, as Ehrenpreis shows, what is at the center of his attention is the *fact* of their not being spoken, the audacity with which Fielding so nearly gives away the riddle of the book. We admire his skill in keeping it dark, but could not do so if we did not at the same time know what it was.

In another way, however, our dual vision of things actually seems to undermine our confidence in the narrator. Since we are left to supply information necessary to the full understanding of a scene, we fancy ourselves better informed than the narrator himself. Often enough, indeed, the narrator professes his inadequacy: "the Fact is true; and, perhaps, may be sufficiently accounted for by suggesting . . ." (V, x). But this, as Eleanor Hutchens shows,[28] is an ironic trick designed to make us attend in exactly the way the author desires. There is, however, a much more pervasive sense that the narrator cannot (or does not) reveal many things that the reader nevertheless is aware of. Of course the reader is aware of them only because he at last appreciates the design the author has had in mind from the beginning. But since the author does not actually write such things into the text of the novel, since he leaves the reader to supply them silently, he gives the impression that in some important ways the novel has written itself.

In the scenes we have been discussing, Fielding observes that Blifil is offended at Tom's riotous behavior so soon after Allworthy's illness and Bridget's death. There is no mistaking Blifil's real feelings and motives; ". . . Mr. *Blifil* was highly offended at a Behaviour which was so inconsistent with the sober and prudent Reserve of his own Temper." Yet, however little sympathy we feel for Blifil, we sense that there is some justice in his attitude: "He bore it too with the greater Impatience, as it appeared to him very indecent at his Season; 'When,' as he said, 'the House was a House of Mourning, on the Account of his dear Mother.'" Jones's ready sympathy and remorse reflect our own response: "he offered to shake Mr. *Blifil* by the Hand, and begged his Pardon, saying 'His excessive Joy for Mr. *Allworthy's* Recovery had driven every other Thought out of his Mind.'" Yet, after all, this does not shake our conviction that Blifil is hateful: he soon reverts to the behavior we expect of him: "Blifil scornfully rejected his Hand; and, with much Indignation, answered, 'It was little to be wondered at, if tragical Spectacles made no Impression on the Blind; but, for his Part, he had the Misfortune to know who his Parents were, and consequently must be affected with their Loss'" (V, ix). These are the terms in which the narrator has constructed the episode. This must be our reading of it as it stands. Yet that is not the way in which we do read it. When Blifil speaks of his mother's death we know that he knows that she is also Tom's mother. Tom's generous sympathy, then, far from helping to justify Blifil, actually heightens our sense of outrage. And Blifil's response, no longer just a gratuitous and insulting sneer at Tom's illegitimacy, becomes a piercing revelation of his utter inhumanity. Not only can he allow Tom to remain ignorant that his mother has just died, he can actually, with staggering impudence, make his words a concealed taunt. He finds it possible to use his knowledge for a cruel secret game: "he had the Misfortune to know who his Parents were, and consequently must be affected with their Loss."

There are, then, areas of meaning which the narrator does not even mention. But his reticence does not prevent us becoming conscious of them. Thus the book begins to escape from the narrow designs imposed on it, from the conscious intention of the narrator. After all, it does seem to acquire something of the "full sense of actual life." Fielding is not always obtrusive; in fact, it is at this deep level, where the authenticity of the book is most in question, that he is least in evidence. We noted that in those instances where he pushed himself forward he was wanting the reader to look elsewhere for the real intention. But though the text is centered on the unpredictable, on the random behavior of Fortune, the full scope of the novel is to be measured in the dual meaning of the plot. The author leaves the book to itself, or rather, to the reader. In other words, Fielding has been able, by means of the plot, to create a reader wise enough to create the book he reads.

The "Pursuit of True Judgment"

The plot of *Tom Jones*, then, may be best understood in terms of the way it is read. Its structure is the structure of successive responses to the novel. It exists in the reader's attention rather than in the written sequences. This means that its effect is epistemological rather than moral. It helps us to see how we acquire our knowledge of human experience; it is a clarification of the processes of understanding. It presents life as a fortuitous sequence of events, as the play of Fortune, and traces the ways in which we come to see these events as a pattern. This certainly does not in any direct way establish a moral sense in the novel. Take, for instance, Tom's affair with Molly Seagrim. His remorse, prompting him to make amends to her, leads him to find her in bed with Square and then to discover that she had been first seduced by Will Barnes. His generous impulse leads to the knowledge that will release him: "*Jones* was become perfectly easy by Possession of this Secret with regard to *Molly*" (V, vi). But this is luck, not morality. His remorse pays dividends, but not because it *is* remorse. To center the plot on Fortune is to lift the moral burden from the behavior of the characters, with the unexpected effect at times of sharpening their conscience. At the point when Tom is least to blame he reproaches himself most bitterly. Hearing of his supposed incest he first exclaims against Fortune and then blames himself: "'Fortune will never have done with me, 'till she hath driven me to Distraction. But why do I blame Fortune? I am myself the Cause of all my Misery. All the dreadful Mischiefs which have befallen me, are the Consequences only of my own Folly and Vice'"(XVIII, ii). This is absurd. Yet there is a truth in it: he *is* responsible in an essential way. But this moral discovery cannot be made through the plot as such.

It is natural to assume that what the plot cannot do will have to be done by the author's explicit comments. Thus Ian Watt holds that Fielding's technique as "deficient at least in the sense that it was unable to convey this larger moral significance through character and action alone" that *Tom Jones* "is only part novel."[29] This kind of distinction between "showing" and "telling" has, at least since the publication of *The Rhetoric of Fiction*,[30] come to seem much less secure. But it is as well to note that in Fielding's time it would have been widely accepted. It was in fact confirmed by just that epic theory that Fielding appealed to. Le Bossu himself, the approved interpreter of Aristotle,[31] takes up the assertion that the poet who speaks in his own person is no imitator: he should seek for "une manière de rendre la Narration agissante."[32] The orator, but not the poet, may enter into a direct relation with his audience. What makes the narrative convincing in an epic poem is the "rapport que le Poète met entre ses Auditeurs et ses Personnages."[33] Thus, as Shaftesbury notes in his "Advice to an Author," the advantages of the Platonic Dialogue are that "the author is annihilated, and the reader, being no way applied to, stands for nobody. . . . You are not only left to judge coolly and with indifference of the sense delivered, but of the character, genius, elocution, and manner of the persons who deliver it." But this unhappily is not the way of the modern writer: "he suits himself on every occasion to the fancy of his reader, whom, as the fashion is nowadays, he constantly caresses and cajoles." This is "the coquetry of a modern author . . . to draw attention from the subject, towards himself."[34]

In this light Fielding's narrative looks like a planned flouting of decorum; he aligns himself with the vain, egotistical "modern" author, in the manner of Swift, but with a more subtle ironic intention. Swift apes the bad writer in order to demolish him; Fielding chooses "bad" art in order to unseat the bad reader. Whilst appearing to ingratiate himself in the "modern" manner, he is actually trying to school the reader, to induce him to attend more closely and to judge well. Fielding is very far from being defeated by his medium. Rather he employs his narrative method with calculated effect, as a means to draw the reader into the action of the book and so clarify its meaning. His method is, in fact, as William J. Farrell has shown, the proper method for a "history."[35] We have seen how Fielding presents the shape of history as a dilemma for the reader; it is important to recognize that conventionally the historian's mode of address also expects the reader's participation. "The narrator-to-audience observations," writes Mr. Farrell, "invariably bring into the work a fairly well-defined character called 'the reader'."[36] In Fielding's novels, of course, the device is used not to authenticate "historical" truth but to enforce "the believability of [the] narrator through whom the reader sees the entire action."[37] Certainly the rhetorical basis of the novels needs this kind of support; insofar as Fielding successfully projects the persona of his narrator we shall be prepared to accept that "telling" is after all a kind of "showing". But an equally important use for the device is to make the reader's role clear. The reader has his responsibility also: he must try to judge well. To encourage him to do so is itself a part of the subject of the book. That is, the book is *about* judgment, and the understanding necessary for good judgment. This is where the moral sense is located, in the analysis and evaluation of diverse judgments. It is epistemological in this way also. It focuses attention, not only on events, but on the mind which perceives and judges them. Fielding is quite aware that his fiction has the same aims as Locke's *Essay*. In one of the *Champion* papers he quotes from Locke's opening chapter: *"The Understanding, like the Eye* (says Mr. *Lock), whilst it makes us see and perceive all other things, takes no Notice of itself; and it requires Art and Pains to set it at a Distance and make it its own Object"* (March 1, 1739–40). But, Fielding continues, the analogy is not perfect, "for the Eye can contemplate itself in a Glass, but no *Narcissus* hath hitherto discovered any Mirrour for the Understanding," and self-knowledge may too easily slide into "self love." To provide such a mirror, to guard against such error is the purpose of *Tom Jones*. To effect it Fielding must establish his relationship with the reader.

In his first chapter he shows what this is to be. "On the image which Fielding produces just here," says Andrew Wright of the offered "bill of fare," "the meaning of the novel depends."[38] This is true, but not, I think, in the way he explains it, as an invitation "to take *Tom Jones* in a festive spirit." We know Fielding's opinion of innkeepers and are hardly surprised that when he poses as one his invitation lacks cordiality. Like "one who keeps a public Ordinary, at which all Persons are welcome for their Money," he is quite prepared to find that the critical reader will be ill-mannered. "Men who pay for what they eat, will insist on gratifying their Palates, however nice and even whimsical these may prove; and if every Thing is not agreeable to their Taste, will challenge a Right to censure, to abuse, and to d————n their Dinner without Controul" (I, i). This is why he publishes his bill of fare: prospective customers may decide either to stay or "depart to some other Ordinary better accommodated to their Taste." This is explicitly not an "eleemosynary Treat."[39] Fielding thus establishes mutual rights of criticism: if my reader is to be allowed freedom of censure, I must be permitted to make fun of him; in this way we may come to respect each other. Empson, taking his cue from Fielding's work as magistrate rather than his role in the book, puts the matter admirably:

> . . . the unusual thing about Fielding as a novelist is that he is always ready to consider what he would do if one of his characters came before him when he was on the bench. . . . As to the reader of a novel, Fielding cannot be bothered with him unless he too is fit to sit on a magistrate's bench, prepared, in literature as in life, to handle and judge any situation. This is why the reader gets teased so frankly.[40]

Actually, Fielding's way of envisaging this relationship has less to do with inns and law-courts than with the theater, and especially with the audience. The usual analogy between the world and the stage is not enough for him: "None, as I remember, have at all considered the Audience at this great Drama" (VII, i). He imagines the reactions of the world's upper-gallery, pit and boxes to the scene in which Black George steals Tom's £ 500. Some are abusive, some offended, some tolerant and others "refused to give their Opinion 'till they had heard that of the best Judges. . . . As for the Boxes, . . . most of them were attending to something else" (VII, i). He is interested more in the audience than the play, as we see also from several other passages in the novel. Partridge, for instance, is seen in the gallery at a performance of *Hamlet*. "*Jones* . . . expected to enjoy much Entertainment in the Criticisms of *Partridge*" (XVI, 5). On another occasion Fielding inserts the story of the murderer of Mr. Derby, one Fisher, who also went to see *Hamlet*, "and with an unaltered Countenance heard one of the Ladies, who little suspected how near she was to the Person, cry out, 'Good God! if the Man that murdered Mr. *Derby* was now present!' Manifesting in this a more seared and callous Conscience than even *Nero* himself" (VIII, i).

This manœuvre, in which the audience becomes the center of interest, exposed to the author's criticism as he was to theirs, is brilliantly illustrated by Hogarth's etching "The Laughing Audience." The ten laughing people are rendered with a touch both subtle and vigorous, both sympathetic and caustic. There is an infectious gaiety in their laughter and at the same time a delicate observation of their different temperaments. We feel a harshness in the drawing and yet a pleasure in the simplicity and naturalness depicted. The one "critic" among them, who is not watching the stage and sits in contemptuous isolation, is made to seem absurdly out of place. In the boxes and unobserved by anyone in the picture there is a scene of foppish affectation and gallantry, theatrical in appearance and more amusing, Hogarth implies, than anything the audience could be laughing at. Who is laughing at whom? This brilliant and complex design, cutting across the usual distinctions between subject and object, observer and observed, is an exact parallel to Fielding's procedure in *Tom Jones*. For he is not, as Andrew Wright suggests, drawing attention primarily to the artificiality of life, trying to make us see it as a play. On the contrary, as Partridge's naiveté reminds us, the best acting is that which most resembles life. And the consummate "actor" who appears in the very next chapter is Blifil, the hypocrite. No, if Fielding is watchful of his readers, interested in the way they take his story, this is because their judgment is in the long run part of that story.

But Fielding is not content merely to observe his audience; he wants to teach them. He looks for intelligent readers. We have already seen his attitude to the ill-natured critic. It remains constant throughout the book: "I must desire all those Critics to mind their own business . . . " (I, ii); "a little Reptile of a Critic" (X, i); "if we judge according to the Sentiments of some Critics, and of some Christians, no Author will be saved in this World, and no Man in the next" (XI, i). Why does Fielding adopt this petulant tone? It looks as if he is trying to keep up the role of the bad writer to whom all critics are a nuisance. But there is a better use for it. The critic's "hungry Appetite for Censure" (XVI, i) is an extreme example of "judgment" in the wrong sense, "in which it is frequently used as equivalent to Condemnation" (XI, i). This applies in life as well as literature: the critic is a type of the "common Slanderer, . . . a Person who prys into the Characters of others, with no other Design but to discover their Faults, and to publish them to the World" (XI, i). He means to remind us of Blifil, of course; but the remarks are actually referred to our own response as readers. He is expecting the reader to know how to judge with generosity, in T. S. Eliot's words to "compose his differences with as many of his fellows as possible, in the common pursuit of true judgment."[41] "All Beauty of Character, as well as of Countenance, and indeed of every Thing human, is to be tried in this Manner" (XI, i). This sounds very generalized, but we have seen how it grows out of an imagined situation, out of what Wayne Booth calls "the 'plot' of our relationship with Fielding-as-narrator."[42] To make us serve his purpose Fielding appropriates us to the world of his fiction.

He also reverses the process and contrives in many ways to suggest that his fictional world is available to us in reality. We could follow Tom's route and, in that case, Fielding would recommend us to stay at the Bell, Gloucester, "an excellent House indeed" (VIII, viii). And we may, says Fielding, "have the Pleasure of riding in the very Coach, and being driven by the very Coachman, that is recorded in this History" (X, vi). He always writes as if we were present at the events narrated: "the reader will, I believe, bear Witness for him" (II, iv); "I question not but the Surprize of the Reader will be here equal to that of *Jones*" (V, v); "Reader, if thou hast any good Wishes towards me, I will fully repay them, by wishing thee to be possessed of this Sanguine Disposition of Mind (i.e. like Tom's), . . . which puts us, in a Manner, out of the Reach of Fortune" (XIII, vi). We are not insulated. We are not only to watch, it seems, but to be subjected to the same hazards as the characters themselves. Fielding does not set us apart from them; indeed, *they* are often made to seem more like audience than actors. Some, like Square and Thwackum, are created just to be observers, to offer opinions. And the design of the story gives equal weight to action and to the discussion it provokes. A transparent example of this is in Book IV, Chapter iv, when the episode of Sophia's little bird is debated by Square, Thwackum, Western, Allworthy, and a "Gentleman of the Law, who was present." But hardly anything happens in the novel that does not create its ripples of comment, discussion, and conflicting judgments. The reader and even the narrator are, in these situations, on an equal footing with the actors. In other words, the story, as distinct from the plot, is really a system of stories within stories, like the house that Jack built. Thus the tale told by the Man of the Hill, often thought to be digressive and disruptive, is actually firmly embedded in the whole design. And, as if to emphasize this, Fielding arranges it in symmetry with the parallel story told by Mrs. Fitzpatrick to Sophia.

Reactions to an event are themselves events. In the same way some of the most important acts in the novel are acts of judgment. We discover and express ourselves in judging others; our moral existence consists in our ability to form moral judgments. Hence the importance of that chapter

(VII, i) in which we have seen "the great audience's" reactions to Black George's theft. For Fielding there goes further than Hogarth, who merely shows the audience its own image. He uses the analogy to discover something about the nature of moral judgments. This audience's opinions are worthless. Theirs is the judgment of the "mob" (i.e., "persons, without Virtue, or Sense, in all Stations," I, ix). They judge superficially and casually, that is, on the isolated scene enacted before them. This is why we must go "behind the Scenes of this great Theatre of Nature," where we shall learn the true character of a man. "A single bad Act no more constitutes a Villain in Life, than a single bad Part on the Stage." This is often taken to mean that we may overlook faults where virtues predominate. But this is certainly not what Fielding intends:

> Indeed, nothing can be of more moral Use than the Imperfections which are seen in Examples of this Kind; since such form a Kind of Surprize, more apt to affect and dwell upon our Minds, than the Faults of very vicious and wicked Persons . . . when we find such Vices attended with their evil Consequence to our favourite Characters, we are not only taught to shun them for our own Sake, but to hate them for the Mischiefs they have already brought on those we love.   (X, i)

So Tom has in the end to face himself. Sophia insists on this, and her insistence has more moral rigor than Allworthy's balancing of "his Faults with his Perfections" (IV, xi). "'I think, Mr. *Jones*,' said she, 'I may almost depend on your own Justice, and leave it to yourself to pass Sentence on your own Conduct'" (XVIII, xii). One must be harsh with oneself, charitable and compassionate to others. Faults will not go undetected but "will raise our Compassion rather than our Abhorrence" (X, i); and, Fielding concludes, having been permitted to look behind the scenes, "the man of Candour and of true Understanding is never hasty to condemn. . . . The worst of Men generally have the Words *Rogue* and *Villain* in their Mouths" (VII, i).

The book, then, is not concerned with judgments made in detachment and isolation. Shaftesbury's ideal reader, judging "coolly and with indifference," will, Fielding implies, only be sinking deeper into his own illusions. For if our judgments are an expression of our own moral identity, they are also an expression of community, of our attitude to others. Any flaw in this feeling for others will imply a flaw in our own being. This is, of course, nominally Shaftesbury's argument also: "That to have the natural, kindly, or generous affections strong and powerful towards the good of the public, is to have the chief means and power of self-enjoyment, . . . to want them is certain misery and ill."[43] Thus Shaftesbury bids "self-love and social be the same." What he does not allow for is the difficulty, the stress of living up to these principles. Fielding has to test Shaftesbury's ideals in the thick of life. He puts the matter with a quite different emphasis: "[Tom] was never an indifferent Spectator of the Misery or Happiness of any one; and he felt either the one or the other in greater Proportion as he himself contributed to either" (XI, viii).

Initially, to be sure, Fielding seems to align himself more closely with Shaftesbury. His book, a tribute to Lyttleton and Ralph Allen (the model for his "Picture of a truly benevolent Mind," [Dedication]), is also a kind of tribute to Shaftesbury, whose image of the Deity has many of the features we discern in Allworthy: " . . . a Deity who is considered as worthy and good, and admired and reverenced as such, . . . In such a presence, 'tis evident that as the shame of guilty actions must be the greatest of any, so must the honour be of well-doing, even under the unjust censure of a world."[44] But Fielding cannot sustain such confidence, as we may gather from his skepticism about the Gipsy King's benevolent despotism. As he says, it has the one defect that it is difficult to find "any Man adequate to the Office of an absolute Monarch" (XII, xii). From the start, therefore, there is something unreal about Allworthy: "a human Being replete with Benevolence, mediating in what Manner he might render himself most acceptable to his Creator, by doing most Good to his Creatures" (I, iv). We can hardly credit that this could be meant seriously, and Fielding does in fact give it an ironic twist: "Reader, take Care, I have unadvisedly led thee to the Top of as high a Hill as Mr. *Allworthy's,* and how to get thee down without breaking thy Neck, I do not well know. However, let us e'en venture to slide down together" (I, iv).

Allworthy has always seemed one of the puzzles of the book. Henry James Pye, writing in 1792, notes him as "a character at opposition with himself, though more perhaps in general with that which the author tells you in his own person he is, than with his own conduct in those parts where the author suffers him to act from himself." The trouble, as Pye sees it, is that Allworthy, offered as "a man of sense and discernment, with a benevolence almost angelic," is actually "the dupe of every insinuating rascal he meets; and a dupe not of the most amiable kind, since he is always led to acts of justice and severity. The consequence of his pliability is oftener the punishment of the innocent than the acquittal of the guilty, and in such punishment he is severe and implacable."[45] Andrew Wright sees more clearly that he could never have been intended as the "moral centre" of the book[46] but errs, I think, in claiming that the existence in the novel of Western is "the strongest of all reasons" for thinking so. No doubt Western is "full of vitality, [and] also playful," but we need not conclude that either Fielding or the reader finds this combination of qualities "irre sistible." There is surely some severity in Fielding's comment that "Men over-violent in their Dispositions, are, for the most Part, as changeable in them" (XVIII, ix). Western is erratic, undependable and tyrannical. A full view of him must include the harsh ironies of Book VII, Chapter iv, in which his love for Sophia is measured against his hatred of his neglected and abused wife. Yet, it appears, Allworthy's detachment and impartiality are not in themselves a protection against profound error. One important way of establishing this is by comparison, not with Western or another character, but with the reader himself.

In Book IV, Chapter xi, Allworthy is at first represented as somewhat arbitrary and harsh in his treatment of Molly Seagrim: "I question, as here was no regular Information before him, whether his Conduct was strictly regular." When Toms pleads for the girl, Allworthy's moral indignation is deflected ("I own, indeed, [the guilt] doth lie principally upon you, and so heavy it is, that you ought to expect it should crush you"). Allworthy fails to see how this rebuke reflects on his judgment of Molly: should he not from the beginning have directed his anger against the principal offender? Fielding has insinuated, in any case, that the house of correction is an ineffectual punishment. And when he seems to wish to salvage Allworthy's reputation for impartiality it is with a curious effect: "he was not so blinded by [the offense], but that he could discern any Virtue in the guilty Person, as clearly, indeed as if there had been no Mixture of Vice in the same Character." This, Fielding asserts, indicates that he has come to "the same Opinion of this young Fellow which, we hope, our Reader may have conceived." But he has not in fact been encouraging us to estimate Tom in terms of this kind of "moral arithmetic." And its inadequacy emerges as soon as it is challenged. Thwackum, admittedly, cannot sway Allworthy. But Square, "a much more artful Man," has no difficulty at all in persuading him that Tom's generosity is the mark of "a depraved and debauched Appetite": "he supported the Father, in order to corrupt the Daughter, and perserved the Family from starving, to bring one of them to Shame and Ruin." To Allworthy these "considerations" (not, we note, new evidence but a new interpretation of the evidence) are "too plausible to be absolutely and hastily rejected" and stamp in his mind "the first bad Impression concerning *Jones*." His judgment throughout the episode is as wrong as it can be. If the arguments advanced by Square have any force, Allworthy should himself have reckoned with them in reaching his first judgment; if they do not, he should not have been affected by them. But his moral failure here is made more glaring by contrast with the kind of judgment Fielding expects from the reader. Before Square states his case, the reader is given the same evidence as Allworthy himself is given. "The Reader must remember the several little Incidents of the Partridge, the Horse, and the Bible, which were recounted in the second Book." They had first enlisted Allworthy's approval. "The same, I believe, must have happened to him with every other Person who hath any Idea of Friendship, Generosity, and Greatness of Spirit; that is to say, who hath any Trace of Goodness in his Mind." The reader will not easily forfeit his claim to such qualities, and Square's speech need not persuade him to do so. But Allworthy, by contrast, is blinded and confused; his very judiciousness saps his power to judge aright.

Furthermore, Allworthy's detachment and impartiality, fallible enough in themselves, all too often forsake him altogether. When he banishes Tom, for instance, we find him unexpectedly egocentric: it becomes obvious to the reader that what most sways him is Tom's supposed disrespect towards him. As this is just what he cannot admit openly, his censure of Tom looks motiveless: "nay, indeed, (Tom) hardly knew his Accusation: for as Mr. *Allworthy*, in recounting the Drunkenness, & *c.* while he lay ill, out of Modesty sunk every Thing that related particularly to himself, which indeed principally constituted the Crime, *Jones* could not deny the Charge" (VI, xi). In fact his judgments are almost always prejudiced: "the poor Game-keeper was condemned, without having any Opportunity to defend himself" (III, x); Molly was to be committed to Bridewell without a hearing; the evidence that Jenny might have given in support of Partridge "would have deserved no Credit," and, when he continues to protest his innocence, "Mr. *Allworthy* declared himself satisfied of his Guilt, and that he was too bad a Man to receive any Encouragement from him" (II, vi). Allworthy is quick to blame, more aware of guilt than innocence. Mrs. Miller finds in Tom "one of the most humane tender honest Hearts that ever Man was blessed with," though he is marred by "Faults of Wildness and of Youth" (XVII, ii). Allworthy maintains rather that there are "few Characters so absolutely vicious as not to have the least Mixture of Good in them" (XVIII, vii). He is, accordingly, slow to see through Blifil, though quick to dismiss Tom.

Allworthy *should* have seen through Blifil. As Fielding says in his "Essay on the Knowledge of the Characters of Men," "the truth is, nature doth really imprint sufficient marks in the countenance, to inform an accurate and discerning eye" (*Works,* viii, p. 166). And in fact Mrs. Miller's simplicity is more penetrating than Allworthy's deliberate and patient judgment: "'Guilty!'", she exclaims, on seeing the change in Blifil's face, "'Guilty, upon my Honour! Guilty, upon my Soul!'" (XVIII, v). With this in mind it is difficult not to suspect Fielding of irony when he appears to be defending Allworthy against possible criticism: "Of readers who . . . condemn the Wisdom or Penetration of Mr. *Allworthy*, I shall not scruple to say, that they make a very bad and ungrateful Use of that Knowledge which we have communicated to them" (III, v). Must we take this to mean that there are no grounds for condemning Allworthy's judgments? Surely it is intended rather as a sharp reminder that but for Fielding's help we would fare no better ourselves. If Allworthy fails, his failure reflects no credit on us. It should in fact engage our admiration. There is something heroic in Allworthy. If Tom is the comic hero, always acting and always in the dark, Allworthy, never allowed to withhold judgment or to be less than his best, is the book's most admired yet poignant figure, its tragic hero in fact. It is through his high-minded failures that we gain some of our clearest impressions of the difficulty of judging well. Yet, in our respect for the stubborn excellence of Allworthy, we are not to reconcile ourselves to judging like him. We are expected to go "behind the scenes," to do in fact what the author has been doing for us. There is no credit in ignorance.

Not that Fielding simply recommends "penetration" and keen discernment. Indeed, it is obvious he likes the opposite qualities—the credulity of Mrs. Miller, or the simplicity of Sophia. Mrs. Western's penetration, on the other hand, or the "sagacity" of the reader, or the innkeeper who thought that Sophia was Jenny Cameron, are comical. Yet, as he argues elsewhere, "Good-nature requires a distinguishing Faculty, which is another Word for Judgment, and is perhaps the sole Boundary between Wisdom and Folly; it is impossible for a Fool, who hath no distinguishing Faculty to be good-natured" (*The Champion*, March 27, 1740). Simplicity is not good-natured (and here we recall Partridge) unless it is combined with keen penetration. But, as we have seen, penetration is often a kind of blindness and folly. We can perhaps resolve the dilemma by recalling the distinction Fielding makes between the two degrees of suspicion. One, arising from the heart, imagines evil where none exists; the other, arising from the head, the understanding, is "no other than the Faculty of seeing what is before your Eyes, and of drawing Conclusions from what you see" (XI, x). Whilst this is a way of detecting guilt, the former can only harm the innocent. But again this is a rather mechanical formula. To see a more vital connection between good nature and understanding, simplicity and discernment, we must turn to Tom.

Tom's good nature is described in terms which ought to apply to All-worthy; the moral principle which governs his conduct is a judicial one, "like the LORD HIGH CHANCELLOR of this Kingdom in his Court; where it presides, governs, directs, judges, acquits, and condemns according to Merit and Justice; with a Knowledge which nothing escapes, a Penetration which nothing can deceive, and an Integrity which nothing can corrupt" (IV, vi). And this is an "active Principle," not arbitrating in remote detach-ment, not content "with Knowledge or Belief only," but prompting good actions and restraining from bad. Here, surely, is the hub of the book's meaning. All that Fielding has to show of the nature of judgment centers here, in these rare moral qualities. They place before us, as a constant point of reference in the book, the high ideal which, in Butler's sermons, is called conscience.

> But there is a superior principle of reflection or conscience in every man, which distinguishes between the internal principles of his heart, as well as his external actions: which passes judgment upon himself and them; . . . which, without being consulted, without being advised with, magisterially exerts itself, and approves or condemns him the doer of them accordingly: . . . It is by this faculty, natural to man, that he is a moral agent, that he is a law to himself.[47]

Thus our approval of Tom is meant to lead us to challenging moral issues. There is much more to him than a good heart and a healthy appetite. What we are to appreciate in his nature is something like the discernment and judgment we ourselves are expected to display in our reading of the novel. The book, by making us conscious of ourselves as readers, by exer-cising our critical faculties, is contributing no less than Butler himself to a philosophical process. Indeed, the terms in which the eighteenth century derived its ethical principles, from the earlier reactions to Hobbes,[48] are strikingly relevant to the novel. Thus Richard Cumberland in 1672, in the act of refuting Hobbes, anticipates many of Fielding's remarks:

> Shall I not reckon among the perfections of the human understanding, that it can *reflect* upon it self? *Consider* its habits, as dispositions arising from past actions? *Remember* and *recollect* its own dictates, and compare them with its actions? *Judge* which way the mind inclines? And *direct* it self to the pursuit of what seems fittest to be done? Our mind is conscious to it self of all its own actions, and both can, and often does, observe what counsels produced them; it naturally sits a *judge* upon its own actions, and thence procures to it self either *tranquillity* and joy, or *anxiety* and sorrow. In this power of the mind, and the

actions thence arising, consists the whole force of *conscience,* by which it *proposes* law to it self, *examines* its past, and *regulates* its future conduct.[49]

Here, as Baumrin points out, we find the "terms and ideas which will become part of the conceptual hardware of rationalism"[50]; Fielding not only shows himself familiar with them, he takes full possession of them in the imaginative world of his novel. And the reader, whose role in that world is so important, is in a position to possess them in the same way.

It may seem, in fact, that it is only in this way and not through the rendering of character and behavior that such a meaning is established. Though Tom's moral sense certainly becomes more urgent as the story unfolds, yet his conduct with Lady Bellaston, for instance, calls for more self-reproach than he can command, and its moral implications remain unresolved. Yet Fielding does drive the narrative to a conclusion where Tom comes face to face with conscience. However lightly, Fielding at last indicates that the book has a religious dimension. Sophia demands of Tom this kind of awareness: "'Sincere Repentance, Mr. *Jones,*' answered she, 'will obtain the Pardon of a Sinner, but it is from one who is a perfect Judge of that Sincerity'" (XVIII, xii). After what we have seen of Fielding's sustained attention to the question of judgment, this ultimate appeal does not seem forced. It provides a way of estimating Allworthy's Shaftesburyan benevolence, and it anchors Tom's conduct firmly to the tougher principles of conscience: "conscience naturally and always of course goes on to anticipate a higher and more effectual sentence, which shall hereafter second and affirm its own."[51]

Yet after all it is by no means because he is morally impeccable that Tom is to be set against Allworthy. Fielding needs someone who can do wrong in order to bring out the hollowness of Allworthy's rectitude. A man who cannot act badly has no business to be judging others. It is in fact Tom, his own affairs tangled and squalid, who is able to persuade Nightingale to do what is right. It seems absurd that he should now "preach," just as earlier Allworthy had read him "a very severe Lecture on Chastity." Nightingale is ready to scoff: "Thou wilt make an admirable Parson" (XIV, iv). But it is because Tom is what he is that he can reply with authority and force: "'Lookee, Mr. *Nightingale,*' said *Jones,* 'I am no canting Hypocrite, nor do I pretend to the Gift of Chastity, more than my Neighbours. I have been guilty with Women, I own it; but am not conscious that I have ever injured any—nor would I, to procure Pleasure to myself, be knowingly the Cause of Misery to any human Being.'" Not even, we are sure, to procure the pleasure of being in the right.

"Judge not, that ye be not judged": the injunction is often in Fielding's mind. *Tom Jones* shows, though, that we cannot choose not to judge. Nor can we avoid being judged, however "prudent" our lives. But we can and should learn to judge with knowledge, that is with full experience and full sympathy; above all we have to learn how to forgive. The last thing to learn is that all this is part of a great comedy: if Fielding anywhere sets out his intentions in the book it is in his invocation to his genius, the genius of comedy:

Teach me, which to thee is no difficult Task, to know Mankind better than they know themselves. Remove that Mist which dims the Intellects of Mortals, and causes them to adore Men for their Art, or to detest them for their Cunning in deceiving others, when they are, in Reality, the Objects only of Ridicule, for deceiving themselves . . . . fill my Pages with humour; 'till Mankind learn the Good-Nature to laugh only at the Follies of others, and the Humility to grieve at their own (XIII, i).

Notes

1. Frank Kermode, "Afterword" to *Tom Jones* (New York: Signet Classics edition, 1963), p. 859.
2. *An Introduction to the English Novel* (1951), I, p. 77.
3. *Henry Fielding: Mask and Feast* (1965), p. 22.
4. Ibid., pp. 72, 30.
5. Henry James, *The Art of the Novel*, introd. by R. P. Blackmur (1947), p. 68.
6. E. M. Forster, *Aspects of the Novel* (Pelican Books, 1962), p. 93.
7. *The Rise of the Novel* (1957), p. 279.
8. *Tom Jones* (Signet Classics), p. 857.
9. Ibid., p. 857.
10. Ibid., p. 859.
11. *Irony in "Tom Jones"* (Alabama, 1965), p. 41.
12. *The English Novel: Form and Function* (New York: Harper Torchbooks, 1961), pp. 80–81.
13. *The Rise of the Novel*, p. 271.
14. "Henry Fielding, Christian Censor," in *The Age of Johnson*, ed. F. W. Hilles, PP. 140–42.
15. *The Works of Henry Fielding*, ed. A. Murphy (1771), VIII, pp. 499–500.
16. *Irony in "Tom Jones"*, p. 67.·
17. Ibid., p. 39.
18. "Fielding and the Meaning of History," *PMLA*, 79 (1964), 561.
19. *Irony in "Tom Jones"*, p. 61.
20. *Fielding: "Tom Jones"* (1964), p. 51.

21. "Fielding's Social Outlook," *Eighteenth-Century English Literature*, ed. J. L. Clifford (New York, 1959), p. 263.

22. Cf. R. S. Crane, "The Concept of Plot and the Plot of *Tom Jones*," *Critics and Criticism, Ancient and Modern* (Chicago, 1952), pp. 637–8.

23. *The English Novel*, p. 72.

24. Ibid., p. 68.

25. *Fielding: "Tom Jones"*, pp. 23–24.

26. Cf. Ehrenpreis, op. cit., p. 66: "Such surprises combine puzzlement with relief"; and p. 65: "The same agent seems repeatedly to save us from perils to which he alone has exposed us; we are continually being lost and found by the same guide."

27. "The Concept of Plot and the Plot of *Tom Jones*," pp. 635–36.

28. *Irony in "Tom Jones"*, p. 56.

29. *The Rise of the Novel*, p. 287.

30. See Wayne C. Booth, *The Rhetoric of Fiction* (Chicago, 1961).

31. See Ethel M. Thornbury, *Henry Fielding's Theory of the Comic Prose Epic* (Wisconsin, 1931), pp. 56ff.

32. René Le Bossu, *Traité du Poëme Epique* (Paris, 1693), p. 239.

33. Ibid., p. 207.

34. Anthony Ashley Cooper, Third Earl of Shaftesbury, *Characteristics*, ed. J. M. Robertson (1900), I, p. 131.

35. "Fielding's Familiar Style," *ELH*, 34 (March 1967), p. 65.

36. Ibid., p. 73.

37. Ibid., p. 76.

38. *Henry Fielding: Mask and Feast*, p. 32.

39. Perhaps Fielding is echoing Burton: "—*ut palata, sic judicia*, our censures are as various as our palats . . . Our writings are as so many Dishes, our Readers Guests. . . . What shall I doe in this case? As a Dutch host, if you come to an Inne in Germany, & dislike your fare, diet, lodging, &c. replies in a surly tone, *aliud tibi quaeras diversorium*, if you like not this, get you to another Inne: I resolue, if you like not my writing, goe read something else." Robert Burton, *The Anatomy of Melancholy* (6th ed., 1632), pp. 9–10.

40. William Empson, *"Tom Jones,"* *The Kenyon Review*, 20 (1958), 249.

41. "The Function of Criticism," *Selected Essays* (1951), p. 25.

42. *The Rhetoric of Fiction*, p. 216.

43. *Characteristics*, I, p. 292.

44. op. cit., I, p. 268.

45. *A Commentary Illustrating the Poetic of Aristotle* (London, 1792), reprinted in *Aristotle's Poetics and English Literature*, ed. Elder Olson (Chicago, 1965), pp. 39–40.

46. op. cit, pp. 159–62.

47. Joseph Butler, *Works*, ed. W. E. Gladstone (Oxford, 1896), II, p. 59.

48. See B. H. Baumrin, the New Introduction to L. A. Selby-Bigge, *British Moralists* (New York, 1964), pp. xff.

49. *De Legibus Naturae* (1672), chap. 2, sect. 12, cited in Selby-Bigge, *British Moralists*, p. xxiii.

50. Ibid., p. xxiv.

51. Butler, op. cit., II, p. 59.

Smollett and the
Old Conventions

MICHAEL ROSENBLUM

Over twenty years ago, Nathalie Sarraute designated the times an "age of suspicion": henceforth the serious novelist could no longer rely on the "warts and waistcoats, characters and plots" of the traditional novel since these could only reveal "a reality, the slightest particle of which we are familiar with already." In the same spirit Robbe-Grillet insisted that any art which wishes to continue the "discovery of reality" must purge itself of its dead and dying conventions.[1] But of course for the demanding writer and the demanding reader it has always been an age of suspicion. Although the suspicion of the modern novelist may seem more far-reaching, what he says in defense of his innovations is only an updated version of Virginia Woolf's defense of the Georgian novelist's attempts to go beyond the "warts and waistcosts" of the Edwardians. Or, to move back to the beginnings of prose fiction, a version of the complaints of Encolpius in the *Satyricon* about the numbing effect of the stock tropes of the rhetoricians.

All writers have a stake in the fight against stale convention; certainly the complaints of poets against poetic diction, or dramatists against the formulas of the well-made play are familiar enough. But perhaps the novelist of all writers is the most militant enemy of the old conventions, since the novel (at least according to Ian Watt's influential account) is the genre most committed to a "fresh exploration of reality" without the reliance upon the literary conventions of the past. As Frank Kermode has argued,

From *Philological Quarterly*, 55 (1976), 389–402.

the history of the novel is a perpetual cycle of novel and anti-novel. The novelist is always trying to evade "the old laws of the land of romance and the old hero," the conventions of the language of fiction that he inherits.[2] It is not surprising then that the "first" great novel should be a sustained attack on the old hero and the old laws of romance. The writers of the eighteenth century in England likewise found it almost obligatory to begin their works with disparaging references to earlier fiction. Smollett was only being blunter than most when he dismissed romance as an embarrassing survival of the Gothic age: "Romance, no doubt, owes its origin to ignorance, vanity, and superstition."[3]

But new starts for fiction are not made so easily. The artist may dream of banishing convention and getting directly at unmediated reality, but there is no such thing as unmediated reality in art. As Roman Jakobson pointed out over fifty years ago, the concept of realism is always relative: not only to the norms of the beholder, but also to the existing system of representation which the artist inherits.[4] Thus it is also not surprising that Cervantes should carry out his attack on the old conventions not by *avoiding* them, but by recalling as many of them as possible in his "new" work. It is now a commonplace that romance is not only Cervantes' target, but his great inspiration as well. Similarly, for all their scorn towards the fictional indulgences of an earlier, more childlike age, it was impossible for Smollett or his fellow novelists to banish the old language of fiction from their works. The question is not so much how to avoid romance as how to come to terms with the romance inheritance in particular and the literary past in general.

For the "naive" but still suspicious novelist like Defoe or Richardson there was no problem. Believing that they were imitating reality directly, they allowed their imaginations free play and produced some of the most conventionalized plot formulas of the old fiction: the romance underpinnings of *Pamela* or the incest motifs of *Moll Flanders*. Moreover, they were not bound to the assumptions of the doctrine of separation of styles which decreed that if the story were to be serious, the protagonist must be some version of the old hero, that is, the more elevated hero of epic, tragedy, or romance.[5] For them it was no breach of decorum to give serious and extended treatment to the affairs of servants or middle-class households. On the other hand, more self-conscious writers like Fielding and Smollett, more aware of the literary past, could not pretend that their works had nothing in common with earlier traditions. Hence the facetious embarrassment about the protagonist's genealogy in *Joseph Andrews* and *Ferdinand Count Fathom*, the fondness of both novelists for the secret-of-birth social promotion by which it turns out that the hero isn't so "low" after all, and the pervasive mock-heroic stance which protects the narrator in his excursions into low life.

In the preface to *Ferdinand Count Fathom* Smollett defensively antici- pates the objections of the reader who may be offended at yet another treat- ment of "the obscene objects of low life." In the preface to *Roderick Ran- dom* he apologizes for his representation of the "mean scenes" in which the hero finds himself. The justification is that the "low state" shows "those parts of life where the humours and passions are undisguised by affectation, ceremony, or education; and the whimsical peculiarities of dis- position appear as nature has implanted them" (I, x). This is very similar to Fielding's claim that "the various callings in lower spheres produce the great variety of humorous characters." For both writers, scenes from ordi- nary life become the material for genre pieces, Empsonian pastorals in which the sophisticated author uses his "primitive" subjects as models for the more complex and therefore more opaque humanity in which he is really interested.

With this outlook, neither Fielding nor Smollett is ready to abandon traditional notions of social and literary decorum, even in what they take to be a new kind of writing. Nor will we be surprised if such novelists constantly and deliberately revert to earlier ways of telling a story. Despite his apparent contempt for romance, Smollett rarely gets away from the old hero and the old plots of the land of romance.[6] Even at the most superficial level, the debt to romance is obvious: the heroes are from the start pre- sented as extraordinary young men, their specialness being indicated by the early-signs-of-future-greatness formula (the precocity of Random and Fathom), the backward hero formula (Greaves and Melville), or an alter- nation between the two, as in the early career of Peregrine Pickle. Only in his last work does Smollet break out of the formula by introducing Humphry Clinker, a backward hero who remains backward. These exam- ples perhaps reveal no more than the persistence of minor narrative fossils. I think, however, that Smollett draws upon earlier ways of telling a story in a more important way: Random, Pickle, Melville, and Greaves share what could be called a romance mentality, a way of conceiving of them- selves and their relation to the outside world that reflects not necessarily their reading of romance (though this is the case with Greaves), but the simple fact that their creator casts his work in the molds of the older lan- guage of fiction.

The best place to begin is the opening pages of Smollet's first work of fiction. Random tells how he is restored to the birthright of which he has been cheated, and brought to that state of felicity prophesied in his mother's dreams—that her son would "return to his native land, where he would flourish in happiness and reputation." All the hero's difficulties begin with the disinheritance of his father by his grandfather for the crime of marrying beneath his rank. The grandfather is "an unnatural and inflexible parent," "a merciless tyrant," whose decrees as a judge are "invariable as the laws of the Medes and Persians." Mother and child are saved by a faithful old maidservant without whose assistance the mother "and the innocent fruit of her womb would have fallen miserable victims to his rigour and inhumanity. By the friendship of this poor woman she was carried up to a garret, and immediately delivered of a man-child, the story of whose unfortunate birth he now relates" (I, 4). After the death of his mother and the disappearance of his father, Roderick is left to face his hostile relatives alone. The more he shows signs of promise, the more Roderick is hated and envied by his cousins and grandfather. The only help that he gets in his early years (aside from Bowling's) comes from the poor tenants who love him because his father was their particular favorite.

Romance archetypes are never far from the surface of Smollett's narrative, but in this account of "the unfortunate birth" they emerge more clearly than usual. The style throughout is hyperbolic:[7] the grandfather becomes an oriental despot, a Pharaoh, a Herod slaughtering the innocents. But for Random, who is telling his own story, the language is not excessive. He sees himself as having the birthright and all the gifts of nature which give him a claim to the hand of Fortune. The typical excess of the language suggests the extraordinary importance being accorded the events—as if Random were indeed the hero of romance, or even of sacred myth. We recognize such classic motifs as the birth in humble circumstances, the help from the lowly in avoiding the wrath of the mighty, the enmity of jealous siblings as it becomes apparent that the hero has been chosen to fulfill a special destiny. The immediate situation, boy cheated of his estate, has been transformed and charged with all the significance of an anointed prince cheated of throne and patrimony by usurpers. In Smollett gentlemanhood becomes mythologized, becoming as precious and singular a condition as being the prince or king in "straight" romance.

Random's experiences in the world are shaped by his gentlemanhood, the simple circumstance that he is his father's son. When he meets Miss Williams for the second time, he tells her he can choose any "scheme of life" "without forfeiting the dignity of my character beyond a power of retrieving it" (I, 192). The essential and permanent part of him, his "dignity of character," is untouched by experience and cannot be compromised whether he turn foot-soldier or fortune-hunter. As Miss Williams tells him, although his circumstances are low, he is still a gentleman. Since the fact of birth is irrevocable, gentlemanhood depends neither on present circumstances, wealth, or conduct. Because the sense of self is prior to and independent of experience, Random's adventures are separate from what he is and do not change him into something different than what he has been. Like most of Smollett's other heroes, Random does not really change in the course of the novel.[8] His adventures begin when he is expelled from the paternal estate, and they end when that lost estate is recovered. The time between is therefore a time of exile, a marking of time until the final return to reclaim the estate to which he is entitled.

The framing plot for *Random*, the fictional shape within which all the episodes are "contained," is a very direct adaptation of the typical romance sequence of disinheritance and exile followed by recognition and restoration,[9] and in one way or another this sequence recurs in all the later novels. In *Peregrine Pickle* the hero is in the curious position of trying to reclaim his patrimony from his own parents. The whole situation is wildly implausible, since the cause of disheritance is Mrs. Pickle's unaccountable aversion for her first-born and her even more unaccountable preference for her second son. The very great lengths to which Smollett goes in order to bring about the disinheritance suggests his dependence on the romance pattern as a way of giving shape to his narratives. In the third novel, *Ferdinand Count Fathom*, it is Count Melville who is cheated out of his estate by his wicked stepfather, Count Trebasi. The novel ends with the recovery of the lost estates of Don Diego de Zelos and Melville. In *Launcelot Greaves* the hero has already come into possession of his estate, and the exile is imposed only by his "madness." In this work, however, it is not necessary for Smollett to insist on the conventions of the romance plot, since Greaves enacts in a literal way the romance assumptions of the heroes of the earlier novels. Only in his last work, *Humphry Clinker*, does Smollett really transform the conventions by parodying them: the social promotion of Clinker is at once unexpected, conventional, and ludicrous since, the revelation of the secret of his birth notwithstanding, Clinker remains a highly unlikely hero. Even though Smollett is being arch about the romance conventions, the point is he still must use them in order to conclude his story.

The protagonist of the romance and the novel may have similar "great expectations," but typically the hero of the novel, unlike his romance counterpart, discovers in the end that his secret dreams of a special destiny are not to be realized.[10] As Ortega puts it, Quixote, the typical hero of the novel, lives in a world in which "the will is real but what is willed is not real." DeFoe's Colonel Jacque knows that he is a bastard and is therefore haunted by the possibility that he is of high birth. Although the memory of the romance dream has not been lost (in which all bastards are potentially princes), no romantic Fortune is going to intervene to validate his secret dreams. Whatever social promotion Jacque, Moll, or Pamela get they must earn by their own efforts. For all their talk about the hand of Providence, we can see clearly that it is their own provident natures that make Robinson Crusoe or Moll Flanders so successful. It is only in the special world of romance that what is willed can be converted without effort into the actual. In narratives that we feel to be more "realistic," no supernatural agent, whether it be the hand of Fortune or Providence, can be allowed to tamper with the machinery of causation, suspending the ordinary laws of probability in order to bring about the happy ending. In comedy and tragedy, as in romance, we see a literary kind of fortune, "a wholly extraordinary concatenation of events,"[11] a view of life made safer or more perilous under the comic or tragic dispensation.

By contrast, the events and system of causation in more realistic genres such as the picaresque (a genre to which Smollett's works are often assigned) are not extraordinary. However unlucky, the picaro does not see his misfortune as singular, since he himself is not important enough to have been singled out for special attention by the gods. Fortune to him is an order of events which results from what Auerbach describes as "the inner processes of the real, historical world." Given the structure of society, the workings of economic cause and effect, the picaro is likely to suffer. But since bad luck is not inexorable, as it would be if it were the expression of the enmity of the gods (as in *The Satyricon* or *The Golden Ass*), it can be sidestepped, and with a little extra effort the picaro can be as successful as a Lazarillo de Tormes. Instead of the image of the relentless wheel of Fortune, we have the mild indifference expressed by Gil Blas when he remembers Epictetus' maxim that Fortune is a whore who dispenses her favors at random.

Although Smollett's heroes may at times have glimpses into the connections between their own fortunes and the structure of society, they more often see themselves as subject to an extraordinary, magical fortune. For them Fortune remains "charged" and personal, the persecution of a cruel Goddess when adverse, and the reward of a kind parent when favorable. When Random finally gets what he wants, he claims that "fortune seems determined to make ample amends for her former cruelty." This imparts a purpose and memory to fortune, as if the probability of a penny landing on heads were to be increased because it had landed on tails for the last forty-nine tosses. Random expects a return of good fortune, a favorable fiftieth toss after the previous consecutive disastrous ones, as no more than his due. The probability of the statistician (who says that the next toss is still just as likely to be tails) is discarded in favor of a universe which keeps track of the tosses. For all the earlier frustrations of the protagonist, the romance fortune in the end implies alignment between will and the world, wish and fulfillment. As in the pathetic fallacy, human feelings are magically projected and reflected in the workings of the external world.

Towards the end of *Roderick Random* and *Peregrine Pickle* both heroes find themselves destitute in prison without any hope of relief. In an education novel this might be the point at which the hero reviews his life and resolves to change. But in both novels there is no introspection and certainly no conversion. On the contrary, the hero does not need to change in order to merit his final reward. Lieutenant Bowling, Roderick's "beneficent kinsman," turns up once more, having in his long absence prospered at sea contrary to all reasonable expectation. He is thus able to convert his beneficence into cash and bail his nephew out. Peregrine Pickle also finds his deliverance from the sea: a ship in which he has invested returns safely. There is no reason why the good luck of Benjamin Chintz the merchant should "reconcile Peregrine to life and predispose him to enjoy human society again," but it does. What reconciles Pickle to life is "this unexpected smile of fortune," the sudden reminder that fortune may be responsive to his wishes after all. One's ship will come in, there are rich uncles, and fortune is neither indifferent nor malign.

Nor is this all. More "magic" is needed to extricate the two young men. Only a completely independent fortune will pass scrutiny and allow Random to marry Narcissa as a gentleman, the only footing on which, by his own vow, he could enjoy her hand. Pickle is equally scrupulous in turning down the offers of assistance made by Pipes, Hatchway, Emilia, and Gauntlet. Only his father's money and estate will serve. Coming into one's own means that the hero is restored to his original condition. He cannot by his own efforts make the restoration come about—he accepts the good fortune as his due. Only with the accession to the paternal estate can the heroes be free, and this can only be accomplished through the most conventional formulas of the world of romance.

The stroke of luck that delivers Peregrine from his perplexity and retrieves his lost estate is the apoplectic stroke that kills his father. Instead of trying to conceal the unlikelihood of his resolutions, Smollet seems to go out of his way to call attention to their artificiality. Nowhere is this clearer than in *Ferdinand Count Fathom*, where the elaborate chivalric strategems inevitably suggest Tom Sawyer's rescue of Jim. By challenging and defeating Count Trebasi in knightly battle, Melville frees his sister and mother and regains his patrimony. The happy ending in *Launcelot Greaves* is equally astonishing: Greaves is fortuitously thrown into the very same madhouse as Aurelia Darnel; Ferret reveals that he is Bridget Marples' secret husband, and thus the entail on Captain Crowe's estate is no longer valid. And finally it is revealed that Dolly Cowslip is the natural child of Jonathan Greaves and thus of sufficiently high birth to be a proper match for Lawyer Clark. As the chapter heading which ushers in all these marvels puts it: "The knot that puzzles human Wisdom, the Hand of Fortune sometimes will untie" (266).

Smollett's favorite means of forcing the hand of fortune is the recognition scene, a staple of literary plots from Homer onwards and one especially favored by writers of romance. Smollett can hardly have been under any illusions as to its novelty, and yet, with the exception of *Peregrine Pickle*, it appears conspicuously in all the novels. Since the first and last (and the most important) of Smollett's novels end with elaborate recognition scenes, it is only a mild exaggeration to say that Smollett's whole achievement in fiction is framed by the recognition scene. And if we can believe the report first given in Moore's *Life*, this was the kind of scene that Smollett liked to stage in his life as well as in his novels.[12] While characters are always reappearing in Smollett, the recognition scene proper is an extraordinary event violating ordinary probability. The most miraculous are those in which two parties related by the closest ties of blood or friendship encounter each other after the greatest possible separation in time and space. The long separation may lead each to assume that the other is dead, and the scene suggests the most dramatic breach of the natural order, the return to life of the dead. The reunion may also bring about a complete reversal of fortune for one or another of the participants. The scene itself is a public spectacle, producing copious tears from participants and spectators alike.

In the recognition scenes between father and son that climax *Roderick Random* and *Humphry Clinker*, Smollett turns his back on the demands of realistic fiction and unequivocally writes a kind of fiction in which wishfulfillment fantasies are not hindered by the reality principle. The reunion between Random and his father in the suitably exotic land of Paraguay has all the improbability of romance; the immediate and mysterious attraction that each feels intimates a hidden relation between them. The revelation that they are father and son is so overwhelming that Random falls into a delirium which brings him to the point of death. He awakens to find his father and uncle hovering over his bed; he has been reborn into a world in which chance is redeemed. The encounter between Clinker and Bramble also conveys the sense that mysterious forces are operating beneath the surface of ordinary events. Because Bramble has saved him from nakedness, hunger, and disease, Clinker promises to "go through fire as well as water" to save Bramble. And he does go through fire and flood to fulfill his vow—even thought the fire at Bullford's is a practical joke and the drowning of Bramble in the ocean is only apparent. But at the very end of the novel Clinker finally gets his chance when the carriage overturns in the stream. As in *Random*, there is a "point of ritual death" after which "a *cognitio* takes place, in the course of which their family relationships are regrouped, secrets of birth brought to light, and names changed."[13]

The recognition scene and other cadence formulas make possible the final return of the estate, the event which concludes or is in prospect in all of the novels. What is said of Pickle's journey back to reclaim his estate— it is "the most delightful of all journies he had ever made"—might be said of other return journeys in the novels. At the end of *Random, Greaves,* and *Pickle,* a party composed of the hero and his bride, secondary couples, parents, and parent surrogates stages a triumphal public procession back to the estate, receiving the homage of the local gentry and the adoration of the common people attached to the estate. The solemnity of these processions and the fervor of the tenants suggest the return of an exiled king to his rightful inheritance rather than just the return of a popular landowner.

The estate as final destination in Smollett's narratives has, I think, relatively little to do with the realities of economic life in the second half of the eighteenth century.[14] Smollett's treatment of economic and social forces is for the most part schematic, conveying little of the novelist's interest in the infinite degrees of dependence and independence in society. For his heroes there are only two conditions, vulnerability and security, which correspond to two social classes, the needy vagabond and the independent gentleman. By means of the legal transactions which end *Random, Fathom,* and *Pickle,* the hero has all the signs of his new (old) status conferred upon him. The estate is as mythologized as the condition of gentlemanhood which it defines and the romance conventions which lead to its retrieval. It is viewed through the filters of classical literary myths of Arcadia, Horatian rural retirement, and what may be described as a conservative mythology about orderly societies of the past.[15]

If we think of the eighteenth century as the time of the "rise of the novel," the development of formal realism and the subsequent break with older ways of telling a story, it will be obvious that in returning to the old hero and the old plots, Smollett is a writer who prefers to look backward to what is in some ways a discredited language. The lazy or inept writer falls back on the old formulas because he knows they will be acceptable to his "unsuspicious" readers—indeed, they might demand them, and they make his task a bit easier. A romantic closing formula like the recognition scene is in the same category as the wedding and funeral bells which E. M. Forster says providentially come to the aid of the tired novelist. Smollett is not entirely innocent on this score, since at times the formulas do seem to be invoked merely to get from one point in the narrative to the next. Often, however, instead of being signs of the perfunctory, the romance language is used to signal the most important transactions in the novel.

The language of romance defines the nature of the journey undertaken in the novels, supplying both starting point and destination. Because of the overall romance shape of the journey, I would suggest that Smollett's affinities with the writers of picaresque have been exaggerated.[16] The picaro can travel indefinitely, since there is no natural stopping point: he has no destination, no quest to fulfill which would provide the climax for his adventures. Gil Blas' return to his birthplace is not for him a significant return, and he is soon on the road again, the homeward journey being for him only one of many possible journeys. There is no fixed indentity to return to, no patrimony to reclaim. In contrast, Smollett's heroes (and romance heroes in general) are their father's sons, and so they do not enjoy, nor would they wish to, the picaro's freedom from the confines of a fixed identity. When they finally return at the end of the novels, they reclaim their proper place in society. For similar reasons, it seems to me unsatisfactory to describe Smollett as a writer of education novels. The education novel usually traces the process by which the hero discovers his identity or vocation. In contrast, Random, Pickle, Greaves, and Melville have a conception of themselves which is prior to their experience rather than the product of continuing experience. Smollett's heroes need not discover who they are, since they already know who they are and who they will always be. If the hero of the education novel is in the process of becoming, Smollett's heroes are from the beginning already themselves. The end of the novel comes when that identity is confirmed.

I have been suggesting that the romance sequence of disinheritance, exile, and restoration provides Smollett with an "extended fiction,"[17] a plot or group of related motifs which serves to unify the total body of an author's work. My next suggestion is one that will be apparent to any reader of Smollett: romance serves mainly as a way of generating a satiric fiction. The romance language brings into focus a world that is the opposite of the idealized and orderly world of romance, the fallen and disorderly world of satire. Smollett updates the old hero and the old plot by insisting upon its anachronism. The heroes are throwbacks to an earlier time, the case of Launcelot Greaves only being a more explicit version of the dislocation of the other heroes. Romance is the language of yesterday which can be made to tell the truth about today only by demonstrating how contemporary reality will not conform to the patterns of romance. The poetic justice required by romance can be secured only by the most outrageous artifice, to demonstrate that gentlemanhood is as anachronistic a condition as the fictional language in which it is expressed. The novelist uses the most contrived of literary devices to make sure that the reader, if not the innocent hero, realizes who it is behind the gifts; only by resorting to an archaic language can one imagine the heroes getting their just deserts. The romance assumptions are exposed to the reader, but not mocked: although romance does not show us how things happen, it does show us the way things ought to happen.

I do not think this sentimentalizes or blunts the force of the satire. Smollett's "realism of assessment" is not compromised by his rejection of "realism of presentation." To the extent that any of the novels make propositions about the world, they are not saying that a young man of merit is likely to be rescued by a rich uncle, but rather that in the world of the novel which is a model for mid-eighteenth century England, nothing short of a rich uncle can help a worthy young man make this way. For the novels imply another fortune, not the charged, mythological fortune of romance, but the "realistic" fortune that is the product of "the inner processes of the real, historical world," to quote Auerbach once more. It is clear that the fate which these forces contrive is very different from the destiny contrived by the hand of the novelist.

The strategy for Smollett's satire is a very traditional one: romance expectations are played off against what the world is willing to give the hero. Smollett holds the world of desire against the world of experience, the order of gentlemanhood and the inherited estate against the disorder of the society which rejects those values. As Frye reminds us, it is characteristic of satire to contrast the romantic mythical forms with the realistic world which they fit only ironically. Smollett's heroes are a version of one of the classic satiric fictions, the traveler from a purer, simpler world who must voyage through an alien, fallen world. After his time of exile the traveler is allowed to retreat back again into the vanished and timeless world of romance.

Smollett is not a neglected, nor for the most part, a misunderstood writer. He is one of the "Big Five" of the eighteenth-century novel (though almost demonstrably the least of them), and as such he is assured a place on the "required reading lists" of the future—as secure though modest a portion of immortality as a writer of the second rank can hope to obtain. There is, however, one aspect of Smollett's reputation which could stand some slight modification. A long critical tradition has seen Smollett as a primitive, unliterary writer: a gifted natural the vigor of whose native woodnote wild doesn't quite disguise the fact that he is also singing slightly out of tune. And for most critics the out-of-tuneness is the result of Smollett's deficient sense of form. The rejoinder to this criticism has been very guarded, since Smollett's formal limitations are obvious. It would be tempting to pretend that Smollett was a more suspicious writer than he was, to fashion him in the mold of the very suspicious writers of our own time who seem to know exactly how to mock and exploit literary convention simultaneously. In other words, make him into a writer much like his twentieth-century admirer John Barth, who cunningly ransacks all the myths of the hero and appropriates them for his own purposes in *Giles Goat Boy* and *Chimera*. The claim for Smollett has to be more modest: if he is not as profoundly self-conscious as Barth, rarely is he a sloppy writer falling back uncritically on any available convention. His reworking of romance conventions to construct a satiric fiction suggests that, like any other serious writer, Smollett had to find a way to use and go beyond the language of fiction that he inherited. Although not as sophisticated as his two contemporaries, the knowing Fielding and the infinitely suspicious Sterne, he nevertheless shares with them a strong sense of the uses to which earlier ways of telling a story might be put.

Notes

1. Nathalie Sarraute, *The Age of Suspicion*, trans. Maria Jolas (New York: Braziller, 1963), p. 60, and Alain Robbe-Grillet, "From Realism to Reality," *For a New Novel*, trans. Richard Howard (New York: Grove Press, 1965), p. 158.

2. Frank Kermode, *The Sense of an Ending* (New York: Oxford University Press, 1966), pp. 128–29.

3. *Roderick Random* I, vii. All citations from the novels given here refer to the Shakespeare Head edition (Oxford: Blackwell, 1925–26).

4. "On Realism in Art," *Reading in Russian Poetics: Formalist and Structuralist Views*, ed. Ladislav Matejka and Krystyna Pomorska (M.I.T. Press, 1971).

5. See Erich Auerbach's description of the separation of styles in *Mimesis: The Representation of Reality in Western Literature* (New York: Doubleday, 1957), p. 27.

6. I am greatly indebted to Sheridan Baker's "*Humphry Clinker* as Comic Romance," in *Essays in the Eighteenth Century Novel*, ed. Robert Spector (Indiana U. Press, 1965), and "The Idea of Romance in the Eighteenth Century Novel," in *Papers of the Michigan Academy of Science, Arts, and Letters*, 49 (1963), 507–23. My concern is somewhat more general than Professor Baker's: to use Smollett as an illustration of the proposition that any fictional language takes off from a previous language or set of conventions.

7. The typical excess of style in all of Smollett's novels has been noted by Philip Stevick in "Stylistic Energy in the Early Smollett," *SP*, 64 (1967), 712. See also Albrecht Strauss, "On Smollett's Language," *English Institute Essays, 1958: Style in Prose Fiction*, ed. Harold Martin (Columbia U. Press, 1959), pp. 25–54.

8. For the opposing view that Smollett's heroes do change significantly in the course of their adventures see Rufus Putney, "The Plan of *Peregrine Pickle*," *PMLA*, 60 (1945), 1051–65 and M. A. Goldberg, *Smollett and the Scottish School* (U. of New Mexico Press, 1959).

9. F. M. Cornford, *The Origins of Attic Comedy* (New York: Doubleday, 1961), p. 133.

10. Maurice Schroeder, "The Novel as a Genre," in *The Theory of the Novel*, ed. Philip Stevick, (New York: Macmillan, 1967), p. 15.

11. Auerbach, p. 24.

12. When returning to Scotland in 1753, Smollett arranged to be introduced to his aged mother as a gentleman from the West Indies: "The better to support his assumed character, he endeavoured to preserve a very serious countenance, approaching to a frown; but while the old lady's eyes were riveted with a kind of wild and eager stare on his countenance, he could not refrain from smiling: she immediately sprung from her chair, and throwing her arms around his neck exclaimed, 'Ah, my son! my son! I have found you at last.'" As quoted in Lewis Mansfield Knapp, *Tobias Smollett: Doctor of Men and Letters* (Princeton U. Press, 1949), p. 161.

13. Northrop Frye, *Anatomy of Criticism: Four Essays* (Princeton U. Press, 1957), p. 179.

14. For an opposing view see David L. Evans, "*Humphry Clinker* and Smollett's Tempered Augustanism," *Criticism*, 9 (1967), 257–74.

15. I have argued that such is the case in "Smollett as Conservative Satirist," *ELH*, 42 (1975), 556–79.

16. For a recent discussion of Smollett as essentially a writer of picaresque see Robert Spector's *Tobias George Smollett* (New York: Twayne, 1968). For a very strong denial that the term "picaresque" is relevant to the understanding of Smollett's fiction, see G. S. Rousseau, "Smollett and the Picaresque: Some Questions about a Label," *Studies in Burke and his Time*, 12 (1971), 1886–1904.

17. I am borrowing the term Maynard Mack has used to describe Pope in *The Garden and the City* (U. of Toronto Press, 1967), p. 236.

Pastoral War in
Tristram Shandy

RICHARD A. LANHAM

Uncle Toby is the great triumph of *Tristram Shandy*, the figure all have applauded, that none could resist loving. In the thin times for Sterne's reputation, when the stock of learned wit was low or self-conscious clowning thought exhibitionistic, Toby carried the novel and the novelist on his sturdy shoulders to the next period of critical appreciation. To the Victorians, he proved that Sterne could feel deeply, that the core of the man was not beyond redemption. And to the modern commentator, he stands for that sentiment that glues together—barely but nobly—the fragmented bits of an existentially absurd world. As humor character, as gamesman par excellence in the novel, he is—exaggerated as his obsession may be—essentially like us all:

> Yet this impossible artifact, Toby, becomes by Sterne's dramatic rhetoric a strangely real and sane man, whose desperate humors we see finally as essentially no different from Walter's, or, indeed, from those of Madam or His Worship the Reader.[1]

Sterne is not urging us to be like Toby,[2] yet we must come to see that in many ways we are like him. He is obsessed by game as we are—only more so. Obversely, he is full of fellow-feeling as we should be—only more so. Hence his humor and his pathetic glory. Toby is, then, crucial to those who find the novel serious and equally so to those who think Sterne a

From *Tristram Shandy: The Games of Pleasure* (Berkeley: University of California Press, 1973), pp. 77–92.

jester, a miniature painter in the pathetic vein. For so important a character in either argument, he has been more often pointed to, smiled with, applauded, loved, than analyzed. Toby is crucial to our argument, too. And since we proceeded, in the case of Walter Shandy, on Kenneth Burke's principle of "perspective by incongruity" and considered him not as philosopher so much as gamesman, here it seems more promising to consider Toby not as gamesman but as philosopher. For this role he is, after all, a natural.

I

Toby begins his fabled hobbyhorse, as a philosopher should, to answer a two-headed question. Where was he wounded? He finds out. And he cures himself in the finding. Thus he starts his cure not by an act of feeling, but by an act of knowing. He does research. He becomes, in fact, the only successful, authentic virtuoso in the novel. He makes of his knowledge first a healing nostrum, then a game, a perfect paradigm for the satisfactions of private life. A. R. Towers points out that the fortifications are given a pronounced sexual character, are Toby's "woman" long before the Widow Wadman comes along.³ And, arguing more generally, Burckhardt maintains that "manifestly the chief structural metaphor of the novel [is] the interchangeability of sex and war."⁴

Thus his game satisfies precisely the drive his wound prevents him from satisfying. And in his satisfaction, he stumbles on—by experience—what Walter Shandy tries to search out in theory—the wellspring of human motive. Walter may be the ideal contemplative man.⁵ But it is Toby who finds the secret of the private life. Although remarkable for the depth of his feeling, not of his thinking, he challenges the reader to think about as well as love him. For his real significance lies, not in how deeply, sincerely he feels—a quality that we can only admire, wonder at—but in how he finds happiness, in his game of pastoral war and *its* relation to his spontaneous fellow-feeling. Although Toby may not be a systematic philosopher, he is a successful one and it is as this that we are first invited to consider him.

One is continually tempted, on the basis of one part or another of *Tristram Shandy*, to make Sterne out a prophet. The temptation is especially strong with Toby, the model for today's private man. Pleasure in private life has more and more been drawn from a carefully controlled virtuosity, from one kind of hobby or another. The pleasure is passive and indirect, the aim contentment. Toby is thus the perfect complement to his brother, who draws his contentment from struggle. Yet the brothers are fundamentally obsessed not by the search for wisdom but by the play attitude. This has not been the common view. Stedmond, for example, contrasts the two brothers this way:

> But Toby is represented as interested in knowledge for its own sake, as a sort of therapy, rather than in any practical application of it. He plays at war in order to undo the damage which war has done to him. . . .
> Walter is something else again. His fence against life is the realm of pure abstraction. In this realm, theory is ostensibly designed to lend order to the flux of existence. In fact, of course, his theories are of as little practical use as Toby's model forts, perhaps even less, since Toby does find ease and contentment in his miniature bowling green world. . . . Neither succeeds in living up to man's full potentiality, and their idiosyncrasies are accordingly comic. Both can succeed only by anaesthetizing parts of themselves, by refusing in their varying ways to accept the full consequence of the human state.[6]

But Walter, too, plays therapeutic games. Both brothers live a pastoral life in a green world. Neither acknowledges the existence of a "reality" outside the range of his possible pleasures. Both are, in our sense of the word as well as Sterne's, "retired." Both, like Shandy Hall itself, reflect the game sphere's absence of economic pressure and of the resulting extrinsic profit. For both, the struggles are over. More so, I think, than any other eighteenth-century novel, *Tristram Shandy* is the novel of private life. Public events are few. Walter Shandy rises and falls from arcane reading, Toby from a gazette, yet both lead, from a public perspective, a private, derived, secondary existence. We may, I suppose, talk about their not accepting "the full consequences of the human state." But those consequences, whatever they are, are nowhere suggested in *Tristram Shandy*. Its sphere *is* the game sphere. This is its reality. Neither brother evades it. And, if Walter's perpetual frustration includes a pleasurable alloy, Toby's placid contentment does not lack its stresses.

He does, after all, feel called upon to defend his hobby, to apologize for making a hobby out of war. The dumb man speaks. This itself is surprising, and we wonder at the end of it whether "Lillabulero" isn't his *forte* after all. Walter has been twitting him about that loss of his hobbyhorse which the peace of Utrecht had occasioned. "My uncle *Toby*," Tristram tells us, "never took this back-stroke of my father's at his hobby horse kindly.— He thought the stroke ungenerous; and the more so, because in striking the horse, he hit the rider too, and in the most dishonorable part a blow could fall."[7] The most dishonorable part is presumably Toby's martial honor, but I suppose we must make it a physical part too, and so symbolical of the hobby as a compensation for the wound and the sexual impotency that the wound brings (if it does) with it. Walter means presumably that Toby is willing to continue a cruel and bloody war so that he may continue his own hobby. Toby takes the criticism far otherwise. He defends real war, his real career as a soldier. A thirst for glory does not equal, he insists, a thirst for blood. "Or because, brother *Shandy*, my blood flew out into the camp, and my heart panted for war,—was it a proof it could not ache for the distresses of war too? O brother! 'tis one thing for a soldier to gather laurels,—and 'tis another to scatter cypress." Toby then defends war as an instrument of national policy:

> Need I be told, dear *Yorick*, as I was by you, in *LeFever's* funeral sermon, *That so soft and gentle a creature, born to love, to mercy, and kindness, as man is, was not shaped for this?*—But why did you not add, *Yorick*,—if not by NATURE— that he is so by NECESSITY?—For what is war? what is it, *Yorick*, when fought as ours has been, upon principles of *liberty*, and upon principles of *honour*—what is it, but the getting together of quiet and harmless people, with their swords in their hands, to keep the ambitious and the turbulent within bounds? And heaven is my witness, brother *Shandy*, that the pleasure I have taken in these things,— and that infinite delight, in particular, which has attended my sieges in my bowling green, has arose within me, and I hope in the corporal too, from the consciousness we both had, that in carrying them on, we were answering the great ends of our creation. [VI, xxxii, 462]

It is not always easy, in *Tristam Shandy*, to separate Sterne from Tristram, and I do not think Sterne kept or wanted to keep a constant distance between them. Here they seem some way apart. Toby is deluded. His delight in war is uncritical, naive, illogical. The English are a quiet and harmless people driven by necessity to curb turbulent ambition. Yet the principal motivation that spurs on these quiet and harmless people, Toby among them, is turbulent ambition and thirst for glory. Toby is defending the *necessity* of war, yet the occasion of his defense is a regret that peace has been made, that war is no longer a necessity. The Utrecht treaty that Toby thought base, made precisely the point Toby addressed himself to— that war was not necessary, was being continued for the reasons of honor that, Toby confesses, are really what gratify him. One can, I think, safely conclude that Toby disproves—and we are intended to see (though Tristram does not see) that he disproves—his own argument. Yet Toby, after all, is hardly a Tamburlaine. What actually charms him at the beginning is the *play* aspect of war—the drums, guns, and ensigns. These he reckons harmless, easily agreeing with his dependable compassion. He is right. But he leaves the aggression out of war, the pleasures taken from it outside the play sphere. He turns a fight into a game. Here is his naiveté, a naiveté his brother cannot understand. Toby remains consistent within his own terms and Tristram accepts these, presumably, and applauds them. At least he never really brings the two opinions together, whereas Sterne, I think— or the novel if you will—insists that we do.

No one, so far as I know, has ever asked why Sterne chose to give a character like Toby a martial hobbyhorse.[8] This incongruity Toby addresses himself to in his apologetical oration: sentimental sympathy versus killing. At the end of the oration, it still confronts us. Toby has been for so long a sentimental darling, one step away from the village idiot perhaps, but loved the more for it, that only temerity might suggest him as allegorizing an unpleasant truth. He is, rather, the redeeming feature of the universe. Watkins, for example, writes of Sterne's conviction, "not unlike that of Coleridge and especially of Wordsworth, that the principal spirit in the Universe is one of joy. . . . The perfect embodiment of this spirit, the perfect child of nature is, of course, Uncle Toby."[9] A child of nature he is, but of a less Romantic nature than this. He reenacts, as homely truth, the powerlessness of sentiment, of humane fellow-feeling, at the hands of the natural, centrally-human propensity for game. Toby is in a very real sense an idiot, *idiōtēs*, obsessed by the private life. On his hobbyhorse, he has no fellow-feelings at all. Stedmond, in a fine discussion of this side of Toby's nature, maintains that "Tristram, in fact, makes a distinction between Toby's *moral* character and his *hobby-horsical* character."[10] Does he not rather shirk the problem and make us put the two together ourselves? We are to conclude, I suspect, that the pleasures of the one are essentially egotistical, that one plays a game for one's own satisfaction, fights a war for the pleasure it gives one. The long diapason of sentiment for Toby has been accompanied by a good deal of praise for him as a humorous character. The mechanical dependability of his responses, his one-track mind, certainly earn him this. But the drastic constriction, the absorption in his game really liberates his feelings, gives them a marvelous freedom and openness. Sterne was, I think, fearful of man's natural propensity to make game of experience because of its power to cut off the flow of feeling at the wellspring. Once one fell into a role, the natural feelings were replaced, the old poseur knew, by others quite different. At the same time, he saw the enormous moral value of Toby's pastoral warfare in draining off the aggressive and aesthetic drives that tend to capitalize on the feelings and put them to nefarious use. For the paradox of Toby's war is a double one. It is both a *peaceful* and an *artistic* war, that constitutes, as Traugott says,[11] Toby's rhetoric, and a very full one too. Only by means of it can Toby feel with the purity and absence of calculation which has made him so loved and eulogized.

A reassembled Toby, the two sides of his character put together, figures forth a character different from that of the popular imagination and more complex. Toby is made to play war because war, better than any other game, illustrates the power of game itself. He would not be the same character if obsessed by, say, ordinary gardening, or if he "followed the turf" in the usual meaning of the phrase, although he perhaps might be as dear to those readers whose ideas of sentimental humor take a Dickensian turn. Game and sentiment conflict in his character as much as war and sentiment. Toby's sentiment, his fellow-feeling, can be as pure and spontaneous as it is because his game—even though it is a game played out, on the real stage, in hideous suffering—so fully satisfies him. The fortifications may be his mistress. If so, he made a lucky choice. She satisfies him completely. And it is the complete satisfaction that liberates his feelings. Toby's feelings appeal because uncontaminated by egotism. Not naturally pure of heart, "a comic version of the saint,"[12] as popular opinion has it, he has become so when his egotism has been drained off. The whole of Toby's character is a purity of feeling bought *at the price of* obsession. Sterne is far, I think, from sentimental gush about Toby. He is emphatically not a lovely person who also is by chance a half-wit with a shell-shocked hobby.[13] He can be the one only because he is the other. And this appears to Sterne a generic verdict. It will always be thus. Perhaps, for Sterne, sentiment redeemed a radically unknowable world. But, looking at Toby, we may doubt it. The price is too high.

We might ask a derivative question. What kind of comment about war, rather than about Toby, does his apologetical oration, and the hobby behind it, really make? The answer is not far to seek. All that is good about war survives transplanting to the bowling green and the sooner the better. For the bowling green war is not less absorbent of aggression than real war but more so. Sterne sees, I think, Toby's war as a kind of applied pastorality, using the mechanism of pastoral to discharge quite unpastoral impulses. Such a pastoral is less a resignation than a working-through of antisocial behavior. Perhaps in this connection we can see the juxtaposition of the two brothers a little more clearly. It is not really a question of either one's realizing his full potential as a human being. Neither stands as the round character of realistic fiction. Sterne uses them in a narrower drama—a drama of sentiment. Toby has managed to liberate his sentiment, can feel spontaneously for others. Walter can feel for others only occasionally and upon specific stimulus. This difference has up to now been accepted as simply a difference in temperament, a *donnée*. Actually, the novel earns it. Toby has managed to invest his game with all the demands of his ego, and it has satisfied them. Walter's games are less completely relied upon and so less successful. They are, at the same time, more pretentious and intellectual. Here is mild satire, if you like. Philosophy, supposed to lead to love, contentment, tranquility, leads to puzzlement instead. War, supposed to lead to hatred, instead takes us to the goals of philosophy. But such an observation can hardly be optimistic in the usual sense. The root of the ethic of fellow-feeling in *Tristram Shandy* is indeed a spontaneous goodness in the heart of man. But that is not all that is at the heart of man. Self and desire share the place and must be satisfied. What satisfies them is pleasure. Even in war, the ultimate antisocial behavior, we find a salve to the self, a satisfaction, which liberates fellow-feeling. Soldiers are, and can be, so sentimental, Sterne tells us, because the other side of their job so fully and satisfactorily orchestrates that part of the psyche that interferes with spontaneous fellow-feeling. As General Lee said, it is good war is so horrible, else we would grow too fond of it.

Perhaps this argument may clarify a final question that remains about Uncle Toby: the relation of his sentiment to his humor, or rather of our sentimental reponse to him and our humorous response. Dilworth, in his illuminating and entertaining (and not very intelligently reviewed) *The Unsentimental Journey of Laurence Sterne,* discriminates between these two absolutely.[14] In the matter of the fly, for example, he is at pains to point (correctly, I think) to the artifice and affectation of the rhetorical structure surrounding the famous liberation scene. The whole, he thinks, is made up as a self-conscious exercise. And, "let it be said flatly . . . and with all possible resolution, that the episode of Uncle Toby and the Fly is not sentimentality but humor."[15] I do not see how the two can be separated, coming as they do from a single source. A distinguished scholar has shown us that the affected side of humor and the eccentric side can yield quite different results: "That humour as imitation and affectation should be ridiculous, while humour as particular inclination, individual uniqueness, or even individual eccentricity should be held above ridicule, will surprise nobody who has read widely in the age of Pope."[16] We can see how Sterne elicits the second and not the first. We trust the spontaneity of Toby's response, whereas in anyone else we would call it affected, because we accept from the beginning not simply the sentimental side of him but the *Kriegspiel* side, and put them together. Toby's "humor" is really two things, his bowling green and his spontaneous goodness. His goodness, his sentimentality, if you will, is as much a part of his humor as his dependable interest in siege works. The success of Toby as a character of the popular imagination surely comes from just this union of a goodness and a frivolity equally dependable and from the same cause. Inevitably, we attribute an equal causality to each side of his nature. Now, we can accept eccentric preoccupation far more easily than we can believe in spontaneous goodness. By yoking them—and providing a *reason* why they should be yoked—Sterne can transfer our acceptance from the one to the other. Suddenly a spontaneous goodness does seem to come from the heart of things. And, because this is as it ought to be, the eccentricity, too, seems to be as it ought to be. Toby as a humor character, then, seems to me explicable, not simply a happy accident, or a random marriage of quirk and sentimental goodness. Perhaps the theoretical relation of the two will be clear if we quote a theorist, Hazlitt, on humor: "The most curious problem of all, is this truth of absurdity to itself. That reason and good sense should be consistent is not wonderful: but that caprice and whim, and fantastical prejudice, should be uniform and infallible in their results, is the surprising thing." People, he goes on, make an aesthetic response to the wholeness and consistency of humor. "The devotion to nonsense, and enthusiasm about trifles, is highly affecting as a moral lesson: it is one of the striking weaknesses and greatest happinesses of our nature. That which excites so lively and lasting an interest in itself, even though it should not be wisdom, is not despicable in the sight of reason and humanity." Sterne, it seems to me, is trying to say, in the case of Toby, just why the absurdity is true to itself. He succeeded: Hazlitt, just after this passage, alludes to Uncle Toby as the kind of character he has in mind.

We face, then, a problem. Hazlitt, if I understand him, thinks humor a far more natural product than wit: "Humour is, as it were, the growth of nature and accident; wit is the product of art and fancy. Humour, as it is shown in books, is an imitation of the natural or acquired absurdities of mankind . . . wit is the illustrating and heightening the sense of that absurdity by some sudden and unexpected likeness or opposition of one thing to another."[17] By this definition, at least, as well as by the analysis we have pursued above, Toby finally challenges not our humor but our wit. Witty he is not. But the relation of his two humors seems to me to be—and to be intended to be—a profoundly witty one.

II

"There are two play-idealizations par excellence," Huizinga tells us, "two 'Golden Ages of Play' as we might call them: the pastoral life and the chivalrous life."[18] Toby, by bringing the arts of war (more properly of the siege, the most ritualized scenario war then provided) into his garden, unites them. And from their union springs the spontaneous sentiment that has made him famous. He is not a great figure of humor because he can feel, but he can feel because he is a great figure of humor. If Walter Shandy shows that the truth of human affairs hides from the purely speculative reason, then Toby shows it hidden from pure feeling too. Once again we are thrown back on the metaphor of drama for society and identity. It alone combines reason and feeling. McKillop reminds us that Sterne was the first novelist to write a *humorous* novel that would be called sentimental.[17] How the humorous and the sentimental find their common ground and their causal connection in pleasure is, I hope, by now clear. We may, then, apply it to some of the critical discussions Toby's characterization has generated. It prompts first an observation on the kind of humor Sterne creates. The best definition of humor I know is Kenneth Burke's:

> Humor is the opposite of the heroic. The heroic promotes acceptance by *magnification*, making the hero's character as great as the situation he confronts, and fortifying the non-heroic individual vicariously, by identification with the hero; but humor reverses the process: it takes up the slack between the momentousness of the situation and the feebleness of those in the situation by *dwarfing the situation*. It converts downwards, as the heroic converts upwards. Hence it does not make for completely well-rounded a frame of acceptance as comedy, since it tends to gauge the situation falsely. In this respect it is close to sentimentality, a kinship that may explain why so many of our outstanding comedians (who are really humorists) have a fondness for antithetical lapses into orgies of the tearful.[20]

A conventional definition like this illuminates the unconventional kind of humor Toby represents. There is little conversion downward; the situation is most artificially dwarfed but scaled at the start to fit Toby. And, he copes very well with what he has gathered from coincidence. Not the *discrepancy* but the *fittingness* between man and situation seems Sterne's target. Toby preserves the Bergsonian mechanized response of the humor character, its inelasticity, but the private life seems made to contain it. He gauges circumstance well, not ill. Thus the final stress falls not on Toby but on Shandy Hall, on the private life. *It* is humorous. The discrepancy finally springs from the relation of public and private worlds and this relation enters only by implication into *Tristram Shandy.*

Toby's hobbyhorse backlights the whole civilizing tendency of game, its ability to metamorphose aggression, to move in on the arena of fight, Stedmond precisely misses the point when he says of Toby's garden war: "The tendency to treat human beings as 'things,' evident in Uncle Toby's dehumanized version of war, is a dominant strand in the book."[21] Humanize, not dehumanize, is surely the right word. Toby's pity finds a precise analogy in his pastoral siege, his movement of warfare from the public sphere to the private.

Toby may also shed ironic wisdom on that great and for him soporific philosopher John Locke. Tristram is holding forth in a Lockian way (II, iii, 85 ff.) when he tells us that Toby's life "was put in jeopardy by words." The double sense of *where* he was wounded is in question. The general reflection is on the dangers of ambiguity inherent in the nature of words. But Toby's experience teaches the opposite lesson—the chance healing words can effect. What they take away, they with equal frequency give. We compare Locke's despair at the absurd world with Toby's mindless, unerring march toward pleasure. Toby may be the mental eunuch he seems, but so what? Not what he knows but what he shows predominates. Here evaporates another perplexity associated with Toby. We are often told of his inarticulateness. He cannot speak. He must gesture. Most of the novel's readers must at one time or another have asked themselves liverishly what he might say could he speak. Expressing nothing, nothing to express. If Sterne's people cannot really understand one another, they do not have much to communicate either. But neither what they have to say nor how they say it is as important in *Tristram Shandy* as how each of the characters pleases himself. Communication, if not irrelevant, hardly preoccupies us.

We might consider what Toby's presence adds to the novel's great scenes of sentiment. There are three levels to those, a critic tells us: the dominant conscious-pathetic; the alternative farcical; the recessive tragic.[22] Clearly Toby supplies the first and Tristram the second. To admit the recessive tragic would drag us back into high seriousness. But we do blend Toby's perspective with Tristram's into a point of view neither can supply alone. Consider, for example, the sentimental pathos in the scene of scenes, the death of Le Fever (VI, vi, 416 ff.). We need not rehearse again the ways Tristram qualifies the scene with obvious irony. The unstated irony clusters round Toby's head. For all of Le Fever's tribulations come from following the greater shadow of Toby's hobby, from going to the wars.

Yet Toby's pity can be qualified precisely for this reason. He accepts the logic of game (Le Fever *must* go to the wars) and the obligation to pity him, with equal openness. He can thus muster a heart-whole pity that the ironical Tristram cannot. It remains for the reader to contrast the two attitudes, to locate the springs of Toby's kind of fellow-feeling and the springs of Tristram's. The debate about whether Sterne wants us to read the pathos straight (as the Victorians did) or ironically (as today) thus seems a false distinction. The passage suggests rather the possibility of *both kinds* of response, the source and nature of each. The scene offers two handles. We grasp whichever suits us. If, grasping neither, we observe both, we can syncretize the Victorian reading of Sterne's sentiment with the modern. Of course he shows us feeling enjoyed for its own sake. And of course he shows Tristram laughing at such enjoyment. Of course he does not laugh at Toby but at us. We must imitate both attitudes—the feeling and the laughter—to hold them together in our minds. Through such artifice lies *the reader's* path to redemption, to spontaneous response. We must fall into neither rhetorical trap, the sentimental nor the ironical. We must see instead, or at least first, the groundwork of sentiment and of irony. If we are simply ironical, we are on the modern road to high seriousness. If simply sentimental, we will shortly fall in love with Toby, and this is fatal. We must keep the two views separate. Stedmond points to similarity:

There is an obvious analogy between this "world" created by Toby, and Tristram Shandy's "world" of words. Tristram, too, fends off the spleen by transforming his trials and tribulations into symbolic form.[23]

But the gross resemblance hides a multitude of differences. They play different, almost antithetical games, and the differences stand out much more boldly than the likenesses. For Tristram is a clerk and the clerical game has always stood aloof from the chivalric.

Notes

1. John M. Traugott, *Tristram Shandy's World: Sterne's Philosophic Rhetoric* (Berkeley and Los Angeles, 1954), p. 33.
2. Ibid, p. 74.
3. A. R. Towers, "Sterne's Cock and Bull Story," *ELH*, XXIV (1957), pp. 20ff.
4. Sigurd Burckhardt, *"Tristram Shandy's* Law of Gravity," *ELH*, XXVIII, I (1961), p. 82.

5. Robert A. Donovan, *The Shaping Vision: Imagination in the English Novel from Defoe to Dickens* (Ithaca, N.Y., 1966), p. 105.

6. John M. Stedmond, *The Comic Art of Laurence Sterne* (Toronto, 1967), pp. 81–83.

7. Laurence Sterne, *The Life and Opinions of Tristram Shandy, Gentleman*, ed. James A. Work (New York, 1940), VI, xxxi, 458.

8. A life-model argument has been suggested. See the letter of Reginald L. Hine, F.S.A., to *TLS* (21 May 1931), p. 408, for the suggestion of Captain Robert Hinde as an original.

9. W. B. C. Watkins, *A Perilous Balance* (Princeton, 1939), pp. 118–119.

10. Stedmond, *Comic Art*, p. 60.

11. Traugott, *Tristram Shandy's World*, p. 18.

12. Stedmond, *Comic Art*, p. 81.

13. Even so ardent an admirer as J. B. Priestley has written: "He is the simplest of mortals, and, indeed, one step further along the path of simplicity and he would be tumbling into idiocy." (*The English Comic Characters* [New York, 1925], p. 145.)

14. Maack's Hegelian resolution of the two gives up and calls it "literary magic"! (Rudolph Maack, *Laurence Sterne im Lichte seine Zeit* [Hamburg, 1936].)

15. Ernest N. Dilworth, *The Unsentimental Journey of Laurence Sterne* (New York, 1948), p. 27.

16. Edward N. Hooker, "Humour in the Age of Pope," *HLQ*, XI (1948), 372.

17. *Lectures on the Comic Writers:* I-"On Wit and Humour," *The Collected Works of William Hazlitt*, ed. A. R. Waller and Arnold Glover (London, 1903), VIII, 11, 15.

18. J. Huizinga, *Homo Ludens* (Boston, 1955), pp. 180–181.

19. Alan D. McKillop, *The Early Masters of English Fiction* (Lawrence, Kan., 1956), p. 182.

20. Kenneth Burke, *Attitudes Toward History* (rev. ed., Boston, 1961), p. 43.

21. Stedmond, *Comic Art*, p. 60.

22. Ben Reid, "The Sad Hilarity of Sterne," *Virginia Quarterly Review*, XXXII (1956), 117–118.

23. Stedmond, *Comic Art*, p. 120.

Learning to Read Johnson:
The Vision of Theodore and
The Vanity of Human Wishes

LAWRENCE LIPKING

We can always learn something about a great writer—I suppose everyone would agree—by considering the work that he himself thought his best. But what can we learn about Samuel Johnson by looking at "The Vision of Theodore, the Hermit of Teneriffe, Found in his Cell"? Very few modern readers, certainly, have wanted to look at this little allegorical sketch for long. "To what use can the work be criticised," Johnson wrote of Akenside, "that will not be read?"[1] And modern eyes somehow slip away from an instructive fable that, forsaking the charms of story or rich allegorical detail, concerns itself with the Path to *Happiness* on the *Mountain* of *Existence*, with the need to follow *Reason* and her greater mistress *Religion* while avoiding the temptations of *Appetites* and *Passions*, and above all with the warning that *Habits*, which properly watched over will smooth the Path, constantly threaten to enchain us with subtle bonds and bring us to the Caverns of *Despair*. The allegory seems all too explicit; the intention of preaching leaves little to the imagination. Nor will any but the most innocent student find much here that he does not suppose himself to know already: virtue should be chosen over vice. Readers of "Theodore," clearly, put themselves "in the Hands of *Education*, a Nymph more severe in her Aspect and imperious in her Commands, who confined them to certain Paths, in their Opinion, too narrow and too rough. . . . But it was easy to discover, by the Alacrity which broke out at her Departure, that her Pres-

From *ELH*, 43 (1976), 517–37.

ence had been long displeasing, and that she had been teaching whose who felt in themselves no want of Instruction."[2]

On the importance of instruction, however, the author himself admits no doubts at all. Those who have strayed from Education's path "proceeded up the Mountain by some miry Road, in which they were seldom seen, and scarcely ever regarded" (519). Indeed, the first lesson of "Theodore" may well be to remind us that Johnson, unlike his modern readers, demands an instructive literature: books that are some *use*. "The only end of writing," according to his famous formulation, "is to enable the readers better to enjoy life, or better to endure it."[3] Johnson recasts the classical injunction on the poet to please and instruct into its effects on the reader, and the grave demand that the reader be helped to endure the pain of existence shows how seriously this author takes his burden as a writer. Even visions must be of use. We are all in want of instruction, and an author who forces truth, however obvious, upon his reader, should feel satisfied that he has done his best.

"The Vision of Theodore" was composed, in fact, expressly for purposes of education. It first appeared in *The Preceptor* (1748), a "general course of education" compiled by Robert Dodsley to enable unschooled or uninstructed youths to grasp "the first principles of polite learning." Johnson wrote the preface for the work as a whole, and "Theodore" (drafted in one night, "after finishing an evening in Holborn")[4] introduces the last part, "On Human Life and Manners." Its allegory is designed for a specific purpose: to exhort the pupil who has made his first entrance into "the Temple of Science," by reading thus far, to make "farther Progress into the sacred Recesses of this glorious Structure" (513). Once the student has finished the book, his mind sowed with "every useful Seed," he must assume responsibility for his own continuing education, and submit to other guides: Reason and Religion, whose dictates will complement his new-won learning. Johnson suits his fable perfectly to the occasion. Not only the context of "Theodore" but its internal point of view, puts every reader in the place of a fledgling scholar. The angel who lectures Theodore lectures us as well. With schoolmasterly rigor, he pictures life as an unending course, from which we graduate into the sky; and we scramble up the *Mountain* of *Existence* like a troop of schoolboys on an outing. No faltering, no truancy is allowed. Again and again the reader must be instructed that the road to happiness is long and hard—the hermit Theodore, to whom this vision is vouchsafed, has already passed forty-eight years in his cell. Nor does the explicit allegory leave room for even the slowest learner to misunderstand his duty.

Johnson also performs his duty. The picture of life as a narrow course
of obstacles tells us a good deal about the way he envisioned his own
career. Both the speed of the writing and its manufacture for an occasion
are characteristic. As a professional author, he wrote to formulas; he wrote
for bread. Nor does such an author waste time on self-pity. If Johnson
remembered "The Vision of Theodore" so fondly, doubtless one reason
was that he thought it a neat and ready piece of work. But the need to fit
the occasion did not absolve him from the claims of conscience. Rather, it
set the terms, throughout his middle years, of a special kind of heroism.
Johnson refuses to charm his audience, or to deviate from his own strict
path. Carlyle's lecture on "The Hero as Man of Letters," overblown as it
is, nevertheless catches a part of the truth that modern scholars tend to
overlook. As an author in his own mid-life, and a reader of "Theodore,"
he appreciates the power of habit. "What we call 'Formulas' are not in
their origin bad; they are indispensably good. Formula is *method*, habitude;
found wherever man is found. Formulas fashion themselves as Paths do, as
beaten Highways, leading towards some sacred or high object, whither
many men are bent. Consider it."[5] To master habit, to walk upright along
the path of necessity, constitutes Johnson's vision of the hero; that is
another lesson of "Theodore."

Indeed, Johnson conceives his life as a course between temptations.
During the decade preceding the publication of the *Dictionary* (1755),
while his career hung in the balance, he consistently assumed the stance of
a defiant moral hero, thrusting unwelcome truth upon his audience. Notice,
for example, the Prologue to *Irene* (1749), where the struggles of Christians against their infidel captors and their own apostasy are specifically
associated with the author's resistance to popular demands.

> Vot'ries of Fame and Worshippers of Pow'r!
> Dismiss the pleasing Phantoms for an Hour.
> Our daring Bard with Spirit unconfin'd,
> Spreads wide the mighty Moral for Mankind.
> Learn here how Heav'n supports the virtuous Mind,
> Daring, tho' calm; and vigorous, tho' resign'd.
> Learn here what Anguish racks the guilty Breast,
> In Pow'r dependent, in Success deprest,
> Learn here that Peace from Innocence must flow;
> All else is empty Sound, and idle Show.[6]

The repeated word "daring," applied to the bard as well as to the virtuous
characters revealed in his play, emphasizes that Johnson, like a true Chris-

tian hero, would rather be a martyr than an apostate to the stage. He imagines the theater allegorically, as a testing ground for the spirit. The trappings of vice, its "pleasing phantoms," "empty sound, and idle show," are specifically associated with the stage illusions of an ordinary theatrical entertainment. Instead, this audience, like a group of reluctant scholars, is repeatedly called upon to "learn." Johnson rejects any success bought at the price of an innocent conscience, and refuses (even verbally) to separate his aesthetic and moral principles. "In Reason, Nature, Truth he dares to trust"; uncompromised, his play must live or die according to poetic justice.

Behind much of Johnson's best work of this period, and even behind his own conception of his life, a familiar classical souce may be discerned: the famous "Choice of Hercules, between Virtue and Pleasure." Not coincidentally, Robert Lowth's verse translation of this brief allegory (ascribed to Prodicus, and preserved in Xenophon's *Memorabilia*) immediately follows "The Vision of Theodore" in *The Preceptor*. Many scholars have studied the consummate influence of the "Choice" in the eighteenth century, especially upon pictorial tradition.[7] But none ever claimed more for it than Johnson himself, who once wrote that no other subject could be chosen (even to take a subject, it may be noted, involves a *choice* for Johnson): "for by this conflict of opposite principles, modified and determined by innumerable diversities of external circumstances, are produced all the varieties of human life; nor can history or poetry exhibit more than pleasure triumphing over virtue, and virtue subjugating pleasure."[8] One story, and one story only, is worth the telling: the reader, like Hercules, must always be persuaded to opt for virtue.

An author too must make his choice. If all the best of history and poetry exhibit only one subject, then the way of a modern poet should be clear: he must take up the subject once more, translating or renewing it for a modern audience. "To supply virtue with argument, and to detect the sophistries of pleasure will, in this world, always be necessary: these topicks, therefore, can never be antiquated; and he that shall enforce truth with new reasons, or adorn it with new illustrations, must always be accounted a benefactor to mankind."[9] Though Johnson expects originality from poets—new reasons, new illustrations—he also believes that literature continuously reflects versions of the same basic truth. Thus poetry, in his practice even more than in his theory, rarely severs its ties to translation and imitation. The author who wishes to be useful to mankind must recapitulate the same great conflict, virtue against pleasure, that the ancients had explored so fully; he must return to their sources, and bring them home.

"The Vision of Theodore," certainly, can help teach us how seriously Johnson took the obligation of the modern writer to bring the classics into present use. The original context makes this intention plain. At the end of *The Preceptor*, "Theodore" is followed first by "The Choice of Hercules," then by another allegorical fable, "The Picture of Human Life"—the so-called "Table of Cebes," translated by Joseph Spence—which closes the whole course of instruction. "Cebes," without question, furnishes the main inspiration for Johnson's own vision. In his early days as a schoolmaster, Johnson had sketched a curriculum in the Greeks for his cousin Samuel Ford, and the name of Cebes heads the list. This celebrated dialogue, attributed to a friend of Socrates,[10] expounds a mythological tablet in the temple of Saturn; an old man explains to some visitors that the picture represents Life, in whose various courts the human multitude attains the virtues or vices, the true or false learning, that each deserves. Upon this model Johnson constructs the panorama of "Theodore": its framing device, in which a great scene is interpreted for a character in the dialogue, and thus for us; its monumental scale; its organization of human life as a journey through successive temptations to a promised, if almost inaccessible, end; its personifications of Reason, Education, Despair. The steep hill of Virtue turns into Teneriffe; the wisdom of the ancients into a modern vision.

The emphasis of the picture is changed, of course, by Christian insight. Johnson's Preface to *The Preceptor* gives the student notice of "three Fables, two of which are of the highest Authority, in the ancient *Pagan World*. But at this he is not to rest, for if he expects to be Wise and Happy, he must diligently study the SCRIPTURES of GOD"; and "Theodore" itself profits from that higher authority. It depicts, not a tablet, but a vision; its interpreter is not a wise old man but a benevolent "Being of more than human Dignity" (517). Its superior goddess, most of all, is *Religion*, who can view an afterlife unknown by *Reason*. "Look upwards, and you perceive a Mist before you settled upon the highest visible Part of the Mountain, a Mist by which my Prospect is terminated, and which is pierced only by the Eyes of *Religion*" (521). (It is not the least of the young enthusiast's mistakes, in *The Vanity of Human Wishes*, to think that he can reach the Throne of Truth "Should Reason guide thee with her brightest Ray, / And pour on misty Doubt resistless Day"; only Faith can dispel the mist.) The Christian dispensation reveals a choice unknown to Prodicus, the choice of Heaven, where life, like art, attains a final harmony—"indeed, if our present state only be taken into the view, virtue will not easily triumph over pleasure."[11] Here pagan conflicts are resolved. Significantly, the pilgrims of "The Vision of Theodore" are directed toward the Temples of *Happiness*, rather than toward the classical Abode of True Learning or the Paths of Glory. Happiness, the deepest of pleasures, also implies the pinnacle of virtue, that ultimate felicity known only to the blest. Theodore sees further than Hercules or Cebes. Beyond the heights of human ambition, he knows, lies a kingdom that no hero can attain without the help of grace.

A conventional interpretation, however, will fail to account for Johnson's vision. "Theodore" does not end, like *Pilgrim's Progress*, by passing beyond the world to Happiness. Its final dream, indeed, is draped in gloom. More than one biographer has noted the powerful emotion, the peculiarly Johnsonian self-reference, through which both the hermit and his creator finally dwell on the Captives of *Indolence:*

> *Discontent* lowered in their Looks, and *Sadness* hovered round their Shades; yet they crawled on reluctant and gloomy, till they arrived at the Depth of the Recess, varied only with Poppies and Nightshade, where the Dominion of *Indolence* terminates, and the hopeless Wanderer is delivered up to *Melancholy:* the Chains of *Habit* are rivetted for ever, and *Melancholy* having tortured her Prisoner for a Time, consigns him at last to the Cruelty of *Despair.*   (526)

Perhaps Theodore deserves this punishment. He has spent forty-eight years, at least, in forgetfulness; and since the first paragraph of "The Vision" tells us that it was written in the fifty-seventh year of his retreat, "lest his solitary Hours should be spent in vain," evidently another nine years passed before he summoned up the energy to transcribe his dream (Johnson regards hermits as especially susceptible to discontent, since he suspects them not only of sloth but of secret longings for "the Scenes of Life").

Yet why should Johnson himself, at this highly productive time in his career, have felt so bound to indolence, melancholy, despair? Part of the answer, doubtless, stems from his stringent religious creed, based principally on William Law's *Serious Call to a Devout and Holy Life* (1728), that every moment, every single talent that one possesses, must be turned to God's account. Johnson fears active vice—the Passions and Appetites—less than *bad Habits*, repeated tiny sins of omission; "like the envenom'd Shirt of *Hercules*," we are told in the preface to "Theodore," in spite of all your Endeavours to shake them off, they will hang upon you to your Destruction" (516). An author who pictures himself as Hercules may expect a similar doom; having prevailed over great temptations, he may be brought down by the petty. Once again Carlyle evokes a proper image for Johnson's spiritual pain. "Like a Hercules with the burning Nessus'-shirt on him, which shoots-in on him dull incurable misery: the Nessus'-shirt not to be stript-off, which is his own natural skin! In this manner *he* had to live."[12] Moreover, Johnson shares one vice with Theodore that seems inseparable from authorship: he is given to dreaming. If the habits of the dreamer lead sometimes to useful allegories, they can also enslave life to idle dreams.

The strongest identification of Johnson with his narrator comes in the final paragraph of the "Vision," when the sleeper wakes.

> While I was musing on this miserable Scene, my Protector called out to me, 'Remember, *Theodore*, and be wise, and let not HABIT prevail against thee.' I started, and beheld myself surrounded by the Rocks of *Teneriffe*; the Birds of Light were singing in the Trees, and the Glances of the Morning darted upon me. (526)

Here Theodore becomes the object of his own allegory; lost in the caves of Melancholy, he wakes to a warning. The effect seems even more exquisite when we remember that Johnson himself is reported to have written the fable in one night: as the vision ends, the morning breaks upon him. (Castiglione's *Courtier*, a work that Johnson much admired, closes with a similar effect.) Rousing himself from the gloomy scene of his own imagining, the author perceives that his real struggle against habit has yet to come, in life. It is morning, he is still in the middle of his journey. Nor do we know whether he and his listeners will make good use of their instruction. In this parable, as in *Rasselas*, the conclusion is that nothing is concluded.

Such a conclusion may leave the reader also hanging. The ancient allegories that Johnson imitated do not end this way: Hercules chooses Virtue, and the old man assures Cebes that Wisdom may be reached in our present life. Johnson draws a harder moral. Both religion and experience teach him that human efforts to reform cannot be trusted; life puts us to daily, grinding tests compared to which the fables of art prove over-simple. Indeed, art itself, for Johnson, seems somewhat less than conclusive. Its usefulness depends on what the reader makes of it. Nor can the poet, captive to his visions, nor the vision itself, avoid the afterthoughts of irony.

Irony is attached, certainly, to the very conception of "The Vision of Theodore." We have already noticed the author's skepticism about hermits, and Theodore resembles Johnson not least in being suspicious of himself. The vision is set in motion by his "Wish to view the Summit of the Mountain, at the Foot of which I had so long resided. This Motion of my Thoughts I endeavoured to suppress, not because it appeared criminal, but because it was new; and all Change, not evidently for the better, alarms a Mind taught by Experience to distrust itself" (517). But Theodore's curiosity overcomes his scruples—"I was always reproaching myself with the Want of Happiness within my Reach"—and at last he sets out on his journey. The climb proves too steep for him. Exhausted, he arrives "at a small Plain, almost inclosed by Rocks and open only to the East," where he sits down to rest, falls asleep, and dreams of a mountain higher than Teneriffe. The vision descends to us, therefore, through a fallible medium: a hermit drawn from his cell by his "Ardour to survey the Works of Nature."

The ascent of Teneriffe had been a favorite subject, in fact, for the publications of the Royal Society. Both in 1667 and 1715 correspondents had described their climbs to the peak, each noting the rocky enclosure on the east where the faintness of the party had forced them to rest for the night. A paper read for the Society on February 6, 1752, mentions that this place is called "La Estancia de los Ingleses, or the English baiting-place."[13] One source for Theodore, evidently, is the literature of exploration; like Johnson, he has a weakness for philosophical transactions. If his vision of the Mountain of *Existence* had not interrupted him, he would probably have gathered materials instead for a scientific paper on the Mountain of Teneriffe.

It is not only irony about Theodore's latent worldliness, however, that prompts Johnson to choose Teneriffe as his locale. Any classically-educated Englishman would have been quick to associate the Canary Islands with the Fortunate Isles, or Elysian Fields, described by Homer and Plutarch.[14] Upon these, Christian tradition had often superimposed the Mountain of Purgatory—a logical connection, if we think of the immense height of the island-mountain Teneriffe, its peak usually misted by clouds, rising out of the Atlantic.

> Doth not a Tenarif, or higher Hill
> Rise so high like a Rocke, that one might thinke
> The floating Moone would shipwracke there, and sinke?[15]

By imperceptible degrees Teneriffe blends with Mount Purgatory, which blends in turn with the Mountain of Existence. Perhaps we shall not go too far in perceiving the plain where Theodore rests, open to the East, where "The Branches spread a Shade over my Head, and the Gales of Spring wafted Odours to my Bosom" (517), as an Earthly Paradise. Here, in this almost-Eden, an angel speaks to him, and paints the vision of a higher summit than that to which he has aspired. No wonder that in such a place a hermit should dream of a more exalted world. The truth he brings back to us, like the etymology of the name Theodore itself, is a "gift of God."

Why then should Johnson undercut Theodore's vision with irony? and why does he not make the Christian background of the allegory more plain? The reason, apparently, is that Johnson does not believe in Paradises on earth. The ancients, as well as some enthusiastic Christians, may have hoped to land on the Fortunate Isles, but Johnson would have approved Frost's "Answer": "But Islands of the Blessèd, bless you, son, / I never came upon a blessèd one."[16] Just as the Happy Valley in *Rasselas*, based on factual accounts of Abyssinia as well as traditions of the false Paradise of Mount Amara, proves on closer inspection to be intolerable to the inhabitants of this world, so the Eden of Teneriffe stays at one remove from life. What practical help in living, after all, can we expect from a hermit? The Gothic overtones of the name Theodore tend to relegate his vision to a more credulous age: a visionary time, fortunate perhaps in its beliefs, but perhaps also a little absurd. The kingdom of God will be found neither on earth nor in a dream, and Johnson will not betray it with a fiction.

Indeed, the allegorical style and mode of "The Vision of Theodore," as well as its meaning, warn us against the danger of succumbing to illusions. Johnson chooses the mode of "Stoic" allegory, epitomized by Cebes, in which each personification directly conveys its didactic significance, without being diverted into an extended story or a code of meanings that need to be deciphered. Allegory is "one of the most pleasing vehicles of instruction" for Johnson, not an entrance into mysteries.[17] Nor will he excuse the allegorical poet from his worst imaginative fault: creating an ideal world where abstractions can live but men cannot. Johnson seldom mentions the golden age, that wishful home of poets, shepherds, and hermits, without some asperity of tone. "The poets have numbered among the felicities of the golden age, an exemption from the change of seasons, and a perpetuity of spring; but I am not certain that in this state of imaginary happiness they have made sufficient provision for that insatiable demand of new gratifications, which seems particularly to characterize the nature of man."[18] Johnson's own allegories dwell less on imaginary happiness than real woes. Fiction and poetry transport us for a brief season to a world elsewhere, he tells us, but only so that we may be wakened to remember ourselves.

In theory and practice, therefore, Johnson specifically opposes the notion—popular in his own day, and even more popular in ours—that poetry at its best is an attempt to recreate the golden age: to build Jerusalem, or infancy again, or Eden. Every poem, W. H. Auden has written, contrives "to present an analogy to that paradisal state in which Freedom and Law, System and Order are united in harmony.... Every beautiful poem presents an analogy to the forgiveness of sins."[19] Johnson, obviously, does not believe that such forgiveness is within our power. His own fables carefully refrain from abandoning themselves to any world where normal laws and morals might be suspended. The task of the imagination, as he defines it, is to come to the aid of reason, not to challenge the Creator; unlike John Dennis, Johnson knows that poetry will not restore the Fall.[20] "The Vision of Theodore" deliberately prevents its readers from giving too much credence to a vision.

Nevertheless, Johnson too would like to think that poems can effect a reconciliation between this world and a better. If charming Stella, playing the harpsichord, could only blend truth with delight, "*Instruction* with her Flowers might spring, / And *Wisdom* warble from her String"; if the audience at Drury-Lane would only "chase the Charms of Sound, the Pomp of Show, / For useful Mirth, and salutary Woe," then Truth would "diffuse her Radiance from the Stage."[21] In this imperfect world of ours, with its actual nymphs and theaters, such hopes inevitably verge upon the comic. There is irony, as well as rue, in Johnson's comment on Gray's "Progress of Poetry": "that Poetry and Virtue go always together is an opinion so pleasing that I can forgive him who resolves to think it true."[22] Yet Johnson asks nothing less of art. The epic poet, he insists, requires "an imagination capable of painting nature and realizing fiction."[23] Johnson hungers for a "realized fiction"; for a world of poetry absolutely golden because it is also absolutely true.

So thinking, he subjects imaginative work to an almost intolerable pressure. At his most heroic, Johnson demands—and trains—an audience of heroes. Relentlessly exposing the fallacies that blind us from the truth, he turns the weapons of poetic metaphor back upon themselves, and makes his own imaginative process function as a warning. "The Vision of Theodore" may serve, finally, as an "entrance into the science" of reading Johnson. All that it teaches us—the central importance of education, the view of life as a heroic journey, the Christian applications of Prodicus and Cebes, the power of habit in the author's mind, and the ambivalent attitude toward vision itself—informs his later work. If "Theodore" was his favorite, it was also his model; it represented the limits of permissible imagination. Later in the same year, composing verses with a similar speed and sureness, he followed that model, and wrote *The Vanity of Human Wishes*. It began, of course, as another exercise in imitation. Many scholars, comparing the poem with Juvenal's tenth Satire, have noticed what Johnson's Christian reading gains and loses. He sets out to save the text, above all from its translators. "The peculiarity of Juvenal is a mixture of gaiety and stateliness, of pointed sentences, and declamatory grandeur. His points have not been neglected; but his grandeur none of the band seemed to consider as necessary to be limited."[24] Johnson, everyone sees, tends to the opposite extreme, and sacrifices gaiety to grandeur. Loading every rift of the poem with ethical ore, he burdens the language and images with multiple compressed meanings. Sometimes, indeed, Juvenal's conversational ironies become lost in reverberations, as grand and unintelligible as voices in a church. *The Vanity of Human Wishes*, Garrick said smartly, "is as hard as Greek."[25]

Indeed, Johnson *wanted* his poem to have the sound of Greek: the Greek of Prodicus and Cebes. Far more than Juvenal, the *Vanity* portrays a march through life, down a narrow path bordered everywhere by tempting illusory personifications of false glory. Its difficulties are difficulties of vision; of seeing the good, in a world where so many phantoms dangle before us. The explicit idealism of Greek allegory, imposed upon Roman worldliness, accounts for much of the density of the poem, its striving to find a useful moral amid such a torrent of deflations and anticlimaxes. Can sight itself be trusted? Johnson's images suggest that it cannot; that sight depends on the untrustworthy generalizations, the grasping after chimeras, painted by the mind.

> Let Observation with extensive View,
> Survey Mankind from *China* to *Peru;*
> Remark each anxious Toil, each eager Strife,
> And watch the busy Scenes of crouded Life;
> Then say how Hope and Fear, Desire and Hate,
> O'erspread with Snares the clouded Maze of Fate,
> Where wav'ring Man, betray'd by vent'rous Pride,
> To tread the dreary Paths without a Guide;
> As treach'rous Phantoms in the Mist delude,
> Shuns fancied Ills, or chases airy Good.

With only a slight hint from Juvenal *(erroris nebula)*, Johnson creates a complete tablet, a picture that summarizes both Cebes' and Theodore's visions. We gaze upon a Scene of Life, where our instructor points out a man lost in a maze. Nor can we perceive a goal, even from this immense distance; the dreary paths, covered with clouds, appear to have no issue. *The Vanity of Human Wishes* opens, then, with an allegorical tableau. Modern readers, unused to visualizing what they read, usually overlook the visual pointing of Johnson's imagination, but even the unschooled eighteenth-century reader—at least the reader who had studied his *Preceptor* some months before—would recognize the scene. Fleshed in personifications, a story is enacted. Out of the crowd (Cebes's courtyard) a man emerges to set out on a journey, but his supposed friends (Passions, with Pride at their head) have tricked him into the wrong road, and he merely wavers between alternatives. The following line, inevitably, introduces both Hercules's predicament and the missing Guide: "How rarely Reason guides the stubborn Choice."

If Johnson paints us a picture, however, he also places remarkable difficulties in the way of our visualizing. The accumulation of personified figures—Toil, Strife, Hope, Fear, Desire, Hate—passes before us too rapidly to allow faces to be singled out. The internal rhyme on *crouded* and *clouded* summarizes most of the passage: a prospect too full, too dark, for clarity of vision. We gaze, indeed, at phantoms, shadows that are not what they seem: fancied Ills (angels in the mist?) or airy Good (the *ignis fatuus* of a demon?). The picture seems fashioned, in fact, to strain our eyes. Johnson induces the reader to re-enact the confusions of Man, surrounded by images that change shape rapidly as clouds. *Observation*, that god in the sky, has a vantage point that no man can share, since Mankind is what He sees. Our own more limited perspectives, unguided, can never stand outside themselves.

The pathos of human short-sightedness, therefore, is built into the very mode of *The Vanity of Human Wishes*, its allegorical sight-lines. We cannot take extensive views; and the reader spends himself, like the characters of the poem, in chasing shadows. Nor does the author stand much better. Involved with illusions, those poetic phantasms that function as his medium of instruction, Johnson shares the dreams of glory that he dispels. Like Theodore, he falls into melancholy visions, from which he starts awake with a warning. At its most moving, then, the poem seems informed by a personal sorrow, less public (and less funny) than Juvenal's tirade. The great passage on the life of the scholar, for instance, has no equivalent in the Tenth Satire. Juvenal (114–32) points out, rather gloatingly, that even bad verses must be preferred to the eloquence of Cicero and Demosthenes, an ambitious public genius that cost them their necks. Johnson, in contrast, clearly writes about himself, in a vision that could make any scholar cry.

When first the College Rolls receive his Name,
The young Enthusiast quits his Ease for Fame;
Resistless burns the Fever of Renown
Caught from the strong Contagion of the Gown;
O'er *Bodley's* Dome his future Labours spread,
And *Bacon's* Mansion trembles o'er his Head.[26]

The imagery brilliantly conveys the confused, subjective point of view that dooms a fanciful author even before he has fairly begun. The young Enthusiast ("One who vainly imagines a private revelation; one who has a vain confidence of his intercourse with God") imagines his name, inscribed with so many others on the college rolls, as a kind of publication (*The Vanity of Human Wishes*, published when Johnson was turning forty, was the first work with his name on its title page). His academic robe poisons him with ambition like Hercules's shirt—and may remind us that *The Preceptor*, not many months before, had used the same image to warn students against the toxic effect of bad habits. This student, however, cannot put Hercules out of mind; he dreams of his future labors. Indeed, his contagious vision heaps the very dome of the Bodleian with his mounds of future writings, and communicates a disease like a fire: the fever of renown that authors catch in libraries and deposit there in turn. And the enthusiast's perspective infects the poem too. We are not told that Bacon's study—which according to tradition "will fall, when a man greater than Bacon shall pass under it"[27]—*seems* to tremble, but that it trembles. Imagination, in this poem, leads to destruction: a disease that burns the veins, a fire that ravishes libraries, a wish that threatens to bring down the mansions of science.

Johnson's affectionate mockery—aimed, of course, at his own heroic younger self—controls his picture of the following triumphal march: the fullest and most splendid of all his versions of Hercules and Cebes.

Are these thy Views? proceed, illustrious Youth,
And Virtue guard thee to the Throne of Truth,
Yet should thy Soul indulge the gen'rous Heat,
Till captive Science yields her last Retreat;
Should Reason guide thee with her brightest Ray,
And pour on misty Doubt resistless Day;
Should no false Kindness lure to loose Delight,
Nor Praise relax, nor Difficulty fright;
Should tempting Novelty thy Cell refrain,
And Sloth effuse her opiate Fumes in vain;

> Should Beauty blunt on Fops her fatal Dart,
> Nor claim the Triumph of a letter'd Heart;
> Should no Disease thy torpid Veins invade,
> Nor Melancholy's Phantoms haunt thy Shade;
> Yet hope not Life from Grief or Danger free,
> Nor think the Doom of Man revers'd for thee.

One after another, as in the Greek tableaux, the demons rise. And each is conquered; or rather, conditionally put aside, for the sake of argument. Yet a rueful irony pervades the whole. For these are the hazards of life as imagined by the young, with youthful pride: the sharply defined, personified hazards pictured by Cebes (the first author in the curriculum). Fresh from his *Preceptor,* fortified by his little draft of learning, the youth thinks himself qualified to withstand all temptations. He has learned to dream rightly—and does not perceive, as Johnson does so clearly, that the very habit of dreaming may lead him at last to melancholy. Once again, as in "Theodore," a familiar demon waits at the end of the road. Mrs. Piozzi records an occasion when Johnson, reading this passage aloud, "burst into a passion of tears." George Lewis Scott, an old friend, "clapped him on the back, and said, What's all this my dear Sir? Why you, and I, and *Hercules,* you know, were all troubled with *melancholy.*"[28] Scott's education has prepared him to understand the lines better than most modern critics; he knew the likely progress of the hero, and the end of his labors.

The young scholar, however, like a hermit, knows little of life. What will happen to such an innocent when his lettered heart encounters, not Beauty, but beauty, the blue angels of this world? What will become of all his dreaming then? The end of the verse paragraph brings a rude awakening.

> Deign on the passing World to turn thine Eyes,
> And pause awhile from Learning to be wise;
> There mark what Ills the Scholar's Life assail,
> Toil, Envy, Want, the Garret, and the Jail.
> See Nations slowly wise, and meanly just,
> To buried Merit raise the tardy Bust.
> If Dreams yet flatter, once again attend,
> Hear *Lydiat*'s Life and *Galileo*'s End.

Johnson adjusts the perspective of the youth—and of the reader—away from bookish visions toward the harsher vistas proved on a scholar's senses. Experience paints a different picture. Personifications, according to eighteenth-century theory, occur spontaneously in moments of high excitement, like the Enthusiast's fever, when the poet *sees* his ideas. But Ills, Toil, Envy, Want offer no exciting prospect, nor do they come alive. *This* progress through life ends with cold, unpersonified realities: garret and jail. Johnson's famous 1755 revision of "Garret" to "Patron," in honor of Lord Chesterfield, improves the theme with a witty double stroke; here is additional evidence that experience forces us to revise our expectations.

The class is not yet dismissed. In the following couplet, dreams and reality subtly contend. "Buried Merit" refers to a specific dead worthy, Milton, to whom a tardy bust had been raised in 1737. But is would also be possible to read the phrase more idealistically, as a "hidden worth" that will eventually be recognized. A young scholar, reading it this way, might well begin to dream of being discovered after his death. Yet this dream too, once raised, is immediately put to flight. Poor worthy Thomas Lydiat, dead for more than a century, has *still* not been recognized (when the *Gentleman's Magazine* excerpted the poem it supplied, with perhaps unconscious irony, a biographical note); and Galileo, despite all his fame, was forced at the last to repudiate his work. The passage ends, not with an idea, but with two exemplary scholarly lives: a poor show. Like a schoolboy roused from his daydreams, the reader is sharply ordered to pay attention, and the lesson for today is harder than Cebes.

At the close of the lesson we pause for questions. One after another, the stately triumphal marches of *The Vanity of Human Wishes* disintegrate in a thunder of anticlimax, to point a moral or adorn a tale. The hope of making a choice fades before the greater difficulty of finding something to choose. Johnson poses a long series of rhetorical questions—"Does Envy seize thee?" "Shall *Wolsey*'s Wealth, with *Wolsey*'s End be thine?" "Are these thy Views?" "But did not Chance at length her Error mend?" "Where then shall Hope and Fear their Objects find?"—whose answers often rebound upon the terms of the question itself. We do not know enough to make the right inquiries, the poem suggests; human expectations are corrupt in their very nature. Hope and Fear shall *not*, in fact, find Objects; they live among phantoms of their own creation, products of the fallacious human need to pretend that dreams are real. "Must dull Suspence corrupt the stagnant Mind?" Yes, so long as the mind remains stagnant. "Enquirer, cease," the poet tells us—at least until we can ask better questions.

The questions Johnson poses, however, are by no means purely rhetorical. They aim at a refinement of the questioning process itself, at a mode of inquiry where "Suspence" will be replaced by "Petitions." As the structure of many modern symphonies is determined by the search for a key, so

The Vanity of Human Wishes derives its structure from a search for a point of view. The god "Observation" with whom the poem begins, that disinterested surveyor in the skies, turns at the last into another kind of far-seer.

> Still raise for Good the supplicating Voice,
> But leave to Heav'n the Measure and the Choice,
> Safe in his Pow'r, whose Eyes discern afar
> The secret Ambush of a specious Pray'r.

The gods, as Juvenal says, know what we need better than we do; unlike Hercules, few of us are strong enough to make a choice. And the gods see further than we do. But Johnson imagines a different God, one whose powers of observation are not indifferent or uninvolved. Like a military leader, He scans the route of Life to prevent an ambush. Moreover, He sees within as well as without, into the hearts of men as well as their scenes. Paradoxically, the ambushes that hypocrites set for heaven threaten only themselves; thinking to capture eternity with strategic prayers, they thwart their own salvation. Prayers that are specious—to read the syntax another way—ambush the would-be supplicant. (Thus Hamlet's attempt to ambush Claudius at his prayers accomplishes less than Claudius' self-ambush, his inability to pray.)[29] God's insight does not stop at observing the motives of human life, but sets the terms by which they will be judged.

As the point of view of the poem alters at the end, so does its geography. Devotion that aspires to the skies will ask for "a happier Seat," not situated over the earth we know,

> For Love, which scarce collective Man can fill;
> For Patience sov'reign o'er transmuted Ill.

The "collective Man" of the opening lines, stretching from China to Peru, cannot crowd the universe of Love as people crowd our little globe; from Love's perspective, all the souls of men can be taken in at a glance. Similarly, the patient man will not delude himself with "fancied Ills," since his rule over himself transmutes Ill back into a recognizable shape. Love, Patience, Faith—

> With these celestial Wisdom calms the Mind,
> And makes the Happiness she does not find.

Juvenal had closed with Fortuna, whom men, with their lack of foresight (*prudentia*), place in the skies. But Johnson evokes a different goddess, celestial Wisdom, who has the power not only to observe life but to change it. All the paths of the righteous lead to Wisdom, because she is located within the mind that seeks her out.

Nevertheless, she remains a celestial being, a gift of God. The last lines of Johnson's *Vanity* offer a consolation mixed with severity; severe partly because the final words, as they echo in the mind, caution us that happiness will not be found on earth, and partly because the ability to understand our fates seems not within our power. Johnson carefully qualifies Juvenal's self-reliance with a submission to higher laws. Happiness can be made, perhaps, only in the afterlife; a healthy perspective can be achieved only through death; questions can only be answered by realizing their futility. Indeed, celestial Wisdom herself, like Boethius' Lady Philosophy, functions as an emissary rather than a goal. The harbinger of a diviner Love, she is the best that a poetic imagination can do when it tries to conceive a deity. *The Vanity of Human Wishes* pauses on the brink of Christian mystery, and refuses to profane the truth of revelation by translating it into the visions of poetry.

If poetry consists of a dream, then all fictions that face the truth must end with an awakening. Theodore wakes to find himself back on the lower slopes of his mountain, in his middle state; the reader of the *Vanity* learns to give over his wishes. Nor can poetic visions themselves—which Johnson associated so strongly with the pagan classics—wholly survive this awakening. Poetry, it often seems, depends on wishes, on the lingering glances we cast back on the earth in spite of heaven. Johnson's version of the Orpheus story, translated from Boethius about 1765, pictures the emblematic poet: betrayed by the same love that had inspired his song, an aspirant to the skies who cannot quit the earth.[30] The choice of Johnson's life was different. A moralist rather than a visionary, he strove to use his talents in total wakefulness; instead of storming heaven with willful heroism, like Hercules, he took Cebes's rugged road to truth.

Yet he could not keep from looking back. In one of the most personal (and most neglected) works Johnson ever wrote, the Latin poem "After revising and correcting the English dictionary" (12 December 1772), he returned once more to an allegory of human life. The Greek title of the poem, Γν ῶθι σεαυτὸ ν, translated elsewhere as "Be acquainted with thyself,"[31] points again to Johnson's habit of visualizing himself as a figure in a moralized Greek landscape. The hero of the story, however, is another dictionary-maker, the great Scaliger.

> Te sterili functum cura, vocumque salebris
> Tuto eluctatum spatiis Sapientia dia
> Excipit aetheris . . .

(You, when you had performed your barren labor, and had safely struggled through the rough roads of language, divine Wisdom welcomed into the expanse of the upper air . . .)[32]

In contrast, Johnson pictures himself as the prisoner of Indolence, Melancholy, and the "bad dreams of an empty mind." His spirit takes no pleasure in its past achievements,

> Sed sua regna videns, loca nocte silentia late
> Horret, ubi vanae species, umbraeque fugaces,
> Et rerum volitant rarae per inane figurae.

(But seeing its kingdom, shudders at the silent regions of the spreading night, where empty visions, and fleeting phantoms, and tenuous images of things flutter through the void.)[33]

Nor does the poet, in his journey through the night, find a path to a better life ("melioris semita vitae"). This allegory, like so many others, concludes with nothing concluded; with a series of questions. What shall I do? Shall I ask for the shades? or weightier studies? or after all, new dictionaries? The mists at the top of the mountain veil the *Lives of the Poets*, and Johnson receives no answer.

He does receive, however, a proper point of view: look to yourself. Nor can allegory, for Johnson, have any better purpose. To survey the self, one needs to set the world at a distance, by such a process of "retirement and abstraction, as may weaken the influence of external objects."[34] The visions of poetry, a preceptor knows, supply that distance. Measuring ourselves against Scaliger, or Hercules, we learn to estimate the true height of our abilities; we view our own troubled hearts, our "sublunary hopes and fears," with a calm that comes from immense perspectives of space and time. Thus Johnson perceives himself under the aspect of Theodore, who lives not in London but Existence, and who draws his wisdom not from a single evening of creation but from fifty-seven years of retirement. And if Existence proves to be a nightmare, we always hold in our own power the chance of coming awake. Learning to read "The Vision of Theodore" and *The Vanity of Human Wishes*, the student learns to read himself. That is one course, at least, where nothing is ever concluded.

Notes

1. *Lives of the Poets,* ed. G. B. Hill (Oxford, 1905), III, 420. Johnson's remark that he thought "Theodore" "was the best thing he ever wrote" was recorded by Thomas Percy in 1760; Boswell's *Life of Johnson,* ed. G. B. Hill and L. F. Powell (Oxford, 1934–50), I, 192, 537.

2. "The Vision of Theodore," Dodsley's *Preceptor* (London, 1748), II, 518–19, 521. Page numbers in the text refer to the first edition.

3. "Review of 'A Free Enquiry into the Nature and Origin of Evil'" (1757), Johnson's *Works* (Oxford, 1825), VI, 66.

4. According to Thomas Tyers, in the *Gentleman's Magazine,* December, 1784. *Johnsonian Miscellanies* (Oxford, 1897), II, 343.

5. "The Hero as Man of Letters. Johnson, Rousseau, Burns" (1840), *On Heroes, Hero-Worship, and the Heroic in History* (Boston, 1901), p. 207.

6. Ll. 5–14. *The Complete English Poems,* ed. J. D. Fleeman (London, 1971), p. 53. The Prologue, exactly contemporary with *The Vanity of Human Wishes,* dates from the end of 1748; *The Preceptor* had been published on April 7.

7. The classic study is Erwin Panofsky, *Hercules am Scheidewege* (Leipzig and Berlin, 1930). The influence of the theme in England has been demonstrated by Jean H. Hagstrum, *The Sister Arts* (Chicago, 1958) and Ronald Paulson, *Hogarth: His Life, Art, and Times,* 2 vols. (New Haven, 1971). Earl R. Wasserman, "The Inherent Values of Eighteenth-Century Personification," *PMLA,* 65 (1950), 435–63, was among the first to emphasize the importance of Prodicus and Cebes for eighteenth-century English literature. At the time of writing the present essay, I had not seen Wasserman's "Johnson's *Rasselas:* Implicit Contexts," *JEGP,* 74 (1975), 1–25, whose use of Prodicus and Cebes as "implicit norms" for Johnson's narrative strategies anticipates my own (cf. his pp. 15–16). Though Wasserman's interesting reading of *Rasselas* complements the readings here, his claim that Prodicus and Cebes furnish "presiding narrative patterns" and "formal expectations" to the eighteenth-century readers seems exaggerated to me; it tends to reduce all Johnson's themes and ironies to a single source. Carey McIntosh, *The Choice of Life: Samuel Johnson and the World of Fiction* (New Haven, 1973), has organized his thoughtful discussion of Johnson around a similar pattern of images (see especially pp. 109–16). The continuing importance of the Hercules theme in American culture (most of all at Princeton) has been thoroughly documented by James McLachlan, "The *Choice of Hercules:* American Student Societies in the Early 19th Century," *The University in Society,* ed. Lawrence Stone (Princeton, 1974), II, 449–94.

8. A review of *Telemachus. A Mask* by George Graham, *Critical Review,* 15 (1763), 314.

9. Ibid. Cf. *Rambler* 129.

10. Modern scholarship assigns it rather to a Stoic philosopher of the first century A.D. The letter to Ford is printed in Johnson's *Letters,* ed. R. W. Chapman (Oxford, 1952), 1, 7.

11. *Critical Review* (1763), p. 317.

12. *On Heroes,* p. 205.

13. "Observations made in going up the *Pic of Teneriffe,*" by Thomas Heberden, communicated by William Heberden, *Philosophical Transactions of the Royal Society,* 47 (1752), 354. William Heberden, who later attended Johnson as a physician, began his London practice in 1748. In the *Philosophical Transactions* for 1715, an account by J. Edens describes "a Cave three or four Miles from the Pike, where are a great many Skeletons and Bones of Men; and

some say there are the Bones of Giants in this Cave" (p. 325); this may have suggested the Caverns of *Despair*.

14. *Odyssey*, IV, 563ff.; *Lives*, "Sertorius," 8. Compare with "Theodore" Pope's *Odyssey*, IV, 773–74: "the Blest inhale / The fragrant murmurs of the western gale." As late as 1869, a popular guide to the Canaries by Eugène Pégot-Ogier was titled *The Fortunate Isles* (Eng. tr. 1871).

15. Donne's *First Anniversary*, ll. 286–88. The context is the encroachment of the earth upon both Heaven and Hell.

16. *The Poetry of Robert Frost* (New York, 1969), p. 363.

17. *Rambler* 121. Edwin C. Heinle, "The Eighteenth-Century Allegorical Essay" (Columbia Diss., 1957), has studied the allegorical conventions behind "Theodore," and Bernard L. Einbond, *Samuel Johnson's Allegory* (The Hague, 1971), pp. 56–64, discusses it in terms of Johnson's allegorical theory.

18. *Rambler* 80; Johnson's *Works* (New Haven, 1969), IV, 56.

19. "The Virgin & the Dynamo," *The Dyer's Hand* (New York, 1962), p. 71.

20. Johnson's doubts about sacred poetry should be compared especially with Dennis' *Advancement and Reformation of Modern Poetry* (1701), Part II, ch. 1, "That the Design of the True Religion and Poetry are the same."

21. "To Miss————," ll. 23–24; "Drury-Lane Prologue" (1747), ll. 59–62. *Complete English Poems*, pp. 70, 82.

22. *Lives of the Poets*, II, 437.

23. *Lives of the Poets* (Milton), I, 170.

24. *Lives of the Poets* (Dryden), I, 447.

25. Boswell's *Life of Johnson*, I, 194.

26. The reading of the first edition. In 1755 the middle couplet became "Through all his Veins the Fever of Renown / Spreads from the strong Contagion of the Gown"; in 1778, at Boswell's urging, Johnson changed "Spreads" to "Burns." Boswell's statement that this alteration "was more poetical, as it might carry an allusion to the shirt by which Hercules was inflamed" (*Life*, III, 358), makes little sense; *all* versions carry that allusion, as "Labours" attests in the following line. It is possible that Boswell confused the burning of Hercules in his pyre with the spreading of his inflammation.

27. Note added in 1755. On the passage as a whole, the best commentary is *Adventurer* 85 (28 August 1753), where Johnson reveals his basic sympathy with young scholarly ambitions: there Francis, rather than Roger, Bacon is made the model for emulation.

28. *Johnsonian Miscellanies*, I, 180.

29. *Hamlet*, III.iii. Cf. Johnson's comments, *Works* (New Haven, 1968), VIII, 989–90.

30. When grasping Bliss th'unsteady mind / Looks back on what She left behind, / She faints and quits her hold." *Complete English Poems*, p. 126.

31. *Rambler* 24; *Works* (New Haven, 1969), III, 130. *Rambler* 24 applies the phrase to the "gay and light" parts of life; *Rambler* 28 to the "grave and solemn."

32. Ll. 19–21; *Complete English Poems*, p. 147 (my translation).

33. Ll. 49–51. The Latin is reminiscent of Juvenal; cf. l. 41, "Res angusta domi," the phrase from the Third Satire that *London* had rendered as "Poverty" but which here seems to refer to a destitution of mind.

34. *Rambler* 28 (23 June 1750); *Works* (New Haven, 1969), III, 156.

Structure and Absence
in Boswell's *Life of Johnson*

WILLIAM C. DOWLING

The problems posed by the structure of the *Life of Johnson* seem to revolve around another problem that we do not at first glance see in structural terms: the tension between various idealized versions of Johnson that dominate the foreground of the biographical story and the darker and more disturbing Johnson we glimpse in its gloomy background. The problem is a problem because neither Johnson is wholly unreal: the image of the revered sage and moralist is not an arbitrary fiction imposed by Johnson's admirers on some gloomy and contrary reality. There is much in Johnson's writings and conversation, in his literary and moral character, to sustain the image, and yet that gloomy and contrary reality exists as well, inhabited by a Johnson quite unlike the image the world has created of him.

Even to speak of the foreground of the biographical story, however, or of a gloomy background occasionally glimpsed, is to impose upon the *Life* itself an illusion of perspective. The implication is that in passing through the foreground—the conversation scenes, say, with their image of Johnson in exuberant good spirits—to the darker realm of existence that lies behind them, we have penetrated through appearances to reality, or at least to a reality more real than what we have passed through. Thus the notion of pictorial perspective translates into moral and existential terms; in the depths of the biographical story we glimpse the Johnson who suffers throughout his life from a dismal malady of the spirit, from the "dejection, gloom, and despair, which made existence misery" (I.63).[1]

From *Language and Logos in Boswell's "Life of Johnson"* (Princeton: Princeton University Press, 1981), pp. 66–97.

There is much in the narrative structure of the *Life* to sustain this illusion, but the reason we do not immediately seek to explain it in structural terms is that it is ultimately sustained by something else. In every biographical narrative perhaps, but in the *Life* overwhelmingly, the illusion of receding perspective derives from an idea of actual or ideal presence: somewhere behind the *Life*, glimpsed only imperfectly in any moment of narration or speech, seen in terms sometimes more real or less superficial than others, lies the presence of a Samuel Johnson not identical with or reducible to the text we are reading. As we seem to pierce through language to the world it describes, we seem to penetrate, or always to be on the point of penetrating, through the *Life* to a Johnsonian presence.

Yet it is not altogether an illusion of visual perspective that imposes this on us, for that perspective is itself an illusion: we gaze into the painted landscape aware that there is, there behind the tiny receding figure trudging into the distance down a disappearing road, nothing but canvas. The illusion perhaps corresponds to a reality in which background becomes foreground, where as we ourselves move down a road the scene changes and a new landscape looms before us, but even this has something in common with what we have been calling illusion; the new landscape too has its foreground and its background, and this, in just the same way as in the landscape on the wall, reaches out to infinity.

The meaning of the analogous illusion in the *Life*, an illusion of ontological rather than visual perspective, lies in that which the illusion exists to shut out or deny. For unless we could in some sense pierce through the *Life* to the actual or ideal presence of Johnson, to a reality at least implied by the illusion of receding perspective, the *Life* would seem to be nothing more than a window on infinity, a biographical portrait of no subject. As the word corresponds to the object it names, biography must correspond to a biographical subject external to its narrative, the *Life* to a Johnson not contained within the pages of the *Life*.

The notion of a Johnsonian presence behind the text of the *Life* may serve to explain an odd confusion in Boswell's mind about the nature of the story he is telling. In a purely conventional sense, Boswell understands Johnson's death as a kind of absence; those who have contributed to his account of Johnson's life, he says in the opening pages, resemble "*the grateful tribes of ancient nations, of which every individual was eager to throw a stone upon the grave of a departed Hero, and thus to share in the pious office of erecting an honourable monument to his memory*" (I.5). Yet this is only absence from the world of men, and biography is another sort of world.

It is always the world of his biography that Boswell has in mind when he writes as though Johnson, though absent through death in some trivial or literal sense, lives on in the *Life*—as though, that is, the soul had departed the corpse only to take up lodging in the Johnsonian presence behind the story: "Had his other friends been as diligent and ardent as I was, he might have been almost entirely preserved. As it is, I will venture to say that he will be seen in this work more completely than any man who has ever yet lived" (I.30). For what is preserved, if we grant the existence of the corpse, is the soul or spirit that once resided in it.

Yet there seems to be something mistaken, too, about dismissing all this as mere illusion, asserting that there is nothing behind the *Life* but the absence of any biographical subject not contained in the text. For while there is nothing we could point to behind the text, as we might utter a word and point to the object it named, there is a stubborn complexity in the illusion of Johnson's presence that invites us to consider it in more detail. What teases us about the notion of absence, of a vacuum at the center of the *Life*, is that it is made meaningful by an earlier notion of presence; it is not absence pure and simple—if that is in any case conceivable—but absence of what the *Life* projects as a presence.

The notion of an ideal or abstract center, that is to say, is something equally posited by the opposing notions of presence and absence; in a manner of speaking they converge on it. For to say that there is a vacuum at the center of the *Life* is to say that that center exists after all. The emptiness of the conjurer's hat when he has completed the trick is defined by the trick itself: hats are normally empty, and emptiness so to speak signifies only when we expect to see a rabbit. The problem of absence in the *Life* is thus simultaneously a problem of presence, and it is this that leads one to explore the problem in terms of narrative and thematic structure.

When we approach the problem through a consideration of structure, we discover that we are regarding from a new angle the puzzle of receding perspective in the narrative, the illusion of a gloomy background occasionally glimpsed behind the conviviality and bustle of the foreground. For what that receding perspective implies is nothing other than the center we wish to locate: if idealized versions of Johnson dominate the foreground of the *Life*, and if behind these we glimpse a bleaker reality inhabited by another Johnson, our very notion of reality, of what is selective and idealized as opposed to complete and substantial, involves the notion of a Johnsonian presence somewhere behind that last reality, a center on which everything in the story somehow converges.

To say that idealized versions of Johnson dominate the foreground of the *Life* is, at the same time, to say that we recognize these as being creations, unreal figments for one or another reason constructed by the inhabitants of Johnson's world. In general terms, we want to say that we recognize these as selective or idealized constructions because they conflict or are at odds with other elements of the story, but this does not account for our sense that they obscure a more substantial reality. It is not a matter of competing versions of an identical reality, as one might hear, say, in courtroom testimony, but of realities competing with one another.

The illusion of receding moral and ontological perspective in the *Life* is created by this competition, or rather by the terms on which it is played out within the structure of the narrative. For every idealized version of Johnson originates in some distinct world of consciousness or perception, and to recognize it as an idealized creation or construction is nothing other than to see that the world to which it belongs is threatened or subverted by antiworlds containing radically different conceptions of Johnson. To isolate the relation of world and antiworld in the *Life*, or to say that its structure exists as a network of antithetical relations, is to represent that structure in frozen or spatial terms; the dynamic element that completes the account lies in the concept of deconstruction.

Our sense of structure and meaning in the *Life*, that is, is not anything frozen or spatial; it is something that emerges only as the narrative assumes its shape as a whole. And it is the dynamics of this process—the narrative logic governing our sense of structure and meaning—that demands to be seem in terms of deconstruction, with one world of consciousness or perception dissolving or giving way to another in the antithetical regions behind it, moving us inward to an implied center in which, or just behind which, we shall discover the Johnsonian presence corresponding to perceptions of Johnson. It is not that one deconstructs the idealized versions of Johnson that dominate the foreground of the story, but that explanation mirrors the process through which they are deconstructed within the text itself.

At this point, perhaps, I should abandon the metaphor of receding or pictorial perspective in the *Life*; it is simply a metaphor, and has only the limited virtue of allowing one to speak about something actually occurring within the structure of the *Life*. Yet explanation must nonetheless begin in what the metaphor led me to call the foreground of the biographical story, with one or another of those idealized perceptions of Johnson that seem to dissolve in the dark light of antithetical relation. This is the significance, for instance, of the long passage from Courtenay's poem of Johnson's moral and literary character that Boswell quotes early in the narrative:

"By nature's gifts ordain'd mankind to rule,
He, like a Titian, form'd his brilliant school;
And taught congenial spirits to excel,
While from his lips impressive wisdom fell.

. . . .

Nor was his energy confin'd alone
To friends around his philosophick throne;
Its influence wide improv'd our letter'd isle,
and lucid vigour mark'd the general style:
As Nile's proud waves, swoln from their oozy bed,
First o'er the neighbouring meads majestick spread;
Till gathering force, they more and more expand,
And with new virtue fertilise the land."

(I.222–23)

The occasion for bringing Courtenay's idealized vision of Johnson into the *Life* at this point is ostensibly Boswell's consideration of Johnson's style: the italicized couplet simply repeats in rhyme and pentameter Boswell's own pedestrian comments on Johnson's prose—"from the influence which he has had upon our composition, scarcely any thing is written now that is not better expressed than was usual before he appeared to lead the national taste." Yet italicization at this moment comes close to reversing its normal significance: if it is *only* that couplet in Courtenay's poem that supports Boswell's point, what is the burden of meaning carried by the unitalicized lines, the image of Johnson that now floats disembodied above Boswell's discussion of prose style?

The answer is that Johnson's prose style is transparently a pretext for establishing, thus early in the story, an image of Johnson that dominates the entire foreground of the *Life*. The true subject of Courtenay's poem is an invisible monarchy of mind and moral vision, a world in which Johnson sits high above ordinary mankind dispensing wisdom, in both speech and writing, from a philosophic throne. And this image, long after it has dissolved in favor of darker and more complex perceptions of Johnson, continues to exert something of its original power. It is why, for instance, we will see Johnson's famous meeting with George III as a meeting between two monarchs—even, when Johnson is speaking, as a meeting between a monarch in the realm of mind and one of his ordinary subjects.

In the metaphor of a circle of congenial spirits surrounding Johnson's philosophic throne we discover too an image that seems to expand and stabilize Courtenay's idealized portrait. For this is a metaphor that the *Life* seems to enact: throughout the story, as kindred spirits like Reynolds, Beauclerk, Langton, and numberless others are drawn toward Johnson's presence as by a moral or intellectual law of gravity, we do see something like a monarchy of intellect emerge. The inhabitants of the *Life*, no matter how talented or considerable in their own right, do revolve around Johnson like greater or lesser bodies around a sun, and from this the image of a philosophic throne, a fixed or stationary point from which the world comes and goes, takes on its significance.

Within the invisible circumference of Johnson's world in the *Life* exist all those who perceive him as an object of awe and veneration. And even when we see that every such conception of Johnson originates in a distinct world of consciousness, the consciousness of a Reynolds, a Langton, a Beauclerk, a Campbell, we still want to say that the foreground of the *Life* is dominated by a galaxy of worlds related to one another by something like the idealizing impulse expressed in pure form in Courtenay's lines. The monarchy of mind and moral vision in this sense exists almost as the poem describes it, and the *Life* is populated by its subjects.

Yet even to say that Courtenay's image of Johnson is idealized is to perceive that it inevitably dissolves in the light of antithetical relation, that his poem exists as a world in relation to antiworlds working towards its deconstruction. Here, once again, the blankness of the page separating Boswell's commentary from Courtenay's verse signals an antithetical system of relations, for Boswell's more complex consciousness of Johnson includes darker elements that Courtenay's image simply denies or excludes, and the same is true of Reynolds, Langton, and the rest of those congenial spirits whom Courteny portrays as the subjects of Johnson's invisible monarchy. The whiteness of the page that surrounds Courtenay's poem signals its isolation with an entire network of darker and more complex conceptions of Johnson, and in its isolation it wavers and begins to fade.

The reason we want to say that the foreground of the *Life* is dominated by a galaxy of worlds that seem to expand and stabilize Courtenay's image, then, is merely because that image corresponds to the unreal figments existing in the minds of those who first know Johnson only through his writings—to Boswell's imaginary sage, living in a state of solemn elevated abstraction in the immense metropolis of London, to Langton's remarkably decorous philosopher, to the magisterial presence Reynolds imagines to exist behind the pages of the *Life of Savage*. Yet these are figments that dissolve in light of the uncouth and troubling reality of Johnson's actual presence, and in the moment of their dissolution there occurs a simultaneous dissolution of Courtenay's image of an invisible monarchy.

Yet throughout the *Life* a shadow of that monarchy remains. To see that Boswell's or Reynolds's consciousness of Johnson contains disturbing elements denied by Courtenay's image—a Johnson who mutters to himself in company, who gesticulates constantly and ludicrously, who eats with such unwholesome voracity that the veins of his forehead swell—is indeed to begin a pursuit of the series of deconstructions that carries us inward toward the center of the *Life*, toward that bleak and gloomy realm of private suffering revealed in the *Prayers and Meditations*. Yet, through all this, the idealizing impulse shared by Courtenay and such congenial spirits as Boswell and Reynolds persists.

To understand why the impulse persists, we must glance in a preliminary way at a principle that organizes the structure of the *Life* as a whole, and that the deconstructive sequence leading to its center brings into ever greater visibility. In brief, the congenial spirits who surround Johnson's philosophic throne in the *Life* are creatures of an age of spiritual disintegration whose own longing for moral certitude impels them to construct a Johnson who does not exist, to hear in Johnson's speech and his writings a tone of magisterial reassurance to which, in this anxiety, they supply a corresponding presence. The imaginary throne of Courtenay's poem is, so to speak, empty throughout the *Life*, and only within the separate consciousness of every congenial spirit does it come to be occupied by an unreal and idealized Johnson.

The *Life* as a whole enacts a drama of presence and absence at least partly because the same drama is played out within the consciousness of those of its inhabitants who perceive Johnson as an object of awe and veneration. To imagine the Johnson who speaks in *Rasselas* or *The Rambler* as an idealized philosopher or sage is to imagine a presence behind the moral voice, and to greet the uncouth figure in unbuckled shoes and shriveled wig is to understand suddenly that that presence is imaginary after all, that there is quite literally nothing there where one had imagined an elevated and serene moralist. And yet the idealizing impulse is not defeated but only thwarted; contrary realities are adjusted to one another, and perceptions of Johnson antithetical in their nature compete within the problematic space of the real.

There is a danger here of seeming to generalize the experience of only a few major characters in the *Life*—Boswell's, certainly, and Reynolds's and Langton's, and perhaps Oglethorpe's or Campbell's or Burney's, but who then? Yet the pattern of their experience is universal for those whom the *Life* counts as subjects of its invisible monarchy: in one way or another, kindred spirits are drawn toward Johnson's actual presence as by a law of moral or intellectual gravity, a process that invariably begins in a reverence for the disembodied voice heard in the writings and ends in the reality of quite another Johnson holding forth in drawing room or tavern. And if this other Johnson gives grounds at all for awe or veneration, it is only as he distantly resembles the wholly imaginary moralist and sage.

What is also universal in the *Life*, dividing its world into an inner and an outer sphere, is the shared sense of spiritual crisis that impels those who venerate Johnson to seek in his presence a refuge from a world of abstract conflict, of growing anxiety and doubt. To perceive Johnson as a heroic spirit fighting a solitary battle against the forces of skepticism and infidelity—the forces of Voltaire and Hume and Holbach and a thousand minor philosophes and freethinkers—and to discover in his writings and his speech a power of gigantic moral reassurance in the midst of overwhelming doubt, is simultaneously to perceive the age in the same light as so many nineteenth-century writers would come to perceive their own, as a time in which "old opinions, feelings—ancestral customs and institutions are crumbling away, and both the spiritual and the temporal worlds are darkened by the shadow of change."[2]

It is this perception of the age, as we shall see when we come to discuss the problem of audience in the *Life*, that sustains the image of an invisible monarchy, and that locates those who perceive Johnson as a moral hero within the inner sphere of its world. For whatever they do not have in common, inhabitants of the outer sphere do share not merely a failure to see Johnson as an object of veneration, but a benign or optimistic view of the age. From the cheerful stoicism of Hume to the vacant cheerfulness of Johnson's schoolfellow Mr. Hector, from the idiosyncratic preoccupation of Lord Monboddo to the pagan insouciance of John Wilkes, those who see Johnson as merely an odd or opinionated creature do so because they are simply oblivious to the moral context in which he figures as a hero.

Since the invisible law of gravity drawing kindred spirits toward Johnson's actual presence begins to operate only at the moment one imagines an idealized and disembodied Johnson as a presence behind his writings, we should expect that those writings, at least, would serve within the structure of the *Life* to sustain the idealized image. For though the uncouth figure who greets Boswell or Langton at the door of his chambers shatters the illusion they had carried in their minds to the encounter, the illusion should at least return with full force when one goes back to the pages out of which it was created. And, on one level, this is precisely what occurs; whenever he rereads *Rasselas,* says Boswell, gazing back over his long acquaintance with Johnson to the first time he read Johnson's works, "I can scarcely believe that I had the honour of enjoying the intimacy of such a man" (I.342).

The Johnson whose intimacy Boswell enjoyed is not, of course, the Johnson whom he rediscovers whenever he opens the pages of *Rasselas,* for at the moment he begins to read, his acquaintance with an actual Johnson, the Johnson of drawing room and tavern, is annihilated. The Johnson whose voice he hears in *Rasselas* is precisely that disembodied sage and moralist who awakens his veneration—grown up in his imagination, as he says, into a kind of superstitious reverence—when he is a young man in Edinburgh. It is a short circuit of the imagination that returns the middle-aged Boswell, a survivor gazing retrospectively on Johnson and the world he has departed, to that state of superstitious reverence in which he came down from Edinburgh to London as a youth of twenty-two.

In the pattern of Boswell's experience, then, we should expect to discover a pattern that serves to explain the structure of the *Life* as a whole. For it is not simply the case that Boswell's experience is the experience of everyone who inhabits the inner sphere of the *Life,* that so many others have been drawn by the disembodied and idealized Johnson of the writings into the presence of an actual Johnson, but rather that the disembodied sage and moralist lives on when the actual Johnson is in the grave. Whenever Johnson's works enter the *Life,* the assumed audience of the biographical story in one sense reenacts just the same experience: like Boswell or Reynolds or Langton before them, its members move from the disembodied moralist into the presence of a Johnson who moves and speaks in actual surroundings, and the idealized presence they imagine to exist behind the writings lingers in the memory, coloring what actually occurs in the drawing room.

To say that Johnson's writings compose a separate world within the *Life* is to see them as allowing an unmediated view of the imaginary philosopher whose magisterial voice provides moral reassurance in an age of spiritual anxiety. Yet the passages from Johnson's writings that Boswell quotes throughout the *Life* do not themselves compose a world. The reason we want to speak of them that way is precisely that we glimpse, as the invisible context of any passage quoted in the *Life,* the unquoted totality of Johnson's writings, a separate and coherent sphere of mind and moral imagination. The passages interpolated in the text are an assemblage of reminders, and we reach through their final configuration to a world.

Always in the *Life*, the mechanics of quotation—quotation marks, textual spacings, margins, differences of type—represent the text calling attention to its own discontinuities. Typography, in itself neutral and meaningless, points to the underlying reality of an antithetical system. For it is the system or structure of antithetical relations that gives the typographical form of the text its meaning, that in a manner of speaking allows the quotation mark or the blankness of the page to signify. And though they signify equally whenever the *Life* interpolates a letter or a secondhand account of Johnson or a passage from the *Prayers and Meditations*, they signify whenever we encounter a passage from *The Rambler* or *Rasselas* or *The Vanity of Human Wishes* the presence of a world not only separate from but alien to the text.

The very meaning of quotation in a narrative like the *Life*, and of the mechanics that set off or signal the otherness of what is quoted, derives from what Hillis Miller has called "the inexorable law which makes the uncanny, 'undecidable,' or 'alogical' relation of host and parasite, heterogeneity within homogeneity . . . reform itself within each separate entity which had seemed, on the larger scale, to be one or the other."[3] Even when we view the *Life* as a single coherent world, we understand that passages from Johnson's writings belong to and have been detached from another world and brought into the text: it is an element of another world that the blank space surrounding the passage proclaims, and that is what is signaled by the marks of quotation in the text.

When we have seen that the world of the *Life* is not single and coherent, that it dissolves into a system of separate worlds existing in antithetical relation to one another, any direct quotation of Johnson's writings within the text raises a more complex problem. To say that a series of lines from *The Vanity of Human Wishes* exists in antithetical relation to Boswell's perception of Johnson, for instance, and that this relation is precisely what is signaled by the blankness of the page separating Boswell's commentary on the poem from Johnson's magnificent lines, is implicitly to assert that *The Vanity of Human Wishes* works to dissolve or deconstruct Boswell's idealizing perception of Johnson. Yet this Johnson, the stern and clairvoyant moralist speaking eloquently of the inevitable misery of human existence, is identical with the disembodied philosopher who awakened Boswell's impulse to veneration long before he made the acquaintance of any other Johnson.

What is true of Boswell in his relation to Johnson's writings, moreover, is true for every other member of the inner circle of the *Life:* the idealized Johnson who dwells in the separate consciousness of a Reynolds or a Langton or a Burke is the moralist of *Rasselas* and *The Vanity of Human Wishes*, the imaginary Johnson whose mind and moral character moved them to seek out the actual Johnson of drawing room and tavern. This is the meaning, for instance, of the passage Boswell quotes not from *Rasselas* or *The Vanity of Human Wishes* but from Johnson's preface to his early translation of Lobo's *Voyage to Abyssinia:*

> "The reader will here find no regions cursed with irremediable barrenness, or blessed with spontaneous fecundity.... Here are no Hottentots without religious polity or articulate language; no Chinese perfectly polite, and completely skilled in all sciences; he will discover, what will always be discovered by a diligent and impartial enquirer, that wherever human nature is to be found, there is a mixture of vice and virtue, a contest of passion and reason; and that the Creator doth not appear partial in his distributions, but has balanced, in most countries, their particular inconveniencies by particular favours." (I.89)

The biographical reason for bringing the passage into the *Life* is obvious enough: here, in a preface written when Johnson is young and impoverished and unknown, working in thankless obscurity as a provincial bookseller's hack, is the same voice that will be heard later in the poetry and the moral writings and the great philosophical passages of the *Lives of the Poets*. Yet the thematic significance of the passage is quite removed from its place in the biographical story, for what it celebrates is the sudden emergence of that idealized moralist who will come to dwell in the consciousness of those who surround the actual Johnson in his world. "Mr. Edmund Burke," says Boswell by way of introducing the passage," . . . was, I remember, much delighted with the following specimen." Burke's delight, like Boswell's, is the delight of a world that has discovered a monarch to set upon a philosophic throne hitherto vacant.

Yet it is not so far obvious why the voice of Johnson the moralist is heard by men like Boswell and Burke as a voice of moral reassurance. There is, to be sure, an evident faith in an ontological order both rational and providential ("the Creator doth not appear partial in his distributions"), but nothing to suggest that this goes beyond a piety wholly conventional. The answer seems to lie, rather, in the power of the moralist to penetrate the shifting appearances of human life, to brush aside delusion and self-delusion and bring into view the permanent and universal reality beneath the surface. What we see, what is seen by Boswell and Burke, is what is always there to be seen by "a diligent and impartial enquirer, that wherever human nature is to be found, there is a mixture of vice and virtue."

Yet this too is an observation wholly conventional in eighteenth-century terms, the central assumption of Pope's *Essay on Man* and *Gulliver's Travels*, of *Tom Jones* and *Tristam Shandy*, of the ethical doctrines of Shaftesbury and the comedies of Goldsmith and Sheridan. What, then, allows Boswell and Burke to hear the voice of the moralist in so unlikely a context as this, a preface to a translation of Lobo in which Johnson is, on the face of it, merely attacking the literary tradition of the fabulous voyage? The answer is that all this has only superficially to do with fabulous books of travel, brutish Hottentots and polite Chinese, for the standard against which they are measured is the universal reality of human nature in all ages and countries—what will *always* be discovered—as seen through study and observation, what a traveler must know before he sets out on his travels.

Whenever Johnson's writings appear in the *Life*, each passage floating in a textual space that compels us to see it as a specimen momentarily detached from the larger body of his thought, we again encounter, whatever the subject, a penetrating moral vision that sweeps aside illusory appearances and insists on a permanent and universal truth. Johnson the moralist is an Augustan survivor, the last great spokesman for a moral and literary tradition reaching back through Renaissance humanism to classical antiquity. Behind every specimen quoted in the *Life* there lies, there in the unquoted totality of Johnson's writings, the entire authority of the Augustan vision:

> A great part of the time of those who are placed at the greatest distance by fortune, or by temper, must unavoidably pass in the same manner; and though, when the claims of nature are satisfied, caprice, and vanity, and accident, begin to produce discriminations and peculiarities, yet the eye is not very heedful or quick, which cannot discover the same causes still terminating their influence in the same effects, though sometimes accelerated, sometimes retarded, or perplexed by multiplied combinations. We are all prompted by the same motives, all deceived by the same fallacies, all animated by hope, obstructed by danger, entangled by desire, and seduced by pleasure. (*Rambler* 60)

The power of reassurance in Johnson's writings, then, and the power of the imaginary and idealized moralist to awaken the veneration of lesser souls, derives in the last analysis from the ontological assumptions underlying the view of human nature embodied in those writings. For in continually reminding humanity that there are no individual hopes and fears, that the disguises of life—social rank, wealth, power, age, country—are separable and adventitious, that the interior existence of man is common to every soul on earth and in history, the disembodied moralist invokes a larger principle of intelligibility, and explanation of the universe for which classical and Christian myth, philosophical and theological systems, are merely grand metaphors.

Unlike the Johnson of drawing room and tavern, moving through the dirty streets of London in an age growing increasingly troubled, Johnson the sage and moralist is a dweller in the city of God, an observer of human existence who seems, amid the anxiety and skepticism and doubt of lesser souls, sustained by the same large sense of spiritual unity that sustained Augustine or Aquinas. And if the moralist draws an uncompromisingly gloomy picture of human life, portrays it as a realm of delusion and misery, his explanation is implicitly the same as theirs: the misery of our existence is a misery of alienation from the divine, that derangement of the will and enslavement to the passions that Christian theology expresses in the doctrine of original sin.

When we perceive Johnson's writings as a separate world within the *Life*, they do suggest in overpowering terms a sense of spiritual coherence and even, at the deepest level, of moral serenity. The disembodied and magisterial Johnson they project is real, and only when we hear the tones of moral serenity in his voice do we fully understand why he so assuages the doubt and anxiety of lesser souls. Thus, for instance, when Boswell comes to discuss *The Vanity of Human Wishes*, he omits altogether to quote the long first part of the poem, that great and gloomy picture of human existence as an unrelieved round of misery and delusion. The page is occupied instead by the conclusion, a picture of the universe as governed by divine love and wisdom: "'These goods he grants, who grants the power to gain; / With these celestial wisdom calms the mind, / And makes the happiness she does not find'" (I.195).

With celestial wisom, too, Johnson the moralist calms the mind; "were all the other excellencies of this poem annihilated," says Boswell, "it must ever have our grateful reverence from its noble conclusion." Yet the *Life* as a whole always insists that we read *The Vanity of Human Wishes* from a reverse perspective, see its gloomy picture of human misery as overwhelming and finally negating the conventional pieties of the conclusion Boswell sees as being so noble. The poem that haunts the *Life* is a *Vanity of Human Wishes* in which the conclusion is what is annihilated, the bleak vision of the suppressed earlier lines moving in to occupy a textual space suddenly vacant. The poem that haunts the *Life* is a poem that simply ends with the lines occurring at the beginning of the specimen Boswell quotes: "'Must helpless man, in ignorance sedate, / Roll darkling down the torrent of his fate?'"

The terrible question posed in those lines must be answered either in the negative or the affirmative, and the answer that pervades the *Life* is the affirmative: we must, in ignorance sedate, roll darkling down the torrent of our fate. It is Johnson's gigantic power of affirmation as a moralist that allows Boswell to dwell serenely on the poem's concluding lines, that allows others in Johnson's world to discover in his writings a voice that annihilates skepticism and doubt, creating at least for the moment a comforting illusion of moral certitude. Yet to do this is to exclude an alternative possibility inexorably suggested by the writings themselves, the possibility that they are written out of a personal sense of misery and despair that wholly overwhelms conventional piety and outworn mythologies of divine and universal order.

In this instance, *The Vanity of Human Wishes* may be seen to stand for the totality of Johnson's writings as they appear—or do not appear—in the *Life*. For what Boswell's discussion, his quotation and commentary, excludes is precisely the terrible possibility that those writings carry within them the seeds of their own deconstruction, that the magisterial philosopher and sage is nothing more than a soul close to despair, vainly attempting to shore against the ruins of his age some fragments of classical wisdom and Christian theology, exploded systems of coherence and belief. To view the moralist in this light is to see him not as an Augustan survivor but as a lonely anachronism, and to see his outworn assumptions as the discarded lenses through which he futilely tries to impose order on a meaningless flux.

To view Johnson's writings in this light is to understand why that other Johnson, the uncouth denizen of the drawing room, appears as a moral hero to those who venerate him. For it is not that Boswell and Burke and Reynolds and the rest have been duped by their veneration of an idealized moralist into a veneration of the actual Johnson who produced the writings, but that the actual Johnson admits in his own life all those dark possibilities that the writings seem to exclude, lives constantly with the fear that existence is meaningless and the universe mindless, and through a gigantic and sustained effort of will denies the haunting specter of what Boswell once calls an eternal necessity without design.

Yet this other Johnson is not the Johnson perceived by Boswell or Burke or Reynolds, and to explain why they see him as a moral hero is to explain precisely what their perceptions shut out or exclude. The uncouth philosopher they venerate is, as much as the disembodied moralist, a creation or construct, a creature of their own deepest anxieties. The Johnson they encounter in life is, so to speak, a moral hero with no context to explain his heroism, a champion battling invisible adversaries in an arena invisible to ordinary men (and this explains, quite as much as Johnson's heroism, the quixotic light in which he so often appears in the *Life*). Yet the arena and the adversaries are not really invisible; they are terrible to contemplate, and focusing solely on the figure of Johnson as hero is a means of denying their existence.

Every idealizing perception of Johnson in the *Life*, then, is subjected to the antithetical pressures—a field of deconstructive force—existing in the space between the world of his moral writings and the gloomy antiworld revealed in the *Prayers and Meditations*. To see that the magisterial moralist of the writings is merely the reverse or positive image of the miserable supplicant of the *Prayers and Meditations* is to see that every conception of Johnson that lies between them, even as it seems to include the complexities of a heroism mingled with despair, is finally precarious and unstable, a conception that wavers and dissolves as we move inward toward the center of the *Life*. And this is true not simply of Boswell and Reynolds and Langton and Burke, but of every member of that circle of veneration that composes the inner sphere of the *Life*.

To see why this is so, it is not necessary to trace in tedious detail the system of antithetical relations that works toward the dissolution or deconstruction of every idealizing perception of Johnson. For what occurs is that the system in its entirety, the *Life* as a whole, insists strongly on the dark possibilities that such perceptions exclude. Thus we see Johnson's melancholy, for instance, not as an occasional illness or disease, but as the retreat of a heroic spirit from the specter of a meaningless universe, a mode of spiritual paralysis:

> He was so ill, as, notwithstanding his remarkable love of company, to be entirely averse to society, the most fatal symptom of that malady. Dr. Adams told me, that, as an old friend, he was admitted to visit him, and that he found him in a deplorable state, sighing, groaning, talking to himself, and restlessly walking from room to room. He then used this emphatical expression of the misery which he felt: "I would consent to have a limb amputated to recover my spirits." (I.483)

When we attempt to explain the meaning of any such scene as this in terms of our conventional model of narrative structure, our impulse is to focus on its complication of perspectives; there is Johnson, living in solitary misery, there is Adams, entering the scene and reporting it later to Boswell, and finally there is Boswell himself, absent at the time but recreating the scene in his imagination in vivid detail ("sighing, groaning, talking to himself") before our eyes. Yet what cuts through all questions of mediation and narrative time is the shared perspective of Adams and Boswell, the perspective of a world that sees any such episode as this as "illness," as a "hypochondraick disorder," as a gloomy interlude in an existence altogether more cheerful and serene.

The *Life* as a whole, on the other hand, insists on an opposite reality, a reality in which Johnson's moments of serenity, even, in company, of hilarity and high glee, are momentary escapes from the despair that makes existence misery. Thus Johnson's lethargy, so often preventing him from exertion for months at a time, must, like his melancholy, be seen as a form of spiritual paralysis inexorably drawing us inward through the middle sphere of idealizing perceptions to the central reality revealed in the *Prayers and Meditations*—"my time has been unprofitably spent, and seems as a dream that has left nothing behind." And thus Johnson's horror at the thought of death, always seen by those who venerate him in terms of orthodox doubts about salvation and damnation, must be seen as a horror of death as mere annihilation; "'when he dies,'" says Johnson of Hume's pagan stoicism in the face of death, "'he at least gives up all he has'" (II.106).

To one degree or another, the consciousness of every inhabitant of the *Life* who perceives Johnson as a moral hero is defined by a denial of the dark and troubled reality revealed in the *Prayers and Meditations*—and this precisely reenacts, on the ordinary level, Johnson's own heroic attempt to deny the terrible reality of a blank material universe. The most prominent example in the *Life*, simply because the world of his consciousness is so prominent among the worlds composing its structure, is Boswell. In any scene where he turns to Johnson for spiritual reassurance in the midst of his own deep anxieties, the impulse to create or construct a Johnson answering his private needs is overwhelmingly visible:

I said, I had reason to believe that the thought of annihilation gave Hume no pain. JOHNSON. 'It was not so, Sir. He had a vanity in being thought easy. It is more probable that he should assume an appearance of ease, than that so very improbable a thing should be, as a man not afraid of going (as, in spite of his delusive theory, he cannot be sure but he may go,) into an unknown state, and not being uneasy at leaving all he knew. And you are to consider, that upon his own principle of annihilation he had no motive to speak the truth.'   (III.153)

The outlines of the spiritual dilemma that moves Boswell to introduce the notion of death as annihilation are visible here as well. On the one side there is Hume, symbolizing the world of Enlightenment skepticism, a world at once powerfully destructive of traditional ideas of order and cheerfully stoical in its pagan acceptance of a universe blind to the existence of men. On the other side there is Johnson, a spokesman for traditional systems of belief so powerful that he can for a moment dispel the dark clouds of doubt that surround Hume's cheerful behavior on the deathbed. And poised between them, in the doubtful position of every ordinary soul unable to sustain his own convictions without external support, is Boswell. Though the reassurance he receives can never be more than partial, it is reassurance nonetheless: "I thought, that the gloom of uncertainty in solemn religious speculation, being mingled with hope, was yet more consolatory than the emptiness of infidelity" (III.154).

The sense of reassurance derives, in all such scenes as this, from an utter denial of the possibility that Johnson's horror of death and Hume's pagan stoicism may be opposite reactions to an identical perception of the universe, that it is the notion of annihilation, so undismaying to Hume, that haunts Johnson's darkest dreams, lies at the source of his lethargy and melancholy, and oppresses his every waking hour. To see Johnson's unrelievedly gloomy view of human existence as having its source only in "the gloom of uncertainty in solemn religious speculation" is to locate him once again in the Augustinian tradition, to see him in all his private misery as a heroic defender of belief in an age of doubt, a spirit offering sustenance to lesser souls beset with fears.

To conceive of Johnson in this way, to create or construct a Johnson answering to the needs of a personal dilemma, is not, as it were, to operate in a void. For there is ample evidence—if one sees selectively, and denial now is nothing other than creation through a selective screening of elements—that some such Johnson exists. Now it is not only Johnson's moral writings but his speech, giving an unmediated view of a mind wholly committed to a vision of order and meaning in the universe, that seems to sustain the reassuring image. Johnson arguing with an overwhelming wit and energy and inventiveness for coherence and belief, as when in the scene above he instantly turns the argument of Hume's essay on miracles against Hume's own infidelity, always creates a powerful illusion of certitude in the midst of doubt.

Yet speech, precisely because it is unmediated, may always expose the illusion, threaten or subvert or deny the unreality one constructs. Thus

372 MODERN ESSAYS ON 18TH CENTURY LITERATURE

there is another sort of scene in the *Life* that always works to subvert Boswell's perception of Johnson as an unfailing source of spiritual reassurance, a type of scene in which the Johnson of the *Prayers and Meditations* lurks gloomily behind the heroic spokesman for order and meaning:

> I told him that David Hume said to me, he was no more uneasy to think he should *not be* after this life, than that he *had not been* before he began to exist. JOHNSON. "Sir, if he really thinks so, his perceptions are disturbed; he is mad: if he does not think so, he lies. He may tell you, he holds his finger in the flame of a candle, without feeling pain; would you believe him? When he dies, he at least gives up all he has." . . . BOSWELL. "But may we not fortify our minds for the approach of death?—Here I am sensible I was in the wrong, to bring before his view what he ever looked upon with horrour; for although when in a celestial frame, in his "Vanity of human Wishes," he has supposed death to be "kind Nature's signal for retreat," from this state of being to "a happier seat," his thoughts upon this awful change were in general full of dismal apprehensions. . . . To my question, whether we might not fortify our minds for the approach of death, he answered, in a passion, "No, Sir, let it alone. It matters not how a man dies, but how he lives. The act of dying is not of importance, it lasts so short a time." He added, (with an earnest look,) "A man knows it must be so, and submits. It will do him no good to whine." (II.106–7)

At any such moment, the precariousness and instability of Boswell's perception of Johnson, its tendency to waver and dissolve under the antithetical pressures of the text, reveals itself in unmistakable terms. What is dissolving just at the moment is Boswell's attempt to see in an identical focus two utterly opposing Johnsons, the disembodied moralist of *The Vanity of Human Wishes*, in whose "celestial frame" is so great a source of spiritual reassurance, and the gloomy Johnson of the *Prayers and Meditations*, whose thoughts on his own death are so "full of dismal apprehensions." The model Boswell attempts to impose on the antithesis, that of a single mind subject to change of mood, is wholly inadequate to the occasion, and the scene itself dissolves in an angry rupture; "he was so provoked, that he said, 'Give us no more of this;' . . . and when I was going away, called to me sternly, 'Don't let us meet tomorrow'" (I.107).

By the antithetical pressures of the text, then, I mean precisely those pressures that at this moment undermine, subvert, and finally dissolve Boswell's idealizing perception of Johnson. For to say that Boswell attempts to see two radically opposing Johnsons in an identical focus is not ourselves to assert an opposition as unstable as Boswell's unstable perception of an unreal identity. It is the text itself that asserts that *The Vanity of*

Human Wishes represents one world—the ultimately serene world of the idealized moralist—the *Prayers and Meditations* another, and the unmediated world of Johnson's speech yet a third, all in antithetical relation to one another. It asserts this through its discontinuities, its obeying of the laws of quotation and narration and dramatic or dialogue form; and in the moment we recognize this assertion we see Boswell's perception of Johnson begin to dissolve.

Antithetical pressures are at work as well within the sphere of idealizing perceptions of Johnson, the sphere of Burke, Reynolds, Goldsmith, Langton, and other members of the inner circle. For every such perception dwells within a separate world of consciousness, and every such world exists in antithetical relation to every other in the *Life*. Thus Boswell, after giving it as his opinion that Johnson's ludicrous convulsions are "of the nature of that distemper called St. Vitus's Dance" (that is, that they are merely physical in origin), introduces the opposing opinion of Sir Joshua Reynolds: "'Those motions or tricks of Dr. Johnson are improperly called convulsions. . . . my opinion is, that it proceeded from a habit which he had indulged himself in, of accompanying his thoughts with certain untoward actions, and those actions always appeared to me as if they were meant to reprobate some part of his past conduct. Whenever he was not engaged in conversation, such thoughts were sure to rush into his mind'" (I.144).

Once again, it is the discontinuity of the narrative, signaled by quotation marks and textual space, that reminds us that Boswell's perception of Johnson, and Reynolds's, exist in the relation of world to antiworld. For it is not simply that Boswell's impulse to explain Johnson's convulsions as a physical disorder follows just the same pattern as his impulse to explain Johnson's private misery as an illness or hypochondriac disorder, or that Sir Joshua's explanation is less idealizing as at least allowing for a darker explanation of Johnson's misery, but that the instability of Boswell's entire conception of Johnson is revealed in the moment that Reynolds gestures, however indirectly, toward the gloomy world of the *Prayers and Meditations*. Yet Reynolds's own conception of Johnson, as denying in its own way the awful reality of that world, is in its turn unstable.

Throughout the *Life*, whenever we encounter one or another of the secondary accounts of Johnson interpolated in the text, our usual model of narrative structure invites us to speak of a multiplication of perspectives, of different angles of perception converging on an identical object. Yet all such accounts (and now Boswell's own narration figures simply as an account of Johnson occupying more space than the others) exist in the same relation to one another as does Boswell's to Reynolds's in this instance, as separate worlds of consciousness in a system of antiworlds. Whether it is the voice of Reynolds we hear, or of Langton or Beauclerk or Campbell or Boswell himself, each threatens the dissolution of all the others.

Yet our sense that we have passed through an intermediate space when we pass through the sphere of idealizing perceptions to the realm of the *Prayers and Meditations* is explained, as we have seen, by a logic of structure that locates these perceptions between the outer periphery occupied by the world of Johnson's moral writings and the central world of the *Prayers and Meditations*. The inner periphery, in a manner of speaking the last point of arrest before we reach the center of the *Life*, is occupied by Johnson's letters and letters to him, an epistolary narrative with no plot beyond the transactions of separate minds in the world. Like a self-contained narrative in epistolary form, like *Clarissa* or *Humphrey Clinker* without the telos of events we call plot, letters in the *Life* embody a separate world.

To speak of an epistolary world within the *Life* is to raise just the sort of problem we encounter in epistolary fiction. For what seems to be a stable structure—consciousness speaking to consciousness through the medium of written language—is in fact radically unstable. Just as Boswell or Dr. Dodd or Mrs. Thrale address their letters not to Johnson but to their own conceptions of Johnson, all enclosed within a dialogue of their own making, Johnson addresses a world of imaginary correspondents, not Boswell or Mrs. Thrale but the Boswell and Mrs. Thrale he imagines to exist. The epistolary world contained within the *Life* does not dissolve but implodes upon itself, leaving us to gaze directly into the world revealed in the *Prayers and Meditations*.

The world of the *Prayers and Meditations* takes as its center the helpless cry of the supplicant on the dark edge of despair. Around this center revolve meditation and prayer in various other forms: prayer, for instance, as occasional utterance, as when Johnson prays before beginning the study of law or going into politics with H———; prayer as resolution, as in Johnson's endless schemes to regulate his life; prayer as self-examination, as in his annual review, usually during the Easter season, of the past year of his life. Through all this there are what Boswell calls "intervals of quiet, composure, and gladness," and in such intervals the gloomy center is obscured to our view. Yet there is a more powerful reason why that center is so often obscure.

Though one can explain the *Prayers and Meditations* only as a separate world with the *Life*, as one world among others in a vast system of antithetical relations, there is a sense in which the *Life* as a whole works to reject, almost as an organism rejects tissue it recognizes as foreign, the world they reveal. This is why, for instance, Boswell so often quotes only a phrase or so from those prayers expressing a naked sense of misery or despair ("in 1777, it appears from this 'Prayers and Meditations,' that Johnson suffered much from a mind 'unsettled and perplexed'" [III.98]) or so often buries in a footnote, at a safe textual distance from the main narrative, some dark hint of Johnson's private suffering. It is also the reason that the space occupied by the *Prayers and Meditations* in the text is so often given over to prayer as occasional utterance, as self-examination, as resolution to better regulate life.

When we perceive the helpless cry of the supplicant as the center of this world, then, we are tempted to say that it is the sheer intensity of Johnson's anguish that overwhelms everything else, cuts through all calm meditation and sober resolution to expose a naked center: *"Have mercy upon me, O GOD, have mercy upon me; years and infirmities oppress me, terrour and anxiety beset me. Have mercy upon me, my Creator and my Judge'"* (III.99, italics mine). In such moments we perceive beyond all else a wasteland of the spirit, for this is not prayer but what Tennyson calls an agony of lamentation, "like a wind that shrills / All night in a waste land, where no one comes, / Or hath come, since the making of the world." Yet for all its intensity, its terrible agony of spirit, this is not why the helpless cry occupies the center of the *Prayers and Meditations*, the *Prayers and Meditations* the center of the *Life* as a whole.

The reason we seek is found, rather, in the nature of prayer itself, in the principle of supplication which, as Kenneth Burke has said, is "the most radically grounded aspect of language as a communicative medium." In prayer, says Burke, we "confront the making of two Absolutes: the cry *ab intra*, the solace *ab extra*. And what are the nearest, most *immediately personal* grammatical substitutes for that relationship? Obviously, an 'I' and a 'Thou.'"[4] The brilliant compression of Burke's remarks on prayer may be seen to expand into an entire explanation of the structure of the *Life*, not simply of the *Prayers and Meditations* as the center of that structure, but of the logic governing the series of deconstructions that draws us through a succession of dissolving worlds to the last reality they expose.

The *Prayers and Meditations* lie at the center of the *Life* because they contain within them the double nature of supplication. There is nothing double about the cry *ab intra* ("'years and infirmities oppress me, terrour and anxiety beset me'"), for the meaning of Johnson's private misery lies precisely in the consciousness of his own mind or soul, and "I" seeking to complete itself in communion with a transcendent Thou. Yet we understand the cry *ad extra* ("'Have mercy upon me, my Creator and my Judge'") only when we see its doubleness, hear that it is not only a prayer to God but a prayer that there be a God to whom to pray. To pray that there *be* a God, a Creator and a Judge, is to have nothing to which to pray, and the terror of the cry *ad extra* is then that it becomes a cry into the blankness of the void.

The *Prayers and Meditations* are able to function as the center of the *Life*, then, only because the *Life* as a whole acknowledges only the first dimension of prayer, what Johnson expresses *in* speech when speaking directly to his Creator. What the *Life* utterly denies is the other dimension deriving from the nature of prayer as symbolic action, the cry *ad extra* revealing through the very form of supplication its radically grounded need to complete itself in transcendent communion. Yet the *Prayers and Meditations* embody both modes of signification, and it is because the meaning of prayer as symbolic action cannot ultimately be denied that it remains to haunt the *Life* as a dark dream of blank meaninglessness, a wind that shrills all night in a wasteland where no one comes.

Even to speak of the *Prayers and Meditations* as lying at the center of the *Life* is to return in a new way to the problem of presence and absence from which we began. For the very notion of a center now implies a notion of presence: if the *Prayers and Meditations* function as the center of the *Life*, it will be because there corresponds to them—exists behind them, so to speak, in the way that a person exists as a presence behind his speech— a Johnson somehow more real than all those Johnsons dwelling as idealized conceptions in the consciousness of others. Should there be, behind the *Prayers and Meditations*, not presence but an absence that they do no more than define, the very notion of a center itself dissolves, and we gaze into the *Life* as into a centerless structure, a system of purely antithetical relations in which every world is defined as a world by every other.

As a literary structure, however, the *Life* exists on just these terms. As much as Johnson's writings or his letters or his speech, the *Prayers and Meditations* are only a system of language or discourse, and behind them there exists no Johnson more or less real than any other—behind them there exists, quite simply, nothing at all. Yet the absence they define is not the same as that defined by Johnson's writings or his letters or his speech, and the question that ultimately demands an answer is how an illusion of presence, of a Johnson more real than any other, ended by drawing us to a nonexistent center, a world of private discourse to which nothing and no one corresponds. The notion of a vacuum at the center of the *Life* remains to tease us even when the notion of a center has dissolved.

The answer may be seen to lie in an alternative notion of what constitutes a center—that is, in something like Derrida's notion of a center as what we arbitrarily posit in order to make sense of an otherwise incomprehensible system of elements. The center once posited, organizing and bringing into fixed relations the elements of an otherwise centerless system, the problem of unintelligibility or incomprehension is solved; the relations we seek to explain are suddenly there, and nothing remains but to explore them. The illusion of a Johnsonian presence behind the *Life*, and the logic of deconstruction that draws us toward the *Prayers and Meditations* as toward a center, can ultimately be explained in these terms alone.

The notion of an outer periphery or foreground in the *Life* begins precisely in an illusion of presence. The invisible monarchy of Courtenay's poem, the disembodied moralist who draws Boswell and Reynolds and Langton into the presence of an "actual" Johnson, are illusions in just the same sense as the notion of a Johnsonian presence behind the *Prayers and Meditations* is an illusion. To say that Boswell's idealizing perception of Johnson as a moralist dissolves in the light of antithetical relation, then, is nothing other than to say that we recognize the illusion as an illusion: the serene and elevated moralist he carries in his mind when he comes down from Edinburgh to London in his twenty-second year exists only because, to understand Johnson's writings as a world of discourse, he has had to supply a presence behind them, to posit an arbitrary center that is not there.

As with Boswell's narration, the separate world of his consciousness, so with every other world in the *Life*. The logic of deconstruction that draws us inward toward the *Prayers and Meditations*, through Boswell's account of Johnson and secondary accounts, through the world represented in Johnson's writings and the world of his speech or conversation, through the epistolary world of Johnson's letters and letters to him, demands at every stage that we recognize the illusion of presence as an illusion, that we see absence where a Boswell or a Reynolds or a Burke has imagined a presence. When we arrive at the *Prayers and Meditations*, at that unmediated center at which the *Life* enacts the agony of an "I" seeking desperately to complete itself in transcendental communion with a Thou, the illusion of presence, never more powerful, remains no less an illusion.

To understand the illusion, however, to see that there is only absence where the text promises a Johnsonian presence lying outside or beyond itself, is ultimately to grasp the meaning of the *Life of Johnson*. For as a biographical narrative the *Life* undertakes an impossible task, to give to the world a Johnson not identical with itself, to "preserve" Johnson, as Boswell says, in its pages, to allow us to penetrate through its structure to a presence that cannot be contained in but only represented by language. To discover at the end of the *Life* that there is nothing but the *Life* itself, that the biographical presence is only absence, is to discover the impossibility of its undertaking.

The subject of the *Life of Johnson*, we have always wanted to say, is Samuel Johnson, and by this we have wanted to mean something uncomfortably like that imaginary presence who exists only in an absence defined by the *Life* as a whole. Our sense of discomfort disappears, perhaps, only when we see that the true subject of the *Life*, as of all biographies, is the impossibility of the biographical enterprise, not presence but the illusion of presence ultimately revealed as an illusion, the dilemma of narrative trying and failing to reach through to a world beyond itself. To say that the *Life* is the greatest of biographies is to say that it confronts this dilemma more directly, works through the impossibility of its task more completely, than any other.

Notes

1. References are to James Boswell, *The Life of Samuel Johnson, LL.D*, 6 vols. ed. G. B. Hill, rev. L. F. Powell (Oxford: Clarendon, 1934, 1950).

2. Edward Bulwer Lytton, *England and the English*, quoted in Walter E. Houghton, *The Victorian Frame of Mind* (New Haven: Yale University Press, 1957) p. 2.

3. J. Hillis Miller, "The Critic as Host," *Critical Inquiry*, 3 (1977), 434.

4. Kenneth Burke, "Post-Poesque Derivation of a Terministic Cluster," *Critical Inquiry*, 4 (1977), 215–16.

"Our Unnatural No-voice":
The Heroic Epistle,
Pope, and Women's Gothic

GILLIAN BEER

Pope's *Eloisa to Abelard* (1717), it has often been noted, presages in its imagery the psychological landscapes of the Gothic novel.

> In these deep solitudes and awful cells,
> Where heav'nly-pensive, contemplation dwells,
> And ever-musing melancholy reigns;
> What means this tumult in a Vestal's veins?[1]

Eloisa, immured in her nunnery, cannot obliterate the images of passionate love which are intensified by her solitude and flare out anew from the symbols of religious ecstasy.

> When from the Censer clouds of fragrance roll,
> And swelling organs lift the rising soul;
> One thought of thee puts all the pomp to flight,
> Priest, Tapers, Temples, swim before my sight,
> In seas of flame my plunging soul is drown'd,
> While Altars blaze, and Angels tremble round.
>
> (l. 271)

From *The Yearbook of English Studies*, Vol. 12, ed. G. K. Hunter and C. J. Rawson (Coventry: Modern Humanities Research Association, 1981), pp. 125–51.

Perception, sensation, and objects collapse into each other. Pope's poem powerfully expands a system of symbolism, necessary to Gothic experience, which makes little distinction between external and internal events. The heroine's identity, always in tumult, finds itself beset equally by the intransigence and the malleability of the objective world: intransigent in its resistance to her desires and needs; malleable in the speed with which objects succumb to symbol and become vagrant elements in her own imaginative ordering, according too closely to offer any stability or any issue out from the self.

The landscape of enclosure, melancholy, and silence in Ann Radcliffe's *The Italian* is like that of Eloisa's "deep solitudes and awful cells": "solitary passages" and "melancholy awe." The architectural features of the imprisoning monastery "seemed as if menacing the unhappy Ellena with hints of future suffering." Once entered, she is conducted by a silent nun:

> The nun, still silent, conducted her through many solitary passages, where not even a distant foot-fall echoed, and whose walls were roughly painted with subjects indicatory of the severe superstitions of the place, tending to inspire melancholy awe. Ellena's hope of pity vanished as her eyes glanced over these symbols of the disposition of the inhabitants, and on the countenance of the nun characterised by gloomy malignity, which seemed ready to inflict upon others some portion of the unhappiness she herself suffered. As she glided forward with soundless step, her white drapery, floating along these solemn avenues, and her hollow features touched with the mingled light and shadow which the partial rays of a taper she held occasioned, she seemed like a spectre newly risen from the grave, rather than a living being.[2]

In Ann Radcliffe's description the malignancy of the nun's privation, of purity withered to spectral whiteness, corresponds to Ellena's unvoiced (and unvoiceable) dreads. She is reft away from her lover, sequestered in a hostile community dedicated to sexual penury. Everything that she perceives in this unspeaking labyrinth "where not even a distant foot-fall echoed" expresses the loss of "living being," the stultification of erotic powers. Light survives only as "the partial rays of a taper."

> The Waxen Taper which I burne by Night,
> With the dull vap'rie dimnesse mocks my Sight,
> As though the Dampe which hinders the cleere Flame,
> Came from my Breath, in that Night of my Shame.[3]

Those lines are from Rosamond's epistle to Henry the Second in Michael Drayton's *Englands Heroicall Epistles* (1619). The qualities of experience and rhetoric which link Pope's poem to Gothic sensibility are not merely his own invention. In this essay I shall argue that we shall better understand the vehemence, the particular kind of licence, and the preoccupation with women's experience, which characterize late eighteenth-century and Romantic Gothic, if we set it in relation to the long-admired but now largely forgotten poetic genre of which Pope's poem is in an outstanding example: the genre of heroic epistle. Already at the beginning of the eighteenth century (1703) David Crauford's *Ovidius Britannicus* moves heroic epistle closer to the flattering obscurity of Gothic romance in his fictional provenance for the six epistles of Hermes and Amestris, two "Persons of Quality." Crauford claims to have discovered their affair in "a great many Musty Papers, very difficult to be read and understood, in an old, dark Closet, that had not been opened twenty years before."[4]

The heroic epistle as an active form has vanished from our literature. Its remote descendants are to be found today, perhaps, in works such as Elizabeth Smart's *By Grand Central Station I sat Down and Wept*, Menotti's one-woman opera *The Telephone*, or in some of Dorothy Parker's short stories and poems, such as the sonnet "I know I have been happiest by your side," with the delicately Gothic innuendo of its conclusion:

> Yet this the need of woman, this her curse:
> To range her little gifts, and give, and give,
> Because the throb of giving's sweet to bear.
> To you, who never begged me vows or verse,
> My gift shall be my absence while I live,
> But after that, my dear, I cannot swear.[5]

In English literature up to the beginning of the nineteenth century, from Chaucer to Byron, the heroic epistle was much practised and admired. During the sixteenth and seventeenth centuries its generative text, Ovid's *Heroides*, was probably the most highly valued of all his works, and valued particularly for its moral as well as its artistic properties. So Henry Peacham in *The Compleat Gentleman* (1622) wrote: "Among his Workes his Epistles are most worthy your reading, being his neatest peeces, every where embellished with excellent and wise sentences."[6] Erasmus had praised the chastity of the work, and it was a school-book for many generations.[7] Thackeray's acute sense of historical period is evident in the little scene in *Henry Esmond* when young Harry comes to "the lady of Castlewood" with his verse-imitation of some of Ovid's *Heroides:*

> About this time young Esmond, who had a knack of stringing verses, turned some of Ovid's epistles into rhymes, and brought them to his lady for her delectation. Those which treated of forsaken women touched her immensely, Harry remarked; and when (Œnone called after Paris, and Medea bade Jason come back again, the lady of Castlewood sighed, and said she thought that part of the verses was the most pleasing. Indeed she would have chopped up the dean, her old father, in order to bring her husband back again. But her beautiful Jason was gone, as beautiful Jasons will go, and the poor enchantress had never a spell to keep him.   (Chapter 9)[8]

But it is not only Thackeray's sense of historical period which is evident here: the commentary grasps the paradox which gave and continues to give heroic epistles their power. They were at once highly eloquent rhetorical artifacts, and the direct, painful representation of human loss and desire, particularly women's loss and desire. If the narrative pattern prepared women for martyrdom, the rhetoric restored power to the powerless. In heroic epistle everything that may be said *is* said, and said well. The one pain the form does not include is that of *esprit d'escalier*. In Gothic, the problem is rather to find a language for what *cannot* be said about sexual knowledge and experience. Heroic epistle offers tropes, signs, gestures, which can be deciphered without the intervention of the Gothic heroine.

Yet there is always something incommensurate between the expressive, endless outpouring of the dramatic character in heroic epistle and the reader's linguistic gratification, and that incommensurateness is in itself disturbing. Daniel's Octavia ends her epistle to Antony by writing:

> But whither am I carried all this while
> Beyond my scope, and know not when to cease?
> Words still with my increasing sorrowes grow:
> I know t'have said too much but not enow.[9]

Drayton's Queene Isabel concludes her epistle to Mortimer:

> What should I say? My Griefes doe still renew,
> And but begin, when I should bid Adiew.
> Few by my Words, but manifold my Woe,
> And still I stay, the more I strive to goe.
>   (I. 159)

"Saying too much but not enough" is the problematic expressed in this poetry: how can the self which has lost mutuality ever discover its own limits or escape its own confines? How can language substitute for the body? What kind of voice can women discover in a world which instructs them to be silent? What language will not be misconstrued?

> Thinke you not then, poore Women had not need
> Be well advis'd, to write what Men should read;
> When being silent, but to move awry,
> Doth often bring us into obliquie?

So writes Alice Countesse of Salisburie to the Blacke Prince in Drayton.[10] Yet although even gesture is dangerous, still they write. They are active and declarative, risking the reification of language, and thereby at least avoiding that other reification described in Butler's *Hudibras!*

> Shee that with *Poetry* is won,
> Is but a *Desk* to write upon.[11]

Here in contrast the women control pen, ink, and utterance.

The heroic epistle may be, for the reader, consolatory more than distressing: our participation in the heroine's extremity allows us to enjoy a commanding rhetoric. Moreover these poems do not admit the diminution of passion. Their heroines are not concerned with survival and the makeshifts of survival. They include rancor and rebellion but resolutely leave out of account that final desuetude of emotion which Thackeray goes on to analyze:

She had been my lord's chief slave and blind worshipper. Some women bear farther than this, and submit not only to neglect but to unfaithfulness too—but here this lady's allegiance had failed her. Her spirit rebelled and disowned any more obedience. First she had to bear in secret the passion of losing the adored object; then to get a further initiation, and to find this worshipped being was but a clumsy idol: then to admit the silent truth, that it was she who was superior, and not the monarch her master: that she had thoughts which his brains could never master, and was the better of the two; quite separate from my lord although tied to him, and bound as almost all people (save a very happy few) to work all her life alone.   *(Henry Esmond*, pp. 96–97)

The sad *extent* of life still to be lived after love has failed is part of a different kind of truthfulness from that of heroic epistle.

Heroic epistle has the obduracy of hope and passion at their final stretch before despair. It never represents the possibility of the woman's whole self reviving after the breakdown of sexual love: it could never, therefore, be called entirely a feminist form of literature. It is, moreover, largely the creation of male authors. It may function as much to exorcise sexual guilt as to sustain it. Nevertheless, the attempt to represent, inhabit, and accord fullest importance to the erotic experience and expressive powers of women means that it is a form of literature peculiarly dedicated to the value of such experience, and one which over the centuries helped to shape women's apprehension of their own potentialities and constraints. If it suggested that women could find the apex of significance for their lives only in love, it suggested too that the experience of the slighted, the abandoned, the powerless, mattered.

During the eighteenth century, the story of Yarico and Inkle was several times celebrated in heroic epistle.[12] This is a tale which tells far more than it knows. It takes the form of a verse-letter written by an innocent Indian maid, Yarico, to her European lover, Inkle. After an idyll on her island when she protected him and he taught her to read and write English, he not only abandons her but sells her into slavery. When she tells him she is pregnant, he raises the slave-price. Her lover gives her his language and takes away her freedom. Her entry into language takes her out of innocence and into contradiction and privation: the colonizing male sells her into slavery. The tale gives form to a double unease and guilt: that concerning the exploitation of women, and that concerning the ransacking and annexing of new dominions and the breaking of faith with the people who lived there. Implicitly, the identity of the two processes is recognized. The black slave-woman is left with nothing but the white man's language, and with that she can protest, but not find freedom.

The quasi-historical fiction of Yarico is a particularly striking example of the way heroic epistle could disturb, and could claim space for those whose experience was usually brushed aside. In Ovid, those left behind when the picaresque hero moved on to his next adventure turned out to have a significance as full (fuller while we read the poem) as the absent hero. Œnone or Ariadne come to mean more than Paris or Theseus. The rhetoric accorded to the women is assertive and assured. This assertiveness is presented without irony or demurral. The heroines are capable of excoriating analysis of their own needs and those of their longed-for lovers. And in Ovid, at least, the language also sustains a sense of the wonderful, of *jouissance,* and of the joyousness in love. Few of his heroines, in contrast to those of Drayton or to Pope's Eloisa, are entrammeled by sexual guilt.

And even in those later writers it is separation which allows guilt to thrive, not what has been shared.

So little is the form now discussed that before going further I should perhaps characterize it more directly: heroic epistles are, most typically, poems written in the form of letters from famous historical or mythological women to their absent lovers.[13] Sometimes there is a pair of letters between woman and man. The poems are never directly autobiographical. They are never spoken to any one present. They are never addressed to confidantes. They are never in prose.

Chaucer had warmed and mediated heroic epistle into a new form by shifting it from first person to third and turning the tales into eulogy. In *The House of Fame* he recommends his reader to read "the Epistle of Ovyde" to discover for himself of Dido "what that she wroot or that she dyde." In Chaucer's summary of the *Heroides* the treachery of men is the motive force, but in Ovid all space is given to the expression of women, so that their emotion is the generative power of the poem. In *The Legend of Good Women* Chaucer makes the telling of women's stories the means by which he defends himself when arraigned before the court of love on the charge of having brought women into disrepute. The rancor and extremity of heroic epistle vanish from his language: the whole is softened towards pathos and regret. Chaucer holds and distances these women's tales by his language of pity and example. Cleopatra, Thisbe, Dido, Hypsipyle and Medea, Lucretia, Ariadne, Phyllis and Hypermnestra, are martyrs for love. In contrast, Ovid's legendary women and Drayton's historical ones are insurgent, breaking out of the bounds of summary and litany into the present. Their passion is unassuageable because it is not yet over. The first-person-present is essential to the meaning of the form.

Dramatic monologue in the nineteenth century is in a curious way a riposte to the older form: almost all the speakers are men (Ulysses or Fra Lippo Lippi or the Bishop ordering his tomb). The speakers address a present listener instead of writing in silence to an absent lover. In dramatic monologue the listener within the poem may be contingent or incidental. In heroic epistle the person to whom the poem is addressed (who may or may not receive and read it) is its longed-for subject. The letter is always a substitute for what is wanted. The whole sequence of the *Heroides* opens with a letter from Penelope to Ulysses which begins thus:

Hanc tua Penelope lento tibi mittit, Ulixe—
nil mihi rescribas tu tamen; ipse veni!

"Do not write back: come yourself!" Drayton's Lady Geraldine ends her letter by referring to this same passage:

> Then, as **ULYSSES** Wife, write I to thee,
> Make no reply, but come thy selfe to mee.[14]

"Come" is the most important word (even, finally, the *only* important word) in heroic epistle. The entire rhetoric seeks to realize its meaning. "Come! with thy looks, thy words, relieve my woe," writes Eloisa (l. 119); "Come thou, my father, brother, husband friend!" (l. 152); "Come *Abelard!* for what hast thou to dread?" (l. 257); "Come, if thou dar'st, all charming as thou art!" (l. 281); "Ah come not, write not, think not once of me" (l. 291). The struggle in Pope's poem to overcome earthly passion reaches its climax when the word "come" ceases to be her cry to Abelard and becomes the ghost's invitation to Eloisa to embrace death:

> Come, sister come! (it said, or seem'd to say)
> Thy place is here, sad sister come away!
>
> (l. 309)

The secondary sexual sense of the word in English remains always secondary. Restored mutual love is the goal always just beyond the possible in these poems. Language is conditional, the outcome of loss and a part of separation: *"Make no reply, but come thy selfe to mee."*

The only major work of criticism on heroic epistle is Heinrich Dörrie's excellent *Der Heroische Brief* (Berlin, 1968) which presents and categorizes the diverse manifestations of the form in European literature since Ovid. Dörrie's work is invaluable, particularly because of the wealth of material that he brings together. Inevitably, in a work of such historical scope, his discussion of individual poems is not extensive, and his account of heroic epistles in English is concerned to describe rather than to quote or analyze. He does not comment on its particular function of giving expression to women. Remarkably few critics of Pope discuss *Eloisa to Abelard* as heroic epistle beyond a bald reference to Ovid. Reuben Brower is an honorable exception, and in his analysis of the poem in *Pope: The Poetry of Allusion* he pays full homage to Pope's alertness to Ovid's prosodic effects. Patricia Meyer Spacks on the other hand ignores both the models for the poem, the Eloisa-Abelard letters and the heroic epistle form, and takes Eloisa personally to task for being over-absorbed in her own experience. With moralizing scepticism she suggests that "the fact that Eloisa finds such enormous emotional power in her own experience may make it difficult for the reader to find as much."[15] Certainly the heroic epistle as a form gives no ground to those readers who demand, as she does, "a judging voice" and think passion "magnification."

The seriousness with which the figures in heroic epistle take their own emotion is the condition of the form's creativity; neither irony nor levity can be used within its reading codes. The irony of the reader's role *as reader* is, however, important: we read a missive not addressed to us and of whose outcome we know more than the writer. This is an irony of situation rather than of language, and one which entraps rather than releases. The rhetoric strives to re-make in language a succession of moments which can never be wrought to happen again. The poems are ceremonies of passion. At times, in the face of the wracked obsessionality of feeling in these works, any reader may feel the need to take refuge in mirth or moralism. But in doing so we obliterate the experience offered.

What is the special nature of that experience and what are its typical conditions? It may be questioned, for example, why I refer to it as a form dedicated to women's feelings, since there occur quite frequently in later heroic epistles exchanges of letters between women and their lovers, and even in the *Heroides* there are examples of such exchanges. But in Ovid the first fifteen epistles are addressed by women to their lovers (Penelope to Ulysses, Phyllis to Demophoon, Briseis to Achilles, Phaedra to Hippolytus, Œnone to Paris, Hypsipyle to Jason, Dido to Aeneas, Hermione to Orestes, Deianira to Hercules, Ariadne to Theseus, Canace to Macareus, Medea to Jason, Laodamia to Protesilaus, Hypermnestra to Lyceus, and Sappho to Phaon). There are no replies. The last six letters are pairs (Paris to Helen, Helen to Paris; Leander to Hero, Hero to Leander; Acontius to Cydippe, Cydippe to Acontius). Paris and Acontius both seek to seduce: the action of the exchange is the delicate revisions of feelings experienced by Helen and Cydippe as they veer between rejection and inclination. These three exchanges may have been a response by Ovid to Sabinus, who had provided replies to his earlier solitary writers.

Pope in *Eloisa to Abelard* returned to the strict Ovidian form. He ignored the rest of the correspondence between Abelard and Eloisa and concentrated on her letters alone, drawing mainly on the first of them but with some material from later ones. The matrix of emotion and language is Eloisa's. The "Preface" to the 1785 edition of John Hughes's translation

(1713) comments on the French translation from the original Latin of the letters:

> This translation is much applauded, but who was the author of it is not certainly known. Monsieur Beyle says he has been informed it was done by a woman: and perhaps he thought no one beside could have entered so thoroughly into the passion and tenderness of such writings, for which that sex seems to have a more natural disposition than the other. This may be judged of by the *Letters* themselves, among which those of Heloise are the most moving. The Master seems in this particular to be excelled by the scholar. (p. iv)

The "natural disposition" to "passion and tenderness" in women was assumed, represented, and also fostered by the long tradition of heroic epistle. These are not expressions of virginal or purely unrequited love. They are poems stemming from sexual experience and mutuality. Though the body and the identity of the beloved are absent, they are *known*. The central topic of heroic epistle is loss of plenitude: the breakdown of mutual love is the point at which language enters.

> Oh happy state! when souls each other draw,
> When love is liberty, and nature, law:
> All then is full, possessing, and possest,
> No craving Void left aking in the breast:
> Ev'n thought meets thought ere from the lips it part,
> And each warm wish springs mutual from the heart.
> This sure is bliss (if bliss on earth there be)
> And once the lot of *Abelard* and me.
>
> (*Eloisa to Abelard*, l. 91)

Opposites are congruous, and the line ignores any sense of paradox: "When love is liberty, and nature, law." The "craving void" must be filled by language. The reciprocity of male and female underlies all these poems; they are lost dialogues. Feeling does not meet response from feeling, and so becomes gigantic, not shaped by reply. The grotesque amplification of heroic epistle shows emotions ballooning outward to fill empty space, language unmitigated by response. These are overweening poems, seeking to encompass what cannot be contained. The unknowability of the other, the loved one, is here given the form of distance, estrangement, removal, silence.

The characters are mythical or historical. We can be assumed already to know roughly what happened to them before we begin to read. The reading transforms the statuesque into the flux of emotion and language. In one way heroic epistles are like proto-historical novels. We are elected to intimacy with the great. In Drayton's *England's Heroicall Epistles*, the most extensive re-working of the form in our literature, each exchange (between, say, Matilda and King John, Henry Howard and the Lady Geraldine, Elinor Cobham and Duke Humphrey) is prefaced by an account of the historical facts and supplemented by end-notes. Drayton said that he hoped to mitigate the "braynish," that is, the erotic, by his accompanying historical commentary. The authenticity of situation is important to the form, in part because, as I have suggested, it closes up and determines our reading. We know what will happen—what has happened—although the writer does not. The paradox of summary fore-knowledge and of participation in the gyrations of expression at once burdens us with double awareness and exempts us from the characters' uncertainty. The heroic epistle has always a dual recipient: the lover within the fiction to whom they are addressed, the anonymous reader outside the fiction who reads them. The pressure of the first-person address is outward, to a named partner. The "writer" occupies the entire space of the poem, and yet these are dramatic, not lyric, poems. The covert author at once declares and conceals himself in the rhetoric with which the single writer is endowed.

Heroic epistle takes, as its occasion, pain, and seeks to represent the most deeply intimate and private knowledge in a highly conscious and achieved rhetoric. But this is not merely a captious super-imposition of language: language is the product of the dramatic dilemma. It has become necessary because the lovers are separated, but it is always a second-best, a substitute. Within the dramatic ordering of the poems the rhetoric is a means to make the past again at one with the present, to make it anew.

> But oh, forgive me Lord, it is not I,
> Nor doe I boast of this, but learne to die:
> Whilst we were as ourselves, conjoyned then,
> Nature to Nature, now an Alien.
> (Drayton, "Lady Jane Gray to Gilford Dudley," l. 91)

The poems are attempts at action in that they are attempts to *move*, to bring the lover back. The reader is the weakened substitute for that lover, as language is for presence. These are not soliloquies. They are acts of invocation, seeking even magically, through eloquence, to seal up the gap between body and language, between enactment and desire, between memory and the present moment. Briseis writes:

> est aliquid, collum solitis tetigisse lacertis,
> praesentisque oculos admonuisse sinu.
> sis licet inmitis matrisque ferocior undis,
> ut taceam, lacrimis conminuere meis.
>
> (*Heroides*, III. 131)

> There is a sweeter eloquence in kisses,
> If I incircle thee within mine armes,
> My close embraces are like powerful charmes:
> My naked breasts being in thy view laid open,
> Will soone perswade thee, though no word be spoken.
> If thou wert like the Sea, voyd of compassion,
> My silent teares would move commiseration.
>
> (Saltonstall's translation)[16]

Medea and Drayton's Eleanor actually practice witchcraft: "carmina" (charms) and "cantata" (incantations), *Heroides*, VI. 83–84. In all these outpourings, moreover, language is used like a charm; the vehement exercise of will by the powerless forces language to be power. But that power is never sufficient. The gap between body and language is not sealed, and the activity of the poems calls attention always to lack as well as to magnificence. The heroic epistle in the hands of Ovid, Drayton, Daniel, Dryden, and Pope, as well as in the hands of less-known figures such as Anne Francis, with her letters from Charlotte to Werther, Leah to Jacob, Dido to Iarbas, or of the anonymous Countess with her epistle from the deserted child of nature Yarico to her treacherous civilized lover Inkle, always has the same basic emphasis: the privation of women and the sumptuousness of their imaginative life. Silent writing and declamatory language figure these qualities. They were to fuel the libertine reading-pleasures of the Gothic.

Samuel Daniel's poem, "A Letter from Octavia to Marcus Antonius," epitomizes one force of feeling explored within the heroic epistle: that of constraint gazing on liberty. Why should women be confined while men range free? "What? are there barres for us, no bounds for you?": Octavia describes not only physical confinement, but the imposed ideal of silence for women. The women in heroic epistle do not speak, they *write;* and they write in the main to correspondents who, they fear, will neither read nor pay attention. Their language acknowledges distance. It is not that of everyday happening, of the circumstantial, but of persuasion and anger. It typically conveys what Geoffrey Tillotson calls "a militant melancholy." Octavia describes men's liberty as opposed to women's *"interdicted"* state:

> Thrices happy you, in whom it is no fault,
> To know, to speake, to doe, and to be wise:
> Whose words have credit, and whose deedes, though naught,
> Must yet be made to seeme farre otherwise:
> You can be onely heard, whilst we are taught
> To hold our peace, and not to exercise
> The powers of our best parts, because your parts
> Have with our freedome robb'd us of our hearts.
>
> (*Works*, I, 126)

Women's words are not credited. Only men are heard. Women are taught to be silent and not to exercise the "powers of their best parts": their minds, imagination, and judgment. Worst of all, their habit of imprisonment has put them in thrall to love. The sense of "parts" in Daniel's lines shifts from intellectual capability to the physical and sexual body. In Ovid, Hero made the same complaint to Leander: men have many activities—hunting, husbanding, dining, fishing, the pleasures of the market-place, (ll. 9–14)—but for the woman, sequestered from all distraction, there is nothing left to *do* but love:

> his mihi summotae, vel si minus acriter urar,
> quod faciam, superest praeter amare nihil.
>
> (*Heroides*, XIX. 15)

The famous stanza in *Don Juan*, "Man's love is of man's life a thing apart," is a deliberate allusion to these earlier statements. Julia's letter to Don Juan in which the stanza appears (Canto I, Stanzas 192–97) is a heroic epistle.

> Man's love is of man's life a thing apart,
>   'Tis woman's whole existence; man may range
> The court, camp, church, the vessel, and the mart,
>   Sword, gown, gain, glory, offer in exchange
> Pride, fame, ambition, to fill up his heart,
>   And few there are whom these can not estrange;
> Men have all these resources, we but one,
> To love again, and be again undone.[17]

Instead of the asperity of Daniel's Octavia or the imaginative participation
of Hero, Julia's letter has a voluptuous and sentimental majesty which sets
women at the service of men. And in *Don Juan* heroic epistle is drained of
its power of protest by being made part of a much longer work, the provenance of the letter diminishing its contents:

> This note was written upon gilt-edged paper
> With a neat little crow-quill, slight and new.

The emphasis upon confinement in earlier heroic epistle was part of its
insurrectionary potential. In another satiric heroic epistle, one which concludes Samuel Butler's *Hudibras*, the lady puts the point with cheerful
militancy:

> If Women had not Interven'd,
> How soon had Mankind had an end?
> And that it is in *Being* yet,
> To us alone, you are *in Debt*.
> Then where's your Liberty of Choyce,
> And our unnatural No-voyce?
>
> (l. 243)

Voice and choice are more than a rhyme: heroic epistle is a way of putting
into language the *"unnatural No-voice"* of silenced women.

A state of physical confinement (in a nunnery, on a desolate island, in the
Tower) is common to the heroines of heroic epistle as it is also later to the
sequestered heroines of Gothic fiction. The bars of the quiescent self,
unable and not daring to express, are figured as cages, caverns, and castles.
Or, more directly, as prisons. Daniel's Octavia continues:

> We, in this prison of ourselves confin'd,
> Must here shut up with our own passions live,
> Turn'd in upon us, and denied to find
> The vent of outward meanes that might relieve:
> That they alone must take up all our mind,
> And no room left us, but to think and grieve:
> Yet oft our narrowed thoughts looke more direct
> Then your loose wisdomes born with wild neglect.
>
> (*Works*, I. 127)

The passionate silence of the oppressed is represented in the word
"prison."

Matilda in Eliza Parson's *The Castle of Wolfenbach* reads an inscription written on a window with a diamond which again sets forth the problem of silence and voice (Matilda in Drayton's *Heroicall Epistles* had taken refuge from the intruding King John in a nunnery and hoped at first "still to have been mute | Onely by Silence to repell thy Sute"). In *The Castle of Wolfenbach* an unknown woman has written on the glass:

> I am dumb, as solemn sorrow ought to be;
> Could my griefs speak, my tale I'd tell to thee.
> In another place these lines were written;
> A wife, a mother—sweet endearing ties!
> Torn from my arms, and heedless of my cries;
> Here I am doomed to waste my wretched life,
> No more a mother—a discarded wife.[18]

The anonymity which distinguishes the Gothic from heroic epistle here creeps further in: the nameless writer offers to an unknown reader a cryptic account of her griefs, which yet must breach the dumbness held to be proper to grief. The room looks out only on blank walls and distant mountains. There is no middle distance in which action could take place.

The impossibility of action, or even of speech, "the vent of outward meanes," gives the obsessional drive to the language of the heroic epistle, a drive which underpins the bravura variety of its rhetorical devices. What Margaret Anne Doody writes of Eloisa could equally apply to all the heroines of heroic epistle: "There is no need to ask about meaning or sense aside from the psychological. Eloisa need not be asked to do anything in the objective world because she cannot. There is no event in the poem: the poem is Eloise, that passive victim and active dreamer."[19]

But "the psychological" is underpinned by abiding social habits and assumptions about women. That is *why* they cannot "do anything in the objective world." The letter and death are the only two possible forms of action: sometimes the two occur almost simultaneously. The illustration to Saltonstall's seventeenth-century translation of Ovid pictures Dido sitting at her desk writing, her pen in her right hand, her dagger in her left. And Canace writes to her brother and lover Macareus that if her words are illegible it is because they are stained with her blood. She describes the triangle typical of the body in the iconography of these poems:

> dextra tenet calamum, strictum tenet altera ferrum,
> et iacet in gremio charta soluta meo.
> *(Heroides*, XI. 3)

("My right hand holds the pen, the other hand a drawn sword, and the paper lies spread out *in my lap*," "in gremio.") Pen, sword, and paper: within this strict geometry a frantic voiding of the self is expressed in the poems, which are simultaneously complaints and elegies. But alongside that wayward eager onrush which is always "saying too much and not enough" there is also the attempt to *stay* experience, to make it hold. This finds expression in a number of ways: through the use of apothegm, through place, and through dreams, all of them gnomic condensations of experience.

For a heroine like Drayton's Rosamond, entrapped by sexual guilt, there is no way out of the toils of emotion: world and self grow equally intricate and disproportionate. She writes to Henry the Second from her hiding-place at Woodstock that all other women avoid her:

> Well knew'st thou what a monster I would be,
> When thou didst build this Labyrinth for me,
> Whose strange meanders turning ev'ry way
> Be like the course wherein my youth did stray;
> Only a clue doth guide me out and in,
> But yet still walke I circular in sinne.
>
> (l. 87)

Drayton's annotation insists upon both physical place and allegorical significance. He says of the Cretan labyrinth: "Some have held it to have been an Allegorie of Mans Life: true it is, that the Comparison will hold; for what liker to a Labyrinth, then the Maze of life? But it is affirmed by Antiquitie, that there was indeed such a Building; though Dedalus being a name applied to the Workmans excellencie, make it suspected: for Dedalus is nothing else but, Ingenious, or Artificiall.... Rosamonds Labyrinth, whose Ruines, together with her Well, being paved with square Stone in the bottome, and also her Tower, from which the Labyrinth did runne" are still remaining (*Works*, II, 138–39). Heroic epistle is always held at a point of equipoise between fiction and history. The highly conscious referential mode of these texts, with their habit of citing models, alluding to forerunners, and referring to other mythical or historical figures as models, reifies experience but also claims a heroic equality for the experience of the individual.

The terror of the reflexive is the central terror of heroic epistle, as it largely is of Gothic literature. The poems attempt to represent and to outgo enclosure, "circular in sinne." In the case of Drayton's Lady Jane

Gray, for example, the enclosure is literal (she is imprisoned in the Tower) and psychic (she is separated from her lover). The poem opens thus:

> Mine owne deare Lord, sith thou art lock'd from me,
> In this disguise my love must steale to thee,
> Since to renue all loves, all kindness past,
> This refuge scarcely left, yet this the last.
> My keeper comming, I of thee inquire,
> Who with thy greeting answeres my desire;
> Which my tongue willing to return againe,
> Griefe stops my words, and I but strive in vaine:
> Wherewith amaz'd in hast he goes,
> When through my lips my heart thrusts forth my woes,
> But then the dores that make a dolefull sound,
> Drive back my words, that in the noyse are drown'd,
> Which somewhat hush'd, the eccho doth record,
> And twice or thrice reiterates my word.

The letter is a substitute, a *disguise,* enforced rather than enjoyed and standing in place of the longed-for reciprocity of present love. Here, very exactly, language substitutes for the body. It is a clothing, or a surreptitious means of contact. And always contact, not touch.

The abstract or removed form is produced by the situation (*contact*); the language attempts to remake the love-experience (*touch*). But that attempt always acknowledges its own insufficiency and insists that language is incommensurate with desire. In this passage speech is stopped with grief. Dumbness seals emotion, then the cavern of the mouth dilates in a shriek. The doors of the prison obliterate the sound with their own doleful noise: inner and outer are commingled, identified, confused. The echo reiterates the unnamed word. Emotions and surroundings, body and prison, grotesquely replicate each other.

Language may be a way out of reflexivity. But the price of this is that it is never fully synchronous with experience. Art succeeds event and in the poems this succession is itself a form of bereavement. The end of a love is the end of a mutual self, a shared and particular identity which cannot be revived in any other relationship. This is one reason why the writers in heroic epistle dwell on *place.* The irreplaceable particularity of place vouches for past event and feeling and recovers instants of undeniable, shared, and secret experience.

Est nemus et piceis et frondibus ilicis atrum;
vix illuc radiis solis adire licet.
sunt in co—fuerant certe—delubra Dianae;
aurea barbarica stat dea facta manu.
noscis? an exciderunt mecum loca? venimus illuc.
(*Heroides*, XII. 67)

("There is a grove and in it there is—or there was certainly—a shrine to Diana.
Do you know it? Or have places fallen out of your mind along with me? We
came there.")

Medea's imagery of the sombre grove into which scarce any rays of sunlight can penetrate and of the golden statue carved by barbaric hand conjure
in the reader immediate memory, a meta-memory which for us is also retrospectively reinforced by the Gothic novel and Keats's poetry. Heroic
epistle is a mode which relies on place and on history because all its experience is articulated as the past. Its enterprise is to recombine through rhetoric the ruptured continuity of past, present, and future, into the storyless
now of love.

Or perhaps it would be truer to call that its humanistic ideal. For in the
language of these poems there is also an acknowledgment of, even a celebration of, the immoveability of language once it has replaced (or
re-placed) experience. The body becomes the world and dilates endlessly,
but it becomes also, and only, language. Drayton's Queene Margaret
writes:

My Brest, which once was Mirths imperiall Throne,
A vast and desart Wildernesse is growne;
Like that bold Region, from the World remote,
On whose breeme Seas the Icie Mountains flote.
(*Queene Margaret*, l. 115)

So the question arises of how far this genre of poetry is about the special
quality of women's experience, or how far the authors are using this experience as a means of analyzing an underlying artistic predicament: that of
language codifying and thereby ousting experience based on bodily
knowledge.

Does the heroic epistle with its insistence on psychological portraiture
and its presentation of women's love as the motive power of its drama
demonstrate a power of empathy? Or is it an opportunity for male authors
to explore a new range and extremity of language, to widen the register
beyond that which would be acceptable for a man using a lyric or bio-

graphic form? If the second were the case, then the form would be rather like the Pindaric Ode, which gave the opportunity to explore the expressivity of madness. By doing so within a designated form it also *contained* the expressivity of madness.

In my view, the form did function to extend the rhetorical possibilities of language for its male authors—but this extension relied upon an appeal to the authority of women, who were assumed to be naturally learned in the realms of erotic knowledge and suffering. So the claims of the art-form have a mimetic basis: the primary "author" or authority is conceived as the experiencer; the actual author-writer casts himself as secondary, a concealed scribe recording the actualities derived from women's experience (the link with Richardson's view of himself as scribe is striking). Heroic epistle takes as its pre-condition the enforced passivity of women: formally and in narrative the poems rely upon sequestration. But the sense of enforcement means that these are poems which sustain a constant protest against the conditions which produce the form. This creates a further paradox.

The form gave authority to the solitary. It historicized hidden feeling and claimed space for sequestered knowledge. It was both formal and expressive: the central consciousness was displayed, analyzed, and shared, rather than judged. Yet it did enclose and separate what it described: the emotions of women in love. And thereby it reinforced even while it protested against "the prison of ourselves." It represents both "voice" and "no-voice." The voice is lost in the silence of writing and must, unnatural no-voice, substitute for the potentialities of the whole body, as Aphra Behn suggests in a brilliantly expressionist phrase: "with outstretched voice I cry'd."[20]

The separation between author and persona is crucial to the form. It never occupies that teasing distance which places Jonson's or Donne's epistles somewhere close at hand to the author but nowhere fully to be identified with him. Nor is it ever bedded in that confidential shared world of feminine knowledge like Eliza Haywood's *Epistles for Ladies* (1755), prose letters mainly between fictional ladies offering moral instruction, humorous accounts, and descriptions of adventure and love: "Erminina to Lady Betty, giving her an account of the brutish treatment she had received from Comus; and the providential escape she had from his intended violence, at the house of a person of quality"; "From Eusebia to the bishop of XXX, on the power of divine music. With some hints of a proposal for the better encouraging it in these kingdoms."[21] The declarative language of the heroines of heroic epistle may well feed Pamela's high sentences, which alternate in the novel with the circumstantial, in a way that Fielding was able to mock in *Shamela*. Richardson's epistolary heroines, however, address very few letters to their lovers. This is mainly because they are seeking to repulse rather than to reclaim the men. Most of their letters are addressed to members of their families, a female confidante, or even (as in the case of Pamela's journal, which she despairs of having delivered) to themselves. The expressions of passion in Richardson's heroines are oblique, unrecognized, uncontrolled—not part of an accepted sense of self. Passion in Richardson, as in the Gothic novel, is a renegade emotion.

By the eighteenth century, an alternative form of heroic epistle was well established, one in which affairs of state rather than of love were described and where the writer or writers were men. Dörrie's study notes in addition a sub-form of religious epistle developed by the Jesuits. But the subject of love, and particularly of women's love, remained central. Moreover, it was held that the heroic epistle was particularly apt for women readers. Dryden stated that Ovid originally intended his Epistles for a readership of women. Dryden caviled at the name *Heroides*, however, because although the topic of the poems is the plight of women abandoned by their lovers, Ovid would hardly have called his poem *The Heroines* when the cast included men! "But, sure, he cou'd not be guilty of such an over-sight, to call his work by the name of Heroines, when there are divers Men, or Heroes, as, namely, Paris, Leander, and Acontius, joyned in it."[22] Saltonstall dedicated his translation "to the Vertuous Ladies and Gentlewomen of Great Britain," explaining that "these Epistles, in regard of their subject have just relation to you, Ladies and Gentlewomen, being the complaint of Ladies and Gentlewomen, for the absence of their Lovers" and claiming that Vertue will appreciate virtue. He ends with a flowery euphemistic compliment.

So much concerning the worke, and the Author Ovid, now you expect a complement for the Dedication.

Ladies and Gentlewomen, since this booke of Ovids, which most Gentlemen could reade before in Latine, is for your sakes come forth in English, it doth at first addresse it selfe a Suiter, to wooe your acceptance, that it may kisse your hands, and afterward have the lines thereof in reading sweetned by the odour of your breath, while the dead letters form'd into words by your divided lips, may receive new life by your passionate expression, and the words marryed in that Ruby coloured Temple, may thus happily united, multiply your contentment. And in a word let this be,

A Servant with you to the Lady Vertue
Wye Saltonstall.[23]

Ladies don't read Latin, but they do read aloud. Pleasingly, the copy of the book now in Cambridge University Library makes it clear that the translation did find its intended audience. It is inscribed: "Grizell Irish Her Book 1706."

So in the seventeenth and eighteenth centuries, it seems, heroic epistle was seen as a women's genre in its subject matter and audience, though not in its authorship. In Dryden's collection of translations, Aphra Behn is the only woman contributor and hers is the only translation described as a paraphrase. But in *Eloisa to Abelard* Pope drew upon a woman's writing and language to fuel his poem. Discussion of the authenticity of the Eloisa/Abelard letters post-dates this period and so forms no part of Pope's artistic situation. He believed in them as a historical document with no edge of dubiety. The woman's voice is the source of his authority. It would be simplistic, however, to suggest that his source brought a whole new range of language within his command, since Eloisa's own language of passion, and certainly Hughes's translation of it from which Pope worked, draw on Ovid. What is striking is how Pope used and transformed these tropes.

The heroines in Ovid persistently conjure up a particular image: a woman on the extreme verge of land gazing out over a stormy sea, chilled, restless, alone. Phyllis, Hero, Dido, Ariadne, Sappho, Œnone, Hypsipyle all share this image. Sometimes they remember the moment of the man's sea-departure as one of trust and mutuality, but sea and land have always since been set at odds:

> Ultimus e sociis sacram conscendis in Argon.
>   illa volat; ventus concava vela tenet;
> caerula propulsae subducitur unda carinae;
>   terra tibi, nobis adspiciuntur aquae.
>   *(Heroides, VI. 65)*

> And while thy ship the blew waves passed o're,
> I lookt unto the sea, thou to the shore.
>   (Saltonstall, p. 41)

The suggestion of human form everywhere persists in this earth-sea landscape. Phaedra writes to Hippolytus:

> Aequora bina suis obpugnant fluctibus isthmon,
> et tenuis tellus audit utrumque mare.
>   *(Heroides, IV. 105)*

("There are two seas that one either side assail an isthmus with their floods, and the slender land hears the waves of both. Here with you will I dwell" [Loeb translation].)

Ariadne is the epitome of these heroines, and it is Ariadne's history which is most frequently taken up by later poets and composers, for the heroic epistle was important to seventeenth-century musicians when the fashion for monody succeeded polyphony.

The solitary voices and emotions of heroic epistle caught the imagination of composers. Monteverdi wrote two settings of Ariadne's epistle, taking up some of Ovid's phrases. The first of them (1614) is in parts, but seven years later he published a new "Lamento d'Ariana" for a single voice. Nicholas Lanier (1588–1666) set Hero's epistle to Leander, "Nor com'st thou yet, my slothful love." And more than a hundred years later the form was still productive, as we can hear in Haydn's great *cantata a voce sola,* "Arianna a Naxos" (1789). Medea's "cantata" or incantations have become Haydn's cantata. This musical transformation of heroic epistle has its importance for our understanding of Pope and the Gothic. Emotion in heroic epistle is intensely declarative. In the seventeenth and eighteenth centuries this merged into actual performance. Saltonstall imagines his readers reading Ovid aloud: "The dead letters form'd into words by your divided lips, may receive new life by your passionate expression." Tillotson says that by 1750 most readers of it knew *Eloisa to Abelard* by heart and could recite it. The language of the poem has sometimes been described as "operatic," and this is more exact than abusive. Pope's *Eloisa* strains the contrary aspects of heroic epistle to their fullest tension: silence and secrecy are essential to the poem but so also are those declamatory and assertive properties which will finally find their grotesque high-Gothic form in the arias of the Queen of Night in Mozart's *Magic Flute,* where women's emotions are figured as freakish, destructive, inordinate.

In Pope, Eloisa's emotions are given their full authority, and our experience of the poem is our entry into her sensations. Ariadne again is the heroine closest to the poem's language, though Sappho's more voluptuous words are used as well. Ariadne remembers her state when she discovered Theseus gone:

> aut ego diffusis erravi sola capillis,
> qualis ab Ogygio concita Baccha deo,
> aut mare prospiciens in saxo frigida sedi,
> quamque lapis sedes, tam lapsis ipsa fui.
> (*Heroides,* X. 47)

("Either I have wandered alone, with hair flying loose, like women roused by the Bacchantian god, or looking out upon the sea I have sat all chilled upon a stone, as much a stone myself as was the stone I sat upon.")

The senses are heightened and tormented as well as frozen. Pope takes up the same febrile intensity of sense-experience and uses, like Ovid, ono-matapoeic effects, to suggest the body abraded, the mind scarified by loss. Warmth and chilling (the shared felicity of the body now grown cold) organizes the experience of both poems:

> et tua, quae possum pro te, vestigia tango
> strataque quae membris intepuere tuis.
>
> (l. 53)

Coming to the couch, in place of you "it a pleasure unto me did seeme / To touch the warme place, where thy limbes had beene" (Saltonstall). Physical touch comforts or presses upon the flayed sensibility:

> Mons fuit—apparent frutices in vertice rari;
> hinc scopulus raucis pendet adesus aquis.
> adscendo—vires animus dabat—atque ita late
> aequora prospectu metior alta meo.
>
> (l. 25)

("There was a mountain with bushes rising here and there upon its top; a cliff hangs over from it, gnawed into by deep-sounding waves. I climb its slope—my spirit gave me strength—and thus with prospect broad I scan the billowy deep.")

The sound of the waves moves through "raucis . . . aquis."

The same emotional force, of a body and mind over-alert with anxiety so that they are naked to the tactile pressures of objects or even of language is evident in the passage where Eloisa's words recall Ariadne's "quamque lapis sedes, tam lapis ipsa fui."

> Ye rugged rocks! which holy knees have worn;
> Ye grots and caverns shagg'd with horrid thorn!
> Shrines! where their vigils pale-eye'd virgins keep,
> And pitying saints, whose statues learn to weep!
> Tho' cold like you, unmov'd, and silent grown,
> I have not yet forgot myself to stone.
>
> (*Eloisa to Abelard*, l. 20)

The language emphasizes both the contrast and the abrasion of animate and inanimate objects. Apart from the rather hefty onomatopoeic harshness of "rugged rocks," there is an emphasis upon tactility which disturbs the picturesque: the weight of knees has "worn" the rocks; the caverns are "shagg'd with horrid thorn"; and Pope brings out the Latin sense of "bristling" in "horrid." Rough and rasping textures drag against the implicit body. Saints' statues weep. The latent suggestion of contrasting temperatures, warm tears against cold stone, is seized in that address: "Tho' cold like you, unmov'd and silent grown." It is addressed to self, landscape, and architecture, but also covertly addresses Abelard, builder of the place, "cold, unmov'd, and silent grown."

Pope takes up a hint from Hughes's translation of the Eloisa/Abelard letters. Abelard writing to a friend describes his depression amidst a melancholy landscape: "I live in barbarous country, the language of which I do not understand. I have no conversation but with the rudest people. My walks are on the inaccessible shore of a sea which is perpetually stormy."[24] This scenery occurs again, associated with Schedoni, in Ann Radcliffe's *The Italian*. In Pope's poem the dead calm of the sea, so much in contrast with the usual iconography in this genre, brings home the impossibility of passionate arousal for Abelard now:

> Thy life a long, dead calm of fix'd repose;
> No pulse that riots, and no blood that glows.
> Still as the sea, ere winds were taught to blow,
> Or moving spirits bade the waters flow.
>
> (l. 251)

In the early editions, up to 1720, the equation of sea and sexuality is made more explicit in a couplet which immediately follows that passage:

> Cut from the root my perish'd joys I see,
> And love's warm tyde for ever stopt in thee.

In Ovid, the interfusion of animate and inanimate world has a significance which is poised between the fanciful and the genetic, and which allows a liberty like that of dream:

> te lapis et montes innataque rupibus altis
>   robora, te saevae progenuere ferae,
> aut mare, quale vides agitari nunc quoque ventis,
>   quo tamen adversis fluctibus ire paras.
>
> (*Heroides*, VII. 37)

Aeneas's behavior suggests his kinship with rocks, mountains, wild beasts: most of all, the sea.

Dreams in heroic epistle, as in the Gothic novel, are of more than allegorical significance. Margaret Anne Doody has excellently analyzed the various ways in which dreams are expressed in Gothic novels, and particularly in eighteenth-century novels by women. But her introductory analysis of Eloisa's dreams makes no mention of the extent to which the landscapes and icons of female dream in literature are established in heroic epistle, nor of how fully Pope was drawing upon the narrative and imagistic resources of the form:

> I pray thee, POOLE, have care how thou do'st passe,
> Never the sea yet halfe so dang'rous was;
> And one fore-told, by Water thou should'st die,
> (Ah! foule befall that foule Tongues Prophesie)
> Yet I by Night am troubled in my Dreames,
> That I doe see thee toss'd in dang'rous Streames;
> And oft-times ship-wrack'd, cast upon the Land,
> And lying breathlesse on the queachy Sand.
>
> (*Queene Margaret*, l. 139)

Hero tells Leander:

> namque sub aurora, iam dormitante lucerna,
>   somnia quo cerni tempore vera solent,
> stamina de digitis cecidere sopore remissis,
>   collaque pulvino nostra ferenda dedi.
> hic ego ventosas nantem delphina perundas
>   cernere non dubia sum mihi visa fide,
> quem postquam bibulis inlisit fluctus harenis.
>   unda simul mierum vitaque deseruit.
>
> (*Heroides*, XIX. 195)

Her dawn-dream shows a dolphin swimming through stormy waters and cast up upon the shore, abandoned first by waves and then by life. These are warning dreams which prove themselves true just beyond the time boundaries of the narrative, and which we, as cognisant readers, *know* will prove themselves true. Their primary function is admonitory and emblematic.

But the *Heroides* includes also dreams which allow a largesse of experience. Dream, like language, is a needed substitute for love when the loved one is absent. Laodamia hopes for false joys at least since she lacks his

ambracing arm: "dum careo veris gaudia falsa iuvant" (*Heroides*, XIII. 108).
But her dream is bleak: his pallid face appears, and she hears his groans.
Instead, she turns aside into day-dreaming of the time when they will lie
together again and story-telling will be part of love-making, "multa tamen
capies oscula, multa dabis," language relaxed and intermittent, instead of
being the strained only means, as in the poems, of keeping continuity
between what has been and may again be:

> semper in his apte narrantia verba resistunt;
> promptior est dulci linga referre mora.
>
> (l. 121)

The profuse and hopeful fantasy (ll. 115–22) with its staying of experience
into apothegm ("The words of well-told tales meet ever with such stops")
is contained and rendered poignant for the reader by our prior and double
knowledge: Protesilaus, the first Greek casualty of the Trojan war, is about
to be killed by Hector, and the Gods will take pity on Laodamia's grief
and allow him to return to life for three hours to visit her. Her daydream
will be enacted not in the timeless spaciousness of return, but in a cramped
three hours of respite after which, unable to bear another parting, she will
kill—has already killed—herself. The double time of heroic epistle
accounts for some of the particular power of dreams in the form: the frozen knowledge of history is dissolved but not lost in the stream of sentiment. We remain vigilant. Both ominous sleeping dream and amorous
waking dream will prove true, but in ways which cancel their manifest
meaning.

In contrast to Laodamia, Eloisa's plight is that there is nothing left to
happen. The foreknowledge of the reader is particularly bleak. Ovid has
room also for dreams of satisfaction. Pope draws upon the language
ascribed to Sappho for Eloisa's description of her dreams of Abelard. Language, Sappho suggests, turns us all into voyeurs, and with erotic decorum
she eschews recounting the climax of her dream: she registers bodily
weight "onerare": and the close caresses of tongues:

> Tu mihi cura, Phaon; te somnia nostra reducunt—
>   somnia formoso candidiora die.
> illic te invenio, quamvis regionibus absis;
>   sed non longa satis gaudia somnus habet
> saepe tuos nostra cervice onerare lacertos,
>   saepe tuae videor supposuisse meos;

oscula cognosco, quae tu committere linguae
aptaque consueras accipere, apta dare.
blandior interdum verisque simillima verba
eloquor, et vigilant sensibus ora meis.
ulteriora pudet narrare, sed omnia fiunt,
et iuvat, et siccae non licet esse mihi.

(*Heroides*, XV. 123)

The only source of *trouble* in this passage is that all must take place in dream and memory, but dream and memory here can almost fill up the space of need. Language here is content to be abandoned for performance and can also satisfyingly revive performance. There is no repudiation of either body or language. When we set this alongside the account of Eloisa's dream, we see more exactly what new elements of feeling Pope brought into heroic epistle and the ways in which his language sets the contraries which Ann Radcliffe can later moralize. In Ovid there is no guilt about sexual feeling, though there may be guilt about its consequences, such as Deianeira feels. But in Pope's language dream and desire are fueled and then fragmented by guilt. The persistent use of zeugma is an attempt to control this fragmentation.

> Far other dreams my erring soul employ,
> Far other raptures, of unholy joy:
> When at the close of each sad, sorrowing day,
> Fancy restores what vengeance snatch'd away,
> The conscience sleeps, and leaving nature free,
> All my loose soul unbounded springs to thee.
> O curst, dear horrors of all-conscious night!
> How glowing guilt exalts the keen delight!
> Provoking Daemons all restraint remove,
> And stir within me ev'ry source of love.
> I hear thee, view thee, gaze o'er all thy charms,
> And round thy phantom glue my clasping arms.
>
> (l. 223)

Conscience sleeps and is succeeded in sleep by libertine "consciousness," the full awakening of the senses. The shared knowledge ("conscious") is guilty, "glowing guilt exalts the keen delight." (Sappho writes just after her dream-description, of woods and grottoes, "conscia deliciis illa fuere meis": they were in the secret of ("conscia") my joys.) The scenery she describes, rugged rocks, deep trees, is denuded of meaning by Phaon's absence but retains the impress of what has been: "the earth was hollowed by our weight." Eloisa's nightmare which succeeds her passionate dream is far more desolate than Sappho's.

> —methinks we wandring go
> Thro' dreary wastes, and weep each other's woe;
> Where round some mould'ring tow'r pale ivy creeps,
> And low-brow'd rocks hang nodding o'er the deeps.
> Sudden you mount! you becken from the skies;
> Clouds interpose, waves roar, and winds arise.
> I shriek, start up, the same sad prospect find,
> And wake to all the griefs I left behind.
>
> (l. 241)

The tall tower, the rocks hanging over the deep, the roaring waves, are all recognizable from the landscape of emotion inhabited by women in the *Heroides*. But the terrifying contrast of horizontal and vertical is not: the fallen pair, like Milton's Adam and Eve leaving paradise "with wandring steps and slow," "wandring go / Thro' dreary wastes, and weep each other's woe." Mutuality sorrows. But the rupture between them is presented in terms of Abelard's *ascension:* "Sudden you mount! you becken from the skies." They are no longer on the same plane. He has been rapt away into god-like authority.

Religious language in Christianity is so intimately interpenetrated with secular eroticism that it requires constant acts of judgement to distinguish them. The particular tensions which hold together the work of novelists like Monk Lewis and Ann Radcliffe are desire and the impossibility of fulfillment. Passion in the Gothic is always roused in comes to grief. To express this they both use religious settings and show the attempt to sequester emotions and language to religious uses. Both emotions and language persistently breach the bounds which should contain them.

The ribald appropriation of religious language back to the language of seduction can readily be placed as evil. Drayton cynically reversed the two domains of language in King John's epistle to Matilda who had fled to a nunnery to avoid his advances:

> Holy MATILDA, Thou the Saint of mine,
> Ile be thy Servant, and my Bed thy Shrine.
> When I doe offer, be thy Brest the Altar,
> And when I pray, thy Mouth shall be my Psalter.
>
> (l. 837)

But for Eloisa the conflict is not easy. Instead of praying to Diana as an alternative to her love for Abelard, she must pray to a God who is to be addressed as Spouse:

> For her the Spouse prepares the bridal ring,
> For her white virgins *Hymenæals* sing.
>
> (l. 219)

God, for Eloisa, figures as a love-rival to Abelard. Yet he has handed her over to this higher husband who demands that she feel guilt for her earlier attachment and that she deny her memories of love. She is sequestered, but her restraint is ineffectual: her fancy riots. The jarring discords of language in the poem represent not only a rupture between past and present but the fracturing of an identity placed under intolerably-opposed demands which figure themselves in identical language. The language of desire and the language of renunciation are the same. For the readers of Gothic fiction, desire, constraint, silence, arousal, and disappointment are set inordinately close, as they were in the practice of heroic epistle.

Women in heroic epistle are figured as victimized yet powerful. The

How committed the form is to a high valuation of women and women's experience can be shrewdly judged by comparing the attitude implicit in one of the satires Pope's poem brought in its wake. *Éloise, en deshabille* (1729) stands in the same relation to *Eloisa to Abelard* as *Shamela* to *Pamela*. Like *Shamela*, it is a reactionary work which assumes that "young ladies" or "ladies-maids" are all of one ilk and can be rapidly seen through, their apparent complexities unknotted, and their self-seeking motives brought to light. It suggests that all we need to do to understand what Eloisa was "really" up to is to change the linguistic register. The author says in his introduction that where he wanders from Pope's text "the reader will be pleased to observe that either Eloisa uses the same sentiment in some other part of the epistle, or he takes the liberty of putting *words into her mouth which might naturally be expected from a young lady in her situation*" (my italics). Women, being known to be venal, frivolous, and low-minded, will "naturally" use the language he assigns to Eloisa, of whom he comments in a footnote: "As Abelard has instructed his fair pupil in philosophy, natural as well as moral, we are not to be surprised at her displaying a degree of knowledge uncommon in the fair sex." The sala-cious comedy of his poem is enforced by printing Pope's poem on the left hand page, his own on the right. The opening lines, which mimic the lines of Pope quoted in the first paragraph of this essay, sufficiently indicate the tone of the pastiche:

> Immur'd in this prison, so dull, and so moping,
> Where vows and high walls bar all hopes of eloping;
> Where close-grated windows scarce shew us the sun,
> What means this strange itch in the flesh of a nun?

He brings out blatantly the urgent but disguised eroticism: there is in this satire no drama, because no complexity. Instead there is a perky, complacent, frequently funny, always demeaning prurience. So Pope's Eloisa's awkward, eager couplet describing her own death when at last Abelard may be present:

> See my lips tremble, and my eye-balls roll,
> Suck my last breath, and catch my flying soul!
>
> (l. 323)

becomes:

> Even then, as you've oft mark'd the roll of my eyes,
> From my quivring lips catch my soul as it flies,
> And to finish the whole, with a spice of thy function
> Give my last languid motion love's ultimate unction.[25]

Eloisa's letters reinforced the authenticity of claims for women's intelligent feelings: the frankness and starkness of Eloisa's language has none of the lubricious monotony of suffering to be found in *Lettres portugaises*, letters supposedly from a young Portuguese nun abandoned by her cavalier lover.

The emphasis upon solitude, enforced silence, rhapsodic feeling, separation, and expressive rhetoric in heroic epistles were all taken up into the work of Ann Radcliffe, there to be explored and, ultimately, moralized. Ovid's Adriadne lies not far behind a description such as this:

She could just distinguish the dark sails of some skiffs turning the cliffs, and entering the little bay, where the hamlet margined the beach. To Ellena, who had believed that no human habitation, except her prison, interrupted the vast solitudes of these forests and shores, the view of the huts, remote as they were, imparted a feeble hope, and even somewhat of joy. . . . It was a lowering evening, and the sea was dark and swelling; the screams of sea-birds too, as they wheeled among the clouds, and sought their high nests in the rocks, seemed to indicate an approaching storm.

But the tone shifts into one unthinkable in heroic epistle at this point. Ellena stabilizes her perceptions and escapes into a sympathetic, selfless fantasy which allows terror to diminish:

Ellana was not so wholly engaged by selfish sufferings, but that she could sympathise with those of others, and she rejoiced that the fishermen, whose boats she had observed, had escaped the threatening tempest, and were safely sheltered in their little homes, where, as they heard the loud waves break along the coast, they could look with keener pleasure upon the domestic circle, and the warm comforts round them. (*The Italian*, pp. 219-20)

"Sympathy" provides a reassuring respite from the self and yet is simply part of fantasy life for the isolated heroine. She turns back "to a sense of her own forlorn and friendless situation" and into a soliloquy cast in the language of heroic epistle: the woman is abandoned, friendless, persecuted. " 'Alas!' said she, 'I have no longer a home, a circle to smile welcomes upon me! I have no longer even one friend to support, to rescue me. I—a miserable wanderer on a distant shore!' " Schedoni, the monk who will seek to rape and murder her and will prove to be her father, appears immediately after this speech.

In these novels there is no longer the possibility of mutuality *and* passion: mutuality is reserved for the chaste and absent hero; passion means rupture and incursion by an alien other. Ann Radcliffe's heroines externalize passion and refuse to recognize it as a part of themselves: it returns therefore in uncontrollably threatening forms. In heroic epistle passion is both internalized and externalized. The figurations of landscape and event correspond with claustrophobic exactness to symbol and feeling. The virginal heroines of Gothic fiction cannot represent women's full experience; the fullness of that experience is not condensed in character, but it permeates the landscapes, solitudes, dreams, and threats. In Eleanor Sleath's *The Orphan of the Rhine*, for example, the heroine's female condition of passivity, isolation, and privation is strongly identified with silence both within and without doors: Julie "wandered for some time in uninterrupted silence through a long extent of desolated chambers" and in the woods "all was melancholy, repose, and silence."

In women's Gothic, the woman author writes while the heroine is mute.

In heroic epistle, the experiencer writes: the emphasis on place is recognized in first-person narrative, but in the Gothic the suggestions are carried by the text independent of the characters' awareness. So a sexually inexperienced central consciousness is surrounded by the erotic iconography we recognize from heroic epistle. The symbolic landscapes and rhetorical tropes form an address which need not impute awareness to the virginal heroine. The unawakened state of Gothic heroines allows them to stir up trouble and to be absolved from responsibility for it. The codes of heroic epistle permit Ann Radcliffe and writers such as Eliza Parsons and Eleanor Sleath to communicate sexual forces without attributing them to any specific source. The Freudian landscape can be dispeopled and particularized: conflict need not be *owned*. In the inner courtyard "wild and grass-grown" (of *The Orphan of the Rhine*) stands a column topped by the statue of a young hero "surrounded by lofty walls, which were overgrown with wild weeds, and the deadly night-shade, whilst the thread moss encrusted the fragments of the fallen ramparts which lay scattered at the base of the pillar, it seemed as if exulting in its strength, and triumphing amid the desolation and ruin it surveyed."[26]

The Gothic women writers share the emphasis of heroic epistle on the enclosure and silencing of women, and they rebel against it *through language*. The process of silent reading and of sensationalist language, of libertine and emblazoned reading-pleasures, gave a new resource to the "unnatural No-voice" of women which alarmed moralists of the period. The tradition of heroic epistle and, in particular, Pope's *Eloisa to Abelard*, offered a language of sensation, an iconography, a grandeur of scale, an emphasis on sequestration and an acceptance of women's extreme emotion which were all essential to the Gothic novelists.

Notes

1. *The Twickenham Edition of the Poems of Alexander Pope*, edited by John Butt and others. II vols (London, 1939–69), II (revised 1954), 275–327, line 1. All subsequent references are to this edition.

2. Ann Radcliffe, *The Italian*, edited by Frederick Garber (Oxford, 1971), pp. 66–67.

3. *The Works of Michael Drayton*, edited by J. William Hebel, 5 vols. (Oxford, 1932), II, 137–38 (l. 175). All subsequent references are to this edition.

4. Cited in Twickenham *Pope*, II, 276.

5 *The Penguin Dorothy Parker*, edited by Brendan Gill (Harmondsworth, 1977), p. 91.

6. Edited by G. S. Gordon (Oxford, 1906), p. 87.

7. Cited in Richard F. Hardin, "Convention and Design in Drayton's *Heroicall Epistles*," *PMLA*, 83 (1968), 35–41, (p. 37).

8. *Henry Esmond,* edited by George Saintsbury (Oxford, 1896).

9. "A Letter sent from *Octavia* to her husband *Marcus Antonius* into Egypt" (1599), *The Complete Works in Verse and Prose of Samuel Daniel,* edited by Alexander Grosart, 5 vols. (London, 1885; reissued New York, 1963), I, 138.

10. Drayton, *Works,* II, 164; II, 182.

11. Samuel Butler, *Hudibras,* edited by John Wilders (Oxford, 1967), p. 117 (Part II, Canto I, l. 591).

12. For example, "Yarico to Inkle," anon. (London, 1736); The Right Hon. the Countess of XXXX. "An Epistle from Yarico to Inkle after he had left her in slavery" (London, 1738); Mrs. Eddell, "Incle and Yarico" (London, 1742); "Yarico to Inkle," anon. (London, 1771). See also the excellent *Inkle and Yarico Album,* selected by L. M. Price (Berkeley, California, 1937).

13. Ellen Moers, in *Literary Women* (London, 1978), takes up the term "Heroides" as a shorthand expression for the theme of women mourning or yearning for love in novels of the eighteenth and nineteenth centuries. Although she discusses "female Gothic" in a lively chapter, she does not make connections between heroic epistle and the Gothic novel nor examine heroic epistle as a representation and a shaping force in women's consciousness.

14. References are to Ovid, *Heroides and Amores* (hereafter *Heroides*), edited by T. E. Page and W. H. D. Rouse, with an English translation by Grant Showerman, Loeb Classical Library (London, 1914), p. 10; Drayton, *Works,* II, 292. Translations of Ovid are my own unless otherwise stated.

15. *An Argument of Images: The Poetry of Alexander Pope* (Cambridge, Mass., 1971), p. 236.

16. *Ovid's Heroicall Epistles,* Englished by W. S. [William Saltonstall] (London, 1639), p. 30.

17. *Byron's Don Juan,* edited by Truman Guy Steffen and Willis W. Pratt, 4 vols (Austin, Texas, 1957), II, 131.

18. Edited by Devendra Varma (London, 1968), p. 26.

19. "Deserts, Ruins and Troubled Waters: Female Dreams in Fiction and the Development of the Gothic Novel," *Genre,* 10 (1977), 529–72 (p. 531).

20. "A Paraphrase on the Foregoing Epistle of Œnone to Paris," in *Ovid's Epistles: With His Amours, translated into English by the Most Eminent Hands,* edited by John Dryden (London, 1776), p. 83.

21. It is perhaps worth noting that Eliza Haywood quotes Drayton in Epistle XCV of this work.

22. *Ovid's Epistles,* p. [vii].

23. Saltonstall, p. [x].

24. *Letters of Abelard and Heloise. To which is prefixed a particular account of their Lives, Amours and Misfortunes. By the late John Hughes Esq.* (London, 1785), p. 64.

25. *Eloise, en déshabille,* by "a celebrated Greek Professor" (London, 1729), pp. 3, 27.

26. Eleanor Sleath, *The Orphan of the Rhine,* edited by Devendra Varma (London, 1968), p. 277.

The Flight from History
in Mid-Century Poetry

JOHN SITTER

It is no doubt too simple to see the novelists of the 1740s and later as marching off in one direction—the road of Hume and historiography — and the poets as taking the "way" of William Law and vision. I will try to complicate this picture enough in the chapters ahead to do near-justice to the shared concerns of novelists and poets alike and to accommodate their influence on each other. Nonetheless, I hope to be able at the same time to preserve some of the simplicity that attends our fork-in-the-road model for the realities of mid-eighteenth-century literary life, merely because it suggests the either/or quality of certain artistic choices or means of finding and telling the appropriate truth. From our vantage point we could list some of these as solitary *or* social perspectives, the use of subliminal suggestion *or* visual "data," expressive description *or* narration of details generally regarded as sociologically accurate, and so on.

But a major problem concerns the extent to which we can trust models which depend on "our vantage point." The next question is whether we have any choice.[1] For example, the term "preromantic," so often applied to the poets of this period, suggests a conspicuous question about retrospective distortion which remains, whether or not we avoid the term. The objections to the concept are obvious, and many of them have been made before. To regard the mid-century poets as "preromantics" is to evaluate their worth primarily in terms of values later established by the achievement of the romantic writers we happen to like most. To regard, say, Col-

From *Literary Loneliness in Mid-Eighteenth-Century England* (Ithaca: Cornell University Press, 1982), pp. 77–103.

lins or Gray as a "preromantic" is to impose a false teleology on the past, one in which the poet is "trying" to be Wordsworth or in which he becomes a sort of John the Baptist heralding the redeemers to come. (Redemption is central enough to romantic mythology to have made this latter version particularly seductive.)

Problems of terminology are not in themselves very interesting, but much has been written during the last generation concerning the preromantic label as well as about designations often used more broadly, such as "classical," "Augustan," "Enlightenment," and of course the "Age of Reason."[2] Why not, if all of these are felt to carry too many preconceptions, throw them all out and start fresh? Terms are sometimes thrown out altogether. The "Age of Reason" is virtually dead now in serious discussions of the eighteenth century except as a phrase in curatorial quotation marks. Others remain, voiced or unvoiced, because they represent a way of generalizing which still seems interesting and plausible. For all its problems, "Augustan" is not only a convenient but a provocative term, suggesting self-conscious wishes and fears on the part of many of the figures grouped under its shade, and it allows (as Howard Weinbrot's work shows) new scrutiny of the historical material.[3] Other terms can be suppressed to occasional good effect, and I will for the most part attempt to suppress the term "preromantic" in favor of "post-Augustan." I do so not in the belief that the latter is without problems but in the simple hope that it calls more attention to the immediate past with which the writers themselves had to deal than to the future which preoccupies later critics. But if such a maneuver is a useful shift of emphasis, it would be wrong to exaggerate its novelty. We are still working with similar sorts of retrospective generalizations which will filter much of what we see in the available past. The alternative—and it exists more clearly in theory than in practice—would be to attempt no discriminations. Thus Josephine Miles's "samples" of poetry of various decades are selected more or less without regard to whether they represent new trends or lingering habits of the time. As soon as we begin to discriminate, to decide, for example, that some poems are more "of" the 1740s or 1750s than others also published then, we naturally begin to look for qualities which we believe to be important in the development of poetry. If we commit ourselves to the concept of preromanticism, in short, we will prize anticipation; if we see the mid-century as "post-Augustan" we will emphasize rejections of previous models. In either case we simplify, and our best method is merely to try to recognize the limits of our categories before we begin. Ernst Cassirer put the problem clearly in defending Burckhardt's generalized "Renaissance" type against the objections of scholars who claimed they could not find this type exemplified anywhere in their source material.

> What we are trying to give expression to here is a unity *of direction*, not *actualization*. The particular individuals *belong together*, not because they are alike or resemble each other, but because they are *cooperating in a common task*, which ... we perceive to be new and to be the era's distinctive "meaning." ... All genuine concepts of style in the humanities reduce ... to such conceptions of meaning. The artistic style of an epoch cannot be determined unless we gather into a unity all its divergent and often patently disparate artistic expressions, unless ... we understand them as manifestations of a specific "artistic will."[4]

Cassirer's formulation may be particularly useful for our purposes not only as a plea for certain kinds of generalizations but because the sense of history to which it appeals—the idea of history as secular "direction"— first became powerful in the middle of the eighteenth century.

The middle and later years of the eighteenth century have been best studied in terms of the vast and sophisticated body of critical theory the period produced. In the following pages I will look more closely at poetic procedures than at critical ones, for the simple reason that we now have more to learn from the shared metaphors and period style or styles of the poetry itself than from the aesthetic territory so well charted by, most prominently, Samuel Monk, W. J. Bate, and M. H. Abrams. When we look directly at the poetic procedures in the middle of the century, those which are often most interesting are procedures of avoidance, and they show that the poets are seeking to avoid history.

This claim requires much illustration to be convincing or of help, but before proceeding to the poetry of the mid-century it will be helpful to recall the single critical work of the period which, while containing little that is profound, best suggests the major discontinuity between the poetic assumptions of the period ending about 1740 and the generation or so following. The work is Joseph Warton's *Essay on the Writings and Genius of Pope*, volume 1 of which appeared in 1756. This book, along with Thomas Warton's study of Spenser, his later history of English literature, and the poems of both Joseph and Thomas—including the several poems they wrote "for" their deceased father—show why the Warton brothers are so often singled out as the exemplars of preromantic taste.[5] Joseph's *Essay* is an attempt to put Pope in his place, which for Warton is clearly second place, behind Shakespeare, Milton, and Spenser. It is true that Warton's

position is often taken to be more heterodox than it was and that his claim
that Pope had not attempted the highest genres would have gone unchal-
lenged by most readers.[6] Nevertheless, the decisiveness and explicitness
with which Warton "places" Pope suggests a polemical stance, in fact a
continuation of the miniature manifesto which had prefaced Warton's *Odes*
a decade before the *Essay*, when he declared his intention to do what he
could to detach poetry from the fashion of moralizing in verse and restore
it to its "proper channel." While Warton would hardly go as far as Arnold
a century later, there is a clear line between his premises and Arnold's
opinion that Pope, like Dryden, is one of the classics not of our poetry but
of our prose. Common to both is the assumption that there is something
essentially unpoetic about Pope's subjects, that many of the poems are too
didactic to enter the kingdom of "pure poetry."[7]

   If we look at Warton's own poetry and much of what he praises in the
newer poetry around him, we find in fact that he could tolerate quite a bit
of didacticism and moralizing in verse, so that we need to push on a little
further to see what the dividing lines really are. We gain a better idea from
the following remarks concerning a poem Pope planned but never wrote,
a nationalistic epic, *Brutus*. It would have been a failure, Warton decides,
because Pope

   would have given us many elegant descriptions and many general characters, well
   drawn, but would have failed to set before our eyes the *Reality* of these objects,
   and the *Actions* of these characters, so that it would have appeared . . . how much,
   and for what reasons, the man that is skillful in painting modern life, and the
   most secret foibles and follies of his contemporaries, is, THEREFORE disqualified
   for representing the ages of heroism, and that simple life, which alone epic
   poetry can gracefully describe, in a word, that this composition would have
   shown more of the *Philosopher* than the *Poet*.   [1756 ed., p. 281]

   This passage is interesting, first, because it is entirely in the subjunctive:
like many present-day critics, Warton rises to high eloquence when unen-
cumbered by a text. Interesting for our inquiry is the assumption that what
disqualifies Pope for the epic is his modernity—his skill in "painting *mod-*
ern life." Warton views Pope as too historical, too much *in* history to rise
above it. Warton does not put the emphasis squarely there and is not usually read the way I am reading him. In fact, he argues that poetry is likely
to be better if it is historical, because "events that have actually happened
are, after all, the properest subjects for poetry." But his examples of great
works "grounded on true history" are revealing: *Oedipus, King Lear, Romeo*

and Juliet, as well as Pope's own *Elegy to the Memory of an Unfortunate Lady*, all works based on very distant, obscure, or private history (253). Anything recent, documentable, and public will not have "poignancy" enough. Pope's later poetry will be judged inferior to his early work by posterity because it is more historically particular. "For Wit and Satire are transitory and perishable, but Nature and Passion are eternal" (333–34).

The oppositions are interesting—Wit versus Nature, Satire versus Passion—and of course sentimental. With too much wit and too little passion, Pope's writing presumably does not come straight enough from the heart, but more is going on here than the simple victory of bourgeois sentimentalism over Augustan satire.[8] Since satiric poetry is nearly always highly *historical* poetry, the battle is in large part over whether poetry should be factual or fictional—that is, "romantic" in the old sense. When Warton says that Pope's epic would have shown more of the Philosopher than of the Poet, he means, I think, that Pope would have been not too logical but too accurate, too verifiable, and the antithesis anticipates Wordsworth's later declaration that the opposite of poetry is not prose but science.[9] Closer to Warton's own day, and closer to the terms of our discussion, we hear Adam Ferguson employing a similar distinction in *An Essay on the History of Civil Society*, published in 1767. The historian, he complains, who invokes a mythical state of nature to prove his points, "substitutes hypothesis instead of reality, and confounds the provinces of imagination and reason, of poetry and science." (Ferguson's zeal in exploding historical myths of societal origins is his generation's counterpart to Locke's zeal in exploding innate ideas.) For Ferguson, as for Hegel, history begins once myth and poetry have been cleared away. History is prose.[10]

And the poets would seem to agree. Whether by decision or default, from the 1740s on, most of the younger poets avoid direct historical treatment of the events of their day, even of their century. We can best appreciate how fundamental a shift occurs here by recalling that one of the deepest connections we can find between Dryden and Pope—and many of the contemporaries of each—is the shared sense of the poet's role as historian of his own times. That Dryden was for a time both poet laureate and historiographer royal was perhaps partially accidental, but it is also perfectly emblematic of his concerns from *Annus Mirabilis* to *Absalom and Achitophel* and beyond.[11] Pope's historical commitment deepens throughout his career, though it is strong even in the resolution of *Windsor Forest* into current prospects for the engaged observation of *The Rape of the Lock*, which, like Gay's *Trivia*, fondly records as it criticizes. Increasingly in Pope's later poetry, the historical role impresses with more urgency; the decision to name names becomes not only a matter of satiric strategy but a determination to leave a record—the true record—for posterity, a record often spilling over into footnotes meant to outlast the pseudohistories of Walpole's propagandists. The catalog of corruption is wearying and perhaps futile, Pope concludes by 1738, "Yet may this Verse (if such a Verse remain) / Show there was one who held it in disdain" (*Epilogue to the Satires*, I, 171–72). The desire to reconcile poetry and history—which in the broadest sense is characteristic of most of what we think of as Augustan poetry from 1660 to 1740—is likewise the warrant for all those details of political history which Swift appends as footnotes for posterity to the *Verses on the Death of Dr. Swift*. Finally, the nightmare lurking behind the *Dunciad* is an Orwellian one of cultural amnesia: "O Muse! relate (for you can tell alone, / Wits have short Memories, and Dunces none)."

The specter which seems to be lurking behind much of the poetry of the generation after Pope's and Swift's, however, is the fear not of the loss of history but of its crushing presence, a subliminal version of Stephen Daedalus's vision where "history is a nightmare from which I am trying to awake."[12] If this is a correct interpretation of the underlying motivation of much mid-eighteenth-century poetry, as I will try to argue satisfactorily in what follows, it should be added at once that it is usually not conscious and that the poets frequently wake from history by turning to sleep. All of the symptoms of sleepiness which Pope attributed ironically to the dunces and to Dulness—lethargy, indolence, inertia, aversion to light, the blurring of perceptual and conceptual boundaries—begin to appear quickly in the 1740s as positive poetic values. One aspect of this change has been characterized by Martin Price as a shift from the "light-centered worlds of Spenser, Milton, and Pope" to the "asylum of darkness."[13] Probably the most popular poem of the forties (and an extremely popular poem for another century) was *Night Thoughts*. Kindred but blessedly less sublime are the evening poems, of which Gray's *Elegy* and Collins's *Ode to Evening* are conspicuously the best.

That an atmosphere of melancholy gloom was cultivated during this period by solitary poetic wanderers has been well known since Eleanor M. Sickels wrote *The Gloomy Egoist* nearly half a century ago. Not explored in much depth since then is what might be regarded as the politics of melancholy, or perhaps more accurately, the politics of sensibility, of which melancholy is simply the commonest form in poetry. We will need to derive such a "politics" in most cases without the aid of the poets' explicit political statements, which are generally either lacking altogether in, or run contrary to what seem to be the likelier implications of, certain poetic decisions. To put these decisions into a context which clarifies their meaning, we need to consider them in continual relation to poetic procedures typified by Pope and Swift. Later I will contrast Swift and Gray in hopes of illustrating different sets of assumptions about the relation of public history and "poetic" privacy, but here the most useful general context may be suggested by considering Pope's career again. As Maynard Mack has pointed out, the vantage point from which Pope is able to tell his modern history is one of retirement.[14] This is a very complex stance, something achieved by living not merely in the country but close enough to the metropolis to be part of it (a sort of Connecticut of the soul); it must be achieved again and again in poem after poem, a vocal vision carefully and naturally "cultivated."

By the mid-century, retirement has hardened into retreat. The poet characteristically longs to be not only far from the madding crowd, which Pope had wanted as much as Gray, but far from everybody. Accordingly, many of the poems that most reflect the 1740s and 1750s are not epistles—that is, not poems with an explicit audience and implicit social engagement—but soliloquies or lyrics, usually blank verse musings or odes addressed to personifications. Conventionality again prevents us from taking this vogue as seriously as we might; personification is sometimes little more than capitalization, the echoes of Milton grow tiresome, and the iconography of melancholy is all too quickly learned in its entirety. (Parodies of melancholy poetry were written as early as the fifties and sixties, many of them as poetic recipes.)[15] But the fashion seems potentially revealing largely because it becomes so fashionable so quickly. Moreover, the melancholy poems seem merely to be part of a larger turning away from the social-historical world to which poetry traditionally belonged, and the deliberate break with and from the past is sometimes just as evident in many of the more cheerful poems of the period.

A signal example is the poem Joseph Warton placed at the front of his volume of odes in 1746, the ode *To Fancy*, which begins by saluting that visionary lady as the "Parent of each lovely Muse" and goes on to celebrate her "magic" and "all-commanding" power to alter the data of reality—for instance, to make gardens bloom in Lapland. Traditionally, however, the mother of the muses is not fancy but memory, whose magic is bounded by mimesis. The link between poetry and memory is of course more vivid in an oral culture than in a literate one, where prose and print carry more of the burden of record keeping, and it is true that the idea did not rest easily with Milton and Blake, who complained of the confusion of true poetic "Inspiration" with the "siren daughters" of "Dame Memory."[16] But I have

JOHN SITTER 419

tried to suggest how for most writers during the late seventeenth and early eighteenth centuries the conception of poetry as a special form of memory is operative: the poet remembers history and remembers it best. To make *fancy* the mother of the muses is to sever by poetic fiat the link between poetry and history and between the poet and the community.

We cannot place so much weight on the shoulders of Joseph Warton, but the pattern is conspicuous elsewhere in the middle years of the century. When, from the late forties on, we find poems in praise of memory, they are likely to praise *private* memory; thus, Shenstone's *Ode to Memory* (1748) is largely an ode to childhood days and to "innocence." Whatever other motives may be involved, the act of prizing private memory and childhood innocence allows the poet to declare his innocence of history, that adult world of public contention. The innocence of childhood is something of a mid-eighteenth-century invention, and we can best grasp its political content by considering that to which it is frequently opposed, namely "Ambition." We will return to the theme of ambition directly below, but for now it is useful to recall that Shenstone uses memory as an explicit vehicle to transport him from the world of ambition, even purely literary ambition, to the careless world of his hobbyhorse and whistle. (It is pleasant to imagine Sterne deliberately placing Toby, his time divided between hobbyhorse riding and whistling, in a world of conventional childhood duties.)

A few years before Shenstone's *Ode to Memory*, Gray wrote the first important eighteenth-century poem which poses childhood scenes against the fallen world of adulthood, the *Ode on a Distant Prospect of Eton College* (1742). Gray's nostalgic praise of childhood joys, the "paths of pleasure" from which the speaker is separated by time and space, is all the more interesting as a period phenomenon, since Gray most likely had spent some miserable years on the edges of those celebrated playing fields. But after the gracefully awkward humor of pliant arms cleaving grassy waves and idle progeny urging the flying ball, the description of childhood is mostly in negative terms, in terms of its difference from the speaker's present condition:

> Gay hope is theirs by fancy fed,
> Less pleasing when possessed;
> The tear forgot as soon as shed,
> The sunshine of the breast. . . .

Only a powerful need to simplify childhood experience could prompt a poet of Gray's intelligence to say that the child's tear is forgotten as soon

as shed or to sum up the world which includes adolescence—Gray himself
left Eton at seventeen—as a guiltless succession:

> The thoughtless day, the easy night,
> The spirits pure, the slumbers light,
> That fly the approach of morn.

It is tempting to compare Gray's generalized "slumbers light" with the
passage in *The Prelude* where Wordsworth describes the haunted slumbers
following the boat-stealing episode:

>   No familiar shapes
> Remained, no pleasant images of trees,
> Of sea or sky, no colours of green fields;
> But huge and mighty forms, that do not live
> Like living men, moved slowly through the mind
> By day, and were a trouble to my dreams.[17]

Thus far the temptation suggests much about the preoccupations of both
poets, but it would not be useful to follow it a step further and to conclude
that Wordsworth's lines are deeper because truer to experience. They are
"truer" psychologically, and they depend less on conventional views of
experience, or else on conventions closer to our own (the uninnocence of
children); but the truth Gray is after here is, I think, more political than
Wordsworth's and in fact more political than Gray himself would be likely
to acknowledge:

>   Alas, regardless of their doom,
>   The little victims play!
> No sense have they of ills to come,
>   Nor care beyond today:
> Yet see how all around 'em wait
>   The ministers of human fate,
> And black Misfortune's baleful train!
> Ah, show them where in ambush stand
> To seize their prey the murtherous band!
>   Ah, tell them, they are men!

Gray's lament would seem to be wholly apolitical, since the woes which
await the children are envisioned as human rather than historical evils, due,

in other words, to the nature of things rather than to the nature of people's allotment of things. The children shall one day be torn by "fury Passions," those "vultures of the mind," which Gray catalogs iconographically ("pallid Fear," "pining Love," "Envy wan," and so on). Then Gray turns to a somewhat more social picture, though the images remain indistinct:

> Ambition this small tempt to rise,
> Then whirl the wretch from high,
> To bitter Scorn a sacrifice,
> And grinning Infamy.
> The stings of Falsehood those shall try,
> And hard Unkindness' altered eye,
> That mocks the tear it forced to flow;
> And keen Remorse with blood defiled,
> And moody Madness laughing wild
> Amid severest woe.

The most accurate thing we could say at this point of the politics of this particular melancholy is that Gray cannot or will not make a distinction between necessary and unnecessary human suffering, just as it is not clear a few lines later whether "Poverty" is as inevitable as "slow-consuming Age" or something which accompanies it because of human "Unkindness."[18] Gray offers no political platform, just as Johnson does not in *The Vanity of Human Wishes*. But what is politically significant from our position is simply the fact that childhood and rural innocence are being used as new norms by which to measure the passionate tragedy of the world adults make. The prepassionate, or innocent, state attributed to the schoolchildren is a kind of internalized Golden Age, a prehistory of the sort which Adam Ferguson later complained belongs more to poetry than to truth. So, at the beginning of *The Seasons*, James Thomson lavishly describes the earliest stage of human life, when all was springtime harmony and vegetarian plenty, as a prepassionate childhood of the race. Now, however, "all / Is off the poise within: the passions all / Have burst their bounds," and the breeze of social feeling has given way to a psychic "storm" of "mixed emotions":

> Senseless and deformed,
> Convulsive Anger storms at large; or, pale
> And silent, settles into fell revenge.
> Base Envy withers at another's joy,

And hates that excellence it cannot reach.
Desponding Fear, of feeble fancies full,
Weak and unmanly, loosens every power.
Even Love itself is bitterness of soul,
A pensive anguish pining at the heart;
Or, sunk to sordid interest, feels no more
That noble wish, that never-cloyed desire,
Which, selfish joy disdaining, seeks alone
To bless the dearer object of its flame.
Hope sickens with extravagance; and Grief,
Of life impatient, into madness swells. . . .

(*Spring*, 281–95)

From this storm of violent and contending passions grows eventually the "listless unconcern" of modern life until (in phrases reminiscent of Book IV of the *Dunciad*) "At last, extinct each social feeling, fell / And joyless inhumanity pervades / And petrifies the heart" (301–7).[19]

One secular version of history which had been available to poets who wanted to retain the idea of a Golden Age was a correspondingly secular version of the Fortunate Fall: being expelled from a cultural Eden, or, as Thomson puts it, from "Nature's ample lap" (*Spring*, 182; cf. 351), leads man to exert his energies, learn, build, make laws, and so on. This is Pope's version of history in epistle 3 of the *Essay on Man*, and it is compatible both with traditional Christian patterns of theodicy and with the desire to posit a Lockean rather than a Hobbesean original state. But increasingly toward the mid-century, the Fall into society and history is seen not as a fortunate fall but as a catastrophe.

To see this development accurately we need to distinguish "official" dogma for many of the poets from what emerges less consciously. Thomson is the best single example of the possible forms of ambivalence, probably because he is literally between the generation of Gay and Pope, for example, and that of Gray and Collins. (Gay was born in 1685, Thomson in 1700, Gray in 1716, Collins, the Wartons, and Akenside in the early 1720s.) What I refer to as the official view in Thomson and later writers is one which endorses vigorous activity, commercial energy, social engagement, "worthy" ambition, and patriotism, which is merely a broadened form of benevolence, which in turn is virtue at its highest. Public life, hard work, technical progress are all good things, according to this view. We can see it embodied in the several mid-century adaptations of "The Choice of Hercules," the episode originally imagined by Prodicus, in which the young Hercules has to choose between Virtue and Pleasure. In Shenstone's rendition, "The Judgment of Hercules," it is clear that pleasure is suspect because it lies in "cloister'd" withdrawal from society, while virtue is tied to "industry," "Fame," "arts," and "arms." Officially, in short, virtue is public.[20]

But the increasingly commercial civilization in which public virtue would find its theater is at best problematic. Thomson is in the awkward position of celebrating the Golden Age, one of the traits of which is the absence of navigation, shortly before turning to praise the British navy and sea-connected empire—and "Navigation bold," that "Mother severe of infinite delights!" (Summer, 1,768–70). But if Thomson's mercantile muse praises the "rising world of trade," sings the city as the "nurse of art," and sees "Industry" as its human prerequisite (Summer, 1,006; Autumn, 113–41), Thomson repeatedly imagines his own inspiration as coming from solitary walks in the hills and longs for the "deepending dale, or inmost sylvan glade" (Summer, 191–99, 560), for such precincts are

> the haunts of meditation, these
> The scenes where ancient bards the inspiring breath
> Ecstatic felt, and, from this world retired,
> Conversed with angels and immortal forms.
> (Summer, 522–25)

The opposition of poetic and political values animates Thomson's most powerful contrast of rural and urban life, contemplation and action, innocence and guilt:

> Let others brave the flood in quest of gain,
> And beat for joyless months the gloomy wave.
> Let such as deem it glory to destroy
> Rush into blood, the sack of cities seek—
> Unpierced, exulting in the widow's wail,
> The virgin's shriek, the infant's trembling cry.
> . . . .
> Let this through cities work his eager way
> By legal outrage and established guile,
> The social sense extinct; and that ferment
> Mad into tumult the seditious herd,
> Or melt them down to slavery. Let these
> Ensnare the wretched in the toils of law,
> Ensnare the wretched in the toils of law,

> Fomenting discord, and perplexing right,
> An iron race! and those of fairer front,
> But equal inhumanity, in courts,
> Delusive pomp, and dark cabals delight. . . .
>
> (*Autumn*, 1,278–96)

Against this catalog of the woes of modern social life Thomson places an image of individual retreat, a stoic figure who detaches himself from the wreckage around him. This image we will find again in Joseph Warton, where, too, the stoic protestations carry overtones of desperation because the "philosophy" is so clearly at odds with the emotionalism prized elsewhere in the poem. Thomson's sage is one who,

> from all the stormy passions free
> That restless men involve, hears, and but hears,
> At distance sage, the human tempest roar,
> Wrapped close in conscious peace. The fall of kings,
> The rage of nations, and the crush of states
> Move not the man who, from the world escaped,
> In still retreats and flower solitudes
> To Nature's voice attends from month to month,
> And day to day, through the revolving year—
> Admiring, sees her in her every shape. . . .
>
> (*Autumn*, 1,299–1,308)

If this sage resembles a Roman philosopher at the beginning of the passage, by its end he seems more like an English poet, specifically, a poet who might write a poem on the "revolving year." And if this poet is the laureate of "Nature's voice," it is clear that Nature here does not include human nature. We have entered the world of modern usage, where "nature" typically means a place without people (or without any people but me) and where "society" is seen as radically "unnatural." This is the complex of assumptions which started becoming conventionally "poetic" during the middle and later years of the eighteenth century and which in Cowper apparently hardened into the axiom that "God made the country, and man made the town" (*The Task*, I, 749). One could add, of course that God made man and so must have something to do with the town and with human society generally, but the addition is not often made by the mid-century poets.

Celebrations of solitary retreat are particularly arresting in Thomson because they are very likely to follow, or be followed quickly by, a call to art and arms, by praise of progress, or by intimations of the providential role of British imperial policy. But Thomson's most starkly ambivalent poem is *The Castle of Indolence*, a work rather indolently composed, beginning sometime in the thirties and ending with its publication a few months before his death in 1748. Although Thomson uses his Spenserian idiom at several points for burlesque, it also calls attention to the similarity between the Castle and Spenserian seductions which must be destroyed or fled. Conceptually as well as chronologically, however, Thomson's Castle is closer to the Palace of Art than to the Bower of Bliss. Although sensually appealing, its lure is more intellectual than erotic: it is a retreat, offering uninterrupted solitude, freedom from any social responsibility, and absolution from all duties and from memory, and it is associated most persuasively with reverie and poetic imagination, "dreams that wave before the half-shut eye" (I, vi; cf. I, xxxvi–xlviii).

The castle is of course eventually broken up by the "Knight of Arts and Industry" in a kind of harrowing of hell, and the prisoners of sloth are set free. But more to the point for our inquiry concerning poetic alignment is the fact that this knightly paragon of social virtue is accompanied by a poet, the "little Druid wight" (II, xxxiii) usually identified as Alexander Pope (which might suggest that the Knight himself, who at his country seat combined the roles of "the chief, the patriot, and the swain," should remind us of Bolingbroke). Since it is the poet's song which breaks the enchanter's spell, Thomson is paying wistful allegiance to the notion of poetry as a political force, idealizing the collaboration of poet and patriot as Pope had done in his later poetry and as he himself had done in his most sustained political-historical poem, *Liberty* (1735–1736), where he commemorates the "recording arts" for their power to "rouse ambition" in a great nation (V, 374ff.).[21] But ambition is, as we have seen in *The Seasons*, likely to be delusive, dirty, and dangerous. In the *Castle of Indolence* there is a crystal ball called the Mirror of Vanity in which one can see the ambitious toiling at their getting and spending, at writing books—

> This globe pourtrayed the race of learned men,
> Still at their books, and turning o'er the page,
> Backwards and forwards: oft they snatch the pen
> As if inspired, and in a Thespian rage;
> Then write, and blot, as would your ruth engage.

> Why, authors, all this scrawl and scribbling sore?
> To lose the present, gain the future age,
> Praised to be when you can hear no more,
> And much enriched with fame when useless worldly store!
>
> (I, lii)

We next see those trying to make their way in the city, and then the politicians whispering and shrugging the "important shoulder" significantly.

> But what most showed the vanity of life
> Was to behold the nations all on fire
> In cruel broils engaged, and deadly strife:
> Most Christian kings, inflamed by black desire,
> With honourable ruffians in their hire,
> Cause war to rage and blood around to pour.
> Of this sad work when each begins to tire,
> They sit them down just where they were before.
> Till for new scenes of woe peace shall their force restore.
>
> (I, lv)

The Castle of Indolence can be read as a debate on the virtues of the stances I have characterized as Augustan retirement and post-Augustan retreat, with retirement the official winner: the rural but industrious Knight lives in "deep retirement" (II, xxvii), and he and his poet destroy the isolated and indolent world of the Castle. But at the same time much of the best energy of the poem is used to paint the futility of "industry" so convincingly that the world of reverie and retreat looks not only comfortable but potentially noble by comparison. Thomson might not agree with this reading of his unofficial sympathies, and some present-day students of his poetry certainly would not.[22] This reading, however, accords not only with much that is in the poem but with much that is around it, in the work of several writers of the mid-eighteenth century for whom the urgings of "ambition" and the promptings of "pure" poetry are felt as antithetical demands. This tension is of course especially difficult for anyone who might ambitiously want to be a pure poet, and we will examine its strains more closely in the next chapter.

In the mid-eighteenth century, history's metonymy is conflict. Very often it is the violent conflict of war, but it can also be the strife of competition. Not surprisingly, the retreat from history occurs in poems most dramatically when historical events and public actors are portrayed as hostile not only to the life of poetry (for example, as antithetical to Thomson's nature-loving solitary) but to the life of the poet himself. The very earliest major poems of William Collins and Thomas Warton the Younger are pastorals in which the youthful poetic speakers are victims of violence perpetrated by older, more public males. The speakers are fugitives from war, appearing in the poems at just the point where they are becoming refugees. The last of Collins's *Persian Eclogues* (published in 1742, but probably written when Collins was seventeen) ends with two shepherds fleeing the invading Tartar army—

> when loud along the vale was heard
> A shriller shriek and nearer fires appeared:
> The afrighted shepherds through the dews of night,
> Wide o'er the moonlight hills, renewed their flight.

Warton's *Pastoral Eclogues* (published anonymously in 1745) are set "during the wars in Germany," and his young swains are continually retreating from the clamor of war to the protection of groves and caves.

But the best example of such a collision between the poet-speaker and the hostile force of history is *The Bard*. Gray's poem is based on the appealing tradition that Edward I executed the Welsh bards once he had conquered that country—an appealing tradition because it suggests the poets were once too potent politically to be ignored—and the poem begins as the bard stands high on a cliff hurling prophetic curses down on the king like so many verbal boulders. Finally he hurls himself:

> " . . . with joy I see
> The different doom over fates assign.
> Be thine despair and sceptered care;
> To triumph, and to die, are mine."
> He spoke, and headlong from the mountain's height
> Deep in the roaring tide he plunged to endless night.

To triumph and to die. The phrase seems more a definition than a paradox in Gray's poetic world, where death, like childhood, can so readily become an emblem of innocence from history. The bard's suicide is both a badge of his sincerity (an association we have since tended to take more literally) and a final exercise of the kind of linguistic power which William Law had attributed to God: "What he speaks he acts."[23] To end his poet's lyric and life in the same breath is Gray's sublime speech act. If we visualize the dramatic moment Gray has frozen in the poem, we may understand better the full significance of the encounter and the redefinition of death as triumph. The fantasy on which it turns is double. On the one hand, history must stop for the poet, since this king, unlike George II, must actually listen to the ode he has occasioned;[24] on the other hand, the forced march of history will go on and, embodied in Edward and his army, will kill the poet.

The collision between poet and history is less violent in the *Elegy Written in a Country Churchyard* but no less fatal. The poem ends with the imagined death of the poet himself, a death related in the subjunctive but converted into virtual fact in the epitaph, which I take to be the poet's own. Once we view the *Elegy* as a poem in which the poet imagines the reaction to his own death, a useful comparison comes to mind with Swift's *Verses on the Death of Dr. Swift*. The poems are so obviously different in intent and effect that most readers, not surprisingly, would not draw the comparison; but it may help clarify some rapid changes in poetry if we attempt to pinpoint some of the differences between these poems of the early 1730s and the late 1740s.

Both the *Verses* and the *Elegy* are poems of moral generalization. Swift's reflections are largely glosses on the maxim from La Rochefoucauld which he translates in the epigraph as, "In the Adversity of our best Friends, we find something that doth not displease us," and versifies as, "In all Distresses of our Friends / we first consult our private Ends." Gray's "maxims," on the other hand, are "The paths of glory lead but to the grave," and "Even from the tomb the voice of nature cries." The moral position implied by the *Elegy* as a whole is almost an inversion of La Rochefoucauld: we are so sympathetic, so tenderly framed, that even the imagined distresses of total strangers affect us feelingly. Not *every*one, exactly, but surely the speaker and the reader will appreciate the moral sentiments carved in the stones and trees of the churchyard in the innocent country.[25]

Distance from town is an important part of the moral atmosphere of Swift's poem, too, and so is the relative solitude of the speaker. If Swift is not quite as explicit about locating his world far from the madding crowd or about isolating his speaker ("And leaves the world to darkness and to me"), the ethos of his *Verses* is quite as dependent on the impression that the speaker is far from the center of power and that he is insulated by his integrity. The obvious difference on this count, however, is one between total and partial solitude. The simple and supposedly neutral speaker who characterizes Swift insists upon his social life: it is a contracted society, to be sure, but the friendships are as essential a part of the man as his pleasant stories of Whigs and Tories. Gray's speaker speaks to no one except the

reader, and for the "hoary-headed swain" who describes him (a nice counterpart to Swift's coffeehouse judge) he is the silent image of "one
forlorn."

The sympathies of Gray's poet are generalized to the whole village and
to the simpler folk everywhere ("mindful of the unhonored dead"), but he
has no specific connection to anyone. The different attitudes toward the
use of particulars is in fact the source of most of the other differences
between the poems. For just as the expression of anger and humor in
Swift's poem depends on the use of historical particulars, so Gray's melancholy and solemnity depend on the generalization of emotions into a
subjunctive world, a world where *"Perhaps . . . is laid"* some potential hero
to be mourned by a poet whom *"Haply* some hoary-headed swain *may"*
describe to *"some* kindred spirit" who comes by "chance" to ask. Swift's
poem is wholly without despondency because its anger so clearly has particular limits; Gray's, like the melancholy it marks as its own, is grief without an object.

While Swift's poem aims to make all of the people and events it names
into part of the historical record, much of the most poignant musing in
Gray's *Elegy* centers on the reflection that the simple villagers buried in
the churchyard are not part of history. The "short and simple annals of the
poor" are contrasted with the public "Memory" left by "Ambition,"
"Grandeur," and the "pomp of power." There is much melancholy in their
obscurity as it is translated into the speculative subjunctive:

> Perhaps in this neglected spot is laid
> Some heart once pregnant with celestial fire;
> Hands that the rod of empire might have swayed,
> Or waked to ecstasy the living lyre. . . .
>
> Some village-Hampden that with dauntless breast
> The little tyrant of his fields withstood;
> Some mute inglorious Milton here may rest,
> Some Cromwell guiltless of his country's blood.

But Gray insists upon having it both ways, as we have ever since the
mid-eighteenth century: the pathos of unrealized potential is balanced emotionally by the triumph of rural innocence.

> The applause of listening senates to command,
> The threats of pain and ruin to despise,
> To scatter plenty o'er a smiling land,
> And read their history in a nation's eyes,

Their lot forbade: nor circumscribed alone
Their growing virtues, but their crimes confined;
Forbade to wade through slaughter to a throne,
And shut the gates of mercy on mankind. . . .

It is the conception of potential—unnurtured or thwarted talent—that is most remarkable in all of these reflections. What, after all, is a mute Milton? The fact that we are likely to read the lines hundreds of times without asking that question suggests how deeply the idea of potential is embedded in modern thought. A blind Milton we know, a deaf Milton we could imagine, but to conceive a mute Milton we need to conceive of the poet in a different manner; before the phrase can have any meaning, the poet must be no longer one who writes poetry but a sensitive person who has a poet's soul. In the *Ode to Fear* Collins prays that he will be allowed not to write like Shakespeare but "once like him to feel," the presumption being that all the rest will then follow.

Just after the stanzas from the *Elegy* which we have been considering, the villagers are idealized for living "far from the madding crowd's *ignoble strife*," a phrase which suggests a vision like the one available in Thomson's little mirror of vanity. The emphasis is less on the crowd as an unruly or destructive mob—a traditional staple of satiric imagery—but on strife, the competition and ambition of city folk as "ignoble" virtually by definition. Gray's poet is not made for such a world, and even the subjunctive intrusion of history into the village where he has sought refuge is enough to kill him off. The mixture of defensive and superior feelings at being out of the public world and the historical mainstream crystallizes in the last line of a later poem, *The Progress of Poesy*, where the poet imagines his eventual place, "Beneath the Good how far—but far above the Great."

The suspicion of greatness is one of the few themes shared by early eighteenth-century satirists and later sentimentalists alike. *A Tale of a Tub, The Beggar's Opera*, and *Jonathan Wild* are largely treatises on the subject. If chronology did not discourage us, we might almost read the mock-heroic *Jonathan Wild* as an ironic commentary on Hegel's conception of heroism in his lectures on history. To juxtapose the two authors helps to measure the distance between either Augustan or post-Augustan attitudes and at least one strain of later romantic preoccupations with titanic figures. Hegel's world-historical individuals "must be called 'heroes,' insofar as they have derived their purpose and vocation not from the calm, regular course of things, sanctioned by the existing order, but from a secret source whose content is still hidden and has not yet broken through into existence." (Cf. Pope's ironic explanation in the *Epistle to Bathurst* that misers act upon "Some Revelation hid from me and you.") "Great men have worked for their own satisfaction and not that of others," Hegel explains, but when we consider their fate we find that

> they were not what is commonly called happy, nor did they want to be .... Thus they attained no calm enjoyment. Their whole life was labor and trouble.... They die early like Alexander, they are murdered like Caesar, transported to St. Helena like Napoleon. This awful fact, that historical men were not what is called happy—for only private life in its manifold external circumstances can be "happy"—may serve as consolation for those people who need it, the envious ones who cannot tolerate greatness and eminence.[26]

These are the terms in which Fielding's Jonathan Wild soliloquizes over his punch on the motives of "priggery" (that is, thievery):

> " 'tis the inward glory, the secret consciousness of doing great and wonderful actions, which alone can support the truly GREAT man, whether he be a CON-QUEROR, a TYRANT, a STATESMAN, or a PRIG.... For what but some such inward satisfaction as this could inspire men possessed of power, wealth, of every human blessing which pride, avarice, or luxury could desire, to forsake their homes, abandon ease and repose, and ... at the hazard of all that fortune hath liberally given them, could send them at the Lead of a multitude of *prigs*, called an army, to molest their neighbours; to introduce rape, rapine, bloodshed, and every kind of misery among their own species? ... let me then hold myself contented with this reflection, that I have been wise though unsuccessful, and am a GREAT though an unhappy man."[27]

A second, briefer pairing of ideas will underscore the difference between pathos based on heroic faith and irony based on a colder estimate of individualistic "greatness." Of heroes Hegel says, "Once their objective is attained, they fall off like empty hulls from the kernel" (41); they are dropped, in other words, when "Reason" no longer needs them. Fielding puts it this way: "There seems to be a certain measure of mischief and iniquity which every great man is to fill up, and then fortune looks on him [as] of no more use than a silkworm whose bottom is spun, and deserts him" (126).

But now let us turn the commentary and allow Hegel to serve as critic of some of the dominant chords in mid-eighteenth-century writing. We can indeed, says Hegel, dwell with melancholy, lamenting the decay of kingdoms and "contemplating history as the slaughter-bench at which the happiness of peoples, the wisdom of states, and the virtues of individuals have been sacrificed." But, he insists, "we have purposely eschewed that method of reflection which ascends from this scene of particulars to general principles. Besides, it is not in the interest of such sentimental reflection really to rise above these depressing emotions and to solve the mysteries of Providence presented in such contemplations. It is rather their nature to dwell melancholically on the empty and fruitless sublimities of their negative result" (27).

Hegel is not but easily could be describing in this meditation on melancholy the "fruitless sublimities" of Gray's *Elegy* or Johnson's *Vanity of Human Wishes*. We have seen how the conflict and violence of public history as it is conceived metonymically by many of the poets leads to images of Retreat, images of shepherds fleeing as they sing, for example, hurrying toward the shelter of shady groves or the protection of caves, and we have seen that these images of seclusion are also metaphors for the solitary poetic imagination itself. In one of the most radical of retreats, Joseph Warton imagines himself at the end of *The Enthusiast* secured from the ravages of historical reality, like Thomson's sage in his distance from disaster but unlike him in that he does not even hear the disturbance:

> So when rude Whirlwinds rouse the roaring Main,
> Beneth fair THETIS sits, in coral Caves,
> Serenely gay, nor sinking Sailors Cries
> Disturb her sportive Nymphs. . . .
>
> (1744)

The imagined shipwreck is suggestive, for it is the image Hegel invoked to characterize one response, an inadequate response, in his view, to historical misery: "And at last, out of the boredom with which this sorrowful reflection threatens us, we draw back into the vitality of the present, into our aims and interests of the moment; we retreat, in short, into the selfishness that stands on the quiet shore and thence enjoys in safety the distant spectacle of wreckage and confusion" (27).

What is the nature of the world into which the poets retreat and which they pose as an alternative history? It is not in general a world of romance, although that is the term usually opposed to "history" in eighteenth-century criticism. The successful assimilation of romance material into poetry really *is* a romantic achievement. The post-Augustan poetic world first evident in the 1740s is typically less rich in narrative analogues and more abundant in detached images of seclusion and protection; it is a world which is often visually indistinct or darkened; and it is a world where consolation is prized over confrontation, stasis over strife.

Notes

1. The question is meant to be not whether final "objectivity" is available but what use is to be made of our own perspective when dealing with a "period of transition." This is much of the subject of Whitehead's *Adventures of Ideas*, written half a century ago, and a preoccupation of later "metahistory," including Hayden White's book by that title (Baltimore: Johns Hopkins University Press, 1973). Whitehead: "Knowledge is always accompanied with accessories of emotion and purpose . . . . In every age of well-marked transition there is the pattern of habitual dumb practice and emotion which is passing, and there is oncoming of a new complex of habit. Between the two lies a zone of anarchy, either a passing danger or a prolonged welter involving misery of decay and zest of young life. In our estimate of these agencies everything depends upon our standpoint of criticism: In other words, our history of ideas is derivative from our ideas of history, that is to say, upon our own intellectual standpoint" (*Adventures of Ideas* [New York: Macmillan, 1933], pp. 5, 8).

2. Donald Greene surveys the problems of these and other categories in "Augustinianism and Empiricism," *ECS*, 1 (1967): 33–68, and *The Age of Exuberance* (New York: Random House, 1970). For "preromantic" see, e.g., Bertrand Bronson, "The Pre-Romantic or Post-Augustan Mode," *ELH*, 20 (1953), reprinted in *Facets of the Enlightenment* (Berkeley: University of California Press, 1968), pp. 159–72; Northrop Frye, "Towards Defining an Age of Sensibility," *ELH*, 23 (1956): 144–52; and Joan Pittock, *The Ascendancy of Taste: The Achievement of Joseph and Thomas Warton* (London: Routledge & Kegan Paul, 1973), pp. 215–20.

3. Weinbrot concludes his deeply provocative study of "Augustan" literature and political writing with the recommendation that the term be discarded: see *Augustus Caesar in "Augustan" England: The Decline of a Classical Norm* (Princeton: Princeton University Press, 1978), esp. pp. 229–41.

4. *The Logic of the Humanities* (New Haven: Yale University Press, 1961), pp. 139–40. For Miles's alternative approach see *The Primary Language of Poetry in the 1740's and 1840's* (Berkeley: University of California Press, 1950).

5. According to David Fairer, "The Poems of Thomas Warton the Elder?" *RES*, n.s., 26 (1975): 287–300, 395–406, Joseph and young Thomas wrote at least ten of the poems published in 1748 in the posthumous collection of their father's verse. The Wartons have been studied recently by Joan Pittock in *The Ascendancy of Taste*, by Arthur Johnston in his admirable brief survey "Poetry and Criticism after 1740," in Roger Lonsdale, ed., *History of Literature in the English Language: Dryden to Johnson* (London: Sphere, 1971), pp. 257–98, and by Wallace Jackson, *The Probable and the Marvelous* (Athens: University of Georgia Press, 1978), pp. 39–88.

6. So argued George Sherburn in *The Early Career of Alexander Pope* (Oxford: Oxford University Press, 1934), p. 10

7. Joseph Warton first used the phrase "pure poetry" in his dedication (to Edward Young) of the *Essay on the Writings and Genius of Pope* (1756): "We do not, it would seem, sufficiently attend to the difference there is, betwixt a MAN of WIT, a MAN OF SENSE, and a TRUE

POET. Donne and Swift were undoubtedly men of wit and men of sense: but what traces have they left of PURE POETRY?"

8. Cf. Thomas Lockwood, "On the Relationship of Satire and Poetry after Pope," *Studies in English Literature*, 14 (1947): 387–402.

9. In a note to the preface to the second edition of *Lyrical Ballads* (1800), Wordsworth remarked that "much confusion has been introduced into criticism by this contradistinction of Poetry and Prose, instead of the more philosophical one of Poetry and Matter of Fact, or Science."

10. Ferguson, *An Essay*, ed. Duncan Forbes (Edinburgh: Edinburgh University Press, 1966), p. 2, cf. pp. 6, 8, 10, 30. Hegel: "Myths, folk songs, traditions are not part of original history; they are still obscure modes and peculiar to obscure peoples. Here we deal with peoples who knew who they were and what they wanted. Observed and observable reality is a more solid foundation for history than the transience of myths and epics" (*Reason in History*, trans. Robert S. Hartman [Indianapolis: Bobbs-Merrill, 1953], p. 3).

11. Earl Miner emphasizes Dryden's personal and public historicism persuasively in *Dryden's Poetry* (Bloomington: Indiana University Press, 1967), pp. 106–43.

12. James Joyce, *Ulysses* (New York: Random House, 1946), p. 35.

13. "The Sublime Poem: Pictures and Powers," *Yale Review*, 58 (1968–69): 194–213.

14. *The Garden and the City: Retirement and Politics in the Later Poetry of Pope, 1731–1743* (Toronto: University of Toronto Press, 1969).

15. Eleanor M. Sickels, *The Gloomy Egoist* (New York: Columbia University Press, 1932), pp. 67–68, 95–98.

16. Milton, introduction to *Reason of Church Government*; Blake, preface to *Milton*; cf. Northrop Frye, *Fearful Symmetry* (Princeton: Princeton University Press, 1947), p. 163.

17. *Prelude* (1850), I, 395–400, in *The Prelude*, ed. Jonathan Wordsworth, M. H. Abrams, and Stephen Gill (New York: Norton, 1979). Quotations from Gray are from *The Poems of Gray, Collins, and Goldsmith*, ed. Roger Lonsdale (London: Longmans, 1969); Collins is quoted from *The Works of W. C.*, ed. Richard Wendorf and Charles Ryskamp (Oxford: Clarendon Press, 1979).

18. Cf. the "common lot" of political and natural ills in *Night Thoughts*, I, 237ff.: "War ... volcano, storm ... Oppression ..."

19. Quotations from *The Castle of Indolence* are from *The Seasons and The Castle of Indolence*, ed. James Sambrook (London: Oxford University Press, 1972); *The Seasons* is quoted from Thomson's *Poetical Works*, ed. J. L. Robertson (1908; reprint ed., London: Oxford University Press, 1965).

20. On the mid-century vogue of *The Choice of Hercules*, see Earl Wasserman, "The Inherent Values of Eighteenth-Century Personification," *PMLA*, 65 (1950): 435–63 (esp. 437–39), and Ronald Paulson, "The Simplicity of Hogarth's *Industry and Idleness*," *ELH*, 41 (1974): 291–320 (esp. 308–11). Shenstone's "The Judgment of Hercules" is quoted from *The Poetical Works of William Shenstone*, ed. George Gilfillan (1854; reprint ed., New York: Greenwood, 1968), pp. 186–201; the phrases are from lines 315–80.

21. *Liberty* has been quoted from the text of Thomson's *Poetical Works*, ed. J. L. Robertson, Oxford Standard Authors (1908; reprint ed.: London, Oxford University Press, 1965).

22. E.g., Donald Greene, "From Accidie to Neurosis: *The Castle of Indolence* Revisited," in Maximillian E. Novak, ed., *English Literature in the Age of Disguise* (Berkeley: University of California Press, 1977).

23. Law, *A Demonstration* ... (1737), in *The Works of W. L.*, 9 vols. (New Forest: G. Moreton, 1892–93), V, 73.

24. Similar fantasies of the poet's access to his king and power over him are enacted in Thomas Warton's *The Crusade* and *The Grave of King Arthur*.

25. The moral appeal of Gray's work has been reconsidered freshly and helpfully by Howard Weinbrot in "Gray's *Elegy*: A Poem of Moral Choice and Resolution," *Studies in English Literature*, 18 (1978): 537–51.

26. Hegel, *Reason in History*, trans. Robert S. Hartman (Indianapolis: Bobbs-Merrill, 1953), p. 41; page numbers in text refer to this edition.

27. Fielding, *Jonathan Wild and a Voyage to Lisbon*, ed. A. R. Humphreys and Douglas Brooks (London: J. M. Dent, 1973), pp. 58–59; page numbers in text refer to this edition.

The Urbane Sublime

MARSHALL BROWN

Ein Geist, heißt es, ist ein Wesen, welches Vernunft hat. So ist es denn also keine Wundergabe, Geister zu sehen; denn wer Menschen sieht, der sieht Wesen, die Vernunft haben.

(Kant, *Träume eines Geistersehers*)

Even the best sublime poetry of the eighteenth century often seems intolerably naive. The style is self-consciously inflated, the formal sense is deficient, and the poets display a fatal attraction to spirits, ghosts, and Muses. As a result, an uncomprehending reader is apt to discount these poems as the effluvia of an epidemic of bad taste. Yet the eighteenth century attached far more importance to matters of taste than the twentieth does, and in its day the poetry gave enjoyment—and not just enjoyment, but often delight, amazement, transport—to countless readers, including many of great knowledge and discernment. Clearly the sensibility of these readers was different from our own. If we wish, then, to explain the success and the historical destiny of the sublime style, we will need to patiently reconstruct the criteria according to which the poets wrote.

George Eliot's notorious destruction of Young is a case in point. By inquiry into Young's sincerity, Eliot arrives directly at the dismissive conclusion that he was (to borrow Hume's phrase) a liar by profession.[1] And to be sure, the widespread use of first person forms in Young, as in other poets of the age, is liable to strike a psychologically sophisticated modern reader as naive or insincere. But this impression is misleading. It may be accurate to call the poets liars, but it is anachronistic to condemn them on that account. Bishop Hurd, for one, quotes Hume's catch phrase with

From *ELH* 45 (1978), 236–54.

approval in order to defend poetic license. Poets should and do lie, he argues, though they have no intention to deceive and are "not so unreasonable [as to] expect to have their lyes believed" (*Letters on Chivalry and Romance*, X). Instead of condemnation, Eliot's brilliant dissection of Young ought thus properly to have led to the insight that all the poetry of the period, even including apparently confessional outpourings, is deliberately and consciously artificial.

From this perspective the sublime poets are seen to have more in common with the satirists than is generally acknowledged. It has been the prevailing, though not universal practice to divide the poets into two opposing camps: the comic and the serious, the clever and the pompous, the critically detached and the uncritically self-involved, or, more simply, the good and the bad. Thus, in a well-known essay, included in a volume significantly entitled *Hateful Contraries*, William Wimsatt wrote that "Augustan poetry at its best . . . was the last stand of a classic mode of laughter against forces that were working for a sublime inflation of ideas and a luxury of sorry feeling."[2] More recently, a provocative essay by Peter Hughes has treated us to the spectacle of a conflict waged between, on the one hand, the rational forces of counter-Reformation and enlightenment, who speak with the tongues of men, and, on the other, the barbarian enthusiasts, who speak with the tongues of heroes or of gods.[3] Such "dualistic" accounts, however important their differences in detail, ultimately all stress the "dissociation" between two poetic modes as well as the "discontinuities" inherent within the sublime mode.[4]

In contrast to this prevailing view, I wish to suggest that the satiric and the sublime poets wrote on the basis of common stylistic presuppositions. They employed similar kinds of verbal artifice, entertained similar conceptions of formal organization, and envisioned similar purposes with respect to much the same audience. There is a continuity between the satiric and sublime modes, as well as between the sublime mode and ordinary experience. Important consequences follow from these observations. They allow us to see the earlier eighteenth century as a unit with its own integrity, rather than as the battleground for competing styles representing incompatible intellectual syntheses. More important, they also allow us to see what the unity of the period consists in. It was a period able to encompass within a single stylistic framework a remarkable and remarkably shifting range of tone and subject matter. Its thought processes are characterized by their continuity, their fluidity, and their reluctance to be polarized, in short, by what might fancifully be called a benevolent latitudinarianism of the understanding. My ultimate purpose in showing the unity within diversity of early eighteenth century verse is thus to make a statement not just about poetic style, but about the eighteenth century mind.

For reasons which will become increasingly clear, I choose to call the dominant style of the period the urbane sublime.[5] I can only present the more difficult half of the case here, showing the urbanity within leading examples of sublime verse. I have also indicated in passing some salient points of contact with Pope, trusting that the elevated seriousness which informs much Tory satire is by now generally recognized.[6] The present essay, then, offers a tripartite analysis of the style of eighteenth century sublime poetry, with the aim of bringing to light the principles governing its composition. The opening section deals with the most obviously troublesome aspect of the style, its artificial and inflated rhetoric, taking as an example one of the century's most palpable and most artful poetic lies, Thomas Gray's *Ode on a Distant Prospect of Eton College*. The second section turns to *The Seasons* and to Collins' *Odes* in order to examine the period's formal sense, and the third to Eliot's *bête noire*, *Night Thoughts*, in order to describe the purpose of the style and to account for its fascination with the supernatural. I am concerned here only with poetry of, roughly, the first half of the century; in a subsequent essay, dealing with Cowper, Kant, and Rousseau, I will discuss the collapse of the urbane sublime style and speculate on the reasons for the post-romantic blindness to its techniques, structures, and purpose.

I

The first obstacle to reading much eighteenth century poetry is the apparent lack of decorum: the style often appears ill assorted to the subject matter. As a result, it becomes difficult to gauge the intended stylistic effect or to evaluate the role played by the poetic and rhetorical artifices in achieving the poetic aims. I have chosen to begin with the *Eton College Ode* because its unusual tonal richness and precision make a determination of the stylistic level relatively easy and therefore render the ode more readily accessible than the other poems which I will discuss.

How ought we to respond to the ode? We are told that Gray disliked sports and suffered through school on that account. Hence there is no biographical justification for treating the poem as the result of a sudden fit of sentimentality or as the spontaneous overflow of powerful feelings. Rather, the tone is set by the closing lines, "Where ignorance is bliss,/'Tis folly to be wise." This is a neatly turned, pointed epigram, which should be attributed neither to the naive spontaneity of the children nor to the deep meditation of the seer; instead, it is a clever reversal which intervenes to ward off the dangers of too much prophecy. In assessing the tone of Gray's "praise of folly," we can hardly forget that this is an erudite poem, written by a poet notoriously intolerant of readers less learned than he was, and that it is prefixed by a cynical motto, in the original Greek, derived from the comic poet Menander. The poem is a little excursion through time toward a pastoral retreat, but at the end Gray has neither become a child nor forgotten the difficulties of the road; instead, he has been enabled to contemplate both his childhood and the perils of life with learned equanimity and ironic detachment.[7] And since the place *where* ignorance is bliss is the abode of "grateful science," Eton College, the ignorance which Gray praises cannot be that of an unlettered village-Hampden, but must rather be the simplicity of a self-sufficient mind unconcerned about past or future and uncontaminated by base and worldly engagements.

The closing lines thus arrive at a mood of disciplined coolness in which we, as readers of the epigram, have already begun. It has been generally overlooked that this tone runs throughout the poem and constitutes Gray's answer to the temptations of time-bound worldliness. The first half describes the ritualized games of the children, unchanged for centuries, in an even more ritualized, distanced rhetoric. The hint of condescension results from a restricted and imitative diction (descending even to echo effects such as "less pleasing—thoughtless—regardless"), from a deceptive and confusing syntax ("While some on earnest business bent/Their murmuring labours ply/'Gainst graver hours that bring constraint/To sweeten liberty"), and from a punning vocabulary (such as "bent" and "ply," which describe the "earnest business" in terms drawn from the world of ball games and boat races). In the second half the "sprightly race" gives way to a race of spirits, yet a certain lightness remains. The poem slides into a different perspective and a larger temporal framework, but it is a carefully prepared, Marvellian shift: quasi-personifications such as "Lively cheer of vigour born" smooth the transition to the only slightly more vivid personifications of the second half.[8] Unlike the similar but more realistic fragment describing an eruption of the Glaurus which Gray had written shortly before, we have here constant reminders that this is but a mock kingdom, inhabited by would-be poets who snatch inspiration "in every wind," set in a landscape which apes the brow of its royal founder, and threatened only by an even more shadowy mock court. It is little more than a continuation of the poem's self-conscious distancing when this cast of theatrical demons erupts out of the "vitals" of the earth to taunt and chase the life out of imaginary victims, for the pathos of distance in the first stanza already suggests a potentially unbridgeable gap between the sophisticated poet and the hieratic setting, and even in the closing aphorism the rhetorical antitheses continue to hint at inevitable separations. To be sure, the pathos does increase as the poem progresses, but this is counteracted by increasingly impersonal grammar, so that as danger closes in on the figures, they in effect progressively retreat from its grasp. The changes of mood are thus more apparent than real, while the subdued wit, the continuities of imagery, and the even tenor of the poetic diction serve to stabilize the tone and to protect against the imminent terrors of experience.

I do not wish to exaggerate the ode's good nature to the exclusion of all else. The poem lends itself to more than one interpretation, for poetic diction is by nature imprecise and therefore generously open to various readings. Moral pathos and psychological conflict are as much a part of the ode as is urbane irony. Yet there is more than just the wit of the closing lines to suggest that Gray's final purpose was to tame his fear of the spirits, to restore simplicity of mind, and to inculcate a stance of urbane detachment. The motto serves as an additional guide, not to the exclusive meaning, but at least to the prevailing attitude of the ode.

῎Ανθρωπος· ἱκανὴ πρόφασις εἰς τὸ δυστυχεῖν

It is tempting to link the Greek πρόφασις to the gloomy predictions of the visionary, as if the phrase meant, "The children are men, and that is sufficient to prophesy their doom." Any reader who makes this link, however, is the unwitting butt of yet another urbane witticism, for πρόφασις means "reason" or "pretext," not "prophecy." The spirit of Menander's adage and the tone which governs the poem are not those of the sublime visionary, but rather those of the venerable and evasive Father Thames, who remains silent, and of the urbane poet who decides at the end, using a word etymologically related to πρόφασις, not to tell the children their "fate." In the modern world, as Collins' *Ode on the Poetical Character* tells us, the "inspired bowers" have been "o'erturned" or at least "curtained close." There should be reasons, but no prophecies.

A chief virtue of the urbane sublime, then, is its discretion. It speaks in generalities and with indirection; it does not descend to particulars. The silence of Father Thames when asked to name the children conforms in this respect to the tenets of the man who, more than any other, set the tone of the age, Joseph Addison.

> If I attack the Vicious, I shall only set upon them in a Body; and will not be provoked by the worst Usage I can receive from others, to make an Example of any particular Criminal. It is not *Lais* or *Silenus,* but the Harlot and the Drunkard, whom I shall endeavour to expose; and shall consider the Crime as it appears in a Species, not as it is circumstanced in an Individual. (*Spectator,* 16)

The urbane stylist refuses either to be teased out of his detachment or, as Addison goes on to say, to be coerced into partisanship. For if the urbane style is discreet, it is also tolerant; it is couched in generalities and therefore leaves the reader great discretionary latitude in his interpretation. The urbane sublime is a liberal style, conducive to ease and familiarity. It reflects an artful effort to domesticate the supernatural and irrational and to deprive them of their terrors. Again the Spectator, that most ubiquitous and genial of all eighteenth century ghosts, defines the stylistic ambition.

> For my own Part, I am apt to join in Opinion with those who believe that all the Regions of Nature swarm with Spirits; and that we have Multitudes of Spectators on all our Actions, when we think ourselves most alone. But instead of terrifying myself with such a Notion, I am wonderfully pleased to think that I am always engaged with such an innumerable Society in searching out the Wonders of the Creation, and joining in the same Consort of Praise and Adoration. (*Spectator,* 12)

In passages like these, "Mr. Specter" (as some of the imaginary correspondents call him) points the way toward a comprehensive style of writing, capable of encompassing an unusually great range of high and low subjects, and even (though much more distantly) toward the conversation poems of Coleridge and Wordsworth and the fully integrated romantic landscape, with its perfect marriage of the sublime and the beautiful, the spiritual and the natural.[9]

Yet in one important respect the poets of mid-century went beyond Addison's example. Like many successful allegorical modes, Gray's poetic diction has what Angus Fletcher has called a cosmic dimension. That is, it is both decorative and inflationary. Common nouns tend to sound like capitalized personifications, dead metaphors revive, and the generalizing diction is apt to treat any action as the emblem of a higher truth. In spite of its detachment, in other words, the style calls attention to the importance of its subject. In Gray's ode, for instance, both the ornate landscape and the elaborate rhetoric have a specifically national function: the hillside school by the Thames near Windsor becomes an image of the ancient aristocratic order of England. Within the "little reign" lie dignity, virtue, and moderation; without lie trespass and extremity, or (in the parallel terms of the *Elegy*) "the paths of glory" and ultimately "the grave." Behind the urbane wit of Gray's style, then, there does lie a sublime message: human passions are irrational demons which can be contained by preserving the native English purity and simplicity of manners. No more Cromwells, even if there are also no more Miltons; better the muteness of Father Thames— or the reticence of Gray himself.[10]

II

Because of its inherent discretion, the urbane sublime is able to tolerate many apparent paradoxes. It is both high and light, sophisticated and primitive, liberal and aristocratic, elevated but capable of describing the most mundane phenomena, innovative and yet doggedly conventional.[11] It is perhaps the presence of these contradictory impulses, rather than its unnatural inflation, which makes a modern reader ill at ease with eighteenth century poetry, and it is certainly the persistence of contradictory impulses which makes the history of eighteenth century poetry so baffling to write. Having used the *Eton College Ode* to illustrate the style, I should like to turn to Thomson's *Seasons* in order to demonstrate the intellectual coherence underneath its superficial inconsistencies and seemingly ill-defined ideology.

Inquiry into the origins of poetic diction can draw attention away from its contextual function. Often, in serious as in satiric verse, a principle of compensation applies. Thus the *Eton College Ode* spends its most rotund Latinity on the children's games and falls back on monosyllabic Anglo-Saxon adjectives for its more sublime and visionary moments. The passage on birds' nests in Thomson's *Spring* (ll. 631–86) offers an even more obvious example of this reverse decorum. On the one hand, there is a clear vertical hierarchy, with "humble" nests on the ground and the various other types sorted by altitude; the sense of propriety is strengthened by the repetition "kind concealment," "kind duty," "kindly care," where "kind" has the connotation, "appropriate to the species." Yet on the other hand, the tree birds build simple "nests"; the somewhat less dignified, thievish swallows erect somewhat more pretentious "habitations," while the ground-nesting species are granted the noblest oratory: "humble texture," "artful fabrics," and even, surprisingly, "domes" (Latin "domus"). Similarly, while the idle male bird, who "takes his stand high," is described in

generally simple diction, his menial better half "assiduous sits," a bad ety-
mological pun which elevates even as it ridicules.[12]

One of Thomson's hesitations illuminates the impulse behind this
reverse decorum. The first version of *Winter* describes how cattle, when
they return at evening, "ask, with meaning Low, their wonted Stalls"
(1726, l. 124). The revision, a few months later, reveals the concealed lex-
ical and grammatical ambiguities so typical of the urbane sublime: it
changes the capitalization to, "with Meaning low," thus inverting the hierarchy of adjective and noun. By means of this metamorphosis the animal
noise is shown to be a meaningful speech act. The transformation is paradigmatic of the style as a whole. The urbane sublime cannot condescend
to an object without elevating it. On the other hand, it also cannot express
sympathy without taking cognizance of difference: the Low may have a
meaning, but it is a "Meaning *low*." No matter how egalitarian the gestures,
the sense of hierarchy is inescapable. Indeed, both leveling and gradation
are implicit in the adjective-noun structure which forms the backbone of
the style. Whether the adjective and noun are related as species to genus,
abstract to concrete, or figurative to literal, the pairing of words almost
always implies a divided perspective and yet also works to moderate the
rigid stratifications of "classical" decorum.

The pacing and structure of *The Seasons* exhibit a comparable differen-
tiated moderation, or "art of discrimination," as Ralph Cohen has called it.
The poem was most carefully composed and the contribution of each word
duly weighed. Yet as methodically as Thomson went to work, the constant
effect is one of wandering and of choices yet to be made; the tone remains
deliberative rather than decisive. The poet sustains his slow progress
through the year by nourishing a permanent sense of anticipation, and he
typically resists temptations toward culmination. Just as the rejection of
prophecy characterizes Gray's poetry from the early *Latin Verses at Eton*
("Fata obstant; metam Parcae posuere sciendi") to the late *Descent of Odin*
(where the prophetess herself commands, "That never shall enquirer
come,/To break my iron sleep again"), so too *The Seasons* regularly retreats
from transcendence. Thus, after finding himself "in airy vision rapt,"
Thomson's "every sense/Wakes from the charm of thought: swift-shrink-
ing back,/I check my steps" (Su 585-89—this version has been toned
down from the earlier, "I stand aghast"). After a passing enthusiasm for
"visionary vales," he draws back with the line, "Or is this gloom too
much?" (Au 1030-37). After hymning nature's stunning impact on his
"ravished eye," he concedes, "But, if to that unequal" (conclusion of
Autumn). Most notably, the end of the whole poem subsides from present

epiphany (Wi 1041–43: "And see!/'Tis come, the glorious morn! the second birth/Of heaven and earth") to merely predicted epiphany (1068–69: "The storms of wintry time will quickly pass,/And one unbounded Spring encircle all"). To the eighteenth century rhymester, even "ecstasies" arrive "by degrees" (Thomas Warton, *Ode on the Approach of Summer*). We are faced with a great intensity of verbal energy at every point, but with a diffuse and enervating whole.

Concomitantly, the forms preferred by the age are the georgic, the progress, and the loco-descriptive poem. Each of these combines steady movement with an affectionate dwelling on particulars, and in consequence a rhetoric develops in which the compactness of the classical period is compromised by excessive itemization. The many diffuse catalogues in *The Seasons* are obviously deficient in rhetorical unity and focus, but even in the *Eton College Ode* the strict triadic cadences of the opening stanzas succumb as the excitement grows: "*This* racks the joints, *this* fires the veins,/*That* every labouring sinew strains,/*Those* in the deeper vitals rage:/*Lo, Poverty* to fill the band,/That numbs the soul with icy hand,/*And* slow-consuming *Age*."[13] In *The Seasons* this technique of discrimination by means of superfluous enumeration is related to an emphasis on gradual, deliberate order, presided over by a host of mild, intermediate divinities, each with its own realm, and with no universal controlling power in evidence. In lieu of the fixed, sculptural "stationing" which Keats praised in Milton, there is a flexible positioning; the mind tries to assign each spirit "to his rank," but the perceptions are indistinct and changing, "ever rising with the rising mind" (conclusion of *Summer*). Evening, that mild spirit which, as Geoffrey Hartman has shown, so entranced men's minds later in the century, best represents Thomson's moderation as well.

> Confessed from yonder slow-extinguished clouds,
> All ether softening, sober Evening takes
> Her wonted station in the middle air,
> A thousand shadows at her beck. First this
> She sends on earth; then that of deeper dye
> Steals soft behind; and then a deeper still,
> In circle following circle, gathers round
> To close the face of things. A fresher gale
> Begins to wave the wood and stir the stream
> Sweeping with shadowy gust the fields of corn,
> While the quail clamours for his running mate.
> Wide o'er the thistly lawn, as swells the breeze,
> A whitening shower of vegetable down

Amusive floats. The kind impartial care
Of Nature naught disdains: thoughtful to feed
Her lowest sons, and clothe the coming year,
From field to field the feathered seeds she wings.
(Su 1647–63)

In so gentle a matriarchy as that of nature, how could life help but be pleasant? Little in Thomson's world is firm and earthbound or surging and fiery;
indeed, even summer's heat is almost always a liquid, "dazzling deluge"
when it is not simply "exuberant spring" (Su 435, 697). Instead, Thomson
is fascinated, as in the lines on Evening, with air and water, the ambient
elements which allow suspended substances to move easily up and down
through the many levels of existence. Above all, as the multiple puns of the
lines on the mock snowfall show, air and water are "amusive," intrinsically
poetical because they imitate the "musing," deliberate course of thought
itself. Thomson's early preface to *Winter* harps on this theme as it
describes the temperate pleasures of his poem's "cool, wide survey" of
nature. Poetry, he says, is associated with "the most charming power of
imagination, the most exalting force of thought, the most affecting touch
of sentiment"; it displays "a finer and more amusing scene of things"; it
can "amuse the fancy, enlighten the head, and warm the heart."[14]

What passes for artifice and inconsistency is thus more adequately
understood, at least in the better poetry of the century, as the easy, "musing" acceptance of shifting orders and fluid hierarchies.[15] This applies to
politics as well as to poetic forms. Thomson, like Gray, Akenside, and the
Wartons, can startle the present-day reader by simultaneously praising
modern liberty and ancient privilege without any sense of strain. "Oh,
Queen of men!/Beneath whose sceptre in essential rights/Equal they live,
though placed for common good/Various, or in subjection or command,/
And that by common choice" (Thomson, *Liberty*, III, 328–32). There is,
of course, no inconsistency to such a political vision; its viability is demonstrated equally by the examples of ancient Rome and of modern Britain
with her "bounded kings" (IV, 1146).[16] Nor is there any greater inconsistency to the century's flexible conception of formal structure and poetic
style. These, like the politics, reflect the poets' view of the nature of society. For if we ask what determines both the tone and the organizational
sense of the urbane sublime, the answer is its social basis.

"Social" is the word which resolves the apparent paradoxes of the
urbane sublime. The Muse, as Thomson says, is "most delighted when she
social sees / The whole mixed animal creation round / Alive and happy"

(Au 381-83). In the best of all possible worlds even the vegetable kingdom would be social: "Great Spring before / Greened all the year; and fruits and blossoms blushed / In social sweetness on the self-same bough" (Sp 320-22). In these lines the very alliterations are sociably sorted, as often in Thomson, into neighboring pairs. The word's range—from the nobly societal to the collegially sociable—reflects the range of the style itself, and yet all the variations are reducible to a single concept, the continuous give-and-take of social intercourse.

Even the poetry of William Collins, the most inward and difficult poet of the century, retains the easy sociality of the urbane sublime. The *Odes on Several Descriptive and Allegorical Subjects* begin, it is true, with an attempt to summon the cognate tragic emotions of pity and fear. However, Collins then turns away from these passions of art and toward the "genuine thought" and "temperate vale" of Simplicity. His "tale," to which the last line of the *Ode to Simplicity* refers, becomes the subject of the following *Ode on the Poetical Character,* which relates a "fairy legend" about the origin of poetry. This ode has often been misread as a sublime allegory on the solitary genius, but Earl Wasserman has demonstrated that its intent was actually to differentiate Collins' more humble aspirations from those of the truly inspired Milton.[17] Nor is the legend so elevated as the Pindaric form and intricate syntax would lead one to expect: the prevailing meter is that of *L'Allegro* and *Il Penseroso* (from which the description of Milton in lines 63-64 derives), and urbane lightening is provided by an epistle-like opening and by a creation myth which portrays God rather as a divine couturier than as a divine artificer. The remaining "musings"—the word occurs five times, beginning in the *Ode to Simplicity*—are all devoted to social virtues. Only in the *Ode to Evening* does the solitary sublime again become a temptation, and then only for a passing instant: whereas in the *Poetical Character* Collins' "trembling feet . . . pursue" the Miltonic bowers, the peremptory violence of nature in *Evening* "forbid[s] my willing feet," thereby repressing the urge to wander alone on high. Collins' refuge "beneath the sylvan shed" and his invocation to "Fancy, Friendship, Science, rose-lipped Health" are often regarded as a break in tone and a betrayal of the poem's romanticism; in fact they fulfill one of the fundamental impulses of his poetry. The intricate daily minutiae of individual observation, which is always capable of being distracted by some passing bat or beetle, are properly absorbed into the more long-ranged and "simple" perspective of seasonal and social regularities. The final diptych of social odes, *The Manners* and *The Passions,* crowns the volume with a palinode to the opening poems. *The Manners* replaces the "buskined Muse" of *Pity* with humor's "comic sock." *The Passions* passes the tragic emotions in review only in order to let each refute itself: thus, Fear recoils in fear, Anger is too impatient to remain, Despair "beguiles" itself, and so forth. The ode concludes by praising the sociability and "native simple heart" of Music.[18]

III

Nowhere is the musing character of eighteenth century consciousness more apparent than in Young's *Night Thoughts*. Though few today would dare to call this poem "captivating," as Percival Stockdale did early in the nineteenth century,[19] and though Young's writing is relatively free from conventional poetic diction, it would be a mistake to overlook his urbanity. The poem is not a silent meditation, but rather a long monologue addressed to a reprobate named Lorenzo, and Young is careful to vary the pacing, to lighten the tone with ironic sallies, and to intersperse frequent parenthetical asides and self-reference, all so as to preserve a conversational feeling. While the poem's theme is the correction of the individual, its standards are social, and its very discursiveness is seen as the best weapon against false pride.

> In *Contemplation* is his proud Resource?
> 'Tis poor, as proud, by *Converse* unsustained.
> Rude Thought runs wild in *Contemplation*'s Field.
> *Converse*, the menage, breaks it to the Bit
> Of due Restraint; and *Emulation*'s Spur
> Gives graceful Energy, by Rivals aw'd.
> 'Tis Converse qualifies for Solitude.
>
> (II, 488–94)

The rhetoric is informal and completely non-periodic; the current of thought never stops, but only ebbs and flows as each sentence funnels into a successor of greater or lesser intensity. The view of life is Heraclitean— "Life glides away, Lorenzo, like a Brook;/For ever changing, unperceiv'd the Change" (V, 401–2)—and the poem's utter formlessness mirrors this view of life. Wherever it is opened—and some early editions are indexed to facilitate browsing—the reader enters into the middle of an elevated, consoling conversation.

This very formlessness, so hard to appreciate today, was the source of the poem's charm in its own day. The great enemy, the great divide, as

Young often says, was death, and by avoiding any divisions or articulations the final reckoning could be postponed indefinitely. It is fitting that the longest night by far is called "The Consolation," for length, expansiveness, and infinite repetition constitute the best anodyne against the fear of death.

> Dost ask, Lorenzo, why so warmly prest,
> By Repetition hammer'd on thine Ear,
> The Thought of *Death?* . . .
> . . . That Thought ply'd home,
> Will soon reduce the ghastly *Precipice*
> O'er hanging Hell, will soften the Descent,
> And gently slope our Passage to the Grave.
>
> (V, 682–89)

Everything described in the poem turns out to be gentle, nothing abrupt; everything is intermediate, nothing absolute; everything is in flux, nothing fixed. "The World's no *Neuter*," says Young (VIII, 376), and he means that there is no impartial, unchanging standard of reference. All things are value-laden, and all values are relative and variable. The poem's theodicy is not based on rational persuasion, but rather on making the reader conscious of the eternal variability of life. Young's most common strategy is easy to paraphrase: things may look bad, but they might be worse, and worse, and worse, and so they come to seem, by contrast, better, and better, and better. The only absolute is that the value of things must be determined by our consciousness of them.

> Worth, conscious Worth! should *absolutely* reign;
> And other Joys ask Leave for their Approach;
> Nor, unexamin'd, ever Leave obtain.
>
> (VIII, 978–80)

The aim of *Night Thoughts* is to examine our feelings and to make us conscious of the variability and relativity of values. But to the eighteenth century mind this is a tautology: all consciousness is consciousness of relative value. Thus Young writes, "So grieve, as conscious, Grief may rise to Joy; / So joy, as conscious, Joy to Grief may fall" (VIII, 763–64). One might therefore just as well say, the aim of *Night Thoughts* is, simply and absolutely, to make us conscious. This is what I meant when I said that the urbane sublime imitated the musing course of thought. In its deliberative ebb and flow, in its indeterminacy, in its hierarchic tendency, in its heightening of experience, the urbane sublime expresses the very form of eighteenth century consciousness.[20]

In his studies of poetic diction, Geoffrey Tillotson pointed out that the word "conscious" was never ethically neutral in eighteenth century usage, but always positively or negatively charged.[21] One spoke of "conscious pride," "conscious shame," "conscious sin," "conscious virtue." Thus Addison writes, "Every Thought is attended with Consciousness and Representativeness; the Mind has nothing presented to it but what is immediately followed by a Reflection or Conscience, which tell you whether that which was so presented is graceful or unbecoming" (*Spectator* 38). For Addison, it must be added, there is also the possibility of excess self-consciousness, which he terms "Affectation." For the sublime poets, on the other hand, consciousness is all: "Is *Conscience*, then, / No part of Nature? Is she not supreme?" (*Night Thoughts*, VII, 841–42). The sublime style is intended to interest and affect the reader, to heighten his moral sensibilities, in sum, to correct and educate his "brute unconscious gaze" (Thomson, *A Hymn on the Seasons*, 28).

In the eighteenth century consciousness is hardly to be distinguished from intuition, knowledge from faith; even Hume, though he exposed this state of affairs to view, despaired of changing it. We do not find the grand oppositions of romantic dialectic—spirit against matter, general against particular, eternal against temporal—and the poetry can only seem incoherent if we look for them. Instead there is nuanced gradation, slow accumulation, and constant flux. At times, indeed, *Night Thoughts* can seem almost Wordsworthian (it is even quoted in *Tintern Abbey*), but it lacks Wordsworth's stoppings and reversals, his overflowings, submergings of consciousness and restorations—in short, the dialectical intensity of Wordsworthian sublime. Indeed, Young's poem, though less discreet and therefore less intriguing than Gray's *Eton College Ode*, is a particularly valuable witness because it so clearly reveals the presuppositions of the age. Death, for instance, is not the annihilation of life, but its culminating stage: "Our Birth is nothing but our Death begun" (V, 719). Immortality is not the opposite of mortal life, nor even simply its perpetuation, but it is an intensification, "the Crown of Life" (III, 526):

> It is but Life
> In stronger Thread of brighter Colour spun,
> And spun for ever.
>   (VI, 77–79)

Death does not terminate our consciousness, but elevates it.

> In Life embark'd, we smoothly down the Tide
> Of Time descend, but not on *Time* intent;
> Amus'd, unconscious of the gliding Wave;
> Till on a sudden we perceive a Shock;
> We start, awake, look out; what see we there?
> Our brittle Bark is burst on *Charon*'s Shore.
>
> (V, 411–16)

This last quotation, to be sure, forces a distinction, but it is a distinction which the poem has already clarified. Death is a shock. But it is only a shock to the "brute unconscious gaze" of the natural savage. It is not a shock to those who have been educated in their lifetime to a conscious, rational faith.

> *Faith* builds a Bridge across the Gulph of Death,
> To break the Shock blind Nature cannot shun.
> And lands Thought smoothly on the *farther* Shore.
>
> (IV, 721–23)

Though Young does give in cursory fashion the customary proofs of religion, he does not view reason primarily as dialectics, but rather as the ground of belief.

> My Heart became the Convert of my Head;
> And made that *Choice*, which one was but my Fate.
> "On Argument alone my Faith is built:"
> *Reason* pursu'd is Faith; and, unpursu'd
> Where Poof invites, 'tis Reason, then no more.
>
> (IV, 740–44)

This last theme is sounded again and again: the head and the heart are allied; thought consciously prolonged is feeling.

> Think you my song too turbulent? too warm?
> Are *Passions*, then, the Pagans of the Soul?
> *Reason* alone baptis'd? alone *ordain'd*
> To touch Things sacred? Oh for warmer still!
> . . . .
> Passion is Reason, Transport Temper, *here*.
>
> (IV, 628–31, 640)

The cool and the warm, reason and passion, urbanity and sublimity are mutually self-sustaining. The apparent inconsistencies of eighteenth century poetry are not contingent facts of an unsuccessful style, but constitutive structures of a particular form of experience. Where consciousness is understood as the elevation of sensation, all things become manifest not in themselves, and not by contrast with their opposites, but by comparison with higher or lower degrees on a scale of intensities. The serious exists only in relation to the more comic, elevation of style only with reference to its potential degradation, the liberal or new only as a relaxed modality of the aristocratic or old; order and formal perfection are inseparable from freedom and formal flexibility; nature and organism are hardly distinguishable from art and mechanism; poetry and prose differ only in degree of intensity. Indeed, even dissolute scheming and divine wisdom are related "as the waning, and the waxing Moon" (V, 352). The very lines most ridiculed by George Eliot—and for good reason—find their explanation as yet one more expression of this creed. "More generous Sorrow, while it sinks, exalts; / And conscious Virtue mitigates the Pang" (I, 301–02). Constant rising and sinking are a part of man's middle state, and consciousness is the force which both recognizes our instability and reconciles us to it.[22]

From this point of view even the fascination with ghosts and muses becomes comprehensible. They are figures of conscious, that is, of heightened perception. Young says as much, using an image which, however much it may seem to anticipate the *Ode to the West Wind*, speaks for a vastly different sensibility.

> *Truth* bids me look on Men, as *Autumn* Leaves,
> And all they bleed for, as the Summer's dust,
> Driv'n by the Whirlwind: Lighted by her beams,
> I widen my Horizon, gain new Pow'rs,
> See Things invisible, feel Things remote,
> Am present with futurities.
>
> (V, 336–41)

Young, like Shelley, speaks of being haunted, but it is a happy haunting which emphasizes the copresence of the spirits and declines to be "the trumpet of a prophecy":

> Pale *worldly Wisdom* loses all her Charms;
> In pompous Promise from her Schemes profound,
> In future Fate she plans, 'tis all in Leaves,

Like *Sibyl,* unsubstantial, fleeting Bliss!
At the first Blast it vanishes in Air.

(V, 345-49)

The personified "Things invisible" which abound in the poetry of the century thus body forth the expanded horizon and broader perspective of the enlightened mind, as opposed to the "heedless," earthbound superstitions of Collins' hermit. The spirits, I would suggest, are the reminders of the social bond, the unviersal intercourse, and the comparability of all things.

Notes

1. Hume calls poets "liars by profession" in the chapter "On the Influence of Belief" in the *Treatise on Human Nature.*

2. "The Augustan Mode in English Poetry," *Hateful Contraries* (Lexington, 1966), p. 164.

3. Language, History and Vision: An Approach to 18th Century Literature," *The Varied Pattern: Studies in the 18th Century,* eds. Peter Hughes and David Williams (Toronto, 1971), pp. 77-96. See also Hughes's sequel "Restructuring Literary History: Implications for the Eighteenth Century," *NLH,* 8 (1977), 257-78. Related, but cruder, is Theodor Adorno's account in Ch. 1 of *Dialektik der Aufklärung.*

4. The words in quotation are all used prominently by Thomas Weiskel in Ch. 1 of *The Romantic Sublime* (Baltimore and London, 1976), a sophisticated restatement of the traditional view, based (as is often the case) on Locke and the theorists rather than on Hume and the poets. More supple, and argued from actual poetic practise, is Martin Price, "The Sublime Poem: Pictures and Power," *Yale Review,* 58 (1968), 213; Price, however, neglects the sociability and the retreat from transcedence which I discuss below.

5. The best description of the urbane style, to my knowledge, is still I. A. Richards's account of a very belated example, Longfellow's elegy *In the Churchyard at Cambridge,* in *Practical Criticism* (New York, 1950), pp. 175-76: "If this interpretation of the poem is right, 'rude' is simply an acknowledgment of the social convention, not in the least a rebuke. . . . The last verse is not a grim warning or an exhortation, but a cheerful realisation of the situation, not in the least evangelical, not at all like a conventional sermon, but on the contrary extremely urbane, rather witty, and *slightly* whimsical. . . . If there is any character in poetry ɩʰat modern readers—who derive their ideas of it rather from the best known poems of Wordsworth, Shelley and Keats or from our own contemporaries, than from Dryden, Pope or Cowper—are unprepared to encounter, it is this social, urbane, highly cultivated, self-confident, temperate and easy kind of humour."

6. For a classic statement of the satirists' seriousness, see Louis Bredvold, "The Gloom of the Tory Satirists," in *Eighteenth-Century Literature: Modern Essays in Criticism,* ed. James L. Clifford (London, 1959), pp. 3-20. Bredvold's account of political history has recently been called into question, but his poetical analysis still seems valid. Ralph Cohen's unsystematic but important essay, "The Augustan Mode in English Poetry," *ECS,* 1 (1967), 3-32, contains some excellent pages on asymmetry and emotional intensification (i.e., movements toward sublimity) within Pope's couplets. On the continuity of seemingly opposing styles,

MARSHALL BROWN

453

see also Cohen's essay, "On the Interrelations of Eighteenth-Century Literary Forms," in *New Approaches to Eighteenth-Century Literature,* ed. Phillip Harth (New York, 1974), pp. 33–78, esp. p. 65: "Distinctness [of species] was a matter of degree rather than of kind."

7. Patricia Meyer Spacks has drawn attention to some additional ironies of the final couplet in *The Poetry of Vision* (Cambridge, Mass., 1967), pp. 101–02; her discussion (pp. 91–95) of the delicate humor of the *Ode on the Spring* is also useful, as is the excellent treatment of the *Elegy* along similar lines by George T. Wright, "Stillness and the Art of Gray's Elegy," *MP*, 74 (1977), 381–89. More generally, cf. Chester Chapin's hesitant conclusion in *Personification in Eighteenth-Century Poetry* (New York, 1968), p. 133: "The use of personified abstractions as figures of vision is never, accordingly, with most eighteenth-century poets, entirely serious."

8. I borrow the observation concerning quasi-personifications in st. 5 from Kurt Schlüter, *Die Englische Ode* (Bonn, 1964), pp. 85–86.

9. Carey McIntosh has a good recent analysis of the Addisonian voice as it pervades eighteenth century prose in *The Choice of Life: Samuel Johnson and the World of Fiction* (New Haven and London, 1973), pp. 122–43. On the genesis of the romantic fusion, see my essay, "Toward an Archaeology of English Romanticism: Coleridge and Sarbiewski," *Comparative Literature,* 30 (1978), 313–37.

10. See Murray Krieger's essay, "Samuel Johnson: The Extensive View of Mankind and the Cost of Acceptance," *The Classic Vision* (Baltimore and London, 1971), pp. 125–45, for a strikingly similar reading of *The Vanity of Human Wishes.* In Johnson, of course, the fabric of assurance (the urbane and witty flexibility) begins to come apart, which may help to account for his resentment of the commonplaceness of the Eton College ode.

11. Cf. Pope's letter to Walsh, July 2, 1706: "To bestow heightening on every part is monstrous: Some parts ought to be lower than the rest" etc., *(Correspondence,* ed. George Sherburn [Oxford, 1956], I, 19). Similarly, on the proper way of translating Homer, in the postscript to the *Odyssey:* "To read thro' a whole work in this strain, is like travelling all along on the ridge of a hill; which is not half so agreeable as sometimes gradually to rise, and sometimes gently to descend, as the way leads, and as the end of the journey directs" *(Works,* Twickenham Edition, X, ed. Maynard Mack [London and New Haven, 1967], 388).

12. There has still not been enought attention paid to the "deeply buried and always reticent" puns in Pope's non-satiric verse. (The phrase is Maynard Mack's, in "Wit and Poetry and Pope: Some Observations on his Imagery," *Eighteenth-Century Literature: Modern Essays in Criticism,* eds. James L. Clifford [London, 1959], p. 32). Like one of Thomson's inverse decorums, for instance, the sublime, neo-Platonizing treatment of nature in the *Essay on Criticism* is prepared by a rarefied pun which suggests the mutuality of high and low: "Would all but *stoop* to what they *under-stand*" (line 67, hyphen added).

13. For some additional remarks on the historical significance of Gray's enumerations see Geoffrey Tillotson, "The Methods of Description in Eighteenth- and Nineteenth-Century Poetry," in *Restoration and Eighteenth-Century Literature: Essays in Honor of Alan Dugald McKillop,* ed. Carroll Camden (Chicago, 1963), pp. 235–38.

14. See Ralph Cohen's valuable discussions of Thomson's punning, which he calls "illusive allusion," in *The Unfolding of "The Seasons"* (Baltimore, 1970), pp. 39–40 and passim (consult index). I cannot detail here all my points of agreement and disagreement with Cohen's commentary, but I would like to call attention to the excellent pages on sociability, pp. 252–92, and to what seems a misleading treatment of summer as a fiery season.

15. Typical of the poets' conscious preference for loose over rigid forms is Gray's criticism of Buffon's "Love of System, . . . the most contrary Thing in the World to a Science,

entirely grounded upon Experiments, & that has nothing to do with Vivacity of Imagination" (letter to Wharton, Aug. 9, 1750, *Correspondence*, ed. Paget Toynbee and Leonard Whibley [Oxford, 1935], I, 329). For more documentation see D. J. Greene's witty essay, 'Logical Structure' in Eighteenth-Century Poetry," *PQ*, 31 (1952), 315–36.

16. Cf. also Goldsmith's *Letters from a Citizen of the World*, 50, which praises the "ductility of the laws" in England. Goldsmith argues that there can be more liberty and looser enforcement of the laws in aristocratic England than in a democracy because the state is stronger by nature.

17. Earl Wasserman, "Collins' Ode on the Poetical Character," *ELH*, 34 (1967), 92–115.

18. On Collins as a light or sociable poet see Wylie Sypher, "The *Morceau de Fantaisie* in Verse: A New Approach to Collins," *UTQ*, 15 (1945); 65–69; Arthur Johnston, *The Poetry of William Collins* (London, 1974); John F. Sitter, "Mother, Memory, Muse and Poetry after Pope," *ELH*, 44 (1977), 312–36 (an important analysis of female personifications throughout the century). It has not been customary to see a unifying plan in the odes; thus Ricardo Quintana, "The Scheme of Collins's *Odes on Several . . . Subjects*," in *Restoration and Eighteenth-Century Literature: Essays in Honor of Alan Dugald McKillop*, ed. Carroll Camden (Chicago, 1963), pp. 371–80, separates the odes into two distinct groups, poems about poetic kinds and patriotic poems.

19. Percival Stockdale, *Lectures on the Truly Eminent English Poets* (London, 1807), I, 587.

20. Pope is again comparable. His form too is social even when the content is at its most personal. Neither he nor Collins could rest content with the pilgrim's heedless hum, and repeated statements in his letters show that even the retreats to the isolation of his garden had a quasi-social function, to "converse with myself." Like Young, who was taken for the author of the anonymous *Essay on Man*, Pope aimed to promote man's self-knowledge as a creature of a "middle state," in his varying relation to higher and lower spheres. Indeed, in his gloomier moods Pope could sound much like a more gifted Young conceding that human reason is nothing more than heightened imagination and that optimism is a corollary of despair, as in the following letter to Caryll, July 13, 1714 *(Correspondence*, I, 236): "Half the things that employ our heads deserve not the name of Thoughts, for they are only stronger dreams or impressions upon the imagination; our schemes of government, our systems of philosophy, our golden words of poetry, are all but so many shadow images and airy prospects, which arise to us but so much the livelier and more frequent as we are more overcast with darkness, wrapt in the night, and disturbed with the fumes of human vanity." See, however, Martin Price, *To the Palace of Wisdom* (Garden City, 1965), pp. 345–51, for a portrait contrasting Pope and Young.

21. Geoffrey Tillotson, *Augustan Poetic Diction* (London, 1964), p. 77.

22. This cardinal principle of eighteenth century thought has of course not gone unnoticed, but the full consequences are rarely drawn. Such, for instance, is the defect of Reuben Brower's "Form and Defect of Form in Eighteenth Century Poetry: A Memorandum," *CE*, 29 (1969), 535–41. On the relation of art and nature see Martin Battestin's excellent essays on 18th century pastoral, *The Providence of Wit* (Oxford, 1974), Ch. 2 and 4; one might also cite lines like Parnell's (in "Hesiod, of the Rise of Woman"), "And all the nature, all the art of love," as well as the same poem's reference to "native tropes," a characteristically fluid notion that would only involve a problematical dialectic if found in an author later than Rousseau. On the admittedly vexed question of the "poetry of statement," Hume's opinion in "Of the Standard Taste" needs to be considered: "Every kind of composition, even the most poetical, is nothing but a chain of propositions and reasonings, not always, indeed, the justest and most exact, but still plausible and specious, however disguised by the colorings of the imagination."

Dynamics of Fear:
Fanny Burney

PATRICIA MEYER SPACKS

As novelist and as writer about herself, Fanny Burney takes a position in every respect opposed to Laurence Sterne. Committed to propriety as he to its opposite, apparently unaware of the formal possibilities or implications of her conventional plots, feeling that the most important question about novels concerned their moral influence, she reminds the reader that Tristram Shandy's conviction of the impossibilities of art does not represent the only conceivable viewpoint. The moral and psychological organization of her fiction and her diaries insists on the order of life itself. Keeping an intermittent record of herself for more than seventy years, she reveals not the chaos of experience but the reiteration of pattern. The rational structure of her prose helps her to assert the significant structure of her life.

A woman's vision? It seems important to say so. *Tristram Shandy* is organized to reveal the pervasiveness of male fear, demonstrating in form and in substance how the terror of impotence spreads through every endeavor. The entire mass of Fanny Burney's writing forms itself as centrally in relation to female fear—not of the absence of power but of failure of goodness and consequent loss of love. Tristram's fears reduce his life to disorder; Miss Burney's (and her heroines') have ordering force, defending against chaotic possibility.

Unique in her century in having left to posterity both a group of novels and the rich private record of voluminous letters and diaries, Miss Burney

From *Imagining a Self: Autobiography and Novel in Eighteenth-Century England* (Cambridge: Harvard University Press, 1976), 158–92.

also provides through her published work a basis for investigating the relationship between avowedly autobiographical and purportedly fictional accounts of experience. Previous critics have perceived this as a rather simple issue in her writing. Thus Ernest Baker writes: "Fanny Burney's importance in the history of the novel is . . . that she came so near to what may be called a direct transcript of life . . . There is only, as it were, a narrow and vanishing margin between literature and life. Scores of pages in her diaries may be put side by side with pages from her novels to illustrate this."[1] Edwine Montague and Louis L. Martz comment about *Evelina:* "People who enjoy the *Diary* enjoy finding Fanny Burney in the novel too; and so the book becomes a kind of appendix to the *Diary.*"[2] But neither novels nor diaries in fact offer anything like a "direct transcript." Both demonstrate the shaping of experience by a special sensibility, the artistry of pattern almost as manifest in letters and journals as in fiction. The pattern of Fanny Burney's life as she perceives and interprets it resembles the structures that shape her fictions, both converting psychological defense into literary tactics.

The two volumes of Fanny Burney's early diary, the six volumes first edited by her niece Charlotte Barrett, and the four volumes that have thus far emerged under Joyce Hemlow's editorship, comprise an enormous mass of disparate material.[3] They record public as well as private events: Miss Burney lived at Court for five years as Second Keeper of the Robes to Queen Charlotte; her subsequent marriage to a French emigré involved her at least peripherally in post-Revolution French politics. They demonstrate the literary and personal virtues with which their author has always been credited: her sharp ear for speech rhythms, her eye for social detail, her sensitivity to manners as an index of moral quality; her devotion to her family; and her extreme propriety. The interpretative structure that forms her account of her life's happenings depends upon strategies of concealment. The idea of virtue provided Fanny Burney—as it has many women—a first line of defense. Goodness has always been a source of female force, a guard against enemies without and within. Miss Burney, hiding behind her impeccable morality, protects her inner life.

Two episodes reported at different times of her life exemplify Fanny Burney's characteristic moral stance. Writing of her beloved husband's death, which took place in 1819 (she was sixty-seven years old), she dwells in retrospect on her inner conflict over whether she would invite the priest to return after a single visit to the dying man's bedside. (D'Arblay, bred a Catholic, had preserved only a nominal allegiance to his church during his English residence. His wife, motivated by a sense of fitness, called a priest to administer the last rites.) She summarizes the dimensions of her psychic struggle: "The fear of doing wrong has been always the leading principle of my internal guidance."⁴ (In this instance, she adds, she finds herself "overpowered" by her inability to decide what was right and consequently unable to resolve on any course of action at all.) More than thirty years before, while she was still at Court, she had talked with the Reverend Charles de Guiffardière (always rferred to in her journal as "Mr. Turbulent") about good conduct. He inquires whether she has ever done something she repents. Sometimes, she replies, but not often, "for it is not very often that I have done anything." What has saved her from misbehavior? Mr. Turbulent suggests prejudice, education, and accident. Miss Burney agrees, but adds *fear*. "I run no risks that I can see—I run—but it is always away from all danger that I perceive." Surely, Mr. Turbulent exclaims, such is not the "rule of right." Once more his interlocutor agrees, concluding the discussion, rather smugly, "I must be content that it is certainly not the rule of wrong" (Jan. 1788; III 392).

Both these encounters, in addition to their psychological interest, suggest the literary possibilities of Miss Burney's principle of self-interpretation, an essentially dramatic view of her experience because it involves imagining goodness as precariously won and preserved and constantly to be defended, rather than as an achieved state of being. The active consciousness of danger that Fanny Burney reports emphasizes the potential drama within her quiet life, despite the fact that, as she confesses, she actually does little. Indeed, her refrainings themselves partake of her drama.

Reading the mass of the journals, one gradually realizes the energy of the decorous woman's verbal self-presentation, structured by her determination to be perceived as good, and her fear of negative judgment. The action of Fanny Burney's vast collections of journals and letters, like that of most women's writing in her century, derives from her attempt to defend—not to discover, define, or assert—the self. Both her choices and her ways of describing them testify to her productive and self-protective solution to unescapable problems of women's existence. That solution provides psychic space for her imaginative life, thus making her literary career possible, and also shapes the operations of her imagination.

The relation between Fanny Burney's loudly proclaimed concern with virtue and her impulse to write was an early theme of her diaries. Virtue and writing, it seemed in her youth, made utterly opposed demands. At the age of fifteen, she consigned to a bonfire all her literary production to date. Almost fifty years later, she explained why. "So early was I impressed myself with ideas that fastened degradation to this class of composition [fiction], that at the age of adolescence, I struggled against the propensity which, even in childhood, even from the moment I could hold a pen, had impelled me into its toils; and on my fifteenth birth-day, I made so resolute a conquest over an inclination at which I blushed, and that I had always kept secret, that I committed to the flames whatever, up to that moment, I had committed to paper."[5] She sounds as though she is reporting a struggle against sexual sin ("propensity," "its toils," "an inclination at which I blushed," "secret") and the language of battle in which she records her suppression echoes the vocabulary in which her fiction relates her heroines' conflicts between reason and passion ("struggled against," "so resolute a conquest"). Writing fiction seemed to her, at the beginning, a fatal self-indulgence and writing fact, only slightly less menacing. Her friend Miss Young warns her that keeping a journal "is the most dangerous employment young persons can have—that it makes them often record things which ought *not* to be recorded, but instantly forgot."[6] A few pages earlier (I, 14), the diarist has inadvertently exposed two other hazards of her literary occupation: keeping a diary encourages a hunger for fresh experience, and it fosters undue reflectiveness about the experience one has. Miss Burney feels apologetic about her literary activity; she spends the morning on needlework, thus proving herself a good little woman, in order to justify an afternoon of reading and writing. But although she has burned her youthful novel, she continues her journalizing: a necessity of her psychic life.

In a letter to her "Daddy" Crisp, one of the older men who played important roles in her life partly as guardians of morality, Fanny, granting the *"general* superiority" of men to women, concludes that women's weakness stems from defects of head rather than heart (1774; I, 272). Women, therefore, must trust their emotions: hence, presumably, Fanny Burney's own adherence to fear as a sufficient guide to conduct. Yet they must also recognize the danger of their feelings. "Talking of happiness and misery, sensibility and a total want of feeling, my mama [i.e., her stepmother] said, turning to me, 'Here's a girl will *never* be happy! *Never* while she lives!—for she possesses perhaps as feeling a heart as ever girl had!'[7] To write a novel, Fanny believes as a girl, is to venture into dangerous realms of feeling and fantasy. To write a journal, on the other hand, may provide a way to deal with feelings as well as to express them. In the *Early Diary*, written for "nobody" (this strategy itself a youthful instance of the writer's defensive self-deprecation), we see the author struggling with moral and emotional dilemmas, using language to construct her defenses. The later journals, composed for various members of her family, show the process at a more advanced stage: writing now a means of consolidating and proclaiming already established defense systems. By the end of the *Early Diary*, Fanny Burney has rejected her first suitor, declaring her intent to live single. No further suitor presented himself, as far as we are told, until the man she accepted. She had defined clear channels for her emotional life.

Fear provided partial solutions for the crucial problem of a woman's relations with others. Twenty-one-year-old Fanny mentally questions the conduct of Miss Bowdler, who "lives exactly as she pleases"; she concludes her account, "I can by no means approve so great a contempt of public opinion" (*Early Diary*, I, 221). Two years earlier, Fanny had encountered another young woman, a Miss Allen, who seemed to her possibly "too sincere: she pays too little regard to the world." The observer cannot decide what to think of such a phenomenon. She disapproves of the woman's ready disdain for *"harmless* folly," but she recognizes how "infinitely tiresome" such folly can seem and applauds the honesty of openly acknowledging the fact (I, 128).

These two sets of observations sketch the issues of social relations as Fanny Burney understood them. Suffering from the impingement of conventional pressures on individual lives, she yearned for freedom. Yet convention, she understood, guarded feelings. The individual who boldly expressed her personal preferences (like Miss Bowdler's for men) or distastes (like Miss Allen's intolerance for folly) might hurt or mislead others. Despite Miss Burney's half-articulated desire to control her own destiny, she could not finally approve "contempt for public opinion." Manners and morals—as her four novels were to testify—reflected one another, in her conviction; the minutiae of socially acceptable conduct provided orthodox means for expressing consideration and concern for others. Fear of offending supplied a more potent principle of action than distaste for being offended.

As Fanny Burney discovered more and more emphatically the uses of fear as a principle of guidance in her life, she found also the way to tell her own story and came to understand the nature of the story she was constructing. "The act of journalizing," a theorist of autobiography writes, "intensifies the conflict in any autobiographer between life and pattern, movement and stasis, identification and definition, world and self."[8] The observation applies hardly at all to Miss Burney as journalizer. Writing down her experience, she seems, on the contrary, to resolve potential conflicts between life and pattern and world and self. Discovering the structures of her life, she finds out how to feel about the world. As a result she contradicts also, essentially if not technically, the common generalization that, however highly wrought its individual entries, a "diary or journal as a complete work will never reflect the conscious shaping of a whole life for one informing purpose."[9] One can speculate about how conscious the diarist's structuring could have been, but the sense of an informing purpose shaping her existence in the living and in the recording becomes increasingly strong. That purpose—to defend the freedom of the self by asserting fear of wrongdoing and commitment to virtue—involved familial, social, and literary relations, dictated action and restraint, and resolved as well as created conflict.

Often, particularly in Miss Burney's adolescence, the desire for freedom appears to clash with the need to avoid offending. The conflict between the two dominates her *Early Diaries*.

O! how I hate this vile custom which obliges us to make slaves of ourselves!—to sell the most precious property we boast, our time;—and to sacrifice it to every prattling impertinent who chooses to demand it!—Yet those who shall pretend to defy this irksome confinement of our happiness, must stand accused of incivility,—breach of manners—love of originality,—and ... what not. But, nevertheless ... they who will nobly dare to be above submitting to chains their reason disapproves, them shall I always honour—if that will be of any service to them! For why should we not be permitted to be masters of our time?—Why may we not venture to love, and to dislike—and why, if we do, may we not give to those we love the richest jewel we own, our time?   (1769; I, 49)

Miss Burney's sequences of reflection, in those early years, repeatedly duplicate the structure of this passage. The strong impulse to reject custom's slavery wavers in the face of anticipated charges of incivility. When the impulse returns to dominance, it has changed form: the author no longer imagines defying convention herself, only honoring those brave enough to do so, with an edge of self-contempt for her own ineffectuality. She can conclude her consideration only in unanswerable questions that express her resentment of the course of conformity she has chosen. Similarly, we find her meditating on love (I, 9–10), confessing that she wishes "truly, really, and greatly ... to be *in love*" and committed to a feeling devoid of rational justification, self-sufficient and satisfying. But soon she condemns such a longing as "foolish and ill-judged!" explaining that she does not really know what she says, she cannot mean it. Feeling leads in opposite directions.

When Mr. Barlow proposes to Fanny, that point becomes painfully apparent. She has long associated marriage with lack of freedom. The prospect of her own marriage reduces her to panic. Manifestly admirable though Thomas Barlow is, her heart tells her that she cannot unite herself with him. Her revered father and her "Daddy" Crisp argue his case; her deep desire always to comply with their wishes wars with her disinclination to marry. She thinks about "the duty of a wife": how hard it must be, "practised without high esteem!" Her reluctance, it seems, is sexual. But she continues, "And I am too spoilt by such men as my father and Mr. Crisp to content myself with a character merely inoffensive" (II, 51). She prefers a father to a husband. Her father, opposing male reason to female emotion, urges serious consideration of Barlow's suit. Fanny, realizing that reason offers her no support, creates a lavish display of emotion, unable to eat, constantly weeping, feeling more misery than ever before "except when a child, upon the loss of my own beloved mother, and ever revered and most dear grandmother!" (II, 69). The prospect of marriage threatens another terrible loss: that of her father and her established dependencies. Unable to face it, she opposes her father's professed wishes, retains her single state, and immediately (twenty-three years old now) begins thinking that no one will ever love her.

In this conflict as in the other internal struggles recorded in the diary of the pre-*Evelina* years, one feels an adolescent uncertainty of identity but little uncertainty of action. Miss Burney possesses already a strong impulse to reject: to push away impropriety and to forestall impingement. The force of public opinion has for her the status of a concrete reality with high potential for personal damage. By avoiding impropriety, she can avoid notice and consequently threat. She wants also to preserve the securities of her protected role as daughter. The issues of her life are already defined. How can a woman evade attention, yet assert her self? How can she protect that self? How can she avoid wrongdoing without resigning herself to total passivity? What can she say without dangerous exposure?

Writing *Evelina* in secrecy and publishing it anonymously, she allowed herself some self-exposing "saying." Her resultant sense of danger and fear dominates her journal and published letters for years after the book's publication. "All that I can say for myself is," she summarizes, "that I have always feared discovery, always sought concealment, and always known that no success should counter-balance the publishing my name" (*Diary and Letters*, I, 166). She has supported this statement in advance with abundant instances of a terror of discovery that seems, like her early guilt about writing, to bear a distinctly sexual aspect. When Mrs. Thrale accuses her of "an over-delicacy that may make you unhappy all your life," she explains that she had thought herself "as safe" with the publisher Lowndes as when her manuscript lay in her own bureau drawer. To be "known as a scribbler" threatens her impregnability (I, 97). She "trembles" and worries about her possible "downfall" as writer (I, 126–7). "I would a thousand times rather forfeit my character as a writer," she explains, "than risk ridicule or censure as a female" (I. 162). At the age of sixty-two, looking back over a successful career, she remarks that "never yet had the moment arrived in which to be marked had not been embarrassing and disconcerting to me, even when most flattering" (VI, 112).

To be marked, discovered, known as a writer, and, therefore, perhaps not a proper female, perhaps a woman unforgivably addicted to self-display: this idea focused Fanny Burney's terror of doing wrong. To make oneself known as a writer invites people to look; to offer one's fantasies for the perusal of others invites violation. For a woman to be looked at or talked of means, at best, loss of dignity, at worst, loss of reputation.[10] Lured into discussion of "learning in woman," Miss Burney confesses her belief that "it has no recommendation of sufficient value to compensate its evil excitement of envy and satire" (IV, 222). When her half sister, Sarah Burney, visits her after her mother's death, Fanny acknowledges her virtues and skills but complains at length about the fact that the young woman (twenty-five years old) wishes her accomplishments recognized. "She has many excellent qualities . . . but she is good enough to make me lament that she is not modest enough to be yet better."[11]

Loss of modesty amounts to loss of virtue; only by strict decorum can a woman protect herself. From 1786 to 1791, her journal and letters make clear, Miss Burney committed herself absolutely to propriety in her service to Queen Charlotte. Her court experience, as she reports it, emphasizes the degree to which her life was assuming what seems in retrospect the symmetrical development of a carefully worked-out drama. First had come the questioning adolescence, in which social fear triumphed over daring impulse without ever quite extinguishing it; then followed a social pattern paralleled by that of Miss Burney's literary life, in which the writing of a second novel (to be published in secret) succeeded the destruction of the first, which she had felt to be entirely impermissible. Finally came the young adult years in which Fanny Burney struggled with the sense of exposure created by successful authorship. She wrote a comedy but withdrew it from public view at her father's suggestion of possible impropriety. She labored over a second publishable novel of unimpeachable morality, explaining, to the point of tedium, her impeccable purposes, soliciting and accepting frequent advice from all her mentors, as if to lessen the potential burden of notoriety and the conceivable imputation of seeking it. But no amount of self-guarding or protestation could resolve her guilt at self-display. Acceptance of the court position represented an attempt to find solution at the opposite extreme. Sinking herself in a role, giving up writing for publication, governing herself entirely by external expectation, she tried by total self-subordination to eliminate all conflict.[12]

She never fancied the court position would provide personal pleasure. In accepting it, she wished above all to please her father, although she realized that her new commitment would involve relinquishing indulgence of her vital private affections. Compliance is the theme of her time at court. She comes to love the Queen, and from the start she adores Mrs. Delany, the old lady who introduced her to the royal family and whom she continues to see in her new position. Subordinating herself to such women, she believes herself thus to escape all danger of wrongdoing. But despite her devotion and her eagerness to serve, to please her father, the Queen, and Mrs. Delany, to be good and avoid evil—despite these forces urging her toward contentment, she feels bitter and unending abhorrence of her lot. She suffers from the capricious tyranny of Mrs. Schwellenberg, her immediate superior, to whom the Queen feels so deeply attached that Fanny cannot complain to her. She suffers from deprivation of real human fellowship, from the boredom of repeated ritual, and from the intense physical strain of her position.

To her sister, Mrs. Phillips, she writes, in August 1786, confessing her misery and outlining her proposed solution to it: "If to you alone I show myself in these dark colours, can you blame the plan that I have intentionally been forming—namely, to wean myself from myself—to lessen all my affections—to curb all my wishes—to deaden all my sensations?" (III, 9). To wean, to lessen, to curb, to deaden: a program of deprivation and reduction. A few months later, in her journal, she puts it in more positive terms.

> Now, therefore, I took shame to myself, and *Resolved to be happy*. And my success has shown me how far less chimerical than it appears is such a resolution.
> To be patient under . . . disappointments . . . to relinquish, without repining, frequent intercourse with those I love;—to settle myself in my monastery, without one idea of ever quitting it;—to study for the approbation of my lady abbess, and make it a principal source of content, as well as spring of action;—and to associate more cheerily with my surrounding nuns and monks;—these were the articles which were to support my resolution.   (16 Jan. 1787; III, 161–2)

Despite the talk of happiness, patience, and cheeriness, she still advocates for herself suppression, submission, and resignation. She knows her absolute dependence on those around her. Struggling to convert it into a fact of positive meaning, she demands of herself something almost equivalent to religious conversion—her metaphor of the monastery suggesting her recognition of exactly this point.

The terms of the conflict between the need for self-assertion and the desire for self-concealment through conformity become more vividly defined during the record of the court years. The conflict itself, in fact, was probably more intense than at any other time of Fanny Burney's life because now her solution could not readily resolve the internal opposition. Before and after her service to the Queen, Miss Burney used her fears and proprieties as a means of guarding her inner life, her writing life. At Court, on the other hand, she did not write to any purpose, although she began several tragedies in an evident effort to express and contain her inner turmoil. As the imbalance increased between the demands of the world and the needs of the self, the solution was in danger of becoming the problem. Previously the young writer had met both demands simultaneously, strategies of self-concealment providing means of self-assertion. Now the strategy no longer worked. Because the journal has already established its clear vision of the personal possibilities implicit in the life of subordination, it can also sharply convey the experience of something going wrong, possibilities closing off. But it conveys, further, the consequent growth of new certainties.

During these years at Court, with their vivid experience of suppression, Fanny Burney appears to have reflected on the essential experience of women. Her own life—like the lives of her fictional heroines—confronted her with severely limited alternatives. What could she do if she left the Queen's service? She could only life with her father, doomed to be his burden unless another man took her off his hands. She could, of course, once more write for publication, but the idea of achieving independence through writing did not yet appear to occur to her. What did occur to her, although perhaps not quite consciously, was that other women in different ways duplicated her fate. She sees around her painful results of arranged marriages and subordinated female lives. In her conversations with "Mr. Turbulent," we learn of her attitudes about women. The Reverend de Guiffardière figures largely in Miss Burney's account of her court years. Apparently happily married, he nevertheless indulges in extravagant flirtation with Miss Burney, his purpose unclear. Deliberately provocative, he challenges her cherished evasions. Thus, when Miss Burney declares her unwillingness to countenance "error" in other women, Mr. Turbulent accuses her of hypocrisy. "This brought me forth. I love not to be attacked for making professions beyond my practice; and I assured him, very seriously, that I had not one voluntary acquaintance, nor one with whom I kept up the smallest intercourse of my own seeking or wilful concurrence, that had any stain in their characters that had ever reached my ears" (III, 116). The dialogues between Mr. Turbulent and Miss Burney dramatize the tensions of "bringing forth" such a woman. She withdraws; he pursues. She shows herself; he triumphs. What she says makes no difference to him, only whether she is willing to say anything at all. Although she prides herself on not engaging in debate, he forces her to participate. Finally she makes the fact of his forcing the source of her victory.

> "And pray, Mr. Turbulent, solve me, then, this difficulty: what choice has a poor female with whom she may converse? Must she not, in company as in dancing, take up with those who choose to take up with her?"
> He was staggered by this question, and while he wavered how to answer it, I pursued my little advantage—
> "No man, Mr. Turbulent, has cause to be flattered that a woman talks with him, while it is only in reply; for though *he* may come, go, address or neglect, and do as he will,—she, let her think and wish what she may, must only follow as he leads." (19 Feb., 1787; III, 215)

In dancing, in company, in life, a woman "must only follow." Given the social demand for such subservience, compliance becomes meaningless; behind her expert cooperation, the woman thinks and wishes as she will. True, she cannot act upon her thoughts and wishes. Equally, she cannot be compelled to expose them. Mr. Turbulent is quite naturally "staggered." No matter what he drives Miss Burney to say, she can claim finally to have said it for his sake, not her own. Her thoughts and wishes remain her own—not to be "brought forth," never shown. Beginning to identify her tactics and her need for them as consequences of her sex, she gains force in her modest self-assertions, now able to claim the power of her privacy without justifying it by literary productivity. Such journal sequences as the account of the conversation with Mr. Turbulent have more profound literary merits than their authentic renditions of speech. They reveal a rich imagining of the conventionally disguised self. Miss Burney convinces the reader, just as she convinces Mr. Turbulent, that much lies beneath her compliance. Without revealing her own depths, she evokes their mysterious existence. Her life of emotional deprivation gradually gives her the survivor's strength. Unhappy, she learns to maintain herself; her diaries evoke the drama of her survival and her strengthening.

Miss Burney's elaborate fears, with the avoidances they generate, create for her in her maturity a rather distinct identity, although one which would require formulation in largely negative terms. She identifies herself as a woman in hiding, the product of a feminine discipline of fear, but this identity does not altogether satisfy her. Her youthful concern with freedom has not vanished. Although she reaps psychic benefits from her flawless conformity, she also pays large costs. Mrs. Schwellenberg insists that she keep the window down on her side of the carriage, to provide air. A sharp wind seriously inflames her eyes. Her father, seeing the consequences of obedience to such authority, orders her to insist that the glass remain raised on subsequent expeditions. "I was truly glad of this permission to rebel, and it has given me an internal hardiness in all similar assaults, that has at least relieved my mind from the terror of giving mortal offence where most I owe implicit obedience, should provocation overpower my capacity of forbearance" (27 Nov., 1787; III, 337). Permission to rebel! Yearning for freedom, Fanny Burney requires that it be given her. She pleads with her father to allow her to abandon court life, which has not only damaged her health but forced her to live "like an orphan—like one who had no natural ties, and must make her way as she could by those that were factitious" (1790; IV, 392). Claiming her entitlement to parental nurturance, her right to a woman's life of feelings, she returns to the original safety of her father's house.

This choice, however, seems not to have been so regressive as it may appear. In some ways it indeed involves a return to the status and the feelings of adolescence. Fanny begins writing again—"merely scribbling what will not be repressed"—thus providing "a delight to my dear Father inexpressibly great."[13] He hardly cares what she writes; neither, apparently, does she. She makes no attempt to publish anything, still fully convinced of the danger of exposure. At the age of forty she writes, "the panics I have felt upon entering to any strange company, or large party even of intimates, has [sic], at times, been a suffering unspeakably, almost incredibly severe to me."[14] Fear continues to provide the principle not only of her conduct but of her very being.

Such a woman, it seems evident, could hardly hope to marry, to make a positive commitment that would separate her from her beloved father. Yet marry she did, uniting herself with a man of different culture and religion, a man capable of providing no economic security, and most startling of all, one whom her father thought an inappropriate match. Her father did not attend her wedding. The psychic process that made it possible involved the rationalization of old patterns into new forms. As feeling urged her in unfamiliar directions, she discovered how the fear of wrongdoing could justify satisfying her desires. M. D'Arblay's position as persecuted victim of political injustice made it seem wrong to cause him further unhappiness by refusing to gratify him. Moreover, the Frenchman, it turned out, could assume a position in Miss Burney's life morally comparable to that of Mrs. Delany and Queen Charlotte. If they had functioned for her as substitute grandmother and mother (she suggests these terms herself), M. D'Arblay could take the moral stance of father—that posture characteristic of all Fanny Burney's novelistic heroes, beginning with Evelina's Lord Orville. In early April 1793, Fanny writes to her sister: "His nobleness of character—his sweetness of disposition—his Honour, Truth, integrity—with so much of softness, delicacy, & tender humanity—except my beloved Father & Mr. Lock, I have never seen such a man in this world, though I have drawn such in my Imagination." The man of her dreams, in short, must be a moral paragon. She has no doubt of her suitor's power to make her happy; she only questions her own reciprocal capacity.[15] The next month, he rebukes her for failing to write her sister frequently enough. "I own I had an odd feel at the sort of authority that might seem implied in the reproof. But this noble Creature will spare no one & no thing that he holds wrong. I vindicated myself . . . He heard my justification with a look of serious attention that made me internally smile & *look forward*—for it said, 'I MUST ALWAYS FULLY understand that you do RIGHT—' 'Tis well I have no intention to do otherwise!—Oh my Susan! if it should, indeed, be my lot to fall into the hands of one so scrupulous in integrity, how thankfully shall I hail my Fate!"[16] Her rhapsodic tone, inspired by his rigorous demands on her, sounds perfectly genuine, as does her formulation of marriage as a commitment requiring only passive acceptance. Because M. D'Arblay assumes the position of moral mentor, she can avoid wrongdoing by marrying him, for she is both helping a needy man (her pension from the Queen supported them both) and submitting to the guidance of one whom she considers her moral superior. Her union with him marks the climax of her story. Reporting it, she emphasizes the degree to which it confirms her identity, while enlarging her sense of possibility.

"Can you conceive any thing equal to my surprise," one of her sisters wrote to another, "at hearing our vestal sister had ventured on the stormy sea of matrimony."[17] Fanny explains that she married in search of happiness, which for her must derive from "Domestic comfort & social affection." Moreover, "M. d'Arblay has a taste for literature, & a passion for reading & writing as marked as my own; this is a simpathy to rob retirement of all superfluous leisure, & ensure to us both occupation constantly edifying or entertaining. He has seen so much of life, & has suffered so severely from its disappointments, that retreat, with a chosen Companion, is become his final desire."[18] Thus she fantasizes an ideal situation (an ideal, incidentally, which she very nearly achieved): retreat from the world and final commitment to the life of avoidance with a husband unable to find employment in England; a life of the affections as well, that existence of feeling and emotional security for which she had yearned; pseudo-parental permission to indulge her passion for reading and writing at the side of a man who shared and condoned it.

Mme. D'Arblay knows the general astonishment at her marriage and professes that her own amazement exceeds that of "all my Friends united."[19] From the new safety of matrimony she asserts a distinct and positive sense of self. Despite, or perhaps because of, her long training and eager participation in the rituals of female compliance, she has developed a "specialness" of character and taste that any conceivable husband must conform to rather than hope to change. Only with such a man would the hazard of marriage diminish, its promise expand, and the likelihood of happiness seem greater than that in a state of such autonomy as a single woman could hope to achieve. In fact autonomy, for Fanny Burney, felt less desirable than sympathy. Liberty of feeling and expression would be infinitely less dangerous if someone shared her feelings and approved her expression. Long accustomed to following external dictates, she could best discover her own will through another. Thus, writing to Mrs. Waddington about her pregnancy, she reveals her physical terror of childbirth and comments, "My Partner, however, who daily encreases the debt I owe him of my life's happiness, rejoices—& I must be a wretch of ingratitude & insensibility to regret whatever he can wish."[20] Still formulating her responsiblities in terms of what she must *not* do, she attributes the wish for parenthood to her husband alone and gains moral strength for her ordeal by interpreting it as something done for the sake of another.

Through the "Social Simpathy" she found with D'Arblay, the writer once more could write for the public, her sense of the potential indecency of such display counteracted by her conviction that her writing, too, served the interests of others, helping to support her husband and son. "I had previously determined," she observes, "when I *changed my state*, to set aside all my innate & original abhorrences, & regard & use as resources MYSELF, what had always been considered as such by others."[21] Others had long valued the products of her fantasy. Now she could value them herself, as the source of economic security, and she expresses openly her desire to drive the best possible bargain for her work. No longer wrongdoing to be avoided and less vividly an inlet for danger, the writing of novels had become virtuous. It provided a way of articulating her own good principles and of exorcising her dangerous impulses, and provided also means of supporting her family.

The mature identity asserted in the journals depends on a rich acceptance of roles. Mme. D'Arblay conveys herself as wife, mother, and writer. The three roles comfortably interchange and merge, the first two creating a screen for the third. Secure in her understanding of her writing as means to a noble end, she need worry no longer about why she feels compelled to write. Her fears of the world are held at bay by the solidity of her domestic position. She writes charmingly and perceptively of her son's development and expresses with increasing ease and freedom her opinions about the vexed affairs of her extended family, rich in disastrous marriages, unexpected elopements, unmentionable adulteries, all of which Fanny contemplates serenely from her domestic retreat. She survives twelve years of post-revolutionary France with aplomb, occupying herself with her last novel, intended to support her son at Cambridge University. Hostile criticism seems less terrifying than it had earlier appeared. Income matters more than praise or blame.

Yet Fanny Burney never outgrew her woman's dependence on the approval of those she loved. She had been right in her premarital assessment of her husband. His sympathy with her wishes and purposes was almost total. But when, in 1800—she was forty-eight years old—her father disapproved an attempt to produce her comedy, "Love and Fashion," she reveals the continued potency of early conflict. Withdrawing the play, she yet movingly begs her father to allow her the liberty he claims for himself. "Leap the pales of your paddock," she urges him to tell her—"let us pursue our career; and, while you frisk from novel to comedy, I, quitting Music and Prose, will try a race with Poetry and the Stars." (Dr. Burney was writing a long poem about astronomy.) Immediately, guilt ensues: "I am sure my dear father will not infer, from this appeal, I mean to parallel our work. No one more truly measures her own inferiority, which, with respect to yours, has always been my pride. I only mean to show, that if my muse loves a little variety, she has a hereditary claim to try it" (V, 461). The same emotional ambivalence (here manifest even in sentence structure: is she comparing her inferiority to his inferiority?) controlled much of her life: on the one hand, the longing to "leap the pales," on the other, the inability to do so without parental permission. Her tone indicates resentment of enforced inferiority although she asserts her pride in the inferiority that has constituted a woman's (or a girl's) security. The devious appeal to parental emotion, with the reference to "hereditary claim," possibly recalls to the reader if not the writer that earlier deviousness by which Miss Burney reminded her father that he had caused her to live "like an orphan" at Court. Playing on her father's guilt and revealing her own, she suggests how she has both used and been controlled by fears that originate in the child's dependent condition.

It may appear that I have been telling the story of Fanny Burney's life. In fact I have been summarizing her story of her life as it emerges through the evolving record of the letters and diaries. Only by the diarist's interpretation do we learn that the important aspect of publishing a novel is that people look at you and that her husband's moral impeccability makes her marriage possible. The story of her life, as the journals and letters tell it, dramatizes the freedoms and the restrictions of fear. Its narrative strength derives from its singleness of interpretation. The principles of self-concealment that appear to have controlled Fanny Burney's life control her telling of that life (and are reinforced by that telling), giving to her story, despite the fact that it is composed of disparate small units, integrity of purpose and coherence of form. The unmastered conflict that muddles Mrs. Pilkington's and Mrs. Charke's literary intent, the self-pity and self-importance that mar the proportions of Mrs. Thrale's story here yield to literary and moral clarity. Although such clarity implies the embracing of limitation, it is a principle of power. At least as consciously as her predecessors, Fanny Burney writes of herself specifically as a woman. Her grasp of a woman's resources, however, extends to their literary possibilities.

Virginia Woolf, reflecting on her own keeping of a diary, wrote:

There looms ahead of me the shadow of some kind of form which a diary might attain to. I might in the course of time learn what it is that one can make of this loose, drifting material of life; finding another use for it than the use I put it to, so much more consciously and scrupulously, in fiction . . . I should like it to resemble some deep old desk, or capacious hold-all, in which one flings a mass of odds and ends without looking them through. I should like to come back, after a year or two, and find that the collection had sorted itself and refined itself and coalesced, as such deposits so mysteriously do, into a mould, transparent enough to reflect the light of our life, and yet steady, tranquil compounds with the aloofness of a work of art.[22]

The mysterious process of "sorting" and "coalescing," the tranquility of a work of art—these descriptions apply also to Fanny Burney's journals, a miscellaneous repository in which dynamism and unity alike derive from the implications of commitment to fear of wrongdoing as an operative principle and as the action of the writer's life and work. Of course, to understand the journals in this way involves ignoring many of their details in an effort to perceive the underlying principle of coherence. But that principle, I would argue (as Virginia Woolf presumably would too), gives to the utterances of diary and letters their fundamental literary strength.

If the collection of Fanny Burney's journals and letters creates the effect of autobiography, a coherent narrative implying an imaginative grasp of experience, her four novels also have aspects of psychic autobiography. One can readily perceive in them versions of the journals' central theme: the discipline and the liberation of a woman's fears of disapproval and of being found wanting—fear, in fact, of the other people who comprise society. But novels, with their capacity to express wish and fantasy as well as reality, allow Fanny Burney to enlarge her communication of her own nature. Her fiction illustrates complex feminine identities of indirection.

Ian Watt, noting that women wrote most novels in the eighteenth century, hints also—in terms more tactful than mine—that most of those novels were bad. In Jane Austen, he suggests, we first encounter an unmistakable example of the fact "that the feminine sensibility was in some ways better equipped to reveal the intricacies of personal relationships and was therefore at a real advantage in the realm of the novel."[23] He does not explain why earlier female writers had proved unable to exploit this advantage. Indeed, the fact—like many facts about literary quality—is profoundly inexplicable. One can describe the aspects of Fanny Burney's novels that make them more moving and more meaningful than Jane Barker's, and it is possible to demonstrate how Jane Austen excels Fanny Burney. *Why* is another matter; *why* reduces one to vaguenesses like *talent* and *genius*.

To define the strengths and weaknesses of Fanny Burney's fictional achievement, however, may lead at least to speculation about the reasons for her superiority to her female contemporaries. Her strengths are more far-reaching than has been generally recognized. *Evelina* has been praised as though it consisted only of a collection of skillful character sketches.[24] Joyce Hemlow has demonstrated its affinities to the "courtesy book," as an effort to outline a scheme of acceptable womanly conduct.[25] It has been admired ever since its own time for the accuracy of its social detail and conversation. But it also manifests a high level of psychological insight closely related to the self-knowledge that emerges from even the youthful diaries. Fanny Burney may write better fiction than other women of her era partly because she has come to terms more fully than they with the realities of the female condition. She is therefore "equipped to revel the intricacies of personal relationships" as they actually exist in the world and is not blinded by wishful fantasy or by anger, although both manifest themselves in her work.

Self-discovery of a woman in hiding constitutes the subject of the novels, as of the journals. Fanny Burney's heroines hide specifically because they are women, driven to concealments in order to maintain their goodness. They do not, except in brief moments, openly resent their fates. Yet the tension suggested by a formulation that asserts the simultaneity of discovery and hiding pervades Miss Burney's fiction. She constructs elaborate happenings to articulate conflict, locate happiness, and apportion blame. Her transformations of life in fiction, while insisting on the essential order of experience, also hint their author's awareness of the psychic costs of such affirmation. Anxiety dominates the Burney novels, despite their happy endings. However minute its pretexts—and often they seem trivial indeed—its weight is real, deeply experienced by the central characters and, to a surprising extent, shared even by readers who can readily dismiss its nominal causes. In fact, the causes lie deep; the heroines suffer profound conflicts.

Evelina, of the four heroines, has the fewest and most trivial real problems. Like Cecilia and Juliet in *The Wanderer*, she is in effect an orphan (her father, though alive, has refused to acknowledge her), but she has a benevolent guardian and devoted friends. A summary of the novel's plot will suggest, though, how profoundly it involves itself with fundamental questions of identity. Evelina is the unacknowledged daughter of an English baronet secretly married to a young woman, half French, who died in childbirth, leaving her infant to the guardianship of a benevolent clergyman until the child's father is willing to admit his marriage as well as his paternity. At the narrative's opening, Evelina, after seventeen years of rural seclusion, goes to visit a friend who soon takes her to London. There she encounters, by chance, her vulgar and disagreeable French grandmother, Mme. Duval, who insists that she associate with equally vulgar English relatives. Evelina, however, feels drawn to the aristocracy. She is sexually attracted to Lord Orville, extravagantly courted by Sir Clement Willoughby. Much of the action concerns her efforts to identify herself with the upper class—her manners are already upper class manners—and to evade her kinship with the bourgeoisie. Finally she claims acknowledgment by her true father, only to face absolute rejection as an impostor, since he believes another young woman to be his daughter. A nurse's confession reveals an earlier baby-switching trick, and the novel ends with Evelina in happy possession of, in effect, three fathers: her paternalistic new husband, Lord Orville; her virtuous guardian, Mr. Villars; and her genuine father, Sir John Belmont. All three confirm her identity of true aristocracy and virtue.

The difficulties the novel nominally concerns itself with, according to its writer's direct assertion, derive mainly from Evelina's social inexperience. Nothing happens except "little incidents," but virtue, feeling, and understanding finally receive their just reward, the heroine's "conspicuous beauty" providing the means to this appropriate end.[26] More obviously than stories such as Jane Barker's tale of a merman and his paramour, this tale represents a familiar female fantasy: a potent vision of virtue recognized and rewarded despite its incidental errors—specifically, in this instance, Fanny Burney's own kind of virtue. But the novel has a level of realism lacking in many other fictions by female writers. It concerns itself with a young woman's entrance into a genuinely imagined social world, dominated, like Fanny Burney's own, by forms and manners, and very real in its pressures, cruelties, and arbitrary benignities. "The right line of conduct," Evelina's guardian, Mr. Villars, tells her, "is the same for both sexes" (p. 217). But Mr. Villars lives quite out of the world. Right though he is in theory, and confirmed in his rightness by the wish fulfillment of the ending, he does not understand the practical problems of a woman's following the right line of conduct. Evelina has to come to terms with the disparity between his ideals (which are also hers) and the way life actually takes place in the world, but she also must avoid relinquishing, or even modifying, the standards that attest her virtue. Like Tom Jones, she must learn prudence.[27] But prudence for her, as for Fanny Burney, constitutes mainly avoidance, and she too is perpetually, and increasingly, dominated by fear of wrongdoing.

Direct comments in the novel about the world emphasize its danger, its superficiality and hypocrisy, and its sinister power. The world threatens individual identity. Mr. Villars, living in retirement, fears its effects on Evelina. He also recognizes the world's inescapable power. Only the frivolous wholeheartedly accept worldly values, but no one escapes them. The choices for women consist mainly of options to refuse or to accept rather than possibilities to act. Evelina acts meaningfully and independently once, when—in an improbable and overwritten scene—she snatches the pistols from a suicidal young man. She then faints. "In a moment, strength and courage seemed lent me as by inspiration: I started, and rushing precipitately into the room, just caught his arm, and then, overcome by my own fears, I fell down at his side, breathless and senseless" (p. 182). Even when the woman possesses and displays strength and courage, she understands (or explains) them as given to her from outside, and her own powerful fears counteract her impulse toward action, reducing her to the passivity more characteristic of the female state and more unarguably blameless. Women aspire to the negative condition of blamelessness. Evelina is constantly beset by fears of being thought bold, or rude, or unwomanly. She fears acting. She writes to Mr. Villars, "Unable as I am to act for myself, or to judge what conduct I ought to pursue, how grateful do I feel myself, that I have such a guide and director to counsel and instruct me as yourself!" (p. 160). And, much later (p. 306), she appeals in similar terms to her lover, Lord Orville. The proper line of conduct is *not* the same for both sexes. Men guide and instruct; women are guided and instructed. Evelina makes quite explicit her desire (which she shares with her creator) to find a lover or husband to fill the same role as father or guardian. She assumes the utter propriety of remaining as much as possible a child: ignorant, innocent, fearful, and irresponsible.

Proving her sagacity, her lover values her for precisely these qualities. Like Evelina's guardian, whom in many respects he resembles, he believes the world is opposed to rationality and values the woman who knows nothing of it. Shortly before he proposes, he summarizes Evelina's character for a group of his fashionable friends, explaining the occasional "strange" elements in her behavior as effects "of inexperience, timidity, and a retiring education," praising her as "informed, sensible, and intelligent," and glorifying "her modest worth, and fearful excellence" (p. 347). Fearfulness has become an index of goodness. Lord Orville recognizes the positive qualities of Evelina's mind, but he praises more the elements of her personality that encourage her to hold back from experience. Strikingly often in all Fanny Burney's novels, the terms of praise applied to women—*artless, blameless*—emphasize the negative: the refrainings induced by fear.

But *Evelina* also contains one minor woman character who does not refrain: the redoubtable Mrs. Selwyn. "She is extremely clever; her understanding, indeed, may be called *masculine*; but, unfortunately, her manners deserve the same epithet; for, in studying to acquire the knowledge of the other sex, she has lost all the softness of her own" (p. 268). No one likes Mrs. Selwyn, and since a woman's fate in the world depends largely on the degree to which she is liked, this fact alone presumably urges negative judgment of a female who feels entitled on the basis of her strong mind to act aggressively in company. She alone, for instance, feels free to remark devastatingly (and accurately) on masculine idiocy in the presence of its perpetrators. Evelina observes that this habit makes enemies; she does not comment on the accuracy of Mrs. Selwyn's judgment. Fanny Burney, disclaiming responsibility for Mrs. Selwyn through her heroine's disapproval, yet allows her to remain a provocative image of female intelligence and force. The novelist thus suggests that she is aware, although she has not yet fully acknowledged it, that Evelina's choices, proper as they are, do not exhaust the tempting possibilities for intelligent women.

Evelina chooses dependency and fear, a choice no less significant for being thrust upon her. It amounts to the declaration of the identity that achieves her social and economic security. The identity she cares about most is given her from without by husband and father. The problem in achieving her woman's identity differs from its male equivalent, from Tom Jones's search for his identity, for example. Her education in society teaches her not to relinquish but to use her innocence and her fears.[28] The discovery of prudence enables her to form new dependency relations. No better solution for women is fully realized in the novel. Yet that disturbing figure, Mrs. Selwyn, who expresses female hostility toward the male without suffering any penalty beyond general dislike, whose mind and money make her sufficiently powerful to resist or endure dislike, suggests an alternative to the dominant fantasy of the woman rewarded for innocence by the dream of scorning the world's judgment while forcing its notice.

But the dominant dream of female withdrawal that preserves individual integrity, protects private feeling, and attracts the perfect lover suggests more clearly than any utterance in her diary the young author's longings and hopes. *Evelina*, like the letters and journals, concentrates on a woman's attempt to preserve and defend herself with the few obvious resources at her disposal. The success of that attempt reaffirms Fanny Burney's personal decisions.

Novels—at least eighteenth-century novels—differ from autobiographies and journals partly in their detailed attention to characters other than the protagonist. Women novelists on the whole had trouble dealing with this aspect of their craft; rarely did they succeed in evoking more than the single female character at the center of their narratives. (In some instances, of course, not even the heroine, paragon rather than recognizable person, was convincingly evoked.) Fanny Burney, on the other hand, seemed to find multiple characterization a vital expressive resource. Through the people she makes Evelina encounter she manages to convey considerable, and rather complicated hostility. Lord Orville and Mr. Villars, both exemplary males, actually engage little of her attention: they remain wooden presences. But the large cast of distasteful aristocrats, the equally unattractive petty bourgeoisie, sadistic Captain Mirvan, and vulgar but vigorous Mme. Duval—these figures come splendidly to life. Their satiric portrayal enables the writer to express and to justify her vivid antagonisms. Mrs. Selwyn provides a direct mouthpiece for aggressive impulses, but Miss Burney also conveys aggression through her derogatory character sketches and through her repeated invention of actions expressing extreme hostility: Captain Mirvan's plot to make Mme. Duval think herself beset by highwaymen, the race of two ancient women arranged by the aristocrats, the scene in which Sir Clement is bitten by a monkey.

As autobiography, in other words, this novel reveals more than the diaries. Allowing Miss Burney to articulate repressed aspects of her personality, it reminds us of the degree to which her constant professions of fear and her insistent withdrawals represent not true timidity but a socially acceptable device of self-protection. The writing and publishing of novels—a public act—also involves self-protection; no one holds the author personally responsible for Captain Mirvan's sadism or Mrs. Selwyn's ferocious commentary. Through imagining such sadism and such commentary, she permits herself the impermissible. She both declares the high value of her own mode of dealing with the world and compensates for the restrictions of her propriety.

After *Evelina* came *Cecilia,* insistently moral, carefully controlled, much too long, and containing some disturbing implications. The power of wealth gives its heroine initial security; her experience teaches her insecurity. Altogether a more sinister fable than *Evelina,* despite its insistent morality, *Cecilia* acknowledges more openly the high psychic cost of female compliance. The permeating sense of anxiety here derives largely from the increasingly explicit recognition of the difficulties and inherent limitations of woman's social position. Cecilia has wealth, intelligence, beauty, adequate social status, and the nominal freedom to do whatever she wants. In fact, as she discovers, she possess all the concomitants, but no real freedom and no power. She must use her energies for self-suppression. "Her passions were under the control of her reason, and she suffered not her affections to triumph over her principles."[29] She must learn to give up, yielding her money as sign and symbol of larger relinquishments. Never does she question—any more than Evelina questions—the necessity to be good. Like Evelina, she is rewarded by marriage. But the diminishment she undergoes in order to achieve it and the torments she endures along the way suggest a dark view of women's fate.

The heroine of *Camilla* suffers yet greater diminishment. Like Evelina, Camilla is inexperienced, powerless, and poor; like Evelina, she learns that she must preserve inexperience, use powerlessness, and emphasize her dependency. Unlike Evelina, she perceives some alternatives to this procedure before discovering their impossibility.

Because of her lack of knowledge of the world, Camilla cannot deal with sophisticated values. Her fiancé Edgar feels that she should not try: she should stay out of the world rather than endeavor to confront it. Knowledge for a woman, from his point of view, constitutes a moral equivalent of rape. Men encourage women to remain ignorant, foolish, and cowardly. They are capitvated by the sight of a beautiful woman agitated by a bull: "What lovely timidity!—What bewitching softness!—What feminine, what beautiful delicacy!—How sweet in terror."[30] *How sweet in terror!* To please a man, a woman, preserving and using her fears and her reluctances, must withdraw. Edgar sees clearly that any "public distinction"—i.e., any social self-assertion—will threaten his plans for Camilla, spoiling "her for private life" (III, 278). The explicit moral of Camilla's experience—the moral she herself accepts—supports Edgar's view. The ideal woman will be neither too beautiful nor too rich; she will be properly humble. Fearful, sweet, ignorant, and utterly dependent, she acknowledges the superior wisdom of the male to whose guidance she eagerly submits. The lessons Camilla learns elaborate the implications of Cecilia's learning and Evelina's. She discovers that apparent sources of power disintegrate in a woman's grasp, that her fears offer more dependable guides than her ambitions, and that only through dependency can she find female success. The world she inhabits contains more multitudinous causes for terror even than Cecilia's: prison, illness, death, betrayal, and poverty. The anxiety, which in *Evelina* issued most often in the heroine's repeated experience of confusion, now has far more serious correlatives.

The balance struck in *Evelina* between acceptance of female self-concealment as a useful strategy and resentment against the world that makes hiding necessary for women becomes with each successive novel more precarious. Yet Fanny Burney's personal life was increasingly happy; her letters state explicitly that marriage brought her unprecedented contentment. *Camilla*, composed in the joyful period after the birth of her son, expresses a jaundiced view of the world. Personal happiness, one may speculate, weakened Miss Burney's commitment to her own discipline of social fear. More and more in the novels she came out of hiding.

None of these first three novels directly protests women's lot, although each more vividly than its predecessor implies the author's awareness that women's fears acknowledge the intolerable dilemmas of their social position. Yet the ideal marriages that conclude the stories suggest that by willing acceptance of fear and restriction women can achieve happiness. Unhappy marriages also exist in these novels, but their moral causes are carefully specified. The heroines have only to avoid the weaknesses that produce them. Fanny Burney glorifies a fugitive and cloistered virtue as uniquely appropriate for women. Still, the strong women of whom she and her heroines disapprove and the trains of disaster that pursue young women aspiring to even mild independence, hint at some resentment of the social necessities apparently so fully accepted.

In 1792 Mary Wollstonecraft published *A Vindication of the Rights of Women*. Some time before 1800, Fanny Burney began writing her last novel, *The Wanderer: or, Female Difficulties*, published in 1814. There is no evidence that she read Mary Wollstonecraft. Yet *The Wanderer* articulates female protest in terms vividly analogous to the social critic's, although nominally only to refute such protest. Mary Wollstonecraft's attack on the existing system of female education and on the assumptions that governed women's conduct focuses on issues already implicit in Fanny Burney's first three novels. Infuriated that a woman should be made to consider her proper function that of pleasing men, Mary Wollstonecraft inveighs particularly against the encouragement of female passivity: "listless inactivity and stupid acquiescence."[31] She remarks that women are "kept in ignorance under the specious name of innocence" (p.23), a comment precisely applicable to Camilla's "education." Men expect of women, she points out, only negative virtues, if any: "patience, docility, good humour, and flexibility—virtues incompatible with any vigorous exertion of intellect" (p. 64). "Kind instructors!" she inquires passionately, "what were we created for? To remain, it may be said, innocent; they mean in a state of childhood. We might as well never have been born" (p. 68).

Concerned with possibilities of social action, Mary Wollstonecraft interests herself in the question of collective female identity: how women can understand themselves as women. Fanny Burney, as a novelist, involves herself rather in the development of individuals, but *The Wanderer* implies some relation between collective and individual possibility through the striking character of Elinor Joddrell, a young and attractive woman of good family who under the influence of revolutionary ideas from France has developed a rather remarkable vision of her own resources and rights. She claims "the Right of woman, if endowed with senses, to make use of them," moving to eloquent questions about larger privileges.[32] "Must even her heart be circumscribed by boundaries as narrow as her sphere of action in life? Must she be taught to subdue all its native emotions? To hide them as sin, and to deny them as shame? . . . Must every thing that she does be prescribed by rule? . . . Must nothing that is spontaneous, generous, intuitive, spring from her soul to her lips?"(I, 405).

These questions, which describe with only slight exaggeration the emotional program followed by Fanny Burney herself, justify Elinor from her own point of view in boldly declaring her love for a man who has indicated no romantic interest in her, claiming her individual right to violate social expectation, and enlarging for herself alone the narrow boundaries of permitted emotional expression. The novel's action makes a fool of her. The man she loves does not reciprocate her feelings. She threatens and attempts suicide repeatedly in increasingly melodramatic fashion but never quite achieves it. She strikes grand attitudes and makes grand speeches, finally to disappear from the scene and reform in quiet obscurity. Juliet, the novel's heroine, concurs in her lover's judgment that Elinor needs to be brought to her senses.

Elinor, like Mrs. Selwyn, exists to be refuted, and like Mrs. Selwyn she survives refutation. However foolish her actions and her extravagant emotional displays, she raises issues that cannot readily be laid to rest. She articulates a point never explicitly acknowledged in Miss Burney's previous books (a point implicit also in the novels by other women treated in an earlier chapter): a woman's individual sense of identity depends necessarily on her generic identity. Men (Mary Wollstonecraft duly noted this fact) have more varied possibilities for action and feeling within the context of their social definition. Woman's nature has been so specifically defined that it largely excludes idiosyncrasy. A girl's individualistic impulses must hide themselves; Elinor must learn on a personal level the inevitable failure of revolutionary hope.

Although Elinor's message rings more powerfully than may be intended, it does not speak unambiguously for the author. Yet, more systematically than *Cecilia* or *Camilla*, *The Wanderer* expresses conscious resentment of the female condition. The "female difficulties" alluded to in the subtitle impede the heroine's attempt to achieve economic and personal independence. Juliet, like Cecilia, is an orphan; like Evelina she suffers from her parents' secret marriage and the resultant mystery about her birth and status; like all the Burney heroines, she falls in love early but faces countless external obstacles to love's fulfillment. Unlike any of her predecessors, though, she must depend on her own resources for emotional and economic survival. An exile from France, where she has been educated, penniless as a result of an accident, forbidden to reveal her origins, background, or even her name, she must make her own way in England. She herself understands her problem, in its particular ramifications, as peculiar to her sex and as illustrating the limitations of social definitions of the female state. "How insufficient, she exclaimed, is a FEMALE to herself! How utterly dependant upon situation—connexions—circumstance!" (II, 197). An ideal of self-sufficiency dominates Juliet throughout the events that demonstrate its impossibility. She finds female experience to involve utter dependency, endless difficulty, and constant negative judgment from without of all attempts at self-assertion. Like Mary Wollstonecraft, she discovers how women's education forestalls their significant accomplishment: women do not learn to do anything. When Juliet laments to Elinor the severe difficulties of a female trying to make her way in the world, Elinor insists that she need only forget that she is "a dawdling woman" and remember that she is an "active human being," and her difficulties will vanish (III, 36). But Elinor has never faced and cannot even recognize the external difficulties that confront Juliet. Juliet is right, as Mary Wollstonecraft is right. But what use is such rightness?

The most interesting aspect of *The Wanderer* is the degree to which Juliet has internalized the social expectations that nullify her continuing struggle. She wins limited social recognition by demonstrating her mastery of the ladylike accomplishments of harp-playing and singing, and her competence in "the useful and appropriate female accomplishment of needlework" (I, 163). Forced against her will to appear in private theatricals, she thus acquires a further opportunity to display the range of her talents and skills. Perhaps more significantly, the play enables her to demonstrate "those fears of self-deficiency . . . which . . . often, in sensitive minds, rob them of the powers of exertion" (I, 199). In its first scene, she shows herself a totally incompetent actress because of her fears; later she rouses herself to triumph (I, 204). Impossible not to think of Miss Burney with her consistent social display of her fears, but one may be surprised, in the particular novelistic context, to find fear glorified as an index of sensitivity. Juliet brings herself to give harp lessons in order to earn a living, but when her ambiguous status and background make her lose pupils, she is unwilling to use her talents in a public musical performance—partly because Harleigh hints that to participate in such an undertaking might obviate the possibility of honorable marriage. Although financial necessity drives the heroine to determine upon performance at last, on the actual occasion she faints before she has to play. She then takes a job as companion to an irascible and tyrannical older woman, effectively dramatizing her social condition of dependency.

Increasingly Juliet finds herself relying—always limited, of course, by considerations of propriety—on financial, emotional, and physical help from men. Money embarrasses her, as it did her creator.[33] She needs it nonetheless, and she needs the self-esteem of winning it by her own efforts, but almost equally she needs the quite opposed self-esteem derived from never even appearing to do wrong. Like Fanny Burney, Juliet comes to recognize that to act as little as possible, if it does not ensure doing right, at least prevents wrong. Her situation forces her to act; her femininity urges her toward passivity.

Elinor points out how inconsistently men—hence, the world—judge women. They declare women unable to act as meaningfully as men because of their natural limitations, although men have in fact barred women from action by controlling their education. On the other hand, while estimating woman below themselves, they also elevate her above, requiring "from her, in defiance of their examples!—in defiance of their lures!—angelical perfection" (III, 42). Juliet, who attempts—largely unsuccessfully—to defy the prohibition of meaningful action, entirely accepts this other impossible standard with its goal of "angelical perfection." For her virtue rather than her action, she wins reward: the man of her choice.

Before the reward, though, apparently hopeless entanglements develop. Juliet, it turns out, is married already. Her commitment to passive virtue has led her to self-sacrifice for the sake of her guardian, when his life is threatened by revolutionaries. One of these wretches demands Juliet, for the sake of her fortune, promising her guardian's life as her price. She marries him; then before consummation she escapes to England, but when he claims her she must acknowledge his right. In this crisis, her passivity markedly increases. Harleigh begs her not to let "your too delicate fears of doing wrong by others, urge you to inflict wrong, irreparable wrong, upon yourself!" (V, 163), but, like her creator, Juliet is dominated by terror of public wrongdoing. She is rescued from her nominal husband, in one instance, by a male friend who commands her "to attend her own nearest relations"; otherwise she would not attempt to evade her fate, controlled as she is "by an overwhelming dread that to resist might possibly be wrong" (V, 326). She can turn only to piety, by which she denies or in fantasy avoids "all present and actual evil," concentrating instead on "an enthusiastic foretaste of the joys of futurity" (V, 208). Her conflicts, multitudinous and irreconcilable, reduce her to total immobility. Her existence becomes one loud plea for help. When her lover describes her as "wholly independent; mistress of her heart, mistress of herself—", she protests: "No, Mr. Harleigh, no! I am not so independent! . . . Had I an hundred hearts,—ten thousand times you must have conquered them all!" (V, 364–5). Her triumph derives from her relinquishment of all claim to self-sufficiency.

On the novel's final pages, the author summarizes Juliet as "a female Robinson Crusoe, . . . reduced either to sink, through inanition, to nonentity, or to be rescued from famine and death by such resources as she could find, independently, in herself" (V, 394–5). But only in brief intervals has her survival depended on herself. Elinor seems right about the limited possibilities for women in existent social conditions, although wrong in her hope of enlarging them. Much earlier, Harleigh has complained of the "dangerous singularity" in Elinor's character (I, 376). In the end, he urges Juliet not to worry about the other young woman, who "has a noble, though, perhaps, a masculine spirit." (Applied to Elinor, as to Mrs.Selwyn, *masculine* is a harsh designation.) She will come to see the error of her ways, he continues, returning "to the habits of society and common life, as one awakening from a dream in which she has acted some strange and improbable part" (V, 370–71). Juliet, too, is recovering from her dream of independence. Fanny Burney's imagining of a female Robinson Crusoe is an imagining of despair. For Juliet as a heroine must struggle not only with the obstacles supplied by a hostile physical and social environment but with those created by her own standard of femininity; no psychic or religious conversion can rescue her. Femininity wins; all else is only a dream. Juliet and Elinor in different ways illustrate a female fantasy of self-realization and self-definition through action rather than avoidance. Testing that fantasy, Juliet discovers its frailty. The fear of doing wrong finally controls her, teaching her her helplessness.

"There is no doubt but that *The Wanderer* is Fanny Burney's poorest novel," Michael Adelstein writes.[34] Virtually all critics have concurred, from the time of first publication to the present. Its elaborate plot, didactically disposed characters, and old-fashioned rhetoric compose a moralistic artifice rather than a realized fiction; it seems an imitation of theory, not of life. Yet its relation to life as Fanny Burney knew it lies deeper than one might suppose. What Joyce Hemlow perceives as a schematic arrangement of virtuous and morally defective characters may be seen also as Fanny Burney's most detailed rendition of the female strategy of virtue, its costs, and its rewards.[35] That strategy involves manipulation rather than simple acceptance of weakness. To use goodness as a stance toward the world (the tactic adopted by the character Juliet as well as by her creator) embodies some claim of strength: Juliet achieves moral superiority if not economic success. But it is an underdog's device, understood explicitly as such by the character who employs it. Goodness amounts to Juliet's only viable resource; her obsessive fear of wrongdoing implies her terror of losing her single weapon for battling the world. And her resentment of being so handicapped in life's struggle expresses itself in her repeated recognition that women know nothing and can do nothing to help themselves. They must allow themselves to be helped and must invite infantilization; they must avoid so much that finally they virtually avoid life itself. Given the detailed realizations along the way of what the female plight means, the happy ending of *The Wanderer* and the novel's artifices of plot and character seem to comprise a bitter mockery, so inadequate are artifices of plot to solve the problems here richly exposed. Fanny Burney was unable to integrate her deep perceptions of the female condition into a believable fiction—perhaps her habits of fear and avoidance made her fear and avoid the implications of her insight. But *The Wanderer* too contains its autobiographical revelations. Less careful than the journals, the novel reveals that the longing for freedom, confessed in moments of despair at the restrictions of Court life, extended farther than Fanny Burney directly acknowledged, vividly reflecting her awareness that fear of wrongdoing as a principle of action itself exemplifies the severe restrictiveness of female possibility.

No one now reads Fanny Burney's novels, except for *Evelina,* where comedy and youthful exuberance qualify the pervasive anxiety and one can even smile at the anxiety, for its causes are, by and large, so trivial. Yet the later novels, creaky of plot and increasingly impenetrable in rhetoric, seriously explore the possibilities for women to assert individual identities. More clearly than Fanny Burney's letters and diaries, the novels betray her anger at the female condition, although she also acknowledges the possibility of happiness within that condition. Imagining female defiance, she imagines also its futility in those heroines dominated, like herself, by fears of doing wrong. The atmosphere of anxiety she vividly evokes suggests what conflicts attend a woman's search for identity. The Burney female characters face endless struggle between what they want to have (independence, specific husbands, friends, pleasure, work) and what they want to be (angelically perfect): between the impulses to action and to avoidance. However important or negligible the specific images of this conflict, it stands behind the action and the characterization of all the novels.

The record of the journals, extending chronologically far beyond the writer's marriage, makes it clear that her commitment to D'Arblay, fulfilling as it was, did not mark the happy ending to her experience as it did for all her fictional heroines. Marriage resolved or simplified conflicts, granting Fanny Burney permission to act (through writing) while yet remaining conspicuously good; it thus provided energy. It also generated new dramas: classic Oedipal struggles, symbolic dilemmas about where and how to live, and conflicts of interest between Fanny's old family and her new—dramas that the journals expose more freely than they had revealed the problems of the author's youth, although in fact the problems remain in many respects essentially the same. The plot of the diaries thus necessarily differs from that of the novels, which never explore post-marital experience.

Yet the fictional inventions uncover the inner realities of the writer's mature as well as her youthful life. Indeed, comparison of Fanny Burney's personal record with her novels suggests the possibility that fiction may more vividly than autobiography delineate the shape of an author's private drama. The external events of Miss Burney's life, as reported in her diaries, supply small excitements, minor clashes, and tiny resolutions. The events of her novels increasingly emphasize important happenings—in *The Wanderer*, political as well as personal happening. Her heroines must cope with grotesque misunderstandings, malicious enemies, and bitter strokes of fate. They suffer more than they can comprehend—more perhaps even than their author comprehends. They express both their creator's wishes and her conviction that such wishes must be punished: the real essence of the inner drama that is more palely reflected in the relatively trivial events she chooses to record in diary and letters.

Fiction is fantasy. Both the strength and the weakness of Fanny Burney's novels derives from this fact. The books betray their author's longing for more grandiose experience than her powerful sense of decorum would allow her even to know she wanted. All except *Cecilia*, that fable of the poor little rich girl, rely on the deeply satisfying fairytale structure in which the hero (in these cases the heroine) with no apparent assets survives a series of demanding tests, winning by the power of goodness, triumphing over those seemingly more advantaged, and finally achieving the royal marriage that symbolizes lasting good fortune. But Fanny Burney betrays conflicting fantasies, which lessen her fiction's energy: on the one hand the dream of self-assertion and success in the face of all obstacles, on the other the fearful fantasy of nemesis for female admission of hostility and female attempts at self-determination. However she heightens happenings to melodramatic impossibility, ignoring logic and straining rhetoric to insist on the importance of her tale, her stories work against themselves. In her direct accounts of herself, with her sense of morality firmly in control the conflict between the impulse to freedom and the commitment to propriety—its resolution in action always predictable and its emotional dynamics often compelling—shapes a persuasive narrative. But the world of fiction holds forth the possibilties of greater freedom, possibilities that Fanny Burney could not adequately handle, although they enabled her to reveal herself.

Fiction is form, and form is fiction. The forms that tempted Miss Burney, in life and in literature, were moral structures that assured her that virtue found its reward. Around her she could see evidence to the contrary, particularly in female fates. Her stepsister Maria and her beloved sister Susanna both married brutes and suffered dire consequences. Susanna died after some years of Irish exile necessitated by her husband's arbitrary decisions. Marriage in real life constituted punishment as often as reward. The structures of fiction, as structures of moral order, made sense of experience. They could be imposed also on records of life. Fanny Burney's narrative of herself, in diary and letters, interpreting all conflict as moral conflict and every choice as an effort to determine the good, rationalizes her relatively quiet life as a struggle for virtue and her happy marriage as virtue's reward. It thus creates shape out of a life's random sequence of events—but a shape, significantly, of conflict.

Fiction is public communication. Fanny Burney's consciousness of this fact expresses itself, characteristically, most often in statements of what she has left out of her novels in order to avoid contaminating young minds. Thus, she boasts that *Camilla* contains no politics because "they were not a *feminine* subject for discussion" and "it would be a better office to general Readers to carry them wide of all politics, to their domestic fire sides."[36] As usual, she is avoiding wrong. But public communication has a positive as well as a negative aspect. In the youthful diaries, writing for "nobody," Fanny expressed a deprecating sense of self; all her letters and diairies insist upon her modesty. The more impersonal expression of fiction enabled her to enlarge her self-image by splitting herself into infinitely virtuous heroines and ingeniously aggressive minor characters, by dramatizing her sense of virtue through those heroines who suffer endlessly in their efforts toward the right, and by expressing ideas that she could not allow herself to endorse through such figures as Mrs. Selwyn and Elinor Joddrell. Only in rare moments of the private record—as when she complains that Mrs. Thrale showers her with too many gifts—does Fanny Burney betray her hostility. The open record of fiction provided greater protection: she could simultaneously convey both anger and her disapproval of anger. Much more successfully than her female contemporaries, she found ways to manipulate and use her own psychic experience, not simply to avoid it through wishful fantasy or ethical didacticism.

Fiction, finally, may constitute autobiography. Through Fanny Burney's novels, through their flaws and their positive achievements, she conveys her private self more emphatically, more explicitly, than she does in the diaries. Not needing to exercise reductive moral control over every character, she can use her fantasies to communicate her feelings and her conflicts, the interior drama that her decorous life largely concealed. She quotes Mme. de Genlis: "The life of every Woman is a Romance!"[37] The remark, implying an interpretation of actual experience in terms of literary categories, suggests a useful way to read the diaries and letters—perceiving the extent to whch, even in her personal record, it is Fanny Burney's fictions that reveal herself. Writing novels, she allows herself to convey the impermissible sides of her nature and to enlarge the permissible. Writing journals, she confines herself largely to the surfaces of her life; yet she uncovers the depths by the unchanging form of her self-interpretation, by her wistful, persistent fantasy of flawless virtue, and by her insistence on shaping her account of all that happens to her in terms of the struggle for virtue. She tells the story of an uneventful life as a romance rich in drama.

Fanny Burney's novels and her journals alike reveal the dynamics of fear in a woman's experience. They also reveal some ways in which the imagination deals with emotion, demonstrating how useful are the disguises of fiction in clarifying the truths of personality and how much the forms and perceptions of fiction become necessary material for the autobiographer.

Notes

1. *The History of the English Novel: The Novel of Sentiment and the Gothic Romance* (London: Witherby, 1942), p. 156.

2. "Fanny Burney's *Evelina*," *The Age of Johnson: Essays Presented to Chauncey Brewster Tinker* (New Haven: Yale University Press, 1949), p. 172.

3. *The Early Diary of Frances Burney, 1768–1778*, ed. Annie Raine Ellis, 2 vols. (London, 1889); *Diary and Letters of Madame D'Arblay*, ed. Austin Dobson (from the edition of Charlotte Barrett), 6 vols. (London: Macmillan, 1904). The new edition of *The Journals and Letters of Fanny Burney* thus far includes Vol. I (1791–1792), ed. Joyce Hemlow with Curtis D. Cecil and Althea Douglas (Oxford: The Clarendon Press, 1972); Vol. II (1793), ed. Joyce Hemlow and Althea Douglas (1972); Vol. III (1793–1797), ed. Joyce Hemlow with Patricia Boutilier and Althea Douglas (1973); Vol. IV (1797–1801), ed. Joyce Hemlow (1973).

4. *Diary and Letters*, VI, 363. Subsequent references to this edition will be incorporated into the text.

5. *The Wanderer: or, Female Difficulties,* 5 vols. (London, 1814), dedication, I, xx–xxi.

6. *Early Diary,* I, 18.

7. *Early Diary,* I, 7. Years later, Richard Owen Cambridge, telling Fanny of his daughter's approaching death, urges her, as he has urged her friend Sally Baker, "to be cheerful." "'You two,' added he, 'and my two girls, have, among you all four but one fault,—and that is too much feeling. You must repress that, therefore, as much as you can'" *(Diary and Letters,* II, 245; 1783).

8. Francis R. Hart, "Notes for an Anatomy of Modern Autobiography," *New Literary History,* 1 (1970), 497.

9. Barrett John Mandel, "The Autobiographer's Art," *Journal of Aesthetics and Art Criticism,* 27 (1968), 222.

10. As in the case of Sophie Streatfield: see *Diary and letters,* II, 39.

11. To Mrs. Phillips, #17, 29 Aug. 1797; *Journals,* III, 352. Sarah subsequently eloped with her married half brother, twenty-two years her senior, thus confirming Miss Burney's dark suspicions of her.

12. She describes her first social encounter with the King in a vivid passage beginning "It seemed to me we were acting a play" *(Diary and Letters,* II, 319). Although her later references are more discreet, her entire account of court life emphasizes the extreme artificiality of its customs and the prescribed nature of all activity.

13. #8, To Mrs. Phillips and Mrs. Locke, Oct. 1791; *Journals,* I, 73.

14. #23, Journal-letter to Mrs. Phillips and Mrs. Locke, May 1792; *Journals,* I, 160.

15. #61, To Mrs. Phillips, [2–3] April [1793]; *Journals,* II, 42.

16. #82, To Mrs. Phillips, 8 May 1793; *Journals,* II, 116–17.

17. Maria Rishton to Susan Phillips, quoted by Joyce Hemlow, *The History of Fanny Burney* (Oxford: The Clarendon Press, 1958), p. 239.

18. #120, To Mrs. Waddington, 2 Aug. [1793]; *Journals,* II, 179.

19. #124, To Mrs. Waddington, [19 Sept.] 1793; *Journals,* III, 9.

20. #154, 16 Oct. 1794; *Journals,* III, 84.

21. #169, To Dr. Burney, 13 June 1795; *Journals,* III, 113.

22. *A Writer's Diary,* ed. Leonard Woolf (London: The Hogarth Press, 1954), entry for 20 April 1919, pp. 13–14.

23. *The Rise of the Novel: Studies in Defoe, Richardson, and Fielding* (London: Chatto and Windus, 1957), p. 310.

24. Kemp Malone, "Evelina Revisited," *Papers on Language and Literature,* 1 (1965), 3–19.

25. *The History of Fanny Burney,* pp. 91–95.

26. See *Evelina, or the History of a Young Lady's Entrance into the World,* ed. Edward A. Bloom (London: Oxford University Press, 1970), preface, pp. 7–8. Subsequent references to this edition will be incorporated in the text.

27. The introduction to Bloom's edition of *Evelina* argues the importance of prudence as a lesson the heroine must learn, pp. xix–xxiii.

28. Michael Adelstein enunciates a commonly accepted view in suggesting that Evelina learns nothing of importance, having "merely exchanged snobbery for sweetness, and sympathy for indifference," and demonstrating "that social education is all." *Fanny Burney* (New York: Twayne, 1968) p. 38. It will be clear that I disagree.

29. *Cecilia: Or, Memoirs of an Heiress,* 2 vols. (London, 1914), I. 244.

30. *Camilla: Or, A Picture of Youth,* 5 vols. (London, 1796), I. 322. Subsequent references to this edition will be incorporated in the text.

31. *The Rights of Women* (London: J. M. Dent & Sons Ltd., 1955), p. 68. Subsequent references to this edition will be incorporated in the text. The book was first printed as *A Vindication of the Rights of Women*, 1792.

32. *The Wanderer*, I, 403. Subsequent references to the edition cited in note 5, above, will be incorporated in the text.

33. See *The Wanderer*, III, 175, where Miss Burney writes directly from her own emotional experience. Compare: "There is something, after all, in money, by itself money, that I can never take possession of it without a secret feeling of something like a degradation: money in its effects, and its product, creates far different and more pleasant sensations" (*Diary and Letters*, III, 142).

34. *Fanny Burney*, p. 129.

35. *The History of Fanny Burney*, p. 342.

36. #198, To Dr. Burney [for 6 July 1796]; *Journals*, III, 186.

37. #410, To Mrs. Waddington, 4 April 1801; *Journals*, IV, 483.